Acknowledgments

To my readers—The IT Pro Solutions series is a new adventure. Thank you for being there with me through many books and many years.

To my wife—for many years, through many books, many millions of words, and many thousands of pages she's been there, providing support and encouragement and making every place we've lived a home.

To my kids—for helping me see the world in new ways, for having exceptional patience and boundless love, and for making every day an adventure.

To everyone I've worked with at Microsoft—thanks for the many years of support and for helping out in ways both large and small.

Special thanks to my son Will for his extensive contributions to this book. You've made many contributions previously, but now I can finally give you the cover credit you've earned and deserved for so long.

—William R. Stanek

Exchange Server 2016:
Server Infrastructure

IT Pro Solutions

William R. Stanek
Author & Series Editor

William R. Stanek, Jr.
Contributor

Exchange Server 2016:
Server Infrastructure

IT Pro Solutions

Published by Stanek & Associates, PO Box 362, East Olympia, WA, 98540-0362, www.williamrstanek.com.

ORGANIZATION OR WEBSITE AS A SOURCE OF FURTHER INFORMATION DOES NOT MEAN THAT THE PUBLISHER OR THE AUTHOR ENDORSES THE INFORMATION THE ORGANIZATION OR WEBSITE MAY PROVIDE OR THE RECOMMENDATIONS IT MAY MAKE. FURTHER, READERS SHOULD BE AWARE THAT WEBSITES LISTED IN THIS BOOK MAY NOT BE AVAILABLE OR MAY HAVE CHANGED SINCE THIS WORK WAS WRITTEN.

Stanek & Associates publishes in a variety of formats, including print, electronic and by print-on-demand. Some materials included with standard print editions may not be included in electronic or print-on-demand editions or vice versa.

Country of First Publication: United States of America.

Cover Design: Creative Designs Ltd.
Editorial Development: Andover Publishing Solutions
Technical Review: L & L Technical Content Services

You can provide feedback related to this book by emailing the author at williamstanek @ aol.com. Please use the name of the book as the subject line.

Version: 1.0.0.9c

> **Note** I may periodically update this text and the version number shown above will let you know which version you are working with. If there's a specific feature you'd like me to write about in an update, message me on Facebook (http://facebook.com/williamstanekauthor). Please keep in mind readership of this book determines how much time I can dedicate to it.

Table of Contents

About This Book

William Stanek has been developing expert solutions and writing professionally for Microsoft Exchange since 1995. In this book, William shares his extensive knowledge of the product, delivering ready answers for day-to-day management and zeroing in on core commands and techniques.

As with all books in the IT Pro Solutions series, this book is written especially for architects, administrators, engineers and others working with, supporting, and managing a specific version of a product or products. Here, the product written about is Exchange Server 2016.

This book, *Exchange Server 2016: Server Infrastructure*, is designed to be used with *Exchange Server 2106 & Exchange Online: Essentials for Administration*. While this book focuses on architecture and server configuration, the latter book focuses on:

- Using Exchange Admin Center
- Working with Exchange Management Shell
- Managing mail boxes, mail contacts and distribution groups
- Setting up address lists and address books
- Configuring Exchange clients
- Implementing Exchange security and role-based permissions

Using the books together, you can answer most of the everyday questions you'll have with Exchange Server 2016 and Exchange Online.

Print Readers

Print editions of this book include an index and some other elements not available in the digital edition. Updates to this book are available online. Visit http://www.williamrstanek.com/exchangeserver/ to get any updates. This content is available to all readers.

Digital Book Readers

Digital editions of this book are available at all major retailers, at libraries upon request and with many subscription services. If you have a digital edition of this book that you downloaded elsewhere, such as a file sharing site, you should know that the author doesn't receive any royalties or income from such downloads.

Already downloaded this book or others? Donate here to ensure William can keep writing the books you need:

https://www.paypal.com/cgi-bin/webscr?cmd=_s-xclick&hosted_button_id=CPSBGLZ35AB26

Support Information

Every effort has been made to ensure the accuracy of the contents of this book. As corrections are received or changes are made, they will be added to the online page for the book available at:

http://www.williamrstanek.com/exchangeserver/

If you have comments, questions, or ideas regarding the book, or questions that are not answered by visiting the site above, send them via e-mail to:

williamstanek@aol.com

Other ways to reach the author:

Facebook: http://www.facebook.com/William.Stanek.Author

Twitter: http://twitter.com/williamstanek

It's important to keep in mind that Microsoft software product support is not offered. If you have questions about Microsoft software or need product support, please contact Microsoft.

Microsoft also offers software product support through the Microsoft Knowledge Base at:

http://support.microsoft.com/

Conventions & Features

This book uses a variety of elements to help keep the text clear and easy to follow. You'll find code terms and listings in `monospace`, except when I tell you to actually enter or type a command. In that case, the command appears in **bold**. When I introduce and define a new term, I put it in *italics*.

The first letters of the names of menus, dialog boxes, user interface elements, and commands are capitalized. Example: the New Mail Contact dialog box. This book also has notes, tips and other sidebar elements that provide additional details on points that need emphasis.

Keep in mind that throughout this book, where William has used click, right-click and double-click, you can also use touch equivalents: tap, press and hold, and double tap. Also, when using a device without a physical keyboard, you are able to enter text by using the onscreen keyboard. If a device has no physical keyboard, simply touch an input area on the screen to display the onscreen keyboard.

Share & Stay in Touch

The marketplace for technology books has changed substantially over the past few years. In addition to becoming increasingly specialized and segmented, the market has been shrinking rapidly, making it extremely difficult for books to find success. If you want William to be able to continue writing and write the books you need for your career, raise your voice and support his work.

Without support from you, the reader, future books by William will not be possible. Your voice matters. If you found the book to be useful, informative or otherwise helpful, please take the time to let others know by sharing about the book online.

To stay in touch with William, visit him on Facebook or follow him on Twitter. William welcomes messages and comments about the book, especially suggestions for improvements and additions. If there is a topic you think should be covered in the book, let William know.

Chapter 1. Getting Started with Exchange Server 2016

You can implement Exchange services in several ways, including:

- **On-premises**   With an on-premises implementation, you deploy Exchange server hardware on your network and manage all aspects of the implementation, including server configuration, organization configuration, and recipient configuration.
- **Online**   With an online (or cloud-only) implementation, you rely on hardware and services provided by Microsoft. All aspects of the server configuration are managed by Microsoft. You manage the service-level settings, organization configuration, and recipient configuration.
- **Hybrid**   With a hybrid implementation, you integrate on-premises and online implementations. The on-premises and Exchange Online organizations use a shared domain namespace, so mail is securely routed between them, and you can easily share data between the implementations.

When you use an online implementation, Microsoft manages the hardware configuration and ensures availability. Otherwise, you are responsible for any on-premises hardware.

In terms of functionality, Exchange Server 2016 is an incremental release, building on the radical changes in Exchange Server 2010 and adding enhancements to the refinements found in Exchange Server 2013. Like Exchange Server 2010 and Exchange Server 2013, Exchange Server 2016 does away with the concepts of storage groups, Local Continuous Replication (LCR), Single Copy Clusters (SCC), and clustered mailbox servers. This means that:

- Databases are no longer associated with storage groups.
- Database availability groups are used to group databases for high availability.
- Databases are managed at the organization level instead of at the server level.

Exchange Server 2016 integrates high availability into the core architecture by enhancing aspects of Cluster Continuous Replication (CCR) and Standby Continuous Replication (SCR) and combining them into a single, high-availability solution for both on-site and off-site data replication.

Exchange Server 2016 also provides for automatic failover and recovery without requiring clusters when you deploy multiple mailbox servers. Because of these changes, building a high-availability mailbox server solution doesn't require cluster hardware or advanced cluster configuration. Instead, database availability groups provide the base component for high availability. Failover is automatic for mailbox databases that are part of the same database availability group.

The basic rules for database availability groups have not changed since implementation in Exchange Server 2010. Each mailbox server can have multiple databases, and each database can have as many as 16 copies. A single database availability group can have up to 16 mailbox servers that provide automatic database-level recovery. Any server in a database availability group can host a copy of a mailbox database from any other server in the database availability group.

This seamless high-availability functionality is possible because mailbox databases are disconnected from servers and the same globally unique identifier (GUID) is assigned to every copy of a mailbox database. Because there are no storage groups, continuous replication occurs at the database level. Transaction logs are replicated to each member of a database availability group that has a copy of a mailbox database and are replayed into the copy of the mailbox database. Failover can occur at either the database level or the server level.

With regard to architecture, Exchange Server 2016 is significantly different from early releases of Exchange and furthers the server role consolidation that began with Exchange 2013. While Exchange 2010 and other earlier releases had components split into different server roles for scaling out Exchange organizations, Exchange 2016 does not have separate server roles for Hub Transport servers, Unified Messaging servers or even Client Access servers. As the related components are all now part of the Mailbox Server role, there are no longer any other roles for internal Exchange servers. That said, although Exchange Server 2013 did not include the Edge Transport role until the release of Service Pack 1, the Edge Transport role also is included with Exchange 2016 and available for deployment in perimeter zones. This means you can use Edge Transport servers running this latest version of Exchange to add a layer of security to the Exchange organization.

These architecture changes mean that Mailbox servers storing the active database copy for a mailbox perform all the data processing, data rendering, and data transformation required. The Mailbox server connects the client and performs authentication. Supported protocols for client connections include HTTP, POP, IMAP,

RPC over HTTP, MAPI over HTTP and SMTP. As RPC is no longer supported as a direct access protocol, all Outlook client connections must take place using either RPC over HTTP or MAPI over HTTP, with the latter being preferred.

It's important to point out that Exchange 2016 is designed to work with Outlook 2010 and higher and also continues to support Outlook Web App for mobile access. Rather than connecting to servers using Fully Qualified Domain Names as was done in the past, Outlook 2010 and higher use Autodiscover to create connection points based on the domain portion of the user's primary SMTP address and each mailbox's Globally Unique Identifier (GUID).

The simplified architecture reduces the namespace requirements for Exchange site designs. If you're coexisting with Exchange 2010 or you're installing a new Exchange 2016 organization, you need only one namespace for client protocols and one namespace for Autodiscover. To continue to support SMTP, you also need an SMTP namespace.

> **REAL WORLD**   As discussed in detail in Chapter 13 "Optimizing Web and Mobile Access," Outlook Web App (OWA) is a browser-based application that is accessed via IIS running on your Mailbox servers. Outlook Web App is also referred to as Outlook on the Web in some documentation from Microsoft and in some parts of the Exchange UI. Outlook on the Web is the new name and branding identity for Outlook Web App. For consistency, this text references Outlook Web App or OWA, which is what you'll see in most parts of the UI until re-branding is complete.

Selecting Hardware for Exchange 2016

Before you deploy Exchange Server 2016, you should carefully plan the messaging architecture. As part of your implementation planning, you need to look closely at preinstallation requirements and the hardware you will use. Exchange Server is a complex messaging platform with many components that work together to provide a comprehensive solution for routing, delivering, and accessing email messages, voice-mail messages, faxes, contacts, and calendar information.

If you're using Exchange Online, Microsoft provides the server hardware. Otherwise, for on-premises implementations, Exchange Server 2016 should run on a system with adequate memory, processing speed, and disk space. You also need an appropriate data-protection and system-protection plan at the hardware level.

Exchange Server 2016 requires two different types of server hardware. You want to select hardware for Mailbox servers with scaling *up* in mind while selecting hardware for Edge Transport servers with scaling *out* in mind. Scaling up typically means adding additional or faster, better CPUs and memory to existing servers to meet capacity needs. Scaling out typically means adding additional servers to meet capacity needs.

Key guidelines for choosing hardware for Exchange Server are as follows:

- **Memory** The minimum random access memory (RAM) is 8 gigabytes (GB) for servers with the Mailbox Server role and 4 GB for Edge Transport servers. In most cases, you'll want to have at least twice the recommended minimum amount of memory. The primary reason for this is performance. Most of the Mailbox server installations I run use 16 GB of RAM as a starting point, even in small installations. In multiple Exchange server installations, the Mailbox server should have at least 2 GB of RAM plus 5 megabytes (MB) of RAM per mailbox (with a minimum of 8 GB regardless). For all Exchange server configurations, the paging file should be at least equal to the amount of RAM in the server plus 10 MB, with a maximum size of 32778 MB if the server has more than 32 GB of RAM.
- **CPU** Exchange Server 2016 runs on the x64 family of processors from AMD and Intel, including AMD64 and Intel 64. You can achieve significant performance improvements with a high level of processor cache. Look closely at the L1, L2, and L3 cache options available—a higher cache can yield much better performance overall. Look also at the speed of the front-side bus. The faster the bus speed, the faster the CPU can access memory.
- **SMP** Exchange Server 2016 supports symmetric multiprocessors, and you'll see significant performance improvements if you use multiple CPUs—not just multiple cores in a single CPU. Although the clock speed of the CPU is important, so are the number of logical processor cores and the number of threads that can be simultaneously processed. That said, if Exchange Server is supporting a small organization with a single domain, one CPU with multiple cores may be enough. If the server supports a medium or large organization or handles mail for multiple domains, you will want to consider adding processors. When it comes to processor cores, I prefer two multicore processors to a single processor with the same number of cores, given current price and performance tradeoffs. As part of the preferred architecture, Microsoft recommends dual socket servers, with 16 to 24 cores each for large organizations.
- **Disk drives** The data storage capacity you need depends entirely on the number and size of the data that will pass through, be journaled on, or stored on the Exchange server. You need enough disk space to store all data and logs, plus workspace, system files, and virtual memory. Input/output (I/O) throughput is just as important as drive capacity. Rather than use one large drive, you should use

several drives, which allows you to configure fault tolerance. As part of your hardware planning, it's important to point out that Exchange 2016 supports multiple databases on the same volume, allowing you to have a mix of active and passive copies on a single volume. Keep in mind, however, the input/output per second (IOPS) capabilities for the underlying physical disks. Also note that even if you've been assigned multiple logical unit numbers (LUNs) for use from storage these different LUNs may be spread over the same physical disks. Make sure your hardware uses battery-backed write cache controllers as this will help prevent data loss during an unexpected loss of power. Finally, serially attached SCSI (SAS) disks are preferred to SATA disks as they provide better IO and a lower failure rate.

- **File formats**   Although Windows Server supports several file systems, only the NTFS and ReFS file system should be used with Exchange Server 2016. Use NTFS for the system partition and for any partition that stores Exchange binary files or files generated by diagnostic logging. Use NTFS or ReFS for partitions containing database files, content indexing files and transaction log files. As discussed in more detail in Chapter 2, "Preparing for Exchange 2016," ReFS is preferred to NTFS as it is a more efficient and more resilient filesystem. If you use ReFS with Exchange, be sure to disable the integrity feature.

- **Data protection**   You can add protection against unexpected drive failures by using redundant storage. For the boot and system disks, use mirroring on internal drives. However, when you use availability groups and other high-availability features of Exchange Server, you might not want to use redundant storage for Exchange data and logs. You also might not want to use expensive disk storage systems either. Instead, deploy multiple Exchange servers in each of your database availability groups. As part of the preferred architecture, Microsoft recommends using disk mirroring (RAID 1) for the operating system volume with the rest of the storage configured as Just a Bunch of Disks (JBOD). This preferred architecture assumes that you have deployed multiple mailbox servers in a highly available configuration.

- **Data encryption**   Consider using BitLocker to encrypt the operating system volume and Exchange data volumes. Data encryption reduces concerns about data theft for those with physical access to the server. If you deploy highly available Exchange servers without BitLocker and later want to add BitLocker, be sure to put the server you are working with in maintenance mode first.

- **Uninterruptible power supply**   Exchange Server 2016 is designed to maintain database integrity at all times and can recover information using transaction logs. This doesn't protect the server hardware, however, from sudden power loss or power spikes, both of which can seriously damage hardware. To prevent this, connect your server to an uninterruptible power supply (UPS). A UPS gives you time to shut down the server or servers properly in the event of a power outage. Proper shutdown is especially important on servers using write-back caching controllers. These controllers temporarily store data in cache. Without proper shutdown, this data can be lost before it is written to disk. To prevent data loss, write-back caching controllers typically have batteries that help ensure that changes can be written to disk after the system comes back online.

If you follow these hardware guidelines, you'll be well on your way to success with Exchange Server 2016. It's important to note that beginning with Windows Server 2012, dynamic disks are being phased out in favor of Storage Spaces. However, for mirroring boot and system volumes on internal disks, Microsoft recommends continuing to use dynamic disks and RAID 1.

If you decide to use software-based redundant storage, remember that storage arrays typically already have an underlying redundant storage configuration and you might have to use a storage array–specific tool to help you distinguish between LUNs and the underlying physical disks. Herein, I focus on software-based redundancy implemented with RAID or Storage Spaces rather than the underlying hardware redundancy implemented in storage arrays.

Windows Server is transitioning to standards-based storage beginning with Windows Server 2012. This transition means several popular tools and favored features are being phased out. Officially, a tool or feature that is being phased out is referred to as *deprecated*. When Microsoft deprecates a tool or feature, it might not be in future releases of the operating system (while continuing to be available in current releases). Rather than not cover popular tools and features, I've chosen to discuss what is actually available in the current operating system, including both favored standbys and newer options. One of these newer options is Storage Spaces. With Storage Spaces:

- Simple volumes can stretch across multiple disks, similar to disk striping with parity (RAID 0).
- Mirrored volumes are mirrored across multiple disks. Although this is similar to disk mirroring (RAID 1), it is more sophisticated in that data is mirrored onto two or three disks at a time. If a storage space has two or three disks, you are fully protected against a single disk failure, and if a storage space has five or more disks, you are fully protected against two simultaneous disk failures.
- Parity volumes use disk striping with parity. Although this is similar to RAID 5, it is more sophisticated in that there are more protections and efficiencies.

Navigating Exchange 2016 Editions

Several editions of Exchange Server 2016 are available, including Exchange Server 2016 Standard and Exchange Server 2016 Enterprise. The various server editions support the same core features and administration tools, which means you can use the techniques discussed throughout this book regardless of which Exchange Server 2016 edition you are using. For reference, the specific feature differences between Standard Edition and Enterprise Edition are as follows:

- **Exchange Server 2016 Standard**   Designed to provide essential messaging services for small to medium organizations and branch office locations. This server edition supports up to five databases.
- **Exchange Server 2016 Enterprise**   Designed to provide essential messaging services for organizations with increased availability, reliability, and manageability needs. This server edition supports up to 100 databases (including all active databases and copies of databases) on a particular server. It's important to note that this is a substantial reduction in the number of supported databases as compared to Exchange 2010.

> **NOTE**   Throughout this book, I refer to Exchange Server 2016 in different ways, and each has a different meaning. Typically, I refer to the software product as *Exchange 2016* or as *Exchange Server*, which you can take to mean *Microsoft Exchange Server 2016*. When necessary, I use *Exchange Server 2016* to draw attention to the fact that I am discussing a feature that's new or has changed in the most recent version of the product. Each of these terms means essentially the same thing. If I refer to a previous version of Exchange Server, I always do so specifically, such as Exchange 2010 or Exchange 2013. Finally, I often use the term *Exchange server* (note the lowercase *s* in server) to refer to an actual server computer, as in "There are eight Exchange servers in this database availability group."

> **REAL WORLD**   Microsoft provides a single binary for x64 systems, and the same binary file is used for both the Standard and Enterprise editions. The license key provided during installation is what determines which edition is established during installation.
>
> You can use a valid product key to upgrade from a trial edition to the Standard edition or the Enterprise edition of Exchange Server 2016 without having to reinstall. Using a valid product key, you can also upgrade from the Standard to the Enterprise edition. You can also relicense an Exchange server by entering a new product key for the installed edition, which is useful if you accidentally used the same product key on multiple servers and want to correct the mistake.
>
> There are several caveats. When you change the product key on a Mailbox server, you must restart the Microsoft Exchange Information Store service to

apply the change. Additionally, you cannot use product keys to downgrade editions. To downgrade editions, you must uninstall Exchange Server and then reinstall Exchange Server.

Exchange 2016 is supported on Windows Server 2012, Windows Server 2012 R2 and Windows Server 2016. You can install Exchange Server 2016 on servers running full-server installations of Windows Server 2012 Standard, Windows Server 2012 Datacenter or later. You cannot install Exchange 2016 on servers running server core or minimal server interface. With Windows Server 2012 or Windows Server 2012 R2, you must convert the server core or minimal server interface installation to a full installation by running the following command from an elevated PowerShell prompt:

```
Install-WindowsFeature Server-Gui-Mgmt-Infra, Server-Gui-Shell -Restart
```

In addition to being able to deploy Exchange 2016 on physical servers, you can deploy Exchange 2016 in a virtualized environment on any version of Windows Server with Hyper-V technology or Microsoft Hyper-V Server as well as other hypervisors that have been validated under the Windows Server Virtualization Validation Program. If you do so, keep in mind that making virtual machine snapshots of an Exchange guest virtual machine isn't supported, as the state of Exchange 2016 would not be fully preserved.

> **REAL WORLD**   There are many arguments for and against using virtualization with Exchange Server. Typically, Microsoft recommends using physical servers as part of the preferred architecture, especially for large organizations. The primary reason for this is that virtualization adds complexity while increasing the management overhead as well.

A client accessing an Exchange server requires a Client Access License (CAL). With either Exchange Server edition, the client can use a Standard CAL, an Enterprise CAL, or both. The Standard CAL allows for the use of email, shared calendaring, contacts, task management, Microsoft Outlook Web App (OWA), and Exchange ActiveSync. The Enterprise CAL allows for the use of unified messaging, advanced mobile management, data loss prevention, and custom retention policies. An Enterprise CAL is sold as an add-on to the Standard CAL. A client must have one Standard CAL and one Enterprise CAL add-on to make full use of all Exchange Server features.

Beyond the editions and CALs, Exchange Server 2016 has several variants. Microsoft offers on-premises and online implementations of Exchange Server. An on-premises

Exchange Server is one that you install in your organization. An online Exchange Server is delivered as a subscription service from Microsoft. In Exchange Server 2016, you can manage both on-premises and online implementations of Exchange Server using the same management tools. These implementations can be separate from each other, or you can configure a hybrid installation that allows single sign-on and easy movement of mailboxes and databases between on-premises and online implementations.

As a prerequisite for installing any server running any on-premises version of Exchange Server 2016, Active Directory must be at Windows Server 2008 forest functionality mode or higher. Additionally, all domain controllers in the Active Directory forest must be running Windows Server 2008 Standard, Enterprise or Datacenter, Windows Server 2012 Standard or Datacenter, or later editions of Windows Server.

> **NOTE** Using Active Directory with Exchange Server 2016 is covered in more detail in the "Using Exchange 2016 with Active Directory" section of this chapter and the "Integrating Exchange with Active Directory" section of Chapter 2.

Additionally, Exchange Server 2016 supports IPv6 only when IPv4 is also installed and enabled. When you deploy IPv6, Exchange servers can send data to and receive data from devices, clients, and servers that use IPv6 addresses. You install Exchange 2016 using Exchange Setup. Exchange 2016 requires:

- Microsoft .NET Framework version 4.5.2 (http://go.microsoft.com/fwlink/p/?linkid=518380)
- Microsoft Unified Communications Managed API 4.0, Core Runtime 64-bit (http://go.microsoft.com/fwlink/p/?linkid=258269)
- Windows Management Framework 4.0 (https://www.microsoft.com/en-us/download/details.aspx?id=40855).

If you don't install these additional components prior to running Exchange Setup, the Readiness Checks will fail and links to these resources will be provided. If this happens, you can use the links provided to obtain and install the components and then simply click Retry to have Setup perform the readiness checks again. Once these checks pass, you'll be able to continue with the installation.

With Edge Transport servers, you must install the Active Directory Lightweight Directory Service (ADLDS) feature of Windows. To install, use the following command:

```
Install-WindowsFeature ADLDS
```

With Mailbox servers, you must install a number of Windows features prior to installing Exchange Server. To install these features, use the following command:

```
Install-WindowsFeature AS-HTTP-Activation, Desktop-Experience, NET-Framework-45-Features, RPC-over-HTTP-proxy, RSAT-Clustering, RSAT-Clustering-CmdInterface, RSAT-Clustering-Mgmt, RSAT-Clustering-PowerShell, Web-Mgmt-Console, WAS-Process-Model, Web-Asp-Net45, Web-Basic-Auth, Web-Client-Auth, Web-Digest-Auth, Web-Dir-Browsing, Web-Dyn-Compression, Web-Http-Errors, Web-Http-Logging, Web-Http-Redirect, Web-Http-Tracing, Web-ISAPI-Ext, Web-ISAPI-Filter, Web-Lgcy-Mgmt-Console, Web-Metabase, Web-Mgmt-Console, Web-Mgmt-Service, Web-Net-Ext45, Web-Request-Monitor, Web-Server, Web-Stat-Compression, Web-Static-Content, Web-Windows-Auth, Web-WMI, Windows-Identity-Foundation
```

If you don't install these Windows features prior to running Exchange Setup, the setup process will try to install these components for you. Some of these components require a server restart. Others may not install completely until you exit Exchange Setup and repeat the Exchange setup process. Either way, you'll likely need to repeat the Exchange setup process. Rather than trying to type the long command from this text, see the companion website for this book at http://www.williamrstanek.com/exchangeserver/ for command text you can copy and paste.

Exchange 2016 has a different set of management tools than its predecessors. When you install a Mailbox server or an Edge Transport server, the management tools are installed automatically. You can use Exchange Setup to install the management tools on domain-joined computers running 64-bit editions of Windows 8.1, Windows 10 as well as Windows Server 2012 or later. Although Exchange 2016 has management tools that can be installed, you can perform most management actions remotely using a standard web browser and Windows PowerShell, and you'll learn more about this later in this chapter.

Exchange Server 2016 uses the Windows Installer (the Installer) and has a fully integrated installation process. This means you can configure Exchange Server 2016 much like you can any other application you install on the operating system. The installation can be performed from a command prompt as well.

Chapter 2 provides detailed instructions for installing Exchange Server 2016. You install Exchange 2016 only on domain-joined computers. Whether you use the Standard or Enterprise edition, you have similar options. You can install an internal messaging server by selecting the Mailbox role or a perimeter zone server by selecting the Edge Transport role. Generally, you will not want an internal Exchange server to also be configured as a domain controller with a global catalog.

When you start an installation, Setup checks the system configuration to determine the local time zone, the operating system, the logged-on user, and the status of the registry keys related to Exchange Server 2016. Installation will fail if you are trying to run Setup on an operating system that isn't supported.

After checking the system configuration, Setup allows you to check for updates to the installation process, provided the server has a connection to the Internet. Setup then checks available space on the %SystemDrive% to ensure a temporary folder under %SystemDrive%\Windows\Temp\ExchangeSetup can be used during the installation process. Before you install Exchange 2016, you should ensure the drive on which you plan to install Exchange has at least 32 GB of disk space.

When done copying its work files to the temporary folder, Setup tries to connect to a domain controller and validate the state of Active Directory. If Setup cannot find a domain controller or encounters other errors when validating Active Directory, the installation process will fail and you'll see related errors during the readiness checks.

> **IMPORTANT** By default, Setup chooses a domain controller in the local domain and site. In order to determine the domain information and contact a domain controller, the computer on which you are installing Exchange 2016 must be domain joined and have properly configured TCP/IP settings, and DNS name resolution must be properly configured in your organization. Because Active Directory site configuration also is important for installing Exchange 2016 and setting up an Exchange organization, ensure Active Directory sites and subnets are properly configured prior to installing Exchange 2016.

Once connected to a domain controller, Setup selects a global catalog server to work with and then looks for an Exchange Configuration container within Active Directory. Setup next determines the organization-level operations that need to be performed, which can include initializing Active Directory, updating Active Directory schema, establishing or updating the Exchange organization configuration, and updating the domain configuration.

As you continue through Setup, you'll be able to select the server roles to install, the install location, and more. With the exception of the working files, which are copied to the temporary folder, no changes are made until the server passes the readiness checks. Normally, even when problems are encountered, Setup will continue all the way to the readiness checks. As part of the readiness checks, Setup checks for required components, such as those listed previously.

Other required components include Windows Features that Setup will install automatically if they aren't already installed. These features include Desktop Experience, many components of IIS, Windows Identity Foundation, and the administrative tools for clustering. Although you can manually install these features, it's a long list; Setup will do the work for you if you let it and don't mind having to repeat the setup process.

Exchange 2016 includes the following anti-spam capabilities:

- **Sender filtering**   Allows administrators to maintain a list of senders who are blocked from sending messages to the organization. Administrators can block individual senders by email address. Administrators also can block all senders from domains and subdomains.
- **Recipient filtering**   Allows administrators to block message delivery to nonexistent recipients, distribution lists for internal users only, and mailboxes for internal use only. Exchange performs recipient lookups on incoming messages and block messages, which prevents certain types of attacks and malicious attempts at information discovery.
- **Sender ID verification**   Verifies that incoming email messages are from the Internet domain from which they claim to come. Exchange verifies the sender ID by examining the sender's IP address and comparing it to the related security record on the sender's public DNS server.
- **Content filtering**   Uses intelligent message filtering to scan message content and identify spam. Spam can be automatically deleted, quarantined, or filed as junk email.

> **TIP** Using the Exchange Server management tools, administrators can manage messages sent to the quarantine mailbox and take appropriate actions, such as deleting messages, flagging them as false positives, or allowing them to be delivered as junk email. Messages delivered as junk email are converted to plain text to strip out any potential viruses they might contain.

- **Sender reputation scoring** Helps to determine the relative trustworthiness of unknown senders through sender ID verification and by examining message content and sender behavior history. A sender can then be added temporarily to the Blocked Senders list.

The way you use these features will depend on the configuration of your Exchange organization. If you've deployed Edge Transport servers, you enable and configure these features on your Edge Transport servers. Otherwise, you enable and configure these features on your Mailbox servers.

Exchange 2016 also has anti-malware capabilities, which are enabled by default. Malware scanning is performed on all messages at the server level as messages are sent or received. When users open and read messages in their mailboxes, the messages they see have already been scanned. Exchange Server checks for updates to malware definitions every hour. Exchange downloads the malware engines and definitions using a TCP connection over port 80 from the Internet.

> **TIP** Normally, you'll manually perform the first download of the anti-malware engine and definition updates prior to placing a server into production so you can verify that the initial process was successful and then configure default anti-malware policy prior to users having access to a server.

Although these anti-spam and anti-malware features are extensive, they are not comprehensive. For comprehensive protection, you can pair these features with a cloud-based service, such as Microsoft Exchange Online Protection. By combining the built-in anti-spam and anti-malware features with a cloud-based protection service you can set up substantial, layered protection. Additionally, if you use a third-party anti-malware solution for Exchange 2016, you can disable the built-in anti-malware filtering.

Using Exchange 2016 with Windows Server

When you install Exchange Server on a server operating system, Exchange Server makes extensive modifications to the environment. These modifications include additional system services, integrated authentication, and additional security groups.

Services for Exchange Server

When you install Exchange Server and Forefront Protection for Exchange Server on Windows, multiple services are installed and configured on the server. A summary of key services, how they are used, and which server components they are associated with follows:

- **IIS Admin**   Enables the server to administer the IIS metabase. The IIS metabase stores configuration information for web applications used by Exchange. Exchange servers need IIS for WinRM and remote Powershell. Mailbox servers need IIS for OWA and Web services.
- **Microsoft Exchange Active Directory Topology**   Provides Active Directory topology information to Exchange services. If this service is stopped, most Exchange services will not be able to start.
- **Microsoft Exchange Anti-Spam Update**   Maintains the anti-spam data for Forefront Protection on an Exchange server.
- **Microsoft Exchange EdgeSync**   Provides EdgeSync services between Mailbox and Edge servers.
- **Microsoft Exchange Frontend Transport**   Proxies inbound and outbound SMTP connections.
- **Microsoft Exchange IMAP4 Backend**   Provides IMAP4 services to mailboxes.
- **Microsoft Exchange IMAP4**   Provides IMAP4 services to clients.
- **Microsoft Exchange Information Store**   Manages the Microsoft Exchange Information Store. This includes mailbox stores and public folder stores.
- **Microsoft Exchange Mailbox Assistants**   Manages assistants responsible for calendar updates, booking resources, and other mailbox processing.
- **Microsoft Exchange Mailbox Replication**   Enables online mailbox moves by processing mailbox move requests.
- **Microsoft Exchange Mailbox Transport Delivery**   Receives mail items from the Transport service and ensures they are processed and then delivered into mailbox.
- **Microsoft Exchange Mailbox Transport Submission**   Receives mail items being sent and ensures they are converted from MAPI to MIME and then submitted to the Transport service.
- **Microsoft Exchange POP3 Backend**   Provides Post Office Protocol version 3 (POP3) services to mailboxes.

- **Microsoft Exchange POP3**   Provides Post Office Protocol version 3 (POP3) services to clients.
- **Microsoft Exchange Replication**   Provides replication functionality used for continuous replication.
- **Microsoft Exchange RPC Client Access**   Manages client remote procedure call (RPC) connections for Exchange Server.
- **Microsoft Exchange Search**   Handles queries and controls indexing of mailboxes to improve search performance.
- **Microsoft Exchange Server Extension for Windows Server Backup**   Provides extensions for Windows Server Backup that allow you to back up and recover Exchange application data using Windows Server Backup.
- **Microsoft Exchange Service Host**   Provides a host for essential Exchange services.
- **Microsoft Exchange Throttling**   Provides throttling functions to limit the rate of user operations.
- **Microsoft Exchange Transport Log Search**   Provides search capability for Exchange transport log files.
- **Microsoft Exchange Transport**   Provides mail transport for Exchange Server.
- **Microsoft Exchange Unified Messaging Call Router**   Provides capabilities necessary for routing calls.
- **Microsoft Exchange Unified Messaging**   Enables voice and fax messages to be stored in Exchange and gives users telephone access to email, voice mail, the calendar, contacts, or an automated attendant.
- **Secure Socket Tunneling Protocol Service**   Provides support for Secure Socket Tunneling Protocol (SSTP) for securely connecting to remote computers.
- **Web Management Service**   Enables remote and delegated management for the web server, sites, and applications.
- **Windows Remote Management**   Implements the WS-Management protocol. Required for remote management using the Exchange console and Windows PowerShell.
- **World Wide Web Publishing Service**   Provides web connectivity and administration features for IIS.

Exchange Server Authentication and Security

In Exchange Server 2016, email addresses, distribution groups, and other directory resources are stored in the directory database provided by Active Directory. Active Directory is a directory service running on Windows domain controllers. When there are multiple domain controllers, the controllers automatically replicate directory data with each other using a multimaster replication model. This model allows any domain controller to process directory changes and then replicate those changes to other domain controllers.

The first time you install Exchange Server 2016 in a Windows domain, the installation process updates and extends Active Directory to include objects and attributes used by Exchange Server 2016. Unlike earlier releases of Exchange Server, you do not use Active Directory Users And Computers to manage mailboxes, messaging features, messaging options, or email addresses associated with user accounts. You perform these tasks using the Exchange Management tools.

Exchange Server 2016 fully supports the Windows Server security model and by default relies on this security mechanism to control access to directory resources. This means you can control access to mailboxes and membership in distribution groups and you can perform other Exchange security administration tasks through the standard Windows Server permission set. For example, to add a user to a distribution group, you simply make the user a member of the distribution group in Active Directory Users And Computers.

Because Exchange Server uses Windows Server security, you can't create a mailbox without first creating a user account that will use the mailbox. Every Exchange mailbox must be associated with a domain account—even those used by Exchange for general messaging tasks. In the Exchange Admin Center, you can create a new user account as part of the process of creating a new mailbox.

You manage Exchange servers according to their roles and the type of information you want to manage using the Exchange Admin Center. You'll learn more about this in Chapter 4, "Exchange 2016 Administration Essentials."

Exchange Server Security Groups

Exchange Server 2016 uses predefined universal security groups to separate administration of Exchange permissions from administration of other permissions. When you add an administrator to one of these security groups, the administrator inherits the permissions permitted by that role.

The predefined security groups have permissions to manage the following types of Exchange data in Active Directory:

- **Organization configuration data** This type of data is not associated with a specific server and is used to manage databases, policies, address lists, and other types of organizational configuration details.

- **Server configuration data** This type of data is associated with a specific server and is used to manage the server's messaging configuration.
- **Recipient configuration data** This type of data is associated with mailboxes, mail-enabled contacts, and distribution groups.

The predefined groups are as follows:

- **Compliance Management** Members of this group have permission to configure compliance settings.
- **Delegated Setup** Members of this group have permission to install and uninstall Exchange on provisioned servers.
- **Discovery Management** Members of this group can perform mailbox searches for data that meets specific criteria.
- **Exchange Servers** Members of this group are Exchange servers in the organization. This group allows Exchange servers to work together.
- **Exchange Trusted Subsystem** Members of this group are Exchange servers that run Exchange cmdlets using WinRM. Members of this group have permission to read and modify all Exchange configuration settings as well as user accounts and groups.
- **Exchange Windows Permissions** Members of this group are Exchange servers that run Exchange cmdlets using WinRM. Members of this group have permission to read and modify user accounts and groups.
- **Help Desk** Members of this group can view any property or object within the Exchange organization and have limited management permissions, including the right to change and reset passwords.
- **Hygiene Management** Members of this group can manage the anti-spam and antivirus features of Exchange.
- **Managed Availability Servers** Every Exchange 2016 server is a member of this group. Managed availability is an internal process that provides native health monitoring and recovery for protocol processes to ensure availability of Exchange services. For more information, see Chapter 6, "Implementing Availability Groups."
- **Organization Management** Members of this group have full access to all Exchange properties and objects in the Exchange organization.
- **Public Folder Management** Members of this group can manage public folders and perform most public folder management operations.
- **Recipient Management** Members of this group have permissions to modify Exchange user attributes in Active Directory and perform most mailbox operations.
- **Records Management** Members of this group can manage compliance features, including retention policies, message classifications, and transport rules.
- **Server Management** Members of this group can manage all Exchange servers in the organization but do not have permission to perform global operations.

- **UM Management**   Members of this group can manage all aspects of unified messaging, including unified messaging server configuration and unified messaging recipient configuration.
- **View-Only Organization Management**   Members of this group have read-only access to the entire Exchange organization tree in the Active Directory configuration container and read-only access to all the Windows domain containers that have Exchange recipients.

Using Exchange 2016 with Active Directory

Exchange Server 2016 is tightly integrated with Active Directory. Not only does Exchange Server 2016 store information in Active Directory, but it also uses the Active Directory routing topology to determine how to route messages within the organization. Routing to and from the organization is handled using transport servers.

Understanding How Exchange Stores Information

Exchange stores four types of data in Active Directory: schema data (stored in the Schema partition), configuration data (stored in the Configuration partition), domain data (stored in the Domain partition), and application data (stored in application-specific partitions). In Active Directory, schema rules determine what types of objects are available and what attributes those objects have. When you install the first Exchange server in the forest, the Active Directory preparation process adds many Exchange-specific object classes and attributes to the schema partition in Active Directory. This allows Exchange-specific objects, such as agents and connectors, to be created. It also allows you to extend existing objects, such as users and groups, with new attributes, such as attributes that allow user objects to be used for sending and receiving email. Every domain controller and global catalog server in the organization has a complete copy of the Schema partition.

During the installation of the first Exchange server in the forest, Exchange configuration information is generated and stored in Active Directory. Exchange configuration information, like other configuration information, is also stored in the Configuration partition. For Active Directory, the configuration information describes the structure of the directory, and the Configuration container includes all of the domains, trees, and forests, as well as the locations of domain controllers and global catalogs. For Exchange, the configuration information is used to describe the structure of the Exchange organization. The Configuration container includes lists of templates, policies, and other global organization-level details. Every domain controller and global catalog server in the organization has a complete copy of the Configuration partition.

In Active Directory, the Domain partition stores domain-specific objects, such as users and groups, and the stored values of attributes associated with those objects. As you create, modify, or delete objects, Exchange stores the details about those objects in the Domain partition. During the installation of the first Exchange server in the forest, Exchange objects are created in the current domain. Whenever you create new recipients or modify Exchange details, the related changes are reflected in the Domain partition as well. Every domain controller has a complete copy of the Domain partition for the domain for which it is authoritative. Every global catalog server in the forest maintains information about a subset of every Domain partition in the forest.

Understanding How Exchange Routes Messages

Within the organization, the Transport service on Mailbox servers use the information about sites stored in Active Directory to determine how to route messages, and they can also route messages across site links. These servers do this by querying Active Directory about its site membership and the site membership of other servers, and then using the information they discover to route messages appropriately. Because of this, when you are deploying an Exchange Server 2016 organization, no additional configuration is required to establish routing in the Active Directory forest.

For mail delivery within the organization, additional routing configuration is necessary only in these specific scenarios:

- If you deploy an Exchange Server 2016 organization with multiple forests, you must install Exchange Server 2016 in each forest and then connect the forests using appropriate cross-forest trusts. The trust allows users to see address and availability data across the forests.
- In an Exchange Server 2016 organization, if you want direct mail flow between Exchange servers in different forests, you must configure SMTP send connectors and SMTP receive connectors on the Mailbox servers that should communicate directly with each other.

You can use two types of Mail Transport servers: Mailbox servers and Edge Transport servers. You deploy Mailbox servers within the organization. The Transport service on Mailbox servers handles mail delivery and receipt of mail. Two services are used to deliver mail items to, and receive mail items from, other servers:

- **Microsoft Exchange Mailbox Transport Delivery service**   Handles inbound mail items. After receiving mail items for delivery to a mailbox on the current server, the service submits the mail items for processing and then delivers them into the appropriate mailbox database on the server.
- **Microsoft Exchange Mailbox Transport Submission service**   Handles outbound mail items. After receiving mail items for submission, the service ensures messages are converted from MAPI to MIME and then passes them along to the Transport service. The Transport service then routes the mail items for delivery.

With Mailbox servers as your transports, no other special configuration is needed for message routing to external destinations. You must configure only the standard mail setup, which includes identifying DNS servers to use for lookups. With Edge Transport servers, you can optimize mail routing and delivery by configuring one-way synchronization from the internal Mailbox servers to the perimeter network's Edge Transport servers. Beyond this, no other special configuration is required for mail routing and delivery.

You deploy Edge Transport servers in the organization's perimeter network for added security. Typically, a perimeter network is a secure network set up outside the organization's private network. When you have Edge Transport servers, mail items from outside the organization are received first by the Edge transport servers, which can perform anti-malware and anti-spam checks before passing along mail items to internal Mailbox servers for delivery. Mail items for submission outside the organization are passed from internal Mailbox servers to Edge Transport servers which then submit the mail items for delivery outside the organization.

Working with Exchange Online and Office 365

Exchange Online is a cloud-based service from Microsoft that allows you to implement an online or hybrid implementation of Exchange. Although Exchange Online can be your only solution for all your enterprise messaging needs, a hybrid implementation gives you an integrated online and on-premises solution.

You can get Exchange Online as a standalone service or as part of an Office 365 plan. Currently, Microsoft offers several Exchange Online plans, including a basic plan and an advanced plan. The key differences between the basic and advanced plan are the inclusion of in-place hold and data loss prevention options that may be needed to meet compliance and regulatory requirements. Both plans support Active Directory integration for single sign-on, synchronization with your on-premises Active Directory infrastructure, and creation of hybrid Exchange organizations.

Microsoft offers a variety of Office 365 plans. Some of these plans include access to Office Web Apps, the full desktop versions of Office, or both, as well as access to Exchange Online. You'll likely want to use an Office 365 midsize business or enterprise plan. These plans include Active Directory integration, which is required if you want to create a hybrid Exchange organization.

Using the Exchange Administration Tools

Exchange Server 2016 includes several types of tools for administration. Exchange Admin Center is the administration tool you'll use the most. Also available are Office Admin Center and Exchange Toolbox.

The Exchange Admin Center, shown in Figure 1-1, replaces Exchange Management Console, which was used in early releases of Exchange Server. Although Exchange Management Console was implemented using Microsoft Management Console (MMC), Exchange Admin Center is web-based and you'll use this console for managing on-premises, online, and hybrid deployments of Exchange 2016.

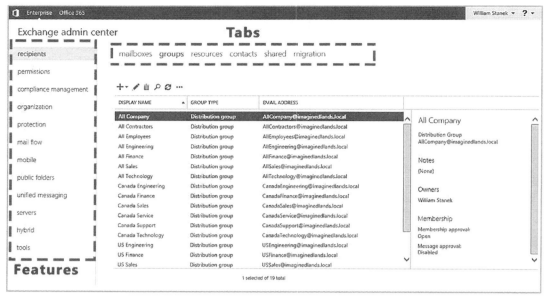

FIGURE 1-1 Exchange Admin Center features and tabs.

The navigation bar at the top of the window has several important options (see Figure 1-2). You use the Enterprise and Office 365 options for cross-premises navigation.

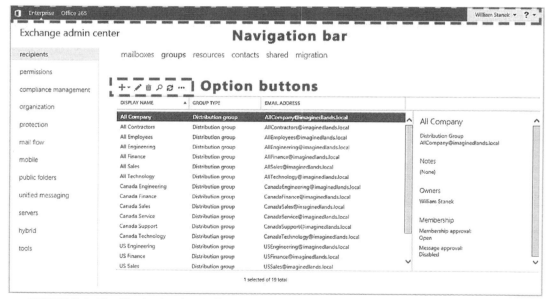

FIGURE 1-2 The Navigation bar in Exchange Admin Center.

When there are notifications, you'll also see a Notification icon on the Navigation bar. Notifications include alerts regarding automated or batch processes and other important information Exchange needs to notify you about. The User button shows the currently logged on user. Clicking the User button allows you to logout or sign in as another user.

A number of Option buttons are displayed under the tabs, including:

New – Allows you to create a new item.

Edit – Allows you to edit a selected item.

Delete – Deletes a selected item.

Search – Performs a search within the current context.

Refresh – Refreshes the display so you can see changes.

More – If available, displays additional options.

When working with recipients, such as mailboxes or groups, you can click the More button (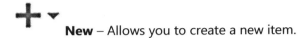) to display additional options that allow you to:

- Add or remove columns
- Export data for the listed recipients to a .csv file
- Perform advanced searches

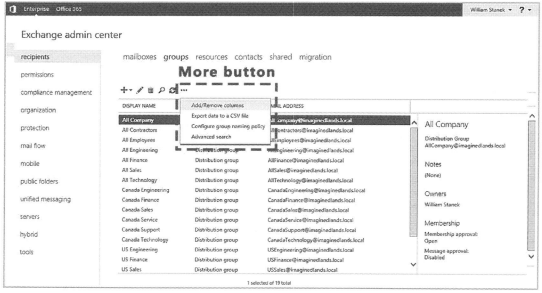

FIGURE 1-3 The More button in Exchange Admin Center.

Customize the view by adding or removing columns. These settings are then saved for the computer that you are using to access Exchange Admin Center. However, because the settings are stored as browser cookies, clearing the browser history will remove any custom settings.

When working with recipients, you typically can select multiple items and perform bulk editing as long as you select like items, such as mailbox users or mail-enabled contacts. Select multiple items using the Shift or Ctrl key and then use bulk editing options in the Details pane to bulk edit the selected items.

Exchange Admin Center runs as a web application on Mailbox servers providing services for the Exchange organization. It is installed automatically when you deploy a Mailbox server. To manage Exchange installations from just about anywhere, you simply need to enter the Uniform Resource Locator (URL) path for the application in your browser's Address field. For on-premises installations, the default internal URL for Exchange Admin Center is *https://MailboxServerName/ecp* and the external URL is *https://yourserver.yourdomain.com/ecp*. For example, if your Mailbox server is named MailServerC, you'd enter https://mailserverc/ecp as the URL for internal access.

When you are accessing an on-premises installation from within your organization (and behind your organization's firewall), you use the internal URL. When you are accessing an on-premises installation outside your organization, you use the external URL. As discussed in Chapter 4, there are many ways to configure access to this app. You can change the default URL, restrict access to the internal URL only, and more.

> **TIP**   If you deploy multiple versions of Exchange Server in the same organization, the version of the web applications you see depends on where your personal mailbox is hosted. When your mailbox is hosted on Exchange 2016, you see the Exchange 2016 version of the applications. When your mailbox is hosted on another version, you see the web applications for that version.
>
> To ensure you always access a particular version of the web applications, add the Exchange version to the access URL. Exchange 2016 is Exchange version 15.1 and Exchange 2103 is Exchange version 15.0. Because both Exchange 2016 and Exchange 2013 have the same major version number, 15, you append **?ExchClientVer=15** to the internal or external URL to access the Exchange version 15 web application. For example, you'd enter the URL as **https://mail.tvpress.com/ecp?ExchClientVer=15** if your external URL is https://mail.tvpress.com.
>
> If your personal mailbox is on Exchange 2016 or Exchange 2013 and you want to access the Exchange Control Panel for Exchange 2010, you can do this as well. Simply, enter the client version as 14 rather than 15, as shown in this example: https://mail.imaginedlands.com/ecp?ExchClientVer=14.

You manage Exchange Online using the cross-premises management options in Exchange Admin Center. With an online or hybrid installation, you'll also be provided an access URL for Office Admin Center, such as *https://portal.microsoftonline.com/admin/default.aspx*. After you log in, you'll see the Office Admin Center dashboard, shown in Figure 1-4.

FIGURE 1-4 The Office Admin Center.

From the Office Admin Center dashboard, you have full access to Exchange Online and Office 365 and can manage the related service-level settings. You'll have options for configuring the Office tenant domain, managing subscriptions and licensing, viewing service health, getting Exchange usage reports, and more. See Chapter 2, "Working with Exchange Online," in *Exchange Server 2016 & Exchange Online: Essentials for Administration* for complete details on working with Exchange Online and Office Admin Center.

The Exchange Toolbox is the only remaining MMC-based console. The Toolbox, shown in Figure 1-5, provides access to a suite of related management tools, including:

- **Details Templates Editor**   Helps administrators customize client-side GUI presentation of object properties accessed through address lists. You can use this tool to customize the presentation of contacts, users, groups, public folders, and more in the client interface.
- **Remote Connectivity Analyzer**   Allows administrators to perform connectivity tests for inbound email, ActiveSync, Exchange Web Services, Outlook Anywhere, and MAPI over HTTP.
- **Queue Viewer**   Allows administrators to track message queues and mail flow. Also allows administrators to manage message queuing and remove messages.

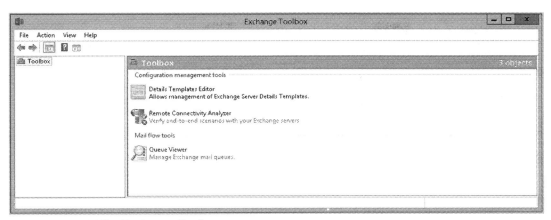

FIGURE 1-5 The Exchange Toolbox.

On any computer where you've installed the Exchange management tools, you can access the Exchange Toolbox from Start. Whether you are working with the Start menu or the Start screen, you can pin the Exchange Toolbox to the desktop taskbar by right-clicking the related icon and then selecting Pin To Taskbar.

Other tools that you might want to use with Exchange Server include:

- **DNS console**   Manages the DNS service.
- **Event Viewer**   Manages events and logs.
- **Failover Cluster Management**   The Failover Cluster Management tools and the related command-line interface must be installed on your Exchange 2016 servers. This allows you to use scripts for managing availability groups.
- **IIS Manager**   Manages Web servers used by Exchange as well as the management service configuration.
- **Server Manager**   Provides setup and configuration options for the local server as well as options for managing roles, features and related settings on remote servers.

You access most of these tools from the Tools menu in Server Manager. Server Manager can be started by clicking the Server Manager icon in the taskbar. With Windows Server 2012 and later, you also can start Server Manager by typing **Server Manager** in the Search box and pressing **Enter**.

Using Exchange Management Shell

Although the graphical tools provide just about everything you need to work with Exchange organizations, there are many times when you might want to work from the command line, especially if you want to automate installation, administration, or maintenance with scripts. To help with all your command-line needs, Exchange Server includes Exchange Management Shell.

Exchange Management Shell is an extension shell for Windows PowerShell that includes a wide array of built-in commands for working with Exchange Server. On any computer where you've installed the Exchange management tools, you'll be able to access Exchange Management Shell from Start. Whether you are working with the Start menu or the Start screen, you can pin Exchange Management Shell to the desktop taskbar by right-clicking the related icon and then selecting Pin To Taskbar. Exchange Management Shell is shown in Figure 1-6.

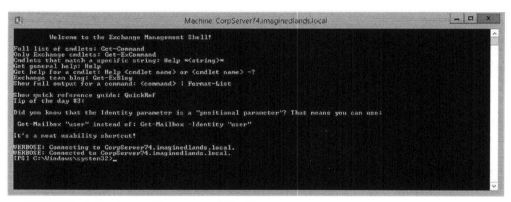

FIGURE 1-6 Exchange Management Shell.

> **REAL WORLD** Exchange Admin Center is a web-based management console that runs as an application on your Mailbox servers. When you install the Mailbox server role for Exchange 2016, the server is configured automatically with a Windows PowerShell gateway that acts as a proxy service. This proxy service allows you to run remote commands in web browsers and in remote sessions. Whenever you work with Exchange Admin Center or Exchange Management Shell, the commands are executed via this proxy—even if you log on locally. Thus, every time you work with Exchange Server, you are using a remote session.
>
> When you log in to the Exchange Admin Center, you are using the Default Web Site running on Internet Information Services (IIS) which processes your actions. Every command you perform in Exchange Admin Center is remotely executed via the Windows PowerShell gateway, as is any command you perform in Exchange Management Shell. Any task you can perform in Exchange Admin Center can be performed in Exchange Management Shell.

Exchange Management Shell is designed to be run only on domain-joined computers. The basics of working with Exchange Management Shell are straightforward:

* Type **get-command** to get a full list of all available cmdlets on the server.
* Type **get-excommand** to get a full list of all Exchange-specific cmdlets available.
* Type **help** *cmdletName* to get help information, where *cmdletName* is the name of the command you are looking up.

> **IMPORTANT** When you are working with Exchange Management Shell, the default recipient scope is set the same as your logon domain. If you are in multi-domain environment and want to work with recipients throughout the Active Directory forest, make sure the Shell session has ViewEntireForest enabled. Enter **Get-ADServerSettings** to view the current Active Directory Server settings. Enter **Set-ADServerSettings -ViewEntireForest $true** to set the recipient scope to the entire forest.

You'll find a comprehensive discussion of Exchange Management Shell in *Exchange Server 2016 & Exchange Online: Essentials for Administration* (Stanek & Associates, 2016). See "Working with Exchange Management Shell" in Chapter 1 and "Using Windows PowerShell with Exchange Online" in Chapter 2. *Essentials for Administration* also has details on troubleshooting and advanced techniques for connecting to Exchange 2016 without installing the management tools or using Exchange Management Shell. See Chapter 11 "Customizing & Troubleshooting the Exchange Shell."

Whenever you remotely manage Exchange services using Powershell, you are relying on the Windows PowerShell remoting features. These features are supported by the WS-Management protocol and the Windows Remote Management (WinRM) service that implements WS-Management in Windows.

Windows Management Framework includes Windows PowerShell and WinRM. Computers running Windows 8 and later, as well as Windows Server 2012 and later, include Windows Management Framework. One way to verify the availability of WinRM services and configure Windows PowerShell for remoting is to follow these steps:

1. Type **PowerShell** in the Search box. Next, right-click the Windows PowerShell shortcut in the search results and select Run As Administrator.

2. The WinRM service is configured for manual startup by default. You must change the startup type to Automatic and start the service on each computer you want to work with. At the PowerShell prompt, you can verify that the WinRM service is running by using the following command:

```
get-service winrm
```

As shown in the following example, the value of the Status property in the output should be Running:

```
Status    Name          DisplayName
------    ----          -----------
Running   WinRM         Windows Remote Management
```

If the service is stopped, enter the following command to start the service and configure it to start automatically in the future:

```
set-service -name winrm -startuptype automatic -status running
```

3. To configure Windows PowerShell for remoting, type the following command:

```
Enable-PSRemoting -force
```

Exchange 2016 is designed to be remotely managed from domain-joined computers. If your computer is connected to a public network, you need to disconnect from the public network, connect to a domain, and then repeat this step. If one or more of your computer's connections has the Public connection type, but you are actually connected to a domain network, you need to change the network connection type in Network And Sharing Center and then repeat this step.

In many cases, you will be able to work with remote computers in other domains. However, if the remote computer is not in a trusted domain, the remote computer might not be able to authenticate your credentials. To enable authentication, you need to add the remote computer to the list of trusted hosts for the local computer in WinRM. To do so, type the following:

```
winrm s winrm/config/client '@{TrustedHosts="RemoteComputer"}'
```

where *RemoteComputer* is the name of the remote computer, such as:

```
winrm s winrm/config/client '@{TrustedHosts="MailServer12"}'
```

If you cannot connect to a remote host, verify that the service on the remote host is running and is accepting requests by running the following command on the remote host:

```
winrm quickconfig
```

This command analyzes and configures the WinRM service. If the WinRM service is set up correctly, you'll see output similar to the following:

```
WinRM already is set up to receive requests on this machine.
WinRM already is set up for remote management on this machine
```

If the WinRM service is not set up correctly, you'll see errors and need to respond affirmatively to several prompts that allow you to automatically configure remote management. When this process completes, WinRM should be set up correctly.

Whenever you use Windows PowerShell remoting features, you must start Windows PowerShell as an administrator by right-clicking the Windows PowerShell shortcut and selecting Run As Administrator. When starting Windows PowerShell from another program, such as the command prompt (cmd.exe), you must start that program as an administrator.

Chapter 2. Preparing for Exchange 2016

Exchange organizations can be deployed in several configurations, including on-premises, online and hybrid implementations. With an on-premises implementation you deploy Exchange server hardware on your network and manage all aspects of the implementation, including server configuration, organization configuration, and recipient configuration. Administrators manage Exchange using Exchange Admin Center and Exchange Management Shell. Users access Exchange using Outlook Web App and a URL provided by your organization or with Microsoft Outlook.

With an online implementation you rely on hardware and services provided by Microsoft. Here, you subscribe to Exchange Online, manage service-level settings using Office 365 Admin Center, and manage the organization and recipient configuration using Exchange Admin Center. Users access Exchange using Outlook Web App and a URL provided by Microsoft or with Microsoft Outlook.

With a hybrid implementation you integrate on-premises and online components. Here, the on-premises and Exchange Online organizations have a shared domain namespace, and mail is securely routed between them. These organizations share a unified global address list, free/busy data, and calendar data. Administrators manage Exchange using a combination of the on-premises and online tools. Users can access Exchange using Outlook Web App and the same URL whether their mailbox is stored on premises or online. Users also can access Exchange using Microsoft Outlook.

When you use an online implementation, Microsoft manages the hardware configuration and ensures availability. Otherwise, you are responsible for any on-premises hardware. Before you deploy an on-premises or hybrid implementation of Exchange 2016, you should carefully plan the messaging architecture. Every Exchange implementation has three layers in its architecture network, directory and messaging.

The network layer provides the foundation for computer-to-computer communications and essential name resolution features. The network layer has both physical and logical components. The physical components include the IP addresses, the IP subnets, local area network (LAN) or wide area network (WAN) links used by messaging systems as well as the routers that connect these links, and firewalls that protect the infrastructure. The logical components are the Domain Name System

(DNS) zones that define the naming boundaries and contain the essential resource records required for name resolution.

The directory layer provides the foundation necessary for authentication, authorization, and replication. The directory layer is built on the Active Directory directory service and has both physical and logical components. The physical components include the domain controllers, Global Catalog servers, and site links used for authentication, authorization, and replication. The logical components include the Active Directory forests, sites, domains, and organizational units that are used to group objects for resource sharing, centralized management, and replication control. The logical components also include the users and groups that are part of the Active Directory infrastructure.

The messaging layer provides the foundation for messaging and collaboration. The messaging layer has both physical and logical components. The physical components include individual Exchange servers that determine how messages are delivered and mail connectors that determine how messages are routed outside an Exchange server's routing boundaries. The logical components specify the organizational boundaries for messaging, mailboxes used for storing messages, public folders used for storing data, and distribution lists used for distributing messages to multiple recipients.

Whether you are deploying Exchange Server for the first time in your organization or upgrading to Exchange Server 2016 from an earlier release of Exchange Server, you need to closely review each layer of this architecture and plan for required changes. As part of your implementation planning, you also need to look closely at the roles your Exchange servers will perform and modify the hardware accordingly to meet the requirements of these roles on a per-server basis. Exchange Server is a complex messaging platform with many components that work together to provide a comprehensive solution for routing, delivering, and accessing email messages, voice-mail messages, faxes, contacts, and calendar information.

Designing the Exchange Server Organization

With Exchange Server Setup, you can deploy servers with the Mailbox or Edge Transport role. Prior to setup and configuration, you need to decide how you will use Exchange Server 2016, what roles you will deploy, and where you will locate those roles. Afterward, you can plan for your deployment and then roll out Exchange Server 2016.

As part of your planning and testing, you can use the Exchange Server Deployment Assistant and the Exchange Remote Connectivity Analyzer. Both are web-based tools that provide step by step guidance. The Deployment Assistant, which can help you plan on-line, on-premises and hybrid deployments, is available at http://go.microsoft.com/fwlink/p/?LinkId=277105 and the Connectivity Analyzer, which can help you diagnose connectivity issues, is available at https://testexchangeconnectivity.com.

On-premises implementations of Exchange Server have three layers in their architecture: a network layer, directory layer, and messaging layer. The messaging layer is where you define and deploy the Exchange Server roles. The Exchange servers at the core of the messaging layer can operate in the following roles:

* **Mailbox Server**   A primary mail server that hosts mailboxes, public folders, and related messaging data, such as address lists, resource scheduling, and meeting items. Mailbox servers accept connections to Exchange Server from a variety of clients and hosts the protocols used by all clients when checking messages. On the local network, Outlook MAPI clients are connected directly to the Mailbox server to check mail using SMTP. Remote users can check their mail over the Internet by using Outlook Anywhere, Outlook Web App, Exchange ActiveSync, POP3, or IMAP4.
* **Edge Transport Server**   An additional mail routing server that routes mail into and out of the Exchange organization. This server is designed to be deployed in an organization's perimeter network and is used to establish a secure boundary between the organization and the Internet. This server accepts mail coming into the organization from the Internet and from trusted servers in external organizations, processes the mail to protect against some types of spam messages and viruses, and routes all accepted messages to a Mailbox server inside the organization.

Exchange 2016 Mailbox servers also host:

* **Client Access services**   Middle-tier services that accept connections to Exchange Server from a variety of clients. These services host the protocols used by all clients when checking messages. On the local network, Outlook MAPI clients are connected directly to the server to check mail using SMTP. Remote users can check their mail over the Internet by using MAPI over HTTP, RPC over HTTP, Outlook Web App, Exchange ActiveSync, POP3, or IMAP4.

- **Unified Messaging services**   Middle-tier services that integrate a private branch exchange (PBX) system with Exchange Server 2016, allowing voice messages and faxes to be stored with email in a user's mailbox. Unified messaging supports call answering with automated greetings and message recording, fax receiving, and dial-in access. With dial-in access, users can use Outlook Voice Access to check voice mail, email, and calendar information; to review or dial contacts; and to configure preferences and personal options. To receive faxes, you need an integrated solution from a Microsoft partner.
- **Transport services**   Mail routing services that handle mail flow, routing, and delivery within the Exchange organization. These services process all mail that is sent inside the organization before it is delivered to a mailbox in the organization or routed to users outside the organization. Processing ensures that senders and recipients are resolved and filtered as appropriate, content is filtered and has its format converted if necessary, and attachments are screened. To meet any regulatory or organizational compliance requirements, the Mailbox server can also record, or journal, messages and add disclaimers to them.

The Mailbox and Edge Transport roles are the building blocks of on-premises Exchange organizations. Table 2-1 provides an overview of the basic processor configurations I recommend for these roles. Processors can have multiple cores. Following the configurations shown in the table, I recommend that you build Edge Transport servers for scaling out and Mailbox servers for scaling up.

TABLE 2-1 Recommended Configurations for Exchange Server Roles

SERVER ROLE	MINIMUM PROCESSORS	RECOMMENDED PROCESSORS	BUILD FOR
Edge Transport	1	2-4	Scale out
Mailbox	1-2	2-8	Scale up

One of the most basic Exchange organizations you can create is one that includes a single Exchange server that provides the Mailbox Server role. A server with this role is the minimum required for routing and delivering messages to both local and remote messaging clients. For added security and protection, you can deploy the Edge Transport server role in a perimeter network on one or more separate servers.

Although a basic implementation of Exchange Server might include only one server, you'll likely find investing in multiple servers is more effective in terms of time, money, and resources. Why? High availability is integrated into the core architecture of Exchange Server 2016 and can be easily enabled.

With the Mailbox Server role, you can configure automatic failover by making the Mailbox servers members of the same database availability group. Each Mailbox server in the group can then have a copy of the mailbox databases from the other Mailbox servers in the group. Each mailbox database can have up to 16 copies, and this means you can have up to 16 Mailbox servers in a database availability group as well.

Planning for High Availability

The underlying functionality of a Mailbox server is similar to that of a database server. Every mailbox-enabled recipient defined in the organization has a mailbox that is used to store messaging data. Groups of related mailboxes are organized using databases, and each database can have one or more database copies associated with it.

With early releases of Exchange, you needed dedicated hardware for clustered Mailbox servers, those servers could not run other roles, and failover occurred at the server level. Microsoft engineered Exchange 2016 to provide continuous availability without the need for dedicated hardware for clustering. Microsoft did this by:

- Integrating key components of Windows clustering into Exchange Server and adding components that allow Exchange Server to automatically manage the clustering functions.
- Integrating key features of Cluster Continuous Replication (CCR) and Standby Continuous Replication (SCR) into Exchange Server and making related features available through database availability groups.

Using the built-in clustering features, you can create a fully redundant Exchange organization using only two Mailbox servers, with each server configured as part of the same database availability group. You would also need a witness server for the database availability group, which doesn't have to be an Exchange server.

The underlying technology built into database availability groups is the key ingredient that makes high availability possible. The related framework ensures failover clustering occurs in the background and doesn't normally require administrator intervention. As a result, Exchange Server 2016 doesn't need, or use, a cluster resource dynamic-link library (DLL) and uses only a small portion of the Windows clustering components, including heartbeat capabilities and a cluster database.

Database availability groups use continuous replication to achieve high availability. With continuous replication, Exchange Server 2016 uses its built-in asynchronous replication technology to create copies of mailbox databases and then keeps the copies up to date using transaction log shipping and replay. Lagged copies can automatically play down log files to automatically recover from certain types of issues. For example, if Exchange detects that a low disk space threshold has been reached, Exchange automatically replays the logs into the lagged copy to play down the log files. If Exchange detects that page patching is required, Exchange automatically replays the logs into the lagged copy to perform page patching. If Exchange detects that there are fewer than three available healthy copies (whether active or passive) for more than 24 hours, Exchange automatically replays the logs into the lagged copy to play down the log files.

Any server in a group can host a copy of a mailbox database from any other server in the group. When a server is added to a group, it works with other servers in the group to provide automatic recovery from failures that affect mailbox databases, including server failure, database corruption, disk failure, and network connectivity failure. Although Exchange 2010 used a scheduled script to alert you that only a single copy of a database was available, this functionality is now integrated into the core architecture along with other managed availability features for internal monitoring and recovery.

When you create a database availability group, Exchange adds an object to Active Directory representing the group. This object stores information about the group, including details about servers that are members of the group. When you add the first server to the group, a failover cluster is created automatically and the heartbeat is initiated. As you add member servers to the group, the heartbeat components and the cluster database are used to track and manage information about the group and its member servers, including server status, database mount status, replication status, and mount location.

Placement and sizing of availability groups is something you should also consider. Focus on whether you need to use a site resilient plan with a datacenter pair as part of your design. Large enterprises that want to achieve high availability and site resiliency will want to deploy an availability group in each of at least two datacenters that are well-connected (meaning you have low, round-trip latency across the network connecting the datacenters).

Generally, you'll want to deploy a single availability group that stretches across the datacenters and scale the number of servers in the group as appropriate. For example, with two datacenters, you deploy two servers in each datacenter and make each server a member of the same availability group. This availability group then has four member servers and you can add servers to each location as the needs of your organization grows.

Although Active Directory sites can stretch across multiple datacenters, you'll usually want each datacenter to have its own Active Directory site. Having servers in different Active Directory sites is required for transport site resilience anyway. Why? Exchange 2016 achieves site resilience using Shadow Redundancy and Safety Net, which both require more than one Active Directory site to achieve transport site resilience. Shadow redundancy ensures that messages are protected from loss the entire time they are in transit by creating a copy of a message and retaining this copy while a message is in transit. Safety Net maintains a queue of messages that were recently delivered to recipients.

Planning Exchange Databases and Storage

Because Exchange databases are represented at the organization level, they are effectively disconnected from the servers on which they are stored, which makes it easier to move databases from one server to another. However, it also means you can work with databases in ways that were not possible with early releases of Exchange and that there are also several requirements when working with databases. Keep the following in mind when working with databases in Exchange Server 2016:

- Database names must be unique throughout your Exchange organization. This means you cannot name two databases identically even if they are on two different Mailbox servers.

- Every mailbox database, except copies, have a different globally unique identifier (GUID). Copies of a database have the same GUID as the original database.
- Mailbox servers that are part of the same database availability group do not require cluster-managed shared storage. However, the full paths for all database copies must be identical on host Mailbox servers.

> **NOTE** Exchange no longer supports public folder databases. Beginning with Exchange 2013, public folder data was moved into specially configured mailboxes that the public folder hierarchy and content. Like traditional mailboxes, these special mailboxes for public folders are stored in mailbox databases and are replicated as part of any database availability group you configure.

For a successful deployment of a Mailbox server, the storage subsystem must meet the storage capacity requirements and must be able to perform the expected number of input/output (I/O) operations per second. Storage capacity requirements are determined by the number of mailboxes hosted on a server and the total storage size allowed per mailbox. For example, if a server hosts 2,500 mailboxes that you allow to store up to 2 gigabytes (GB) each, you need to ensure the storage system capacity can be scaled up to support this.

I/O performance of the storage subsystem is measured in relation to the latency (delay) for each read/write operation to be performed. The more mailboxes you store on a specific drive or drive array, the more read/write operations there are performed and the greater the potential delay. To improve performance, you can use multiple mailbox databases on separate disks. You might also want to store databases with their transaction log files on separate disk drives, such that database A and related logs are on disk 1, database B and related logs are on disk 2, and so on. In some scenarios, you might want the databases and logs to be on separate disks.

Exchange 2016 supports either NTFS or ReFS for partitions containing databases, content indexes and transaction logs. The on-disk storage engine for ReFS is very different from the on-disk storage engine for NTFS. ReFS uses B+ tree structures to represent all information on a disk. B+ tree structures scale well and simplify the architecture. ReFS has many other enhancements over NTFS, including improved reliability and failure recovery. Although ReFS is designed to be used with Storage Spaces, you don't have to use Storage Spaces to gain many of the benefits of this enhanced architecture.

I/O performance in Exchange Server 2016 running on 64-bit architecture is improved substantially over 32-bit architecture. On Mailbox servers, a 64-bit architecture enables a database cache size of up to approximately 90 percent of total random access memory (RAM). A larger cache increases the probability that data requested by a client will be serviced out of memory instead of by the storage subsystem.

Because Exchange 2016 allows a server to host multiple databases on the same volume, you don't need separate volumes for each database copy. As part of your planning, look closely at the input/output per second (IOPS) capabilities of your storage architecture and place database copies appropriately. Because active copies will use more IOPS than passive copies, you'll typically want no more than one active database copy on a volume while allowing multiple passive copies. For example, if you're configuring a four-server database availability group, you could configure storage so that each server has a primary storage volume for the active database copy and passive copies of the databases from the other servers.

As part of the preferred architecture, Microsoft recommends that active database copies are distributed equally across the availability group. This configuration helps to ensure that the workload is distributed across all servers and that the full stack of client connectivity, transport and replication services are being validated during normal operations.

Exchange 2016 is optimized so that servers can use large disks with 2 to 8 terabytes of storage efficiently. With very large volumes like these, you'll want to consider using ReFS rather than NTFS. ReFS uses 128-bit file identifiers which support a larger number of files and directories, and hierarchical allocators which can optimally allocate storage more quickly than NTFS.

If you use ReFS with Exchange Server, you'll also want to:

- Ensure the integrity feature is disabled. Use the Get-FileIntegrity cmdlet to check the status of the integrity feature and the Set-FileIntegrity cmdlet to change the status of the integrity feature.
- Ensure Mailbox servers configured in availability groups are configured so that the auto reseed feature formats disks with ReFS. Use the command Set-DatabaseAvailabilityGroup *DagName* -FileSystem ReFS, where *DagName* is the name of the availability group.

As part of your planning, you also need to understand how Exchange 2016 uses automatic reseed to recover from disk failure, database corruption events, and other issues that require a reseed of a database copy. With automatic reseed, Exchange can automatically restore database redundancy using spare disks that have been pre-provisioned.

The larger the database, the longer it takes Exchange to reseed it. If a database is too large, it can't be reseeded in a reasonable amount of time. With a typical reseed rate of 20 MB per second, it would take Exchange:

- About 28 hours to reseed a 2-terabyte database.
- About 42 hours to reseed a 3-terabyte database.
- About 56 hours to reseed a 4-terabyte database.

Because of this, the total reseed time may be the most important limiting factor for sizing databases. When configuring disks, at least one disk should be reserved as a hot spare to allow auto reseed to restore database redundancy. In the event of a disk failure, auto reseed activates the hot spare and initiates a database copy to reseed the database.

Planning for Client Access

As part of the architecture changes for Exchange 2016, Mailbox servers handle all of the client-related messaging tasks in an Exchange implementation. This means that not only do Mailbox servers perform all mail processing and content conversion, but they also perform authentication, proxying and redirection of client connections as appropriate.

Clients don't connect directly to back-end services on Mailbox servers. In a basic configuration, clients connect to Client Access services running on a Mailbox server and then are routed via local or remote proxy to the back-end endpoint on the Mailbox server that hosts the active copy of the mailbox database storing the user's mailbox. More typically, clients connect to your Exchange organization using the load-balanced virtual IP address of the protocol being used, which involves a series of steps:

1. After the client resolves the namespace to a load-balanced virtual IP address, the load balancer assigns the session to a Mailbox server in the load-balanced server pool.

2. Client Access services running on the Mailbox server authenticate the request and perform a service discovery by accessing Active Directory to identify the Mailbox version and location details.

3. After Client Access services running on the Mailbox server locate the user's mailbox and the active copy of the associated mailbox database, the server either proxies the request or redirects the request to the appropriate Mailbox server within the same forest.

When you are configuring Exchange 2016, you need to determine the client protocols that you want to implement. Exchange Server 2016 allows local access using Microsoft Outlook with Simple Mail Transfer Protocol (SMTP) and remote access using MAPI over HTTP, Outlook Anywhere (RPC over HTTP), Outlook Web App, and Exchange ActiveSync.

Internet Message Access Protocol 4 (IMAP4) and Post Office Protocol 3 (POP3) are available as alternatives to standard protocols. IMAP4 is a protocol for reading mail and accessing public and private folders on remote servers. POP3 is a protocol for retrieving mail from remote servers. Client Access servers provide access to free/busy data by using the Availability service, and they enable clients to download automatic configuration settings from the Autodiscover service.

Each client protocol that you want Exchange to support requires a namespace configuration. For example:

- For autodiscover: autodiscover.tvpress.com
- For HTTP clients: mail.tvpress.com
- For IMAP clients: imap.tvpress.com
- For POP3 clients: pop3.tvpress.com
- For SMTP clients: smtp.tvpress.com

Thus, you will need to configure each of these namespaces as appropriate for your organization. When you are operating Exchange out of two or more datacenters, namespaces can be said to be either:

- **Bound**   With bound namespaces, users are associated with a specific datacenter and there typically are multiple namespaces: a primary and a failback namespace which generally correspond to the primary datacenter and a secondary datacenter used only during failure events. Here, when the organization has a datacenter pair, there typically are separate database availability groups operating in each datacenter with each group containing a set of mailboxes for that datacenter.

- **Unbound** With unbound namespaces, users are not associated with a specific datacenter and there is a single namespace, allowing user requests to be serviced out of any available datacenter. Here, when the organization has a datacenter pair, there typically is a single database availability group with member servers operating in each datacenter.

With unbound namespaces, you deploy a unified namespace and the virtual IP address assigned to the namespace is load balanced to distribute the workload between datacenters. In contrast, with a bound namespace, you deploy a dedicated namespace for each datacenter. Generally, unbound namespaces are preferred to bound namespaces as any available datacenter can service user requests. If you have multiple datacenters and use an unbound model, you can load balance across the datacenters using a layer 7 configuration without session affinity. Session affinity isn't required because sessions are maintained directly with the Mailbox server hosting the active copy of the mailbox database storing the user's mailbox.

Exchange 2016 uses the Active Directory infrastructure to determine its site membership and the site membership of other servers. The Microsoft Exchange Active Directory Topology service running on an Exchange server is responsible for updating the site attribute of an Exchange server in the directory.

Once a server determines its site membership, the server identifies which domain controllers and global catalogs to use for processing Active Directory queries. Because this information is available in the directory, Exchange servers don't need to use DNS to resolve a server address to a subnet associated with an Active Directory site.

Exchange 2016 Mailbox servers interact directly with Outlook clients and Active Directory. Mailbox servers use Lightweight Directory Access Protocol (LDAP) to obtain recipient, server, and organization configuration information from Active Directory. Mailbox servers accept client connections over the local network and over the Internet, returning data to clients as appropriate, including online address book files, free/busy data, calendar schedules, and client profile settings.

Some clients use POP3 or IMAP4 connections to communicate with the Exchange server. Other clients use SMTP, POP3, or IMAP4 to communicate with the Exchange server. The IIS server host running on each Mailbox server manages the web applications for Outlook Web App, Exchange Active Sync, Exchange Admin Center, and PowerShell.

Outlook clients on the corporate network access the Mailbox server to send and retrieve messages. Outlook clients outside the corporate network can use Outlook Anywhere (RPC over HTTP) or MAPI over HTTP to access Mailbox servers. Regardless of whether they are on or outside the corporate network, Outlook clients access public folder data using either RPC over HTTP or MAPI over HTTP. To retrieve a user's Active Directory information, Mailbox servers use LDAP or Name Service Provider Interface (NSPI). By default, communications with domain controllers and global catalogs are encrypted.

> **NOTE** RPC connections are made directly to the MAPI RPC connection point on the Mailbox server and the NSPI endpoint on the Mailbox server. For directory information, Outlook communicates with an NSPI endpoint located on the Mailbox server. NSPI communicates with the Active Directory driver, which then communicates with Active Directory.

It's important to point out that Microsoft recommends using a split-brain approach to DNS infrastructure with Exchange. Split-brain DNS enables different IP addresses to be returned for a particular namespace depending on where the clients is located. If the client is on the internal network, internal IP addresses are used. If the client is outside the internal network, external IP addresses are used. Using split-brain DNS also simplifies the configuration of Exchange virtual directories, as you can use the same values for internal and external URLs. If you don't use split-brain DNS, you will need to specify different internal and external URLs.

Planning to Support Transport Services

The Transport services on Mailbox servers and the Edge Transport role perform similar tasks. You use both for messaging routing, and both have a similar set of filters to protect an organization from spam and viruses. The key difference is in where you place servers with these roles. You place a Mailbox server in the internal network and configure it as a member of the organizational domain. If you use a server with the Edge Transport role, you place it in the organization's perimeter network, and you do not configure it as a member of the organizational domain.

Mailbox servers and Edge Transport servers cannot have the SMTP or Network News Transfer Protocol (NNTP) service installed separately. Although you install Edge Transport servers outside the Active Directory forest, the server must have a DNS suffix configured, and you must be able to perform name resolution from the Edge Transport server to any Mailbox servers.

> **TIP**   Transports store all incoming mail in a database file called mail.que until the transport verifies that all of the next hops for that message have been completed. This database has an associated transaction log in which changes are first committed. If you are using an Exchange Server's internal drive(s) for storage in a high-volume environment in which one million or more messages are persisted, you should consider placing the database and the transaction log on separate disks for optimal performance and fault tolerance. With Storage Area Networks (SANs), it might not be immediately apparent whether disks are physically separate. This is because the volumes you see are logical references to a portion of the storage subsystem. In this case, you might be able to use the Storage Manager For SANs console or a similar tool to help you select logical unit numbers (LUNs) that are on physically separate disks.
>
> **MORE INFO**   Transports have many different queues for messages. These queues are all stored in a single Extensible Storage Engine (ESE) database called mail.que. By default, this database is located in %ExchangeInstallPath%\TransportRoles\data\Queue. Thanks to shadow redundancy, the deletion of a message in the database is delayed until the transport verifies that all of the next hops for that message have completed delivery. If any of the next hops fail before reporting back successful delivery, the message is resubmitted for delivery to that next hop.

Both Mailbox servers and Edge Transport servers can perform protocol logging and message tracking. Only Mailbox servers perform content conversion to format messages for recipients. Protocol logging allows you to verify whether a protocol is performing as expected and whether any issues need attention. Because this feature is designed for troubleshooting, it is disabled by default. Message tracking creates logs that track messages sent and received. Incoming mail from the Internet is converted to Summary Transport Neutral Encoding Format (STNEF) prior to being delivered. STNEF messages are always MIME-encoded and always have a Content-Transfer-Encoding value of Binary. Because content conversion is performed in the temp folder, you can improve performance by ensuring that the temp folder is not on the same physical disk as the paging file and operating system.

The transport pipeline used by Exchange 2016 is different from the transport pipeline for Exchange 2010 and has the following key components:

- Front End Transport service
- Transport service
- Mailbox Transport Submission service
- Mailbox Transport Delivery service

The Front End Transport service is a client access service that proxies all inbound and outbound SMTP traffic for Exchange 2016. Mailbox servers also have a separate Transport service, which handles back-end tasks for SMTP mail flow as well as message categorization and message content inspection. The Transport service doesn't communicate directly with mailbox databases. Instead, the Mailbox Transport Submission and Mailbox Transport Delivery services are used to provide separate mail submission and delivery processes.

The basic submission process works like this:

1. The Mailbox Transport Submission service receives SMTP messages from the Transport service on the local Mailbox server or on other Mailbox servers
2. The Mailbox Transport Submission service connects to the local mailbox database.
3. The Mailbox Transport Submission service uses RPC to deliver the message.

The basic delivery process works like this:

1. The Mailbox Transport Delivery service connects to the local mailbox database using RPC to retrieve messages.
2. The Mailbox Transport Delivery service submits messages over SMTP to the Transport service on the local Mailbox server or on other Mailbox servers.
3. The Transport service routes messages using SMTP.

Messages from inside the organization enter the transport pipeline through a Receive connector, from the Mailbox Transport Delivery service, from the Pickup or Replay directories, or from agent submission. Messages from outside the organization enter the transport pipeline through a Receive connector in the Front End Transport service and are then routed to the Transport service.

Planning for Unified Messaging

Unified messaging allows you to integrate voice mail, fax, and email functionality so that the related data can be stored in a user's Exchange mailbox. To implement unified messaging, your organization must have a PBX that is connected to the LAN, and you must deploy Mailbox servers running Exchange Server 2016. After deployment, the Unified Messaging service running on a Mailbox server has the job of providing call answering, fax receiving, subscriber access, and auto-attendant features that allow access to content over the telephone and storage of content received from the PBX. However, it is the job of the Unified Messaging Call Router service running on Mailbox servers to provide call routing and proxy services that allow calls to be connected.

Although some current PBXs, referred to as *IP-PBXs*, are Internet Protocol–capable, all other PBXs require a separate Internet Protocol/Voice over Internet Protocol (IP/VoIP) gateway to connect to the LAN. After you connect a PBX to the LAN, you can link it to Exchange by deploying and appropriately configuring the Unified Messaging service. The Desktop Experience feature, which is required to install Exchange server, provides the Microsoft Speech service, Microsoft Windows Media Encoder, and Microsoft Windows Media Audio Voice Code components used by the Unified Messaging service.

The Unified Messaging service doesn't perform a great deal of I/O operations, and the primary potential bottlenecks for this service are the processors, memory, and network. Disk I/O operations for this service are primarily limited to accessing routing details and dial plans, which include auto-attendant and mail policy settings.

If you are planning to use Unified Messaging in a hybrid Exchange implementation, you'll also need to configure session board controllers (SBCs). SBCs have two IP interfaces: one for your network and another that connects over the Internet. Your VoIP, IP-PBX, and SBC components must be configured to communicate with your Mailbox servers. You also must create and configure a Unified Messaging IP gateway to represent each deployed device.

Integrating Exchange with Active Directory

Exchange 2016 makes extensive use of Active Directory. Each Exchange server must access Active Directory to retrieve information about recipients and the Exchange organization. Exchange 2016 only works with read-writeable domain controllers.

How Mailbox Servers use Active Directory

Mailbox servers are service locations for email messages, voice-mail messages, and faxes. For outgoing mail, Mailbox servers can access Active Directory to retrieve information about the location of Mailbox servers in their site. Then they can use this information to forward messages for routing.

The Transport service running on Mailbox servers contacts Active Directory for message categorization. The Categorizer queries Active Directory to perform recipient lookup, retrieves the information needed to locate a recipient's mailbox (according to the mailbox store in which it is created), and determines any restrictions or permissions that might apply to the recipient. The Categorizer also queries Active Directory to expand the membership of distribution lists and to perform the LDAP query processing when mail is sent to a dynamic distribution list.

After the Categorizer determines the location of a mailbox, the Transport service uses Active Directory site configuration information to determine the routing topology and locate the site of the mailbox. If the mailbox is in the same Active Directory site as the Mailbox server, the Transport service delivers the message directly to the user's mailbox. If the mailbox is in a different Active Directory site from the Mailbox server, the Transport service delivers the message to a Mailbox server in the remote Active Directory site.

Mailbox servers store all configuration information in Active Directory. This configuration information includes the details of any transport or journaling rules and connectors. When this information is needed, a Mailbox server accesses it in Active Directory.

Mailbox servers also store configuration information about mailbox users, mailbox stores, agents, address lists, and policies in Active Directory. Mailbox servers retrieve this information to enforce recipient policies, mailbox policies, system policies, and global settings.

Client Access services running on Mailbox servers receive connections from local and remote clients. At a high level, when a user connection is received, the Client Access services contacts Active Directory to authenticate the user and to determine the location of the user's mailbox. If the user's mailbox is in the same Active Directory site as the originating Mailbox server, the user is connected to the mailbox. If the user's mailbox is in an Active Directory site other than the one the originating Mailbox server is located in, the connection is redirected to a Mailbox server in the same Active Directory site as the user's mailbox.

At least one of your Mailbox servers in each site must be designated as Internet-facing. The Internet-facing server proxies requests from Outlook Web App, Exchange ActiveSync, and Exchange Web Services to the Mailbox server closest to the user's mailbox.

When deployed, the Unified Messaging service running on Mailbox servers accesses Active Directory to retrieve global configuration information, such as dial plans and IP gateway details. When a message is received by the Unified Messaging service, the service searches for Active Directory recipients to match the telephone number to a recipient address. When the service has resolved this information, it can determine the location of the recipient's mailbox and then submit the message to the appropriate Mailbox server for submission to the mailbox.

How Edge Transports use Active Directory

You deploy Edge Transport servers in perimeter networks to isolate them from the internal network. As such, they are not members of the internal domain and do not have direct access to the organization's internal Active Directory servers for the purposes of recipient lookup or categorization. Thus, unlike the Transport service on Mailbox servers, Edge Transport servers cannot contact an Active Directory server to help route messages.

To route messages into the organization, an administrator can configure a subscription from the Edge Transport server to the Active Directory site that allows it to store recipient and configuration information about the Exchange organization in its AD LDS data store. After an Edge Transport server is subscribed to an Active Directory site, it is associated with the Mailbox servers in that site for the purpose of message routing. Thereafter, Mailbox servers in the organization route messages being delivered to the Internet to the site associated with the Edge Transport server, and Mailbox servers in this site relay the messages to the Edge Transport server. The Edge Transport server, in turn, routes the messages to the Internet.

The EdgeSync service running on Mailbox servers is a one-way synchronization process that pushes information from Active Directory to the Edge Transport server. Periodically, the EdgeSync service synchronizes the data to keep the Edge Transport server's data store up to date. The EdgeSync service also establishes the connectors needed to send and receive information that is being moved between the organization and the Edge Transport server and between the Edge Transport server and the Internet. The key data pushed to the Edge Transport server includes:

- Accepted and remote domains
- Valid recipients
- Safe senders
- Send connectors
- Available Mailbox servers
- Available SMTP servers
- Message classifications
- TLS Send and Receive Domain Secure lists

After the initial replication is performed, the EdgeSync service synchronizes the data periodically. Configuration information is synced once every hour, and it can take up to one hour for configuration changes to be replicated. Recipient information is synced once every four hours, and it can take up to four hours for changes to be replicated. If necessary, administrators can initiate an immediate synchronization using the Start-EdgeSynchronization cmdlet in Exchange Management Shell.

> **NOTE**   During synchronization, objects can be added to, deleted from, or modified in the Edge Transport server's AD LDS data store. To protect the integrity and security of the organization, no information is ever pushed from the Edge Transport server's AD LDS data store to Active Directory.

Integrating Exchange 2016 Into Existing Organizations

Existing Exchange Server 2010 and Exchange Server 2013 installations can coexist with Exchange Server 2016 installations. Generally, you do this by integrating Exchange Server 2016 into your existing Exchange Server 2010 or Exchange Server 2013 organization. Integration requires the following:

- Preparing Active Directory and the domain for the Active Directory changes that will occur when you install Exchange Server 2016.
- Configuring Exchange Server 2016 so that it can communicate with servers running Exchange Server 2010 and Exchange Server 2013.
- Ensuring any installations of Exchange 2010 are running Service Pack 3 with RU11 at a minimum and any installations of Exchange 2013 are running Cumulative Update 10 or later.

You cannot upgrade existing Exchange 2010 or Exchange 2013 servers to Exchange 2016. You must install Exchange Server 2016 on new hardware, and then move the mailboxes from your existing installations to the new installation. See the "Moving to Exchange Server 2016" section later in this chapter for more details.

As an alternative to coexistence, you can deploy a new Exchange 2016 organization. After you deploy a new Exchange 2016 organization, you can't add servers that are running earlier versions of Exchange to the organization. Adding earlier versions of Exchange to a new Exchange 2016 organization is not supported.

Coexistence and Active Directory

As Exchange Server 2016 contains schema changes and other Active Directory updates, you might want to prepare Active Directory and the domain for these changes prior to installing Exchange 2016 for the first time, especially in a large enterprise.

To do this, follow these steps:

1. Prepare the schema by running the following command prior to executing the Exchange 2016 Setup:

   setup.exe /PrepareSchema /IAcceptExchangeServerLicenseTerms

   This command connects to the schema master and imports the LDAP data interchange format files that are used to updates the schema with Exchange 2016 specific attributes. Optionally, use the /DomainController parameter to specify the name of the schema master. You must run this command on a 64-bit computer in the same domain and site as the schema master. If schema needs to be updated and you haven't previously prepared schema, you must ensure the account you use is delegated membership in the Schema Admins group. Wait for the changes to replicate before continuing.

2. Prepare Active Directory for Exchange 2016 by running the following command prior to executing the Exchange 2016 Setup:

setup.exe /PrepareAD /IAcceptExchangeServerLicenseTerms
You must run this command in the same domain and site as the schema master. This computer must be able to connect to all domains in the forest on TCP port 389. To run this command, you must be a member of the Domain Admins groups for the local domain or the Enterprise Admins group. Wait for the changes to replicate before continuing.

The PrepareAD option performs a number of tasks:

- Creates the Microsoft Exchange container and the Exchange organization container in the directory if they don't exist, such as when you are installing a new Exchange organization. Here, you must set a name for the organization using the /OrganizationName parameter.
- Verifies that the schema has been updated for Exchange 2016. It does this by checking objectVersion property for the Exchange configuration container and ensuring the value is 16210 or higher. The command also sets the Exchange product ID of the Exchange organization to that of the version you are installing. The base value for Exchange 2016 RTM is 15.01.0225.042. This value is incremented when you deploy Cumulative Updates to Exchange. Here, 15 is the major version number, 1 is the minor version number and 225.42 is the build.
- Creates any containers that are required in Active Directory for Exchange 2016, creates the default Accepted Domains entry if a default was not previously set, and imports the Rights.ldf file to add the extended rights required for Exchange to the directory.
- Creates the Microsoft Exchange Security Groups organizational unit in the root domain of the forest and then creates the following management role groups used by Exchange to this organizational unit if these haven't been previously created: Compliance Management, Delegated Setup, Discovery Management, Help Desk, Hygiene Management, Organization Management, Public Folder Management, Recipient Management, Records Management, Server Management, UM Management, and View-Only Organization Management. As necessary, also adds these groups to the otherWellKnownObjects attribute on the Exchange Services Configuration container.
- Creates the Unified Messaging Voice Originator contact in the Microsoft Exchange System Objects container of the root domain and then prepares the local domain for Exchange 2016.

3. The domain in which you ran **setup.exe /PrepareAD** is already prepared. For all other domains that will have mail-enabled users or in which you will install Exchange 2016, you must log in and run **setup.exe /PrepareDomain /IAcceptExchangeServerLicenseTerms**. You also can specify the name of the domain in which you want to run the command, such as **setup.exe /PrepareDomain:Tech.Imaginedlands.com /IAcceptExchangeServerLicenseTerms**. Alternatively, you can run **setup.exe /PrepareAllDomains /IAcceptExchangeServerLicenseTerms** to

prepare all domains in the forest. To run this command, you normally must be a member of the Domain Admins groups for the local domain or the Enterprise Admins group. However, if the domain was created after running /PrepareAD, the account you use must be a member of the Exchange 2016 Organization Management role group and the Domain Admins groups in the domain.

For new organizations, this command creates the Microsoft Exchange System Objects container and sets its permissions. For all organizations, this command:

* Sets the objectVersion property in the Microsoft Exchange System Objects container so that it references the version of domain preparation for Exchange 2016, which is 16210 or higher.
* Creates a domain global group in the current domain called Exchange Install Domain Servers and adds this group in the Microsoft Exchange System Objects container as well as the Exchange Servers group in the root domain.
* Assigns permissions in the domain for the Exchange Servers group and the Organization Management group.

NOTE Want to determine the Exchange version number? Use Exchange Management Shell with either of the following commands:

Get-Command ExSetup.exe | % {$_.FileVersionInfo}

Get-ExchangeServer | Format-List Name, Edition, AdminDisplayVersion

---

Although Exchange Server 2016 Setup can perform these processes for you during the upgrade, the changes can take some time to replicate throughout a large organization. By performing these tasks manually, you can streamline the upgrade process. You also can ensure the tasks are run with accounts that have appropriate permissions.

To verify that schema was updated for Exchange 2016, you can use ADSI Edit to check the following properties:

* In the Schema naming context, confirm that the rangeUpper property on ms-Exch-Schema-Version-Pt is set to 15317 or higher.
* In the Configuration naming context, confirm that the objectVersion property in the CN=*OrganizationName*,CN=Microsoft Exchange,CN=Services,CN=Configuration,DC=*DomainName* container is set 16210 or higher.

- In the Default naming context, confirm that the objectVersion property in the Microsoft Exchange System Objects container under DC=*RootDomainName* is set to 16210 or higher.

As a prerequisite for installing Exchange 2016, Active Directory must be at Windows Server 2008 forest functionality mode or higher. Additionally, the schema master for the Active Directory forest along with at least one global catalog server and at least one domain controller in each Active Directory site must be running one of the following operating systems:

- Windows Server 2008 Standard, Enterprise or Datacenter
- Windows Server 2012 Standard or Datacenter
- Windows Server 2012 R2 Standard or Datacenter
- Windows Server 2016 Standard or Datacenter

When you deploy IPv6, Exchange 2016 servers can send data to, and receive data from, devices, servers, and clients that use IPv6 addresses. However, Exchange 2016 only supports IPv6 when IPv4 is also installed and enabled. Exchange requires that IPv4 be enabled even if you don't use IPv4 addressing.

Configuring Exchange 2016 for Coexistence

When managing Exchange servers, you should use the administrative tools for that Exchange Server version. The Exchange Admin Center and Exchange Management Shell are the primary management tools for Exchange 2016. Mailboxes located on Exchange 2010 and Exchange 2013 servers are also displayed in the Exchange Admin Center.

You can manage the Exchange 2010 or 2013 mailbox properties using the Exchange Admin Center or Exchange Management Shell. You can use either tool to move mailbox recipients from Exchange 2010 or Exchange 2013 to Exchange 2016.

Beginning with Exchange 2016, MAPI over HTTP is the preferred access protocol for Outlook clients. MAPI over HTTP includes enhancements that make connections more reliable and stable, and also makes it easier for clients to recover from transport errors. Built-in pause and resume functions as well as other features allow clients to change networks and resume from sleep mode while maintaining the same server context.

Although Exchange 2016 is designed so that Outlook clients can use either Outlook Anywhere (RPC over HTTP) or MAPI over HTTP, keep the following in mind:

* Outlook 2016 clients use MAPI over HTTP by default and can also use RPC over HTTP.
* Outlook 2013 clients must have Service Pack 1 or later to use MAPI over HTTP, and otherwise can only use RPC over HTTP.
* Outlook 2010 clients must have Service Pack 2 or later as well as KB2956191 and KB2965295 to use MAPI over HTTP, and otherwise can only use RPC over HTTP.

MAPI over HTTP is enabled by default in most Exchange 2016 deployments, including new deployments, when upgrading to Exchange 2016 from Exchange 2010 and mixed environments with Exchange 2010 and Exchange 2016 servers. However, MAPI over HTTP is not enabled automatically when you have previously deployed Exchange 2013. As shown in the following example, you can use the Set-OrganizationConfig cmdlet with -MapiHttpEnabled to enable MAPI over HTTP:

```
set-organizationconfig mapihttpenabled $true
```

As with other protocols, MAPI over HTTP relies on internal and external virtual directories to be created. These virtual directories act as endpoints for client connections. You can use the Set-MapiVirtualDirectory cmdlet to specify the internal and external URLs. You can determine whether MAPI over HTTP is working properly using -ProbeIdentity OutlookMapiHttpSelfTestProbe with Test-OutlookConnectivity as shown in the following example:

```
test-outlookconnectivity -probeidentity outlookmapihttpselftestprobe
```

MAPI over HTTP is working properly when "Succeeded" is listed as the result.

If you need to control whether a client can use MAPI over HTTP, use the Set-CasMailbox cmdlet with -MapiHttpEnabled to enable or disable the option for the associated mailbox user. The basic syntax is:

```
set-casmailbox userormailboxname -mapihttpenabled {$true | $false}
```

In the following example, you disable MAPI over HTTP for williams@imaginedlands.com:

```
set-casmailbox williams@imaginedlands.com -mapihttpenabled $false
```

As the mailbox setting has precedence over organization settings, the user won't be able to use MAPI over HTTP even if the protocol is enabled in the organization.

Setting the Default Offline Address Book

A new Offline Address Book (OAB) will be created when you deploy the first Exchange 2016 Mailbox server in an existing Exchange organization. All existing clients that use OAB will see this new OAB by default the next time they perform an OAB update, and they also will perform a full OAB download. If you don't want this to happen, you must configure existing mailbox databases to explicitly point to the current default OAB before you deploy the first Exchange 2016 server.

With Exchange 2010, you can do this by following these steps:

1. In Exchange Management Console, navigate to Organization Configuration, Mailbox, Database Management and then open the Mailbox Database Properties dialog box for the mailbox database you want to work with.
2. On the Client Settings tab of the Mailbox Database Properties dialog box, you'll see an entry for the Offline Address Book and a related Browse button. Use this option to explicitly set the default OAB.
3. Repeat this process for each mailbox database that you want to update.

With Exchange 2013, you can do this by following these steps:

1. In Exchange Admin Center, click Servers in the Features pane and then click Databases. Double-click the mailbox database you want to work with to open its Properties dialog box.
2. Select Client Settings. You'll see an entry for the Offline Address Book and a related Browse button. Use this option to explicitly set the default OAB.
3. Repeat this process for each mailbox database that you want to update.

You also can use Exchange Management Shell to view all mailbox databases without a default OAB explicitly set on them and then explicitly set a default OAB. Start by entering the following command:

```
Get-MailboxDatabase | Where {$_.OfflineAddressBook -eq $Null} |
FT Name,OfflineAddressBook -AutoSize
```

If no values are returned, a default OAB is already explicitly set throughout the organization. If values are returned, you need to configure some databases with an explicitly defined default OAB. The following commands locate all mailbox databases with no default OAB defined at the database level and then set these mailbox databases to the current default OAB in the organization:

```
Get-MailboxDatabase | Where {$_.OfflineAddressBook -eq $Null} |
Set-MailboxDatabase -OfflineAddressBook (Get-OfflineAddressBook |
Where {$_.IsDefault -eq $True})
```

Confirm that all mailbox databases now have an explicitly defined default OAB, by re-running the first command: Get-MailboxDatabase | Where {$_.OfflineAddressBook -eq $Null}. The command should return no values.

Moving to Exchange Server 2016

Most organizations have existing Exchange installations. When moving Exchange 2010 or Exchange 2013 installations to Exchange Server 2016, you cannot perform an in-place upgrade. Instead, you must install new Exchange Server 2016 servers into the existing organization and then migrate to Exchange Server 2016.

Migration from Exchange 2010 or Exchange 2013 to Exchange 2016 involves installing Exchange Server 2016 on new servers and then moving the mailboxes and public folders from your existing installations to the new installation. In a migration, only mailbox and public folder data is moved, and any Exchange configuration data is not maintained.

The steps you perform to migrate from Exchange 2010 or Exchange 2013 to Exchange 2016 are as follows:

1. Plan to migrate all Exchange servers in a particular site to Exchange 2016 at the same time. You should start with Internet-accessible Active Directory sites and then migrate internal Active Directory sites. For each Exchange 2016 Mailbox server, you can configure only one Outlook Web App URL for redirection.

2. Install Exchange 2016 on new hardware and make it a member of the appropriate domain in the forest. You should install Mailbox servers first and then any Edge Transports.

3. Move Internet mail flow from Exchange 2010 or Exchange 2013 to Exchange 2016 by creating appropriate send connectors and accepted domains. You'll also need to configure default email address policy, SSL certificates and URLs for client protocols.

4. Move mailboxes and public folders from your existing Exchange 2010 or Exchange 2030 installations to the new Exchange 2016 Mailbox servers. If you move a mailbox that is part of an email address policy, the email address for the mailbox is automatically updated based on the settings in the email address policy. In this case, the new email address becomes the primary address, and the old email address becomes the secondary address.

During a migration, the version of an Exchange feature that a user sees, such as Outlook Web App, depends on where the user's mailbox is located. If the mailbox is on an Exchange 2013 server, the user sees Exchange 2013 versions of CAS features. When you move the mailbox to Exchange 2016, the user will see Exchange 2016 versions of CAS features.

REAL WORLD You move mailboxes from Exchange 2010 or Exchange 2013 to Exchange 2016 by using an online move. Perform the move from the Exchange 2016 server by using move mailbox requests, either with Exchange Management Shell or the Exchange Admin Center. You can't use the Exchange Management tools for Exchange 2010 or Exchange 2013 to move the mailboxes.

5. Once you've complete the move and have validated the configuration, you can remove unneeded Exchange 2010 or Exchange 2013 servers from the organization.

CAUTION Before removing the last Exchange 2010 or Exchange 2013 server with a particular role, you must be sure that you will never need to introduce an Exchange 2010 or Exchange 2013 server with the role again. Once you remove the last Exchange 2010 or Exchange 2013 server with a particular role, you can never add another one with that role.

Chapter 3. Deploying Exchange Server 2016

You use Exchange Server 2016 Setup to install Exchange Server roles and the Exchange management tools. You can install Exchange 2016 from media or from a download. The same media or download is used for both Exchange Server 2016 Enterprise and Exchange Server 2016 Standard.

Downloads are packaged, self-extracting, executable files. When you access the download page, click Download to start the download process. Next, copy the download to your computer for installation at a later time by clicking Save. After you copy the download to the computer on which you plan to install Exchange, you can double-click the executable file to extract the Exchange 2016 Setup components to a folder. When prompted, be sure to specify an exact folder to put all the setup components in one place. Within this folder, you'll find a program called Setup.exe. This is the Exchange Server 2016 Setup program.

You use Setup to install Exchange Server 2016 on Windows servers and to add the management tools to desktop computers. If you want to uninstall Exchange 2016, you use Programs And Features in Control Panel.

Installing New Exchange Servers

For servers deployed within the organization, you can install the Mailbox role to handle messaging transport and client access needs. While some organizations may be able to use only a single Exchange server, most organization will want to install at least two Exchange servers. Why? You can achieve high availability for the Mailbox role simply by installing two or more Mailbox servers, creating a database availability group, adding mailbox databases to this group, and then adding database copies.

You can achieve high availability for message transport simply by installing multiple Mailbox servers. Thanks to the shadow redundancy feature, a message that is submitted to a Mailbox server is stored in the transport database until the transport server verifies that all of the next hops for that message have completed delivery. If the next hop doesn't report successful delivery, the message is resubmitted for delivery. In addition, when messages are in the transport dumpster, they aren't removed until they are replicated to all the appropriate mailbox databases.

For message transport, install at least one Mailbox server for each group of Active Directory sites that are well connected on a common LAN. For example, if the organization consists of sites A and B, which are well connected on a common LAN, and sites C and D, which are well-connected on a common LAN, with wide area network (WAN) links connecting sites A and B to sites C and D, a minimal implementation would be to have Mailbox servers only in site A and site C. However, Microsoft recommends that you have Mailbox servers in each Active Directory site with mail-enabled clients.

Because you install Edge Transport servers outside the Active Directory forest, you can deploy additional Edge Transports at any time. By configuring multiple Edge Transport servers, you can ensure that if one server fails, Edge Transport services continue. If you also configure your Edge Transport servers with round-robin DNS, you can load balance between them.

> **REAL WORLD**   If you are installing Exchange Server on a new network, such as one for a new company or a development environment, be sure that you've properly configured Active Directory and DNS before installing Exchange Server. You need to create a domain. Typically, you do this by installing a server and establishing the server as a domain controller in a new forest.
>
> When you set up DNS, be sure you configure the appropriate reverse lookup zones. You should have one reverse lookup zone for each subnet. If you forget to set up the reverse zones and do this after installing your servers, be sure that the appropriate PTR records have been created for your domain controllers and Exchange servers. In Active Directory Sites And Services, check that the sites and subnets are configured appropriately. You need to create a subnet in Active Directory to represent each of the subnets on your network. If DNS reverse zones and Active Directory subnets are not configured properly, you will likely experience long startup times on your servers, and Exchange services will likely not start properly.

Installing Exchange Server

Before you run Exchange Server 2016 Setup, make sure that the server meets the system requirements and prerequisites as discussed in "Navigating Exchange 2016 Editions" in Chapter 1, "Getting Started with Exchange Server 2016." You can only run Exchange Server 2016 on full installations of Windows Server 2012, Windows Server 2012 R2 and Windows Server 2016. You cannot install Exchange Server 2016 on a server running in Windows Server Core mode. Instead, you must convert the Core mode to a full installation.

> **NOTE** You can use Setup to install the Exchange Server 2016 management tools on domain-joined computers running 64-bit editions of Windows 8.1 or Windows 10.

You can run Exchange Server 2016 Setup in one of several modes, including:

* **Install** Used when you're installing a new server role or adding a server role to an existing installation.
* **Upgrade** Used when you have an existing installation of Exchange and you're installing a service pack or cumulative update.
* **Uninstall** Used when you're removing the Exchange installation.

> **IMPORTANT** Exchange Server 2016 doesn't support in-place upgrades from any previous version of Exchange. Further, after you install Exchange Server 2016, you won't be able to rename the server.

Generally, you should install Exchange Server 2016 on member servers rather than on domain controllers. This will ensure Exchange operates with strictest security allowed and has optimal performance. If you do install Exchange Server 2016 on a domain controller, you won't be able to demote the server. Once Exchange 2016 is installed, changing a server's role from a member server to a directory server, or vice versa, isn't supported.

If something goes wrong with the installation and re-running Setup and following the prompts doesn't help you resolve the problem, you have several options. You can restore the server from backup or you can run Exchange Server 2016 Setup in recovery mode by running setup /m:RecoverServer at a command prompt. If you are recovering to a different server, the server must use the same fully qualified domain name (FQDN) as the failed server.

When you recover a server, you don't specify the roles to restore. Setup detects the Exchange Server object in Active Directory and installs the corresponding files and configuration automatically. After you recover the server, you can restore databases and reconfigure any additional settings.

When you are ready to run Setup, you can begin the installation and install an Exchange server by completing the following steps:

1. Log on to the server using an administrator account. When you install the Mailbox role, you must use a domain account that is a member of the Enterprise Administrators group. If you've already prepared Active Directory, this account must also be a member of the Exchange Organization Administrators group.

IMPORTANT   Before beginning setup, you should close any open Windows PowerShell or Microsoft Management Console (MMC) windows. Otherwise you will see a warning during the readiness checks that you need to close these windows. The installation process makes updates to Windows PowerShell and MMC and typically requires exclusive access.

REAL WORLD   Ensure the server's TCP/IP settings are properly configured before beginning setup. Also, ensure that the server is a member of the domain in which you want the Exchange organization to be configured. During setup, the server will try to identify the Active Directory site in which it is located. The server will try to connect with a domain controller and global catalog sever in this site.

---

2. Do one of the following:

- If you are using installation media, insert the Exchange Server 2016 media. If Autorun is enabled, Exchange Server 2016 Setup should start automatically. Otherwise, double-click **Setup.exe** on the root folder of the installation media.
- If you are using a download, access the folder where you extracted the Exchange setup files and then start Exchange 2016 Setup by double-clicking **Setup.exe**.

3. On the Check For Updates page, you can specify whether to check for updates to the setup process. If you don't want to check for updates, select **Don't Check For Updates Right Now** before you click **Next** to continue. Setup will then copy files and initialize resources. The server also tries to validate the state of Active Directory.

Check for Updates?

You can have Setup download Exchange Server 2016 updates from the Internet before you install Exchange. If updates are available, they'll be downloaded and used by Setup. By downloading updates now, you'll have the latest security and product updates. If you don't want to check for updates right now, or if you don't have access to the Internet, skip this step. If you skip this step, be sure to download and install any available updates after you've completed Setup.

Select one of the following options:

- ⦿ Connect to the Internet and check for updates
- ◯ Don't check for updates right now

NOTE   If the server is unable to validate the state of Active Directory and choose a domain controller to work with, Setup will log errors and may also report that a domain controller could not be located. If errors are reported, do not continue with the installation. Instead, exit Setup and resolve the communication problem.

4. Setup copies files that are required to the server and then prepares resources.

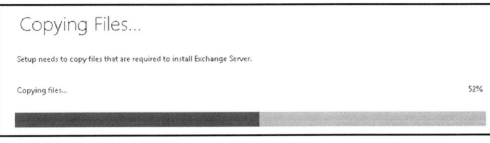

Copying Files...

Setup needs to copy files that are required to install Exchange Server.

Copying files...   52%

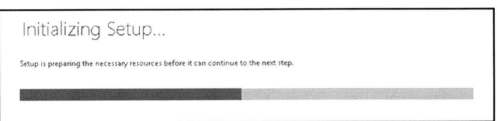

Initializing Setup...

Setup is preparing the necessary resources before it can continue to the next step.

5. The Introduction page begins the installation process. Click **Next** to continue.

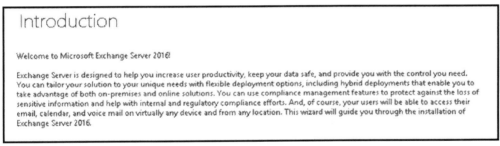

Introduction

Welcome to Microsoft Exchange Server 2016!

Exchange Server is designed to help you increase user productivity, keep your data safe, and provide you with the control you need. You can tailor your solution to your unique needs with flexible deployment options, including hybrid deployments that enable you to take advantage of both on-premises and online solutions. You can use compliance management features to protect against the loss of sensitive information and help with internal and regulatory compliance efforts. And, of course, your users will be able to access their email, calendar, and voice mail on virtually any device and from any location. This wizard will guide you through the installation of Exchange Server 2016.

6. On the License Agreement page, review the software license terms. If you agree to the terms, select **I Accept The Terms In The License Agreement**, and then click **Next**.

◉ I accept the terms in the license agreement

○ I do not accept the terms in the license agreement.

🄴🄱 Exchange   next

7. On the Recommended Settings page, select whether you want to use the recommended settings. If you select Use Recommended Settings, Exchange will automatically send error reports and information about your computer

hardware and how you use Exchange to Microsoft. If you select Don't Use Recommended Settings, error and usage reporting are disabled but you can enable them at any time after Setup completes. Click **Next** to continue.

Recommended Settings

◉ Use recommended settings

Exchange server will automatically check online for solutions when encountering errors and provide usage feedback to Microsoft to help improve future Exchange features.

○ Don't use recommended settings

Manually configure these settings after installation is complete (see help for more information).

---

8. On the Server Role Selection page, choose whether you want to install the Mailbox role or the Edge Transport role. The management tools are installed automatically if you install any server role.

Server Role Selection

Select the Exchange server roles you want to install on this computer:

☐ Mailbox role

☐ Management tools

☐ Edge Transport role

☐ Automatically install Windows Server roles and features that are required to install Exchange Server

---

9. Select **Automatically Install Windows Server Roles And Features That Are Required To Install Exchange Server** to have Setup install any required Windows prerequisites. You may need to reboot the computer to complete the installation of some Windows features. If you don't select this option, you must install the required Windows features manually. Click **Next** to continue.

10. On the Installation Space And Location page, note the space required for the installation. Click **Browse** to choose a location for the installation. Ensure you have enough disk space available on the related drive. Click **Next** to continue.

Installation Space and Location

Disk space required: 8696.2 MB

Disk space available: 92985.9 MB

Specify the path for the Exchange Server installation:

```
C:\Program Files\Microsoft\Exchange Server\V15        [ browse ]
```

11. If this is the first Exchange server in your organization, on the Exchange Organization page, type a name for your Exchange organization or accept the default value of First Organization. The Exchange organization name must be 64 characters or less and can contain only the characters A through Z, a through z, 0 through 9, space (as long as the space is not leading or trailing), and hyphen or dash. You can't leave the organization name blank. Click **Next** to continue.

REAL WORLD Exchange 2016 supports shared permissions and split permissions. Split permissions allow organizations to separate Exchange management and Active Directory management. Role Based Access Control (RBAC) are the recommended split permissions model used with Exchange. If you want to use shared permissions or split permissions that use RBAC, do not select the Apply Active Directory Split Permissions… check box. If your organization has strict requirements for separate management of Active Directory and Exchange Server and RBAC will not meet your needs, select the Apply Active Directory Split Permissions… check box. However, you will then be unable to create users, groups, contacts, and other Active Directory objects using the Exchange management tools

---

Exchange Organization

Specify the name for this Exchange organization:

```
First Organization
```

☐ Apply Active Directory split permissions security model to the Exchange organization

---

12. If you're installing the Mailbox role, on the Malware Protection Settings page, choose whether you want to enable or disable malware scanning. If you disable malware scanning, it can be enabled later.

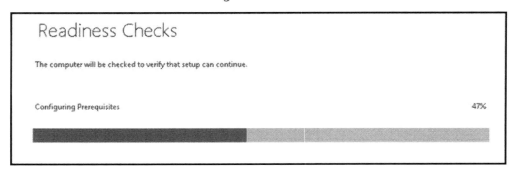

Malware Protection Settings

Malware scanning helps protect your messaging environment by detecting messages that may contain viruses or spyware. It can be turned off, replaced, or paired with other premium services for layered protection.

Malware scanning is enabled by default. However, you can disable it if you're using another product for malware scanning. If you choose to disable malware scanning now, you can enable it at any point after you've installed Exchange.

Disable malware scanning.

○ Yes
◉ No

Internet access is required to download the latest anti-malware engine and definition updates.

13. When you click **Next**, Setup will verify that all prerequisites have been installed and that Exchange 2016 can be installed.

Readiness Checks

The computer will be checked to verify that setup can continue.

Configuring Prerequisites   47%

14. Note any errors. You must resolve any reported errors before you can install Exchange Server 2016. For most errors, you don't need to exit Setup. After resolving a reported error, click **Retry** to run the prerequisite checks again.

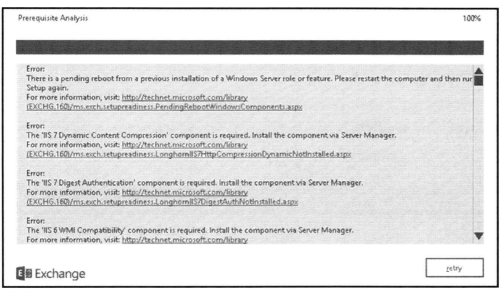

15. When all readiness checks have completed successfully, note any warnings and then click **Install** to install Exchange 2016. The installation process can take up to 1 hour.

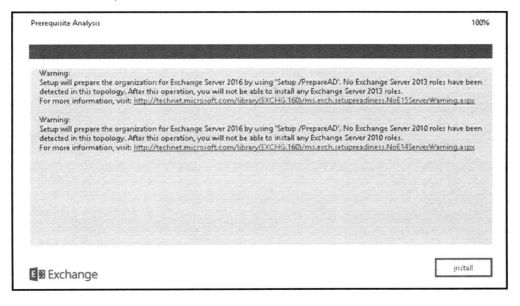

The Setup Progress page, tracks the progress of the installation. The installation is performed in a series of steps, with the progress for the current step tracked with a progress bar and as a percentage of completion.

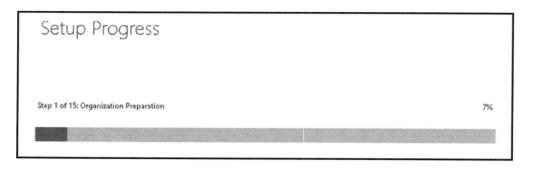

The number of steps varies, depending on the tasks Setup must perform to prepare the environment as well as the options you selected. Typically, the steps see will include:

1. Organization preparation
2. Preparing setup
3. Stopping services
4. Exchange files... Language files
5. Restoring services
6. Languages
7. Management tools
8. Transport service.
9. Client Access service
10. Unified Messaging service
11. Mailbox service
12. Front End Transport service
13. Front End service
14. Finalizing setup

Finally, you'll see the Setup Completed page, when Setup completes the installation. Although you must restart the server to finalize the installation, you may want to select the Launch Exchange Administration Center checkbox before selecting Finish and then set the product key.

> **NOTE** Alternatively, you can manually start the Exchange Administration Center by opening Internet Explorer and entering the Exchange Administration Center. By default, this URL is https://*ServerName*/ecp/ where *ServerName* is the name of the server, such as: https://mailserver35/ecp/.

Setup Completed

Congratulations! Setup has finished successfully. To complete the installation of Exchange Server 2016, reboot the computer.

You can view additional post-installation tasks online by clicking the link: http://go.microsoft.com/fwlink/p/?LinkId=255372. You can also start the Exchange Administration Center after Setup is finished.

☐ Launch Exchange Administration Center after finishing Exchange setup.

By default, Exchange 2016 runs in trial mode. To get out of trial mode, you must validate the installation. In the left pane of the Exchange Admin Center, click Servers and then select Servers as the feature you want to work with. As shown in Figure 3-1, each installed Exchange server is listed by name, role and version. Click the server you want to work with. In the details pane, a link is provided for entering a product key.

FIGURE 3-1 Viewing installed servers in Exchange Admin Center.

Clicking the Enter Product Key link opens the properties dialog box for the mail server with the General page displayed. Enter a valid product key in the boxes provided and then click Save.

CORPSERVER74

▶ general

databases and database
availability groups

POP3

IMAP4

unified messaging

DNS lookups

transport limits

transport logs

Outlook Anywhere

Version number:

Version 15.1 (Build 225.42)

Roles:

Mailbox, Client Access

This Exchange server is currently licensed as a Trial Edition. You
can add a new license by entering a product key below. Learn
more

Enter a valid product key.

[ ] - [ ] - [ ] - [ ]

Save   Cancel

You can change the product key at any time on the general page. Select Change
Product Key, enter a valid product key, and then click Save.

You can upgrade a Standard edition to an Enterprise edition using the options on
the General page as well. Select Change Product Key, enter a valid product key for
Enterprise edition and then click Save.

Verifying and Completing the Installation

You can verify that Exchange Server 2016 installed successfully by running the Get-
ExchangeServer cmdlet in Exchange Management Shell. This command displays a list
of all Exchange 2016 server roles that are installed on a specified server.

During installation, Exchange Setup logs events in the Application log of Event
Viewer. You can review the Application log to make sure there are no warning or
error messages related to Exchange setup. Typically, these events have event IDs
1003 and 1004, with the source as MSExchangeSetup.

You also can learn more about the installation by reviewing the setup log file created
during the setup process. This log file is stored in the
%SystemDrive%\ExchangeSetupLogs folder with the name ExchangeSetup.log. The
%SystemDrive% variable represents the root directory of the drive where the
operating system is installed. Because these logs contain standard text, you can
perform a search using the keyword *error* to find any setup errors that occurred.

As discussed previously, Setup must be able to contact Active Directory. If Setup is unable do this, errors will be logged and the Exchange organization will not be prepared properly. In the following example, Setup couldn't validate the state of Active Directory and couldn't locate a domain controller:

```
[02/14/2016 11:05:31.0253] [0] Setup is choosing the domain controller to use
[02/14/2016 11:05:42.0630] [0] Setup is choosing a local domain controller...
[02/14/2016 11:05:45.0033] [0] [ERROR] Setup encountered a problem while
validating the state of Active Directory: Could not find any Domain
Controller in domain imaginedlands.com.
[02/14/2016 11:05:45.0158] [0] [ERROR] Could not find any Domain Controller
in domain imaginedlands.com.
[02/14/2016 11:05:45.0205] [0] [ERROR] Domain controller not found in the
domain "imaginedlands.com".
[02/14/2016 11:05:45.0205] [0] Setup will use the domain controller ''.
[02/14/2016 11:05:45.0205] [0] Setup will use the global catalog ''.
[02/14/2016 11:05:45.0955] [0] No Exchange configuration container was found
for the organization. Message: 'Could not find any Domain Controller
in domain imaginedlands.com.'.
```

Because of this problem, Setup didn't fully prepare the organization and had problems configuring the Mailbox role: Transport service and the other services as well. When Setup is able to validate the state of Active Directory, the log records a very different set of events as shown in the following example:

```
[02/14/2016 12:11:07.0115] [0] Setup is choosing the domain controller to use
[02/14/2016 12:11:14.0135] [0] Setup is choosing a local domain controller...
[02/14/2016 12:11:24.0729] [0] Setup has chosen the local domain controller
CorpServer24.imaginedlands.com for initial queries
[02/14/2016 12:11:24.0885] [0] PrepareAD has either not been run or has not
replicated to the domain controller used by Setup. Setup will attempt to
use the Schema Master domain controller CorpServer24.imaginedlands.com
[02/14/2016 12:11:24.0885] [0] The schema master domain controller is
available
[02/14/2016 12:11:24.0901] [0] The schema master domain controller is in
the local domain; setup will use CorpServer24.imaginedlands.com
[02/14/2016 12:11:24.0901] [0] Setup is choosing a global catalog...
```

```
[02/14/2016 12:11:24.0917] [0] Setup has chosen the global catalog server
CorpServer24.imaginedlands.com.
[02/14/2016 12:11:24.0932] [0] Setup will use the domain controller
'CorpServer24.imaginedlands.com'.
[02/14/2016 12:11:24.0932] [0] Setup will use the global catalog
'CorpServer24.imaginedlands.com'.
[02/14/2016 12:11:24.0948] [0] No Exchange configuration container was
found for the organization. Message: 'Could not find the Exchange
Configuration Container'.
```

Here, Setup was able to select a domain controller to work with, locate the schema master, and choose a global catalog server. Note that Setup reports that PrepareAD was not run or replicated and that no Exchange configuration container was found. This is normal for a new installation of Exchange 2016. Shortly after validating the state of Active Directory, Setup will determine the organization-level operations to perform. For a new installation of Exchange 2016, related entries should look similar to the following:

```
[02/14/2016 12:11:26.0339] [0] Setup is determining what organization-level
operations to perform.
[02/14/2016 12:11:26.0339] [0] Setup has detected a missing value. Setup is
adding the value PrepareSchema.
[02/14/2016 12:11:26.0339] [0] Setup has detected a missing value. Setup is
adding the value PrepareOrganization.
[02/14/2016 12:11:26.0339] [0] Setup has detected a missing value. Setup is
adding the value PrepareDomain.
```

Here, Setup reports that it will prepare the Active Directory schema, the Exchange organization, and the domain. You can confirm each by looking for the elements that should have been created or configured as discussed in the section titled "Coexistence and Active Directory" earlier in Chapter 2.

To complete the installation for an initial deployment of Exchange into an organization, you need to perform the following tasks:

For Client Access services:

- If you plan to use ActiveSync for mobile messaging clients, configure direct push, authentication, and mobile devices.
- Configure internal and external URLs for the Outlook web applications, Exchange ActiveSync, Exchange Admin Center, and Offline Address Book.
- Configure internal and external URLs for autodiscover, SMTP and HTTP.
- Configure authentication and display options, as appropriate.
- Enable the server for POP3 and IMAP4, as appropriate.
- Enable the server for MAPI over HTTP, as appropriate.
- A self-signed digital certificate is created by default but won't be automatically trusted by clients. You can either establish trust or obtain a certificate from a third party that the client trusts.

For Mailbox servers:

- Configure domains for which you will accept email. You need an accepted domain entry for each SMTP domain for which you will accept email.
- Configure Send connectors as appropriate. If you are unsure about the Send connectors that are needed, create an Internet Send connector at minimum. Use the address space of "*" to route all outbound mail to the Internet.
- If you also deployed the Edge Transport server role, you need to subscribe to the Edge Transport server so that the EdgeSync service can establish one-way replication of recipient and configuration information from Active Directory to the AD LDS store on the Edge Transport server.
- Configure DNS MX resource records for each accepted domain.
- Configure OAB distribution for Outlook 2010 and later clients.
- Configure database availability groups and mailbox database copies, as appropriate.

For Unified Messaging service:

- Configure a unified messaging dial plan, and add the server to it.
- Configure Unified Messaging hunt groups.
- Enable users for unified messaging, as appropriate.
- Configure your IP/VoIP gateways or IP-PBXs to work with Exchange Server.
- Configure a Unified Messaging IP gateway in Exchange Server.
- As desired, create auto-attendant and mailbox policies and configure additional dial plans, gateways, and hunt groups.

Uninstalling Exchange 2016

The Exchange Server 2016 installation process uses Windows Installer. Using Windows Installer helps to streamline and stabilize the installation process, and it makes modification of installation components fairly easy. Thanks to Windows Installer, you also can resume a failed installation or modification simply by re-running Exchange Setup.

If you no longer need an Exchange server, you can uninstall Exchange 2016 to remove Exchange services. Before you can uninstall Exchange 2016, you must disable, move or remove all mailboxes, archive mailboxes, public folder mailboxes and arbitration mailboxes from the server. To help you with this process, use the following techniques:

* Get a list of all mailboxes in all available databases hosted on the server by running the command **Get-MailboxDatabase -Server *ServerName* | Get-Mailbox**. These are the user mailboxes that must be moved or removed.
* Get a list of all archive mailboxes in all available databases hosted on the server by running the command **Get-MailboxDatabase -Server *ServerName* | Get-Mailbox -Archive**. These are the archive mailboxes that must be moved or removed.
* Get a list of all arbitration mailboxes in all available databases hosted on the server by running the command **Get-MailboxDatabase -Server *ServerName* | Get-Mailbox -Arbitration**. These are the arbitration mailboxes that must be moved or removed.
* Disable a non-arbitration mailbox so that you can delete the mailbox database by running the command **Disable-Mailbox *MailboxId***.
* Disable an archive mailbox so you can delete the mailbox database by running the command **Disable-Mailbox *MailboxId* -Archive**.
* Disable a public folder mailbox so that you can delete the mailbox database by running the command **Disable-Mailbox *MailboxId* -PublicFolder**.
* Rather than removing arbitration mailboxes, you should move them to another server using New-MoveRequest. If this is the last server in the organization, disable the arbitration mailbox instead by running the command **Disable-Mailbox ArMailboxID -Arbitration -DisableLastArbitrationMailboxAllowed**.

Although Exchange Setup doesn't allow you to uninstall a server, you can use Programs And Features to do this. Follow these steps:

1. Log on to the Exchange server either locally or remotely. Close any local instances of Exchange Management Shell that are open.

2. In Control Panel, click the **Uninstall A Program link** under Programs. In Programs And Features, select the **Microsoft Exchange Server 2016** entry to display the Uninstall button.

3. Click the **Uninstall** button to start Exchange Setup. When Setup finishes initializing, click **Next** to continue.

Remove Exchange Server

By clicking next, you'll remove Exchange Server 2016 from this computer. Continue only if you're sure that you want to remove Exchange from this computer.

E Exchange

next

4. Setup will then perform readiness checks to determine whether Exchange 2016 can be removed from the server. If there are errors, you will need to correct the error conditions. Perform the recommended tasks and then click Retry to have Setup repeat the readiness checks.

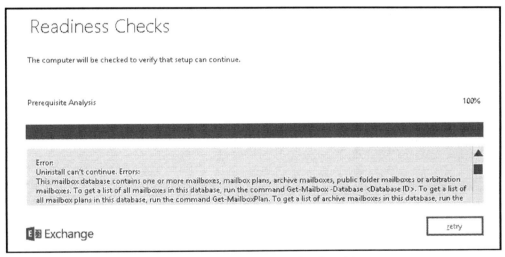

Readiness Checks

The computer will be checked to verify that setup can continue.

Prerequisite Analysis   100%

Error:
Uninstall can't continue. Errors:
This mailbox database contains one or more mailboxes, mailbox plans, archive mailboxes, public folder mailboxes or arbitration mailboxes. To get a list of all mailboxes in this database, run the command Get-Mailbox -Database <Database ID>. To get a list of all mailbox plans in this database, run the command Get-MailboxPlan. To get a list of archive mailboxes in this database, run the

E Exchange

retry

5. When Setup completes the readiness checks without error, you can complete the removal process by clicking **Uninstall**.

Using Cumulative Updates

With Exchange Server 2013 and later, Microsoft decided to start delivering routine product updates and security updates separately. Under this servicing model, routine product updates are delivered periodically as a single, cumulative update, and security updates are delivered separately. While this allows you to install security updates as they are released without having to install a cumulative update, cumulative updates themselves will contain security updates. As with earlier releases of service packs in Exchange Server, cumulative updates are delivered as full product updates and installed as an upgrade.

To better align on-premises Exchange and Exchange Online, Microsoft tries to release cumulative updates on a fixed schedule and applies cumulative updates to their hosted Exchange servers prior to official release of an update. Thus, when an update is released you know it has been applied to all Exchange Online servers and all of the mailboxes stored in the cloud.

> **IMPORTANT** Microsoft is releasing cumulative updates for other products, including Lync and SharePoint, on separate fixed schedules as well. Ideally, this will be a quarterly release schedule with four cumulative updates released each year during the product's lifecycle.

What's in Cumulative Updates?

Cumulative updates more closely resemble service packs than rollup updates. Not only may cumulative updates contain hotfixes and security updates, they may also contain new features, product enhancements, and other changes that affect the way the product works. While language modifications were previously limited to Service Pack releases, cumulative updates may contain updates to language resources. A cumulative update also may contain Active Directory schema updates. If so, the schema changes will be additive and backwards compatible with previous release and product versions.

> **IMPORTANT** Cumulative updates do not replace service packs. Microsoft will continue to release service packs for Exchange Server.

Every cumulative update and service pack is a full release of the product. This means, you install cumulative updates and service packs as a product upgrade and that each update package will be larger than the previous product or update package. Because you install cumulative updates and service packs as an upgrade, any customizations you've made to Exchange Server (using web.config files on Mailbox servers, EdgeTransport.exe.config files on Edge Transport servers, registry changes, or other custom configuration options on servers) are not preserved. This means you will lose any customizations. To prevent this, you must save your customizations and then re-apply them after applying a cumulative update or service pack.

> **REAL WORLD** Don't forget that it is possible the upgrade process will fail. If this happens, you can recover from the failed upgrade like you would recover from a failed service pack installation, which may include running Exchange Server 2016 Setup with a special recovery option. To do this, you enter the command SETUP /m:RecoverServer.
>
> In the unlikely event that the upgrade fails and is unrecoverable, you will need to re-install Exchange Server. This re-installation process will create a new server object and should not result in the loss of mailbox or queue data. However, you will need to re-seed or re-attach existing databases after the re-installation process.

How Are Cumulative Updates Applied?

You apply cumulative updates and service packs using Exchange Server Setup. Because each cumulative update and service pack is a new build of Exchange Server 2016, you don't need to apply cumulative updates or service packs in sequence. You can apply the latest cumulative update or service pack at any time. For example, if you deployed Exchange Server 2016 RTM but didn't upgrade to Cumulative Update 1, you could upgrade the original installation directly to Cumulative Update 2.

> **IMPORTANT** When you are deploying Exchange servers, you don't need to deploy Exchange Server 2016 RTM and then upgrade to a cumulative update or service pack later. As each cumulative update or service pack is a complete build, you can fully deploy the Exchange server using only the current cumulative update or service pack.

In a Database Availability Group configuration, all servers should be running the same cumulative update or service pack of Exchange Server 2016—except during an upgrade. During an upgrade, individual servers within a Database Availability Group can have different cumulative update or service pack versions. This mixed state is expected to be only temporary. Database Availability Group should not operate in a mixed state for long periods of time.

Cumulative updates and service packs are published at the Microsoft Download Center. Because staying current with cumulative updates and service packs may present a particular challenge for some Exchange installations, it is important to note that cumulative updates are supported only for three months after the release of the subsequent cumulative update. With Microsoft's goal of delivering cumulative updates quarterly, this typically means that a prior cumulative update is supported for about six months.

How Do I Track Exchange Version Numbers?

Versioning with Exchange Server 2016 gets a little tricky. The official release of Exchange Server 2016 is referred to as Exchange Server 2016 RTM. Cumulative updates for this release are referred to using the full release name plus the cumulative update number. Thus, Exchange Server 2016 with Cumulative Update 1 is referred to as Exchange Server 2016 CU1.

As Microsoft releases service packs for Exchange Server 2016, those service packs will be full product rollups that include prior cumulative updates of the product and become part of the release cycle in place of a particular cumulative update. This is why Exchange 2013 had a CU1, CU2, CU3 and then an SP1, followed by a CU5.

Keep in mind the version of Exchange Server is updated when you install a cumulative update or service pack. This means that one way to determine what cumulative update or service pack is applied is to check the version number of the Exchange server. The build number for Exchange 2016 RTM is 225.42 and the build number is incremented for each cumulative update and service pack. You can determine the Exchange version number by entering either of the following commands:

```
Get-Command ExSetup.exe | % {$_.FileVersionInfo}
```

```
Get-ExchangeServer | Format-List Name, Edition, AdminDisplayVersion
```

Installing Cumulative Updates and Service Packs

As discussed previously, cumulative updates and service packs are full builds of Exchange Server 2016. You install a cumulative update or service pack as an upgrade, and there is no rollback process should installation fail. Because of this, you should ensure you have a full recovery plan in place prior to applying a cumulative update. Typically, this means having server backups and other backup plans in place prior to installing an update.

You'll find cumulative updates and service packs for Exchange Server 2016 on the Microsoft Download Center. A single download is provided for both Exchange Server 2016 Enterprise and Exchange Server 2016 Standard. When you access the download page, click Download to start the download process. Next, copy the download to your computer for installation at a later time by clicking Save. Copy the download to your server if necessary.

When you run the executable, Windows verifies the file, and you'll then be able to extract the download to a folder. Be sure to specify an exact folder to put all the setup components in one place. Within this folder, you'll find a program called Setup.exe. This is the Exchange Server 2016 Setup program.

Preparing to Install a Cumulative Update or Service Pack

Before you run Exchange Setup make sure you read the release notes for the cumulative update or service pack. Also make sure that any server on which you plan to install the cumulative update or service pack meets the system requirements and prerequisites for Exchange Server 2016.

You can run Exchange Server 2016 only on full installations of Windows Server 2012 and later. Exchange Server 2016 doesn't support in-place upgrades from any previous version of Exchange. After you install a cumulative update or service pack, you cannot uninstall the cumulative update or service pack to revert to an earlier version of Exchange Server 2016. If you uninstall a cumulative update or service pack, Exchange Server 2016 is removed from the server.

As cumulative updates and service packs may contain Active Directory schema changes and other Active Directory updates, you may want to update Active Directory prior to deploying a cumulative update or service pack on any server in your organization, especially in a large enterprise. Here, keep the following in mind:

- If the update contains schema changes, run the following command prior to executing the Exchange Server 2016 Setup.exe: **setup.exe /PrepareSchema /IAcceptExchangeServerLicenseTerms**.
- If the update contains enterprise Active Directory changes (such as role-based Access Control updates), run the following command prior to executing the Exchange Server 2016 Setup.exe: **setup.exe /PrepareAD /IAcceptExchangeServerLicenseTerms**.
- If the update contains changes to the permissions within the Active Directory domain partition, run **setup.exe /PrepareDomain /IAcceptExchangeServerLicenseTerms** in each domain containing Exchange servers or mailboxes.

Although Exchange Server 2016 Setup can perform these processes for you during the upgrade, the changes can take some time to replicate throughout a large organization. By performing these tasks manually, you can streamline the upgrade process. You also can ensure the tasks are run with accounts that have appropriate permissions. Keep the following in mind:

- If schema needs to be updated and you haven't previously prepared schema, you must ensure the account you use is delegated membership in the Schema Admins group.
- If you're installing the first Exchange 2016 server in the organization, the account you use must have membership in the Enterprise Admins group.

- If you've already prepared the schema and aren't installing the first Exchange 2016 server in the organization, the account you use must be a member of the Exchange 2016 Organization Management role group.

> **NOTE** Administrators who are members of the Delegated Setup group can deploy Exchange 2016 servers that have been previously provisioned by a member of the Organization Management group.

After you install a cumulative update or service pack, you must restart the server so that changes can be made to the registry and operating system. If something goes wrong with the installation and re-running Setup and following the prompts doesn't help you resolve the problem, you have several options. You can restore the server from backup or you can run Exchange Server 2016 Setup in recovery mode by running **setup /m:RecoverServer** at a command prompt. If you are recovering to a different server, the server must use the same FQDN as the failed server.

When you recover a server, Setup detects the Exchange Server object in Active Directory and installs the corresponding files and configuration automatically. After you recover the server, you can restore databases and reconfigure any additional settings.

Installing a Cumulative Update or Service Pack

When you are ready to run Setup and install an update, you can begin the installation. If you are installing a new server using a current cumulative update or service pack, follow the procedure as discussed previously under "Installing Exchange Server." Otherwise, to update an existing installation of Exchange 2016, complete the following steps:

1. Log on to the server using an administrator account. When you install the Mailbox role, you must use a domain account that is a member of the Enterprise Administrators group and a member of the Exchange Organization Administrators group.

> **IMPORTANT** Before beginning setup, you should close any open Windows PowerShell or MMC windows. Otherwise you will see a warning during the readiness checks that you need to close these windows. The installation process may make updates to Windows PowerShell and MMC which requires exclusive access.

> **CAUTION** If you are applying a cumulative update or service pack to an existing Exchange 2016 server, any customized per-server settings you made

in Exchange configuration files will be overwritten. To prevent this, save your customized settings before you run Setup. This will help you easily re-configure your server after the update.

2. Access the folder where you extracted the Exchange setup files and then start Exchange 2016 Setup by double-clicking **Setup.exe**. If you've enabled User Access Control (UAC), you must right-click Setup.exe and select Run As Administrator.

3. On the Check For Updates page, you can specify whether to check for updates to the setup process. If you don't want to check for updates, select **Don't Check For Updates** before you click **Next** to continue. Setup will then copy files and initialize resources.

    The server also tries to validate the state of Active Directory. If the server is unable to validate the state of Active Directory and choose a domain controller to work with, Setup will log errors and may also report that a domain controller could not be located. If errors are reported, do not continue with the installation. Instead, exit Setup and resolve the communication problem.

4. If you are installing a new server, you'll see the Introduction page. If you are updating an existing server, you'll see the Upgrade page. Click **Next** to continue.

> **IMPORTANT**   Seeing the Upgrade page is a confirmation that Setup identified the existing Exchange 2016 installation on the server. There is a problem if you are applying an update or service pack to a server already running Exchange 2016 and don't see the Upgrade page at this point. You may need to restart the server or resume Exchange services that have been stopped and then re-run Setup.

5. On the License Agreement page, review the software license terms. If you agree to the terms, select **I Accept The Terms In The License Agreement**, and then click **Next**.

6. On the Readiness Checks page, ensure the prerequisite checks completed successfully. If they haven't, you must resolve any reported errors before you can update Exchange Server 2016. For most errors, you don't need to exit Setup. After resolving a reported error, click **Retry** to run the prerequisite checks again.

> **NOTE**   A cumulative update or service pack may require additional Windows components.

7. When all readiness checks have completed successfully, click **Install** to update Exchange 2016. The installation process should take about 60 minutes.

The Setup Progress page tracks the progress of the installation. The installation is performed in a series of steps, with the progress for the current step tracked with a progress bar and as a percentage of completion. The number of steps varies, depending on the tasks Setup must perform to prepare the environment as well as the options you selected.

As part of the update, Setup removes existing Exchange files from the installation and then copies new files into the appropriate directories. Finally, you'll see the Setup Completed page, when Setup completes the installation.

You must restart the server to finalize the installation. You can verify that the update to Exchange 2016 installed successfully by running the following command to confirm the version has been updated:

```
Get-ExchangeServer | Format-List Name, Edition, AdminDisplayVersion
```

During installation, Exchange Setup logs events in the Application log. You can review the Application log to make sure there are no warning or error messages related to Exchange setup. You also can learn more about the installation by reviewing the setup log file created during the setup process. This log file is stored in the %SystemDrive%\ExchangeSetupLogs folder with the name ExchangeSetup.log. The %SystemDrive% variable represents the root directory of the drive where the operating system is installed. Review any error entries in the log file.

Chapter 4. Exchange 2016 Administration Essentials

To work effectively with Exchange 2016, you need to master a number of key concepts, including:

- How to access and work with Exchange Admin Center
- How connections are authenticated and proxied
- How Exchange uses virtual directories
- Why Exchange requires SSL certificates
- Which Windows processes are used with Exchange Server

For troubleshooting or deeper work with Exchange, you also need to know how to bypass Exchange Admin Center and Exchange Management Shell so that you can work directly with Exchange Server. These topics are all covered in this chapter.

Working with Exchange Admin Center

Whether you are working with on-premises, online, and hybrid Exchange organizations, you'll use one graphical tool for administration: Exchange Admin Center. Exchange Admin Center is a browser-based application that you access via the Mailbox servers deployed in your Exchange organization. This application can be configured with an internal access URL and an external access URL. However, as only an internal access URL is configured by default, you can initially only access Exchange Admin Center when you are on the corporate network. To access this application when working outside the organization, you'll need to configure an external access URL.

Accessing Exchange Admin Center

Although Exchange Admin Center replaces Exchange Management Console and Exchange Control Panel (ECP), ECP continues to be the name for the related virtual directory. You access Exchange Admin Center by following these steps:

1. Exchange Admin Center works with most browsers, as long as you are using a current version. In your browser, enter the secure URL for Exchange Admin Center. If you are outside the corporate network, enter the external URL, such as *https://mail.tvpress.com/ecp*. If you are inside the corporate network, enter the internal URL, such as https://mailserver48/ecp.

The version of Exchange Admin Center you see depends on the version of

Exchange running on the Mailbox server hosting your personal mailbox. Exchange 2016 runs version 15, and you can specify this version explicitly by appending **?ExchClientVer=15** to the internal or external URL. For example, if your external URL is https://mail.tvpress.com, you could enter **https://mail.tvpress.com/ecp?ExchClientVer=15** as the URL.

> **NOTE** By default, you must use HTTPS to connect. If you don't, you'll see an error stating "Access is denied." Using HTTPS ensures data transmitted between the client browser and the server is encrypted and secured.

2. If your browser displays a security alert stating there's a problem with the site's security certificate or that the connection is untrusted, proceed anyway. This alert is displayed because the browser does not trust the self-signed certificate that was automatically created when the Exchange server was installed.

- With Internet Explorer, the error states "There's a problem with this website's security certificate." Proceed by selecting the Continue To This Web Site (Not Recommended) link.
- With Google Chrome, the error states "Your connection is not private." Continue by clicking the Advanced link and then clicking the Proceed To ... link.
- With Mozilla Firefox, the error states "This connection is untrusted." Proceed by selecting I Understand The Risks and then selecting Add Exception. Finally, in the Add Security Exception dialog box, select Confirm Security Exception.

3. You'll see the logon page for Exchange Admin Center. Enter your user name and password, and then click **Sign In**.

    Be sure to specify your user name in DOMAIN\username format. The domain can either be the DNS domain, such as imaginedlands.com, or the NetBIOS domain name, such as imaginedlands. For example, the user JoeH could specify his logon name as imaginedlands.com\joeh or imaginedlands\joeh.

4. If you are logging on for the first time, select your preferred display language and time zone, and then click **Save**.

After you log in to Exchange Admin Center, you'll see the list view with manageable features listed in the Feature pane (see Figure 4-1). When you select a feature in the Feature pane, you'll then see the related topics or "tabs" for that feature. The manageable items for a selected topic or tab are displayed in the main area of the browser window. For example, when you select Recipients in the Feature pane, the topics or tabs that you can work with include: Mailboxes, Groups, Resources, Contacts, Shared and Migration.

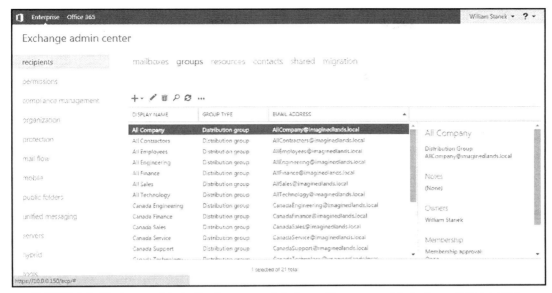

FIGURE 4-1 Exchange Admin Center uses a list view with manageable features listed on the left.

Working with Exchange Server Certificates

When you install an Exchange server, the setup process creates several self-signed security certificates that are used for authentication. The default certificates available for Mailbox servers include:

- **Microsoft Exchange**   A self-signed certificate used by IMAP, POP, IIS, and SMTP. If Autodiscover is configured, this certificate is also used for Autodiscover. This is the primary certificate used by Exchange.
- **Microsoft Server Auth Certificate**   A self-signed certificate for authenticating SMTP connections.
- **Exchange Delegation Federation**   A self-signed certificate used when federated sharing is configured in the Exchange organization.
- **WMSVC**   A self-signed certificate used by the Windows Management service.

As Figure 4-2 shows, you can view these certificates in Exchange Admin Center by selecting Servers in the Feature pane and then selecting Certificates. Because the default certificates are not issued by a trusted authority, you see a related error message whenever you use HTTPS to access services hosted by your Mailbox servers, including Exchange Admin Center, the PowerShell application, and Microsoft Outlook Web App.

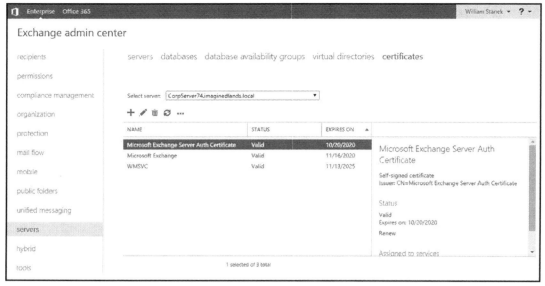

FIGURE 4-2 Viewing the SSL certificates installed on Exchange servers.

One way to eliminate this error message is to install a certificate from a trusted authority on your Mailbox servers. Web browsers should already be configured to trust certificates issued by your organization's certification authority (CA) or by a trusted third-party authority. Typically, browsers need additional configuration only when you use your own CA with non-domain-joined machines.

The services a certificate can be used with include Internet Message Access Protocol (IMAP), Post Office Protocol (POP), SMTP, Internet Information Services (IIS), and Unified Messaging (UM). The default self-signed certificates are assigned services automatically during setup based on the roles installed on the Exchange server.

When you work with certificates, it's critical that you ensure the certificate is used for the right subject name and alternative names. As an example, the Microsoft Exchange certificate created by default has the Subject set as cn=ServerName, where ServerName is the name of the server, such as cn=MailServer21, and the Subject Alternative Names is set as DNS Name=ServerName, DNS NAME=FullyQualifiedServerName, and DNS Name=DomainName. If Autodiscover is configured, there's also a Subject Alternative Name entry for DNS Name=Autodiscover.DomainName. For example, MailServer21 in the Imaginedlands.com domain means the subject name is set as:

```
cn=MailServer21
```

and the Subject Alternative Name entries typically are:

```
DNS Name = MailServer21
DNS Name = MailServer21.imaginedlands.com
DNS Name = imaginedlands.com
DNS Name = Autodiscover.imaginedlands.com
```

> **REAL WORLD**   Outlook Web App (OWA) and Exchange Admin Center can become inaccessible as a result of a required SSL certificate becoming corrupted or being invalidated. If this happens, you will need to access Exchange directly and re-create the required certificate or certificates. One way to safeguard yourself against this problem is to create copies of the original certificates using the Certificates snap-in. When you add this snap-in to a Microsoft Management Console, specify that you want to manage certificates for a computer account. You'll then find the certificates under the Personal node. Export each certificate in turn using the Certificate Export Wizard. To start this wizard, right-click a certificate, select All Tasks, and then select Export.

If your organization has a CA, have your security administrator issue a certificate. Generate the certificate by completing the following steps.

1. In a web browser, open Certificate Services by entering the appropriate URL, such as **https://CertServer03/certsrv**.

2. Specify that you want to create a new request and then choose the advanced creation option.

3. Submit a certificate request by using a base 64 encoded PKS #7 or PKS #12 file.

4. Once the certificate request file is generated, open the file in a text editor.

5. While you are working with Certificate Services in your browser, access the request. Copy the contents of the certificate request file and paste them into the request.

6. Select web server as the server type, and leave all other attributes blank.

7. Save the certificate.

After you create the certificate, you must make it available on the designated Exchange server. To do this, access the Exchange server and then import the certificate using Import-ExchangeCertificate. Next, use Enable-ExchangeCertificate to enable the certificate for specific Exchange services.

If you can purchase a certificate from a trusted third-party authority, you also must make the certificate available on the designated Exchange server. To do this, access the Exchange server and then import the certificate using Import-ExchangeCertificate. Next, use Enable-ExchangeCertificate to enable the certificate for specific Exchange services. Finally, ensure that the new certificate is in use and test web services using Test-OutlookWebServices as shown in the following example:

```
test-outlookwebservices | fl
```

By default Test-OutlookWebServices verifies the Availability service, Outlook Anywhere, Offline Address Book, and Exchange Web Services. Test MAPI over HTTP using -ProbeIdentity OutlookMapiHttpSelfTestProbe with Test-OutlookConnectivity. Test connectivity to the OWA and ECP virtual directories using Test-OwaConnectivity and Test-EcpConnectivity respectively. However, before you can use any of the Test cmdlets, you must create a test account by running the Scripts\New-TestCasConnectivityUser.ps1 script. You'll find this script in the %ExchangeInstallPath%, which by default is C:\Program Files\Microsoft\Exchange Server\V15\. The password you set for the test account is temporary and will be automatically changed every 7 days.

Once you've imported and enabled the certificate, you can then view the certificate in Exchange Admin Center or by using Get-ExchangeCertificate to confirm it is configured as expected. You'll want to ensure the status is valid, the expiration date is appropriate, the subject name is correct, the subject alternative names are correct, and that the assigned services are appropriate.

Configuring Exchange Admin Center

You can configure Exchange Admin Center for single-server and multiserver environments. In a single-server environment, you use one Mailbox server for all of your remote management needs. In a multiple-server environment, you can instruct administrators to use different URLs to access different Mailbox servers, or you can use load-balancing and give all administrators the same access URL.

> **IMPORTANT**   You should work out a plan for Exchange namespaces as part of your deployment and configuration. You will need a namespace for autodiscover, HTTP, SMTP and other technologies you've deployed in the Exchange organization, such as IMAP or POP3. If you have a large Exchange organization, each Exchange namespace can be load balanced across your

datacenters in a layer 7 configuration that doesn't rely on session affinity. With a datacenter pair, you could achieve an approximately 50/50 traffic split between the datacenters using round robin DNS or a similar technique.

NOTE You can use Exchange Admin Center with firewalls. You configure your network to use a perimeter network with firewalls in front of the designated Mailbox servers and then open port 443 to the IP addresses of your Mailbox servers. If Secure Sockets Layer (SSL) is enabled and you want to use SSL exclusively, you only need port 443, and you don't need to open port 80.

You can manage the Exchange Admin Center application using Internet Information Services (IIS) Manager or Exchange Management Shell. The related commands for Exchange Management Shell are as follows:

- **Get-ECPVirtualDirectory** Displays information about the ECP application running on the Web server providing services for Exchange. By default, only front-end virtual directories are listed. Add –ShowMailboxVirtualDirectories to also display the back-end virtual directories.

```
Get-ECPVirtualDirectory [-Identity AppName]
[-ADPropertiesOnly <$true | $false>]
[-ShowMailboxVirtualDirectories <$true | $false>]
[-DomainController DomainControllerName]

Get-ECPVirtualDirectory -Server ExchangeServerName
[-ADPropertiesOnly <$true | $false>]
[-ShowMailboxVirtualDirectories <$true | $false>]
[-DomainController DomainControllerName]
```

- **New-ECPVirtualDirectory** Creates a new ECP application running on the Web server providing services for Exchange. You should use this command only for troubleshooting scenarios where you are required to remove and re-create the ECP virtual directory.

```
New-ECPVirtualDirectory [-AppPoolId AppPoolName]
[-DomainController DomainControllerName] [-ExternalUrl URL]
[-InternalUrl URL] [-WebSiteName SiteName]
```

- **Remove-ECPVirtualDirectory** Use the Remove-ECPVirtualDirectory cmdlet to remove a specified ECP application providing services for Exchange.

```
Remove-ECPVirtualDirectory -Identity AppName
[-DomainController DomainControllerName]
```

- **Set-ECPVirtualDirectory**   Modifies the configuration settings for a specified ECP application providing services for Exchange. Set -AdminEnabled to $false to turn off Internet access to the Exchange Admin Center.

```
Set-ECPVirtualDirectory -Identity AppName
[-AdminEnabled <$true | $false>]
[-BasicAuthentication <$true | $false>] [-DomainController
DomainControllerName] [-ExternalAuthenticationMethods Methods]
[-DigestAuthentication <$true | $false>]
[-FormsAuthentication <$true | $false>]
[-ExternalUrl URL] [-GzipLevel <Off | Low | High | Error>]
[-InternalUrl URL] [-LiveIdAuthentication <$true | $false>]
[-WindowsAuthentication <$true | $false>]
```

- **Test-ECPConnectivity**   Displays information about the ECP application running on the Web server providing services for Exchange.

```
Test-ECPConnectivity [-ClientAccessServer ServerName]
[-MailboxServer ServerName] [-DomainController DomainControllerName]
[-RTSEndPoint EndPointID] [-TestType <Internal | External>]
[-MonitoringContext <$true | $false>]
[-ResetTestAccountCredentials <$true | $false>]
[-Timeout NumSeconds] [-TrustAnySSLCertificate <$true | $false>]
[-VirtualDirectoryName DirectoryName]
```

At Exchange Management Shell prompt, you can confirm the location of the Exchange Admin Center application by typing **get-ecpvirtualdirectory**.

Get-ECPVirtualDirectory lists the name of the application, the associated webwsite, and the server on which the application is running, as shown in the following example:

```
Name                           Server
-------                        -------
ecp (Default Web Site)         MailServer62
```

In this example, a standard configuration is being used in which the application named ECP is running on the Default Web Site on MailServer62. You can use Set-ECPVirtualDirectory to specify the internal and external URL to use as well as the permitted authentication types. Authentication types you can enable or disable include basic authentication, Windows authentication, and Live ID basic authentication. You can use New-ECPVirtualDirectory to create or re-create an ECP application on a Web server providing services for Exchange and Remove-ECPVirtualDirectory to remove an ECP application. You can verify that Exchange Admin Center is working properly using Test-ECPConnectivity.

The PowerShell application has a similar set of commands. In Exchange Management Shell, the related commands are New-PowerShellVirtualDirectory, Get-PowerShellVirtualDirectory, Set-PowerShellVirtualDirectory, and Test-PowerShellConnectivity. If you enter **Get-PowerShellVirtualDirectory | Format-List,** you'll get configuration details for each Exchange server in the Exchange organization. You can use Set-PowerShellVirtualDirectory to enable or disable authentication mechanisms, including basic authentication, certificate authentication, Live ID basic authentication, Live ID NTLM negotiate authentication, and Windows authentication. You can also specify the internal and external URLs for the PowerShell virtual directory on a per-server basis. By default, servers have only internal URLs for PowerShell. For troubleshooting issues related to the PowerShell virtual directory, enter **Test-PowerShellConnectivity** followed by the URL to test, such as https://mailer1.tvpress.com/powershell.

You'll also find commands for working with virtual directories related to:

- Outlook Web App, including New-OwaVirtualDirectory, Get-OwaVirtualDirectory, Set-OwaVirtualDirectory, and Remove-OwaVirtualDirectory
- Offline Address Books, including New-OabVirtualDirectory, Get-OabVirtualDirectory, Set-OabVirtualDirectory, and Remove-OabVirtualDirectory
- Autodiscover, including New-AutodiscoverVirtualDirectory, Get-AutodiscoverVirtualDirectory, Set-AutodiscoverVirtualDirectory, and Remove-AutodiscoverVirtualDirectory
- Exchange ActiveSync, including New-ActiveSyncVirtualDirectory, Get-ActiveSyncVirtualDirectory, Set-ActiveSyncVirtualDirectory, and Remove-ActiveSyncVirtualDirectory
- MAPI over HTTP, including New-MapiVirtualDirectory, Get-MapiVirtualDirectory, Set-MapiVirtualDirectory, and Remove-MapiVirtualDirectory

Keep in mind that there are separate but interconnected virtual directories representing front-end and back-end services. Typically, front-end virtual directories are used for authentication and proxying while back-end virtual directories are used for actual processing. Although the front-end and back-end virtual directories have different components and configurations, the Exchange cmdlets for creating these virtual directories are designed to configure the appropriate settings and components for either front-end or back-end use as appropriate.

You should specify explicitly whether you want to work with the front-end or back-end components. You do this by specifying the related website name. The Default Web Site is used by the front-end components and the Exchange Back End website is used by back-end components.

Bypassing Exchange Admin Center and Troubleshooting

Exchange makes extensive use of IIS. Front-end apps for each essential client service are configured on the Default Web Site. Back-end apps for each essential client service are configured on the Exchange Back End website. This means you'll find front-end and back-end apps for ActiveSync, Autodiscover, ECP, EWS, MAPI, OAB, PowerShell and RPC connections made over HTTP.

Understanding Remote Execution in Exchange Admin Center

When you access OWA in a web browser, you are performing remote operations via the PowerShell application running on the Web server providing Exchange services whether you are logged on locally to an Exchange server or working remotely. The same is true for ECP, but the process is a little more complex, as shown in the following high-level view of the login and workflow process:

1. Generally, OWA handles the initial login for ECP. Thus, when you access ECP using a URL such as https://mailserver17/ecp, the browser actually is redirected to OWA with a URL such as https://mailserver17/owa/auth/logon.aspx?replaceCurrent=1&url=https%3a%2f%2fmailserver17%2fecp%2f.

2. Once you log in to Exchange, you are connected to the designated Mailbox server using the ECP app running on the Default Web Site.

3. ECP performs authentication checks that validate your access to the Exchange 2016 server and determine the Exchange role groups and roles your account is a member of. You must be a member of at least one management role.

4. ECP creates a remote session with the Exchange 2016 server. A remote session is a runspace that establishes a common working environment for executing commands on remote computers.

5. By default, you are connected to the Mailbox server on which your user mailbox resides with the front-end ECP app on that server acting as proxy for the backend ECP app on that server.

6. As you perform tasks, these tasks are executed via the PowerShell app, which also has front-end and back-end components.

IMPORTANT Every step of the login and workflow process relies on properly configured SSL certificates. HTTPS uses SSL certificates to establish and encrypt connections. SSL certificates are also used to initialize and validate remote sessions. Although you could disable the requirement for HTTPS and allow HTTP to be used for connections, the remote sessions themselves would still rely on properly configured SSL certificates.

Thus, many interconnected components must be functioning correctly for you to connect to and work with Exchange Server.

Bypassing Exchange Admin Center and Exchange Management Shell

Because Exchange Management Shell uses remote sessions that run via the PowerShell application running on IIS, you often need a way to work directly with Exchange Server, especially when you are trying to diagnose and resolve problems. Intuitively, you might think that you should do this in the same way you establish a remote session with Exchange Online. For example, if you want to connect to Server21, you might want to use the following code:

```
$Session = New-PSSession -ConfigurationName Microsoft.Exchange
-ConnectionUri https://server21/powershell/ -Authentication Basic
-Credential wrstanek@imaginedlands.com -AllowRedirection

Import-PSSession $Session
```

However, if there any configuration problems, including issues with SSL certificates, you won't be able to connect to or work with Exchange Server in this way. Instead, you'll have to bypass the web-based management interfaces and connect directly to Exchange server using the following technique:

1. Log on to the Mailbox server you want to work with—either at the console or using a remote desktop connection.

2. Open an administrative PowerShell window by right-clicking **Windows PowerShell** and then clicking **Run As Administrator**.

3. Import all Exchange-related snapins for Windows PowerShell by entering **Add-PSSnapin *exchange***. You'll then be able to work directly with Exchange and any related cmdlets.

Because Exchange has separate front-end and back-end components, you'll often need to perform troubleshooting tasks on both. Rather than log on locally to a server, you may want to work remotely. You can invoke commands, establish direct remote sessions, or execute commands remotely using the -ComputerName parameter available with certain cmdlets. (For more information, see Chapters 4 and 5 in *Windows PowerShell: The Personal Trainer. [Stanek & Associates, 2015]*)

To invoke commands on remote servers or establish a direct remote session, use the following technique:

1. Log on to any workstation or server where you've installed the Exchange management tools. (Doing so ensures the Exchange related snap-ins are available.)

2. Open an administrative PowerShell window by right-clicking **Windows PowerShell**, and then clicking **Run As Administrator**.

3. Import all Exchange-related snapins for Windows PowerShell by entering **Add-PSSnapin *exchange***.

4. Either invoke commands on the remote Exchange server or establish a remote session with the remote Exchange server. In your remote sessions, be sure to connect directly, as shown in the following example:

```
$Session = New-PSSession -computername mailserver26
-Credential imaginedlands\williams


Import-PSSession $Session
```

> **IMPORTANT**   When you work with Exchange in this way, you establish connections via the Windows Remote Management (WinRM) service. On an Exchange server, WinRM and related services are set up automatically. On your management computer, you may need to install the required components and configure WinRM as discussed previously in "Using Exchange Management Shell" in Chapter 1, "Getting Started with Exchange

Server 2016." See also "Customizing Remote Management Services" later in this chapter.

Troubleshooting OWA, ECP, Powershell, and More

Sometimes users and administrators see a blank page or an error when they try to log in to OWA or ECP. This problem and other connection issues, such as those related to OAB, Autodiscover, and PowerShell, can occur because of a wide variety of configuration issues, including:

* Invalid or missing TCP/IP settings
* Corrupted or improperly configured virtual directories
* Missing, expired, invalid, or improperly configured SSL certificates

However, before you look at specific issues, ensure required services are running as discussed in "Maintaining Exchange Services" later in this chapter. Be sure to examine the services related to both front-end and back-end services.

Typically, the next logical step is to validate the TCP/IP settings of your Mailbox servers. Not only do servers need to communicate with each other and clients, they also need to communicate with domain controllers.

If Exchange Server can't communicate properly with a domain controller, you may see an error similar to the following when you open Exchange Admin Center or Exchange Management Shell:

```
The LDAP server is unavailable.
Description: An unhandled exception occurred during the execution of the
current web request. Please review the stack trace for more information
about the error and where it originated in the code.

Exception Details: System.DirectoryServices.Protocols.LdapException: The
LDAP server is unavailable.


Source Error:


An unhandled exception was generated during the execution of the current
web request. Information regarding the origin and location of the exception
can be identified using the exception stack trace below.
```

```
Stack Trace:


[LdapException: The LDAP server is unavailable.]
    System.DirectoryServices.Protocols.LdapConnection.Connect() +160015
    System.DirectoryServices.Protocols.LdapConnection.BindHelper
(NetworkCredential newCredential, Boolean needSetCredential) +264
    Microsoft.Exchange.Data.Directory.PooledLdapConnection.BindWithRetry
(Int32 maxRetries) +702
```

Resolve the problem by doing the following:

- Ensure the server has the proper TCP/IP settings and is connected to the network.
- Ensure a domain controller is available for the server to communicate with.

Users or administrators may see a blank page when they try to log on to OWA or ECP as a result of a configuration or certificate problem. If you've determined that required services are running and that the TCP/IP settings are correct, next try to isolate and identify the specific issue.

FIGURE 4-3 An error related to an improperly configured virtual directory or a misconfiguration in IIS.

Try to log on to OWA or ECP in a browser. Sometimes when you log on to OWA or ECP, you'll see a runtime error that indicates an improperly configured virtual directory or an application error due to misconfiguration in IIS (see Figure 4-3). Other times, the browser window may simply be empty or blank as mentioned previously.

For deeper troubleshooting, log on to the Mailbox server hosting the mailbox for the users or administrators experiencing the problem and open Exchange Management Shell. If there's a problem with SSL certificates rather than virtual directory configuration, you'll see an error similar to the following:

```
New-PSSession : [mailserver08] Connecting to remote server mailserver08
failed with the following error message : The server certificate on the
destination computer (mailserver08:443) has the following errors:
The SSL certificate is signed by an unknown certificate authority. For more
information, see the about_Remote_Troubleshooting Help topic.
At line:1 char:12
+ $Session = New-PSSession -ConfigurationName Microsoft.Exchange
-ConnectionUri http ...
+ ~~~~~~~~~~~~~~~~~~~~~~~~~~~~~~~~~~~~~~~~~~~~~~~~~~~~~~~~~~~~~~~~~~~~~~~
~~~~~~~~~~~~~~~~
    + CategoryInfo          : OpenError
 (System.Manageme....RemoteRunspace:RemoteRunspace) [New-PSSession],
PSRemotingTransportException
    + FullyQualifiedErrorId : 12175,PSSessionOpenFailed
```

If there's a problem with virtual directory configuration, you may see another type of error, such as:

```
New-PSSession : [mailserver55.imaginedlands.com] Processing data from
remote server mailserver55.imaginedlands.com failed with the following
error message: The WinRM Shell client cannot process the request. The shell
handle passed to the WSMan Shell function is not valid. The shell handle is
valid only when WSManCreateShell function completes successfully. Change
 the request including a valid shell handle and try again. For more
information, see the about_Remote_Troubleshooting Help topic.
At line:1 char:1
```

```
+ New-PSSession -ConnectionURI "$connectionUri" -ConfigurationName
Microsoft.Excha ... + ~~~~~~~~~~~~~~~~~~~~~~~~~~~~~~~~~~~~~~~~~~~~~~~~
~~~~~~~~~~~~~~~~~~~~~~~~~~~~~~
   + CategoryInfo         : OpenError:
(System.Manageme....RemoteRunspace:RemoteRunspace) [New-PSSession],
PSRemotingTransportException
+ FullyQualifiedErrorId : -2144108212,PSSessionOpenFailed
```

To help diagnose the problem, you can test services using Test-OutlookWebServices. By default, Test-OutlookWebServices verifies the Availability service, Outlook Anywhere, Offline Address Book, and Unified Messaging. You can test OWA, ECP, and PowerShell using Test-OwaConnectivity, Test-EcpConnectivity, and Test-PowerShellConnectivity respectively.

Resolving SSL Certificate Issues

To resolve a certificate issue, you'll need to restore or recreate the primary SSL certificate on the Mailbox server. By default, the self-signed certificate named Microsoft Exchange is the certificate used for authentication and encrypting communications whenever you use OWA, ECP, or the management tools to work with Exchange. If you backed up the certificates on the server or exported the certificates as discussed previously in this chapter in "Working with Exchange Server certificates," you can restore the original certificate to restore services.

If you don't have a backup or an export of the primary SSL certificate, you'll need to re-create the certificate. You can create a new self-signed certificate using New-ExchangeCertificate. The following example shows how to configure services, the subject name, and subject alternative names for MailServer08 in the Imaginedlands.com domain:

```
New-ExchangeCertificate -SubjectName "cn=MailServer08"
-DomainName imaginedlands.com -IncludeServerFQDN
-Services IIS, IMAP, POP, SMTP
```

> **IMPORTANT** If there's a problem preventing you from using Exchange Admin Center and Exchange Management Shell, you'll need to bypass the web-based management interfaces and connect directly to Exchange Server using the technique discussed earlier in the chapter.

With certificates issued by a local CA or a third-party CA, you can use the original certificate file. Import the certificate using Import-ExchangeCertificate and then use Enable-ExchangeCertificate to enable the certificate for IIS, IMAP, POP, and SMTP services. You can ensure that the certificate is in use and test services as discussed previously.

Resolving OWA, ECP, or Other Virtual Directory Issues

To resolve a virtual directory issue, you can remove and then re-create the virtual directory. You won't always know whether the problem exists in the front-end configuration, the back-end configuration, or both, so you may need to remove and re-create both virtual directories. I recommend removing and re-creating the front-end virtual directory first and then checking to see if this resolves the problem before removing and re-creating the back-end virtual directory.

As an example, if you've determined the OWA virtual directory is misconfigured, you can remove it using Remove-OwaVirtualDirectory and then re-create it using New-OwaVirtualDirectory. For example, the following commands remove and then re-create the OWA virtual directory from the Default Web Site on MailServer08:

```
remove-owavirtualdirectory -identity "mailserver08\owa (Default Web Site)"
```

```
new-owavirtualdirectory -server mailserver08
-websitename "Default Web Site"
```

> **IMPORTANT**   Keep in mind that if there's a problem preventing you from using Exchange Admin Center and Exchange Management Shell, you'll need to bypass the web-based management interfaces and connect directly to Exchange Server using the technique discussed earlier in the chapter. You'll then be able to remove the virtual directory and then re-create it. When you are logged on to the server you are configuring, you don't need to use the -Server parameter with New-OwaVirtualDirectory.

By default, the New-OwaVirtualDirectory and New-EcpVirtualDirectory commands enable basic authentication and forms authentication but do not enable Windows authentication. Because Windows authentication is required for OWA and ECP, you must use the Set-OwaVirtualDirectory and Set-EcpVirtualDirectory commands to modify the default authentication settings. The following example enables Windows authentication and disables basic and forms authentication:

```
set-owavirtualdirectory -identity "mailserver08\owa (Default Web Site)"
-WindowsAuthentication $True -Basicauthentication $false
-Formsauthentication $false
```

After you re-create a virtual directory you should restart IIS services. You can do this in IIS Manager or by entering the following command at an elevated command prompt or shell:

```
iisreset
```

You can then test the service using Test-OwaConnectivity, or you can try to log in to OWA. If this doesn't resolve the problem, you can remove, re-create, and configure the OWA virtual directory for the back-end services, as shown in this example:

```
remove-owavirtualdirectory -identity "mailserver55\owa (Exchange Back End)"

new-owavirtualdirectory -server mailserver55
-websitename "Exchange Back End"

set-owavirtualdirectory -identity "mailserver55\owa (Exchange Back End)"
-WindowsAuthentication $True -Basicauthentication $false
-Formsauthentication $false
```

Complete the process by restarting IIS services and then check to ensure the problem is resolved. If the problem isn't resolved, look to related services. For example, remote PowerShell must be properly configured for OWA and ECP to work. If you suspect the PowerShell virtual directory is misconfigured, you can remove and re-create it as well.

Validating Exchange Server Licensing

With Exchange Server 2016, you do not enter a product key during initial setup. Instead, you provide the product key after installation using Exchange Admin Center. Until you enter a product key, Exchange Server 2016 runs in trial mode.

The product key you provide determines which edition is established on an Exchange server. You can use a valid product key to go from a trial edition to

Standard Edition or Enterprise Edition of Exchange Server 2016 without having to reinstall the program.

To determine the established edition and licensing for an Exchange server complete the following steps:

1. In Exchange Admin Center, select **Servers** in the Feature pane.

2. In the main pane, select the server you want to work with.

3. Look in the Details pane to see the server roles, version, established edition, and license details.

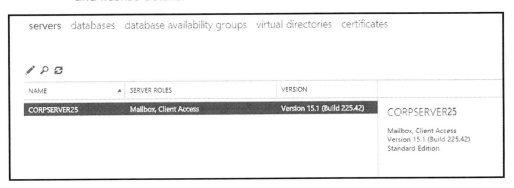

To enter a product key complete the following steps:

1. In Exchange Admin Center, select **Servers** in the Feature pane.

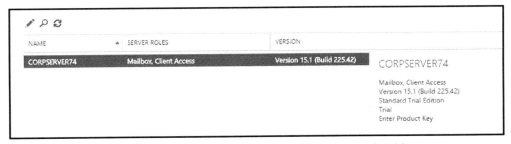

2. In the main pane, select the server you want to work with.

3. In the details pane, select **Enter Product Key**. This opens the Exchange Server dialog box.

CORPSERVER74

general
databases and database
availability groups
POP3
IMAP4
unified messaging
DNS lookups
transport limits
transport logs
Outlook Anywhere

Version number:

Version 15.1 (Build 225.42)

Roles:

Mailbox, Client Access

This Exchange server is currently licensed as a Trial Edition. You can add a new license by entering a product key below. Learn more

Enter a valid product key.

[ ] - [ ] - [ ] - [ ] - [ ]

Save   Cancel

4.   Enter the product key for the Exchange Server 2016 edition you want to establish, either Standard or Enterprise, and then click **Save**.

NOTE The product key is a 25-character alphanumeric string, grouped in sets of five characters separated by hyphens. You can find the product key on the Exchange Server 2016 media or license.

5.   You should see a dialog box stating the product key has been validated and the product ID has been created. If there's a problem with the product key, you'll see an invalid key warning. Click **OK**. Re-enter or correct the product key and then click Save again. Keep the following in mind:

■ Whenever you set or change the product key on a Mailbox server, you must restart the Microsoft Exchange Information Store service to apply the change. In PowerShell, you can do this by entering **restart-service msexchangeis**.

■ While you can upgrade from Standard to Enterprise edition simply by entering a key for Enterprise edition, you cannot use product keys to downgrade editions. To downgrade editions, you must uninstall Exchange Server and then reinstall the older version.

Using Exchange Management Shell, you can enter a server's product key using the Set-ExchangeServer cmdlet. Sample 4-1 shows the syntax and usage. For the identity parameter, use the server's name, such as MailServer55.

SAMPLE 4-1 Setting the Exchange product key syntax and usage

Syntax

```
Set-ExchangeServer -Identity 'ServerName'
-ProductKey 'ProductKey'
```

Usage

```
Set-ExchangeServer -Identity 'MailServer55'
-ProductKey 'AAAAA-BBBBB-CCCCC-DDDDD-EEEEE'
```

> **TIP** By using a valid product key, you can change from the Standard to the Enterprise edition. You also can relicense an Exchange server by entering a new product key for the installed edition, which is useful if you accidentally used the same product key on multiple servers and want to correct the mistake. The best way to do this is to enter the product key using the Set-ExchangeServer cmdlet.

Using and Managing Exchange Services

Each Exchange server in the organization relies on a set of services for routing messages, processing transactions, replicating data, and much more. "Services for Exchange Server" in Chapter 1, "Getting Started with Exchange Server 2016" lists these services.

> **TIP** Of all the Exchange services, the one service that relies on having a network connection at startup is the Microsoft Exchange Information Store service. If you start an Exchange server and the server doesn't have a network connection, the Microsoft Exchange Information Store service might fail to start. As a result, you might have to manually start the service. Sometimes, you'll find the service has a Stopping state. In this case, you have to wait until the server completely stops the service before you restart it.

Working with Exchange Services

To manage Exchange services, use the Services node in the Computer Management console, which you start by completing the following steps:

1. Start Computer Management. Type **compmgmt** in the Search box, and then select **Computer Management**. Or, on the Tools menu in Server Manager, select Computer Management.

2. To connect to a remote Exchange server, right-click the Computer Management entry in the console tree, and then select **Connect To Another Computer** from the shortcut menu. You can now choose the Exchange server for which you want to manage services.

3. Expand the Services And Applications node, and then select **Services**.

Figure 4-4 shows the Services view in the Computer Management console. The key fields of this window are as follows:

- **Name** The name of the service.
- **Description** A short description of the service and its purpose.
- **Status** The status of the service as started, paused, or stopped. (Stopped is indicated by a blank entry.)
- **Startup Type** The startup setting for the service.

> **NOTE** Automatic services are started when the computer is started. Manual services are started by users or other services. Disabled services are turned off and can't be started. To start a disabled service, you must first enable it and then start it.

- **Log On As** The account the service logs on as. The default, in most cases, is the local system account.

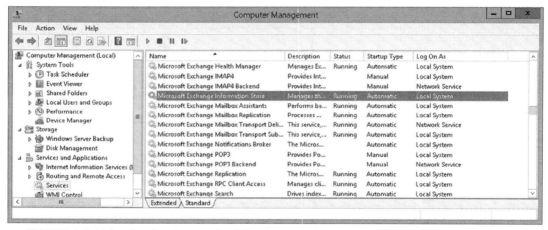

FIGURE 4-4 Using the Services node of the Computer Management console to manage Exchange Server services.

Checking Required Services

You can use Test-ServiceHealth to determine whether all Windows services that Exchange requires are running. As shown in the following example and sample output, the command output lists required services that are running as well as required services that aren't running for each configured Exchange role:

test-servicehealth

```
Role                  : Mailbox Server Role
RequiredServicesRunning : True
ServicesRunning       : {IISAdmin, MSExchangeADTopology,MSExchangeDelivery,
MSExchangeIS, MSExchangeMailboxAssistants, MSExchangeRepl, MSExchangeRPC,
MSExchangeServiceHost, MSExchangeSubmission, MSExchangeThrottling,
MSExchangeTransportLogSearch,W3Svc, WinRM}
ServicesNotRunning    : {}


Role                  : Client Access Server Role
RequiredServicesRunning : True
ServicesRunning       : {IISAdmin, MSExchangeADTopology, MSExchangeIMAP4,
MSExchangeMailboxReplication, MSExchangePOP3, MSExchangeRPC,
MSExchangeServiceHost, W3Svc, WinRM}
ServicesNotRunning    : {}


Role                  : Unified Messaging Server Role
RequiredServicesRunning : True
ServicesRunning       : {IISAdmin, MSExchangeADTopology,
MSExchangeServiceHost, MSExchangeUM, W3Svc, WinRM}
ServicesNotRunning    : {}


Role                  : Hub Transport Server Role
RequiredServicesRunning : True
ServicesRunning       : {IISAdmin, MSExchangeADTopology,MSExchangeEdgeSync,
MSExchangeServiceHost, MSExchangeTransport, MSExchangeTransportLogSearch,
W3Svc, WinRM}
ServicesNotRunning    : {}
```

> **IMPORTANT** Although these roles are no longer separate, Mailbox servers perform each role and continue to view each role as separate though interconnected. If there's a problem preventing you from using Exchange Admin Center and Exchange Management Shell, you'll need to bypass the web-based management interfaces and connect directly to Exchange Server using the technique discussed earlier in the chapter.

Maintaining Exchange Services

As an administrator, you'll often have to start, stop, or pause Exchange services. You manage Exchange services through the Computer Management console or through the Services console.

To start, stop, or pause services in the Computer Management console, follow these steps:

1. If necessary, connect to the remote Exchange server for which you want to manage services, as discussed earlier in this section.

2. Expand the Services And Applications node, and then select **Services**.

3. Right-click the service you want to manipulate, and then select Start, Stop, or Pause, as appropriate. You can also choose Restart to have Windows stop and then start the service after a brief pause. Also, if you pause a service, use the Resume option to resume normal operation.

> **TIP** When services that are set to start automatically fail, the status is listed as blank, and you usually receive notification in a pop-up window. Service failures can also be logged to the system's event logs. You can configure recovery actions to handle service failure automatically. For example, you can have Windows attempt to restart the service for you. See the section of this chapter titled "Configuring Service Recovery" for details.

Configuring Service Startup

Essential Exchange services are configured to start automatically and normally shouldn't be configured with another startup option. That said, if you're

troubleshooting a problem, you might want a service to start manually or you might
want to temporarily disable a service.

Configure service startup by completing the following steps:

1. In the Computer Management console, connect to the Exchange server for
   which you want to manage services.
2. Expand the Services And Applications node, and then select **Services**.
3. Right-click the service you want to configure, and then select **Properties**.
4. On the General tab, use the Startup Type drop-down list to choose a startup
   option. Select Automatic to start a service when the computer starts. Select
   Manual to allow services to be started manually. Select Disabled to disable
   the service. Click **OK**.

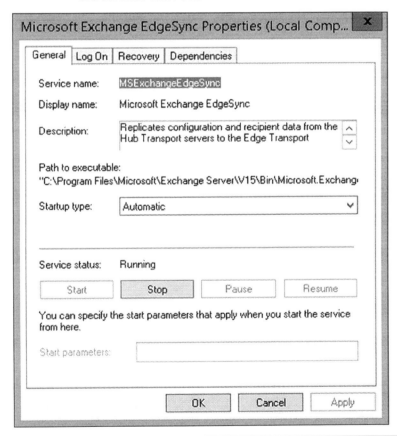

NOTE The Disabled option doesn't stop the service if it's currently running.
It just prevents the service from starting the next time you start the server. To
stop the service, you must click Stop.

Configuring Service Recovery

You can configure Windows services to take specific actions when a service fails. For example, you can attempt to restart the service or reboot the server. To configure recovery options for a service, follow these steps:

1. In the Computer Management console, connect to the computer for which you want to manage services.
2. Expand the Services And Applications node, and then select **Services**.
3. Right-click the service you want to configure, and then select **Properties**.

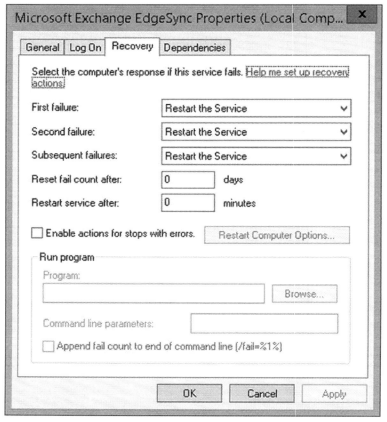

4. On the Recovery tab, you can configure recovery options for the first, second, and subsequent recovery attempts. The available options are as follows:

- Take No Action
- Restart The Service
- Run A Program

* Restart The Computer

    5. Configure other options based on your previously selected recovery options.
        If you elected to restart the service, you need to specify the restart delay.
        After stopping the service, Windows Server waits for the specified delay
        period before trying to start the service. In most cases, a delay of one to two
        minutes should be sufficient. Click **OK**.

When you configure recovery options for critical services, you might try to restart the
service on the first and second attempts and then reboot the server on the third
attempt. If you notice that a service keeps failing, do some troubleshooting to
diagnose and resolve the underlying issue causing the failure.

Customizing Remote Management Services

The Exchange management tools use the Microsoft .NET Framework, Windows
Remote Management (WinRM), and Windows PowerShell for remote management.
WinRM is implemented in the Windows Remote Management service, which is also
referred to as the WS-Management Service or simply the Management Service. To
remotely manage Exchange, your management computer must run this service and
be configured to use the transports, ports, and authentication methods that your
Exchange servers use. The Exchange server you want to connect to must also run this
service. If this service isn't running on your management computer and on the
server, remote connections will fail. For remote management, you normally connect
to the PowerShell virtual directory configured in IIS on a Mailbox server.

By default, the Management Service connects to and listens on TCP port 80 for HTTP
connections and on TCP port 443 for secure HTTP connections. Because firewalls and
proxy servers might affect your ability to connect to remote locations over these
ports, talk with your company's network or security administrator to determine what
steps need to be taken to allow administration over these ports. Typically, the
network/security administrator will have to open these TCP ports to allow remote
communication between your computer or network and the remote server or
network.

The Management Service is preconfigured to share ports with IIS when it runs on the
same computer, but it does not depend on IIS. To support remote management, you
need to install basic authentication and Windows authentication for IIS on your

Exchange servers. These authentication techniques are used when you work remotely.

When you are working with an elevated, administrator command prompt, you can use the WinRM command-line utility to view and manage the remote management configuration. Type **winrm get winrm/config** to display detailed information about the remote management configuration. As Listing 4-1 shows, this lists the configuration details for every aspect of WinRM.

LISTING 4-1 Sample configuration for WinRM

```
Config
 MaxEnvelopeSizekb = 500
 MaxTimeoutms = 60000
 MaxBatchItems = 32000
 MaxProviderRequests = 4294967295
 Client
  NetworkDelayms = 5000
  URLPrefix = wsman
  AllowUnencrypted = false
  Auth
   Basic = true
   Digest = true
   Kerberos = true
   Negotiate = true
   Certificate = true
   CredSSP = false
  DefaultPorts
   HTTP = 5985
   HTTPS = 5986
  TrustedHosts
 Service
  RootSDDL = O:NSG:BAD:P(A;;GA;;;BA)(A;;GR;;;IU)S:P(AU;
FA;GA;;;WD)(AU;SA;GXGW;;;WD)
  MaxConcurrentOperations = 4294967295
  MaxConcurrentOperationsPerUser = 1500
  EnumerationTimeoutms = 240000
```

```
   MaxConnections = 300
   MaxPacketRetrievalTimeSeconds = 120
   AllowUnencrypted = false
   Auth
    Basic = false
    Kerberos = true
    Negotiate = true
    Certificate = false
    CredSSP = false
    CbtHardeningLevel = Relaxed
   DefaultPorts
    HTTP = 5985
    HTTPS = 5986
   IPv4Filter = *
   IPv6Filter = *
   EnableCompatibilityHttpListener = false
   EnableCompatibilityHttpsListener = false
   CertificateThumbprint
   AllowRemoteAccess = true
  Winrs
   AllowRemoteShellAccess = true
   IdleTimeout = 7200000
   MaxConcurrentUsers = 10
   MaxShellRunTime = 2147483647
   MaxProcessesPerShell = 25
   MaxMemoryPerShellMB = 1024
   MaxShellsPerUser = 30
```

If you examine the listing, you'll notice there is a hierarchy of information. The base of this hierarchy, the Config level, is referenced with the path winrm/config. Then there are sublevels for client, service, and WinRS, referenced as winrm/config/client, winrm/config/service, and winrm/config/winrs, respectively. You can change the value of most configuration parameters by using the following command:

```
winrm set ConfigPath @{ParameterName="Value"}
```

where *ConfigPath* is the configuration path, *ParameterName* is the name of the parameter you want to work with, and *Value* sets the value for the parameter, such as:

```
winrm set winrm/config/winrs @{MaxShellsPerUser="4"}
```

In this example, the MaxShellsPerUser parameter is set under WinRM/Config/WinRS. Keep in mind that some parameters are read-only and cannot be set in this way.

WinRM requires at least one listener to indicate the transports and IP addresses on which management requests can be accepted. The transport must be HTTP, HTTPS, or both. With HTTP, messages can be encrypted only using NTLM or Kerberos encryption. With HTTPS, Secure Sockets Layer (SSL) is used for encryption. You can examine the configured listeners by typing **winrm enumerate winrm/config/listener**. As Listing 4-2 shows, this lists the configuration details for configured listeners.

LISTING 4-2 Sample configuration for listeners

```
Listener
    Address = *
    Transport = HTTP
    Port = 5985
    Hostname
    Enabled = true
    URLPrefix = wsman
    CertificateThumbprint
    ListeningOn = 192.168.1.225, 127.0.0.1, ::1, fe80::5efe:10.0.0.150%13
```

By default, your computer is likely to be configured to listen on any IP address. If so, you won't see any output. To limit WinRM to specific IP addresses, the computer's local loopback address (127.0.01) and assigned IPv4 and IPv6 addresses can be explicitly configured for listening. You can configure a computer to listen for requests on HTTP on all configured IP addresses by typing:

```
winrm create winrm/config/listener?Address=*+Transport=HTTP
```

You can listen for requests on HTTPS on all IP addresses configured on the computer by typing:

```
winrm create winrm/config/listener?Address=*+Transport=HTTPS
```

In this case, the * indicates all configured IP addresses. Note that the CertificateThumbprint property must be empty for the SSL configuration to be shared with another service.

You can enable or disable a listener for a specific IP address by typing:

```
winrm set winrm/config/listener?Address=IP:192.168.1.225+Transport=HTTP
@{Enabled="true"}
```

or

```
winrm set winrm/config/listener?Address=IP:192.168.1.225+Transport=HTTP
@{Enabled="false"}
```

You can enable or disable basic authentication on the client by typing:

```
winrm set winrm/config/client/auth @{Basic="true"}
```

or

```
winrm set winrm/config/client/auth @{Basic="false"}
```

You can enable or disable Windows authentication using either NTLM or Kerberos (as appropriate) by typing:

```
winrm set winrm/config/client @{TrustedHosts="<local>"}
```

or

```
winrm set winrm/config/client @{TrustedHosts=""}
```

In addition to managing WinRM at the command line, you can manage the service by using Group Policy. Keep in mind that Group Policy settings might override any other settings you enter.

Chapter 5. Managing Exchange Organizations

Although components of early Exchange releases were split into different server roles for scaling out Exchange organizations, later releases of Exchange Server streamlined the server roles and architecture incrementally while still allowing you to fully scale Exchange organizations to meet the needs of enterprises of all sizes. The end result of this streamlining is that Mailbox servers now perform all role services, except for Edge Transport services. Thus, not only do Mailbox servers store the active database copy for a mailbox performs all the data processing, rendering, and transformation required, they also provide authentication, redirection, and proxy services as needed.

For connections, the supported protocols include HTTP, POP, IMAP, MAPI over HTTP, RPC over HTTP, and SMTP, but no longer include RPC. Exchange 2016 is designed to work with Microsoft Outlook 2010 and higher and also continues to support the Outlook Web App for mobile access. Rather than connecting to servers by using Fully Qualified Domain Names (FQDN) as was done in the past, Outlook 2010 and higher use Autodiscover to create connection points based on the domain portion of the user's primary SMTP address and the GUID of a user's mailbox.

Navigating Exchange 2016 Organizations

An *organization* is the root of an Exchange environment. It's the starting point for the Exchange hierarchy, and its boundaries define the boundaries of any Exchange environment.

Organizational Architecture

When you install Exchange Server 2016, you install your Exchange servers within the organizational context of the domain in which the server is a member. The physical site boundaries and subnets defined for Active Directory Domain Services are the same as those used by Exchange Server 2016, and the site details are determined by the IP address assigned to the server. If you are installing the first Exchange server in a domain, you set the name of the Exchange organization for that domain. The next Exchange server you install in the domain joins the existing Exchange organization automatically.

Exchange 2016 organizations natively have only two server types: Mailbox servers on the internal network and Edge Transport servers on a perimeter network. Typically, client connections are load balanced with your Mailbox servers acting as the front end for Exchange services, and also acting as the back end servicing the connections (see Figure 5-1).

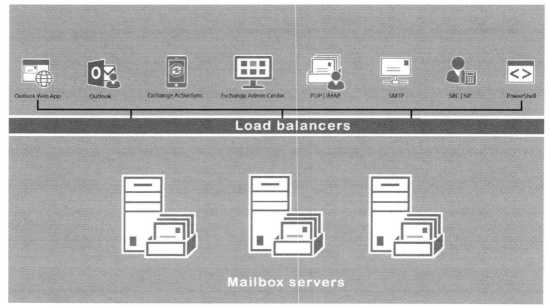

FIGURE 5-1 A basic Exchange organization with load balancers.

Clients connect to Exchange using several different techniques (see Figure 5-2). All Outlook connections take place using either MAPI over HTTP or Outlook Anywhere (RPC over HTTP). Using these technologies simplifies the protocol stack and required namespaces. POP3/IMAP and Unified Messaging connections are handled by dedicated services, as are SMTP connections, which are handled by the Transport stack. All other client connections, such as those for Outlook Web App (OWA), are managed via the IIS instance running on your Mailbox servers and then directed as appropriate.

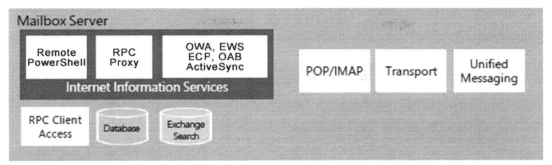

FIGURE 5-2 Connections points into Mailbox servers.

Front End Transport

Mail transport is provided by the Front End Transport service, which provides mailbox locator services and proxies incoming and outgoing SMTP messages, as shown in Figure 5-3.

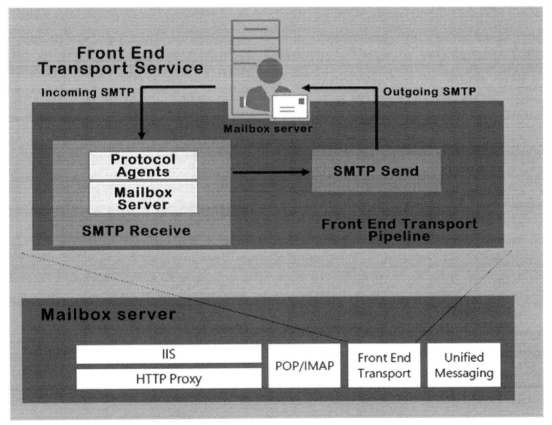

FIGURE 5-3 Front End Transport architecture

The Front End Transport service loads routing tables based on information from Active Directory and uses this information to route messages to the Transport service on Mailbox servers. The Mailbox server is selected based on the location of mailbox databases associated with the recipients.

A recipient is an entity that can receive Exchange mail and includes users, contacts, distribution groups, public folders, and resources (such as rooms and equipment used for scheduling). You refer to recipients as either *mailbox-enabled* or *mail-enabled*. Mailbox-enabled recipients (users and resources) have mailboxes for sending and receiving email messages. Mail-enabled recipients (contacts, distribution groups, and public folders) have email addresses but no mailboxes, which allow users in your organization to send messages to mail-enabled recipients. Keep in mind that when you mail-enable a public folder and grant a user Send As permission on the folder, the user can send mail on behalf of the public folder.

In addition to users, contacts, groups, resources, and public folders, Exchange Server 2016 has two unique types of recipients: linked mailboxes and dynamic distribution groups. Basically, a linked mailbox represents a mailbox that is accessed by a user in a separate, trusted forest. A dynamic distribution group is a type of distribution group that you can use to build a list of recipients whenever mail addressed to the group is received, rather than having a fixed member list.

To manage recipients in your organization, you need to know these key concepts:

* **How address lists are used** Address lists are used to organize recipients and resources, making it easier to find the ones that you want to use, along with their related information. During setup, Exchange creates a number of default address lists, the most common of which is the global address list, which includes all the recipients in the organization. You can create custom address lists as well.
* **How email policies are used** Email address policies define the technique Exchange uses to create email addresses for users, resources, contacts, and mail-enabled groups. For example, you can set a policy that creates email addresses by combining an email alias with @tvpress.com. Thus, during setup of an account for William Stanek, the email alias *williams* is combined with *@tvpress.com* to create the email address *williams@tvpress.com*.
* **How retention policies are used** Retention policies are used to specify how long mail items remain in mailboxes and the actions to be taken when mail items reach their specified retention age. During setup, Exchange creates a default retention policy and this policy is applied automatically when you create an in-

place archive mailbox for a user, providing no other retention policy is already applied.

The Routing tables used by the Front End Transport service contain a special list of Mailbox servers in the local Active Directory site. This list is based on the mailbox databases of message recipients. Routing in the front-end revolves around resolving message recipients to mailbox databases. For each mailbox database, the Front End Transport services looks up the routing destination.

Each routing destination has a delivery group, which is generally either a routable Database Availability Group (DAG), a Mailbox delivery group, or an Active Directory site, but can also be a group of connector source servers or a list of expansion servers for dynamic distribution groups. A Mailbox delivery group is a collection of one or more transport servers that are responsible for delivering messages to that routing destination. When the routing destination is a Mailbox delivery group, the delivery group may contain Exchange 2016 Mailbox servers, Exchange 2013 Mailbox servers, or Exchange 2010 Hub Transport servers.

The process by which the message is routed depends on the relationship between the source transport server and the destination delivery group. If the source transport server is in the destination delivery group, the routing destination itself is the next hop for the message. The message is delivered by the source transport server to the mailbox database or connector on a transport server in the delivery group.

On the other hand, if the source transport server is outside the destination delivery group, the message is relayed along the least-cost routing path to the destination delivery group. In a complex Exchange organization, a message may be relayed either to other transport servers along the least-cost routing path, or directly to a transport server in the destination delivery group.

For an incoming message, the Front End Transport service selects a single Mailbox server to receive the message regardless of the number or type of recipients. If the message has a single recipient, a Mailbox server in the target delivery group is selected, with a preference based on the proximity of the Active Directory site. If the message has multiple recipients, the Front End Transport service uses the first 20 recipients to select a Mailbox server in the closest delivery group. If the message has no mailbox recipients, such as when the message is addressed to a distribution group, a Mailbox server in the local Active Directory site is randomly selected.

Back End Transport

The Back End Transport service runs on all Mailbox servers and is responsible for all mail flow within an Exchange organization, as shown in Figure 5-4.

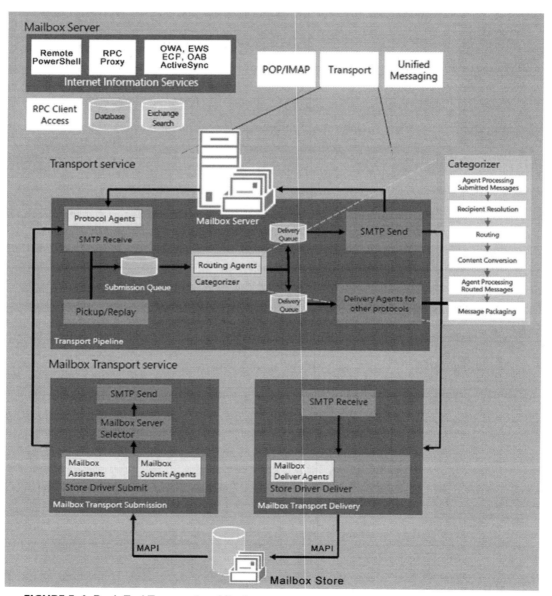

FIGURE 5-4 Back End Transport architecture

The Transport service relies on the Mailbox Transport service, which consists of two separate helper services: the Mailbox Transport Delivery service used with incoming messages and the Mailbox Transport Submission service used with outgoing messages. The transport service receives SMTP messages from the Transport service and establishes an RPC MAPI connection with the local mailbox database to deliver a message. The delivery service connects to the local mailbox database using RPC MAPI to retrieve messages and submits messages over SMTP to the Transport service.

The Mailbox Transport service only communicates with the Transport service and local mailbox databases. When this service receives a message for delivery it accepts the message if the recipient resides in an active copy of a local mailbox database. Otherwise, the service rejects the message and returns a non-delivery response to the Transport service for retrying delivery, generating a non-delivery report or rerouting the message.

When the Mailbox Transport service receives a message for submission, the service resolves the message recipients to mailbox databases. For each mailbox database, the service looks up the routing destination. Each routing destination has a delivery group, which is either a routable DAG, a Mailbox delivery group, or an Active Directory site--and the rest of the process continues as with the Front End Transport service.

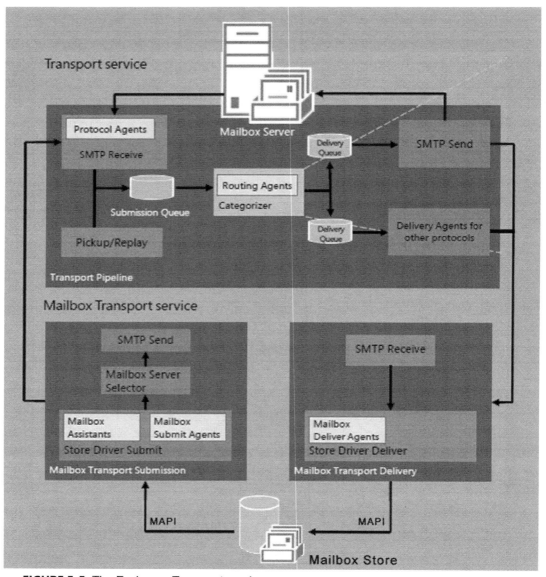

FIGURE 5-5 The Exchange Transport services

Exchange 2016 uses directory-based recipient resolution for all messages that are sent from and received by users throughout an Exchange organization. The Exchange component responsible for recipient resolution is the Categorizer. The Categorizer processes all email messages and uses the final recipient to determine what journaling policies, Information Rights Management policies, data loss prevention rules, and transport rules should be applied (see Figure 5-6).

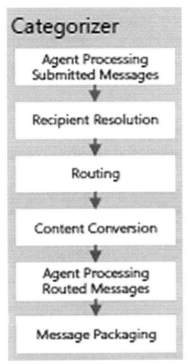

FIGURE 5-6 The Exchange Categorizer

The Categorizer must be able to associate every recipient in every message with a corresponding recipient object in Active Directory. All senders and recipients must have a primary SMTP address. If the Categorizer discovers a recipient without a primary SMTP address, it will determine what the primary SMTP address should be or replace a non-SMTP address. Replacing a non-SMTP address involves encapsulating the address in a primary SMTP address that will be used while transporting the message.

Understanding Exchange Routing

For routing messages, Exchange Server 2016 uses either Active Directory site-based routing or routing based on Database Availability Group (DAG) membership. The use of these routing approaches substantially changes the way you configure and manage Exchange Server 2016.

With Exchange Server 2016, site-based routing is possible because Exchange servers can determine their own Active Directory site membership and that of other servers by querying Active Directory. Using Active Directory for routing eliminates the need for Exchange to have its own routing infrastructure.

Routing Boundaries

Active Directory sites and DAGs are delivery group boundaries. When Mailbox servers aren't part of a DAG, they use site membership information to determine whether other Mailbox servers are located in the same site. This allows the Mailbox server to submit messages for routing and transport to another Mailbox server that has the same site membership. Site-based routing is also used for interoperability with Exchange 2013 and Exchange 2010.

When the destination delivery group is a collection of Mailbox servers in a single Active Directory site, the mailbox databases on those servers are the routing destinations. After a message is routed to the Transport service on a Mailbox server in the site, the Transport service routes the message to the Mailbox Transport service on the Mailbox server in the site that has the active copy of the destination mailbox database. The Mailbox Transport service in this server then delivers the message to the local mailbox database.

As routing destinations and delivery groups are separated by the major release version of Exchange, the Active Directory site may contain multiple Mailbox delivery groups. Specifically, each major release version of Exchange deployed in a particular site will have one delivery group. Regarding routing and delivery, keep the following in mind:

* Mailbox databases on Exchange 2010 Mailbox servers are serviced by Exchange 2010 Hub Transport servers in the site. After a message is routed to a random Hub Transport server in the site, the store driver on that server uses RPC to deliver the message into the mailbox database.
* Mailbox databases on Exchange 2013 Mailbox servers are serviced by the Transport service on Exchange 2013 Mailbox servers in the site. After a message is routed to the destination Mailbox server in the site, the Transport service uses SMTP to transfer the message to the Mailbox Transport service, which then uses RPC to deliver the message into the local mailbox database.
* Mailbox databases on Exchange 2016 Mailbox servers are serviced by the Transport service on Exchange 2016 Mailbox servers in the site. After a message is routed to the destination Mailbox server in the site, the Transport service uses SMTP to transfer the message to the Mailbox Transport service, which then uses RPC to deliver the message into the local mailbox database.

When the destination delivery group is a routable DAG, the mailbox databases in the DAG are the routing destinations. After a message is routed to the Transport service on a Mailbox server in the DAG, the Transport service routes the message to the Mailbox Transport service that has the active copy of the destination mailbox database. The Mailbox Transport service in this server then delivers the message to the local mailbox database. As the DAG itself is the delivery group boundary rather than the Active Directory site associated with a particular Mailbox server, Mailbox servers may be physically located in more than one site even though they are members of the same delivery group.

IP Site Links

Exchange servers determine site membership by matching their assigned IP address to a subnet that is defined in Active Directory Sites and Services and associated with an Active Directory site. The Exchange server then uses this information to determine which domain controllers, Global Catalog servers, and other Exchange servers exist in that site, and it communicates with those directory servers for authentication, authorization, and messaging purposes. Exchange 2016 always tries to retrieve information about recipients from directory servers that are in the same site as the Exchange 2016 server.

TIP In Active Directory, you can associate a site with one or more IP subnets. Each subnet that is part of a site should be connected over reliable, high-speed links. You should configure any business locations connected over slow or unreliable links as part of separate sites. Because of this, individual sites typically represent well-connected local area networks (LANs) within an organization, and wide area network (WAN) links between business locations typically mark the boundaries of these sites. Sites cannot have overlapping subnet configurations because replication and message routing would not work correctly.

As Figure 5-7 shows, Active Directory sites are connected through IP site links, which can connect two or more sites. Each site link has a specific schedule, interval, and cost. The schedule and interval determine the frequency of Active Directory replication, and the cost value determines the cost of using the link relative to other links that might be available. Active Directory replication uses the link with the lowest cost when multiple paths to a destination exist. The cost of a route is determined by adding together the cost of all site links in a transmission path. Administrators assign the cost value to a link based on relative network speed, available bandwidth, and reliability compared to other available connections. By default, IP site links always allow traffic to flow into or out of a site.

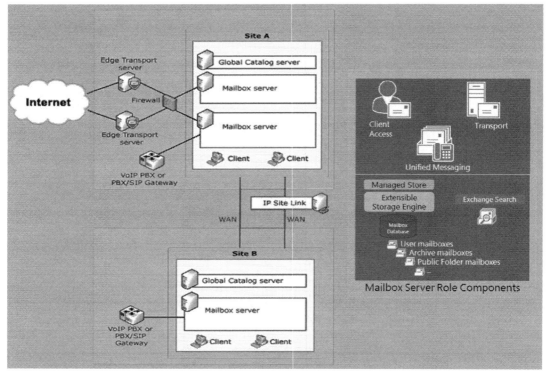

FIGURE 5-7 Message traffic between sites is routed over IP site links.

In large enterprises, message traffic might have to travel through multiple sites to get from the source site to a destination site. When transferring messages from one site to another through other sites, a transport server always tries to connect directly to a transport server in the destination site; therefore, messages are not relayed through each transport server in each site in the link path. Instead, the messages go directly from the transport server in the originating site across the link to the transport server in the destination site.

If the originating server cannot connect directly to a transport server in the destination site, the originating transport server uses the link cost to determine the closest site at which to queue the message. Messages queue until they are processed by the transport server and relayed to their destination. When Edge Transport servers are subscribed to an Active Directory site, the subscribed Edge Transport servers aren't accessible from other Active Directory sites.

The transport server can also use the site link information to optimize the routing of messages that users send to multiple recipients. The transport server expands a distribution list and creates multiple copies of a message only when multiple paths are in the routing topology. This feature is called *delayed fan-out*.

Delayed fan-out is used only when the delivery group is an Active Directory site. When multiple recipients share part of the routing path, delayed fan-out tries to reduce the number of message copies, thereby reducing the number of message transmissions.

Cross-Premises Routing

Exchange Online is a cloud service, meaning the service is provided via the Internet, and it allows you to outsource all or part of your Exchange services. Exchange Online differs from Exchange on-premises (the standard implementation) in several fundamental ways. The Exchange Online hardware resides elsewhere and users access their mailboxes over the Internet; however, administrators still retain control and management over the outsourced mailboxes.

You can simultaneously connect to and manage both online and on-premises configurations in the Exchange Admin Center. Exchange Online has some advantages over an Exchange on-premises implementation, but has disadvantages as well. For users, Exchange Online provides:

- Mailbox hosting
- ActiveSync
- Microsoft Outlook Anywhere
- Microsoft Outlook Web App
- Spam filtering

For administrators, Exchange Online provides:

- Service Level Agreements
- Storage quotas
- Automatic backups
- Automatic archiving

It's important to point out that what Exchange Online doesn't provide is immediacy of access. Users must always be connected to the Internet to get their mail.

Messages typically are routed and transferred across the Internet, which can cause delays. Exchange Online also does not offer Exchange voice mail as well as some other popular features.

As you work to configure your Exchange organization, it's important to keep in mind that Exchange Online is not an all-or-nothing implementation. You can host some mailboxes online and others on-premises. Exchange Server 2016 makes it easy to manage mailboxes regardless of where they are located. Before you transition mailboxes off-site, however, you'll probably want to perform a trial with a limited subset of users while keeping mailboxes for executives and most managers in house. In fact, it's a good idea to always keep mailboxes for executives and other high-level managers in house.

Exchange Server 2016 uses cross-premises routing to transfer messages between on-premises and hosted mailboxes. If you send a message to a user with a hosted mailbox, your organization's transport servers will route the message across the Internet to the hosted Exchange server. If you send a message to a user with an on-premises mailbox, your organization's transport servers will route the message across your organization to the appropriate Exchange server.

Exchange provides features for migrating mailboxes from online to on-premises environments and vice versa. During the migration, a mailbox might temporarily exist in both locations but when Exchange completes the migration, the mailbox exists only in the destination environment. Outlook 2010 and higher include an Autodiscover feature that automatically connects messaging clients to the correct Exchange server. This feature utilizes the user's SMTP email address during automatic discovery to determine where the mailbox is currently located.

Normally, Autodiscover works very well; however, a conflict could occur if a user has a mailbox both in Exchange Online and in Exchange on-premises or if a user has the same primary SMTP email address in Exchange Online and Exchange on-premises. In these scenarios, the Autodiscover feature normally does not configure Outlook for the Exchange Online environment and instead uses Exchange on-premises, which has priority over Exchange Online when there is a conflict and the user's computer is connected to the Active Directory domain. To resolve the problem, delete the original mailbox from its first location as soon as possible after a mailbox migration.

If a user needs both an online and on-premises mailbox, do not use the same primary SMTP email address for both Exchange Online and Exchange on-premises.

Understanding Data Storage in Exchange Server 2016

Exchange Server stores information in several locations, including:

* Active Directory data store
* Exchange Server store
* Exchange Server queues

Working with the Active Directory Data Store

The Active Directory data store contains most directory information for Exchange configurations and recipients as well as other important directory resources. Domain controllers maintain the data store in a file called Ntds.dit. The location of this file is set when Active Directory is installed and should be on an NTFS file system drive formatted for use with Windows Server. Domain controllers save some directory data separately from the main data store. Two key concepts on which to focus when looking at Active Directory are multimaster replication and Global Catalog servers.

Using Multimaster Replication

Domain controllers replicate most changes to the data store by using multimaster replication, which allows any domain controller to process directory changes and replicate those changes to other domain controllers. Replication is handled automatically for key data types, including the following:

* **Configuration data**   Describes the topology of the directory, and includes a list of important domain information
* **Domain data**   Contains information about objects within a domain, such as users, groups, and contacts
* **Schema data**   Describes all objects and data types that can be stored in the data store

Using Global Catalogs

Active Directory information is also made available through global catalogs. Global catalogs are used for information searches and, in some cases, domain logon. A domain controller designated as a Global Catalog server stores a full replica of all objects in the data store (for its host domain).

The first domain controller installed in a domain is designated as the Global Catalog server by default. Consequently, if only one domain controller is in the domain, the domain controller and the global catalog are on the same server; otherwise, the global catalog is on the domain controller configured as such.

Global catalogs are primarily used for information searches. Searches in the global catalog are efficient and can resolve most queries locally, thus reducing the network load and allowing for quicker responses. With Exchange, the global catalog can be used to execute Lightweight Directory Access Protocol (LDAP) queries for dynamic distribution groups. The members of the distribution group are based on the results of the query sent to the Global Catalog server rather than being fixed.

Why use LDAP queries instead of a fixed member list? The idea is to reduce administrative overhead by being able to dynamically determine the members of a distribution group. Query-based distribution is most efficient when the member list is relatively small (fewer than 100). If the member list has potentially hundreds or thousands of members, however, dynamic distribution can be inefficient and might require a great deal of processing to complete.

At a high-level, dynamic distribution works like this:

1. When email messages that are addressed to the group are received, the Exchange Categorizer (a transport component) sends the predefined LDAP query to the Global Catalog server for the domain.
2. The Global Catalog server executes the query and returns the resulting address set.
3. The Exchange Categorizer then uses the address set to generate the recipient list and deliver the message. If the Categorizer is unable to generate the list for any reason—for instance, if the list is incomplete or an error was returned—the Categorizer might start the process over from the beginning.

Using Dedicated Expansion Servers

To make the dynamic query process more efficient, Exchange 2016 shifts the processing requirements from Global Catalog servers to dedicated expansion servers by specifying a collection of one or more expansion servers as a delivery group. Unlike Mailbox delivery groups, this special delivery group can contain a mix of Exchange 2016 Mailbox servers, Exchange 2013 Mailbox servers and Exchange 2010 Hub Transport servers.

The routing destination is still the ultimate destination for a message. A distribution group expansion server is the routing destination when a distribution group has a designated expansion server that's responsible for expanding the membership list of the group. As with other types of routing, how the message is routed depends on the relationship between the source transport server and the destination delivery group. Keep in mind that when a distribution group expansion server is the routing destination, the distribution group is already expanded when a message reaches the routing stage of categorization on the distribution group expansion server. Therefore, the routing destination from the distribution group expansion server is always a mailbox database or a connector.

By default, Exchange 2016 uses the closest Exchange server that has the Mailbox server role installed as the dedicated expansion server. Because routing destinations and delivery groups can also include Exchange 2013 Mailbox servers and Exchange 2010 Hub Transport servers in mixed environments, Exchange 2013 and Exchange 2010 servers could perform distribution group expansion in mixed Exchange organizations.

On occasion, you might want to explicitly specify the dedicated expansion server to handle expansion processing for some or all of your dynamic distribution groups in order to manage where the related processing occurs thereby shift the processing overhead from other servers to this specified server. You can specify a dedicated expansion server for a dynamic distribution group using the -ExpansionServer Parameter of the Set-DynamicDistributionGroup cmdlet.

Navigating the Exchange Information Store

The Exchange store is the core storage repository for managing Exchange databases. Unlike previous releases of Exchange, Exchange 2016 has only one type of database: the mailbox database. Mailbox databases contain the data, data definitions, indexes, flags, checksums, and other information that comprise mailboxes in your Exchange organization.

Data Storage Components

Exchange 2016 supports many types of mailboxes, including:

- **Arbitration mailbox**   An arbitration mailbox is used to manage approval requests, such as handling moderated recipients and distribution group membership approval.
- **Archive mailbox**   An alternative mailbox used to store historical mail items.
- **Discovery mailbox**   A resource mailbox that is the target for Discovery searches.
- **Equipment mailbox**   A resource mailbox for equipment scheduling.
- **Forwarding mailbox**   A mailbox that can receive mail and forward it off-site.
- **Linked mailbox**   A mailbox for a user from a separate, trusted forest.
- **Public folder mailbox**   A shared mailbox for storing public folder data.
- **Room mailbox**   A resource mailbox for room scheduling.
- **Shared mailbox**   An alternative mailbox that is shared by multiple users, such as a general mailbox for customer inquiries.
- **User mailbox**   The primary mailbox type for users to store mail items.

The Information Store (Microsoft.Exchange.Store.Service.exe) is written in C# and is fully integrated with the Microsoft Exchange Replication service (MSExchangeRepl.exe). Officially, the store is referred to as the Managed Store. Although the Microsoft Exchange Information Store service hosts the Exchange store, which uses the Extensible Storage Engine (ESE) as the database engine, the management of the store is divided between the store service and the replication service. As you'd expect, the store service handles the primary store functions while the replication service provides replication and ancillary functions, including log shipping, log replay, log truncation and database seeding operations. The replication service also is responsible for all service availability for Mailbox servers.

The Active Manager component of the replication service is responsible for failure monitoring and failover within DAGs. The Active Manager is also responsible for message resubmissions from the shadow redundancy safety net. As examples, automatic resubmission of messages can occur after you activate the lagged copy of a mailbox database as well as after failover of a mailbox database in a DAG. Every Mailbox server runs Active Manager inside the replication service. If a Mailbox server isn't part of a DAG, the server has a single, Standalone Active Manager. In a DAG, there are two Active Manager roles: Primary Active Manager and Standby Active Manager. The Primary Active Manager determines which database copies are active and which are passive and also handles failover and notifies other members of topology changes.

The VSS writer in the replication service, named the Microsoft Exchange Writer, is responsible for backing up active and passive mailbox database copies and for restoring backed up database copies. Although this writer runs within the replication service, it is the store service that advertises the availability of the VSS writer. Thus, both the store service and the replication service must be running to back up and restore Exchange databases.

After a database backup, the transaction logs are usually truncated as the data is no longer needed for recovery; however, if backups aren't being taken, logs aren't truncated and you can prevent a buildup of logs by enabling circular logging for replicated databases. Exchange can use standard circular logging or continuous replication circular logging.

With standard circular logging, which is performed and managed by the store service, the Extensible Storage Engine (ESE) doesn't create additional log files because the current log file is overwritten when needed.

Combining standard circular logging with continuous replication is referred to as continuous replication circular logging. This type of logging is performed and managed by the replication service with a goal of maintaining log continuity. Logs are deleted only when they are no longer needed for replication.

The Managed Store

The Managed Store uses the worker process model. To isolate any issues with the Managed Store to a particular database, each database runs under its own process. Exchange Server uses transactions to control changes in databases and as with traditional databases, these transactions are recorded in a transaction log. Exchange Server then commits or rolls back changes based on the success of the transaction. The facility that manages transactions is the store service.

When working with databases, keep the following in mind:

- Each enterprise-level Mailbox server can have up to 100 databases (including both active and passive databases), with a maximum size per database of 64 terabytes (TB) — limited only by hardware.
- Each Mailbox server can be a member of only one database availability group and can host only one copy (either the active or passive copy) of a particular database. Because each group can have up to 16 copies of a database, up to 16 different servers can be part of a database availability group.

To create a new mailbox database, you need about 50 megabytes (MBs) of free disk space. The files required by the database use a minimum of 23 MBs of disk space, and you'll need the extra space during creation and for read/write operations.

Other key concepts to focus on when working with the Exchange store and databases are the following:

- How Exchange server data files are used
- How data is stored in Exchange database files

Exchange Server Data Files

With Exchange Server 2016, Mailbox servers have a single database file for each mailbox database. Exchange 2016 stores all messages and attachments in the primary data file. Because attachments are encapsulated and written in binary format, you don't need to convert them to Exchange format. Exchange Server uses a link table within the database to reference the storage location of attachments within it.

As Figure 5-8 shows, each database has a primary data file and several other types of shared working files and transaction logs.

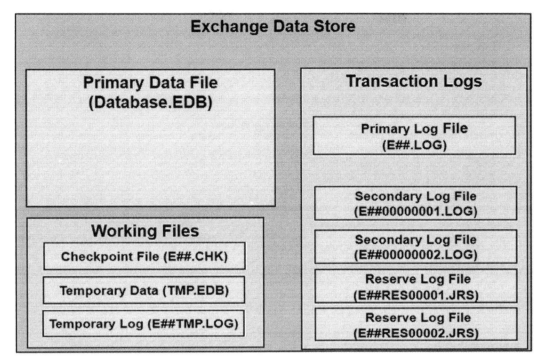

FIGURE 5-8 The Exchange data store has primary data files for each database as well as working files.

The file types are used as follows:

- **Primary data file (Database.edb)**   A physical database file that holds the contents of the data store. By default, the name of the data file is the same as the name of the associated data store with the .edb file extension added; however, you can rename a database without renaming the database file.
- **Checkpoint file (E##.chk)**   A file that tracks the point up to which the transactions in the log file have been committed to databases in the storage group. Generally, the name of the checkpoint file is derived from the database prefix.
- **Temporary data (Tmp.edb)**   A temporary workspace for processing transactions.
- **Current log file (E##.log)**   A file that contains a record of all changes that have yet to be committed to the database. Generally, the name of the log file is derived from the database prefix.
- **Preprovisioned log file (E##tmp.log)**   The next preprovisioned log, which is created in advance.

- **Secondary log files (E##00000001.log, E##00000002.log, ...)** Additional log files that are used as needed. Up to a billion unique log files can be created for each database.
- **Reserve log files (E##Res00001.jrs, E##Res00002.jrs, ...)** Files that are used to reserve space for additional log files if the current log file becomes full.
- **Temporary log (E##tmp.log)** A temporary workspace for logging.

By default, the primary data file, working files, and transaction logs are all stored in the same location. On a Mailbox server, you'll find these files in a per-database subfolder of the %SystemRoot%\Program Files\Microsoft\Exchange Server\V15\Mailbox folder. Although these are the main files used for the data store, Exchange Server uses other files, depending on the roles for which you have configured the server.

Data Storage in Exchange Databases

Exchange uses object-based storage. The primary data file contains several indexed tables, including a data table that contains a record for each object in the data store. Each referenced object can include object containers, such as mailboxes, and any other type of data that is stored in the data store.

Think of the data table as having rows and columns; the intersection of a row and a column is a field. The table's rows correspond to individual instances of an object, and the table's columns correspond to folders. The table's fields are populated only if a folder includes stored data. The data stored in fields can be a fixed length or a variable length.

Records in the data table are stored in data pages that have a fixed size of 32 kilobytes (KBs, or 32,768 bytes). The 32-KB page file size was changed from the 8-KB data pages used with Exchange Server 2007 to improve performance.

In an Exchange database, each data page has a page header, data rows, and free space that can contain row offsets. The page header uses the first 96 bytes of each page, leaving 32,672 bytes for data and row offsets. Row offsets indicate the logical order of rows on a page, which means that offset 0 refers to the first row in the index, offset 1 refers to the second row, and so on. If a row contains long, variable-length data, the data might not be stored with the rest of the data for that row. Instead, Exchange can store an 8-byte pointer to the actual data, which is stored in a collection of 32-KB pages that are written contiguously. In this way, an object and all its stored values can be much larger than 32 KB.

Changes to the mailbox database are written first to the transaction log and then committed to the database. The current active log file (E##.log) has a fixed size of 1 MB. When this log file fills up, Exchange closes the current active log file (E##.log) and renames it as E##*NNNNNNNN*.log (except when you are using circular logging). E##tmp.log is then renamed E##.log and becomes the current active log file.

The secondary log files are also limited to a fixed size of 1 MB. Exchange uses the reserve log files to reserve disk space for log files that it might need to create. Because several reserve files are already created, the transactional logging process is not delayed when additional logs are needed.

Exchange Server Message Queues

Exchange Server message queues are temporary holding locations for messages that are waiting to be processed. Two general types of queues are used:

* **Nonpersistent**   Nonpersistent queues are available only when messages are waiting to be processed.
* **Persistent**   Persistent queues are always available even if no messages are waiting to be processed.

With Exchange Server 2016, both Mailbox servers and Edge Transport servers store messages waiting to be processed in nonpersistent and persistent queues. The list that follow provides an overview of the queues used:

* A nonpersistent primary and shadow Safety Net / Transport dumpster queue on Mailbox and Edge Transports for each Active Directory site
* Nonpersistent *Delivery/Relay* queues found on Mailbox servers with one for each unique destination Mailbox server, connector, designated expansion server, non-SMTP gateway, etc.
* One nonpersistent Remote delivery queue on Edge Transport servers for each unique destination SMTP domain and smart host
* One nonpersistent Shadow redundancy queue on Mailbox and Edge Transport servers for each hop to which the server delivered the primary message
* One persistent Poison message queue found on Mailbox and Edge Transport servers
* One persistent Submission queue on Mailbox and Edge Transport servers
* One persistent Unreachable queue on Mailbox and Edge Transport servers

You can view top-level queues by clicking Queue Viewer in the Exchange Toolbox. You'll learn more about queues in Chapter 17, "Maintaining Exchange Server 2016."

When working with queues, Shadow redundancy and Safety Net are two important concepts that you need to understand. While shadow redundancy keeps a redundant copy of messages in transit, Safety Net keeps a redundant copy of a message after the message is successfully processed. Thus, in effect, Safety Net takes over where shadow redundancy finishes.

Exchange Server 2016 implements shadow redundancy for queued messages. In the event of an outage or server failure, this feature works to prevent the loss of messages that are in transit by storing queued messages until the next transport server along the route reports a successful delivery of the message. If the next transport server doesn't report successful delivery, the message is resubmitted for delivery.

Shadow redundancy eliminates the reliance on the state of any specific Mailbox or edge server and eliminates the need for storage hardware redundancy for transport components. As long as redundant message paths exist in your routing topology, any transport component is replaceable and you don't have to worry about emptying a server's queues or losing messages due to transport failure.

In Exchange 2016, the Transport service makes a redundant copy of a message as soon as it receives it and then acknowledges receipt. In Exchange 2010, the Transport service would acknowledge receipt and then make a redundant copy of a message. Finally, it's important to note that it doesn't matter whether the sending server supports shadow redundancy. If Exchange 2016 determines that a message was lost in transit, Exchange delivers the messages using the redundant copy.

> **TIP**   Shadow redundancy uses less bandwidth than creating duplicate copies of messages on multiple servers. The only additional network traffic is the exchange of discard status between transport servers. Discard status indicates when a message is ready to be discarded from the transport database.

Exchange Server 2016 also implements Safety Net for queued messages. Safety Net replaces and enhances the transport dumpster available in Exchange 2010. By default, Safety Net stores copies of messages that were successfully processed by a

Mailbox server for two days. For Mailbox servers that aren't part of DAGs, Safety Net stores copies of messages delivered to other Mailbox servers in the local Active Directory site. For Mailbox servers that are part of DAGs, Safety Net stores copies of messages delivered to other Mailbox servers in the DAG.

Since Safety Net uses shadow redundancy, it is always fully redundant. The Primary Safety Net queue stores the primary copy of a delivered message. The Shadow Safety Net queue stores a shadow copy of a delivery message. If the Primary Safety Net queue is unavailable for more than 12 hours, any messages that need to be redelivered are redelivered from the Shadow Safety Net queue.

When Mailbox servers are part of a DAG, Safety Net is used for some shadow redundancy functions. Previously, in a DAG, shadow redundancy would keep a copy of messages in the shadow queue until they were replicated to passive copies of the database. As Safety Net already has a copy of delivered messages, shadow redundancy doesn't need to keep another copy of these messages and messages can be resubmitted from Safety Net if necessary.

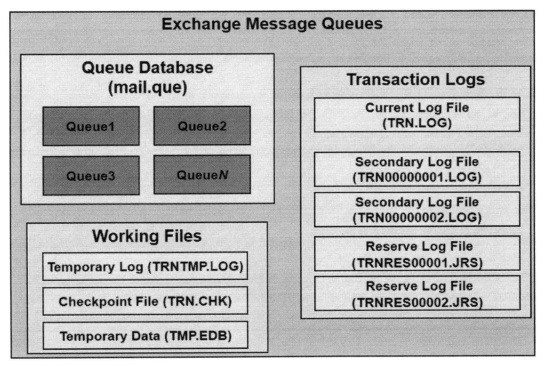

FIGURE 5-9 The Exchange message queues are all stored in a single database.

The various message queues are all stored in a single database (see Figure 5-9). Like the Exchange store, the message queues database uses the ESE for message storage as well as for data pages.

The database has a single data file associated with it and several other types of working files and transaction logs. These files are used as follows:

- **Primary data file (Mail.que)**   A physical database file that holds the contents of all message queues.
- **Checkpoint file (Trn.chk)**   A file that tracks the point up to which the transactions in the log file have been committed to the database.
- **Temporary data (Tmp.edb)**   A temporary workspace for processing transactions.
- **Current log file (Trn.log)**   A log file that contains a record of all changes that have yet to be committed to the database.
- **Preprovisioned log file (Trntmp.log)**   The next preprovisioned log, which is created in advance.
- **Secondary log files (TRN00000001.log, TRN00000002.log, ...)**   Additional log files that are used as needed.
- **Reserve log files (TRNRes00001.jrs, TRNRes00002.jrs, ...)**   Files that are used to reserve space for additional log files if the current log file becomes full.

The facility that manages queuing transactions is the Microsoft Exchange Transport service (MSExchangeTransport.exe). Because logs used with message queues are not continuously replicated, these log files have a fixed size of 5 MB. Changes to the queue database are written first to the transaction log and then committed to the database. When the current active log (trn.log) file fills up, Exchange closes the file and renames it as TRN*NNNNNNNN*.log. Trntmp.log is then renamed Trn.log and becomes the current active log file.

Exchange uses the reserve log files to reserve disk space for log files that might need to be created. Because several reserve files are already created, this speeds up the transactional logging process when additional logs are needed.

By default, the data file, working files, and transaction logs are all stored in the same location. On a Mailbox server or Edge Transport server, you'll find these files in the %SystemRoot%\Program Files\Microsoft\Exchange Server\V15\TransportRoles\data\Queue folder.

Chapter 6. Implementing Availability Groups

Managing the information store is one of your most important tasks as a Exchange 2016 administrator. The Information Store (Microsoft.Exchange.Store.Service.exe) is written in C# and is fully integrated with the Microsoft Exchange Replication service (MSExchangeRepl.exe) and the Microsoft Exchange DAG Management service (MSExchangeDagMgmt.exe).

Every Mailbox server that is deployed in your organization has an information store, which can contain databases and information about database availability groups (DAGs). This chapter introduces databases and focuses on the management of database availability groups. After completing this chapter, you should know how to:

- Enable, create, and use database availability groups
- Manage databases and their related transaction logs
- Improve Mailbox server availability
- Manage full-text indexing of Exchange databases

See Chapter 7, "Configuring Exchange Databases," to learn how to manage databases.

Building Blocks for High Availability

Microsoft built high availability and messaging resilience into the core architecture of Exchange 2016, providing a simple unified framework for high availability, management, and disaster recovery. This approach allows Exchange 2016 to improve continuous replication, provide a robust solution that doesn't require expensive clustering hardware, and reduce maintenance overhead.

The Extensible Storage Engine

Exchange Server 2016 uses Extensible Storage Engine (ESE) databases for mailbox storage. When you install a Mailbox server in an Exchange 2016 organization, this server's information store has a single, default mailbox database. Mailbox databases have a single, dedicated log stream, which is represented by a series of sequentially named log files. Each log file is 1 megabyte (MB) in size. In addition to log files, databases have several other types of files associated with them, including one or more checkpoint files, a temporary working file, and one or more transaction log files. Depending on the state of Exchange Server, you might see other working files as well.

> **NOTE** Exchange 2016 does not use public folder databases. Public folders are now stored in a special type of mailbox.

When you create a mailbox database, you can specify separate folder locations to use for database files and transaction logs. Each database has content-indexing files associated with it as well. These files are generated by the Exchange Search service, which is enabled by default and running on all Mailbox servers. Exchange Search indexes new mail items in the transport pipeline or immediately after the items are created and delivered to a mailbox.

You use Exchange databases to ease the administrative burden that comes with managing large installations. For example, instead of having a single 10-terabyte (TB) database for the entire organization, you can create ten 1-TB databases that you can manage more easily.

> **TIP** As a best practice, 2 TB is the largest recommended size for Exchange Server 2016 databases. Often you'll find that large databases make it easier to support the large mailboxes that might be required by your organization's managers and executives. Still, most mailboxes should be limited to between 2 GB and 10 GB in size.

When you create a mailbox database, you specify the name for the database, and this name sets the name of the primary database file as well. For example, if you create a mailbox database called EngineeringDept, the primary database file is set as EngineeringDept.edb. With Exchange Server 2016, the default location for database files is the same as the log folder. If you want a database to be in a different location, you can specify the location you want to use.

Separating database files and log files from the same database and putting them on different volumes backed by different physical disks can help you scale your organization while ensuring high performance and recoverability. When you are formatting volumes, be sure to consider using ReFS as opposed to NTFS as ReFS is more efficient and resilient than NTFS.

> **TIP** Recoverability is a key reason for separating database files and log files. For example, in the case of a failure on a drive where a database is stored, the transaction logs needed for complete recovery would then be on a

different (and probably functioning) drive. Whether you want to use this approach depends on the size and configuration of your Exchange Mailbox servers as well as the service level agreements with which you need to comply.

The many files associated with databases provide granular control over Exchange Server, and if you configure the data files properly, they can help you scale your Exchange organization efficiently while ensuring optimal performance. In a small implementation of Exchange, you might want to place all the data files on the same drive. As you scale from a small organization to a larger organization, you'll generally want to organize data according to databases, placing all the data for each database on physically separate drives. You can't always do this, however, in a small-to-medium sized organization with limited resources. For example, if you have ten 1-TB databases and only five data drives, you might want to have the five data drives configured as follows:

- Drive 1 with Database 1 and Database 2 and all related data files.
- Drive 2 with Database 3 and Database 4 and all related data files.
- Drive 3 with Database 5 and Database 6 and all related data files.
- Drive 4 with Database 7 and Database 8 and all related data files.
- Drive 5 with Database 9 and Database 10 and all related data files.

In a storage area network (SAN) implementation in which you are using logical unit numbers (LUNs) and don't know about the underlying disk structure, placing the databases on separate LUNs should be sufficient. To protect the data, you might want to consider using hardware RAID (redundant array of inexpensive disks), which is likely already implemented if you are using a SAN. However, if you configure a database availability group with multiple member servers that each have one or more copies of mailbox databases, you likely don't need to use any type of RAID, and you likely won't need daily backups either. Just remember that Microsoft recommends having at least three database copies in addition to the active copy.

REAL WORLD   When you have multiple copies of your data on separate servers, you really might not need to create daily backups of your Exchange data. This doesn't mean that you won't need to create backups ever—it just means you might not need daily backups of Exchange data. You will probably still want to create regular backups of your Exchange servers and still create periodic full backups of all server and Exchange data to rotate to off-site storage as a safeguard against catastrophe.

Database available groups can also make you rethink your use of SANs. Rather than having a single, massive (and likely very expensive) storage device, you might want to rely on a server's internal drives or multiple smaller (and likely much less complex) storage devices. One reason to use internal drives is that reliable, multiple-TB hard drives are becoming increasingly available, and several servers with multiple, large internal hard drives will likely cost a fraction of the price of a single massive SAN. If you use SANs, you might find that multiple smaller storage devices are better than a single, massive storage device because you'll then be protected against a single source of failure (the storage device) causing an outage on all your mailbox servers. I know, I know…the SAN should never go down, but it can (and does) happen.

The High Availability Framework

Exchange 2016 allows you to protect mailbox databases and the data they contain by configuring your mailbox databases for high availability automatically when you use database availability groups (DAGs) . Database availability groups allow you to group databases logically according to the servers that host a set of databases.

Each Mailbox server can have multiple databases, and each database can have as many as 16 copies. A single database availability group can have up to 16 Mailbox servers that host databases and provide automatic database-level recovery from failures that affect individual databases. Any server in a database availability group can host a copy of a mailbox database from any other server in the database availability group.

Exchange 2016 integrates high availability and messaging resilience into the core architecture, providing a simple unified framework for both high availability and disaster recovery. This approach reduces the cost and complexity of deploying a highly available solution. How does this work? Exchange 2016 has enhanced continuous replication and has replaced clustering features in early releases of Exchange with a more robust solution that doesn't require expensive hardware and also requires less maintenance.

In early versions, Exchange was a clustered application that used the cluster resource management model for high availability. In contrast, Exchange 2016 is not a clustered application and therefore does not use the cluster resource model for high availability. Instead, Exchange 2016 uses its own internal high-availability model.

Although some components of Windows Failover Clustering are still used, these components are now managed exclusively by Exchange 2016.

Early versions of Exchange supported continuous replication through several approaches, including Local Continuous Replication (LCR), Cluster Continuous Replication (CCR), and Standby Continuous Replication (SCR). LCR was a single-server solution for asynchronous log shipping, replay, and recovery. CCR combined the asynchronous log shipping, replay, and recovery features with the failover and management features of the Cluster service, and it was designed for configurations in which you had clustered Mailbox servers with dedicated active and passive nodes. SCR was an extension of LCR and CCR that used the same log shipping, replay, and recovery features of LCR and CCR but was designed for configurations in which you used or enabled the use of standby recovery servers.

Some aspects of the continuous replication technology previously found in CCR and SCR are built into Exchange 2016, but the technology has changed substantially. Because storage groups have been removed from Exchange 2016, continuous replication operates at the database level. Exchange 2016 still uses an Extensible Storage Engine (ESE) database that produces transaction logs that are replicated and replayed into copies of mailbox databases. Because each mailbox database can have as many as 16 copies, you can have one or more database copies on up to 16 different servers.

When a Mailbox server is added to DAG, the server works with other members of the DAG to provided automatic recovery from failures that affect mailbox databases, including disk failures, server failures, and other critical failures. When a failure affecting a database occurs and a new database becomes the active copy automatically, this process is known as a failover. When an administrator establishes a database copy as the active mailbox database, this process is known as a switchover.

Failover and switchover occur at the database level for individual databases and at the server level for all active databases hosted by a server. When either a switchover or failover occurs, other Exchange 2016 server roles become aware of the switchover almost immediately and redirect client and messaging traffic automatically as appropriate.

For site resiliency, you use availability groups and deploy Mailbox servers in two or more Active Directory sites. If the sites are located in different datacenters with different network infrastructure, you can ensure mailbox data is protected from software, hardware and datacenter failures. When you use datacenter pairs, you'll want to deploy a single availability group with member servers located in each datacenter. For example, if you have two datacenters, you could deploy two servers in each datacenter and make each server a member of the same availability group. You would then have a single availability group with four member servers. To ensure full protection, each database would have four copies, with two copies in each datacenter. Of the four copies:

* 1 would be active and highly available
* 2 would be passive and highly available
* 1 would be passive and lagged

Lagging a database is an important concept to understand. When you lag a database copy, you configure Exchange to delay processing of log files for a designated database copy. Exchange then processes (or plays down) the log files with a preset time delay, such as 3 days. Because of the delay in processing, the log files of the lagged copy can be used to automatically recovery from broken page references and other issues that would otherwise require administrator intervention for recovery. For example, if Exchange detects that page patching is required, Exchange automatically replays the logs into the lagged copy to perform page patching.

With Exchange Server 2016, Replay Lag Manager is enabled by default and lagged database copy play down can be delayed based on disk latency to ensure active users aren't impacted. In most circumstances, you lag the database copy with the highest activation preference number to protect against catastrophic logical corruption of the database. As a best practice, you should use a replay lag time of at least 7 days and enable the Replay Lag Manager to provide dynamic log file play down of lagged copies when availability is compromised.

You can perform most management tasks for availability groups in the Exchange Admin Center. However, you have additional options when you work with Exchange Management Shell. Commands you can use to manage availability groups and their various features include:

- **Database availability group management**
  Get-DatabaseAvailabilityGroup
  New-DatabaseAvailabilityGroup
  Remove-DatabaseAvailabilityGroup
  Set-DatabaseAvailabilityGroup

- **Database copy management**
  Add-MailboxDatabaseCopy
  Get-MailboxDatabaseCopyStatus
  Remove-MailboxDatabaseCopy
  Resume-MailboxDatabaseCopy
  Set-MailboxDatabaseCopy
  Suspend-MailboxDatabaseCopy
  Update-MailboxDatabaseCopy

- **Database management**
  Dismount-Database
  Get-MailboxDatabase
  Move-DatabasePath
  New-MailboxDatabase
  Remove-MailboxDatabase
  Set-MailboxDatabase

- **Network configuration**
  Get-DatabaseAvailabilityGroupNetwork
  New-DatabaseAvailabilityGroupNetwork
  Remove-DatabaseAvailabilityGroupNetwork
  Set-DatabaseAvailabilityGroupNetwork

- **Switchover management**
  Move-ActiveMailboxDatabase
  Start-DatabaseAvailabilityGroup
  Stop-DatabaseAvailabilityGroup
  Restore-DatabaseAvailabilityGroup

- **Server membership**
  Add-DatabaseAvailabilityGroupServer
  Remove-DatabaseAvailabilityGroupServer

When planning database availability groups, keep in mind that you can create database copies only on Mailbox servers in the same database availability group that do not host the active copy of a database. An active copy differs from a passive copy in that it's in use and being accessed by users rather than offline. You cannot create two copies of the same database on the same server. Other guidelines to keep in mind when working with database copies include the following:

- All Mailbox servers in a database availability group must be in the same Active Directory domain. Database copies can be created in the same or different Active Directory sites and on the same or different network subnets. However, database copies are not supported between Mailbox servers with roundtrip network latency greater than 250 milliseconds (by default).
- You cannot replicate a database outside a database availability group. This means Mailbox databases can be replicated only to other Mailbox servers in the same database availability group.
- All copies of a database use the same path on each server containing a copy. The database and log file paths for a database copy on each Mailbox server must not conflict with any other database paths.

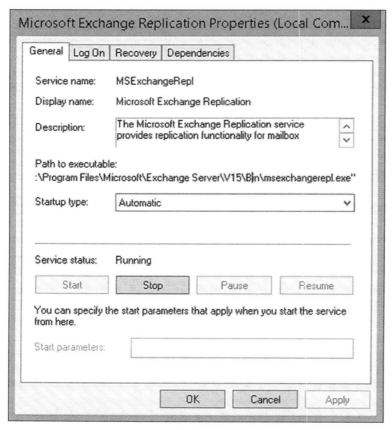

The service responsible for replicating databases is the Microsoft Exchange Replication (MSExchangeRepl) service. The replication service and components that run within the service, including Active Manager, the TCP listener, and the Volume Shadow Copy Service writer, write results to the event logs.

In Event Viewer, you can find these logs by navigating to Applications and Services Logs > Microsoft > Exchange > High Availability. In these logs, you'll find details on database actions, such as database mount operations, log truncation, and cluster action within DAGs. Events related to failures that affect replicated mailbox databases are written to the logs under Applications and Services Logs > Microsoft > Exchange >MailboxDatabaseFailureItems.

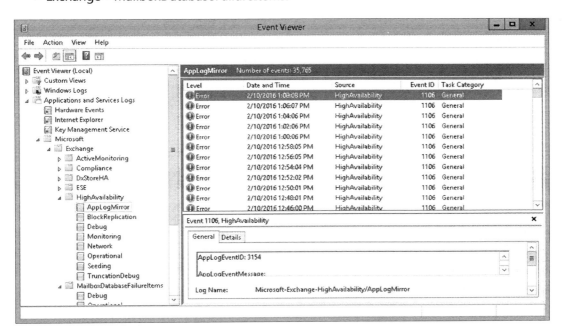

Cluster Components

In Exchange 2016, Active Manager provides the resource model and failover management features previously provided by the Cluster service. When you create your first database availability group in an Exchange organization, Exchange creates a Windows Failover Cluster, but there are no cluster groups for Exchange and no storage resources in the cluster.

Failover Cluster Manager shows only basic information about any cluster, which includes the cluster name and networks, and the quorum configuration. Cluster nodes and networks will also exist, and their status can be checked in Failover

Cluster Manager; however, Exchange manages all cluster resources, including nodes and networks.

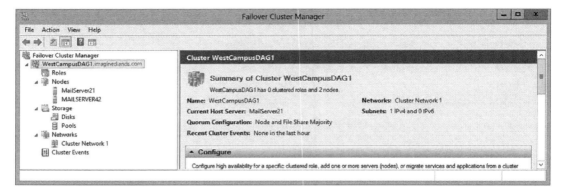

> **REAL WORLD**   Failover Cluster Manager is the primary management tool for working with the Cluster service. Although you need to use the Exchange Management tools to view and manage database availability groups and related features, Failover Cluster Manager does show the status of clustering.

- By selecting the cluster name in the left pane, you get a quick overview of the cluster configuration, including the current quorum configuration, which can be either Node Majority or Node and File Share Majority depending on the number of nodes in the database availability group.
- By selecting the Nodes entry in the left pane, you can quickly check the status of all the nodes in the database availability group.
- By expanding the Networks entry in the left pane and then selecting available cluster networks, you can check the status of the network as well as individual network connections.
- By selecting the Cluster Events node, you can check the event logs on all cluster nodes for errors and warnings.

Exchange makes use of the cluster's node and network management functions. You can check the node and network status in Exchange Admin Center by selecting Servers > Database Availability Groups.

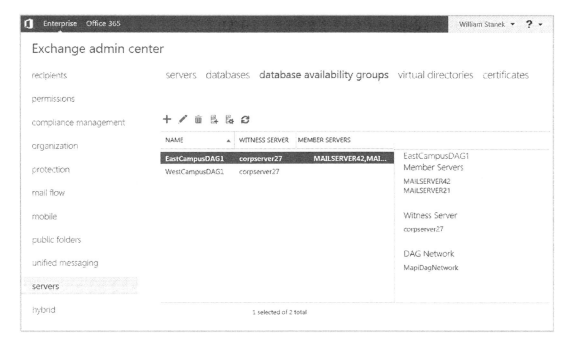

Active Manager Framework

Active Manager runs on all Mailbox servers as a subcomponent of the Microsoft Exchange Replication service. On Mailbox servers that aren't part of a DAG, Active Manager operates as a Standalone Active Manager. On Mailbox servers that are members of a DAG, Active Manager operates as either a primary role holder or a standby secondary role holder with respect to a particular database. The primary role holder, referred to as the Primary Active Manager, decides which database copies will be active and which copies to activate. It also receives topology change notifications and reacts to server failures. Only one copy of a database can be active at any given time, and that copy can be mounted or dismounted.

The group member that holds the primary role is always the member that currently owns the cluster quorum resource and the default cluster group. If the server that owns the cluster quorum resource fails, the primary role automatically moves to another server in the group and that server takes ownership of the default cluster group. Before you take the server that hosts the cluster quorum resource offline for maintenance or an upgrade, you must first move the primary role to another server in the group.

Secondary role holders, referred to as Standby Active Managers, provide information about which server hosts the active copy of a mailbox database to other Exchange components. The secondary role holder detects failures of replicated, local databases and the local information store, and it issues failure notifications to the primary role holder and asks the primary role holder to initiate a failover. The secondary role holder does not determine which server takes over, nor does it update the database location state with the primary role holder. With respect to its local system, the primary role holder also performs the functions of the secondary role by detecting local database and local information store failures and issuing related notifications.

Active Manager determines which database copy should be activated by attempting to locate a mailbox database that has characteristics similar to the following:

- The database has a status of Healthy, DisconnectedAndHealthy, DisconnectedAndResynchronizing, or SeedingSource.
- The database has a content index with a status of Healthy.
- The database has a copy queue length that is less than 10 log files.
- The database has a replay queue length of less than 50 log files.
- The server hosting the database has all components in a healthy state.

If no database copy meets all of these criteria, Active Manager continues looking for the best choice by lowering the selection requirements through successive iterations. Active Manager uses the managed availability framework to perform health checks. After one or more copies have been selected, Active Manager attempts to copy any missing log files from the original source to a potential new active copy by using a process called attempt copy last logs (ACLL). Once the ACLL process is complete, Active Manager compares the value of the AutoDatabaseMountDial property for Mailbox servers hosting copies of the database to the copy queue length of the database being activated. If the value of the AutoDatabaseMountDial property is greater than the number of missing log files, the Primary Active Manager tries to activate the next best copy (if one is available).

If the value of the AutoDatabaseMountDial property is equal to or less than the number of missing log files, the Primary Active Manager issues a mount request. At this point, either the database mounts and is made available to clients or the database doesn't mount and the Primary Active Manager tries to activate the next best copy (if one is available).

Managed Availability Components

In Exchange 2016, the active monitoring and high availability functions are integrated into a single architecture called managed availability, which is implemented on Mailbox servers. Managed availability is a framework that includes a probe engine for taking measurements and collecting data, a monitor engine for determining the status of Exchange components, and a responder engine for taking recovery actions.

Managed availability is implemented using:

- **Exchange Health Manager Worker process (MSExchangeHMWorker.exe)**   A working process that performs the runtime management tasks.
- **Exchange Health Manager Service (MSExchangeHMHost.exe)**   A controller process used to execute and manage the work process. If the worker process becomes nonresponsive or otherwise fails, the controller process is used to recover the worker process.

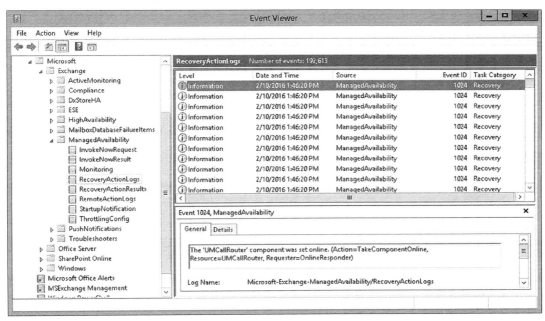

During startup, the health manager worker process reads XML configuration files and initializes the probes, monitors, and responders used by the managed availability framework. The worker process stores runtime data in the registry and writes results to the event logs as well. In Event Viewer, you can find these logs by navigating to Applications and Services Logs > Microsoft > Exchange > ManagedAvailability.

As discussed further in Chapter 18, "Troubleshooting Exchange Server 2016," in the "Tracking Server Health" section, you can use Get-HealthReport and Get-ServerHealth to check the state and health of Exchange resources. Each tracked resource has customized sets of probes, monitors, and responders that help to ensure its availability. Probe definitions identify the Exchange resource to track and the time interval in which the resource is checked. Monitor definitions identify the specific state of the resource based on the collected data. In Event Viewer, you can find definitions and results for probes, monitors, and responders under Applications and Services Logs > Microsoft > Exchange > ActiveMonitoring.

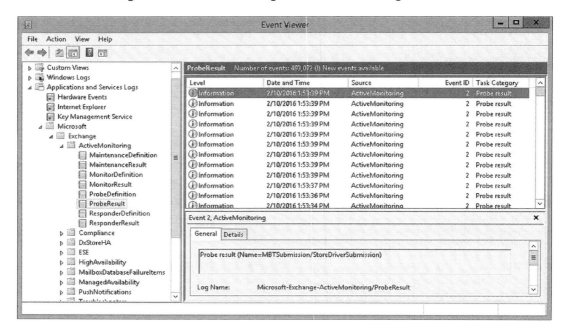

Exchange tracks the transition state internally by using the TargetHealthState property associated with a responder, where

- 0 indicates an alert threshold is no longer met
- 1 indicates a healthy state
- 2 indicates a degraded state
- 3 indicates an unhealthy state
- 4 indicates an unrecoverable state
- 5 indicates a Degraded1 state

- 6 indicates a Degraded2 state
- 7 indicates an Unhealthy1 state
- 8 indicates an Unhealthy2 state
- 9 indicates an Unrecoverable1 state
- 10 indicates an Unrecoverable2 state

When a resource transitions from one state to another is determined by the monitor definition. As soon as the monitor engine detects an unhealthy or degraded state for a responder, the transition state of that resource is shown as Unhealthy or Degraded respectively, which will trigger a recovery action. Whether a resource is shown as Unhealthy or Degraded depends on the data collected. For example, if a resource is unavailable, the resource may be listed as Unhealthy. If a resource is available but is slow to respond due to high latency or a high level of activity, the resource may be listed as Degraded.

Once in an Unhealthy state, the health manager may transition the resource to another state. For example, after 30 seconds in an unhealthy state, the resource may be transitioned to an Unhealthy1 state. After 300 seconds in an unhealthy state, the resource may be transitioned to an Unhealthy2 state. After 3000 seconds in an unhealthy state, the resource may be transitioned to an Unrecoverable state. Once in an Unrecoverable state, the health manager may transition the resource through the related Unrecoverable, Unrecoverable1, and Unrecoverable2 states.

Responder definitions detail the specific recovery actions to take based on the transition state of the Exchange resource. The exact response to an unhealthy state depends on the affected resource. Although the initial response to an unhealthy state might be to restart the related service or application pool, a subsequent response might be to restart the server, and a final response might be to take the server offline so that it no longer accepts traffic.

Creating and Managing Database Availability Groups

Database availability groups are a container in Active Directory and a logical layer on top of Windows Clustering. You can create and manage database availability groups in a variety of ways. Establishing a database availability group and making it operational requires the following at a minimum:

1. Preparing for deployment
2. Creating a database availability group
3. Adding member servers to the group
4. Designating a witness server
5. Creating an availability group network

These tasks and general management tasks for database availability groups are discussed in the sections that follow.

Preparing for DAGs

A database availability group defines a set of servers that provide automatic database-level recovery from database failures. Only members of the Organization Management group or the Database Availability Groups Role can create database availability groups. Only members of the Organization Management group or the Database Copies Role can manage mailbox database copies.

When you create a database availability group, you can specify a witness server or let Exchange choose one for you. The witness server's role is to help maintain the state of the group. It does this by maintaining the quorum when there is an even number of members in the group. On the witness server, you can designate a directory, called the witness directory, for use by the database availability group, or you can let Exchange create a default directory for you. By default, the witness directory is created as a subdirectory of %SystemDrive%\DAGFileShareWitnesses with the name set the same as the fully qualified domain name of the DAG.

Exchange creates and secures the witness directory automatically as part of configuring the witness server for use. The witness directory should not be used for any purpose other than for the database availability group witness server. The requirements for the witness server are as follows:

- The witness server cannot be a member of the database availability group.
- The witness server must be in the same forest as the database availability group.
- The witness server must be running a current version of Windows Server.

To be sure that Exchange administrators are aware of the availability of the witness server and that the server remains under the control of an Exchange administrator, Microsoft recommends using an Exchange 2016 server to host the witness directory.

Using an Exchange 2016 server as the witness also ensures that Exchange has sufficient permissions to remotely create and share the witness directory. The preferred witness server is a Mailbox server in the same Active Directory site as the majority of the members of the database availability group.

A single server can act as a witness for multiple database availability groups; however, every database availability group must have a separate witness directory. When your organization has multiple datacenters, placement of the witness server is especially important. While your organization may have two datacenters, a third location with a separate network infrastructure is needed for automatic failover from a site-level event. If your organization has a datacenter pair but doesn't have an alternate location with separate network infrastructure, you should:

- Consider placing the witness server in an Azure deployment, which would then be your alternate location for ensuring site failover is automatic.
- Or place the witness server in the datacenter where the majority of users are physically located and also make sure the Primary Active Manager for each availability group is located in this same datacenter.

The witness directory doesn't need to be fault tolerant and doesn't require any other special considerations. If you need to reset permissions on the witness directory or recreate the witness directory in its original location, you can use Set-DatabaseAvailabilityGroup as long as the cluster quorum is intact.

> **NOTE** Cluster quorum ensures consistency of the DAG. Quorum represents a shared view of members and resources and also is used to describe the shared physical configuration within the DAG. Having quorum ensures that only one subset of cluster members is functioning in the DAG.
>
> **TIP** Ideally, you'll locate the witness server in the same datacenter as DAG members. Although a server cannot act as a witness server for a DAG of which it is a member, a DAG member can act as a witness server for another DAG.

If the witness server isn't running Exchange 2016, Exchange 2013 or Exchange 2010, you must add the Exchange Trusted Subsystem group to the local Administrators group on the witness server prior to creating the DAG. Adding this group ensures that Exchange 2016 can create and share the witness directory. To add the Exchange Trusted Subsystem group to the local Administrators group, follow these steps:

1. In Control Panel, select **User Accounts**, and then select **Give Other Users Access To This Computer**.

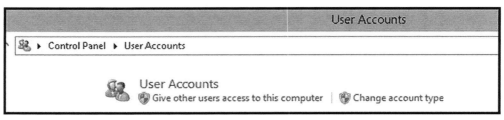

2. In the User Accounts dialog box, on the Advanced tab, click **Advanced**.

3. In the Local Users And Groups console, select **Groups**, and then double-click **Administrators**.

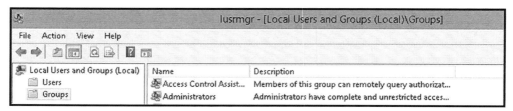

4. In the Administrators properties dialog box, select **Add**.

5. In the Select Users, Computers, Service Accounts, Or Groups dialog box, enter **Exchange Trusted Subsystem** and then click OK. The Exchange Trusted Subsystem is then added to the local Administrators group.

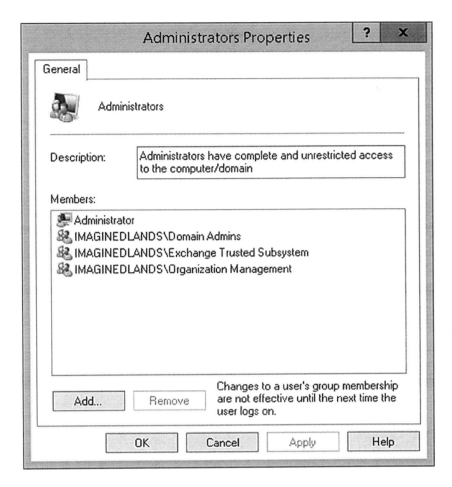

Beginning with Exchange 2016, you can now deploy a DAG with or without an administrative access point for the failover cluster. A failover cluster for the DAG is created without an administrative access point by default. Although a recommended best practice, this configuration is only supported when all member servers are running Windows Server 2012 R2 or later. Alternatively, you can specify one or more static IPv4 addresses for the DAG to use for dynamic IP addressing.

There are important differences between DAGs that have or don't have administrative access points for their failover clusters:

- A DAG with a cluster administrative access point uses a cluster name object (CNO). The CNO must be pre-staged and provisioned by assigning appropriate permissions.

- A DAG without a cluster administrative access point does not have a cluster name object (CNO). This also means you don't need to pre-stage or pre-provision a CNO.

To set up the database availability group, Exchange creates an msExchMDBAvailabilityGroup object and related objects in Active Directory Domain Services (AD DS). These objects represent the database availability group, its members, networks, and attributes. The msExchMDBAvailabilityGroup directory object is used to store information about the database availability group, such as server membership information. Information about the included databases is stored in the cluster database. When you add the first server to a database availability group, a failover cluster is automatically created for the database availability group and failover monitoring is initiated. The failover cluster heartbeat mechanism and cluster database are then used to track and manage information about the database availability group.

After a database availability group has been created, you can add or remove member servers. When the first Mailbox server is added to a database availability group, the following occurs:

- The Windows Failover Clustering component and related management tools are installed, if they are not already installed.

> **IMPORTANT**   Windows Failover Clustering is available on servers that are running Windows Server 2012, Windows Server 2012 R2 and Windows Server 2016. Each Mailbox server in the database availability group should have at least two network interface cards in order to have separate replication and messaging networks.

- A failover cluster is created using the name of the database availability group. For the purposes of authentication and access permissions, the cluster is represented by a computer account that is created in the default container for computers. This computer account is referred to as the cluster virtual network name account or the cluster network object.
- The server is added to the msExchMDBAvailabilityGroup object in Active Directory. When you create a database availability group that has an administrative access point, an IP address is assigned to the group. Then when you add the first server to the group, the name and IP address of the database availability group are registered in Domain Name System (DNS) using a Host (A) record. The name must be no longer than 15 characters and must be unique within the Active Directory forest. Otherwise, when you create a group without an administrative access point,

only a corresponding Cluster Network Object (CNO) is created in Active Directory with the name of the DAG.

- The cluster database is updated with information about the databases that are mounted on the server.
- Exchange examines the current network configuration, as presented by the cluster. If the server has a properly configured network card, the configuration of that network card is used to create the replication network. If the server has two network cards, the configuration settings of those network cards are used to create separate replication and messaging networks.
- A base directory is created on the witness server. If you specified a directory during DAG creation, this directory is created. Otherwise, the %SystemDrive%\DAGFileShareWitnesses directory is created. Permissions are set so that the local Administrators group has full control.

> **NOTE** The witness directory and witness file share aren't created until needed. Permissions are set so that the network name account representing the cluster has full control.

When you add the second and subsequent servers to the DAG, the following occurs:

- The server is joined to the failover cluster for the DAG.
- The server is added to the msExchMDBAvailabilityGroup object in Active Directory Domain Services.
- The cluster database is updated with information about the databases that are mounted on the server.

When a database availability group has a single member server, the failover cluster initially uses the Node Majority quorum mode. When you add the second Mailbox server to the database availability group, Exchange changes the cluster quorum to the Node and File Share Majority quorum model and begins by using the Universal Naming Convention (UNC) path and directory for the cluster quorum. If the witness directory does not exist, Exchange automatically creates it at this point and configures its security with full control permissions for local administrators and the cluster network computer account for the database availability group.

> **REAL WORLD** Every failover cluster has a resource that is responsible for maintaining the witness logs. This resource is called the quorum or witness resource. The quorum resource writes information about all cluster database changes to the witness logs, ensuring that the cluster configuration and state data can be recovered. When you create a database availability group, Exchange automatically determines the appropriate quorum configuration for your cluster based on the number of member servers. When a DAG has an odd number of members, Exchange uses the Node Majority quorum model.

> When a DAG has an even number of members, Exchange uses a Node and File Share Majority quorum model.
>
> In a Node Majority cluster configuration, servers have a local quorum device. This device stores the cluster configuration information. In a Node and File Share Majority cluster configuration, servers use a witness file share rather than a quorum (witness) device. Otherwise, the Node and File Share Majority configuration works like the Node Majority configuration. The change from one model to the other should happen automatically. If it doesn't, run Set-DatabaseAvailabilityGroup with only the -Identity parameter, which will update the quorum settings for the DAG.

Before you create a database availability group that will use an administrative access point, you should pre-stage and prepare the cluster name object. You pre-stage the cluster name object by creating a computer account that will be used as the cluster's name resource. The name resource is a Kerberos-enabled object that acts as the cluster's identity and provides the cluster's security context.

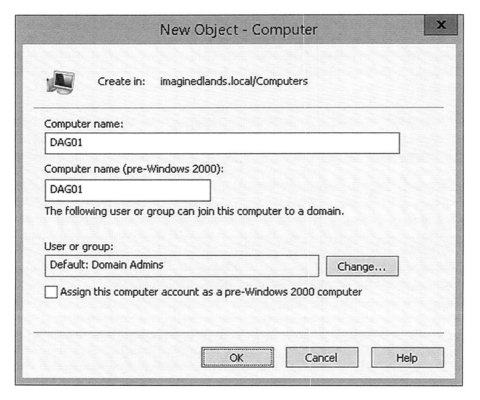

To pre-stage the cluster name object for a DAG with an administrative access point, complete the following steps:

1. In the Active Directory Users And Computers console tree, right-click the container in which you want to place the computer account, click New, and then click Computer.

2. In the Computer Name text box, enter the name that you want to use for the DAG. For example, if you are creating the first DAG in the Active Directory forest, you may want to enter **DAG01** as the name. The name can be up to 15 characters. The name must be unique in the Active Directory forest and cannot contain spaces or other special characters.

3. If Windows Deployment Services are not installed, click OK to create the computer account. Otherwise, click Next twice, and then click Finish.

Next, prepare the cluster name object for the DAG containing the administrative access point. You prepare the cluster name object by completing the following steps:

1. Open Active Directory Users And Computers. If Advanced Features aren't enabled, enable them by selecting **Advanced Features** on the View menu.

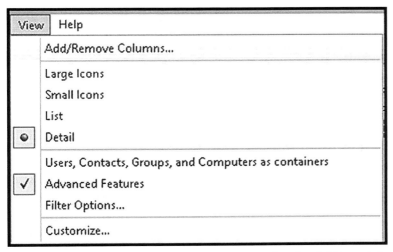

2. Right-click the computer account for the DAG, and then select **Disable Account**.

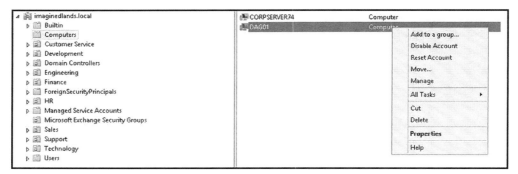

3. When prompted to confirm that you want to disable the account, select **Yes** and then select **OK**.

4. Right-click the computer account for the DAG, and then select **Properties**. In the properties dialog box, select the Security tab and then select **Add**.

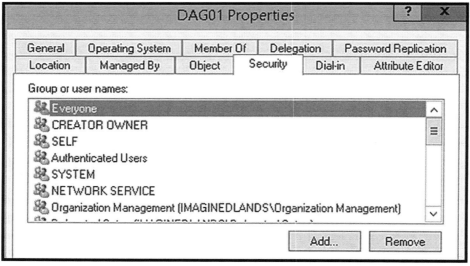

5. In the Select User, Computer, Service Account, Or Group dialog box, enter **Exchange Trusted Subsystem** as the name of the group to which you want to grant privileges, and then click OK.

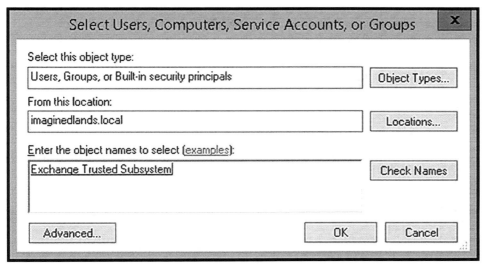

6. With Exchange Trusted Subsystem selected in the Group Or User Names list, select **Full Control** in the **Allow** column, and then select **OK** to grant full control permissions on the cluster name object to the Exchange Trusted Subsystem.

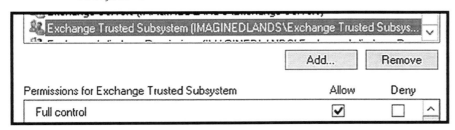

SECURITY ALERT   The Exchange Trusted Subsystem group has as members all the machine accounts for Exchange servers in the domain and as such, this group can be used to manage the cluster name object. Alternatively, you can enter the name of the first Mailbox server you are adding to the DAG and then grant full control permissions to the related computer object to ensure that the LOCAL SYSTEM security context on that server will be able to manage the cluster name object.

REAL WORLD   When Windows Firewall is enabled, you must enable inbound exceptions for Windows Management Instrumentation (WMI) and File And Printer Sharing on the witness server. Keep in mind that if you don't specify a witness server, Exchange searches the local Active Directory site for an Exchange server that isn't a member of the DAG and configures this server as the witness server. To create the required inbound exceptions for Windows Firewall, follow these steps:

1. In Control Panel, select System And Security, and then select Windows Firewall.

2. In the left pane, select Allow An App Or Feature Through Windows Firewall.

3. If File And Printer Sharing is not selected for the Domain profile, select it under Allowed Apps And Features.

4. If Windows Management Instrumentation (WMI) is not selected for the Domain profile, select it under Allowed Apps And Features.

5. If you made changes to the Windows Firewall configuration, select OK.

If Windows Firewall is enabled and these exceptions are not created, you may see error messages warning that Exchange wasn't able to create the default witness directory or that Exchange is unable to access file shares on the witness server. You may see an error message stating: The network path was not found. Or you may see an error message stating: WMI exception occurred on the server. The RPC server is unavailable.

Creating Database Availability Groups

Once you've performed any necessary preparatory steps, you can create the database availability group by completing the following steps:

1. In the Exchange Admin Center, select Servers in the feature pane, and then select Database Availability Groups.

2. Select the New button to create the DAG. You should now see the New Database Availability Group dialog box, as shown in Figure 6-1.

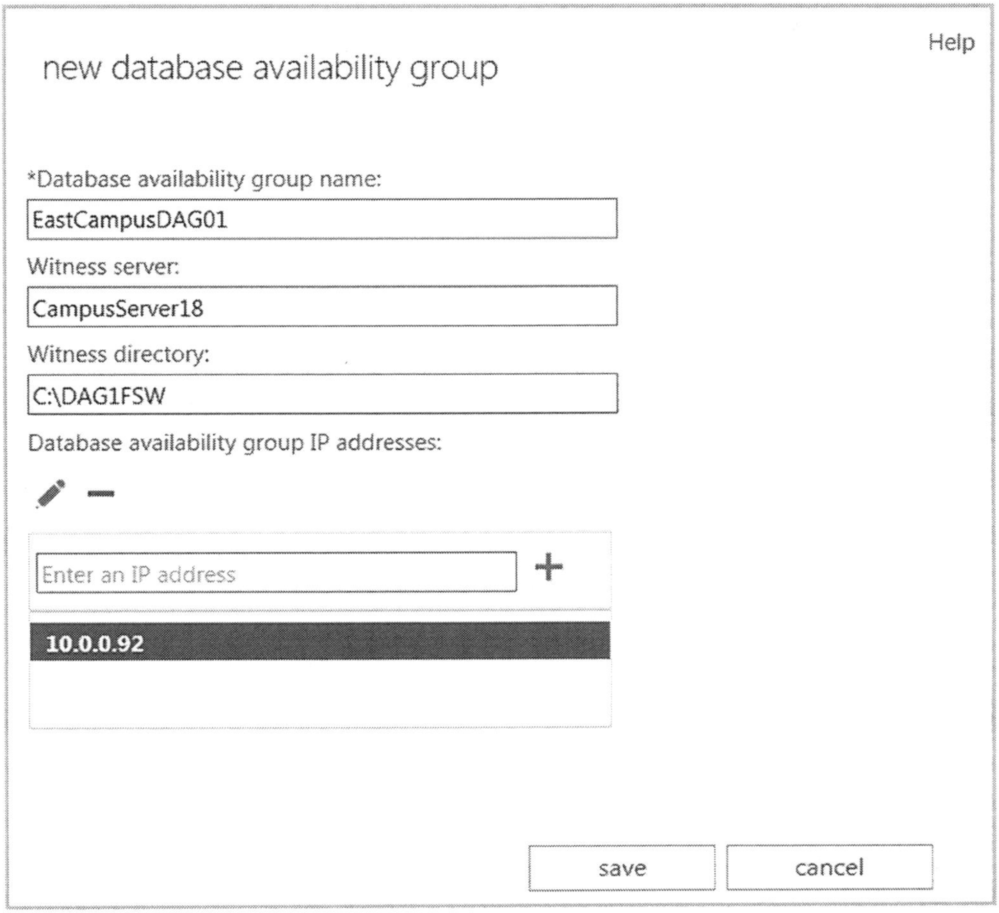

FIGURE 6-1 Set the database availability group name and file locations.

3. In the Database Availability Group Name text box, enter the name of the pre-staged computer account for the DAG.

4. Optionally, provide the name of a server in the same Active Directory forest as the DAG to act as the witness server. Because this server cannot be a member of the database availability group, be sure that you don't select servers that will be members of the database availability group you are configuring. The witness server must be running a current version of Windows Server, but doesn't need to be running Microsoft Exchange. However, if the witness server isn't running Microsoft Exchange, you'll need to modify the local Administrators group on the witness server prior to creating the DAG and add the Exchange Trusted Subsystem security group as a member.

> **NOTE** The server you select as the witness server can be a member of a different database availability group. Also note that if you don't specify a witness server, Exchange attempts to automatically select a witness server by looking in the same Active Directory site as the majority of the DAG members for a Mailbox server that isn't part of the DAG.

5. Optionally, provide the local folder path for a directory that will be used to store witness data, such as C:\WitnessDir. If the directory does not exist, Exchange attempts to create it for you on the witness server. If you don't specify a witness directory, Exchange attempts to create a directory named relative to the database availability group on the witness server's system drive.

> **NOTE** Exchange must have appropriate permissions on the server to create and then share the witness directory. Although you can set the local directory path, the share name is set automatically in the form DAGName.DomainName, such as WestCampusDag1.IMAGINEDLANDS.COM. This share is configured so that the cluster name object has full control.
>
> **TIP** As long as the witness server is an Exchange server in the same forest, Exchange should be able to create and share the directory. If Exchange is unable to create and share the directory, you'll see an error message and will need to take appropriate corrective actions. You can use the Set-DatabaseAvailabilityGroup with the –WitnessDirectory parameter to specify a new directory to use at any time. You also can set a new directory by double-clicking the DAG in the Exchange Admin Center, entering a new directory path in the Witness Directory field, and then clicking OK.
>
> If the witness server is not an Exchange 2016 server, you have to add the Exchange Trusted Subsystem security group to the local Administrators group on the witness server.

6. IP address assignment controls whether the DAG will have an administrative access point:

* To create a DAG without an administrative access point, either provide no IPv4 address or enter 255.255.255.255 as the IPv4 address. Remember, all DAG members must be running Windows Server 2012 R2 or later.
* To create a DAG with an administrative access point and static IP addressing, enter an IP address to use, and then select Add. Repeat this process to specify other static IP addresses to use.
* To create a DAG with an administrative access point and dynamic IP addressing, enter 0.0.0.0 as the IP address to use.

7. Select Save to create the database availability group. If an error occurred, you'll need to take the appropriate corrective action. Otherwise, you can now add member servers to the database availability group.

In Exchange Management Shell, you can create database availability groups by using the New-DatabaseAvailabilityGroup cmdlet. Listing 6-1 provides the syntax and usage. Set DAG name using the -Name parameter. To control whether the DAG has an administrative access point and IPv4 addressing, do the following:

*   Create a DAG without an administrative access point by using the value 255.255.255.255 for the -DatabaseAvailabilityGroupIpAddresses parameter. Ensure all DAG members are running Windows Server 2012 R2 or later.
*   Create a DAG with an administrative access point and static IP addressing by setting the -DatabaseAvailabilityGroupIpAddresses parameter to the specific IPv4 addresses to use.
*   Create a DAG with an administrative access point and dynamic IP addressing by setting the -DatabaseAvailabilityGroupIpAddresses parameter to 0.0.0.0.

> **NOTE** Don't confuse the local witness directory with the witness file share. The local witness directory has a local file path on the witness server, such as C:\WitnessShare. When you specify the witness directory, Exchange creates the base directory and then creates and shares a subdirectory within this directory as appropriate.

LISTING 6-1 New-DatabaseAvailabilityGroup cmdlet syntax and usage

Syntax

```
New-DatabaseAvailabilityGroup -Name DAGName

[-DatabaseAvailabilityGroupIpAddresses IPAddress1, IPAddress2, IPAddressN]

[-WitnessServer ServerName]

[-WitnessDirectory LocalDirOnWitnessServer]

[-DomainController FullyQualifiedName]

[-ThirdPartyReplication <Disabled | Enabled>]
```

Usage

```
New-DatabaseAvailabilityGroup -Name "EastCampusDAG1"

-WitnessServer "WinServer19"

-WitnessDirectory "C:\EastCampusDAG1"


New-DatabaseAvailabilityGroup -Name "WestCampusDAG1"

-WitnessServer "WinServer19"
```

```
-WitnessDirectory "C:\WestCampusDAG1"
-DatabaseAvailabilityGroupIpAddresses 255.255.255.255


New-DatabaseAvailabilityGroup -Name "NorthCampusDAG1"
-DatabaseAvailabilityGroupIpAddresses 0.0.0.0
```

Managing Availability Group Membership

When you add a server to a database availability group, the server works with the other servers in the group to provide automatic, database-level recovery from database, server, and network failures. When member servers have only one network adapter card, the DAG uses the same network for both messaging and replication traffic. When member servers have two network cards, the DAG uses one network card primarily for messaging traffic and the other network card is typically dedicated to replication traffic. If you add more than two network cards to member servers, these additional network cards can be configured for replication, giving the DAG additional replication networks to handle increased workloads.

> **NOTE** Member servers in a DAG can have zero or more replication networks but only one messaging network. For optimal operation, servers should have at least two network interface cards with each network interface card configured to use a different subnet.

Keep the following in mind when planning database availability group membership:

- All servers in a DAG must be running the same operating system, which can be Windows Server 2012, Windows Server 2012 R2 or Windows Server 2016.
- When you add the first Mailbox server to a database availability group, the group must be assigned an IP address. If no IP address is assigned, Exchange uses DHCP to obtain an IP address for the group.
- If you no longer want a server to be a member of a group, you can remove it from the group and the server will no longer be automatically protected from failures. Keep in mind that you must remove all replicated database copies from the server before you can remove it from the group.

You can add a Mailbox server to or remove a Mailbox server from a database availability group by completing the following steps:

1. In the Exchange Admin Center, select Servers in the feature pane, and then select Database Availability Groups to view existing availability groups, as shown in Figure 6-2.

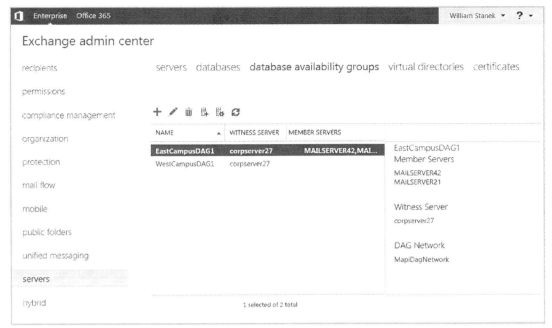

Enterprise   Office 365

William Stanek ▼   ? ▼

Exchange admin center

recipients

permissions

compliance management

organization

protection

mail flow

mobile

public folders

unified messaging

servers

hybrid

servers   databases   **database availability groups**   virtual directories   certificates

NAME	▲	WITNESS SERVER	MEMBER SERVERS
EastCampusDAG1		**corpserver27**	**MAILSERVER42,MAI...**
WestCampusDAG1		corpserver27	

EastCampusDAG1

Member Servers

MAILSERVER42
MAILSERVER21

Witness Server

corpserver27

DAG Network

MapiDagNetwork

1 selected of 2 total

FIGURE 6-2 View configured database availability groups.

2. Select the DAG you want to configure, and then select the Manage DAG Membership button. In the Manage Database Availability Group Membership dialog box, shown in Figure 6-3, any current DAG members are listed by name. You can now:

- Click the Add button to add a server to the database availability group. In the Select Server dialog box, select a server, click Add, and then repeat as necessary to select other servers.
- Select a server and then click the Remove button to remove a server from the database availability group.

3. When you are finished selecting servers, choose OK and then choose Save. For each server you added, Exchange Admin Center will install the required Windows Failover Clustering components, and then add the server to the DAG. Subsequently, Exchange Admin Center will create and configure the witness directory and file share. For each server you removed, Exchange Admin Center will attempt to remove the server from the DAG. If an error occurs during these tasks, you will need to take the appropriate corrective action; otherwise, click Close when these tasks have completed successfully.

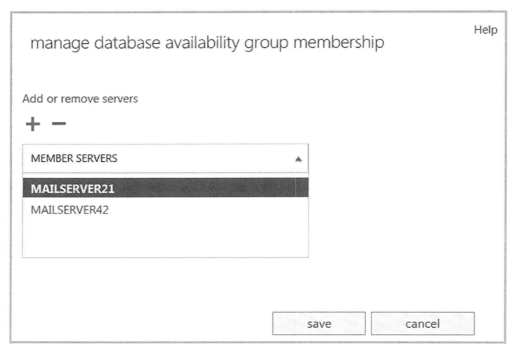

FIGURE 6-3 Add group members.

In Exchange Management Shell, you can list database availability groups by using Get-DatabaseAvailabilityGroup. If you enter Get-DatabaseAvailabilityGroup without additional parameters, you'll see a list of all availability groups in the current Active Directory forest as well as the member servers and operational servers for those groups, as shown in the following example and sample output:

```
Get-DatabaseAvailabilityGroup

Name            Member Servers              Operational Servers
----            --------------              -------------------
EastCampusDAG1  MailServer42, MailServer21  MailServer42, MailServer21
WestCampusDAG1  MailServer44, MailServer96  MailServer44, MailServer96
```

Use the –Identity parameter to specify the name of the database availability group to query. Add –Status to any query to include real-time status information.

You add or remove group members by using Add-DatabaseAvailabilityGroupServer and Remove-DatabaseAvailabilityGroupServer. Listings 6-2 and 6-3 provide the syntax and usage.

LISTING 6-2 Add-DatabaseAvailabilityGroupServer cmdlet syntax and usage

Syntax

```
Add-DatabaseAvailabilityGroupServer -Identity DAGName
-MailboxServer ServerToAdd [-DomainController FullyQualifiedName]
[-SkipDagValidation {$true | $false}]
```

Usage

```
Add-DatabaseAvailabilityGroupServer -Identity "EastCampusDAG1"
-MailboxServer "MailServer62"
```

LISTING 6-3 Remove-DatabaseAvailabilityGroupServer cmdlet syntax and usage

Syntax

```
Remove-DatabaseAvailabilityGroupServer -Identity DAGName
-MailboxServer ServerToRemove [-ConfigurationOnly <$true | $false>]
[-DomainController FullyQualifiedName] [-SkipDagValidation {$true|$false}]
```

Usage

```
Remove-DatabaseAvailabilityGroupServer -Identity "EastCampusDAG1"
-MailboxServer "MailServer62"
```

Managing Database Availability Group Networks

Each database availability group should have a minimum of two networks: one for replication traffic, referred to as the group's *replication network*, and one for MAPI and other traffic, referred to as the group's *messaging network*. Although a DAG can have only one messaging network, you can create additional replication networks in a database availability group and configure them by using the Exchange Management tools. Having multiple replication networks helps scale the DAG to meet increasing requirements.

> **REAL WORLD**   Although highly available servers have multiple logical networks, you can use a single, non-teamed network interface to handle both replication network and messaging network traffic. This configuration is in fact recommended as part of the preferred architecture to simplify the network stack and remove the requirement to manually eliminate heartbeat cross-talk.

By default, Exchange 2016 automatically creates DAG networks based on the configuration of network adapter cards installed on member servers. If a DAG member has multiple network cards and those cards are configured on separate networks, Exchange normally will configure the DAG members with one messaging network and one or more dedicated replication networks automatically. You can manually configure DAG networks as well but must first disable automatic network configuration.

You can enable manual network configuration for a DAG by completing the following steps:

1. In the Exchange Admin Center, select Servers in the feature pane, and then select Database Availability Groups to view existing availability groups.
2. Double-click the DAG you want to manually configure.
3. In the properties dialog box, on the General page, select the Configure Database Availability Group Networks manually check box, and then select Save.
4. You can now manually configure and manage the networks for the DAG. Keep in mind that if you later disable manual configuration, any manually created networks and related settings will be removed and Exchange Admin Center will create new DAG networks based on the current configuration of DAG members.

> **NOTE** Use the –ManualDagNetworkConfiguration parameter of the Set-DatabaseAvailabilityGroup cmdlet to enable a manual network configuration. Set the parameter to $true to enable or $false to disable manual network configuration.

Once you enable manual network configuration, you can manually create and manage network settings for the DAG. Each database availability group network must have a unique name of up to 128 characters, one or more subnet associations, and an optional description of up to 256 characters. When you configure a network, you can dedicate the network to replication traffic or dedicate the network to MAPI traffic.

> **NOTE** Disabling replication does not guarantee that Exchange will not use a network for replication. If all configured replication networks are offline, failed, or otherwise unavailable, and only a nonreplication network remains, Exchange will use that network for replication until a replication-enabled network becomes available.

> **REAL WORLD** Every network address has a network identifier that identifies the network and a host identifier that identifies the individual host on the

network. The network ID is seen as the prefix of an IPv4 or IPv6 address, and the host ID is the suffix. When you define an availability group network, you need to identify the network and then specify the number of bits in the network number that are part of the network ID (and the remaining bits are understood to be part of the host ID). To write a block of IPv4 addresses and specify which bits are used for the network ID, you write the network number followed by a forward slash and the number of bits in the network ID, as follows:

NetworkNumber/# of bits in the network ID

The slash and the number of bits in the network ID are referred to as the network prefix. By default, Class A IPv4 networks have 8 bits in the network ID, Class B IPv4 networks have 16 bits, and Class C IPv4 networks have 24 bits.

IPv6 doesn't use subnet masks to identify which bits belong to the network ID and which bits belong to the host ID. Instead, each IPv6 address is assigned a subnet prefix length that specifies how the bits in the network ID are used. The subnet prefix length is represented in decimal form. If 48 bits in the network ID are used, the subnet prefix length is written as FEC0:1234:5678::/48 to represent the IPv6 addresses FEC0:1234:5678:: through FEC0:1234:5678::FFFF:FFFF:FFFF:FFFF.

You can create a network for a database availability group by completing the following steps:

1. In the Exchange Admin Center, select Servers in the feature pane, and then select Database Availability Groups to view existing availability groups.

2. Select the DAG you want to configure and then select the New DAG Network button.

3. In the New Database Availability Group Network dialog box, shown in Figure 6-4, enter a unique name for the database availability group network of up to 128 characters and then provide an optional description for the database availability group network of up to 256 characters.

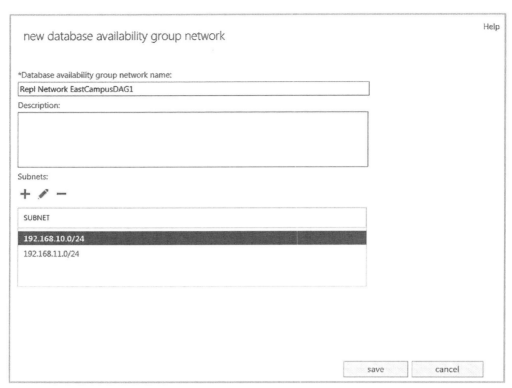

FIGURE 6-4 Create a network for the availability group.

4. Under Subnets, click Add to add a network subnet to the database availability group network. Subnets should be entered by using a format of *IPv4Address/Bitmask,* such as 192.168.15.0/24, or *IPv6Address/NetworkSubnetPrefix,* such as FEC0:1234:5678::/48. The subnet must match the subnet used by one or more DAG members. If you add a subnet that is currently associated with another database availability group network, the subnet is removed from the other database availability group network and associated with the network being created.

5. Click Save. If an error occurred, you need to take the appropriate corrective action before you can create the network. If a warning is displayed, Exchange Admin Center will create the network but the network might not be operational until your correct the problem that prompted the warning. Otherwise, click Close when the task completes.

When the DAG is selected in Exchange Admin Center, the details pane lists the networks associated with the DAG. If manual configuration of networks is enabled, you'll see options for managing each network in the details pane, as shown in Figure 6-5, and these options include:

- **Disable Replication** Configures the network with a preference for messaging; however, the DAG will use the network for replication if necessary. Note also that a DAG can have only one dedicated messaging network.
- **Remove** Removes a DAG network, providing the network doesn't have any active subnets. Before you can remove a network with active subnets, you must assign the subnets to other networks.
- **View Details** Opens the properties dialog box for the network. You can use the options in this dialog box to change the network name, network description, and associated subnets. By selecting or clearing the Enable Replication checkbox, you can enable or disable replication on the network.

The properties dialog box for a DAG network also shows the status of subnets and network interfaces. Subnets and interfaces listed as Up are active. Subnets and interfaces listed as Down are inactive.

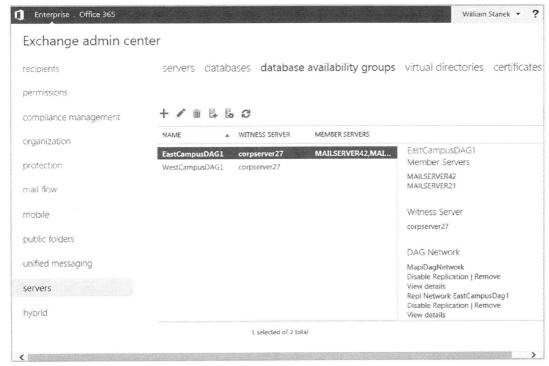

FIGURE 6-5 View the networks configured for a DAG.

In Exchange Management Shell, you can list availability DAG networks and their status by using Get-DatabaseAvailabilityGroupNetwork. If you enter Get-DatabaseAvailabilityGroupNetwork without additional parameters, you see a list of all configured networks for all availability groups. Use the –Identity parameter to specify the name of the network to query. Use the –Server parameter to obtain health information for the network from a specific Mailbox server. The following example lists detailed information for all the networks associated with EastCampusDAG1:

```
Get-DatabaseAvailabilityGroupNetwork -Identity EastCampusDAG1 | fl
```

The following example lists detailed information for network associated with EastCampusDAG1 that have names starting with Repl:

```
Get-DatabaseAvailabilityGroupNetwork -Identity EastCampusDAG1\Repl* | fl
```

The detailed information is helpful as it lists the status of associated subnets and interfaces as shown in the following sample:

```
Name                : Repl Network EastCampusDAG1
Description         :
Subnets             : {{10.0.0.0/24,Up}}
Interfaces          : {{MailServer21,Up,10.0.0.50},
                      {MAILSERVER42,Up,10.0.0.60}}
MapiAccessEnabled   : True
ReplicationEnabled  : True
IgnoreNetwork       : False
Identity            : EastCampusDAG1\Repl Network EastCampusDAG1
IsValid             : True
```

You create or remove group networks by using New-DatabaseAvailability GroupNetwork and Remove-DatabaseAvailabilityGroupNetwork. Listings 6-4 and 6-5 provide the syntax and usage.

LISTING 6-4 New-DatabaseAvailabilityGroupNetwork cmdlet syntax and usage

Syntax

```
New-DatabaseAvailabilityGroupNetwork -Name NetworkName
-DatabaseAvailabilityGroup DAGName
[-Description Description] [-DomainController FullyQualifiedName]
[-IgnoreNetwork <$true | $false>] [-ReplicationEnabled <$true | $false>]
[-Subnets SubnetIds]
```

Usage

```
New-DatabaseAvailabilityGroupNetwork -DatabaseAvailabilityGroup
"EastCampusDAG1" -Name "Primary DAG Network" -Description ""
-Subnets "{192.168.10.0/24, 192.168.15.0/24}" -ReplicationEnabled $true
```

LISTING 6-5 Remove-DatabaseAvailabilityGroupNetwork cmdlet syntax and usage

Syntax

```
Remove-DatabaseAvailabilityGroupNetwork -Identity NetworkName
[-DomainController FullyQualifiedName]
```

Usage

```
Remove-DatabaseAvailabilityGroupNetwork
-Identity "EastCampusDAG1\Primary DAG Network"
```

Changing Availability Group Network Settings

Database availability group networks have several properties that you can configure, including the network name, description, associated subnets, and replication status. The replication status determines whether the network is used as the replication network for the group or the messaging network for the group. When replication is enabled, the network is used as the replication network for the group. When replication is disabled, the network is used as the messaging network for the group.

When manual network configuration is enabled, you can manage the settings for a group network by completing the following steps:

1. In the Exchange Admin Center, select Servers in the feature pane, and then select Database Availability Groups to view existing availability groups.

2. When you select the DAG you want to work with, the details pane lists the associated networks. Each network has a related set of management options. Select the **View Details** option for the network you want to configure.

DAG Network

MapiDagNetwork
Disable Replication | Remove
View details
Repl Network EastCampusDag1
Disable Replication | Remove
View details

3. In the properties dialog box for the network, enter a new name if desired and optionally change the network description.

Repl Network EastCampusDAG1

*Database availability group network name:

Repl Network EastCampusDAG1

Description:

4. Each network must contain at least one subnet. Subnets must be added by using a format of *IPAddress/Bitmask*, such as 192.168.15.0/24, or *IPv6Address/NetworkSubnetPrefix*, such as FEC0:1234:5678::/48. Use the options provided to add, edit, or remove subnets for the network.

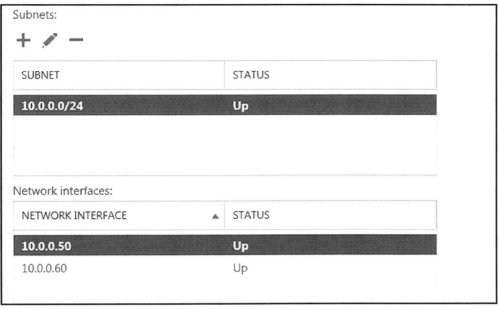

Subnets:

+ ✏ –

SUBNET	STATUS
10.0.0.0/24	Up

Network interfaces:

NETWORK INTERFACE ▲	STATUS
10.0.0.50	Up
10.0.0.60	Up

5. To establish the network as the replication network for the group, select the Enable Replication check box. Otherwise, clear the check box to use the network as the messaging network for the group.

6. Click **Save** to apply your settings.

☑ Enable replication

save   cancel

You can use Set-DatabaseAvailabilityGroupNetwork to configure basic settings for availability group networks. Listing 6-6 provides the syntax and usage for Set-DatabaseAvailabilityGroupNetwork.

LISTING 6-6 Set-DatabaseAvailabilityGroupNetwork cmdlet syntax and usage

Syntax

```
Set-DatabaseAvailabilityGroupNetwork -Identity NetworkName
[-Description Description] [-DomainController FullyQualifiedName]
[-IgnoreNetwork <$true | $false>] [-Name NewName]
[-ReplicationEnabled <$true | $false>] [-Subnets Subnets]
```

Usage

```
Set-DatabaseAvailabilityGroupNetwork
-Identity "EastCampusDAG1\Primary DAG Network"
-ReplicationEnabled $False
```

Advanced options for the networks associated with availability groups are set at the group level. Advanced options you can configure include encryption, compression, and the TCP port used for replication. Database availability groups support data encryption by using the built-in encryption capabilities of the Windows Server operating system. When you enable encryption, database availability groups use Kerberos authentication between Exchange servers to encrypt and decrypt messages. Encryption helps maintain the integrity of the data. Network encryption is a property of the database availability group and not a property of a database availability group network.

You can configure database availability group network encryption by using the –NetworkEncryption parameter of the Set-DatabaseAvailabilityGroup cmdlet in Exchange Management Shell. The possible encryption settings are as follows:

- **Disabled**   Network encryption is not used for any database availability group networks.
- **Enabled**   Network encryption is used on all database availability group networks for replication and seeding.
- **InterSubnetOnly**   Network encryption is used only with database availability group networks on the same subnet.
- **SeedOnly**   Network encryption is used on all database availability group networks for seeding only.

Database availability groups also support built-in compression. You configure network compression by using the –NetworkCompression parameter of the Set-DatabaseAvailabilityGroup cmdlet in Exchange Management Shell. The possible compression settings are as follows:

- **Disabled**   Network compression is not used for any database availability group networks.
- **Enabled**   Network compression is used on all database availability group networks for replication and seeding.
- **InterSubnetOnly**   Network compression is used only with database availability group networks on the same subnet.

- **SeedOnly** Network compression is used on all database availability group networks for seeding only.

You can specify the TCP port to use for replication by using the –ReplicationPort parameter of the Set-DatabaseAvailabilityGroup cmdlet in Exchange Management Shell.

Configuring Database Availability Group Properties

You can use the Exchange Admin Center or Exchange Management Shell to configure the properties of a database availability group, including the witness server and witness directory used by the database availability group. By using Exchange Management Shell, you can configure additional properties, such as encryption and compression settings, network discovery, the TCP port used for replication, alternate file share witness settings, and data center activation coordination mode.

To view or modify the properties of an availability group, complete the following steps:

1. In the Exchange Admin Center, select Servers in the feature pane, and then select Database Availability Groups to view existing availability groups.

2. Double-click the database availability group with which you want to work. This opens the Properties dialog box for the DAG.

3. On the General page, you'll see a list of member servers, the witness server's fully qualified domain name, and the location of the witness directory on the witness server.

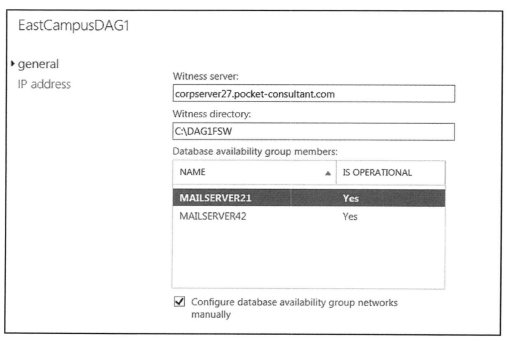

EastCampusDAG1

▸ general
  IP address

Witness server:

corpserver27.pocket-consultant.com

Witness directory:

C:\DAG1FSW

Database availability group members:

NAME ▲	IS OPERATIONAL
MAILSERVER21	Yes
MAILSERVER42	Yes

☑ Configure database availability group networks manually

4. Using the Witness Server text box, you can specify a new witness server by entering the fully qualified domain name of the new witness server. This server should be in the same Active Directory forest as the member servers and cannot be a current or future member of the database availability group.

5. Using the Witness Directory text box, you can specify a new witness directory on the witness server. If the directory does not exist, it will be created on the witness server.

6. Click **Save**.

In Exchange Management Shell, you can configure properties of database availability groups by using the Set-DatabaseAvailabilityGroup cmdlet. Listing 6-7 provides the syntax and usage.

LISTING 6-7 Set-DatabaseAvailabilityGroup cmdlet syntax and usage

Syntax

```
Set-DatabaseAvailabilityGroup -Identity DAGName
[-DatabaseAvailabilityGroupIpAddresses IPAddresses]
[-DatacenterActivationMode {"Off"|"DagOnly"}]
[-DiscoverNetworks] [-DomainController FullyQualifiedName]
[-NetworkCompression {"Disabled"|"Enabled"|"InterSubnetOnly"|"SeedOnly"}
```

```
[-NetworkEncryption {"Disabled"|"Enabled"|"InterSubnetOnly"|"SeedOnly"}
[-ReplicationPort TCPPort] [-AlternateWitnessServer ServerName]
[-AlternateWitnessServerDirectory DirectoryPath]
[-WitnessServer ServerName] [-WitnessServerDirectory DirectoryPath]
```

Usage

```
Set-DatabaseAvailability -Identity "EastCampusDAG1"
-NetworkCompression "Enabled" -NetworkEncryption "Enabled"
-ReplicationPort 33898 -DatacenterActivationMode "Off"
```

Options for working with encryption, compression, and replication ports were discussed previously in "Changing Availability Group Network Settings." Options that weren't discussed include the datacenter activation coordinator mode, the alternate witness server, and alternate witness server directory. These options can be used as part of a datacenter switchover process. The alternate witness server must not be a part of the database availability group.

The data-center coordinator mode should be set for all database availability groups with three or more members that are extended to two or more physical locations. This mode cannot be enabled for groups with less than three members. When the datacenter coordinator is enabled, you can start, stop, and restore member servers in an availability group individually or collectively by using the following:

* **Start-DatabaseAvailabilityGroup**   Activates member Mailbox servers in a recovered data center after a data-center switchover, as part of the failback process to the recovered data center. This command sets the configuration and state so that the servers are incorporated into the operating database availability group and joined to the group's cluster. You use the –MailboxServer parameter to start a specific member server or the –ActiveDirectorySite parameter to start all members in a particular site.

```
Start-DatabaseAvailabilityGroup -Identity DAGName
[-MailboxServer ServerName | -ActiveDirectorySite SiteName]
[-ConfigurationOnly <$true | $false>]
[-DomainController FullyQualifiedName]
```

> **NOTE**   You can also reactivate servers from a previously failed datacenter that has been restored to service. Before you can reactivate member Mailbox servers in a primary data center, the servers must first be integrated back into the operational database availability group. You reintegrate servers by

> running the Start-DatabaseAvailabilityGroup cmdlet and then using the Move-ActiveMailboxDatabase cmdlet to activate databases in the primary data center.

- **Stop-DatabaseAvailabilityGroup** Deactivates member Mailbox servers after a datacenter switchover. You use the –MailboxServer parameter to deactivate a specific member server or the –ActiveDirectorySite parameter to deactivate all members in a particular site.

```
Stop-DatabaseAvailabilityGroup -Identity DAGName
[-MailboxServer ServerName | -ActiveDirectorySite SiteName]
[-ConfigurationOnly <$true | $false>]
[-DomainController FullyQualifiedName]
```

- **Restore-DatabaseAvailabilityGroup** Activates member Mailbox servers in a standby data center. Typically, this process is performed after the failure or deactivation of the active member servers in a primary data center. To activate all members in a particular site, you can use the –ActiveDirectorySite parameter.

```
Restore-DatabaseAvailabilityGroup -Identity DAGName
[-ActiveDirectorySite SiteName]
[-AlternateWitnessServer ServerName]
[-AlternateWitnessDirectory DirectoryPath]
[-DomainController FullyQualifiedName]
[-UsePrimaryWitnessServer <$true | $false>
```

Removing Servers from a Database Availability Group

Before you can remove a server from a database availability group, you must also remove all database copies from the server. To remove member servers from a DAG, select the DAG you want to manage, and then select the Manage DAG Membership button. In the Manage Database Availability Group Membership dialog box, select a server on the list of current members, and then select the Remove button. Repeat as necessary to remove members. Click Save to apply the changes. If an error occurs during these tasks, you will need to take the appropriate corrective action. Otherwise, click Close when these tasks have completed successfully.

After you remove the member servers, you can remove the database availability group by selecting it and selecting the Delete button. When prompted to confirm, click Yes.

Removing Database Availability Groups

You can remove a database availability group only if it has no member servers. Therefore, before you can remove a database availability group, you must first remove any member servers from the group.

You can remove an empty availability group by completing the following steps:

1. In the Exchange Admin Center, select Servers in the feature pane, and then select Database Availability Groups to view existing availability groups.

2. On the Database Availability Group tab, select the database availability group you want to remove, and then select the Delete button.

3. When prompted to confirm the action, click Yes.

In Exchange Management Shell, you can remove database availability groups by using the Remove-DatabaseAvailabilityGroup cmdlet. Listing 6-8 provides the syntax and usage.

LISTING 6-8 Remove-DatabaseAvailabilityGroup cmdlet syntax and usage

Syntax

```
Remove-DatabaseAvailabilityGroup -Identity DAGName
[-DomainController FullyQualifiedName]
```

Usage

```
Remove-DatabaseAvailabilityGroup -Identity "EastCampusDAG1"
```

Maintaining Database Availability Groups

The Microsoft Exchange Information Store service manages the active and passive databases configured on a Mailbox server. To improve performance, the service running on each server maintains a database cache of changes to active databases that haven't been applied to passive copies. In the event of a failover or switchover, the service can apply the changes in the cache to a passive copy and then make the passive copy the active copy. Most of the time, failover completes in about 30 seconds.

The difference between failover and switchover is important. When Exchange detects a failure of an active database, regardless of whether it is from database failure, server failure, or network failure, Exchange uses failover processes to mark the active database as inactive and dismount it and then mount and mark a passive database copy as the active copy. Prior to performing maintenance on a server or for testing or troubleshooting, you might want Exchange to switch from one database to another by marking an active database as inactive and then marking a passive database copy as the active copy.

Switching Over Servers and Databases

Failover and switchover occur at the database level for individual databases and at the server level for all active databases hosted by a server. When either a switchover or failover occurs, other Exchange 2016 server roles become aware of the switchover almost immediately and redirect client and messaging traffic automatically as appropriate.

You can switch over all active databases on a server by completing the following steps:

1. In the Exchange Admin Center, select Servers in the feature pane, and then select Servers. In the main pane, select the server that you are performing maintenance on, testing, or troubleshooting.

2. In the details pane, select Server Switchover. In the Server Switchover dialog box, shown in Figure 6-6, the default option is to allow Exchange to handle the switchover and select a server to take over the databases from the source server automatically. To accept the default, select Save. Otherwise, select Specify A Server As Target For Switchover and then select Browse. In the Select Server dialog box, select the server to take over, select OK. Keep in mind that you can select only a server that is already a member of the database availability group. You can't have copies outside the group either.

3. Select Save to apply the changes. When prompted to confirm the action, click Yes.

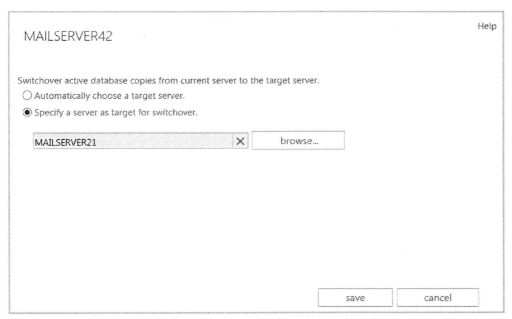

FIGURE 6-6 Switch over the active databases.

You can perform a switchover of an individual database by completing the following steps:

1. In the Exchange Admin Center, select Servers in the feature pane, and then select Databases.

2. In the main pane, select the database you want to work with. In the details pane, you see the available database copies, which are listed according to their copy status and health. Only the active copy will have a status of Active Mounted. All other database copies will display the current status of replication for the database copy, such as Passive Healthy.

3. Using the management options for the passive copy you want to activate, you can select View Details to display detailed information about the database copy, including the content index status, the overall status, the copy queue length, the replay queue length, and error messages.

4. To activate the copy, click the related Activate option. When you click Yes to confirm that you want to activate this copy, Exchange will dismount the current active mailbox database and establish the selected database copy as the active mailbox database.

5. If an error occurred, you need to take the appropriate corrective action before you can create the network. If a warning is displayed, Exchange Admin Center will create the network but the network may not be

operational until your correct the problem that prompted the warning. Otherwise, click Close when the task completes.

When you are working with Exchange Management Shell, you can initiate switchover by using Move-ActiveMailboxDatabase. Listing 6-9 shows the syntax and usage.

LISTING 6-9 Move-ActiveMailboxDatabase cmdlet syntax and usage

Syntax

```
Move-ActiveMailboxDatabase -Identity DatabaseName
[-SkipClientExperienceChecks <$true | $false>] [-SkipHealthChecks
<$true | $false>] [-SkipLagChecks <$true | $false>] {AddtlParams}


Move-ActiveMailboxDatabase -Server ServerName {AddtlParams}


{AddtlParams}
[-ActivateOnServer ServerOnWhichToActivate] [-MountDialOverride
{"Lossless" | "GoodAvailability" | "BestAvailability"
"BestEffort" | "None"} [-DomainController FullyQualifiedName]
[-MoveComment Comment] [-SkipActiveCopyChecks <$true | $false>]
[-SkipClientExperienceChecks <$true | $false>]
[-SkipHealthChecks <$true | $false>] [-SkipLagChecks <$true | $false>]
[-TerminateOnWarning <$true | $false>]
```

Usage

```
Move-ActiveMailboxDatabase -Identity "Engineering Primary Database"
-ActivateOnServer "MailServer86" -MountDialOverride "Lossless"
```

The –MountDailOverride parameter of the Move-ActiveMailboxDatabase cmdlet controls the way databases mount on switchover or failover. Every Mailbox server has a database automount setting and the default is Best Availability. Values you can select to control the database mount behavior include:

- **None**   The database uses the currently configured setting for automatically mounting.
- **Lossless**   The database does not automatically mount until all logs that were generated on the original source server have been copied to the target node.
- **Good Availability**   The database automatically mounts if the copy queue length is less than or equal to 6. If the queue length is greater than 6, Exchange attempts

to replicate the remaining logs to the target server and mounts the databases once the queue length is less than or equal to 6.

- **Best Availability** The database automatically mounts if the copy queue length is less than or equal to 12. The copy queue length is the number of logs that need to be replicated. If the queue length is greater than 12, Exchange attempts to replicate the remaining logs to the target server and mounts the databases once the queue length is less than or equal to 12.
- **Best Effort** The database automatically mounts regardless of the length of the copy queue. As this option essentially forces the database to mount with any amount of log loss, I don't recommend using this value unless you are certain you want to accept what could be a large amount of data loss.

REAL WORLD You can set the default database automount setting for a Mailbox server by using the –AutoDatabaseMountDail parameter of the Set-MailboxServer cmdlet. If you specify either Best Availability or Good Availability and all of the data has not been replicated to the target server, you might lose some mailbox data; however, the transport dumpster feature (which is enabled by default) helps protect against data loss by resubmitting messages that are in the transport dumpster queue. Because of latency problems or other issues, specifying one of these values can result in a database not being mounted, and you might need to use the -AcceptDataLoss parameter with Mount-Database to force the database to mount after a specified amount of time.

Checking Continuous Replication Status

You can use Test-ReplicationHealth to monitor continuous replication and determine the health and status of the underlying cluster service, quorum, and network components. By default, Test-ReplicationHealth performs the following tests:

- **ActiveManager** Verifies that the instance of Active Manager is running on the server.
- **ClusterNetwork** Verifies that all cluster-managed networks on the server are available.
- **ClusterService** Verifies that the Cluster service is running and reachable on the server.
- **DagMembersUp** Verifies that all DAG members are available, running, and reachable.
- **DBCopyFailed** Checks whether any mailbox database copies are in a state of Failed on the server.
- **DBCopySuspended** Checks whether any mailbox database copies are in a state of Suspended on the server.
- **DBDisconnected** Checks whether any mailbox database copies are in a state of Disconnected on the server.

- **DBInitializing**   Checks whether any mailbox database copies are in a state of Initializing on the server.
- **DBLogCopyKeepingUp**   Verifies that log copying and inspection by the passive copies of databases on the server are able to keep up with log generation activity on the active copy.
- **DBLogReplayKeepingUp**   Verifies that replay activities for the passive copies of databases on the server are able to keep up with log copying and inspection activity.
- **FileShareQuorum**   Verifies that the witness server and witness directory and share configured for the DAG are reachable.
- **QuorumGroup**   Verifies that the default cluster group (quorum group) is in a healthy and online state.
- **ReplayService**   Verifies that the Microsoft Exchange Replication service is running and reachable on the server.
- **TasksRpcListener**   Verifies that the tasks remote procedure call (RPC) server is running and reachable on the server.
- **TcpListener**   Verifies that the TCP log copy listener is running and reachable on the server.

Listing 6-10 shows the syntax and usage for Test-ReplicationHealth. You can include monitoring events and performance counters in the results if desired. To do this, set the -MonitoringContext parameter to $true. Use -OutputObjects to output an array of results.

LISTING 6-10 Test-ReplicationHealth cmdlet syntax and usage

Syntax

```
Test-ReplicationHealth [-Identity MailboxServerToCheck]
[-ActiveDirectoryTimeout Timeout] [-DomainController DCName]
[-MonitoringContext <$true | $false>] [-OutputObjects]
[-TransientEventSuppressionWindow Timeout]
```

Usage

```
Test-ReplicationHealth -Identity MailServer15 -ActiveDirectoryTimeout 30
-OutputObjects
```

Restoring Operations After a DAG Member Failure

If a Mailbox server has failed and cannot be recovered, you can recover operations in one of two ways:

- You can remove the configuration settings for the Mailbox server from the database availability group.
- You can install a new server and then restore the roles and settings for the original server.

Before you can remove the configuration settings for a Mailbox server, you'll need to remove any mailbox database copies that the server hosted. Use Get-MailboxDatabaseCopyStatus to list mailbox database copies and then use Remove-MailboxDatabaseCopy to remove the copies. Next, use the Remove-DatabaseAvailabilityGroupServer cmdlet to remove the configuration settings for the Mailbox server from the database availability group. After you remove the configuration settings, all settings associated with the Mailbox server are gone.

REAL WORLD Before you install a new server and then restore the roles and settings of the original server, you should confirm the install location for Exchange 2016 on the original server. If Exchange 2016 is installed in a location other than the default location, you can use the /TargetDir option during the setup of the new server to specify an install location. Otherwise, setup will use the default location for the installation. You can determine the install location for the original server by completing the following steps:

1. In ADSIEdit.msc or LDP.exe, navigate to CN=ExServerName,CN=Servers,CN=First Administrative Group,CN=Administrative Groups,CN=ExOrg Name,CN=Microsoft Exchange,CN=Services,CN=Configuration,DC=DomainName,CN=Com.

2. Right-click the Exchange server object for the failed server, and then select Properties.

3. The value of the msExchInstallPath attribute shows the installation path for the failed server.

To install a new server and then restore the roles and settings of the original server, complete the following steps:

1. Use Get-MailboxDatabase to list any replay lag or truncation lag settings for mailbox database copies that were hosted on the server being recovered. Enter the following command to list the databases associated with a specific server by their display name and lag settings:

```
Get-MailboxDatabase -server ServerName
```

Where *ServerName* is the name of the failed server. After you list the databases associated with the server, list the lag settings for each database in turn by entering the following command:

```
Get-MailboxDatabase DatabaseName | fl *lag*
```

Where *DatabaseName* is the name of a database hosted on the failed server.

> **NOTE** Alternatively, you can list all the databases associated with a specific server by their display name and lag settings by entering the following:
>
> Get-MailboxDatabase -server **Name** | Get-MailboxDatabase | fl name, *lag*
>
> Where *Name* is the name of the failed server. In this example, you examine the mailbox databases on MailServer24:
>
> Get-MailboxDatabase -server MailServer24 | Get-MailboxDatabase | fl name, *lag*

2. After you list the databases associated with the server by name and lag times, you need to remove any mailbox database copies the server hosted by entering:

```
Remove-MailboxDatabaseCopy DatabaseName\ServerName
```

Where *DatabaseName* is the name of the database copy to remove and *ServerName* is the name of the failed server, such as:

```
Remove-MailboxDatabaseCopy EngDatabase\MailServer24
```

3. Remove the failed server's configuration from the DAG by entering the following command:

```
Remove-DatabaseAvailabilityGroupServer -Identity DagName
 -MailboxServer ServerName -ConfigurationOnly
```

Where DagName is the name of the DAG and ServerName is the name of the failed server, such as:

```
Remove-DatabaseAvailabilityGroupServer -Identity EastCampusDag1
-MailboxServer MailServer24 -ConfigurationOnly
```

4. In Active Directory Users And Computers, locate and select the computer account for the failed server. On the Action menu, select Reset Account. When prompted to confirm, select Yes and then select OK.

5. Rename the new server so that it has the same name as the failed server. On the new server, run Exchange 2016 Setup with the /m:RecoverServer switch to have Setup read the failed server's configuration information from Active Directory. After Setup gathers the server's configuration information from

Active Directory, Setup installs the original Exchange files and services on the server, restoring the roles and settings that were stored in Active Directory.

6. When the setup of the new server is complete, add the server to the DAG by entering the following command:

```
Add-DatabaseAvailabilityGroupServer -Identity DagName
-MailboxServer ServerName
```

Where *DagName* is the name of the DAG and *ServerName* is the name of the failed server, such as:

```
Add-DatabaseAvailabilityGroupServer -Identity EastCampusDag1
-MailboxServer MailServer24
```

7. Add mailbox database copies to the server by entering the following command for each database copy to add:

```
Add-MailboxDatabaseCopy -Identity DatabaseName -MailboxServer ServerName
```

Where *DatabaseName* is the name of the database copy to add and *ServerName* is the name of the server you are configuring, such as:

```
Add-MailboxDatabaseCopy -Identity EngDatabase
-MailboxServer MailServer24
```

If any of the database copies had replay lag or truncation lag times greater than 0, you can set those lag times by using the -ReplayLagTime and -TruncationLagTime parameters.

8. After the database copies have been configured, you can check their status by entering the following command:

```
Get-MailboxDatabaseCopyStatus -Server ServerName
```

Where *ServerName* is the name of the server you are configuring, such as:

```
Get-MailboxDatabaseCopyStatus -Server MailServer24
```

The databases and their content indexes should have a healthy status.

9. Verify replication health for the server by entering the following command:

```
Test-ReplicationHealth -Identity ServerName
```

Chapter 7. Configuring Exchange Databases

Microsoft Exchange Server 2016 stores mailboxes and associated user data in mailbox databases. The information stored in a particular database isn't exclusive to mailboxes and their associated user data, however. Exchange Server maintains other related information within databases as well, including information about Exchange logons and mailbox usage. Exchange also maintains information about full-text indexing in mailbox databases, although the actual content indexes are stored in separate files.

Mailbox databases can be either active databases or passive copies of databases. Users access active databases to get their mailbox data. Passive copies of databases are not actively being used and are the subject of the section, "Creating and Managing Database Copies" later in this chapter. You create passive copies of databases as part of a high-availability configuration as discussed in Chapter 6, "Implementing Availability Groups."

Getting Started with Active Mailbox Databases

Every Mailbox server deployed in the organization has an information store. The information store operates as a service and manages the server's databases. Each mailbox database has a database file and multiple log files associated with it. These files are stored in a location that you specify when you create or modify the mailbox database.

Planning for Mailbox Databases

Within an Exchange organization, mailboxes are the normal delivery location for messages. Mailboxes contain messages, attachments, and other types of information that the user might have placed in the mailbox. Mailboxes, in turn, are stored in mailbox databases.

When you deploy a Mailbox server, Setup creates a default mailbox database. The default mailbox database is meant to be a starting point, and most Exchange organizations can benefit from having additional mailbox databases, especially as the number of users in the organization grows. Additional mailbox databases are created for many reasons, but the following reasons are the most common:

- **To provide a smaller unit of management**   Exchange has a practical limit of 2 TB on the size of databases, though you may find it easier to work with databases between 1 TB and 1.5 TB. Large databases require more time to move, restore, and recover compared to smaller databases. Additionally, when you establish database availability groups and create copies of a database, the entire database must be replicated from the source database to the database copies. During recovery, you can restore individual databases without affecting the performance or uptime of other databases on the system.
- **To impose a different set of mailbox rules on different sets of users**   Each additional mailbox database can have its own property settings for maintenance, storage limits, deleted item retention, indexing, security, and policies. By placing a user's mailbox in one mailbox database instead of another, you can apply a different set of rules.
- **To optimize Exchange performance**   Each mailbox database can have its own storage location. By placing the mailbox databases on different physical drives, you can improve the performance of Exchange Server 2016.
- **To create separate mailbox databases for different purposes**   For example, you might want to create a mailbox database called General In-Out to handle all general-purpose mailboxes being used throughout the organization. These general-purpose mailboxes could be set up as shared mailboxes for Postmaster, Webmaster, Technical Support, Customer Support, and other key functions.

When you create a mailbox database, you can specify the following information:

- What the name of the database should be
- Where the database file is to be located
- When maintenance on the database should occur
- Any limitations on mailbox size
- Whether deleted items and mailboxes should be retained

Each mailbox database has a default offline address book (OAB). Microsoft Office Outlook 2010 and later clients access the default OAB and default public folder hierarchy on your organization's Mailbox servers. Exchange 2016 uses the mailbox provisioning load balancer to automatically select a database to use when you create or move a mailbox and do not explicitly specify the mailbox database to use. As the name implies, the purpose of the load balancer is to try to balance the workload across mailbox databases in the organization.

Although the load balancer uses multiple criteria to try to determine where a mailbox should be created or moved, the selection criteria does not take into account the proximity of the Mailbox server on which a database is stored to the computer or computers used by the user. Instead, the load balancer uses the Active Directory site where the mailbox task is being performed to determine which mailbox databases should be selected and only includes databases that are in the local site.

You can control the way automatic distribution works in several ways. You can temporarily or permanently exclude databases from the distribution process by using the -IsSuspendedFromProvisioning and -IsExcludedFromProvisioning parameters of the Set-MailboxDatabase cmdlet respectively. When either of these parameters is set to $True, Exchange excludes the related database from the automatic distribution process.

When selecting a database to use, the mailbox provisioning load balancer also checks the database management scopes of the administrator creating a mailbox. Database management scopes are part of the role-based access control (RBAC) permissions model and are a way to limit the databases administrators can view and manage.

> **NOTE** By default, all administrators in an Exchange organization can see all the mailbox databases in the organization. When you create database management scopes in the organization, administrators will only be able to see databases included in a scope applied to them.

If you create custom scopes, Exchange uses these scopes to select databases. Specifically, the load balancer only selects mailbox databases included in a scope applied to the administrator creating a mailbox. Therefore, if a database isn't included in a scope applied to an administrator, the database won't be selected for automatic distribution.

Preparing for Automatic Reseed

Automatic reseed allows you to quickly restore database redundancy after a disk failure, database corruption event, or other event that requires a reseed of a database to recover operations. For automatic reseed to work, however, you must pre-provision one or more spare disks. These spare disks are then used during the automatic reseed to recover the database copy. Here's how automatic reseed works:

1. The Microsoft Exchange Replication service scans the Information Store periodically for database copies that have a status of FailedAndSuspended.

2. If the replication service finds a database copy with the FailedAndSuspended status, it performs prerequisite checks to evaluate the situation, which includes determining whether spares are available, whether anything could prevent the system from performing an automatic reseed, whether only a single copy of the database is available, and more.

3. If the prerequisite checks pass successfully, the Microsoft Exchange Replication service allocates and remaps an available spare before starting the seed operation.

4. After the seed has been completed, the Microsoft Exchange Replication service verifies that the new copy has a Healthy status.

To prepare spare volumes on a server, you must complete the following steps:

1. Mount the volumes that will contain databases under a single mount point, such as C:\PrimaryVols.

2. Mount the volumes to mount points under this volume. For example, you could mount the first volume as C:\PrimaryVols\Volume1, the second volume as C:\PrimaryVols\Volume2, and so on.

3. Create databases on the server in locations within the specified volumes, ensuring that there are fewer databases than mounted volumes.

Consider the following scenario to see how this would work in practice:

You have 5 volumes mounted under C:\PrimaryVols as C:\PrimaryVols\Volume1, C:\PrimaryVols\Volume2, C:\PrimaryVols\Volume3, C:\PrimaryVols\Volume4, and C:\PrimaryVols\Volume5.

You create 3 databases, locating the first database under C:\PrimaryVols\Volume1, the second under C:\PrimaryVols\Volume2, and the third under C:\PrimaryVols\Volume3.

You then have 2 spare volumes, mounted as C:\PrimaryVols\Volume4 and C:\PrimaryVols\Volume5.

If a disk fails, a database copy becomes corrupted, or another event requiring reseed occurs, the failed database is automatically reseeded to one of the spare volumes.

You can identify the failure and automatic reseed tasks by reviewing the event logs. Related events are logged in the event logs under Applications and Services Logs >

Microsoft > Exchange > High Availability and under Applications and Services Logs > Microsoft > Exchange >MailboxDatabaseFailureItems.

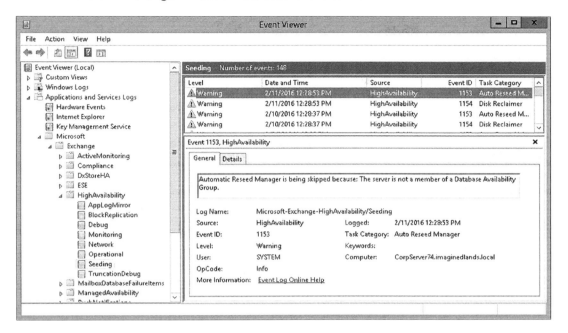

Creating and Managing Active Databases

In the Exchange Admin Center, select Servers in the feature pane, and then select Databases to view the currently available databases in the organization. Database are listed by name, active server, servers with copies, status and bad copy count.

Creating Mailbox Databases

You use the New Mailbox Database wizard to create mailbox databases. Each database has an associated database file path for its .edb file and an associated log folder for its logs. Any new mailbox databases you create using the Exchange Admin Center are configured to use the mailbox provisioning load balancer by default. If you create databases using the shell, you can set the –IsExcludedFromProvisioning parameter to $True to specify that the database should not be considered by the mailbox provisioning load balancer.

Excluding a database from provisioning means new mailboxes are not automatically added to this database. Rather than excluding a database from provisioning, you can set the –IsSuspendedFromProvisioning parameter to $True to specify that a database temporarily not be considered by the mailbox provisioning load balancer. Keep in mind that whether you exclude or suspend a database from provisioning is semantics as in either case the database won't be used for provisioning.

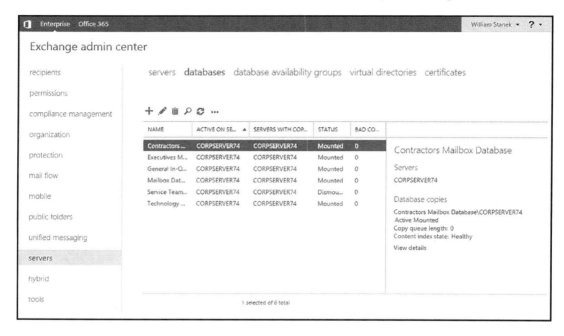

You can create a mailbox database by completing the following steps:

1. In the Exchange Admin Center, select Servers in the feature pane, and then select Databases. In the main pane, you should see a list of active databases that are available in the Exchange organization.

2. Click New ( ) to open the New Database dialog box.

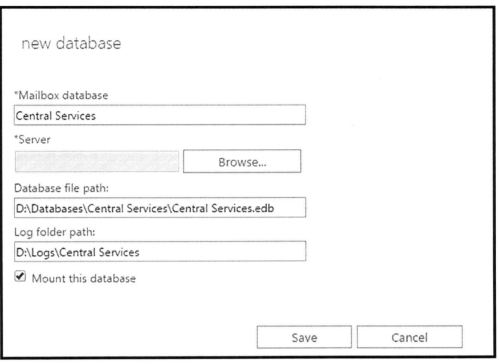

new database

*Mailbox database

Central Services

*Server

[   ]   Browse...

Database file path:

D:\Databases\Central Services\Central Services.edb

Log folder path:

D:\Logs\Central Services

☑ Mount this database

Save   Cancel

3. In the Mailbox Database text box, type a name for the mailbox database. The database name must be unique within the Exchange organization. Although the database name can contain spaces and special characters, it'll be easier to work with the database if the name uses standard characters.

4. Click Browse to the right of the Server text box to open the Select Server dialog box. Mailbox servers are listed by name, version, and exact build as well as associated database availability group, if applicable.

5. Select the Mailbox server that will host the mailbox database, and then click OK. Only Mailbox servers in the Active Directory forest to which you are connected are available.

6. The database file path and log folder path are set to the default location for Exchange data on the selected server. A subfolder with the mailbox database name will be created under the default database file path and the name of the .edb file for the database will be set the same as the database name. Similarly, a subfolder with the same name as the database name is created under the default log folder path. If you don't want to use the default locations, enter the paths you want to use for the database file and the related logs in the text boxes provided.

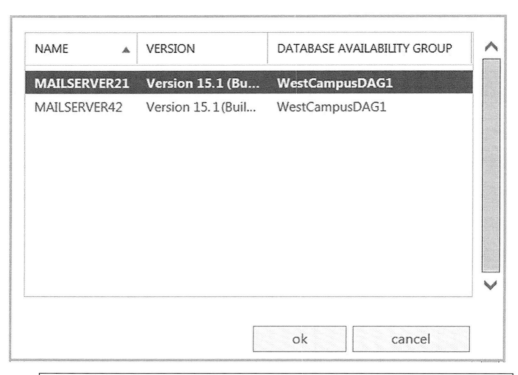

NAME ▲	VERSION	DATABASE AVAILABILITY GROUP
MAILSERVER21	Version 15.1 (Bu...	WestCampusDAG1
MAILSERVER42	Version 15.1 (Buil...	WestCampusDAG1

ok   cancel

REAL WORLD   Exchange creates folders if they do not exist, which is a good thing except when you mistype the intended path. Rather than type in a long file path, you might want to use copy and paste. In Windows Explorer, navigate to the exact folder path you want to use. Click in the folder path on the Address bar to display and automatically select the folder path. Press Ctrl+C to copy the path. In the New Database dialog box, click in the path text box, press Ctrl+A and then press the Delete key. Finally, press Ctrl+V to paste in the path you copied previously.

7. Select the Mount This Database check box if you want to mount this database. Mounting a database puts it online, making it available for use.

8. Click Save to create the mailbox database, and then click OK. If an error occurred, you need to take the appropriate corrective action. Otherwise, you can now modify the properties of the mailbox database as necessary. To make the new database accessible to mailbox users, you must restart the Microsoft Exchange Information Store service.

NOTE   In Exchange Admin Center, you may need to click Refresh ( ) to see the newly created database under Servers > Databases.

Exchange Server 2016 Standard edition supports up to five databases. Exchange Server 2016 Enterprise edition supports up to 100 databases. However, if you install Exchange Server 2016 Enterprise edition but forget to enter the product key, the server runs in Trial mode and only supports up to five databases as well.

Exchange Server can't mount more databases than are supported by the edition you are using. When you create more databases than are supported, Exchange will be unable to mount the database. In the error details, you'll also see a message stating MapiExceptionTooManyMountedDatabases: Unable to mount database.

error

Failed to mount database "Service Teams Mailbox Database".
Error: An Active Manager operation failed. Error: The database
action failed. Error: Operation failed with message:
MapiExceptionTooManyMountedDatabases: Unable to mount
database. (hr=0x8004060e, ec=-2147219954) Diagnostic
context: Lid: 65256 Lid: 10722 StoreEc: 0x8004060E Lid: 1494 --
-- Remote Context Beg ---- Lid: 37952 dwParam: 0x856587F7
Lid: 39576 StoreEc: 0x977 Lid: 35200 dwParam: 0x75B0 Lid:
58864 StoreEc: 0x8004060E Lid: 43248 StoreEc: 0x8004060E
Lid: 35388 StoreEc: 0x8004060E Lid: 54336 dwParam:
0x856587F7 Lid: 35200 dwParam: 0x75B0 Lid: 1750 ----
Remote Context End ---- Lid: 1047 StoreEc: 0x8004060E
[Database: Service Teams Mailbox Database, Server:
CorpServer74.imaginedlands.local]

OK

You can resolve the too many databases problem by reducing the number of databases on the server or simply creating the database on a different server. If the server is running a standard or trial edition of Exchange Server 2016, you can upgrade the server to Enterprise edition to resolve the problem by completing these steps:

1. In Exchange Admin Center, select Servers on the feature pane, and then select Servers.

2. Double-click the server you want to upgrade. In the properties dialog box, on the General page, the current edition should be listed as Trial Edition or Standard Edition.

CORPSERVER74

general
databases and database availability groups
POP3
IMAP4
unified messaging
DNS lookups
transport limits
transport logs
Outlook Anywhere

Version number:

Version 15.1 (Build 225.42)

Roles:

Mailbox, Client Access

This Exchange server is currently licensed as a Trial Edition. You can add a new license by entering a product key below. Learn more

Enter a valid product key.

[ ] - [ ] - [ ] - [ ] - [ ]

Save   Cancel

3. If the server is running Trial Edition, upgrade by entering a valid Enterprise product key in the text boxes provided, and then selecting Save. If the server is running Standard Edition, upgrade by selecting Change Product Key, entering a valid Enterprise product key in the text boxes provided, and then selecting Save.

4. Click OK. For the change to take effect, you must restart the Microsoft Exchange Information Store service.

In Exchange Management Shell, you can create mailbox databases by using the New-MailboxDatabase cmdlet. Listing 7-1 provides the syntax and usage.

> **NOTE** You use a separate cmdlet to mount the database. See the section "Mounting and Dismounting Databases" later in this chapter for details.

LISTING 7-1 New-MailboxDatabase cmdlet syntax and usage

Syntax

```
New-MailboxDatabase -Name DatabaseName -Server ServerName
[-EdbFilePath DbFilePath] [-LogFolderPath FolderPath] {AddtlParams}

{AddtlParams}
[-DomainController FullyQualifiedName][-IsExcludedFromProvisioning <$true
| $false}] [-IsSuspendedFromProvisioning <$true | $false>]
```

```
[-OfflineAddressBook OfflineAddressBook]
```

```
New-MailboxDatabase -Recovery <$true | $false> -Server ServerName
[-DomainController FullyQualifiedName] [-EdbFilePath DbFilePath]
[-LogFolderPath FolderPath]
```

Usage

```
New-MailboxDatabase -Server "CorpServer88" -Name "Accounting Database"
-EdbFilePath "C:\Databases\Accounting\AccountingMail.edb"
-LogFolderPath "D:\DatabaseLogs\Accounting"
```

Setting the Default Offline Address Book

Mailbox databases can have different types of information associated with them,
including a default OAB. You set related options for mailbox databases by using the
Client Settings page of the related Properties dialog box. To view this dialog box and
update the messaging options, follow these steps:

1. In the Exchange Admin Center, select the Servers feature, and then select
    Databases. Next, double-click the database you want to configure.

2. In the Properties dialog box, click the Client Settings page.

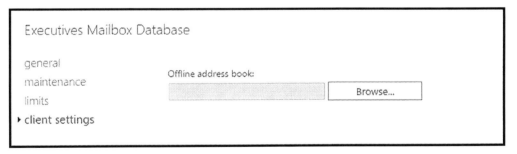

> **NOTE**   If you can't update the text boxes on the Client Settings page, it
> means that a policy has been applied to the mailbox database. You must
> directly edit or remove the policy and then make the necessary changes.

3. The Offline Address Book text box shows the OAB for the mailbox database.
    OABs contain information regarding mail-enabled users, contacts, and
    groups in the organization, and they are used when users aren't connected
    to the network. If the text box is empty, the global default is used. If you've
    created additional OABs beyond the global default, you can specify one of
    these additional OABs as the default for the mailbox database. Click Browse,

select the OAB you want to use, and then click OK. Click Save to apply the changes.

In Exchange Management Shell, you can set the default OAB for mailbox databases by using the Set-MailboxDatabase cmdlet. Listing 7-2 provides the syntax and usage.

LISTING 7-2 Using the Set-MailboxDatabase cmdlet to set the default OAB

Syntax

```
Set-MailboxDatabase -Identity MailboxDatabase
[-OfflineAddressBook OABIdentity
```

Usage

```
Set-MailboxDatabase -Identity "Accounting Mail"
-OfflineAddressBook "\US Corporate"
```

Setting Mailbox Database Limits and Deletion Retention

Mailbox database limits are designed to control the amount of information that users can store in their mailboxes. Users who exceed the designated limits might receive warning messages and might be subject to certain restrictions, such as the inability to send messages. Deleted item retention is designed to ensure that messages and mailboxes that might be needed in the future aren't deleted inadvertently. If retention is turned on, you can retain deleted messages and mailboxes for a specified period before they are permanently deleted and are nonrecoverable.

An average retention period for messages is about 14 days. The minimum retention period for mailboxes should be about seven days. In most cases, you'll want deleted messages to be maintained for a minimum of five to seven days and deleted mailboxes to be maintained for a minimum of three to four weeks. An interval of five to seven days is used for messages because users usually realize within a few days that they shouldn't have deleted a message. A three-week to four-week interval is used for mailboxes because several weeks can (and often do) pass before users realize that they need a deleted mailbox or messages within a deleted mailbox. To understand why, consider the following scenario.

Sally leaves the company. A coworker is given permission to delete Sally's user account and mailbox. Three weeks later, Sally's boss realizes that she was the only person who received and archived the monthly reports sent through email from corporate headquarters. The only way to get reports for previous years is to recover Sally's mailbox, and you can do this if you've set a sufficiently long retention period.

> **NOTE** Exchange has several features to ensure that mailbox items are retained according to policies set forth by an organization for legal reasons, including automatic archiving of old messages and retention policies. Deletion settings on the Limits page control the minimum length of time deleted items are retained if no retention tags specifically apply to deleted items.

To view or set limits and deletion retention for a mailbox database, follow these steps:

1. In the Exchange Admin Center, select the Servers feature, and then select Databases. Next, double-click the database you want to configure.

2. In the Properties dialog box, on the Limits page, use the following options to set storage limits and deleted item retention:

- **Issue A Warning At (GB)**   Sets the size limit, in gigabytes, that a mailbox can reach before Exchange Server issues a warning to the user. The warning tells the user to clear out the mailbox. If you don't want Exchange to issue warnings, set the value to 0 or Unlimited.
- **Prohibit Send At (GB)**   Sets the size limit, in gigabytes, that a mailbox can reach before the user is prohibited from sending any new mail. The restriction ends when the user clears out the mailbox and the total mailbox size is under the limit. If you don't want Exchange to prohibit sending mail, set the value to 0 or Unlimited.
- **Prohibit Send And Receive At (GB)**   Sets the size limit, in gigabytes, that a mailbox can reach before the user is prohibited from sending and receiving mail. The restriction ends when the user clears out the mailbox and the total mailbox size is under the limit. If you don't want Exchange to prohibit sending and receiving mail, set the value to 0 or Unlimited.

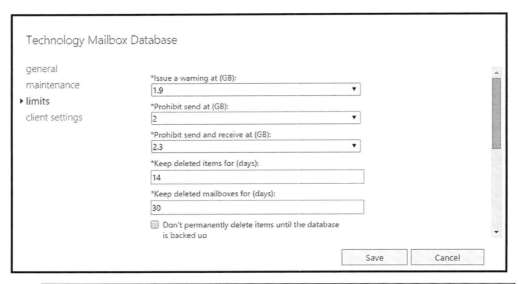

Technology Mailbox Database

general
maintenance
▸ limits
client settings

*Issue a warning at (GB):
1.9

*Prohibit send at (GB):
2

*Prohibit send and receive at (GB):
2.3

*Keep deleted items for (days):
14

*Keep deleted mailboxes for (days):
30

☐ Don't permanently delete items until the database
is backed up

Save   Cancel

> **CAUTION**   Prohibiting send and receive might cause users to lose email.
> When a user sends a message to a user who is prohibited from receiving
> messages, a nondelivery report (NDR) is generated and delivered to the
> sender. The recipient never sees the email. Because of this, you should
> prohibit send and receive only in very rare circumstances. Your organizational
> policy will likely spell out those circumstances. To remove this restriction, set
> Prohibit Send And Receive to Unlimited or enter a value of 0.

- **Keep Deleted Items For (Days)**   Sets the number of days to retain deleted
  items. An average retention period is 14 days. If you set the retention period to 0,
  deleted messages aren't retained, and you can't recover them in the same way
  you could if retention was enabled.
- **Keep Deleted Mailboxes For (Days)**   Sets the number of days to retain deleted
  mailboxes. The default setting is 30 days. You'll want to keep most deleted
  mailboxes for at least seven days to allow the administrators to extract any data
  that might be needed. If you set the retention period to 0, deleted mailboxes are
  retained only if you select the next option, and then only until the database has
  been backed up. If a mailbox is backed up, you can recover it only by restoring it
  from backups.
- **Don't Permanently Delete Items Until The Database Is Backed Up**   Ensures
  that deleted mailboxes and items are archived into at least one backup set before
  they are removed.

  3. The Warning Message Interval sets the interval for sending warning
      messages to users whose mailboxes exceed the designated limits. To change
      this setting, select Customize. You can now set the warning interval using
      the Customize Quota Notification Schedule dialog box.

- Times that are used for quota notification are filled in with a dark bar.

- Times that aren't used for quota notification are blank.

> **IMPORTANT** The default interval for sending warning messages is daily between 1 A.M. and 1:15 A.M., which is an acceptable initial interval for small deployments. As your organization grows, however, you'll want to optimize this interval to ensure that servers aren't overburdened and that servers have enough time to process all the mailboxes.

4. Show the time in hours or in 15-minute intervals by using the options provided. Click the time interval to change the setting.

- Hourly or 15-minute interval buttons are used to select or clear a particular interval for all the days of a week.
- Days of the week buttons allow you to clear or select all the hours in a particular day.
- The All button allows you to clear or select all the time periods.

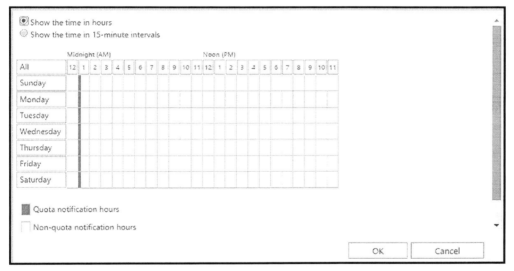

5. If you customized the notification schedule, click OK to close the Customize Quota Notification Schedule dialog box.

6. Click Save to apply your settings.

In Exchange Management Shell, you can set limits for mailbox databases by using the Set-MailboxDatabase cmdlet. Listing 7-3 provides the syntax and usage. When you set a limit, you can specify the value with KB (for kilobytes), MB (for megabytes), or GB (for gigabytes). The default value type is bytes. Additionally, it's important to point out that the -MaintenanceSchedule and -QuotaNotificationSchedule parameters are not used with Exchange 2016.

LISTING 7-3 Using the Set-MailboxDatabase cmdlet to set limits

Syntax

```
Set-MailboxDatabase [-Identity MailboxDatabase]
[-AllowFileRestore <$true | $false>] [-BackgroundDatabaseMaintenence <$true
| $false>] [-CircularLoggingEnabled <$true | $false>]
[-DataMoveReplicationConstraint <None | SecondyCopy | SecondDatacenter |
AllDatacenters | AllCopies>] [-DeletedItemRetention NumberDays]
[-DomainController DCName] [-EventHistoryRetentionPeriod NumberDays]
[-IndexEnabled <$true | $false>] [-IsExcludedFromProvisioning <$true |
$false>] [-IssueWarningQuota Limit] [-JournalRecipient RecipientId]
[-MailboxRetention NumberDays] [-MountAtStartup <$true | $false>]
[-Name Name] [-OfflineAddressBook OABId] [-ProhibitSendQuota Limit]
[-ProhibitSendReceiveQuota Limit] [-RecoverableItemsQuota Limit]
[-RecoverableItemsWarningQuota Limit]
[-RetainDeletedItemsUntilBackup <$true | $false>]
```

Usage

```
Set-MailboxDatabase -Identity "Accounting Mail"
 -IssueWarningQuota 1.9GB
 -DeletedItemRetention 14
 -MailboxRetention 30
 -ProhibitSendQuota 2GB
 -ProhibitSendReceiveQuota 2.4GB
 -RetainDeletedItemsUntilBackup $true
```

Recovering Deleted Mailboxes

When you delete a mailbox from a user account, the mailbox is retained as a
disconnected mailbox according to the mailbox retention setting. You can reconnect
the mailbox to the original user account or another user account if necessary.
Similarly, when you delete a user account and the related mailbox, the mailbox is
retained as a disconnected mailbox according to the mailbox retention setting. You
can connect the mailbox to an existing user account if necessary.

When you move mailboxes between databases, mailboxes in the original (source)
database are soft deleted. This means they are disconnected, marked as soft deleted,
but retained in the original database until the deleted mailbox retention period

expires. In Exchange Management Shell, you can use a DisconnectReason of "SoftDeleted" to find soft-deleted mailboxes.

To recover a deleted mailbox, complete the following steps:

1. In the Exchange Admin Center, select Recipients in the feature pane, and then select Mailboxes.

2. Click the More button (•••), and then select Connect A Mailbox. The Connect A Mailbox dialog box shows all mailboxes marked for deletion but currently retained regardless of whether those mailboxes were disabled, deleted, or soft deleted.

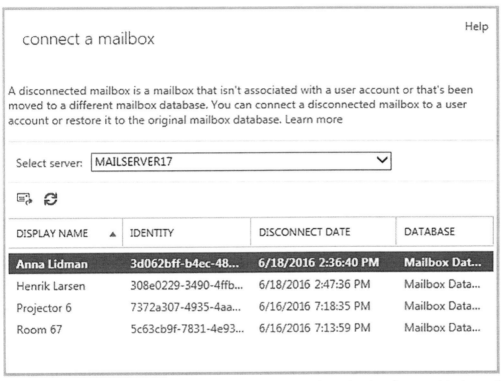

3. In the Connect A Mailbox dialog box, use the selection list provided to select the server in which you want to look for disconnected mailboxes.

4. Click the mailbox to restore it, and then click Connect. Connect the mailbox to the user account to which it was connected previously or to a different user account. If the original user account is available, select the Yes option to reconnect the mailbox to the original user account. If the original user isn't available or you want to associate the mailbox with a different user, select the No option and follow the prompts.

> **NOTE** Deleted mailboxes aren't necessarily marked as such immediately. It can take 15 minutes to an hour before the mailbox is marked as deleted and listed accordingly.

> **IMPORTANT** If you previously removed the mailbox rather than disabling it, the user account associated with the mailbox was deleted as well. Because each user account has a unique security identifier associated with it, you can't simply re-create the user account to get back the same set of permissions and privileges. That said, if you want to connect the mailbox to a user account with the same name, you can do this by recovering the deleted account from Active Directory before garbage collection has occurred or by recreating the account in Active Directory Users And Computers. The account will then be available for selection but when you're connecting the mailbox to an account, you'll need to choose the No option because Exchange and Active Directory see this as a different account.

You can use the Connect-Mailbox cmdlet to perform the same task following the syntax shown in Listing 7-4.

LISTING 7-4 Connect-Mailbox cmdlet syntax and usage

Syntax

```
Connect-Mailbox -Identity OrigMailboxIdentity
-Database DatabaseIdentity
-User NewUserIdentity
[-ActiveSyncMailboxPolicy PolicyId] [-Alias Alias]
[-DomainController DCName] [-ManagedFolderMailboxPolicy PolicyId]
[-ManagedFolderMailboxPolicyAllowed <$true | $false>]
[-Archive <$true | $false>] [-Equipment <$true | $false>]
[-Room <$true | $false>] [-Shared <$true | $false>]
[-ValidateOnly <$true | $false>]


[-LinkedCredential Credential] [-LinkedDomainController DCName]
[-LinkedMasterAccount UserId]
```

Usage

```
Connect-Mailbox -Identity "Don Harmon"
-Database "Accounting Mail" -User "TVPRESS\donh" -Alias "donh"


Connect-Mailbox -Identity "Don Harmon"
```

```
-Database "Accounting Mail" -LinkedDomainController CorpServer72
-LinkedMasterAccount "TVPRESS\donh"
```

Recovering Deleted Items from Servers

You can recover deleted items from mailbox servers as long as you've either set a deleted item retention period for the database from which the items were deleted and the retention period hasn't expired, or you have specified that Exchange should not permanently delete items from mailboxes until the database has been backed up and Exchange hasn't been backed up yet. If either of these conditions are met, you can recover deleted items from mailbox databases.

To use Outlook 2010 or higher to recover deleted items from a Mailbox server, complete the following steps:

1. Log on as the user who deleted the message, and then start Outlook.

2. In the email folder list, select Deleted Items.

3. With Home selected on the navigation pane, select Recover Deleted Items From Server. If this option isn't available, make sure you've access the Exchange account in Outlook and are using online mode.

4. The Recover Deleted Items From dialog box appears. Select the items you want to recover, and then click the Recover Selected Items button.

5. Items you've recovered are copied to the Deleted Items folder. In the left pane, click Deleted Items.

6. In the Deleted Items folder, right-click items you want to keep, select Move, and then click Other Folder.

7. In the Move Items dialog box, select the folder to which the item should be moved, such as Inbox, and then click OK.

To use Outlook Web App (OWA) for recovery, complete these steps:

1. In a Web browser, type ***https://servername.yourdomain.com/owa***, where *servername* is a placeholder for the HTTP virtual server hosted by Exchange Server 2016 and *yourdomain.com* is a placeholder for your external domain name, such as https://mail.tvpress.com/owa.

2. Next, log on as the user (or have the user log on). Type the user name in *domain\username* format, such as **imaginedlands\bertk,** or *user@domain* format, such as **bertk@imaginedlands.com**. Type the password, and then click Sign In.

3. In the left pane, right-click Deleted Items, and then select Recover Deleted Items.

4. In the Recover Deleted Items dialog box, you'll see a list of recoverable items. Each listed item will have a selection check box. Select this checkbox for items you want to recover.

5. Click the Recover button, and then click OK. Items you select will be restored to their default folders.

Creating and Managing Database Copies

Mailbox databases are either active or passive. When your Exchange organization uses database availability groups, Exchange replicates transaction logs from an active mailbox database on a source Mailbox server to other Mailbox servers in the database availability group that have passive copies of the database. On these servers, Exchange replays the transaction logs into the passive copy of the mailbox database by using either file mode or block mode replication. You can monitor the health and status of replication and database copies by using the Exchange Management tools.

The Mailbox server that hosts the active copy of a database is referred to as the *mailbox database primary* for that database. A Mailbox server that hosts a passive copy of a database is referred to as a *mailbox database secondary* for that database. You can move the active database to another Mailbox server in the database availability group by using the switchover process discussed in "Switching Over Servers and Databases" in Chapter 6, "Implementing Availability Groups." In a switchover, the active copy of a database is dismounted on the current Mailbox server and a passive copy of the database is activated and mounted on another Mailbox server in the database availability group.

Creating Mailbox Database Copies

Once you create a database availability group and add Mailbox servers to the group, you can create copies of mailbox databases to initiate replication. Within the group,

replication occurs between the active mailbox database on a source Mailbox server and other Mailbox servers that host copies of the database. You cannot replicate a database outside of a database availability group, nor can you replicate an Exchange 2016 mailbox database to a server running an earlier version of Exchange.

A database availability group can have up to 16 member servers, and you can create up to 16 instances of a database, including one active instance and 15 passive instances. You can create mailbox database copies only on Mailbox servers that do not host the active copy of a mailbox database, and you cannot create two copies of the same database on the same server.

Because all copies of a database use the same path on each server containing a copy, the database and log file paths for a database copy on each Mailbox server must not conflict with any other database paths. You need to ensure the database and log file paths for the database copy can be created in the same location as all other copies and that the paths do not conflict with any other database paths on the target server.

With respect to Active Directory, the member servers in an availability group must all be in the same Active Directory domain. You can create database copies on Mailbox servers in the same or different Active Directory sites, and on the same or different network subnets. However, database copies are not supported between Mailbox servers with roundtrip network latency greater than 250 milliseconds (by default). Database copies are automatically assigned an identity in the format *DatabaseName\HostMailboxServerName*, such as Engineering Primary Database\MailServer36.

To create a copy of a mailbox database, complete the following steps:

1. In the Exchange Admin Center, select Servers in the feature pane, and then select Databases. In the main pane, you should see a list of active databases that are available in the Exchange organization.

2. Select the mailbox database that you want to copy to see a list of all copies of that database in the details pane. Whereas the active copy of a database normally is listed with a status of Active Mounted or Active Dismounted, passive copies are normally listed with a status of Passive Healthy.

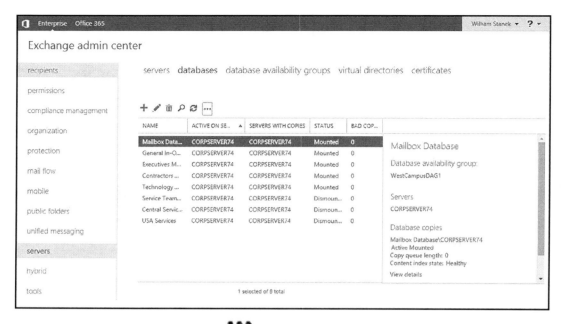

3. Click the More button (••••), and then select Add A Database Copy. This opens the Add Mailbox Database Copy dialog box, which lists the servers that already have a copy of the database and sets the activation preference number to the next value for the next database instance. You can set a lower preference value if desired.

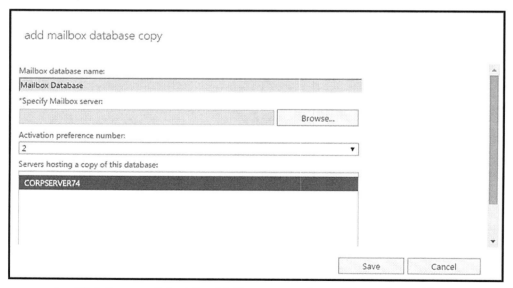

4. Click Browse. Select the Mailbox server that will host the mailbox database copy, and then click OK. Although servers outside the database availability group and servers running earlier versions of Exchange may be listed in the

Select Server dialog box, you'll only want to select an Exchange 2016 Mailbox server in the same database availability group that doesn't have a copy of the database already. Each Mailbox server in a database availability group can host only one copy of a database.

5. Optionally, in the Activation Preference Number text box, specify the preference value for the database copy. The activation preference number represents the order of activation preference for a database copy after a failure or outage of the active copy. The preference value is a number equal to or greater than 1, where 1 has the highest preference. The preference value cannot be larger than the total number of database copies.

> **NOTE** Active Manager uses the preference value only to break ties in the best-copy selection process. If two or more database copies are seen as the best choice for activation, the database copy with the highest preference is selected. Following this, when there is a tie, a database copy with a preference value of 3 would be selected before a database copy with a preference value of 4. For more information on Active Manager, see "Active Manager Framework" in Chapter 6.

6. If you want to configure replay lag time or postpone seeding, select More Options. You'll then be able to specify a replay lag time in days and postpone seeding. If you postpone seeding of the database, you'll need to manually seed the database later.

7. Click Save to create the mailbox database copy, and then click Close when the process completes. If an error occurred, you need to take the appropriate corrective action. Otherwise, you can now work with the database copy.

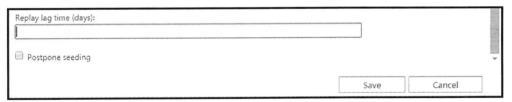

In Exchange Management Shell, you can create mailbox database copies by using the Add-MailboxDatabaseCopy cmdlet. Listing 7-5 provides the syntax and usage. Use the –ReplayLagTime parameter to specify how long the Exchange Replication Service should wait before replaying log files. Use the –TruncationLagTime parameter to specify how long the Exchange Replication Service should wait before truncating logs that have been replayed.

> **NOTE** The new database copy will remain in a Suspended state if you use the –SeedingPostponed parameter. When the database copy status is set to Suspended, the SuspendMessage is set to "Replication is suspended for database copy '<Name>' because database needs to be seeded." You can seed the database as discussed in the "Updating Mailbox Database Copies" section.
>
> **TIP** Different database copies can have different lag times. If you want logs to be replayed immediately, set a relatively short replay lag time or none at all. If you want a cushion for protection against inadvertent changes, set a longer replay lag time. As an example, if you have three database copies, you might want two copies to have short replay lag times and one copy to have a long replay lag time.

LISTING 7-5 Add-MailboxDatabaseCopy cmdlet syntax and usage

Syntax

```
Add-MailboxDatabaseCopy -Identity SourceDatabase
-MailboxServer TargetServer [-ActivationPreference PrefValue]
[-ReplayLagTime Days.Hours:Minutes:Seconds]
[-SeedingPostponed <$true | $false>]
[-TruncationLagTime Days.Hours:Minutes:Seconds]
[-DomainController FullyQualifiedName]
```

Usage

```
Add-MailboxDatabaseCopy -Identity "Engineering Primary Database"
-MailboxServer "MailServer36" -ReplayLagTime 00:03:00
-TruncationLagTime 00:10:00 -ActivationPreference 2
```

Configuring Database Copies

Database copies have associated replay, truncation, and preference values. Replay and truncation values are designed to let you fine-tune the way replication works for each database copy. Replay lag time is the amount of time to delay log replay. Truncation lag time is the amount of time that you want to delay log truncation after a log has been successfully replayed. You can also set a relative preference value for database copies. The preference value sets the order of activation preference after a failure or outage affecting the active database, with a value of 1 indicating the highest preference, a value of 2 the next highest preference, and so on. You cannot set a database copy to a value higher than the number of database copies. Active

Manager uses the preference value in the case of a tie during the best-copy selection process.

To set preference values for a database copy, complete the following steps:

1. In the Exchange Admin Center, select Servers in the feature pane, and then select Databases. In the main pane, you should see a list of active databases that are available in the Exchange organization.

2. Select the mailbox database with the copy that you want to manage. In the details pane, you'll see a list of active and passive copies of the database, along with separate management options for each. Click the View Details option for the database copy you want to modify.

3. The current activation preference number and replay lag time are listed. Change the values as necessary, and then click Save.

In Exchange Management Shell, you can set replay, truncation, and preference values for mailbox database copies by using the Set-MailboxDatabaseCopy cmdlet. Listing 7-6 provides the syntax and usage.

LISTING 7-6 Set-MailboxDatabaseCopy cmdlet syntax and usage

Syntax

```
Set-MailboxDatabaseCopy -Identity Database\Server
[-ActivationPreference PrefValue]
[-ReplayLagTime Days.Hours:Minutes:Seconds]
[-TruncationLagTime Days.Hours:Minutes:Seconds]
[-DomainController FullyQualifiedName]
```

Usage

```
Set-MailboxDatabaseCopy -Identity "Tech Mail Database\MailServer36"
-ReplayLagTime 00:02:00 -TruncationLagTime 00:05:00
-ActivationPreference 6
```

In Exchange 2016, lagged copies automatically play down log files as necessary to accommodate adverse conditions, such as the following:

- If Exchange 2016 detects that page patching is required for a lagged copy, the logs will be automatically replayed into the lagged copy to perform page patching.

- If Exchange 2016 detects that a low disk space threshold has been reached or that no other log copies are available, the logs will be automatically replayed into the lagged copy.
- If Exchange 2016 detects that there are too few available healthy copies (active and passive) of a database for more than 24 hours, the logs will be automatically replayed into the lagged copy.

However, you must enable these options specifically. You enable lagged copy replay for all lagged copies in a particular database availability group by using the following command:

```
Set-DatabaseAvailabilityGroup DAGName -ReplayLagManagerEnabled $true
```

Where DAGName is the name of the database availability group to configure.

You specify the low diskspace threshold as a percentage of free disk space before log replay occurs by using the registry value:

HKLM\Software\Microsoft\ExchangeServer\v15\Replay\Parameters\ReplayLagPlayDownPercentDiskFreeSpace

For example, if you want Exchange to automatically play down lagged copies when the free disk space on the volume used by the active database reaches 10 percent, you'd edit the ReplayLagPlayDownPercentDiskFreeSpace value in the registry and set it to 10.

You specify the number of available healthy copies that triggers replay by using the following registry value:

HKLM\Software\Microsoft\ExchangeServer\v15\Replay\Parameters\ReplayLagManagerNumAvailableCopies

By default, this value is set to 3, meaning replay is triggered whenever there are fewer than 3 copies of a database available for a 24-hour period. Although this value may work well in large deployments of Exchange, this value is not ideal for small deployments. Specifically, in deployments in which you have three or fewer Mailbox servers in a DAG, setting this value to 3 will cause lagged logs to play down every 24 hours whether you want them to or not.

> **NOTE** As lagged copies can use SafetyNet, recovery or activation of lagged copies is much easier than in Exchange 2010. Exchange 2016 also issues

> single copy alerts as part of the managed availability architecture. Previously, single copy alert was implemented as a script that ran periodically as a scheduled task.

Suspending and Resuming Replication

You may need to suspend replication for a database copy as part of planned maintenance or for other reasons.. In addition, prior to performing some administrative tasks, you need to suspend replication activity before you can complete the task—for example, before performing seeding. You can suspend and resume database copy activity by completing the following steps:

1. In the Exchange Admin Center, select Servers in the feature pane, and then select Databases. In the main pane, you should see a list of active databases that are available in the Exchange organization.

2. Select the mailbox database with the copy that you want to manage. In the details pane, you'll see a list of active and passive copies of the database. Whereas the active copy of a database is normally listed with a status of Active Mounted or Active Dismounted, passive copies are normally listed with a status of Passive Healthy.

3. Select the Suspend option for the passive database copy (not an active database) for which you want to suspend replication.

4. In the Suspend Database Copy dialog box, enter a comment as to why you are suspending replication. If you want to ensure replication can only be activated by you or another administrator, select This Copy Can Be Activated Only By Manual Intervention.

5. Click Save to suspend continuous replication.

To resume replication later, click the Resume option in the details pane. If a suspend comment was provided, you can read the comment. Then click Yes to resume continuous replication.

In Exchange Management Shell, you can suspend and resume replication by using Suspend-MailboxDatabaseCopy and Resume-MailboxDatabaseCopy, respectively. Listings 7-7 and 7-8 provide the syntax and usage. If you use the –ActivationOnly parameter to suspend activation only, the database cannot be activated until you resume replication without specifying the –ReplicationOnly parameter. You can use the –ReplicationOnly parameter to resume replication without affecting the activation setting. For example, if the –ActivationSuspended parameter was set to $True, the parameter remains set to $True.

LISTING 7-7 Suspend-MailboxDatabaseCopy cmdlet syntax and usage

Syntax

```
Suspend-MailboxDatabaseCopy -Identity Database\Server
[-ActivationOnly <$true | $false>] [-EnableReplayLag <$true | $false>]
[-DomainController FullyQualifiedName]
[-SuspendComment Comment]
```

Usage

```
Suspend-MailboxDatabaseCopy -Identity "Tech Mail Database\MailServer36"
-ActivationOnly
```

LISTING 7-8 Resume-MailboxDatabaseCopy cmdlet syntax and usage

Syntax

```
Resume-MailboxDatabaseCopy -Identity Database\Server
[-DisableReplayLag <$true | $false>] [-DisableReplayLagReason "Comment"]
[-ReplicationOnly <$true | $false>] [-DomainController FullyQualifiedName]
```

Usage

```
Resume-MailboxDatabaseCopy -Identity "Tech Mail Database\MailServer36"
```

Activating Lagged Database Copies

Lagged database copies have a replay lag time great than 0. You can activate a lagged copy by recovering the database copy from SafetyNet, by replaying all uncommitted log files, or by performing a point in time activation.

Before you activate a lagged copy, you may want to preserve the original files for the lagged copy. If so, you need to create a snapshot of the volumes containing the database copy and its log files by suspending replication of the lagged copy you want to activate, and then creating a shadow copy of these volumes as detailed in the steps that follow:

1. Suspend replication of the lagged copy you want to activate using the following command:

```
Suspend-MailboxDatabaseCopy Database\Server -SuspendComment "Comment"
-Confirm $False
```

Where Database is the name of the lagged copy, Server is the name of the server hosting the lagged copy, and Comment is a descriptive comment, such as:

```
Suspend-MailboxDatabaseCopy "Engineering DB\MailServer96"
-SuspendComment "Suspending replication to take a db snapshot"
-Confirm $False
```

2. Create a snapshot of the database and log folders by using the following command:

```
Vssadmin create shadow /For="c:\Databases\Engineering DB"
Vssadmin create shadow /For="c:\Logs\Engineering DB"
```

3. Optionally, copy the database and log files to another volume where you want to perform the recovery.

To recover a lagged copy from SafetyNet, complete the following steps:

1. Because you don't want the log files to replay when the database is mounted, move the log files for the database copy to an archive folder. This preserves the log files in case they are subsequently needed.

2. To allow the database to mount without all the necessary transaction logs files, you'll need to confirm that you accept the data loss. To do this, mount the database with the -AcceptDataLoss parameter as shown in this example:

```
Mount-Database "Engineering DB" -AcceptDataLoss
```

3. Exchange will mount the database and then request redelivery of missing messages from SafetyNet. You can confirm that the lagged copy was successfully activated by viewing the database properties. In Exchange Admin Center, select Servers in the feature pane, and then select Databases. Next, select the database copy you activated. In the Details pane, click View Details.

4. Once you verify that the database copy was successfully activated, you can delete the log files you moved to an archive folder, as these logs are no longer needed.

To activate a lagged copy by replaying all uncommitted log files, complete the following steps:

1. Activate the lagged copy on a specified server by using the following command:

```
Move-ActiveMailboxDatabase Database -ActivateOnServer Server -SkipLagChecks
```

Where *Database* is the name of the lagged copy and *Server* is the name of the server hosting the lagged copy, such as:

```
Move-ActiveMailboxDatabase "Engineering DB" -ActivateOnServer MailServer96 -SkipLagChecks
```

2. Exchange will mount the database on the designated server and replay all the log files. The duration of the replay process depends on the amount of data to replay and the speed at which your server hardware can replay the logs.

3. You can confirm that the lagged copy was successfully activated by viewing the database properties. In Exchange Admin Center, select Servers in the feature pane, and then select Databases. Next, select the database copy you activated. In the Details pane, click View Details.

To activate a lagged copy to a point in time, complete the following steps:

1. Before you can activate a lagged copy to a point in time, you must first determine which log files are required to meet your recovery requirements. Use the log file date and time to identify which log files you need and which log files should be moved to an archive directory until the recovery process is successfully completed. Specifically, any log file created after your recovery time should be moved to the archive directory.

2. Next, you need to delete the checkpoint file for the lagged copy. This file has the .chk extension.

3. At an elevated command prompt, use Eseutil to perform the recovery operation. The basic syntax is:

```
Eseutil /r ENN /a
```

Where ENN is the log generation prefix for the database, such as E00 or E01. This prefix is used with all the database files, so it's easily identified when you access the database folder for the lagged copy.

4. When all the logs have been replayed, the database will be in a clean state and you can optionally copy the database and log files to another volume where you want to perform the recovery. Keep in mind that the duration of the replay process depends on the amount of data to replay and the speed at which your server hardware can replay the logs.

5. You can confirm that the lagged copy was successfully activated by viewing the database properties. In Exchange Admin Center, select Servers in the feature pane, and then select Databases. Next, select the database copy you activated. In the Details pane, click View Details.

Updating Mailbox Database Copies

Seeding is the process of initially replicating an active or passive database into a database copy. This creates a baseline passive copy of a database. Normally, seeding occurs automatically, and the length of time required to completely seed a database depends on the size of the source database, the available bandwidth on the network, and the level of activity on the servers involved. However, automatic seeding can fail, and in this case, you then need to manually initiate seeding.

> **REAL WORLD** An automatic seed produces a copy of an active or passive database on a target Mailbox server. Automatic seeding occurs only during the creation of a new database or for a database that has never been backed up.
>
> You can identify a problem with seeding by checking the state of the database copy. When you create a database copy, the database should enter the Initializing state and then the Seeding state. When seeding is complete, the database copy should be in the Healthy state. If the database remains in a Suspended state and does not complete initialization or seeding, there is a problem. Note also that if you are seeding when creating the copy, the task will not complete successfully until the seed is completed. So, you simply watch the task progress and do not need to check copy status.

You can reseed a mailbox database copy anytime you suspect divergence has occurred. However, divergence isn't necessarily a problem because incremental reseed (incremental resync) takes care of resolving the divergence. You would not need to do a full reseed except in circumstances in which resync isn't possible—for example, when there is no overlap in log files between diverged copies, or when you've done something you shouldn't have, like an offline defragmentation of a copy that causes uncorrectable divergence.

When you reseed a database, Exchange empties the database copy and replicates a new passive database copy. Typically, you won't need to reseed database copies after the initial seeding has occurred; however, in some situations you might need to reseed a database copy. One state you can check for is the FailedAndSuspended state. In this state, Exchange has detected a failure and suspended replication replay because resolution of the failure explicitly requires administrator intervention. For example, if Exchange detects an unrecoverable divergence between the active mailbox database and a database copy, Exchange marks the database copy as FailedAndSuspended. If an incremental resync doesn't eventually resolve the problem, you need to resolve the underlying cause of the failure before the database copy can be transitioned to a healthy state, which includes reseeding the database.

Before you can seed or reseed a database, you must suspend replication. For very large databases—that is, those that are multiple terabytes (TB) in size—the preferred technique for seeding the initial passive copy of the database, if service level agreements allow or such an outage is acceptable, is to dismount the active copy of the database and copy the database file to the same location on the target Mailbox server in the same database availability group. Rather than copying the database over the network, which could take several days for a multiterabyte database, you should consider the following:

* Copying the database to one or more disk drives, preferably hot-swappable drives that can be moved between the source and target servers
* Copying the database to one or more logical unit numbers (LUNs) in your storage array that can be assigned to or is assigned to the target server

With this approach, the database will be unavailable until seeding is completed and you can mount the database. Alternatively, you can leave the active database online and use the Exchange Management tools to initiate the seeding process. Once you've created at least one baseline passive copy of a database, you can seed new passive copies from the baseline passive copy at any time by using an online or offline approach.

The size of the database, the available network bandwidth, network latency, and the activity levels on the source and target servers determine how long an over-the-network transfer or update takes. After the seeding process has started, don't close the Exchange Admin Center or Exchange Management Shell until the process has completed. If you do, the seeding operation will be terminated and will need to be restarted.

Keep the following in mind when you are considering updating database copies:

- When you seed a database using the Exchange Admin Center, both the database copy and the content index catalog are seeded. In Exchange Management Shell, you can specify that only the database copy should be seeded using the –DatabaseOnly parameter or that only the context index catalog should be seeded using the –CatalogOnly parameter.
- Before you seed the database copy, you may want to manually remove existing files on the server that hosts the database copy. You can delete existing files in Exchange Management Shell by using the –DeleteExistingFiles parameter; however, these options remove only the files Exchange checks for and might fail if other files are present.
- When seeding is complete, Exchange automatically resumes replication. If you want to resume replication manually instead, you can use the –ManualResume parameter in Exchange Management Shell.
- By default, seeding data is transferred over the replication network for the database availability group, unless you are seeding to a remote site, in which case it will default to the messaging network. You can override the defaults by using the –Network parameter. The network compression and encryption settings are used and determine whether the transferred data is compressed, encrypted, or both. You specify the networks to use by name in both management tools. In Exchange Management Shell, use –NetworkCompressionOverride and –NetworkEncryptionOverride to override the network compression and encryption settings, respectively.

You can seed a database manually by completing the following steps:

1. In the Exchange Admin Center, select Servers in the feature pane, and then select Databases. In the main pane, you should see a list of active databases that are available in the Exchange organization.

2. Select the mailbox database with the copy that you want to manage. In the details pane, you'll see a list of active and passive copies of the database.

3. Select the Update option for the passive database copy (not an active database) that you want to update.

> **TIP** The Exchange Admin Center won't let you reseed a database that's in a healthy or other normal state. However, you can force a reseed by suspending the database, copying it, and then updating the database copy.

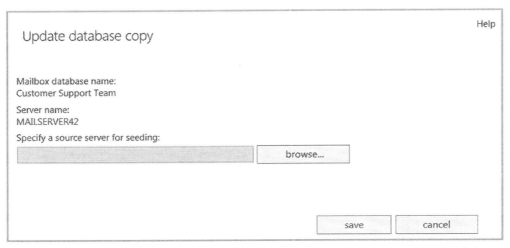

Update database copy

Help

Mailbox database name:
Customer Support Team

Server name:
MAILSERVER42

Specify a source server for seeding:

browse...

save   cancel

4. By default, Exchange will seed the database from the active copy of the database. If you want to use a passive copy for seeding, click Browse. In the Select Mailbox Server dialog box, select the source server hosting the passive copy you want to use and then click OK.

5. Click Save to begin seeding. If an error occurred, you need to take the appropriate corrective action. Click Close.

To seed a database copy in Exchange Management Shell, you use the Update-MailboxDatabaseCopy cmdlet. Listing 7-9 provides the syntax and usage. You can use the –Force parameter when seeding programmatically, and you will not be prompted for administrative input.

LISTING 7-9 Update-MailboxDatabaseCopy cmdlet syntax and usage

Syntax

```
Update-MailboxDatabaseCopy -Identity Database\Server
-SourceServer ServerName [-CancelSeed <$true | $false>]
[-BeginSeed <$true | $false>] [-CatalogOnly <$true | $false>]
[-DatabaseOnly <$true | $false>] [-DeleteExistingFiles <$true | $false>]
[-DomainController FullyQualifiedName] [-Force <$true | $false>]
[-ManualResume <$true | $false>] [-MaximumSeedsInParallel MaxNumSeeds]
[-NetworkCompressionOverride {"UseDAGDefault"|"Off"|"On"}]
[-NetworkEncryptionOverride {"UseDAGDefault"|"Off"|"On"}]
[-Network NetworkID] [-SafeDeleteExistingFiles <$true | $false>]
```

Usage

```
Update-MailboxDatabaseCopy -Identity "CS Mail\MailServer25"
-CatalogOnly -Force


Update-MailboxDatabaseCopy -Identity "CS Mail\MailServer25"
-DatabaseOnly


Update-MailboxDatabaseCopy -Identity "CS Mail\MailServer25"
-Network "EastCampusDAG1\Primary DAG Network"
-NetworkCompressionOverride "On" -NetworkEncryptionOverride "Off"
```

Monitoring Database Replication Status

Monitoring the health and status of database copies is important to ensure that they are available when needed. You can view key health and status information for a database copy by completing the following steps:

1. In the Exchange Admin Center, select Servers in the feature pane, and then select Databases. In the main pane, you should see a list of active databases that are available in the Exchange organization.

2. Select the mailbox database with the copy that you want to manage. In the details pane, you'll see a list of active and passive copies of the database along with the current status of each.

3. Click the View Details option for the database copy with which you want to work. This opens a properties dialog box.

4. Use the information provided to determine the health and status of replication for the database copy. The information provided includes

- **Database** Displays the name of the selected database.
- **Mailbox Server** Displays the name of the Mailbox server that hosts the database copy.
- **Content Index State** Displays the status of content indexing for the database copy.
- **Status** Displays the current health and status of replication for the database copy.
- **Copy Queue Length** Shows the number of log files waiting to be copied and checked.
- **Replay Queue Length** Shows the number of log files waiting to be replayed into this copy of the database.

- **Error Messages**   Displays any current error status or error message for the database copy.
- **Latest Available Log Time**   Shows the time associated with the latest available log generated by the active database copy.
- **Last Inspected Log Time**   Shows the modification time of the last log that was successfully validated by the Mailbox server hosting the database copy.
- **Last Copied Log Time**   Shows the modification time of the last log that was successfully copied.
- **Last Replayed Log Time**   Shows the modification time of the last log that was successfully replayed by the Mailbox server hosting the database copy.
- **Activation Preference Number**   Shows the activation preference value for the database copy.
- **Replay Lag Time**   Shows the current replay lag time in days, if any.

When you are working with database copies, the Copy Status shows the current health and status of replication for the database copy. The possible status values as well as any corrective action that might be required include:

- **Activation Suspended**   The copy has been manually blocked from activation by an administrator. To correct this status, allow activation, if appropriate.
- **Disconnected And Healthy**   The copy has been disconnected, and was in the Healthy state when the loss of connection occurred. This state can be reported during network failures between the active copy and the database copy.
- **Disconnected And Resynchronizing**   The copy is no longer connected to the active database copy, and was in the Resynchronizing state when the loss of connection occurred. This state can be reported during network failures between the active copy and the database copy.
- **Dismounted**   The copy is offline and not accepting client connections. Applies only to the active mailbox database. To correct this status, mount the database if maintenance is complete.
- **Dismounting**   The copy is going offline and terminating client connections. Applies only to the active mailbox database.
- **Failed**   The copy is in a failed state because it is not suspended, and is not able to copy or replay log files. Exchange periodically checks to see whether the problem that caused the copy status to change to Failed has been resolved. If so, and barring no other issues, the copy status automatically changes to Healthy.
- **Failed And Suspended**   The copy is in the Failed And Suspended state because a failure was detected and because resolution of the failure explicitly requires administrator intervention. Take corrective action as appropriate. Exchange does not periodically check to see whether the problem has been resolved and does not automatically recover.
- **Healthy**   The copy is successfully copying and replaying log files, or has successfully copied and replayed all available log files.

- **Initializing**   The copy is being created, or the Microsoft Exchange Replication service is starting up or has just been started, or the Mailbox Database copy is transitioning to another state. While the copy is in this state, Exchange is verifying that the database and log stream are in a consistent state. It should generally not be in this state for longer than 30 seconds.
- **Mounted**   The copy is online and accepting client connections. Applies only to active mailbox database.
- **Mounting**   The copy is coming online and not yet accepting client connections. Applies only to active mailbox database.
- **Resynchronizing**   The copy is being checked for any divergence between the active copy and this passive copy. The copy status remains in this state until any divergence is detected and resolved.
- **Seeding**   The copy is being seeded, the related content index is being seeded, or both. Upon successful completion of seeding, the copy status should change to Initializing.
- **Service Down**   The copy cannot connect to the replication service. To correct this status, start or restart the Microsoft Exchange Replication service on the server that hosts the mailbox database copy.
- **Single Page Restore**   The copy had a single page error, and this error is being corrected automatically.
- **Suspended**   The copy is in a suspended state as a result of an administrator manually suspending the database copy. To correct this status, resume replication if appropriate

In Exchange Management Shell, you can check the health and status of replication by using the Get-MailboxDatabaseCopyStatus cmdlet. Listing 7-10 provides the syntax and usage.

LISTING 7-10 Get-MailboxDatabaseCopyStatus cmdlet syntax and usage

Syntax

```
Get-MailboxDatabaseCopyStatus -Server ServerName {AddtlParams}


Get-MailboxDatabaseCopyStatus [-Identity LocalDatabaseName]
[-Active <$true | $false>] [-Local <$true | $false>]] {AddtlParams}


{AddtlParams}
[-ConnectionStatus <$true | $false>] [-DomainController FullyQualifiedName]
[-ExtendedErrorInfo <$true | $false>] [-UseServerCache <$true | $false>]
```

Usage

```
Get-MailboxDatabaseCopyStatus -Server "MailServer35"
-ConnectionStatus -ExtendedErrorInfo
```

```
Get-MailboxDatabaseCopyStatus
```

```
Get-MailboxDatabaseCopyStatus -Identity "Accounting Mail"
```

Removing Database Copies

You can remove a passive database copy at any time by using the Exchange Management tools. After removing a database copy, you need to manually delete any database and transaction log files from the server.

> **NOTE**   You cannot use these procedures to remove the active copy of a mailbox database. To remove a database that is an active copy, you must first switch the database over to a new active copy. Alternatively, if you no longer want a database and its copies, you first need to remove all passive copies, and then you need to remove all mailboxes from the active database before you can delete it.
>
> **TIP**   You can remove mailbox database copies only from a database availability group with a Healthy status. If the database availability group doesn't have a Healthy status, you won't be able to remove any mailbox database copies.

To remove a database copy, complete the following steps:

1. In the Exchange Admin Center, select Servers in the feature pane, and then select Databases. In the main pane, you should see a list of active databases that are available in the Exchange organization.

2. Select the mailbox database with the copy that you want to manage. In the details pane, you'll see a list of active and passive copies of the database along with the current status of each.

3. Click the Remove option for the database copy you want to remove.

4. When prompted to confirm, click Yes. If an error occurred, you need to take the appropriate corrective action. Click Close.

In Exchange Management Shell, you can remove a database copy by using the Remove-MailboxDatabaseCopy cmdlet. Listing 7-11 provides the syntax and usage.

LISTING 7-11 Remove-MailboxDatabaseCopy cmdlet syntax and usage

Syntax

```
Remove-MailboxDatabaseCopy -Identity DatabaseName\ServerName]
[-DomainController FullyQualifiedName]
```

Usage

```
Remove-MailboxDatabaseCopy -Identity "CS Mail Database\MailServer24"
```

Before you remove a database using the shell, you may need to identify available copies of the database. To do this, enter the following command:

```
Get-MailboxDatabase DatabaseName | fl DatabaseCopies
```

Where *DatabaseName* is the name of the database you want to work with, such as:

```
Get-MailboxDatabase Development | fl databasecopies
```

As shown in this example, the output lists where copies of the database are available:

```
DatabaseCopies : {Development\MAILSERVER42, Development\MAILSERVER21}
```

Maintaining Mailbox Databases

After exploring how to create and use databases, let's look at some general techniques you'll use to manage databases. Keep in mind that these techniques apply only to active mailbox databases. Passive copies of mailbox databases are managed as discussed in the "Creating and Managing Database Copies" section earlier in this chapter.

You can only access databases that are mounted. If a database isn't mounted, the database isn't available for use. If a database isn't mounted it means that an administrator has probably dismounted the database or that the drive on which the database is located isn't online. It could also mean that the Exchange Information Store service is not running or that the drive, log drive, or both are online but out of disk space.

REAL WORLD A dismounted database can also indicate that there are problems with the database, transaction log, and system files used by the database. During startup, Exchange Server 2016 obtains a list of database files registered in Active Directory and then checks for the related files before mounting each database. If files are missing or corrupted, Exchange Server 2016 will be unable to mount the database. Exchange Server 2016 then generates an error and logs it in the application event log on the Exchange server. A common error is Event ID 9547. An example of this error follows:

The Active Directory indicates that the database file D:\Exchsrvr\mdbdata\Marketing.edb exists for the Microsoft Exchange Database; however, no such files exist on the disk.

This error tells you that the Exchange database (Marketing.edb) is registered in Active Directory but Exchange Server 2016 is unable to find the file on the disk. When Exchange Server 2016 attempts to start the corrupted mailbox database, you'll see an additional error as well. The most common error is Event ID 9519. An example of this error follows:

Error 0xfffffb4d starting database Marketing on the Microsoft Exchange Information Store.

This error tells you that Exchange Server 2016 couldn't start the Marketing database. You can try to restore the database to recover its data. If you are unable to restore the database file, you can create a copy of all database files and store them elsewhere and then recreate the database structures in the Exchange Admin Center by mounting the database. When you mount the database, Exchange Server 2016 creates a new database file. As a result, the data in the original database files (and not the copies) is lost and cannot be recovered. Exchange Server 2016 displays a warning before mounting the database and recreating the database file. Click Yes only when you are absolutely certain that you cannot recover the database.

Be sure you don't overwrite the database files containing the data you want to try to recover. You can still work on the database while users access the newly created empty database. This is effectively a dial-tone database that you are creating. Then, take the damaged database file elsewhere, run repair, make the database consistent, and then use it to complete the dial-tone recovery process.

If you can't restore or repair a database and you need as much of the data as you can get back, you might have clients in cached or offline mode with viable copies of the data that can be exported and imported.

Checking Database Status

Mailbox databases have several associated states, including

* Mounted
* Backup In Progress
* Background Database Maintenance

You can determine the status of a database by following these steps:

1. In the Exchange Admin Center, select Servers in the feature pane, and then select Databases. In the main pane, you should see a list of active databases that are available in the Exchange organization.

2. Select the mailbox database that you want to work with to see a list of all copies of that database in the details pane. The status of each database copy also is listed in the details pane.

In Exchange Management Shell, you can determine the status of all databases or specific databases by using the Get-MailboxDatabase. Listing 7-12 provides the syntax and usage for this cmdlet. To see status details, you can specify the status flags associated with each state you want to see as part of the formatted output. In the example, the Mounted, Backup In Progress, and Background Database Maintenance status values are listed as True or False.

LISTING 7-12 Getting database status details

Syntax

```
Get-MailboxDatabase [-Identity MailboxDatabase | -Server Server]
[-DomainController DCName] [-DumpsterStatistics <$true | $false>]
[-IncludePreExchange2013 <$true | $false>]
[-Status <$true | $false>] | format-table Name, Mounted, BackupInProgress,
BackgroundDatabaseMaintenance
```

Usage for specific database

```
Get-MailboxDatabase -Identity "Eng DB" -Status | format-table Name,
Mounted, BackupInProgress, BackgroundDatabaseMaintenance
```

Usage for all databases on a server

```
Get-MailboxDatabase -Server "CORPSVR127" -Status | format-table
Name, Mounted, BackupInProgress, BackgroundDatabaseMaintenance
```
Usage for all databases

```
Get-MailboxDatabase -Status | format-table Name,
Mounted, BackupInProgress, BackgroundDatabaseMaintenance
```

Setting the Maintenance Interval

You should run maintenance routines against databases on a daily basis. The maintenance routines organize the databases, clear out extra space, and perform other essential housekeeping tasks. By default, the automatic background maintenance does some of this work, and Exchange Server runs extended, foreground maintenance tasks daily from 1:00 A.M. to 5:00 A.M. If this conflicts with other scheduled administrative tasks or activities on the Exchange server, you can change the maintenance settings by following these steps:

1. In the Exchange Admin Center, select Servers in the feature pane, and then select Databases. In the main pane, you should see a list of active databases that are available in the Exchange organization.

2. Double-click the database with which you want to work. This opens a properties dialog box for the database.

3. On the Maintenance page, note the current Maintenance Schedule, and then select Customize. You can now set the times when maintenance should occur by using the options in the Customize Maintenance dialog box.

- Times that are used for maintenance are filled in with a dark bar.
- Times that aren't used for maintenance are blank.

> **IMPORTANT** Ideally, you want to schedule background maintenance to occur during off-peak hours. As the size of databases and activity levels change, you'll want to optimize this schedule to ensure that servers aren't overburdened and that servers have enough time to perform necessary maintenance tasks.

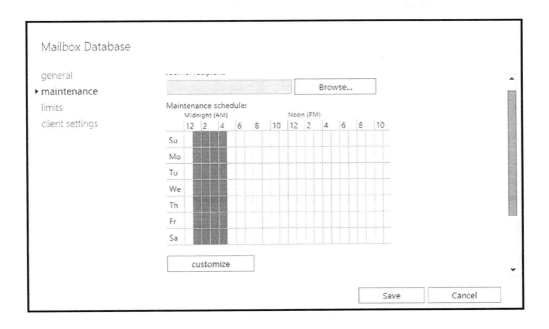

4. Show the time in hours or in 15-minute intervals using the options provided. Change the setting for a time interval by clicking it.

- Hourly or 15-minute interval buttons are used to select or clear a particular interval for all the days of a week.
- Days of the week buttons allow you to clear or select all the hours in a particular day.
- The All button allows you to clear or select all the time periods.

5. Click OK to close the Customize Maintenance Schedule dialog box.

6. By default, Exchange performs background maintenance tasks by scanning the ESE 24 hours a day, 7 days a week. Select or clear the related check box as appropriate. Note that if you change this setting, you must dismount and then remount the database for the change to take effect. Click OK.

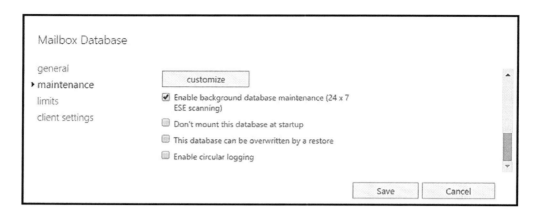

In Exchange Management Shell, you can configure the maintenance schedule for a database by using Set-MailboxDatabase. Listing 7-13 provides the syntax and usage. In the example, replication is configured to occur between Friday at 9:00 P.M. and Monday at 1:00 A.M.

LISTING 7-13 Setting the maintenance schedule

Syntax

```
Set-MailboxDatabase –Identity DatabaseIdentity
[–MaintenanceSchedule Schedule]
[–BackgroundDatabaseMaintenance <$true | $false>]
```

Usage

```
Set-MailboxDatabase –Identity "Eng DB"
 –MaintenanceSchedule "Fri.9:00 PM-Mon.1:00 AM"
```

Renaming Databases

To rename a database, follow these steps:

1. In the Exchange Admin Center, double-click the database with which you want to work. This opens a properties dialog box for the database. The General page is selected by default.

2. In the Name text box, type the new name for the database. Click Save.

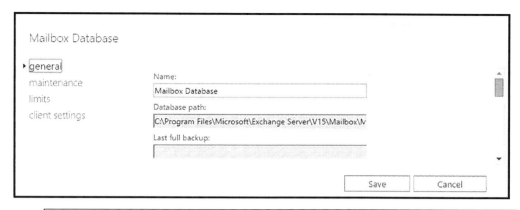

In Exchange Management Shell, you can rename databases by using the –Name parameter of the Set-MailboxDatabase. Listing 7-14 provides the syntax and usage.

LISTING 7-14 Renaming a database

Syntax

```
Set-MailboxDatabase -Identity DatabaseIdentity
 -Name NewName
```

Usage

```
Set-MailboxDatabase -Identity "Eng DB"
 -Name "Engineering Mail Database"
```

Mounting and Dismounting Databases

Before you perform maintenance on a Mailbox server in a database availability group, you should perform a server switchover so that the server's active databases are transitioned and made active on one or more additional servers in the group. You might also want to suspend replication or block activation of passive copies on the server being maintained. For mailbox databases that are not part of an availability group, you should rarely dismount an active database, but if you need to do so, follow these steps:

1. In the Exchange Admin Center, select Servers in the feature pane, and then select Databases. In the main pane, you should see a list of active databases that are available in the Exchange organization.

2. Select the mailbox database that you want to copy to see a list of all copies of that database in the details pane. Note the status of the active database copy. If the copy is mounted, the status normally is listed as Active Mounted.

3. Click the More button (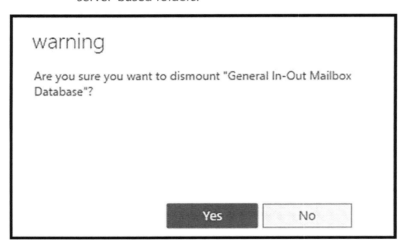), and then select Dismount. When prompted, confirm the action by clicking Yes. Exchange Server dismounts the database. Users will no longer be able to access the database and work with their server-based folders.

---

warning

Are you sure you want to dismount "General In-Out Mailbox Database"?

[**Yes**] [No]

After you've dismounted a database and performed maintenance, recovery, or other procedures as necessary, you can remount the database by selecting the database, clicking the More button, and then selecting Mount. When prompted, confirm the action by clicking Yes.

In Exchange Management Shell, you can dismount and mount databases by using the Dismount-Database and Mount-Database cmdlets, respectively. Listing 7-15 provides the syntax and usage for these cmdlets.

LISTING 7-15 Dismounting and mounting databases

Syntax

```
Dismount-Database -Identity DatabaseIdentity
[-DomainController FullyQualifiedName]
```

```
Mount-Database –Identity DatabaseIdentity
[-AcceptDataLoss <$true | $false>] [-DomainController FullyQualifiedName]
[-Force <$true | $false>]
```

Usage for dismounting a database

```
Dismount-Database –Identity "Eng DB"
```

Usage for mounting a database

```
Mount-Database –Identity "Eng DB"
```

Configuring Automatic Mounting

Normally, Exchange Server automatically mounts databases on startup. You can, however, change this behavior. For example, if you're recovering an Exchange server from a complete failure, you might not want to mount databases until you've completed recovery. In this case, you can disable automatic mounting of databases.

To enable or disable automatic mounting of a database, complete the following steps:

1. In the Exchange Admin Center, select Servers in the feature pane, and then select Databases. In the main pane, you should see a list of active databases that are available in the Exchange organization.

2. Double-click the database with which you want to work.

3. On the Maintenance page, do one of the following and then click Save:

- To ensure that a database isn't mounted on startup, select the Don't Mount This Database At Startup check box.
- To mount the database on startup, clear the Don't Mount This Database At Startup check box.

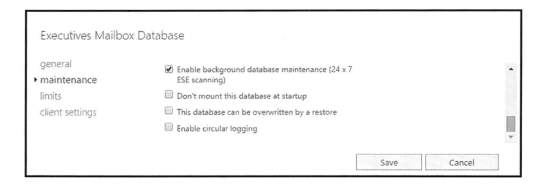

In Exchange Management Shell, you can enable or disable automatic mounting at startup by using the Set-MailboxDatabase. Listing 7-16 provides the syntax and usage for controlling automatic mounting.

LISTING 7-16 Controlling automatic mounting

Syntax

```
Set-MailboxDatabase –Identity DatabaseIdentity
 –MountAtStartup <$true | $false>
```

Usage

```
Set-MailboxDatabase –Identity "Eng DB"
 –MountAtStartup $false
```

Moving Databases

Each database has a database file associated with it, and the location of this file has an important role in managing Exchange Server performance. You can view the current file and folder paths the database is using by entering:

```
Get-MailboxDatabase DatabaseName | fl *path
```

Where *DatabaseName* is the name of the database to check, such as:

```
Get-MailboxDatabase "Engineering" | fl *path
```

In the command output, the database file path is listed as EdbFilePath, the log folder path is listed as LogFolderPath and any associated temporary data folder is listed under TemporaryDataFolderPath, as shown in this example:

```
EdbFilePath            : G:\Databases\Engineering\Engineering.edb
LogFolderPath          : H:\Logs\Engineering
TemporaryDataFolderPath :
```

In Exchange Management Shell, you can move databases by using the Move-DatabasePath cmdlet. Listing 7-17 provides the syntax and usage. If the specified database is mounted, the database is automatically dismounted and then remounted, and it is unavailable to users while it's dismounted. Additionally, you can perform a database move only while logged on to the affected Mailbox server, with one exception. If you are performing a configuration-only move, you can perform the configuration-only move from your management computer.

LISTING 7-17 Move-DatabasePath cmdlet syntax and usage

Syntax

```
Move-DatabasePath -Identity DatabaseIdentity
[-ConfigurationOnly <$true | $false>] [-EdbFilePath EdbFilePath]
[-DomainController DCName] [-Force <$true | $false>]
[-LogFolderPath FolderPath]
```

Usage

```
Move-DatabasePath -Identity "Engineering"
-EdbFilePath "K:\Databases\Engineering\Engineering.edb"
-LogFolderPath "L:\Logs\Engineering"
```

You cannot move a database that is being backed up or a replicated mailbox database. To move a replicated mailbox database, you must disable circular logging if enabled, remove all replicated copies, and then perform the move operation. After the move is complete, you can add copies of the mailbox database and re-enable circular logging. You'll also want to rebuild the content indexes for each copy of the database. To perform these and other related tasks, complete the following steps:

1. Identify any replay lag or truncation lag settings for all copies of the mailbox database being moved by entering the following command:

```
Get-MailboxDatabase DatabaseName | fl *lag*
```

Where *DatabaseName* is the name of the database that you want to move.

2. Disable circular logging if the option is enabled by entering the following command:

```
Set-MailboxDatabase DatabaseName -CircularLoggingEnabled $false
```

3. Identify all copies of the database by entering the following command:

```
Get-MailboxDatabase DatabaseName | fl DatabaseCopies
```

4. Remove the mailbox database copies by entering the following command for each copy:

```
Remove-MailboxDatabaseCopy DatabaseName\ServerName
```

> Where *DatabaseName* is the name of the database copy to remove and *ServerName* is the name of the server.

5. On each server that hosted a copy of the database, move the data files and log files for the database copy to a local archive folder, such as C:\Archives\Database for the database files and C:\Archives\Logs for the log files. This preserves the files on the server so that the database copies don't need to be reseeded after they have been recreated.

6. Use the Move-DatabasePath cmdlet to move the database path and log path to a new location. The syntax is:

```
Move-DatabasePath -Identity DatabaseName
-EdbFilePath EdbFilePath -LogFolderPath FolderPath
```

> During the move operation, the database will be dismounted. When Exchange finishes moving the database, Exchange will automatically mount the database.

7. On each server that hosted a passive copy of the database, create the required folders for the database and logs. For example, if you moved the database to K:\Databases\Engineering\Engineering.edb, you must create the K:\Databases\Engineering folder on each server. If you moved the log folder to L:\Logs\Engineering, you must also create the L:\Logs\Engineering folder on each server. As the active copy of the database was moved already, you don't need to create folders for the active copy.

8. On each server that hosted a passive copy of the database, move the preserved database files to the database folder and then move the preserved log files to the log folder. As the active copy of the database was moved already, you don't need to move the preserved files for the active database.

9. Use the Add-MailboxDatabaseCopy cmdlet to add a passive copy of the database to each server that previously hosted a passive copy of the database. The basic syntax is:

```
Add-MailboxDatabaseCopy -Identity SourceDatabase
-MailboxServer TargetServer
```

Don't set any replay lag or truncation lag times yet because you want to ensure the databases are recovered using the local files (and without reseeding).

10. Recreate the context indexes on each server that hosts an active or passive copy of the database. To do this, use the following commands to stop and then start the Microsoft Exchange Search service:

```
Stop-Service MSExchangeSearch
Start-Service MSExchangeSearch
```

11. If you want to enable circular logging of the active copy of the database, enter the following command:

```
Set-MailboxDatabase DatabaseName -CircularLoggingEnabled $true
```

12. Use the Set-MailboxDatabseCopy cmdlet to reconfigure replay lag and truncation lag times, as appropriate. The basic syntax is:

```
Set-MailboxDatabaseCopy -Identity Database\Server
[-ReplayLagTime Days.Hours:Minutes:Seconds]
[-TruncationLagTime Days.Hours:Minutes:Seconds]
```

Once you've completed all these tasks, you should use the Get-MailboxDatabaseCopyStatus cmdlet to confirm that replication is working as expected. You also should use the Test-ReplicationHealth cmdlet to verify the health and status of the database availability group.

Deleting Databases

Before deleting a mailbox database, you must disable, move or remove all mailboxes, archive mailboxes, public folder mailboxes and arbitration mailboxes from the database. To help you with this process, use the following techniques:

- Get a list of all mailboxes in the database by running the command **Get-MailboxDatabase -Database *DatabaseName* | Get-Mailbox**. These are the user mailboxes that must be moved or removed.

- Get a list of all archive mailboxes in the database by running the command **Get-MailboxDatabase -Database *DatabaseName* | Get-Mailbox -Archive**. These are the archive mailboxes that must be moved or removed.
- Get a list of all arbitration mailboxes in the database by running the command **Get-MailboxDatabase -Database *DatabaseName* | Get-Mailbox -Arbitration**. These are the arbitration mailboxes that must be moved or removed.
- Disable a non-arbitration mailbox so that you can delete the mailbox database by running the command **Disable-Mailbox *MailboxId***.
- Disable an archive mailbox so you can delete the mailbox database by running the command **Disable-Mailbox *MailboxId* -Archive**.
- Disable a public folder mailbox so that you can delete the mailbox database by running the command **Disable-Mailbox *MailboxId* -PublicFolder**.
- Rather than removing arbitration mailboxes, you should move them to another database using New-MoveRequest. If this is the last database in the organization, disable the arbitration mailbox instead by running the command **Disable-Mailbox ArMailboxID -Arbitration -DisableLastArbitrationMailboxAllowed**.

After you've moved items that you might need and deleted items you don't need, you can delete the database by completing the following steps:

1. In the Exchange Admin Center, select the database you want to delete, and then select the Delete button.

2. When prompted, confirm the action by clicking Yes. If the database contains any mailboxes, you'll see an error and will need to disable, move or remove the mailboxes before you can remove the database.

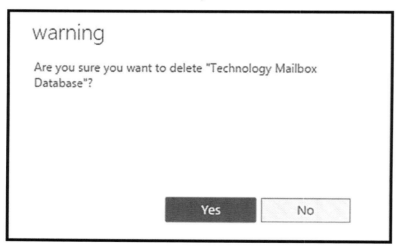

3. After removing the database, you need to delete any database and transaction log files from the server.

In Exchange Management Shell, you can delete databases by using the Remove-MailboxDatabase. Listing 7-18 provides the syntax and usage.

LISTING 7-18 Removing databases

Syntax

```
Remove-MailboxDatabase -Identity DatabaseIdentity
[-DomainController FullyQualifiedName]
```

Usage

```
Remove-MailboxDatabase -Identity "Eng DB"
```

Managing Content Indexing

Every Exchange server in your organization supports and uses some type of indexing. To manage indexing more effectively, use the techniques discussed in this section.

Indexing Essentials

Content indexing enables fast searches and lookups through server-stored mailboxes. Exchange Server 2016 uses the content indexing engine from the Microsoft Search Foundation. The Exchange Server storage engine automatically implements and manages Exchange Search. Exchange Search is used with searches for common key fields, such as message subjects. Users take advantage of Exchange Search every time they use the Find feature in Microsoft Office Outlook. With server-based mail folders, Exchange Search is used to quickly search To, From, Cc, and Subject fields. With public folders, Exchange Search is used to quickly search From and Subject fields.

As you probably know, users can perform advanced searches in Office Outlook as well. For example, in Office Outlook 2010, all users need to do is click in the Search box or press Ctrl+E to access the Search tools, click Search Options, and then click Advanced Find. In the Advanced Find dialog box, users can enter their search parameters and then click Find Now.

When Exchange Server receives an advanced query for personal folders, it searches through every message in every folder. This means that as Exchange mailboxes grow, so does the time it takes to complete an advanced search. With standard searching, Exchange Server is unable to search through message attachments.

With server-based folders, Exchange Server builds an index of all searchable text in a particular mailbox database before users try to search. The index can then be updated or rebuilt at a predefined interval. Then, when users perform advanced searches, they can quickly find any text within a document or attachment.

A drawback of content indexing is that it can be resource-intensive. As with any database, creating and maintaining indexes requires CPU time and system memory, which can affect Exchange performance. Full-text indexes also use disk space. A newly created index uses approximately 10 to 20 percent of the total size of the Exchange database (and is directly related to what's in the database's mailboxes). This means that a 1-TB database would have an index of about 100 to 200 GB.

Each time you update an index, the file space that the index uses increases. Don't worry—only changes in the database are stored in the index updates. This means that the additional disk space usage is incremental. For example, if the original 1-TB database grew by 1 GB, the index could use up to 201 GB of disk space (up to 200 GB for the original index and 1 GB for the update).

Maintaining Exchange Store Search

Exchange Server 2016 doesn't allow administrators to configure how indexing works. Full-text indexes are stored as part of the Exchange data files. Because of this, whatever folder location you use for Exchange data files will have an indexing subfolder, which contains all the Exchange Search data for the related database and all its related databases. By default, you'll find full-text index files for a database in the %SystemDrive%\Program Files\Microsoft\Exchange Server\V15\Mailbox*DatabaseName**GUID* folder where GUID is the database's globally unique identifier.

> **NOTE** Exchange maintains full-text indexes as part of the database maintenance schedule. See the "Setting the Maintenance Interval" section earlier in this chapter for more information.

Each database has an index. If you make a database copy, you are also making an index copy. There's often no need to rebuild an index. That said, as part of the recovery process for a mailbox database, you might want to rebuild the related full-text index catalog to ensure it's current. You might also want to rebuild the full-text index after you've made substantial changes to a database or if you suspect the full-text index is corrupted.

You can rebuild an index manually at any time. Exchange Server rebuilds an index by recreating it. This means that Exchange Server takes a new snapshot of the database and uses this snapshot to build the index from scratch. To manually rebuild an index, enter the following commands to stop and then start the Exchange Search service:

```
Stop-Service MSExchangeFastSearch
Start-Service MSExchangeFastSearch
```

Exchange Discovery relies on Exchange Search for databases and mailboxes within databases. You can enable or disable indexing for individual databases by setting the -IndexEnabled parameter of the Set-MailboxDatabase cmdlet to $true or $false, respectively. The following example disables indexing of the Engineering database:

```
Set-MailboxDatabase "Engineering Database" -IndexEnabled $false
```

When you disable indexing of a database, you also prevent the Exchange 2016 Discovery feature from returning messages from the database or server.

You can disable indexing for all databases on a server by stopping and disabling the Microsoft Exchange Search service. Here's an example using Exchange Management Shell in which you stop and disable the Exchange Search service on a remote server named Server18:

```
Stop-Service MSExchangeFastSearch -ComputerName Server22

Set-Service MSExchangeFastSearch -StartupType Disabled -ComputerName Server22
```

You can enable indexing for all databases on a server by enabling the Microsoft Exchange Search service for automatic startup and starting the service. An example using Exchange Management Shell follows:

```
Set-Service MSExchangeFastSearch -StartupType Automatic
-ComputerName Server18
```

```
Start-Service MSExchangeFastSearch -ComputerName MailServer11
```

When you disable indexing on a server, you also prevent Exchange Discovery for all databases on the server.

Resolving Indexing Issues

You can quickly determine which databases have indexing enabled by using the following command:

```
Get-MailboxDatabase | ft Name,IndexEnabled
```

You can determine whether content indexing has a healthy status by using the following command:

```
Get-MailboxDatabaseCopyStatus | ft Identity, ActiveDatabaseCopy,
ContentIndexState -Auto
```

If you find that the context index for a passive database copy is outdated, you can rebuild or reseed the index. To reseed the index, enter the following command:

```
Update-MailboxDatabaseCopy -Identity Database\Server -CatalogOnly
```

Where Database is the name of the database and Server is the name of the server hosting the database, such as:

```
Update-MailboxDatabaseCopy -Identity Engineering\MailServer12
-CatalogOnly
```

If you need to troubleshoot Exchange Search issues, you can use Test-ExchangeSearch. When you use the -Server parameter to specify the name of a server to check, the cmdlet tests all mailbox databases on the server simultaneously. If the server is a member of a DAG and has a passive copy of a database, the test is automatically performed against the server that has the active database copy.

Chapter 8. Managing SMTP Connectors

SMTP connectors, Active Directory sites, and Active Directory links all have important roles to play in determining how Exchange routes and delivers messages in your organization. You can work with connectors, sites, and links in a variety of ways, but first you need to have a strong understanding about how connectors are used.

Send and Receive Connectors: The Essentials

In Exchange Server 2016, SMTP connectors are used to logically represent the connection between a source server and a destination server. Only transport servers have SMTP connectors and in an Exchange 2016 organization there are two primary types of transport servers:

- Mailbox servers
- Edge Transport servers

> **NOTE** As Exchange 2016 can interoperate with Exchange 2013 and Exchange 2010, Exchange 2013 Mailbox servers and Exchange 2010 Hub Transport servers can also act as transports. Thus, in a mixed environment the transport servers can include Exchange 2010 Hub Transports as well as Mailbox servers and Edge Transports running Exchange 2013 and Exchange 2016.

How you configure an SMTP connector determines how Exchange Server transports messages using that connection. Because each SMTP connector represents a one-way connection, Exchange Server uses both Send and Receive connectors.

Understanding Send and Receive Connectors

Send connectors are logical gateways through which Exchange servers send all outgoing messages. When you create a Send connector, it is stored in Active Directory Domain Services or in Active Directory Lightweight Directory Services as a connector object.

Send connectors are not scoped to a single server; in fact, multiple servers can use a single Send connector for sending messages. Send connectors deliver mail by looking up a mail exchanger (MX) record on a DNS server, by looking up an Address (A) record, or by using a smart host as a destination. With DNS records, the DNS server settings you configure on the transport server are used for name resolution.

You can configure different settings for internal and external DNS lookups if necessary. See the "Configuring Send Connector DNS Lookups" section of this chapter.

Receive connectors are logical gateways through which all incoming messages are received. When you create a Receive connector, it is stored in AD DS or in AD LDS as a connector object. Unlike Send connectors, Receive connectors are scoped to a single server and determine how that server listens for connections.

The permissions on a Receive connector determine from which other servers the connector will accept connections. The authentication mechanisms you configure for a Receive connector determine whether anonymous connections are allowed and the types of authentication that are permitted.

When you install your Mailbox servers, Exchange 2016 creates the connectors required for mail flow within your organization; however, to send mail outside your domain, you must create a Send connector to send mail to the Internet.

If your organization also uses Edge Transport servers, Exchange creates the additional Send and Receive connectors during the Edge Subscription process. You also can explicitly create Send and Receive connectors or automatically compute them from the organization topology by using Active Directory sites and site-link information.

REAL WORLD   To enhance security and prevent malicious users from trying to determine internal infrastructure components, Exchange 2016 applies the header firewall feature to remove X-headers and routing headers from inbound and outbound messages automatically. *X-headers* are user-defined, unofficial headers added to messages during processing, filtering, or virus/spam checking that detail how a message was processed, filtered, or checked. *Routing headers* are standard SMTP headers that provide information about the various messaging servers used to deliver a message.

The exact headers removed from a message depend on the connector type. Receive connectors with the Internal type remove organization and forest X-headers from messages. Receive connectors with the Custom type remove routing headers (as long as permissions groups are not assigned). Internal or Partner type Send connectors remove organization and forest X-headers from messages. Custom type Send connectors remove routing headers (as long as permissions groups are not assigned).

Routing Messages within Sites

Exchange 2016 determines the ultimate destination for a message when routing messages and then uses a least-cost method to determine how to route the message. By default, Mailbox servers use Active Directory sites and the costs that are assigned to the Active Directory Internet Protocol (IP) site links to determine the least-cost routing path to other Mailbox servers in the organization. You can also specify an Exchange cost for links.

After a Mailbox server determines the least-cost routing path, the server routes messages over the link or links in this path, and in this way, a source Mailbox server relays messages to target Mailbox servers. By default, when there are multiple Active Directory sites between the source and destination server, the Mailbox servers along the path between the source server and the target server don't process or relay the messages in any way—with the following exceptions:

- If you want messages to be processed en route, you can configure an Active Directory site as a hub site so that Exchange routes messages to the hub site to be processed by the site's Mailbox servers before being relayed to a target server. The hub site must exist along the least-cost routing path between source and destination Mailbox servers.
- If a message cannot be delivered to the target site, the Mailbox server in the closest reachable site along the least-cost routing path of the target site queues the message for relay. The message is then relayed when the destination Mailbox server becomes available.

Sometimes during routing, messages must pass through transport servers in a hub site that isn't the ultimate destination but is part of the least-cost routing path. All transport servers in a hub site are considered part of the delivery group for that hop and a transport server is randomly selected to handle the message. As a message passes through a hub site, the randomly selected transport server queues and processes the message, routing the message along the least-cost path.

In cases in which a subscribed Edge Transport server is accessible only from the Active Directory site to which it is subscribed, messages must pass through a specific hub site to get to an Edge Transport server to be routed to the Internet or across premises. This happens because a subscribed Edge Transport server is only accessible from the Active Directory site to which it is subscribed.

Each routing destination has a delivery group that handles its message delivery. As discussed in Chapter 5, "Managing Exchange Organizations," in the "Front End Transport" section," an Active Directory site can be a delivery group but so can a routable DAG, a Mailbox delivery group, a group of connector source servers, or a list of expansion servers for dynamic distribution groups. When a DAG is the delivery group, the DAG itself is a routing boundary and the mailbox databases in the DAG are the routing destinations services by the related delivery group. Thus, a message can be sent from a mailbox on any transport server in the DAG to a mailbox on that server or on any other server in the DAG directly. As site boundaries don't apply, the member servers can be in different sites as well.

When a site is the delivery group, Exchange 2016 can use delayed fan-out to reduce the number of message transmissions by identifying recipients that share part of the routing path. On the other hand, when a site isn't the delivery group, Exchange 2016 selects one site in the destination delivery group with the least-cost routing path as the primary site. If multiple least-cost routing paths are available, the path with the fewest number of hops is chosen. If multiple paths are still available, the site nearest the destination is chosen based on the site name. Specifically, Exchange 2016 selects the site with the lowest alphanumeric sort order. For example, Seattle Site 1 is chosen before Seattle Site 2 and Alpha Site is chosen before Beta Site.

To display the configuration details of an Active Directory site, you can use the Get-AdSite cmdlet. If you don't provide an identity with this cmdlet, configuration information for all Active Directory sites is displayed.

Listing 8-1 provides the syntax and usage, as well as sample output, for the Get-AdSite cmdlet. Note that the output specifies whether the site is enabled as a hub site.

LISTING 8-1 Get-AdSite cmdlet syntax and usage

Syntax

```
Get-AdSite [-Identity 'SiteIdentity'] [-DomainController 'DCName']
```

Usage

```
Get-AdSite -Identity 'First-Seattle-Site' | fl
```

Output

```
RunspaceId          :
HubSiteEnabled      : False
InboundMailEnabled  : True
PartnerId           : -1
MinorPartnerId      : -1
ResponsibleForSites : {}
Name                : First-Seattle-Site-Name
AdminDisplayName    :
ExchangeVersion     : 0.0 (6.5.6500.0)
DistinguishedName   : CN=First-Seattle-Site-Name,CN=Sites,CN=Configuration
,DC=pocket-consultant,DC=com
Identity            : imaginedlands.com/Configuration/Sites/
First-Seattle-Site-Name
Guid                :
ObjectCategory      : imaginedlands.com/Configuration/Schema/Site
ObjectClass         : {top, site}
WhenChanged         : 2/15/2016 8:55:33 PM
WhenCreated         : 2/15/2016 8:55:33 PM
WhenChangedUTC      : 2/16/2016 4:55:33 AM
WhenCreatedUTC      : 2/16/2016 4:55:33 AM
OrganizationId      :
OriginatingServer   : CorpServer27.imaginedlands.com
IsValid             : True
ObjectState         : Unchanged
```

To configure an Active Directory site as a hub site and override the default message routing behavior, you can use the Set-AdSite cmdlet with the -HubSiteEnabled parameter. To enable a site as a hub site, set the –HubSiteEnabled parameter to $true. To disable a site as a hub site, set the –HubSiteEnabled parameter to $false. You must have Enterprise Administrator rights to use the –Name parameter to change a site's name.

Listing 8-2 provides the syntax and usage, for the Set-AdSite cmdlet. Keep in mind that when a hub site exists along the least-cost routing path between source and destination Mailbox servers, messages are routed to the hub site for processing before they are relayed to the destination server.

LISTING 8-2 Set-AdSite cmdlet syntax and usage

Syntax

```
Set-AdSite -Identity 'SiteIdentity'
 [-HubSiteEnabled <$true | $false>] [-InboundMailEnabled <$true | $false>]
 [-DomainController 'DCName']  [-Name 'NewSiteName']
```

Usage

```
Set-AdSite -Identity 'First-Seattle-Site' –HubSiteEnabled $true
```

Routing Messages Across Site Links

To view the configuration information about an Active Directory IP site link, you can use the Get-AdSiteLink cmdlet. This configuration information includes the value of the Exchange-specific cost, the cost assigned to the Active Directory IP site link, and a list of the sites in the IP site link.

Listing 8-3 provides the syntax and usage, as well as sample output, for the Get-AdSiteLink cmdlet. Use the –Identity parameter to retrieve the configuration information about a specific IP site link. If you do not provide an identity, the configuration information about all IP site links is returned.

LISTING 8-3 Get-AdSiteLink cmdlet syntax and usage

Syntax

```
Get-AdSiteLink [-Identity 'SiteIdentity']
 [-DomainController 'DCName']
```

Usage

```
Get-AdSiteLink -Identity 'PORTLANDSEATTLELINK' | fl
```

Output

```
RunspaceId     :
Cost           : 100
ADCost         : 100
ExchangeCost   :
```

```
MaxMessageSize     : Unlimited
Sites              : {imaginedlands.com/Configuration/Sites/
First-Seattle-Site}
AdminDisplayName   :
ExchangeVersion    : 0.0 (6.5.6500.0)
Name               : PORTLANDSEATTLELINK
DistinguishedName  : CN=PORTLANDSEATTLELINK,CN=IP,CN=Inter-Site
                     Transports,CN=Sites,CN=Configuration,
DC=pocket-consultant,DC=com
Identity           : imaginedlands.com/Configuration/Sites/Inter-Site
Transports/IP/PORTLANDSEATTLELINK
Guid               :
ObjectCategory     : imaginedlands.com/Configuration/Schema/Site-Link
ObjectClass        : {top, siteLink}
WhenChanged        : 2/15/2016 8:55:33 PM
WhenCreated        : 2/15/2016 8:55:33 PM
WhenChangedUTC     : 2/16/2016 4:55:33 AM
WhenCreatedUTC     : 2/16/2016 4:55:33 AM
OrganizationId     :
OriginatingServer  : CorpServer27.imaginedlands.com
IsValid            : True
ObjectState        : Unchanged
```

By default, Exchange Server 2016 determines the least-cost routing path by using
the cost that is assigned to the Active Directory IP site links. You can change this
behavior by using the Set-AdSiteLink cmdlet to configure an Exchange-specific cost
for Active Directory IP site links. After you configure it, the Exchange-specific cost is
used to determine the Exchange routing path rather than the Active Directory–
assigned cost.

Listing 8-4 provides the syntax and usage, for the Set-AdSiteLink cmdlet. When there
are multiple wide area network (WAN) paths between sites, you can set a higher site-
link cost to reduce the likelihood that a link will be used and a lower site-link cost to
increase the likelihood that a link will be used. You must have Enterprise
Administrator rights to use the –Name parameter to change the name of a site link.

You can use the –MaxMessageSize parameter to set the maximum size for messages that are relayed across a specified link. The default value is "unlimited," which allows messages of any size to be relayed. You can specify the units for values by using B for bytes, KB for kilobytes, MB for megabytes, or GB for gigabytes. The valid range for maximum size is from 64 KB to the largest value in bytes that can be set using a 64-bit integer (9,223,372,036,854,775,807).

LISTING 8-4 Set-AdSiteLink cmdlet syntax and usage

Syntax

```
Set-AdSiteLink -Identity 'SiteIdentity'
 [-DomainController 'DCName']
 [-ExchangeCost Cost]
 [-MaxMessageSize <'Size' | 'Unlimited'>]
 [-Name 'NewSiteLinkName']
```

Usage

```
Set-AdSiteLink -Identity 'PORTLANDSEATTLELINK'
 -ExchangeCost 20


Set-AdSiteLink -Identity 'LASACRAMENTOLINK'
 -MaxMessageSize 'Unlimited'


Set-AdSiteLink -Identity 'LASACRAMENTOLINK'
 -MaxMessageSize '256MB'
```

Managing Send Connectors

Send connectors are the gateways through which transport servers send messages, and only transport servers have Send connectors. Exchange automatically creates the Send connectors required for internal mail flow but does not create the Send connectors required for mail flow to the Internet. Send connectors are stored in Active Directory and are available to all transport servers in the Exchange organization by default.

Creating Send Connectors

As an administrator, you can explicitly create Send connectors for Internet mail flow and other necessary connectors, and then manage the configuration of these explicitly created Send connectors as needed. You cannot, however, manage the configuration of Send connectors created implicitly by Exchange to enable mail flow. The key reasons for creating Send connectors are to:

- Control explicitly how message routing works within domains or between domains.
- Control explicitly the hosts used as destinations or the way messages are routed over the Internet.
- Send mail to systems that are not Exchange servers.

When you create Send connectors, you can encrypt message traffic sent over the link and require strict authentication. You can transmit messages to a designated internal server—called a *smart host*—or you can use DNS records to route messages. If you use a smart host, Exchange Server 2016 transfers messages directly to the smart host, which then sends out messages over an established link. The smart host allows you to route messages on a per-domain basis. If you use DNS records, Exchange Server 2016 performs a DNS lookup for each address to which the connector sends mail.

As part of the new architecture in Exchange 2016, Mailbox servers handle the front-end and back-end processing for mail transport, including the Transport service and the Front End Transport service. The Transport service is responsible for all mail flow, and the Front End Transport service acts as a stateless proxy for all external SMTP traffic. The Transport service on a Mailbox server can use a Send connector to route outbound messages through the Front End Transport service. Mail routing occurs internally. When an Active Directory site has subscribed Edge Transport servers, outbound mail is passed directly from a Mailbox server to an Edge Transport server.

When you create a Send connector, you must define the address space, which determines when the Send connector is used as well as the domain names to which the connector sends messages. For example, if you want to connect two domains in the same Exchange organization—dev.tvpress.com and corp.tvpress.com—you can create a Send connector in dev.tvpress.com, and then add an SMTP address type for the email domain corp.tvpress.com.

Send connectors can be used by multiple transport servers. When you create a Send connector within an Exchange organization, you can specify the transport servers that are permitted to use the Send connector. When you create a Send connector on an Edge Transport server, the connector is configured only for that server.

Typically, the first Send connector you'll create in an Exchange organization is one that enables mail flow to the Internet. To create a Send connector for Internet mail flow, follow these steps:

1. In Exchange Admin Center, select Mail Flow in the Feature pane and then select Send Connectors.

2. Click New. This starts the New Send Connector Wizard, shown in Figure 8-1.

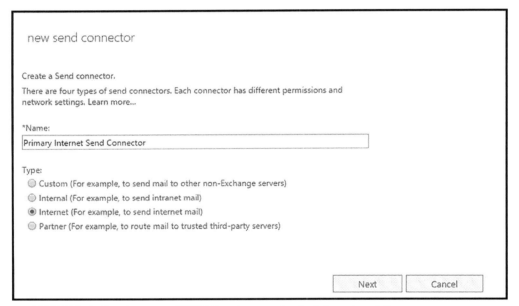

FIGURE 8-1 Create a new SMTP Send connector for Internet mail flow.

3. In the Name text box, type a descriptive name for the connector, such as Primary Internet Send Connector, and then set the connector type as Internet. Click Next.

4. Confirm that MX Record Associated With Recipient Domain is selected, and then click Next.

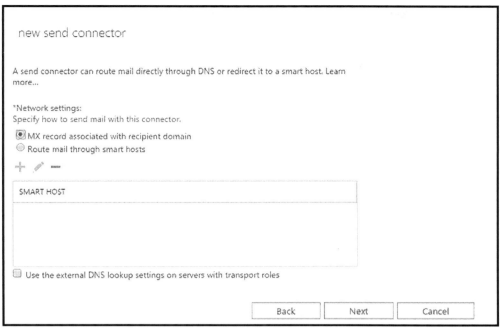

new send connector

A send connector can route mail directly through DNS or redirect it to a smart host. Learn more...

*Network settings:
Specify how to send mail with this connector.

◉ MX record associated with recipient domain
○ Route mail through smart hosts

╋ ✎ ━

SMART HOST

☐ Use the external DNS lookup settings on servers with transport roles

Back   Next   Cancel

5. You next need to define the address space for the send connector. Click the Add button (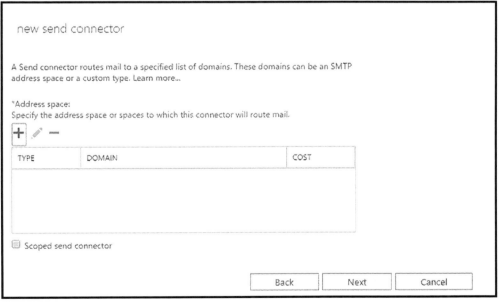).

new send connector

A Send connector routes mail to a specified list of domains. These domains can be an SMTP address space or a custom type. Learn more...

*Address space:
Specify the address space or spaces to which this connector will route mail.

╋ ✎ ━

TYPE	DOMAIN	COST

☐ Scoped send connector

Back   Next   Cancel

6. In the Add Domain dialog box, SMTP is set as the address space type. In the Fully Qualified Domain Name box, enter * to specify that you are creating the connector for routing outbound mail to all external domains. By default,

the address space cost is set to 1, which assigns the highest preference to the connector. If you plan to create other Send connectors, you may want to assign a higher cost to ensure mail is routed appropriately. For example, if you set the cost to 100 and the cost of other Send connectors to a value less than 100, this connector will be used only when no other connector would otherwise apply. Click Save to close the Add Domain dialog box. Click Next.

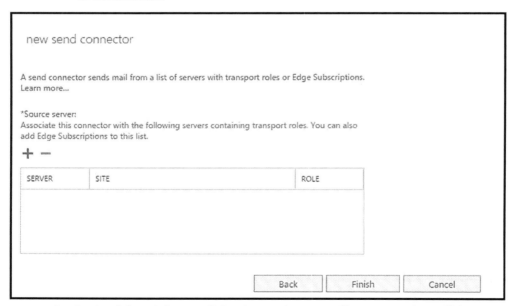

7. On the Source Server page, click the Add button ( ) to associate the connector with the Mailbox server or servers that will be used to send mail to the Internet.

8. In the Select A Server dialog box, select a Mailbox server that will be used as the source server, and then click Add. Repeat as necessary to add more

Transport servers. If you make a mistake, click the Remove link next to the server name.

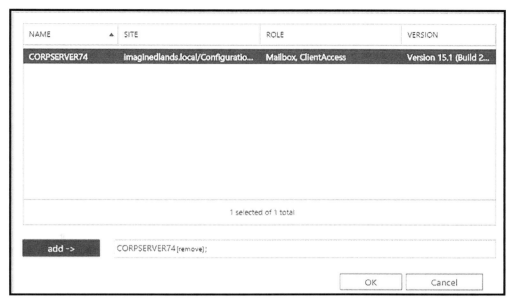

NAME		SITE	ROLE	VERSION
CORPSERVER74	▲	imaginedlands.local/Configuratio...	Mailbox, ClientAccess	Version 15.1 (Build 2...

1 selected of 1 total

add ->   CORPSERVER74 [remove];

OK   Cancel

9. When you are finished selecting servers, click OK to close the Select A Server dialog box, and then click Finish to create the connector. You can verify that the connector is configured properly by sending mail to an external recipient and confirming that the message arrives.

10. By default, the new Send connector is enabled and configured to allow a maximum message size of 35 MB. To change the default maximum message size, open the related properties dialog box by double-clicking the connector's entry in Exchange Admin Center. Next, enter the desired Maximum Send Message Size in the combo box provided and then click Save. Valid maximum send message sizes range from 1 to 2096128 MB. If you don't want the connector to have a specific limit, set the maximum size to 0.

To create other Send connectors, complete the following steps:

1. In Exchange Admin Center, select Mail Flow in the Feature pane, and then select Send Connectors.

2. Click New to start the New Send Connector Wizard, shown in Figure 8-2.

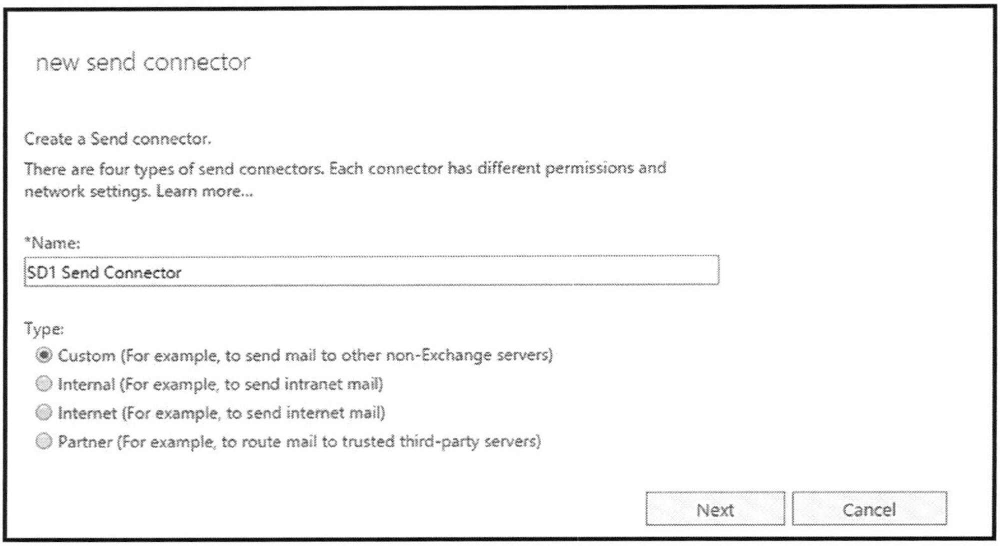

new send connector

Create a Send connector.

There are four types of send connectors. Each connector has different permissions and network settings. Learn more...

*Name:

SD1 Send Connector

Type:
- ◉ Custom (For example, to send mail to other non-Exchange servers)
- ○ Internal (For example, to send intranet mail)
- ○ Internet (For example, to send internet mail)
- ○ Partner (For example, to route mail to trusted third-party servers)

[Next]   [Cancel]

FIGURE 8-2 Create a new SMTP Send connector.

3. In the Name text box, type a descriptive name for the connector, and then set the connector type. The available options are as follows:

- **Custom** Creates a customized Send connector for connecting with systems that are not Exchange servers.
- **Internal** Creates a Send connector for sending mail to another transport server in the organization, and sets the default permissions so that the connector can be used by Exchange servers. This connector will be configured to route mail using smart hosts.
- **Internet** Creates a Send connector that sends mail to external users over the Internet. This connector will be configured to use DNS records to route mail.
- **Partner** Creates a Send connector that sends mail to partner domains. Partner domains cannot be configured as smart hosts. Only connections that authenticate with Transport Layer Security (TLS) certificates are allowed by default. Partner domains must also be listed on the TLS Send Domain Secure list, which can be set by using the –TLSSendDomainSecureList parameter of the Set-TransportConfig command.

4. On the Network Settings page, select how you want to send email with the Send connector. If you select MX Record Associated With Recipient Domain, the Send connector uses the DNS client service on the Transport server to query a DNS server and resolve the destination address. Skip steps 5–9 if you select the MX Record option.

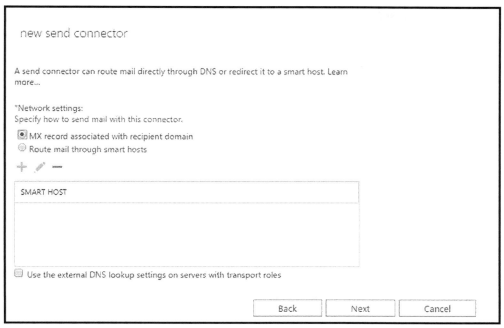

new send connector

A send connector can route mail directly through DNS or redirect it to a smart host. Learn more...

*Network settings:
Specify how to send mail with this connector.

◉ MX record associated with recipient domain
◯ Route mail through smart hosts

✛ ✎ ━

| SMART HOST |
| |

☐ Use the external DNS lookup settings on servers with transport roles

| Back | Next | Cancel |

5. If you select Route Mail Through Smart Host, you have to specify the smart hosts to which mail should be forwarded for processing. Click the Add button (✚).

Add smart host

Specify the smart host's fully qualified domain name (FQDN) or IPv4 address.
*Example: myhost.contoso.com or 192.168.3.2

192.10.10.58

| Save | Cancel |

6. In the Add Smart Host dialog box, enter the IP address or the Fully Qualified Domain Name (FQDN) of the smart host. The Transport server must be able to resolve the FQDN.

7. Click Save to close the Add Smart Host dialog box. Repeat steps 5–7 as necessary to add more smart hosts to this connector. If you make a mistake, select the smart host, and then click Edit or Remove as appropriate. When you are finished, click Next to continue.

8. Optionally, specify that you want the connector to use the external DNS lookup settings of the Mailbox server.

9. After you've configured smart hosts, you'll see the Configure Smart Host Authentication Settings page. On this page, select the method that you want to use to authenticate your servers to the smart host. Choose one of the following options, and then click Next:

- **None**   No authentication.   Use this option only if the smart host is configured to accept anonymous connections.
- **Basic Authentication**   Standard authentication with wide compatibility. With basic authentication, the user name and password specified are passed as cleartext to the remote domain.
- **Offer Basic Authentication Only After Starting TLS**   When you use Basic Authentication, you can select this checkbox to enable basic authentication over TLS. In this case, TLS authentication is combined with basic authentication to allow encrypted authentication for servers with smart cards or X.509 certificates.
- **Exchange Server Authentication**   Secure authentication for Exchange servers. With Exchange Server authentication, credentials are passed securely.
- **Externally Secured**   Secure authentication for Exchange servers. With externally secured authentication, credentials are passed securely using an external security protocol for which the server has been separately configured, such as Internet Protocol security (IPSec).

> **NOTE**   With the Basic Authentication, you must provide the user name and password for the account authorized to establish connectors to the designated smart hosts. All smart hosts must use the same user name and password.

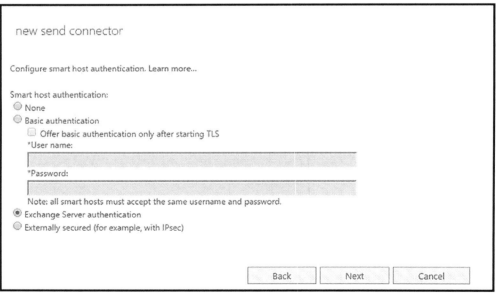

10. Click Next. On the Address Space page, click the Add button (✚).

A Send connector routes mail to a specified list of domains. These domains can be an SMTP address space or a custom type. Learn more...

*Address space:
Specify the address space or spaces to which this connector will route mail.

TYPE	DOMAIN	COST

☐ Scoped send connector

| Back | Next | Cancel |

11. In the Add Domain dialog box, you can use the following options to specify the domain names to which this connector will send mail:

- **Type**   SMTP is the default address space type. Use this type for connectors routing mail to Exchange server and other SMTP servers. For routing mail directly to non-SMTP servers, specify the address space type of the server, such as X400, X500, or MSMAIL.
- **Fully Qualified Domain Name**   The domain or domains to which this connector will send mail, such as imaginedlands.com. With SMTP addresses, you can enter the wildcard character (*) directly in the address space as defined in RFC 1035. For example, you can enter * for all domains, ***.com** for all .com domains, or ***.imaginedlands.com** for the imaginedlands.com domain and all subdomains of imaginedlands.com. With X.400 addresses, you must specify the address space as defined in RFC 1685.
- **Cost**   The address space cost is used for relative weighting. Valid address space costs range from 1, which assigns the highest possible preference, to 100, which assigns the lowest possible preference. When you create a Send connector, the default address space cost is 1. If you set all address spaces to this cost, all address spaces have equal preference for routing mail.

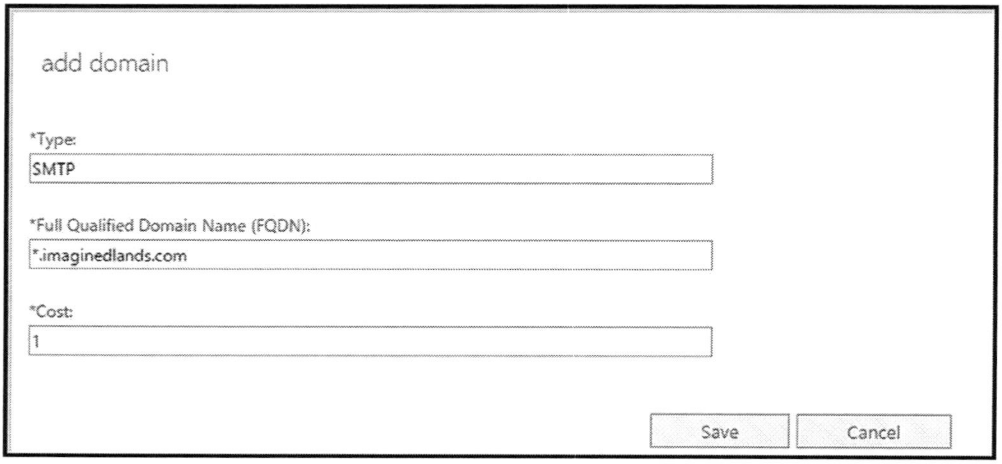

add domain

*Type:

SMTP

*Full Qualified Domain Name (FQDN):

*.imaginedlands.com

*Cost:

1

| Save | Cancel |

12. Click Save to close the SMTP Address Space dialog box. Repeat as necessary to add more address spaces to this connector. If you make a mistake, select the address space and then click Edit or Remove as appropriate.

13. If you'd like to scope the Send connector to the current site, select the Scoped Send Connector check box. When a Send connector is scoped, only Mailbox servers in the same Active Directory site as the Send connector's source servers consider that Send connector in routing decisions. Click Next to continue.

14. Next, you see the Source Server page, allowing you to associate this connector with other transport servers. Click the Add button (**+**) to associate the connector with Mailbox servers and Edge subscriptions.

15. In the Select A Server dialog box, select a Mailbox server or an Edge subscription that will be used as the source server for sending messages to the address space that you previously specified, and then click Add. Repeat as necessary to add more Transport servers. If you make a mistake, click the Remove link next to the server name.

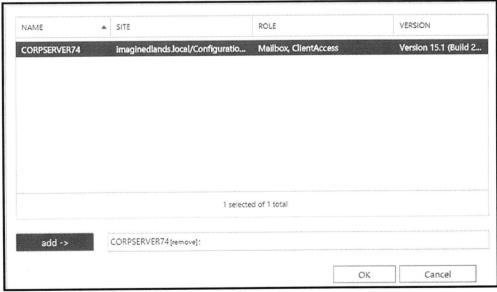

16. When you are finished, click OK to close the Select A Server dialog box, and then click Finish to create the connector. You can verify that the connector is

configured properly by sending mail to an external recipient in a domain associated with the connector and confirming that the message arrives.

17. By default, the new Send connector is enabled and configured to allow a maximum message size of 35 MB. To change the default maximum message size, open the related properties dialog box by double-clicking the connector's entry in Exchange Admin Center. Next, enter the desired Maximum Send Message Size in the combo box provided, and then click Save. Valid maximum send message sizes range from 1 to 2048 MB. If you don't want the connector to have a specific limit, set the maximum size to 0 or select Unlimited in the dropdown list.

18. When you create a Send connector, you can also enable front-end proxying to allow destination specific routing, such as by DNS or IP address. If you want to enable front-end proxying and route outbound messages through the Client Access services running on a Mailbox server in the local Active Directory site, open the related properties dialog box by double-clicking the connector's entry in Exchange Admin Center. Next, select the Proxy Through Client Access Services check box, and then click Save.

In Exchange Management Shell, you can create Send connectors by using the New-SendConnector cmdlet. The –Usage parameter sets the Send connector type as Custom, Internal, Internet, or Legacy. The –AddressSpaces parameter sets the address spaces for the Send connector by FQDN or IP address. Additionally, the –DNSRoutingEnabled parameter determines whether DNS records or smart hosts are used for lookups. To use DNS records, set DNSRoutingEnabled to $true. To use smart hosts, set –DNSRoutingEnabled to $false, and then use the –SmartHosts parameter to designate the smart hosts. To enable front-end proxying, set the –FrontEndProxyEnabled parameter to $true.

Listing 8-5 provides the syntax and usage for the New-SendConnector cmdlet. With basic authentication or basic authentication over TLS, you will be prompted to provide credentials. To scope the Send connector to the current Active Directory site, set the –IsScopedConnector parameter to $true.

LISTING 8-5 New-SendConnector cmdlet syntax and usage

Syntax

```
New-SendConnector -Name Name -AddressSpaces Addresses
  [-AuthenticationCredential Credentials]
  [-CloudServicesMailEnabled <$true | $false>]
```

```
[-Comment Comment]

[-ConnectionInactivityTimeout TimeSpan]

[-Custom <$true | $false>]

[-DNSRoutingEnabled <$true | $false>]

[-DomainController DCName]

[-DomainSecureEnabled <$true | $false>]

[-ErrorPolicies <Default|DowngradeDnsFailures|DowngradeCustomFailures>]

[-Enabled <$true | $false>]

[-Force <$true | $false>]

[-ForceHELO <$true | $false>]

[-Fqdn FQDN]

[-FrontEndProxyEnabled <$true | $false>]

[-IgnoreStartTLS <$true | $false>]

[-Internal <$true | $false>]

[-Internet <$true | $false>]

[-IsScopedConnector <$true | $false>]

[-MaxMessageSize <Size | Unlimited>]

[-Partner <$true | $false>]

[-Port PortNumber]

[-ProtocolLoggingLevel <None | Verbose>]

[-RequireTLS <$true | $false>]

[-SmartHostAuthMechanism <None|BasicAuth|BasicAuthRequireTLS
                         |ExchangeServer|ExternalAuthoritative>]

[-SmartHosts SmartHosts]

[SmtpMaxMessagesPerConnection MaxMessages]

[-SourceIPAddress IPAddress]

 [-SourceTransportServers TranportServers]

[-TlsAuthLevel <EncryptionOnly|CertificateValidation|DomainValidation>]

[-TlsCertificateName "X509:<I>Issuer<S>CommonName"]

[-TlsDomain DomainNameForVerificationofTLSCert]

[-Usage <Custom|Internal|Internet|Partner>]

[-UseExternalDNSServersEnabled <$true | $false>]
```

Usage for DNS MX records

```
New-SendConnector -Name "Imaginedlands.com Send Connector"
 -Usage "Custom"
```

```
-AddressSpaces "smtp:*.imaginedlands.com;1"

-IsScopedConnector $true

-DNSRoutingEnabled $true

-UseExternalDNSServersEnabled $false

-SourceTransportServers "CORPSVR127"
```

Usage for smart hosts

```
New-SendConnector -Name "Cohovineyards.com"
 -Usage "Custom"
 -AddressSpaces "smtp:*.cohovineyards.com;1"
 -IsScopedConnector $false
 -DNSRoutingEnabled $false
 -SmartHosts "[192.168.10.52]"
 -SmartHostAuthMechanism "ExternalAuthoritative"
 -UseExternalDNSServersEnabled $false
 -SourceTransportServers "CORPSVR127"
```

Viewing and Managing Send Connectors

The Exchange Management tools provide access only to the Send connectors you've explicitly created. On Mailbox servers, Send connectors created by Exchange Server are not displayed or configurable. On Edge Transport servers, you can view and manage the internal Send connector used to connect to the Mailbox servers in your Exchange organization, as shown in Figure 8-3.

FIGURE 8-3 Viewing Send connectors in your on-premises Exchange organization.

In Exchange Admin Center, you can view the Send connectors and manage their configuration. When you select Mail Flow in the Feature pane and then select Send Connectors, Send connectors you've created are listed by name and status. You can now do the following:

- **Change a connector's properties** To change a connector's properties, double-click the connector entry, and then use the Properties dialog box to manage the connector's properties. You'll also be able to specify the maximum message size and protocol logging level. By default, the maximum message size is set to 35 MB and the protocol logging level is set to None.
- **Enable a connector** To enable a connector, select it, and then select Enable in the details pane.
- **Disable a connector** To disable a connector, select it, and then select Disable in the details pane.
- **Remove a connector** To remove a connector, select it in Exchange Admin

Center, and then select Delete (   ).

In Exchange Management Shell, you can view, update, or remove Send connectors by using the Get-SendConnector, Set-SendConnector, or Remove-SendConnector cmdlets, respectively. Listings 8-6 through 8-8 provide the syntax and usage. With

Get-SendConnector, if you don't specify an identity, the cmdlet returns a list of all administrator-configured Send connectors.

LISTING 8-6 Get-SendConnector cmdlet syntax and usage

Syntax

```
Get-SendConnector
```

```
Get-SendConnector –Identity ConnectorIdentity
[-DomainController DCName]
```

Usage

```
Get-SendConnector –Identity "Imaginedlands.com Send Connector"
```

LISTING 8-7 Set-SendConnector cmdlet syntax and usage

Syntax

```
Set-SendConnector –Identity ConnectorIdentity
 [–Name NewName]
 [-AddressSpaces Addresses]
 [-AuthenticationCredential Credentials]
 [-CloudServicesMailEnabled <$true | $false>]
 [-Comment Comment]
 [-ConnectionInactivityTimeout TimeSpan]
 [-DNSRoutingEnabled <$true | $false>]
 [-DomainController DCName]
 [-DomainSecureEnabled <$true | $false>]
 [-ErrorPolicies <Default|DowngradeDnsFailures|DowngradeCustomFailures>]
 [-Enabled <$true | $false>]
 [-Force <$true | $false>]
 [-ForceHELO <$true | $false>]
 [-Fqdn FQDN]
 [-FrontEndProxyEnabled <$true | $false>]
 [-IgnoreStartTLS <$true | $false>]
 [-IsScopedConnector <$true | $false>]
 [-MaxMessageSize <Size | Unlimited>]
 [-Port PortNumber]
 [-ProtocolLoggingLevel <None | Verbose>]
```

```
[-RequireTLS <$true | $false>]

[-SmartHostAuthMechanism <None|BasicAuth|BasicAuthRequireTls
                         |ExchangeServer|ExternalAuthoritative>]

[-SmartHosts SmartHosts]

[-SourceIPAddress IPAddress]

[-SourceTransportServers TranportServers]

[SmtpMaxMessagesPerConnection MaxMessages]

[-TlsAuthLevel <EncryptionOnly|CertificateValidation|DomainValidation>]

[-TlsCertificateName "X509:<I>Issuer<S>CommonName"]

[-TlsDomain DomainNameForVerificationofTLSCert]

[-UseExternalDNSServersEnabled <$true | $false>]
```

Usage

```
Set-SendConnector -Identity "Imaginedlands.com Send Connector"
 -AddressSpaces "smtp:*.imaginedlands.com;1"
 -DNSRoutingEnabled $true -SmartHosts 10.10.2.205
 -SmartHostAuthMechanism "None"
 -SourceTransportServers "CORPSVR127"
```

LISTING 8-8 Remove-SendConnector cmdlet syntax and usage

Syntax

```
Remove-SendConnector -Identity ConnectorIdentity
 [-Confirm <$true | $false>] [-DomainController DCName]
```

Usage

```
Remove-SendConnector -Identity "Imaginedlands.com Send Connector"
```

Configuring Send Connector DNS Lookups

You can configure different settings for internal and external DNS lookups by configuring a Transport server's External DNS Lookups and Internal DNS Lookups properties. External DNS Lookup servers are used to resolve the IP addresses of servers outside your organization. Internal DNS Lookup servers are used to resolve IP addresses of servers inside the organization.

In Exchange Admin Center, you can specify enable or disable external DNS lookups for each Send connector by selecting Mail Flow in the Feature pane, and then selecting Send Connectors. Next, double-click the Send connector you want to configure. In the properties dialog box, select Delivery to display the Delivery options. The Use The External DNS Lookup... checkbox controls whether external DNS lookups are permitted. To allow external DNS lookups when the selected connector is used, select this checkbox, and then click Save.

If you've enabled external DNS lookups for Send connectors, you can specify how external lookups should be performed for each Mailbox server in the organization. You also can configure internal DNS lookups for each Mailbox server in the organization. To configure DNS Lookup servers, complete these steps:

1. In Exchange Admin Center, select Servers in the Feature pane, and then select Servers. Next, double-click the server you want to manage.

2. In the properties dialog box, select DNS Lookups to display DNS lookup options.

3. On the External DNS Lookups panel, shown in Figure 8-4, specify how external lookups should be performed:

- To use DNS settings from the server's network card or cards for external lookups, choose either All Network Adapters (All Available IPv4) to use all configured IPv4 settings or a specific network card to use the configured IPv4 settings of that card.
- To use a custom list of DNS servers for external lookups, select Custom Settings. Next, click Add. In the Add IP Address dialog box, type the IPv4 or IPv6 address of a DNS server to use for external lookups, and then click Save. Repeat this process to specify multiple servers. Keep in mind that Mailbox servers perform lookups in the order the DNS servers are listed.

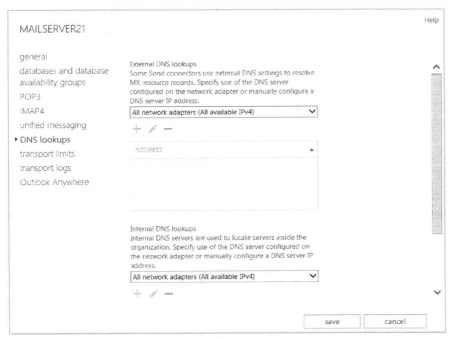

FIGURE 8-4 Configure external DNS lookups.

4. On the Internal DNS Lookups panel, specify how internal lookups should be performed:

- To use DNS settings from the server's network card or cards for internal lookups, choose either All Network Adapters (All Available IPv4) to use all configured IPv4 settings or a specific network card to use the configured IPv4 settings of that card.
- To use a custom list of DNS servers for internal lookups, select Custom Settings. Next, click Add. In the Add IP Address dialog box, type the IPv4 or IPv6 address of a DNS server to use for internal lookups, and then click Save. Repeat this process to specify multiple servers.

5. Click Save to apply your settings.

Setting Send Connector Limits

Send connector limits determine how mail is delivered after a connection has been established and the receiving computer has acknowledged that it's ready to receive the data transfer. After a connection has been established and the receiving computer has acknowledged that it's ready to receive the data transfer, Exchange Server attempts to deliver messages queued for delivery to the computer. If a message can't be delivered on the first attempt, Exchange Server tries to send the message again after a specified time. Exchange Server keeps trying to send the message at the intervals you've specified until the expiration time-out is reached. When the time limit is reached, the message is returned to the sender with a non-delivery report (NDR). The default expiration time-out is two days.

After multiple failed attempts to deliver a message, Exchange Server generates a delay notification and queues it for delivery to the sender of the message. Notification doesn't occur immediately after failure; instead, Exchange Server sends the delay notification message after the notification delay interval and then only if the message hasn't already been delivered. The default delay notification is four hours.

With SMTP, you have much more control over outgoing connections than you do over incoming connections. You can limit the number of simultaneous connections and the number of connections per domain. These limits set the maximum number of simultaneous outbound connections. By default, the maximum number of connections is 1,000 and the maximum number of connections per domain is 20.

You can view or change the Send connector limits by completing the following steps:

1. In Exchange Admin Center, select Servers in the Feature pane, and then select Servers. Next, double-click the server you want to manage.
2. On the Transport Limits page, shown in Figure 8-5, use the following options for retrying unsuccessful outbound connections:

- **Outbound Connection Failure Retry Interval (Seconds)**   Sets the retry interval for subsequent connection attempts to a remote server where previous connections have failed. The default is 600 seconds.
- **Transient Failure Retry Interval (Minutes)**   Sets the interval at which the server immediately retries when it encounters a connection failure with a remote server. The default is five minutes.
- **Transient Failure Retry Attempts**   Sets the maximum number of times that the server immediately retries when it encounters a connection failure with a remote server. The default is six. If you enter 0 as the number of retry attempts or the maximum number of attempts has been reached, the server no longer immediately retries a connection and instead waits according to the outbound connection failure retry interval.

3. When messages that cannot be delivered reach the Maximum Time Since Submission value, they expire, and Exchange Server generates a Non-delivery report. To set the expiration time-out for messages, enter the desired message expiration value in the Maximum Time Since Submission (Days) text box. The default expiration time-out for messages is two days.

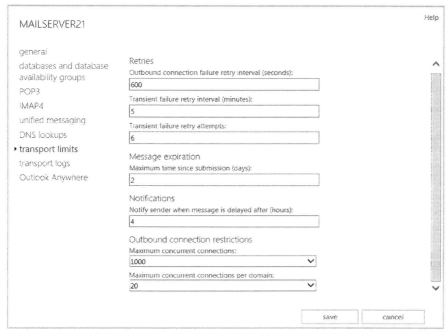

FIGURE 8-5 Configure connection limits.

4. When messages are delayed longer than the allowed delay interval, Exchange Server sends a delay notification to the sender. To set the amount of time to wait before notifying senders of a delay, enter the desired wait time in the Notify Sender When Message Is Delayed After (Hours) text box. The default wait time is four hours.

5. To set an outgoing connection limit, select the Maximum Concurrent Outbound Connections check box, and then type the limit value. The default limit is 1,000 outbound connections. To remove outgoing connection limits, set the value to 0 or select Unlimited in the drop-down list.

6. To set an outgoing connection limit per domain, select the Maximum Concurrent Outbound Connections Per Domain check box, and then type the limit value. The default limit is 20 outbound connections per domain. To remove the outgoing connection limit per domain, set the value to 0 or select Unlimited in the drop-down list.

7. Click Save to apply your settings.

Managing Receive Connectors

Receive connectors are the gateways through which transport servers receive messages. Exchange creates the Receive connectors required for mail flow automatically. The receive permissions on a Receive connector determine who is allowed to send mail through the connector.

Two Receive connectors are created for front-end transport and two for hub transport on each Exchange 2016 Mailbox server:

- The Default connector for hub transport accepts connections from Mailbox servers running the Transport service as well as from Edge Transport servers
- The Client Proxy connector for hub transport accepts connections from Client Access services.
- The Default front-end connector accepts connections from SMTP senders over port 25.
- The Client front-end connector accepts secure connections over TLS
- The Outbound Proxy front-end connector accepts connections from Mailbox servers when front-end proxying is enabled.

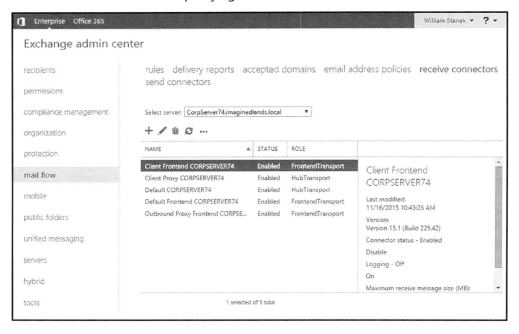

As these default Receive connectors are created automatically, you generally don't need to create Receive connectors to receive mail from the Internet. That said, as an administrator, you can explicitly create Receive connectors, and then manage the configuration of those Receive connectors as necessary. You cannot, however, manage the configuration of connectors created implicitly by Exchange to enable mail flow. The key reasons for creating SMTP connectors are when you want to:

- Control explicitly how messages are received within domains or between domains.
- Control explicitly the permitted incoming connections.
- Receive mail from systems that are not Exchange servers.

Unlike Send connectors, Receive connectors are used by only a single, designated Transport server. When you create a Receive connector within an Exchange organization, you can select the Mailbox or Edge Transport server with which the connector should be associated and configure the specific binding for that connector. A binding is a combination of local IP addresses, ports, and remote IP address ranges for the Receive connector. You cannot create a Receive connector that duplicates the bindings of existing Receive connectors. Each Receive connector must have a unique binding.

> **NOTE** Exchange Server 2016 uses standard SMTP or Extended SMTP (ESMTP) to deliver mail. Because the ESMTP standard is more efficient and allows for extensions, SMTP connectors always try to initiate ESMTP sessions before trying to initiate standard SMTP sessions. SMTP connectors initiate ESMTP sessions with other mail servers by issuing an EHLO start command. SMTP connectors initiate SMTP sessions with other mail servers by issuing the HELO start command.
>
> SMTP was originally defined in RFC 821, and ESMTP was originally defined in RFC 1869. With SMTP, the MAIL FROM and RCPT TO fields are limited to a maximum of 512 characters. With ESMTP, these fields can have more than 512 characters. Additionally, EHLO replies can include a status code, domain, and a list of keywords that indicate supported extensions.
>
> Because the ESMTP standard is more efficient and allows for extensions SMTP connectors always try to initiate ESMTP sessions before trying to initiate standard SMTP sessions. SMTP connectors initiate ESMTP sessions with other mail servers by issuing an EHLO start command. SMTP connectors initiate SMTP sessions with other mail servers by issuing the HELO start command.

Creating Receive Connectors

Receive connectors can be configured for either front-end transport or hub transport. Generally, when you want to control mail flow from external sources, you configure the Receive connector for front-end transport rather than hub transport. Thus, you normally would:

- Configure a Receive connector for receiving messages from the Internet or an external partner as a front end transport.
- Configure a Receive connector for receiving messages from an internal messaging appliance or an internal Exchange server as a hub transport.

You can create a Receive connector for front-end or hub transport by completing the following steps:

1. In Exchange Admin Center, select Mail Flow in the Feature pane, and then select Receive Connectors. On the Receive Connectors page, use the Select Server list to choose the server on which you want to create the Receive connector.

2. Click New (**+**) to start the New Receive Connector Wizard, shown in Figure 8-6. In the Name text box, type a descriptive name for the connector, and then specify the connector role as either Hub Transport or Frontend Transport.

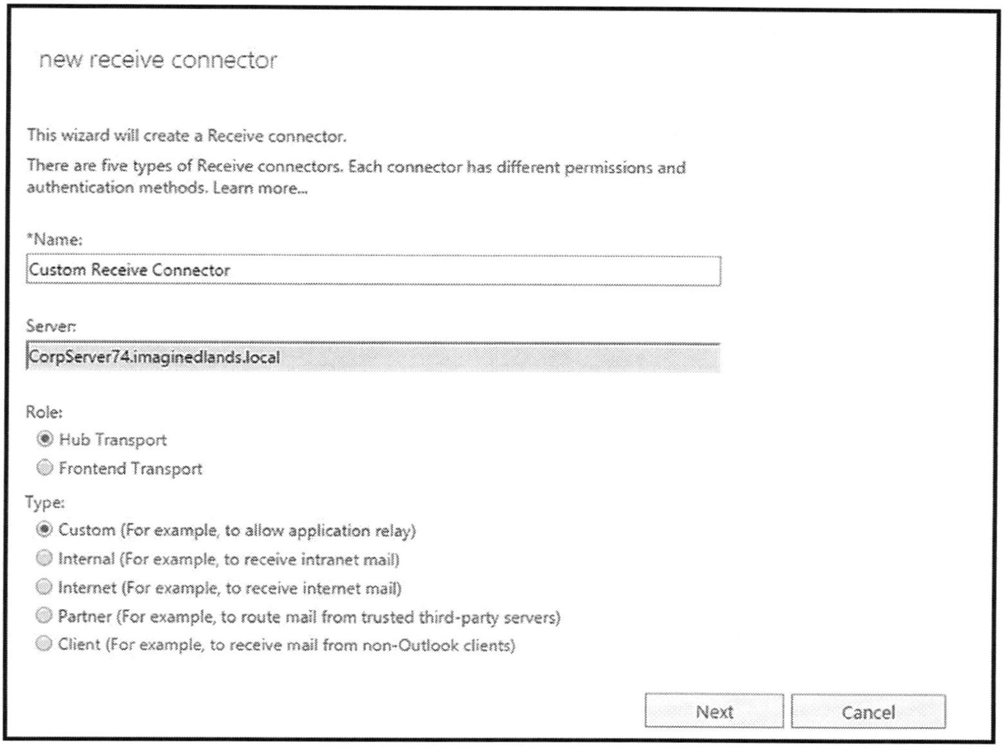

FIGURE 8-6 Create a new SMTP Receive connector.

3. Set the connector type. The available options are as follows:

- **Custom**   Creates a Receive connector bound to a specific port or IP address on a server with multiple receive ports or IP addresses. It can also be used to specify a remote IP address from which the connector receives messages. Generally, a custom Receive connector is used to connect with systems that are not Exchange servers. You also can use custom Receive connectors to receive mail from a Mailbox server in another forest or from an SMTP transfer agent.
- **Internal**   Creates a Receive connector to receive messages from another Transport server in the organization, such as may be necessary for communication between Mailbox servers or between Mailbox servers and third-party transfer agents. For Edge Transport servers, the Internal connector type sets the default permissions so that the connector can be used by Exchange servers. For Mailbox servers, it sets the default permissions so that the connector is configured to accept connections from Exchange servers.
- **Internet**   Creates a Receive connector that accepts incoming connections from the Internet. This connector accepts connections from anonymous users.
- **Client**   Creates a Receive connector used to receive mail from Exchange users. Only connections from authenticated Microsoft Exchange users are accepted by default. Typically used to connect clients not using Microsoft Office Outlook.

- **Partner** Creates a Receive connector used to receive mail from partner domains. Partner domains cannot be configured as smart hosts. Only connections that authenticate with Transport Layer Security (TLS) are allowed by default. Partner domains must also be listed on the TLS Receive Domain Secure list, which can be set by using the –TLSReceiveDomainSecureList parameter of the Set-TransportConfig command.

4. Click Next. For Custom, Partner, and Internet Receive connectors, you can specify the local IPv4 and IPv6 addresses and the port on which mail can be received. By default, Custom and Internet Receive connectors are configured to receive mail over port 25 on all available IPv4 addresses configured for the server. Port 25 is the default TCP port for SMTP. To use a different configuration for IPv4 addresses, select the default entry on the Local Network Settings page, and then click Remove (   ).

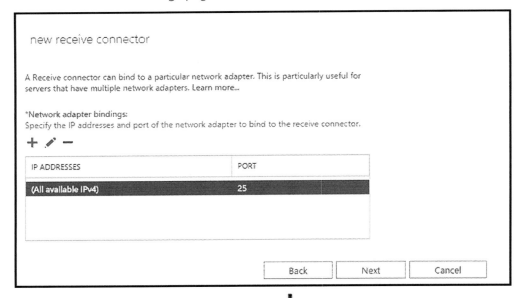

5. To create a new entry, click Add (   ). In the Add IP Address dialog box, select All Available IPv4 Addresses to have the connector listen for connections on all the IPv4 addresses that are assigned to the network adapters on the local server. Alternatively, you can select all available IPv6 addresses or you can select Specify An IPv4 Address Or an IPv6 Address if you want to type an IP address that is assigned to a network adapter on the local server and have the connector listen for connections only on this IP address. As necessary, modify the listen port value. Click Save. Repeat this process as necessary. When you are ready to continue, click Next.

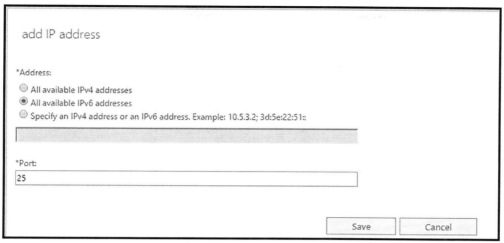

add IP address

*Address:
- ○ All available IPv4 addresses
- ● All available IPv6 addresses
- ○ Specify an IPv4 address or an IPv6 address. Example: 10.5.3.2; 3d:5e:22:51::

*Port:

25

Save   Cancel

6. On the Remote Network Settings page, you can specify the remote IP addresses from which the server can receive mail. By default, Receive connectors are configured to accept mail from all remote IP addresses, which is why the IP address range 0.0.0.0–255.255.255.255 is set as the default entry. You'll only want to change this behavior if you want to limit the servers that are permitted to send mail to the Transport server. To use a different configuration, select the default entry on the Remote Network Settings page, and then click Remove (▬).

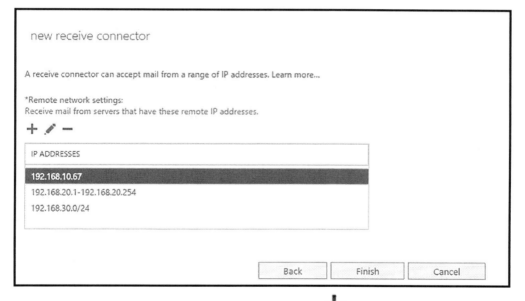

new receive connector

A receive connector can accept mail from a range of IP addresses. Learn more...

*Remote network settings:
Receive mail from servers that have these remote IP addresses.

+ ✎ −

IP ADDRESSES
192.168.10.67
192.168.20.1-192.168.20.254
192.168.30.0/24

Back   Finish   Cancel

7. To specify the remote servers, click Add (✚). Next, in the Add IP Address dialog box, enter an IP address, an IP address range, or an IP address range

in Classless Internet Domain Routing (CIDR) notation. Repeat this process as necessary to specify other acceptable IP addresses. Click Save.

8. When you're finished, click Finish to create the connector. You can verify that the connector is configured properly by confirming that messages arrive from a sending server to which the connector applies.

9. By default, the new Receive connector is enabled and configured to allow a maximum message size of 35 MB. To change the default maximum message size, open the related properties dialog box by double-clicking the connector's entry in Exchange Admin Center. Next, enter the desired Maximum Receive Message Size in the combo box provided, and then click Save. Valid maximum receive message sizes range from 1 to 2047 MB--and you can't specify that there is no limit.

10. When you create a Receive connector, you can also specify the maximum hops that a message can take before it's rejected by the Receive connector. By default, a message can have a maximum of 12 local hops and a maximum of 60 hops in total. If you want to change the default maximum hop counts, open the related properties dialog box by double-clicking the connector's entry in Exchange Admin Center. After you set the maximum number of local hops and the maximum number of hops in total, click Save. The valid range for local hops is 1 to 50 and the valid range for hops in total is 1 to 500. If you don't want the connector to have a specific limit for local hops, set the maximum local hops to 0. You can't set the maximum hops in total to unlimited.

In Exchange Management Shell, you can create Receive connectors by using the New-ReceiveConnector cmdlet. The –Usage parameter sets the Receive connector type as Client, Custom, Internal, Internet, or Partner. The –Bindings parameter sets the internal IP addresses and ports on which to listen. The –FQDN parameter sets the FQDN to advertise in response to HELO or EHLO messages. The –RemoteIPRanges parameter provides a comma-separated list of acceptable IP address ranges. To specify the server on which to create the Receive connector, use the –Server parameter.

As Listing 8-9 shows, the required parameters for the New-ReceiveConnector cmdlet depend on the type of Receive connector you are creating. After you provide the required parameters, the remaining parameters can be used in the same way regardless of which type of Receive connector you are creating. To specify the authentication type, use –AuthMechanism. With Basic Authentication or Basic Authentication Over TLS, you will be prompted to provide credentials. Also, you can use -TransportRole to specify the role with which the Receive connector should be associated.

LISTING 8-9 New-ReceiveConnector cmdlet syntax and usage

Syntax

```
New-ReceiveConnector -Name Name
-Usage <Custom | Internet | Internal | Client | Partner> {AddtlParams}
[-TransportRole <FrontEndTransport | HubTransport>]


New-ReceiveConnector -Name Name -Bindings Bindings
-RemoteIPRanges IPRange1, IPRange2, . . . {AddtlParams}
[-TransportRole <FrontEndTransport | HubTransport>]


New-ReceiveConnector -Name Name -Bindings Bindings
-Internet <$true | $false >  {AddtlParams}
[-TransportRole <FrontEndTransport | HubTransport>]


New-ReceiveConnector -Name Name -Client <$true | $false >
-RemoteIPRanges IPRange1, IPRange2, . . . {AddtlParams}
[-TransportRole <FrontEndTransport | HubTransport>]


New-ReceiveConnector -Name Name -Internal <$true | $false >
-RemoteIPRanges IPRange1, IPRange2, . . . {AddtlParams}
[-TransportRole <FrontEndTransport | HubTransport>]


New-ReceiveConnector -Name <String> -Bindings Bindings
-Partner <$true | $false > -RemoteIPRanges IPRange1, IPRange2, . . .
[-TransportRole <FrontEndTransport | HubTransport>]
{AddtlParams}


{AddtlParams}
[-AdvertiseClientSettings <$true | $false>]
[-AuthMechanism <None | Tls | Integrated | BasicAuth |
BasicAuthRequireTLS | ExchangeServer | ExternalAuthoritative>]
[-Banner Banner]
[-BinaryMimeEnabled <$true | $false>]
```

[-Bindings **Bindings**]

[-ChunkingEnabled <$true | $false >]

[-Comment **Comment**]

[-ConnectionInactivityTimeout **TimeSpan**]

[-ConnectionTimeout **TimeSpan**]

[-Custom <$true | $false >]

[-DefaultDomain **DefaultDomain**]

[-DeliveryStatusNotificationEnabled <$true | $false>]

[-DomainController **DCName**]

[-DomainSecureEnabled <$true | $false>]

[-EightBitMimeEnabled <$true | $false>]

[-EnableAuthGSSAPI <$true | $false>]

[-Enabled <$true | $false>]

[-EnhancedStatusCodesEnabled <$true | $false>]

[-ExtendedProtectionPolicy <none | allow | require>]

[-Fqdn **FQDN**]

[-LiveCredentialEnabled <$true | $false>]

[-LongAddressesEnabled <$true | $false>]

[-MaxAcknowledgementDelay **MaxDelay**]

[-MaxHeaderSize **MaxHeaderBytes**]

[-MaxHopCount **MaxHops**]

[-MaxInboundConnection <**MaxConn** | Unlimited>]

[-MaxInboundConnectionPercentagePerSource **MaxPercentage**]

[-MaxInboundConnectionPerSource <**MaxConnPerSource** | Unlimited>]

[-MaxLocalHopCount **MaxHops**]

[-MaxLogonFailures **MaxLogonFailures**]

[-MaxMessageSize **MaxMessageSize**]

[-MaxProtocolErrors <**MaxErrors** | Unlimited>]

[-MaxRecipientsPerMessage **MaxRecipients**]

[-MessageRateLimit <**RateLimit** | Unlimited>]

[-MessageRateSource <User | IPAddress | Both>]

[-OrarEnabled <$true | $false>]

[-PermissionGroups <None | AnonymousUsers | ExchangeUsers | ExchangeServers | ExchangeLegacyServers | Partners | Custom >]

[-PipeliningEnabled < $true | $false>]

[-ProtocolLoggingLevel <None | Verbose>]

```
[-RemoteIPRanges IPRange1, IPRange2, . . .]
[-RequireEHLODomain <$true | $false>]
[-RequireTLS < $true | $false>]
[-Server Server]
[-ServiceDiscoveryFqdn ServiceFqdn]
[-SizeEnabled <Disabled | Enabled | EnabledWithoutValue>]
[-SuppressXAnonymousTls < $true | $false>]
[-TarpitInterval TimeSpan]
[-TlsCertificateName "X509:<I>Issuer<S>CommonName"]
[-TlsDomainCapabilities DomainName:Capability]
```

Usage

```
New-ReceiveConnector -Name "Custom Receive Connector"
-Usage "Custom" -Bindings "0.0.0.0:425"
 -Fqdn "mailserver85.tvpress.com"
 -RemoteIPRanges "0.0.0.0-255.255.255.255"
 -Server "CORPSVR127"
 -TransportRole HubTransport
```

Configuring Receive Connectors

To view all available Receive connectors for a server, select Mail Flow in the Feature pane, and then select Receive Connectors. Next, on the Receive Connectors page, use the Select Server list to choose the server you want to work with. As shown in Figure 8-7, Receive connectors for the selected server are then listed by name, status, and role.

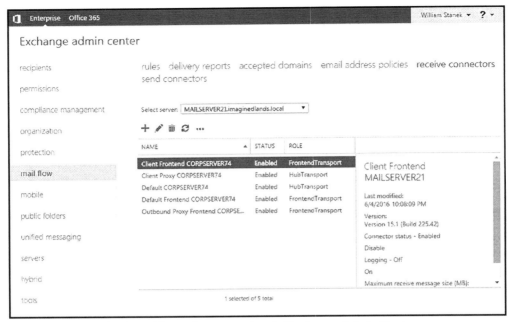

FIGURE 8-7 Working with receive connectors in Exchange Admin Center.

You can now:

- **Enable a connector**   To enable a connector, select it, and then select Enable in the details pane.
- **Disable a connector**   To disable a connector, select it, and then select Disable in the details pane.
- **Remove a connector**   To remove a connector, select it in Exchange Admin Center, and then select Delete (   ).

To change a connector's properties, double-click the connector entry, and then use the Properties dialog box to manage the connector's properties, including protocol logging level, maximum receive size and maximum hop counts.

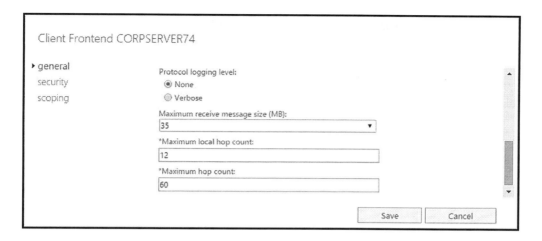

When configuring Receive connector properties, you can specify the security mechanisms that can be used for incoming connections on the Security page. Use any combination of the following:

- **Transport Layer Security**   Allows encrypted authentications with TLS for servers with smart cards or X.509 certificates.
- **Enable Domain Security (Mutual Auth TLS)**   When TLS is enabled, you can also enable domain security to require mutual authentication.
- **Basic Authentication**   Allows basic authentication. With basic authentication, the user name and password specified are passed as base64-encoded text to the remote domain. Base64-encoding is cleartext and should not be confused with encryption.
- **Offer Basic Authentication Only After Starting TLS**   Allows basic authentication only within an encrypted TLS session.
- **Integrated Windows Authentication**   Allows secure authentication by using NT LAN Manager (NTLM) or Kerberos.
- **Exchange Server Authentication**   Allows secure authentication for Exchange servers. With Exchange Server authentication, credentials are passed securely.
- **Externally Secured**   Allows secure external authentication. With externally secured authentication, credentials are passed securely by using an external security protocol for which the server has been separately configured, such as IPsec.

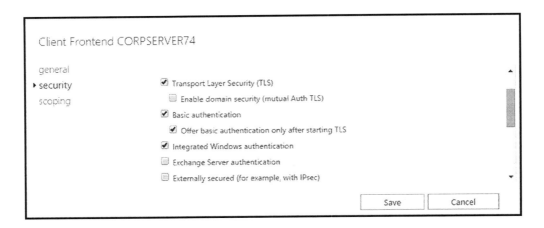

Also when configuring Receive connector properties, you can specify the security group that is allowed to connect on the Permission Groups panel of the Security page. Use any combination of the following:

- **Anonymous Users**   Allows unauthenticated, anonymous users to connect to the Receive connector.
- **Exchange Users**   Allows connections by authenticated users who are valid recipients in the organization (Mailbox servers only).
- **Exchange Servers**   Allows connections by authenticated servers that are members of the Exchange Server Administrator group.
- **Legacy Exchange Servers**   Allows connections by authenticated servers that are members of the ExchangeLegacyInterop group.
- **Partners**   Allows connections by authenticated servers that are members of partner domains, as listed on the TLS Receive Domain Secure list.

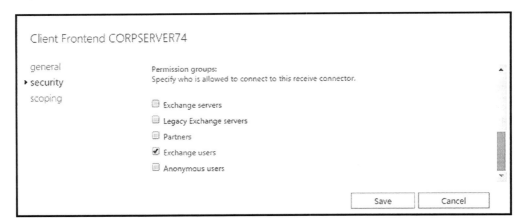

In Exchange Management Shell, you can view, update, or remove Receive connectors by using the Get-ReceiveConnector, Set-ReceiveConnector, or Remove-

ReceiveConnector cmdlets, respectively. Listings 8-10 through 8-12 provide the syntax and usage. With Get-ReceiveConnector, you can return a list of all available Receive connectors if you don't specify an identity or server. If you want to see only the Receive connectors configured on a particular server, use the –Server parameter.

LISTING 8-10 Get-ReceiveConnector cmdlet syntax and usage

Syntax

```
Get-ReceiveConnector [-Identity Server\ConnectorIdentity]
  [-Server Server] [-DomainController DCName]
```

Usage

```
Get-ReceiveConnector
```

```
Get-ReceiveConnector -Identity "Corpsvr127\Imaginedlands.com Receive
Connector"
```

```
Get-ReceiveConnector -Server "Corpsvr127"
```

LISTING 8-11 Set-ReceiveConnector cmdlet syntax and usage

Syntax

```
Set-ReceiveConnector -Identity Identity
  [-AdvertiseClientSettings <$true | $false>]
  [-AuthMechanism <None | Tls | Integrated | BasicAuth |
  BasicAuthRequireTLS | ExchangeServer | ExternalAuthoritative>]
  [-Banner Banner]
  [-BareLineFeedRejectionEnabled <$true | $false>]
  [-BinaryMimeEnabled <$true | $false>]
  [-Bindings Bindings]
  [-ChunkingEnabled <$true | $false >]
  [-Comment Comment]
  [-ConnectionInactivityTimeout TimeSpan]
  [-ConnectionTimeout TimeSpan]
  [-DefaultDomain DefaultDomain]
  [-DeliveryStatusNotificationEnabled <$true | $false>]
  [-DomainController DCName]
  [-DomainSecureEnabled <$true | $false>]
```

```
[-EightBitMimeEnabled  <$true | $false>]
[-EnableAuthGSSAPI <$true | $false>]
[-Enabled <$true | $false>]
[-EnhancedStatusCodesEnabled <$true | $false>]
[-ExtendedProtectionPolicy <none | allow | require>]
[-Fqdn FQDN]
[-LiveCredentialEnabled <$true | $false>]
[-LongAddressesEnabled <$true | $false>]
[-MaxAcknowledgementDelay MaxDelay]
[-MaxHeaderSize MaxHeaderBytes]
[-MaxHopCount MaxHops]
[-MaxInboundConnection <MaxConn | Unlimited>]
[-MaxInboundConnectionPercentagePerSource MaxPercentage]
[-MaxInboundConnectionPerSource <MaxConnPerSource | Unlimited>]
[-MaxLocalHopCount MaxHops]
[-MaxLogonFailures MaxLogonFailures]
[-MaxMessageSize MaxMessageSize]
[-MaxProtocolErrors <MaxErrors | Unlimited>]
[-MaxRecipientsPerMessage MaxRecipients]
[-MessageRateLimit <RateLimit | Unlimited>]
[-MessageRateSource <None | User | IPAddress | All>]
[-Name Name]
[-OrarEnabled <$true | $false>]
[-PermissionGroups <None | AnonymousUsers | ExchangeUsers |
ExchangeServers | ExchangeLegacyServers | Partners | Custom>]
[-PipeliningEnabled < $true | $false>]
[-ProtocolLoggingLevel <None | Verbose>]
[-RemoteIPRanges IPRange1, IPRange2, . . .]
[-RequireEHLODomain <$true | $false>]
[-RequireTLS < $true | $false>]
[-ServiceDiscoveryFqdn ServiceFqdn]
[-SizeEnabled <Disabled | Enabled | EnabledWithoutValue>]
[-SuppressXAnonymousTls < $true | $false>]
[-TarpitInterval TimeSpan]
[-TlsCertificateName "X509:<I>Issuer<S>CommonName"]
[-TlsDomainCapabilities DomainName:Capability]
```

```
[-TransportRole <None | Cafe | Mailbox | ClientAccess | UnifiedMessaging |
HubTransport | Edge | All | Monitoring | CentralAdmin |
CentralAdminDatabase | DomainController | WindowsDeploymentServer |
ProvisionedServer | LanguagePacks | FrontendTransport | CafeArray |
FfoWebService | OSP | ARR | ManagementFrontEnd | ManagementBackEnd | SCOM>]
```

Usage

```
Set-ReceiveConnector -Identity "Corpsvr127\Custom Receive Connector"
 -Bindings "0.0.0.0:425"
 -Fqdn "mailserver85.tvpress.com"
 -RemoteIPRanges "0.0.0.0-255.255.255.255"
```

Listing 8-12 Remove-ReceiveConnector cmdlet syntax and usage

Syntax

```
Remove-ReceiveConnector -Identity ConnectorIdentity
 [-Confirm <$true | $false >]
 [-DomainController DCName]
```

Usage

```
Remove-ReceiveConnector -Identity "CorpSvr127\Imaginedlands.com Receive
Connector"
```

Creating Connectors with Exchange Online

Exchange Online uses Inbound and Outbound connectors, rather than Receive and
Send connectors. Inbound connectors control mail flowing from the Internet, a
partner, or a specific server. Outbound connectors control the flow of mail sent by
recipients in the organization. When mailbox users in the online organization are
sending mail, you can use Outbound connectors to direct messages to a server that
applies additional processing before delivering the mail to its destination.

When you run the Hybrid Configuration Wizard to create a hybrid organization that
combines an on-premises Exchange organization with an online Exchange
organization, a Send connector is created automatically in the on-premises Exchange
organization to route mail to Exchange Online and a Receive connector is created
automatically to receive mail from Exchange Online. Similarly, an Outbound
connector is created automatically in the online Exchange organization to route mail

to on-premises Exchange, and an Inbound connector is created automatically to receive mail from on-premises Exchange.

The automatically created Inbound and Outbound connectors have the connector type set as On-Premises. To view and manage inbound or outbound connectors, access Exchange Admin Center for Exchange Online. Next, select Mail Flow in the Feature pane, and then select Connectors, as shown in Figure 8-8.

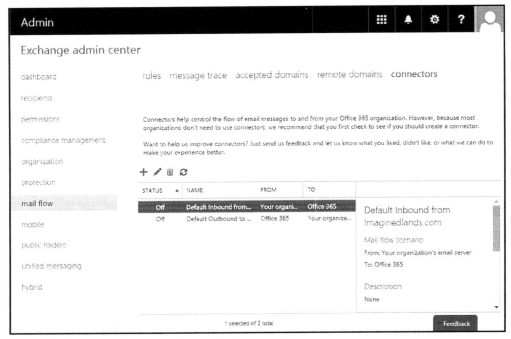

FIGURE 8-8 Viewing connectors in Exchange Online.

You can create additional Inbound and Outbound connectors to control mail flow from and to trusted partners. These additional connectors have the connector type set as Partner, rather than On-Premises. By default, connectors use opportunistic TLS for connection security. This means connectors try to use TLS security for connections but if TLS cannot be used, they establish a standard SMTP connection instead.

To create Inbound or Outbound connectors, click Add (＋). Use the selection lists provided to specify where messages are being routed from and to, such as from Internet to Office 365 or from a partner organization to Office 365. Next, use the options provided to configure the connectors much as you would configure Send and Receive connectors.

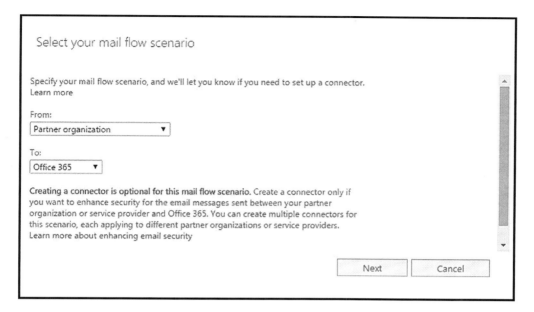

You also can connect to Exchange Online in Windows PowerShell and then use the New-InboundConnector or New-OutboundConnector cmdlet to create a connector. Each connector type has corresponding Set, Get, and Remove cmdlets as well. These are Set-InboundConnector, Get-InboundConnector, and Remove-InboundConnector as well as Set-OutboundConnector, Get-OutboundConnector, and Remove-OutboundConnector.

Chapter 9. Configuring Transport Services

You can configure your Microsoft Exchange Server 2016 organization with only Mailbox servers for message routing and delivery, or you can configure it with Mailbox servers and Edge Transport servers. When you use only Mailbox servers, these servers are responsible for:

- Messaging routing and delivery within the organization.
- Receiving messages from outside the organization and delivering them to Mailbox servers within the organization.
- Receiving messages from Mailbox servers within the organization and routing them to destinations outside the organization.

When you use both Mailbox servers and Edge Transport servers, message routing and delivery works like this:

- Mailbox servers handle message routing and delivery within the organization.
- Edge Transport servers receive messages from outside the organization and route them to Mailbox servers within the organization which, in turn, deliver them to other Mailbox servers if necessary.
- Mailbox servers receive messages from Mailbox servers within the organization and route them to Edge Transport servers, which, in turn, route them to destinations outside the organization.

> **NOTE** In a mixed environment where Exchange 2010 Hub Transports are deployed, the Hub Transport servers work with Mailbox servers and Edge Transport servers to route and deliver messages.

When you use Edge Transport servers in a hybrid deployment, your Edge Transport servers can be configured to handle communications between on-premises Exchange and Exchange Online. Here, the Edge Transport servers act as relays between your internal Exchange servers and Exchange Online, as long as the Edge Transport servers are externally accessible from the Internet on port 25. Additionally, at this time, only Edge Transport servers running Exchange 2010 Service Pack 2 or later support hybrid deployments.

The primary mail protocol used by Exchange Server 2016 is Simple Mail Transfer Protocol (SMTP). This chapter discusses how transport servers use SMTP for routing and delivery, as well as how you can view and manage transport server configurations.

> **REAL WORLD**   Microsoft recommends that you install the Edge Transport server role on a computer that is not part of the internal Active Directory domain. The server can, however, be part of an external Active Directory domain, which isolates the computer and is the most secure implementation. Although you can install the Edge Transport server on a domain-joined computer, the Edge Transport server role will always use Active Directory Lightweight Directory Services (AD LDS) to store recipient and configuration information for the Edge stack, and the underlying Windows stack will use Active Directory Domain Services (AD DS). To send and receive messages from your organization to the Internet, Edge Transport servers use Send connectors and Receive connectors.
>
> Prior to installing the Edge Transport role, you need to set the Domain Name System (DNS) suffix for the server and install the AD LDS role. Generally, you'll want to use a DNS suffix for your organization's primary domain. To install the AD LDS role, use the Add Roles Wizard in the Server Manager. Accept the default settings during installation with one exception: you do not need to create an application partition because AD LDS will be configured for the Edge Transport server role when you install the role, and the required application partition will also be created at that time.

Optimizing Transport Limits

Exchange Server 2016 automatically places receive size, send size, and other limits on messages being routed through an Exchange organization. The limits you can control include:

- Message header limits control the total size of all message header fields in a message. Header limits primarily apply to Receive connectors, although they also apply to messages in the pickup directory used by the Transport service. Header fields are plain text, and so the size of the header is determined by the total number of header fields and characters in each header field. Each character of text is 1 byte.
- Message receive size limits control the total size of messages that can be received, which includes the message header, message body, and any attachments. Exchange uses a custom message header (X-MS-Exchange-Organization-OriginalSize:) to record the original size of a message when it enters the Exchange organization. Although content conversion, encoding, and agent processing can change the size of the message, Exchange uses the lower value of the current or original message size to determine whether the limit applies.
- Message send size limits control the total size of messages that can be sent, which includes the message header, message body, and any attachments.
- Attachment size limits control the maximum size of each individual attachment within a message.

- Recipient limits control the total number of message recipients, with an unexpanded distribution group counted as a single recipient. When a message is composed, recipients are listed in the To:, Cc:, and Bcc: header fields. When a message is submitted for delivery, these recipients are converted into Rcpt To: entries in the message.

> **NOTE** Unlike other limits, exceeding a recipient limit doesn't automatically mean a message will be rejected. The message may be accepted for the first N recipients and then resent by the SMTP server in groups of N recipients until the message is delivered to all recipients.

A message that exceeds any applicable limit is rejected and a non-delivery report is issued to the sender with an error code, status, and description. Transport limits are configured for the organization as a whole, for individual send and receive connectors, for specific servers, for specific users, and for specific Active Directory site links.

As part of your planning for message size limits, you need to consider that base64 encoding will be applied to attachments and any binary data in messages. Base64 encoding increases the size of the attachments and the binary data by approximately 33 percent and in this way increases the total size of a message. Thus, attachments with a total original size of 27 MB could cause a message to exceed a send or receive limit of 35 MB.

Setting Organizational Transport Limits

Organizational transport limits apply to all transport servers in the organization, which includes Exchange 2016 Mailbox servers, Exchange 2010 Hub Transport servers and Exchange 2007 Hub Transport servers. By default, the maximum message size that can be received or sent by recipients in the organization is 10,240 KB and messages can have no more than 500 recipients.

You can view or change the default limits for the Exchange organization by completing the following steps:

1. In the Exchange Admin Center, select Mail Flow in the Feature pane, and then select either Receive Connectors or Send Connectors.

2. In the main pane, select the More button (**•••**), and then click Organization Transport Settings. In the Organization Transport Settings dialog box, the Limits page is selected by default, as shown in Figure 9-1.

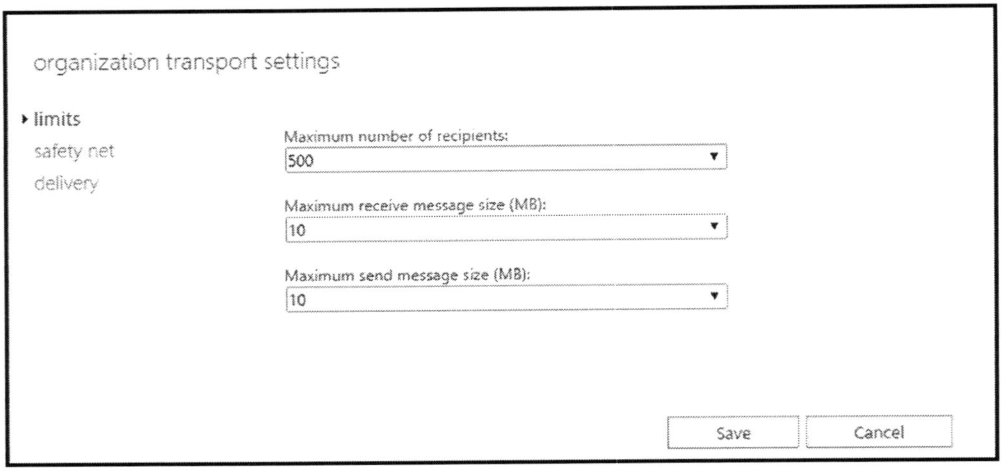

organization transport settings

▸ limits
  safety net
  delivery

Maximum number of recipients:
[500 ▾]

Maximum receive message size (MB):
[10 ▾]

Maximum send message size (MB):
[10 ▾]

[Save]　[Cancel]

FIGURE 9-1 Set transport limits for the Exchange organization.

3. To set a maximum number of recipients limit, type the desired limit in the Maximum Number Of Recipients combo box. The valid input range is 0 to 2,147,483,647. If you use a value of 0, no limit is imposed on the number of recipients in a message. Note that Exchange handles an unexpanded distribution group as one recipient.

4. To set a maximum receive size limit, type the desired receive limit in the related combobox. The valid input range is 0 to 2047.999 MB. If you use a value of 0 or select Unlimited in the dropdown list, no limit is imposed on the message size that can be received by recipients in the organization.

5. To set a maximum send size limit, type the desired send limit in the related combobox. The valid input range is 0 to 2047.999 MB. If you use a value of 0 or select Unlimited in the dropdown list, no limit is imposed on the message size that can be sent by senders in the organization.

6. Click Save to apply your settings.

In Exchange Management Shell, you assign the desired transport limits by using the Set-TransportConfig cmdlet, as shown in Listing 9-1. The –MaxReceiveSize and –MaxSendSize parameters set the maximum receive size and maximum send size, respectively. The -MaxRecipientEnvelopeLimit parameter sets the maximum number of recipients in a message. When you use the –MaxReceiveSize and –MaxSendSize parameters, you must specify the units for values by using KB for kilobytes, MB for megabytes, or GB for gigabytes. Your changes are made at the organization level and apply to the entire Exchange Server 2016 organization.

LISTING 9-1 Setting transport limits

Syntax

```
Set-TransportConfig [-Identity OrgId] [-DomainController DCName]
[-MaxReceiveSize <'MaxSize' | 'Unlimited'>]
[-MaxSendSize <'MaxSize' | 'Unlimited'>]
[-MaxRecipientEnvelopeLimit <'MaxRecipients' | 'Unlimited'>]
```

Usage

```
Set-TransportConfig -MaxReceiveSize '15MB' -MaxSendSize '15MB'
 -MaxRecipientEnvelopeLimit '1000'
```

You can control the maximum message size and maximum attachment size for all Mailbox servers in the organization by using transport rules. To do this, use the -MessageSizeOver and -AttachmentSizeOver parameters of New-TransportRule or Set-TransportRule.

Setting Connector Transport Limits

The transport limits of a connector apply to any message that uses a specified connector for message delivery. Exchange 2016 automatically sets transport limits on Send and Receive connectors. Most connectors have a maximum message size limit of 35 MB by default. The exceptions are the Default Frontend and Outbound Proxy Frontend Receive connectors, which have a 36 MB limit by default.

You can view the current maximum message size limits for all send connectors by entering the following command in Exchange Management Shell:

```
get-sendconnector | fl name, maxmessagesize
```

To view the current maximum size of all receive connectors, enter:

```
get-receiveconnector | fl name, maxmessagesize
```

You can modify the default maximum message size limit by using the -MaxMessageSize parameter of the New-ReceiveConnector, Set-ReceiveConnector, New-SendConnector, and Set-SendConnector cmdlets.

Receive connectors also have default limits on the maximum number of recipients and the maximum header size. Most of the default Receive connectors have a limit of 200 recipients by default. The exception is the Default Receive connector which has a limit of 5,000 recipients by default.

The default Receive connectors and any other Receive connectors you create automatically have a 128 KB maximum header size limit. Although Exchange adds headers to messages during content conversion, encoding, and agent processing, the number of recipients in a message is the most common reason a message exceeds the maximum header size limit. Each character in a recipient's name and email address counts against the limit. If a message is rejected because it exceeds the maximum header size limit, the sender should receive a non-delivery report. This non-delivery report may contain an error status code of 4.4.7, which can help you identify the problem as relating to the maximum header size limit.

In the shell, you can view the current recipient and header size limits for all receive connectors by entering:

```
get-receiveconnector |fl name, maxheadersize, maxrecipientspermessage
```

You can modify the recipient and header limits by using the -MaxRecipientsPerMessage and -MaxHeaderSize parameters of the New-ReceiveConnector and Set-ReceiveConnector cmdlets.

Setting Server Transport Limits

The transport limits of a server apply to any message processed by the server. If a user's mailbox is on a particular Mailbox server, the maximum header size and maximum number of recipient limits for the pickup directory apply. You can configure these limits on a per-server basis as discussed in Chapter 10, "Maintaining Mail Flow" in the "Configuring Messaging Limits for the Pickup Directory" section.

Per-server transport limits also apply to the front-end transport services. The maximum message size for Outlook Web App is 33 MB. Exchange ActiveSync and

Exchange Web Services have maximum message size limits of 10 MB and 64 MB respectively. To change these values, you must edit the appropriate web.config configuration file on each Mailbox server. The configuration files are formatted with XML and can be edited in any standard text editor, including Notepad.exe.

> **IMPORTANT**   Before you make any changes, you might want to create a copy of each of the original configuration files. In Notepad, you can use the Find feature on the Edit menu to search. As the default search starts at the current position, make sure you start your searches at the top of the document. One way to ensure you are at the top of the document is to press Ctrl+Home while working in Notepad.

Setting Exchange Activesync Limits

The %ExchangeInstallpath% variable is an environment variable set when you installed Exchange server. You'll find the web.config file for Exchange ActiveSync in the %ExchangeInstallpath%\ClientAccess\Sync folder. In this web.config file, the MaxDocumentDataSize key sets the maximum size of data that can be received by the ActiveSync protocol, and the MaxRequestLength value sets the maximum size of data that can be received from an ActiveSync client.

You can open the configuration file for editing in Notepad by entering the following command at a command prompt:

```
Notepad %ExchangeInstallpath%\ClientAccess\Sync\web.config
```

Or entering the following at the PowerShell prompt:

```
Notepad $env:ExchangeInstallpath\ClientAccess\Sync\web.config
```

> **REAL WORLD**   If you're using Exchange Management Shell rather than a standard PowerShell prompt, keep in mind Exchange Management Shell does not run in elevated, administrator mode by default because your login credentials are used to create an implicit remoting session. Although you can run Exchange Management Shell in administrator mode, a new session for remoting won't be implicitly established until you run the first Exchange command.

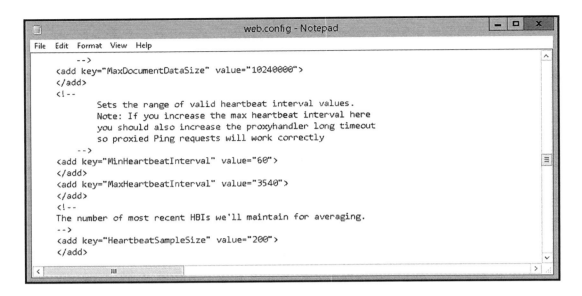

```
                -->
        <add key="MaxDocumentDataSize" value="10240000">
        </add>
        <!--
                Sets the range of valid heartbeat interval values.
                Note: If you increase the max heartbeat interval here
                you should also increase the proxyhandler long timeout
                so proxied Ping requests will work correctly
        -->
        <add key="MinHeartbeatInterval" value="60">
        </add>
        <add key="MaxHeartbeatInterval" value="3540">
        </add>
        <!--
        The number of most recent HBIs we'll maintain for averaging.
        -->
        <add key="HeartbeatSampleSize" value="200">
        </add>
```

After you open the web.config file, search for MaxDocumentDataSize, and then set the related value to the desired maximum size in kilobytes (KB). Next, search for MaxRequestLength to set the related value to the desired maximum size in bytes.

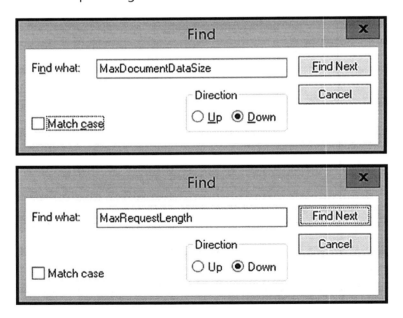

The related entries are:

```
<add key="MaxDocumentDataSize" value="10240000">
… </add>
<httpRuntime maxRequestLength="10240" />
```

When you are finished making changes, save and close the configuration file. Keep in mind that when you save the changes to the configuration file, the related web application is restarted automatically.

Confirm that Exchange ActiveSync is working as expected by entering **Test-ActiveSyncConnectivity** at the shell prompt. If there's a problem with Exchange ActiveSync, check your edits or restore the original configuration file.

Setting Exchange Web Services Limits

You'll find the web.config file for Exchange Web Services in the %ExchangeInstallpath%\ClientAccess\exchweb\ews folder. In this web.config file, the MaxAllowedContentLength value sets the maximum size of HTTP content requests and the MaxReceivedMessageSize value sets the maximum size of messages that can be accepted by Exchange Web Services.

You can open the configuration file for editing in Notepad by entering the following command at a command prompt:

```
Notepad %ExchangeInstallpath%\ClientAccess\exchweb\ews\web.config
```

Or entering the following at the shell prompt:

```
Notepad $env:ExchangeInstallpath\ClientAccess\exchweb\ews\web.config
```

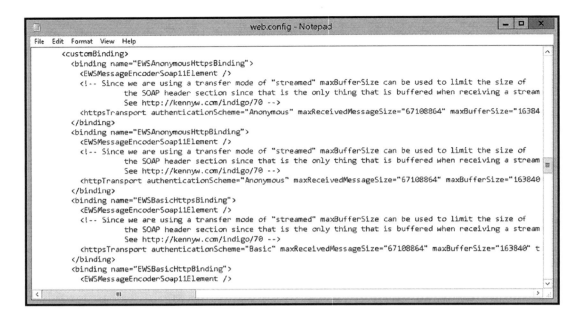

```
web.config - Notepad

File  Edit  Format  View  Help

        <customBinding>
            <binding name="EWSAnonymousHttpsBinding">
                <EWSMessageEncoderSoap11Element />
                <!-- Since we are using a transfer mode of "streamed" maxBufferSize can be used to limit the size of
                        the SOAP header section since that is the only thing that is buffered when receiving a stream
                        See http://kennyw.com/indigo/70 -->
                <httpsTransport authenticationScheme="Anonymous" maxReceivedMessageSize="67108864" maxBufferSize="16384
            </binding>
            <binding name="EWSAnonymousHttpBinding">
                <EWSMessageEncoderSoap11Element />
                <!-- Since we are using a transfer mode of "streamed" maxBufferSize can be used to limit the size of
                        the SOAP header section since that is the only thing that is buffered when receiving a stream
                        See http://kennyw.com/indigo/70 -->
                <httpTransport authenticationScheme="Anonymous" maxReceivedMessageSize="67108864" maxBufferSize="163840
            </binding>
            <binding name="EWSBasicHttpsBinding">
                <EWSMessageEncoderSoap11Element />
                <!-- Since we are using a transfer mode of "streamed" maxBufferSize can be used to limit the size of
                        the SOAP header section since that is the only thing that is buffered when receiving a stream
                        See http://kennyw.com/indigo/70 -->
                <httpsTransport authenticationScheme="Basic" maxReceivedMessageSize="67108864" maxBufferSize="163840" t
            </binding>
            <binding name="EWSBasicHttpBinding">
                <EWSMessageEncoderSoap11Element />
```

After you open the web.config file, search for each occurrence of MaxReceivedMessageSize to set the related value to the desired maximum size in bytes. You must set a MaxReceivedMessageSize value for each HTTP and HTTPS binding and authentication combination.

> **IMPORTANT** Although there are 16 entries for MaxReceivedMessageSize that you want to edit in total, you don't want to modify the two entries for UM bindings.

Next, search for MaxAllowedContentLength and then set the related value to the desired maximum size in bytes. When you're finished making changes, save and close the configuration file. Keep in mind that when you save the changes to the configuration file, the related web application is restarted automatically.

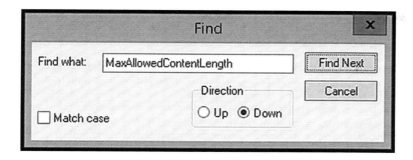

Confirm that Exchange Web Services are working as expected by entering **Test-WebServicesConnectivity** at the shell prompt. If a problem occurs with Exchange Web Services, check your edits or restore the original configuration file.

Setting Outlook Web App Limits

You'll find the web.config file for Outlook Web App in the %ExchangeInstallpath%\ClientAccess\Owa folder. In this web.config file, the MaxAllowedContentLength value key sets the maximum size of HTTP content requests, MaxReceivedMessageSize value sets the maximum size of messages that can be accepted by Outlook Web App and MaxRequestLength value sets the maximum size of data that can be received from an Outlook Web App client.

You can open the configuration file for editing in Notepad by entering the following command at a command prompt:

```
Notepad %ExchangeInstallpath%\ClientAccess\Owa\web.config
```

Or entering the following at the shell prompt:

```
Notepad $env:ExchangeInstallpath\ClientAccess\Owa\web.config
```

```
┌─────────────────────────────────────────────────────────────────────────────┐
│ ▣                          web.config - Notepad                    _ □ X      │
├─────────────────────────────────────────────────────────────────────────────┤
│ File  Edit  Format  View  Help                                               │
│       <requestFiltering>                                                   ▲  │
│         <requestLimits maxAllowedContentLength="35000000" />                  │
│       </requestFiltering>                                                     │
│     </security>                                                               │
│     <staticContent>                                                           │
│       <remove fileExtension=".manifest" />                                    │
│       <mimeMap fileExtension=".manifest" mimeType="text/cache-manifest" />    │
│       <remove fileExtension=".crx" />                                         │
│       <mimeMap fileExtension=".crx" mimeType="application/x-chrome-extension" />│
│       <remove fileExtension=".woff" />                                        │
│       <mimeMap fileExtension=".woff" mimeType="application/x-font-woff" />     │
│     </staticContent>                                                          │
│     <caching>                                                                 │
│       <profiles>                                                              │
│         <add extension=".manifest" policy="DisableCache" kernelCachePolicy="DontCache" />│
│ ◀    III                                                                ▶ .:  │
└─────────────────────────────────────────────────────────────────────────────┘
```

After you open the web.config file, search for MaxAllowedContentLength, and then set the related value to the desired maximum size in bytes. Next, search for MaxReceivedMessageSize, and then set the related value to the desired maximum size in bytes. There are two entries for MaxReceivedMessageSize: one for HTTP and one for HTTPS. Finally, search for MaxRequestLength to set the related value to the desired maximum size in kilobytes. The related entries are:

```
<requestLimits maxAllowedContentLength="35000000" />
...
<binding name="httpsBinding" maxReceivedMessageSize="35000000">
...
<binding name="httpBinding" maxReceivedMessageSize="35000000">
...
<httpRuntime maxUrlLength="500" maxRequestLength="35000"
requestValidationMode="2.0" enableVersionHeader="false" />
```

When you are finished making changes, save and close the configuration file. Keep in mind that when you save the changes to the configuration file, the related web application is restarted automatically. Confirm that Outlook Web App is working as expected by entering **Test-OwaConnectivity** at the shell prompt. If a problem with Outlook Web App occurs, check your edits or restore the original configuration file.

┌───┐
│ **REAL WORLD**   By default, IIS uses overlapping recycling of worker   │
│ processes when restarting applications and application pools. With   │
│ overlapping recycling, new worker processes are started to accept new   │
│ requests from HTTP.sys while current worker processes are marked for   │
│ recycling but continue handling existing requests. When all existing requests │
│ are handled, the original worker processes shut down.   │
└───┘

Managing Message Transport

After you install Mailbox servers running Exchange Server 2016, you need to finalize the configuration of Transport services by creating and configuring a postmaster mailbox and performing any other necessary tasks. For Exchange organizations with only Mailbox servers, you should optimize anti-spam features. For Exchange organizations with Edge Transport servers, you need to subscribe the Edge Transport servers to your Exchange organization.

Configuring the Postmaster Address and Mailbox

Every organization that sends and receives mail should have a postmaster address. This is the email address listed on nondelivery reports and other delivery status notification reports created by Exchange Server. The postmaster address is not set by default; therefore, you must manually set it.

To view your Exchange organization's postmaster address, enter the following command at Exchange Management Shell prompt:

```
Get-TransportConfig | Format-List Name,ExternalPostMasterAddress
```

This command lists the postmaster address for the organization, as shown in this sample output:

```
Name:                     Transport Settings
ExternalPostmasterAddress : postmaster@tvpress.com
```

If you don't set the postmaster address, the address typically is set to $null, except when you have an Edge Transport server that hasn't been through the Edge Sync process. To change the postmaster address, you can use the –ExternalPostMasterAddress parameter of the Set-TransportServer cmdlet, as shown in this example:

```
Set-TransportConfig -ExternalPostMasterAddress "nondelivery@tvpress.com"
```

If you want the postmaster address to be able to receive mail, you must either create a mailbox and associate it with the postmaster address or assign the postmaster address as a secondary email address for an existing mailbox.

You also can view or change the organization's postmaster address by completing the following steps:

1. In the Exchange Admin Center, select Mail Flow in the Feature pane, and then select either Receive Connectors or Send Connectors.

2. In the main pane, select the More button (•••), and then click Organization Transport Settings to display the Organization Transport Settings dialog box.

3. On the Delivery page, the current postmaster email address is listed (if any). If you want to change the postmaster address, enter the address you want to use, and then click Save.

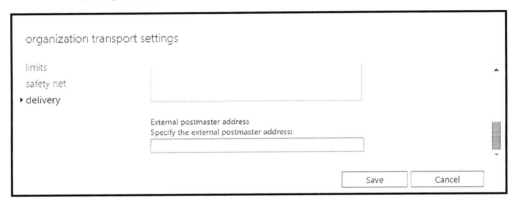

On the Delivery page, you also can specify the delivery status notification (DSN) codes that should be monitored. The postmaster receives a copy of any non-delivery reports delivered to internal senders with these codes. Codes you may want to have monitored include:

- **4.3.1** Issued when there are insufficient resources on the Mailbox server, usually as a result of a resource problem. Note that the report may state an out-of-memory error when the actual error that occurred was caused by a full disk.
- **4.3.2** Issued when the system is not accepting network messages often caused by a frozen queue. To resolve the problem, unfreeze the queue.
- **4.4.7** Issued when a message expires before it can be relayed or delivered, typically occurring as a result of a time-out during communication with a remote server. It also can indicate a message header limit has been reached, so the sender may need to reduce the number of recipients in the message.
- **5.3.5** Issued when a server is improperly configured, specifically when the server is configured to loop mail back to itself. To resolve the problem, check the server's connectors for loops.

- **5.4.6** Issued when a routing loop is detected, specifically when the delivery of a message generates another message and that message then generates another message, and so forth. If the message generating loop continues more than 20 times, this error is issued. To resolve the error, check the mailbox rules associated with the recipients and senders to determine how automatic message forwarding is configured.

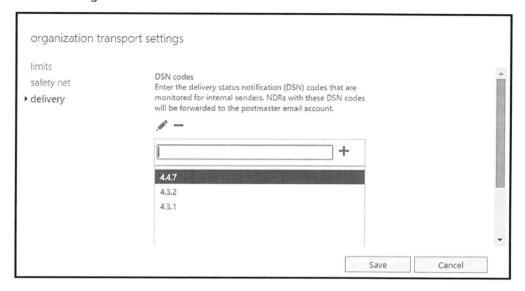

Configuring Shadow Redundancy

Shadow redundancy ensures that messages are protected from loss the entire time they are in transit by creating a copy of a message and retaining this copy while a message is in transit. If any transport server along the route fails to report a successful delivery, Exchange resubmits the message for delivery to ensure that the message continues through to its destination.

By default, shadow redundancy is enabled in the Transport service on all Mailbox servers. Exchange 2016 makes a redundant copy of any message it receives before acknowledging receipt. This approach ensures the message will be delivered even if the receiving server were to shut down immediately after acknowledging receipt of a message. Prior to this approach, a message could possibly be lost if the receiving server were to shut down after acknowledging receipt of a message but before creating a copy of the message.

Thanks to shadow redundancy, as long as you have multiple transport servers (and multiple Edge Transports if you've deployed Edge Transport servers), you can remove any transport server that fails and not have to worry about emptying its queues or losing messages. You also can upgrade or replace a Mailbox or Edge Transport server at any time without the risk of losing messages. If you have a single Mailbox server, you should drain all SMTP queues on the server before performing maintenance. The same is true if you have a single Edge Transport. This ensures that there is no risk of message loss, even without shadow redundancy. Keep in mind that if you have a single transport server, and it fails and must be replaced, you've likely lost data if you can't restore the mail.que file.

> **IMPORTANT** Shadow redundancy requires multiple servers. Your Mailbox servers can be standalone servers or they can be part of a database availability group. However, with standalone servers, each Active Directory site with Mailbox servers must have two or more standalone servers. Although there must be multiple members of a database availability group for shadow redundancy to work, the members of that group can be in different Active Directory sites.

When you work with shadow redundancy, a key concept to understand is that the primary transport server has ownership of the messages in its shadow queue. The first primary owner is always the server on which the message originates. As the message travels through the transport pipeline, different transport servers may become the primary owner of a message. In addition, if a primary owner fails, another server can take over as the primary.

Shadow redundancy is implemented according to high availability transport (HAT) boundaries in the organization. Each Active Directory site with Mailbox servers in the organization is a HAT boundary, as is each Database Availability group in the organization. Within a HAT boundary, two copies of a message are always in transit: the original and the redundant copy.

It's important to point out that the original copy and the redundant copy exist on different servers. When a Mailbox server receives a message, it makes a redundant copy of the message on another Mailbox server in the HAT boundary before acknowledging receipt of the message. With database availability groups, the Transport service prefers creating the redundant copy in a remote site to ensure site resilience.

The basic process works like this:

1. The primary server transmits a copy of the message to the Transport service on another Mailbox server, and the Transport service on the other Mailbox server acknowledges that the copy of the message was created successfully. The copy of the message is the shadow message, and the Mailbox server that holds it is the shadow server for the primary server. The message exists in a shadow queue on the shadow server.

2. After the primary server receives acknowledgement from the shadow server, the primary server acknowledges the receipt of the primary message to the original SMTP server in the original SMTP session, and the SMTP session is closed.

3. The primary server transmits the message. If the primary server transmits the message outside the HAT boundary and the receiving SMTP server acknowledges successful receipt of the message, the primary server moves the primary message into its Safety Net queue. Otherwise, if the ultimate destination for the message is within the HAT boundary, the primary message is moved into the Safety Net queue when the message is accepted by the Transport service on a Mailbox server that holds the ultimate destination for the message.

4. The shadow server moves the shadow message to its Safety Net queue.

This process is complex and can be difficult to understand, so let's take another look at the process. Step-by-step, the process works like this:

1. An SMTP server transmits a message to the Transport service on a Mailbox server in the Exchange organization. The receiving Mailbox server becomes the primary server for the message, and the original message is the primary message.

2. While the original SMTP session with the SMTP server is still active, the Transport service on the primary server opens a new, simultaneous SMTP session with the Transport service on another Mailbox server in the HAT boundary.

3. The primary server transmits a copy of the message to the Transport service on the other Mailbox server. The copy of the message is the shadow message, and the Mailbox server that holds it is the shadow server for the primary server. The message exists in a shadow queue on the shadow server.

4. After the primary server receives an acknowledgement from the shadow server that confirms the copy of the message was created, the primary server acknowledges the receipt of the primary message to the original SMTP server in the original SMTP session, and the SMTP session is closed.

5. The primary server transmits the message. The primary server and the shadow server stay in contact with each other to track the progress of the message.

6. When the primary server successfully transmits the message and the receiving SMTP server acknowledges successful receipt of the message, the primary server updates the discard status of the message to show delivery is complete and relays this to the shadow server.

7. The shadow server moves the shadow message from the shadow queue to its Safety Net queue.

In Exchange Management Shell, you configure shadow redundancy for the on-premises Exchange organization by using the Set-TransportConfig cmdlet, as shown in Listing 9-2. The related parameters are used as follows:

- **MaxDumpsterTime**   Only used by Hub Transport servers in a coexistence scenario. Specifies the maximum amount of time that a delivered message will remain in the transport dumpster for possible resubmission. The default is seven days.
- **MaxRetriesForLocalSiteShadow**   When member servers in a database availability group span multiple Active Directory sites and ShadowMessagePreferenceSetting is configured to prefer remote sites, you can use this option to control how many times the primary server tries to create the shadow copy on a server in the local site after failing to create the copy in a remote site. By default, this option is set to 2. If the preference is for LocalOnly, this option controls the number of times the primary server tries to create the shadow copy on a server in the local site before failing and rejecting the message with a transient error.
- **MaxRetriesForRemoteSiteShadow**   When member servers in a database availability group span multiple Active Directory sites and ShadowMessagePreferenceSetting is configured to prefer remote sites, you can use this option to control how many times the primary server tries to create the shadow copy on a server in a remote site before trying to create the shadow copy on a server in the local site. By default, this option is set to 4. If the preference is for RemoteOnly, this option controls the number of times the primary server tries to create the shadow copy on a server in a remote site before failing and rejecting the message with a transient error.
- **RejectMessageOnShadowFailure**   Determines whether a primary message can be accepted or acknowledged without a shadow copy being created first. This option is disabled by default. If you enable this option and a shadow copy cannot be created, the primary message will be rejected with a transient error. Enable this option only when you must ensure a shadow copy of a message is always created and multiple Mailbox servers exist in each HAT boundary.

- **ShadowHeartbeatFrequency**   Sets the amount of time a transport server waits before establishing a connection to the primary server to check the discard status of shadow messages. The default value is two minutes. Set this value according to the size of your Exchange implementation, the level of messaging traffic, and the relative latency on the network. For example, in a large global organization where transport servers handle an extremely high volume of messages, you might want to set a longer time interval, although the default may suffice for a smaller organization.

- **ShadowMessageAutoDiscardInterval**   Sets the amount of time a server retains discard events for successfully delivered shadow messages. Primary servers queue discard events until they are checked by the shadow server or until the discard interval has elapsed, whichever comes first. The default value is two days. Set the value according to the size of your Exchange implementation, the level of messaging traffic, and the relative reliability of your network. For example, in a large global organization where transport servers handle an extremely high volume of messages on a highly reliable network, you might want to set a shorter discard interval, whereas the default may suffice for a smaller organization.

- **ShadowMessagePreferenceSetting**   When member servers in a database availability group span multiple Active Directory sites, you can use this option to control remote site preferences. By default, this option is set to PreferRemote. Here, the primary server attempts to create a shadow copy on a server in a remote site. If this fails, the primary server attempts to create a shadow copy on a server in the local site. Alternatively, you can specify that the copy should only be made in the local site or only in a remote site. To do this, set the value to LocalOnly or RemoteOnly respectively.

- **ShadowRedundancyEnabled**   Enables or disables shadow redundancy. If you don't use shadow redundancy, you can use this parameter to disable the feature. Ideally, you'd only disable the feature temporarily or in situations in which you have a single Exchange server implementation and are experiencing problems related to this feature. By default, shadow redundancy is enabled.

- **ShadowResubmitTimeSpan**   Specifies how long a shadow server waits before deciding that the primary server has failed and assumes ownership of messages in the shadow queue for that server. The default value is three hours. Set this value according to the size of your Exchange implementation and the relative amount of latency on the network. For example, a large global organization might want to set a longer time span, whereas the default may suffice for a smaller organization.

LISTING 9-2 Setting shadow queue options

Syntax

```
Set-TransportConfig [-Identity OrgId] [-DomainController DCName]
[-MaxDumpsterTime <TimeSpan>]
[-MaxRetriesForLocalSiteShadow RetryCount]
```

```
[-MaxRetriesForRemoteSiteShadow RetryCount]

[-RejectMessageOnShadowFailure <$true | $false>]

[-SafetyNetHoldTime <TimeSpan>]

[-ShadowHeartbeatFrequency <TimeSpan>]

[-ShadowMessageAutoDiscardInterval <TimeSpan>]

[-ShadowMessagePreferenceSetting <PreferRemote | LocalOnly | RemoteOnly>]

[-ShadowRedundancyEnabled <$true | $false>]

[-ShadowResubmitTimeSpan <TimeSpan>]
```

Usage

```
Set-TransportConfig -MaxRetriesForLocalSiteShadow 3

-MaxRetriesForRemoteSiteShadow 4

-RejectMessageOnShadowFailure $false

-SafetyNetHoldTime "3.00:00:00"

-ShadowHeartbeatFrequency "00:05:00"

-ShadowResubmitTimeSpan "02:00:00"

-ShadowMessageAutoDiscardInterval "3.00:00:00"
```

When working with shadow redundancy, Safety Net, and queues, you also want to consider:

- **ConnectionInactivityTimeout** Configured for each Send and Receive connector by using Set-SendConnector and Set-ReceiveConnector. Sets the maximum time that an open SMTP connection between servers can remain idle before timing out. This value must be smaller than the ConnectionTimeout value. For Send connectors, the default is 10 minutes. For Receive connectors, the default is five minutes for both the Transport service and the Front End Transport service on Mailbox servers, but only one minute for Edge Transport servers.
- **ConnectionTimeout** Configured for each Receive connector using Set-ReceiveConnector. Sets the maximum time that an SMTP connection can be open between servers, even if the source server is transmitting data. The default is 10 minutes for both the Transport service and the Front End Transport service on Mailbox servers, but only five minutes for Edge Transport servers.
- **MessageExpirationTimeout** Configured for the Transport service on each Mailbox server using Set-TransportService. Specifies how long a message can remain in a queue before it expires. The default value is two days.

When configuring these settings, you'll want to consider the relative latency and speed of the network as well as level of messaging traffic. If a slow or congested network has high latency, you may need to configure higher timeout values. Keep in mind, however, that each open connection uses resources and that each connector allows a finite number of open connections. By default, with Send connectors, the maximum number of connections is 1,000 and the maximum number of connections per domain is 20.

Configuring Safety Net

All Mailbox servers use Safety Net to maintain a queue of messages that were recently delivered to recipients. As discussed in "Exchange Server Message Queues" in Chapter 5, "Managing Exchange Organizations," and in the previous section of this chapter, this feature works in conjunction with shadow redundancy. The primary server that sends a message maintains the primary Safety Net queue while a second server, called the shadow server, maintains the shadow Safety Net queue.

In Exchange Management Shell, you configure Safety Net with these parameters in mind:

- **SafetyNetHoldTime**   An organization-wide option configured for Set-TransportConfig. Specifies how long a successfully processed message is retained in the Safety Net queue. The default value is two days. Unacknowledged shadow messages expire after the sum of the SafetyNetHoldTime and the MessageExpirationTimeout elapses. Set this value according to the size of your Exchange implementation and the relative amount of latency on the network. For example, a large global organization might want to set a longer time span, although the default may suffice for a smaller organization.
- **ReplayLagTime**   Configured on individual mailbox database copies for Set-MailboxDatabaseCopy. Specifies how long the Exchange Replication service waits before replaying log files that have been copied to the passive database copy. By default, this option is not set. To ensure no data is lost and messages are available for resubmittal from the Safety Net queue, the replay lag time must be less than or equal to the safety net hold time.
- **MessageExpirationTimeout**   Configured for the Transport service on each Mailbox server using Set-TransportService. Specifies how long a message can remain in a queue before it expires. The default value is two days.
- **ShadowRedundancyEnabled**   Set using the Set-TransportConfig cmdlet. Enables or disables shadow redundancy for the Exchange organization. As Safety Net relies on shadow redundancy, you also disable Safety Net if you disable shadow redundancy.

You can use Exchange Admin Center to view or change the Safety Net hold time as well:

1. Select Mail Flow in the Feature pane, and then select either Receive Connectors or Send Connectors.

2. In the main pane, select the More button (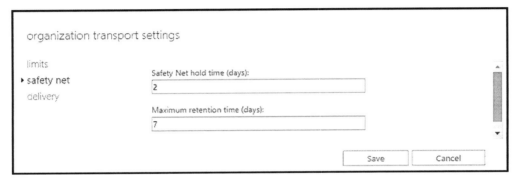), and then click Organization Transport Settings. This displays the Organization Transport Settings dialog box.

3. Click Safety Net. Finally, in the Safety Net Hold Time text box, enter the number of days that messages should be held in Safety Net queues and then click Save.

Enabling Anti-Spam Features

By default, Edge Transport servers have anti-spam features enabled and Mailbox servers do not. In an Exchange organization with Edge Transport servers, this is the desired configuration: you want your Edge Transport servers to run anti-spam filters on messages before they are routed into the Exchange organization. After Edge Transport servers have filtered messages, you don't need to filter them again, which is why Mailbox servers have this feature disabled.

If your organization doesn't use Edge Transport servers and has only Mailbox servers, you can enable the anti-spam features on Mailbox servers that receive messages from the Internet so that you can filter incoming messages for spam. However, if incoming mail has any prior anti-spam filtering, you don't need to filter messages again.

The following anti-spam agents are available for the Transport service on Mailbox servers to use:

- Content Filter agent
- Protocol Analysis agent
- Recipient Filter agent
- Sender Filter agent
- Sender ID agent

You can install and configure these agents by doing the following:

1. Log on to the Mailbox server you want to configure.

2. In Exchange Management Shell, run the following command:

`& $env:ExchangeInstallPath\Scripts\Install-AntiSpamAgents.ps1`

3. After you install the anti-spam agents, you must restart the Exchange Transport service. In the shell, you can do this by running the following command:

`Restart-service MSExchangeTransport`

4. Repeat Steps 1 - 3 for each Mailbox server that should filter messages.

5. Configure organization-wide transport settings that identify any internal SMTP servers that should be ignored by the Sender ID agent. Typically, this includes any Mailbox server in which you've enabled the anti-spam features. Use the -InternalSMTPServers parameter of Set-TransportConfig to identify each server by its IPv4 address. Here are examples:

`Set-Transportconfig -InternalSMTPServers @{Add="192.168.10.52"}`

`Set-Transportconfig -InternalSMTPServers @{Add="192.168.10.52","192.168.10.64"}`

6. You can verify that the servers were added by running the following command:

`Get-TransportConfig | fl InternalSMTPServers`

Once you've installed the anti-spam agents, you can enable or disable the anti-spam features on Mailbox servers by using the Set-TransportService cmdlet. To enable these features, set the –AntispamAgentsEnabled parameter to $true. To disable these features, set the –AntispamAgentsEnabled parameter to $false.

The following example shows how you can enable anti-spam features on a Mailbox server named CorpSvr127:

```
Set-TransportService –Identity 'CorpSvr127' –AntispamAgentsEnabled $true
```

Next you need to restart the Microsoft Exchange Transport service on the server. In the shell, you can do this by running the following command:

```
Restart-service MSExchangeTransport
```

You can now configure the transport server's anti-spam features as discussed in the "Enabling Anti-Spam Features" section in Chapter 9. When you turn on anti-spam features, a transport server can automatically get updates for spam signatures, IP reputation, and anti-spam definitions through automatic updates, as long as you've done the following:

- Conformed to Microsoft's licensing requirements
- Enabled Automatic Updates for use on the server
- Specifically enabled and configured anti-spam updates

To obtain anti-spam updates through automatic updates, Microsoft requires an Exchange Enterprise Client Access License (CAL) for each mailbox user. You can configure automatic updates by using the Windows Update utility in Control Panel. Press Windows key + I, click Control Panel\Security, and then click Windows Update to start this utility. You can also configure Automatic Updates through Group Policy.

Subscribing Edge Transport Servers

When your Exchange organization uses Edge Transport servers and you want to use the Edge Synchronization feature, you must subscribe the Edge Transport server to your Exchange organization prior to performing other configuration tasks on the Edge Transport server. Creating a subscription allows the Microsoft Exchange EdgeSync service running on designated Mailbox servers to establish one-way replication of recipient and configuration information from your internal Active Directory database to the AD LDS database on an Edge Transport server. After you create an Edge subscription, synchronization is automatic. If problems occur, however, you can force synchronization or remove the Edge subscription.

Creating an Edge Subscription

A subscribed Edge Transport server receives the following from the EdgeSync service:

- Send connector configurations
- Accepted domain configurations
- Remote domain configurations
- Safe Senders lists
- Recipients

Any manually configured accepted domains, message classifications, remote domains, and Send connectors are deleted as part of the subscription process, and the related Exchange management interfaces are locked out as well. To manage these features after a subscription is created, you must do so within the Exchange organization and have the EdgeSync service update the Edge Transport server.

Also as part of the subscription process, you must select an Active Directory site for the subscription. The Mailbox server or servers in the site are the servers responsible for replicating Active Directory information to the Edge Transport server.

You can create a subscription for an Edge Transport server by completing the following steps:

1. Log on to the Edge Transport server for which you are creating a subscription by using an administrator account.

2. At Exchange Management Shell prompt, run the following command:

New-EdgeSubscription -filename "C:\EdgeSubscriptionExport.xml"

3. When prompted, confirm that it's okay to delete any manually configured accepted domains, message classifications, remote domains, and Send connectors by pressing A (which answers Yes to all deletion prompts).

4. Copy the EdgeSubscriptionExport.xml file to a Mailbox server in your Exchange organization.

5. Log on to a Mailbox server in your Exchange organization by using an account with Exchange administration privileges.

6. On the Mailbox server, import the Edge Subscription file by running the following command:

New-EdgeSubscription -filename *FilePath*

Where FilePath specifies the full file path to the Edge Subscription file, such as:

New-EdgeSubscription -filename "C:\EdgeSubscriptionExport.xml"

Initial synchronization will begin, as discussed in "Synchronizing Edge Subscriptions." Note that Mailbox servers in the Active Directory site must be able to resolve the IP addresses for the Edge Transport server. You need to ensure that subnets have been created in Active Directory Sites And Services and that DNS is configured to resolve the fully qualified domain name of the Edge Transport server. Mailbox servers in the site must also be able to connect to the Edge Transport server over TCP port 50636.

Listing 9-3 provides the syntax and usage for using the New-EdgeSubscription cmdlet to start a subscription. By default, the –CreateInboundSendConnector parameter is set to $true, which ensures that a Send connector from the Edge Transport server to Mailbox servers is created. By default, the –CreateInternetSendConnector parameter is set to true, which ensures that a Send connector to the Internet is created.

LISTING 9-3 New-EdgeSubscription cmdlet syntax and usage

Syntax

```
New-EdgeSubscription -FileName FilePath
 -Site SiteName [-AccountExpiryDuration <TimeSpan>]
[-CreateInboundSendConnector <$true | $false>]
[-CreateInternetSendConnector <$true | $false>]
[-DomainController DCName] [-FileData ByteStr] [-Force <$true | $false>]
```

Usage

```
New-EdgeSubscription -FileName "Z:\EdgeSubscriptionExport.xml"
-Site "Default-First-Site-Name"
-CreateInboundSendConnector $true
-CreateInternetSendConnector $true
```

Getting Edge Subscription Details

You get information about Edge subscriptions using the Get-EdgeSubscription cmdlet. Each Edge subscription is listed by Edge Transport server name and associated Active Directory site. If you do not provide an identity with this cmdlet, configuration information for all Edge Subscriptions is returned.

LISTING 9-4 Get-EdgeSubscription cmdlet syntax and usage

Syntax

```
Get-EdgeSubscription -Identity EdgeTransportServerName
[-DomainController DCName]
```

Usage

```
Get-EdgeSubscription -Identity "EdgeSvr04"
Get-EdgeSubscription -Identity "EdgeSvr04" | fl
```

Synchronizing Edge Subscriptions

During the configuration of an Edge subscription, you specified an Active Directory site to associate with the subscription. Mailbox servers in this site run the EdgeSync service and are responsible for synchronizing configuration data between Active Directory Domain Services and AD LDS on the Edge Transport server. By default, the EdgeSync service synchronizes configuration data hourly and recipient data every four hours.

If you've just created a new subscription and synchronization has occurred, you should verify that replication is taking place as expected by completing the following steps:

1. On the Edge Transport server, start Exchange Management Shell.
2. Verify that a Send connector was created to send Internet mail by typing the command **get-sendconnector.** As shown in the following example and sample output, you should see an Inbound connector and an Internet connector for EdgeSync:

```
get-sendconnector

Identity                      AddressSpaces      Enabled
--------                      -------------      -------

Primary Send Connector        {SMTP:*.tvpress.com;1}   True
SD1 Send Connector            {SMTP:*.imaginedlands.com;1}   True
```

```
EdgeSync - Seattle-First-Site to Int   {smtp:*;100}        True
EdgeSync - Inbound to Seattle-First-   {smtp:--;100}        True
```

3. Verify that there is at least one entry for accepted domains by typing get-accepteddomain as shown in the following example and sample output:

```
get-accepteddomain
```

Name	DomainName	DomainType	Default
tvpress.com	tvpress.com	Authoritative	True

If you suspect there is a problem with synchronization and you want to start immediate synchronization of configuration data for all Edge subscriptions, complete the following steps:

4. Start Exchange Management Shell.

5. At the prompt, type the following command

```
start-edgesynchronization –Server ServerName
```

where **ServerName** is the name of the Mailbox server on which you want to run the command, such as:

```
start-edgesynchronization –Server mailserver25
```

If you are running the command on the Mailbox server, you can omit the –Server parameter.

Verifying Edge Subscriptions

The easiest way to verify the subscription status of Edge Transport servers is to run the Test-EdgeSynchronization cmdlet. This cmdlet provides a report of the synchronization status, and you also can use it to verify that a specific recipient has been synchronized to the Active Directory Lightweight Directory Service on an Edge Transport server.

Listing 9-5 provides the syntax and usage for the Test-EdgeSynchronization cmdlet. By default, the cmdlet verifies configuration objects and recipient objects. To have the cmdlet verify only configuration data, set –ExcludeRecipientTest to $true. Use the –VerifyRecipient parameter to specify the email address of a recipient to verify.

LISTING 9-5 Test-EdgeSynchronization cmdlet syntax and usage

Syntax

```
Test-EdgeSynchronization [-ExcludeRecipientTest <$true | $false>]
  [-DomainController DCName] [-FullCompareMode <$true | $false>]
  [-MaxReportSize <MaxNumberofObjectsToCheck | Unlimited>]
  [-MonitoringContext <$true | $false>] [-TargetServer EdgeServer]


Test-EdgeSynchronization -VerifyRecipient RecipientEmailAddress
[-DomainController DCName]
```

Usage

```
Test-EdgeSynchronization -ExcludeRecipientTest


Test-EdgeSynchronization -MaxReportSize 500


Test-EdgeSynchronization -VerifyRecipient "williams@tvpress.com"


Test-EdgeSynchronization -TargetServer CorpServer73.tvpress.com
```

Example and sample output

```
test-edgesynchronization

RunspaceId                :
UtcNow                    : 3/18/2016 3:11:22 PM
Name                      : CORPSERVER73
LeaseHolder               : CN=MAILSERVER25,CN=Servers,CN=Exchange
Administrative Group (FYDIBOHF23SPDLT),CN=Administrative Groups,
CN=First Organization,CN=Microsoft Exchange,CN=Services,CN=Configuration,
DC=cpandl,DC=com
LeaseType                 : Option
ConnectionResult          : Succeeded
FailureDetail             :
LeaseExpiryUtc            : 3/18/2016 3:06:30 PM
LastSynchronizedUtc       : 3/18/2016 3:11:59 PM
CredentialStatus          : Synchronized
TransportServerStatus     : Synchronized
```

```
TransportConfigStatus          : Synchronized
AcceptedDomainStatus           : Synchronized
RemoteDomainStatus             : Synchronized
SendConnectorStatus            : Synchronized
MessageClassificationStatus    : Synchronized
RecipientStatus                : Synchronized
CredentialRecords              : Number of credentials 85
CookieRecords                  : Number of cookies 27
```

Removing Edge Subscriptions

If you replace or decommission an Edge Transport server, you no longer need the related Edge subscription and can remove it. Removing an Edge subscription

- Stops synchronization of information from the Active Directory Domain Service to AD LDS.
- Removes all the accounts that are stored in AD LDS.
- Removes the Edge Transport server from the source server list of any Send connector.

In Exchange Management Shell, you can remove an Edge Subscription by passing the identity of the subscription to remove to the Remove-EdgeSubscription cmdlet. Listing 9-6 provides the syntax and usage.

SAMPLE 9-6 Remove-EdgeSubscription cmdlet syntax and usage

Syntax

```
Remove-EdgeSubscription -Identity EdgeTransportServerName
[-DomainController DCName] [-Force <$true | $false>]
```

Usage

```
Remove-EdgeSubscription -Identity "EdgeSvr04"
```

Chapter 10. Maintaining Mail Flow

With Exchange 2016, mail flow occurs through a collection of services, connections, components, and queues that work together as part of the transport pipeline. The Front End Transport service acts as a stateless proxy for all inbound and outbound external SMTP traffic. The Microsoft Exchange Transport service (running as a back-end component) categorizes messages, inspects their content, and queues them for delivery or submission.

Message delivery is handled by the Mailbox Transport Delivery service, and message submission is handled by the Mailbox Transport Submission service—both of which are components of the Microsoft Exchange Transport service. Although the transport pipeline is critical to mail flow, many other factors also affect mail flow in an Exchange organization, including the configuration of message processing speeds, message throttling, accepted domains, email address policies, journal rules, remote domains, filters, and transport rules.

Managing Message Routing and Delivery

To support message routing and delivery, Mailbox and Edge Transport servers maintain a few special directories:

- **Pickup**   A folder to which users and applications can manually create and submit new messages for delivery.
- **Replay**   A folder for messages bound for or received from non-SMTP mail connectors.

The sections that follow discuss how the Pickup and Replay directories are used and configured and also look at the related concepts of message throttling and back pressure.

Understanding Message Pickup and Replay

When a Mailbox or an Edge Transport server receives incoming mail from a server using a non-SMTP connector, it stores the message in the Replay directory and then resubmits it for delivery using SMTP. When a Mailbox or an Edge Transport server has a message to deliver to a non-SMTP connector, it stores the message in the Replay directory and then resubmits it for delivery to the foreign connector. In this way, messages received from non-SMTP connectors are processed and routed, and messages to non-SMTP connectors are delivered.

Your Transport servers automatically process any correctly formatted .eml message file copied into the Pickup directory. Exchange considers a message file that is copied into the Pickup directory to be correctly formatted if it meets the following conditions:

- Is a text file that complies with the basic SMTP message format and can also use Multipurpose Internet Mail Extension (MIME) header fields and content
- Has an .eml file name extension, zero or one email address in the Sender field, and one or more email addresses in the From field
- Has at least one email address in the To, Cc, or Bcc fields and a blank line between the header fields and the message body

Transport servers check the Pickup directory for new message files every five seconds. Although you can't modify this polling interval, you can adjust the rate of message file processing by using the –PickupDirectoryMaxMessagesPerMinute parameter on the Set-TransportServer cmdlet. The default value is 100 messages per minute. When a transport server picks up a message, it checks the message against the maximum message size, the maximum header size, the maximum number of recipients, and other messaging limits.

For the Pickup directory, the maximum message size is 10 megabytes (MB), the maximum header size is 64 kilobytes (KB), and the maximum number of recipients is 100 by default. As may be necessary to meet the needs of your organization, you can change these limits by using the Set-TransportServer cmdlet. If a message file doesn't exceed any assigned limits, the Transport server renames the message file by using a .tmp extension, and then converts the .tmp file to an email message. After the message is successfully queued for delivery, the Transport server issues a "close" command and deletes the .tmp file from the Pickup directory.

REAL WORLD   Header fields are plain text, and each character of text is 1 byte. The size of the header is determined by the total number of header fields and characters in each header field. Organization X-headers, forest X-headers, and routing headers are removed from messages in the Pickup directory. On the other head, routing headers are preserved in the Replay directory, and organization X-headers and forest X-headers also are preserved if an X-CreatedBy header field indicates the headers were created by Exchange 2016 (meaning the field value is set to MSExchange15).

Your Transport servers automatically process any correctly formatted .eml message file copied into the Replay directory. Exchange considers a message file that is copied into the Replay directory to be correctly formatted if it meets the following conditions:

- Is a text file that complies with the basic SMTP message format and can also use MIME header fields and content.
- Has an .eml file name extension, and its X-header fields occur before all regular header fields.
- Has a blank line between the header fields and the message body.

Transport servers check the Replay directory for new message files every five seconds. Although you can't modify this polling interval, you can adjust the rate of message file processing by using the –PickupDirectoryMaxMessagesPerMinute parameter of the Set-TransportServer cmdlet. This parameter controls the rate of processing for both the Pickup directory and the Replay directory. The Transport server renames the message file by using a .tmp extension, and then converts the .tmp file to an email message. After the message is successfully queued for delivery, the server issues a "close" command and deletes the .tmp file from the Replay directory.

Exchange considers any improperly formatted email messages received in the Pickup or Replay directory to be undeliverable and renames them from the standard message name (*MessageName*.eml) to a bad message name (*MessageName*.bad). Because this is considered a type of message-processing failure, a related error is also generated in the event logs. In addition, if you restart the Microsoft Exchange Transport service when .tmp files are in the Pickup directory, Replay directory, or both directories, all .tmp files are renamed as .eml files and are reprocessed, which can lead to duplicate message transmissions.

Configuring and Moving the Pickup and Replay Directories

Because of the way message pickup and replay works, Transport servers do not perform security checks on messages submitted through these directories. This means that if you've configured anti-spam, antivirus, sender filtering, or recipient filtering actions on a Send connector, those checks are not performed on the Pickup or Replay directory. To ensure that the Pickup and Replay directories are not compromised by malicious users, specific security permissions that must be tightly controlled are applied.

For the Pickup and Replay directories, you must configure the following permissions:

- Full Control for Administrator
- Full Control for Local System
- Read, Write, and Delete Subfolders and Files for Network Service

When you have a need to balance the load across a server's disk drives or ensure ample free space for messages, you can move the Pickup and Replay directories to new locations. By using Set-TransportServer with the –PickupDirectoryPath parameter, you can move the location of the Pickup directory. Move the location of the Replay directory by using the –ReplayDirectoryPath parameter on the Set-TransportServer cmdlet. With either parameter, successfully changing the directory location depends on the rights that are granted to the Network Service account on the new directory location and whether the new directory already exists. Keep the following in mind:

- If the new directory does not already exist and the Network Service account has the rights to create folders and apply permissions at the new location, the new directory is created and the correct permissions are applied to it.
- If the new directory already exists, the existing folder permissions are not checked or changed. Exchange assumes you've already set the appropriate permissions.

Listing 10-1 provides the syntax and usage for moving the Pickup and Replay directories. If you want to move both the Pickup and Replay directories, you should do so in two separate commands.

LISTING 10-1 Changing the Pickup directory

Syntax

```
Set-TransportServer -Identity ServerIdentity
 [-PickupDirectoryPath LocalFolderPath]
 [-ReplayDirectoryPath LocalFolderPath]
```

Usage

```
Set-TransportServer -Identity "CorpSvr127"
 -PickupDirectoryPath "g:\Pickup"
```

Changing the Message Processing Speed

By default, Transport servers simultaneously and separately process the Pickup and Replay directories. Transport servers scan the Pickup and Replay directories for new message files once every five seconds (or 12 times per minute), and they process messages copied to either directory at a rate of 100 messages per minute, per directory. Because the polling interval is not configurable, the maximum number of messages that can be processed in either the Pickup or Replay directory during each polling interval, by default, is approximately eight (100 messages per minute divided by 12 messages processed per minute).

Although the polling interval is not configurable, the maximum number of messages that can be processed during each polling interval is configurable. You assign the desired processing rate by using the –PickupDirectoryMaxMessagesPerMinute parameter, because this processing speed is used with both the Pickup and Replay directories. You might want to adjust the message processing rate in these situations:

* If the server is unable to keep up with message processing, you might want to decrease the number of messages processed per minute to reduce processor and memory utilization.
* If the server is handling message transport for a large organization and you are seeing delays in message transport because of an abundance of messages in the Pickup directory, Replay directory, or both directories, you might want to increase the number of messages processed per minute, as long as the server can handle the additional workload.

You assign the desired processing rate by using the –PickupDirectoryMaxMessagesPerMinute parameter of the Set-TransportServer cmdlet, as shown in Listing 10-2, and this processing speed is used with both the Pickup and Replay directories. Your Transport server then attempts to process messages in each directory independently at the rate specified. You can use a per-minute message processing value between 1 and 20,000.

LISTING 10-2 Changing the message processing speed

Syntax

```
Set-TransportServer -Identity ServerIdentity
  [-PickupDirectoryMaxMessagesPerMinute Speed]
```

Usage

```
Set-TransportServer -Identity "CorpSvr127"
 -PickupDirectoryMaxMessagesPerMinute "500"
```

Configuring Messaging Limits for the Pickup Directory

The Pickup directory is used by administrators to test mail flow and by applications that create and submit their own messages. If applications are generating messages with expanded headers, such as when there are many recipients in To:, Cc:, and Bcc: header fields, you may need to modify the messaging limits for the Pickup directory.

You can set messaging limits for the Pickup directory for message header sizes and maximum recipients per message. The default message header size is 64 KB, which allows for 65,536 characters in the header. To change this setting, you can set the –PickupDirectoryMaxHeaderSize parameter of the Set-TransportServer cmdlet to the desired size. The valid input range for this parameter is 32,768 to 2,147,483,647 bytes. When you specify a value, you must qualify the units for that value by ending with one of the following suffixes:

- B for bytes
- KB for kilobytes
- MB for megabytes
- GB for gigabytes

The following example sets the maximum header size to 256 KB:

```
Set-TransportServer -Identity MailServer48
-PickupDirectoryMaxHeaderSize "256KB"
```

The default maximum recipients per message is 100. To change this setting, you can set the –PickupDirectoryMaxRecipientsPerMessage parameter of the Set-TransportServer cmdlet to the desired size. The valid input range for this parameter is 1 to 10,000. The following example sets the maximum recipients to 500:

```
Set-TransportServer -Identity MailServer48
-PickupDirectoryMaxRecipientsPerMessage "500"
```

Configuring Message Throttling

Message throttling sets limits on the number of messages and connections that can be processed by a Mailbox or an Edge Transport server. These limits are designed to prevent the accidental or intentional inundation of transport servers and help ensure that transport servers can process messages and connections in an orderly and timely manner. Throttling works in conjunction with size limits on messages that apply to header sizes, attachment sizes, and number of recipients. Although the default throttling settings work in a typical messaging environment, you may need to modify these settings as your organization grows, especially if users or applications create and send a lot of email messages.

On Mailbox and Edge Transport servers, you can set some message throttling options in the Exchange Admin Center by using the options on the Transport Limits page in the transport server's Properties dialog box. In Exchange Management Shell, you can configure all message throttling options by using Set-TransportServer and related parameters.

- **MaxConcurrentMailboxDeliveries**   Sets the maximum number of delivery threads that can be open at the same time to deliver messages to mailboxes. The default value is 20.
- **MaxConcurrentMailboxSubmissions**   Sets the maximum number of delivery threads that can be open at the same time to accept messages from mailboxes. The default value is 20.
- **MaxConnectionRatePerMinute**   Sets the maximum rate at which new inbound connections can be opened to any Receive connectors that exist on the server. The default value is 1,200 connections per minute.
- **MaxOutboundConnections**   Sets the maximum number of concurrent outbound connections that can be open at the same time for Send connectors. The default value is 1,000.
- **MaxPerDomainOutboundConnections**   Sets the maximum number of connections that can be open to any single remote domain for any available Send connectors. The default value is 20.

With Set-SendConnector, you can configure throttling by using ConnectionInactivityTimeOut. This parameter sets the maximum idle time before an open SMTP connection is closed. The default value is 10 minutes.

With Set-ReceiveConnector, you can configure throttling by using the following parameters:

- **ConnectionInactivityTimeOut** Sets the maximum idle time before an open SMTP connection is closed. The default value is five minutes for a Mailbox and one minute for an Edge Transport.
- **ConnectionTimeOut** Sets the maximum time that an SMTP connection can remain open, even if it is active. The default value is 10 minutes for a Mailbox and five minutes for an Edge Transport. ConnectionTimeout must be longer than ConnectionInactivityTimeout.
- **MaxInboundConnection** Sets the maximum number of simultaneous inbound SMTP connections. The default value is 5,000.
- **MaxInboundConnectionPercentagePerSource** Sets the maximum number of simultaneous inbound SMTP connections from a single source server. The value is expressed as the percentage of available remaining connections on a Receive connector (as defined by the –MaxInboundConnection parameter). The default value is 2 percent.
- **MaxInboundConnectionPerSource** Sets the maximum number of simultaneous inbound SMTP connections from a single source messaging server. The default value is 100.
- **MaxProtocolErrors** Sets the maximum number of SMTP protocol errors allowed before a Receive connector closes a connection with a source messaging server. The default value is five.
- **TarpitInterval** Sets artificial delay in SMTP responses in cases in which unwelcome messages are being received from anonymous connections. The default value is five seconds.

Understanding Back Pressure

Back pressure limits overutilization of system resources on a Mailbox or an Edge Transport server. Transport servers monitor key system resources to determine usage levels. If usage levels exceed a specified limit, the server stops accepting new connections and messages to prevent server resources from being completely overwhelmed and to enable the server to deliver the existing messages. When usage of system resources returns to a normal level, the server accepts new connections and messages. Resources monitored as part of the back pressure feature include:

- Free space on hard disk drives that store the message queue database transaction logs.
- Free space on the hard disk drives that store the message queue database.
- The amount of memory used by all processes.
- The amount of memory used by the Edgetransport.exe process.
- The number of uncommitted message queue database transactions that exist in memory.

Levels of usage are defined as normal, medium, or high. With the normal level, the resource is not overused, and the server accepts new connections and messages. With the medium level, the resource is slightly overused, and limited back pressure is applied, allowing mail from senders in the authoritative domain to continue being sent while the server rejects new connections and messages from other sources. With the high level, the resource is severely overused and full back pressure is applied, meaning message flow stops and the server rejects all new connections and messages.

You have limited control over how back pressure is applied. Some related settings can be configured in the Edgetransport.exe.config file on Edge Transport servers; however Microsoft recommends that you don't change the default settings.

Creating and Managing Accepted Domains

Any SMTP namespace for which an Exchange organization sends or receives email is an accepted domain. Accepted domains include domains for which the Exchange organization is authoritative, as well as domains for which the Exchange organization relays mail.

Understanding SMTP Domains

An Exchange organization can have more than one SMTP domain, and the set of email domains your organization uses are its authoritative domains. An accepted domain is considered authoritative when the Exchange organization hosts mailboxes for recipients in this SMTP domain. Transport servers should always accept email that is addressed to any of the organization's authoritative domains. By default, when you install the first Mailbox server, one accepted domain is configured as authoritative for the Exchange organization, and this default accepted domain is based on the FQDN of your forest root domain.

Often an organization's internal domain name might differ from its external domain name. You must create an accepted domain to match your external domain name. You must also create an email address policy that assigns your external domain name to user email addresses. For example, your internal domain name might be tvpress.local, whereas your external domain name is tvpress.com. When you configure DNS, the DNS MX records for your organization will reference tvpress.com, and you will want to assign this SMTP namespace to users by creating an email address policy.

When email is received from the Internet by a Transport server and the recipient of the message is not a part of your organization's authoritative domains, the sending server is trying to relay messages through your Transport servers. To prevent abuse of your servers, Transport servers reject all email that is not addressed to a recipient in your organization's authoritative domains. However, at times you might need to relay email messages from another domain, such as messages from a partner or subsidiary, in which case, you can configure accepted domains as relay domains. When your Transport servers receive the email messages for a configured relay domain, they will relay the messages to an email server in that domain.

Two options are available for configuring relay domains:

- Internal relay domain
- External relay domain

You configure an internal relay domain when there are contacts from the relay domain in the global address list. If your organization contains more than one forest and has configured global address list synchronization, the SMTP domain for one forest can be configured as an internal relay domain in a second forest. Messages from the Internet that are addressed to recipients in internal relay domains are received and processed by your Edge Transport servers. These messages are then relayed to your Mailbox servers, which, in turn, route the messages to the Mailbox servers in the recipient forest. Configuring an SMTP domain as an internal relay domain ensures that all email addressed to the relay domain are accepted by your Exchange organization.

You configure an external relay domain when you want to relay messages to an email server that is both outside your Exchange organization and outside the boundaries of your organization's network perimeter. For this configuration to work, your DNS servers must have an MX record for the external relay domain that references a public IP address for the relaying Exchange organization. When your Edge Transport servers receive the messages for recipients in the external relay domain, they route the messages to the mail server for the external relay domain. You must also configure a Send connector from the Edge Transport server to the external relay domain. The external relay domain can also be using your organization's Edge Transport server as a smart host for outgoing mail.

You also can configure accepted domains for Microsoft Exchange Online. In this case, accepted domains can either be authoritative or internal relay domains. Although you manage previously defined domains in Exchange Admin Center under Mail Flow>Accepted Domains, you must initially define domains in Office 365 Admin Center by using the Domains > Add A Domain option.

If you are working in a hybrid organization, you'll find that the Hybrid Configuration Wizard adds an accepted domain to the on-premises organization to enable hybrid mail flow. This domain, called the coexistence domain, is added as a secondary proxy domain to any email address policies that have primary SMTP address templates for domains selected in the wizard. By default, the coexistence domain is *YourDomain*.mail.onmicrosoft.com.

Viewing Accepted Domains

To view the accepted domains configured for your organization, complete the following steps:

1. In the Exchange Admin Center, select Mail Flow in the Feature pane, and then select Accepted Domains.
2. In the main pane, accepted domains are listed by name, SMTP domain name, and domain type. The domain type is listed as Authoritative, External Relay, or Internal Relay as shown in Figure 10-1.

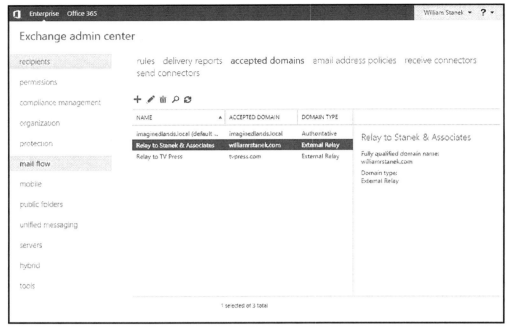

FIGURE 10-1 View accepted domains.

You can use the Get-AcceptedDomain cmdlet to list accepted domains or to get information on a particular accepted domain as well. If you do not provide an identity with this cmdlet, configuration information for all accepted domains is displayed. Listing 10-3 provides the syntax and usage, as well as sample output, for the Get-AcceptedDomain cmdlet.

LISTING 10-3 Get-AcceptedDomain cmdlet syntax and usage

Syntax

```
Get-AcceptedDomain [-Identity DomainIdentity]
[-DomainController DCName] [-Organization OrganizationId]
```

Usage

```
Get-AcceptedDomain
Get-AcceptedDomain -Identity "imaginedlands.local"
Get-AcceptedDomain | Where{$_.DomainType -eq 'Authoritative'}
```

Example Output

Name	DomainName	DomainType	Default
imaginedlands.local	imaginedlands.local	Authoritative	True
Relay to TV Press	tvpress.com	ExternalRelay	False
Relay to Stanek & Associates	williamrstanek.com	ExternalRelay	False

Creating Accepted Domains

To create accepted domains for your organization, complete the following steps:

1. In the Exchange Admin Center, select Mail Flow in the Feature pane, and then select Accepted Domains. Next, click Add (➕) to open the New Accepted Domain dialog box, as shown in Figure 10-2.

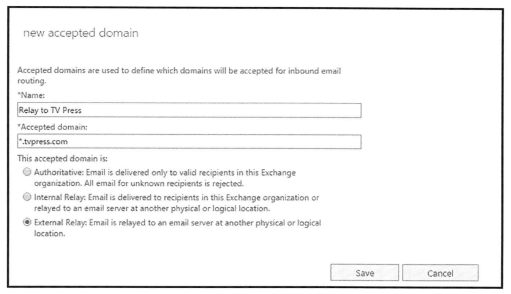

FIGURE 10-2 Create a new accepted domain.

2. Use the Name text box to identify the accepted domain. You can use a descriptive name that identifies the purpose of the accepted domain or simply enter the actual SMTP domain name.

3. In the Accepted Domain text box, type the SMTP domain name for which the Exchange organization will accept email messages. If you want to accept email for the specified domain only, enter the full domain name, such as **imaginedlands.com.** If you want to accept email for the specified domain

and child domains, type * (a wildcard character), then a period, and then the domain name, such as ***.imaginedlands.com.**

> **NOTE** Only domain names you specify can be used as part of an email address policy. Because of this, if you want to use a subdomain as part of an email address policy, you must either explicitly configure the subdomain as an accepted domain or use a wildcard character to include the parent domain and all related subdomains.

    4.   Select one of the following options to set the accepted domain type:

- **Authoritative Domain**   Email is delivered to a recipient in this exchange organization.
- **Internal Relay Domain**   Email is relayed to an email server in another Active Directory forest in the organization.
- **External Relay Domain**   Email is relayed to an email server outside the organization by the Edge Transport server.

    5.   Click Save to create the accepted domain.

In Exchange Management Shell, you can use the New-AcceptedDomain cmdlet to create accepted domains. Listing 10-4 provides the syntax and usage.

LISTING 10-4 New-AcceptedDomain cmdlet syntax and usage

Syntax

```
New-AcceptedDomain -Name Name
 -DomainName DomainName
 -DomainType <Authoritative|InternalRelay|ExternalRelay>
[-Organization OrganizationId]
```

Usage;

```
new-AcceptedDomain -Name "Relay to TV Press"
 -DomainName "*.tvpress.com"
 -DomainType "ExternalRelay"
```

Changing The Accepted Domain Type and Identifier

You can change an accepted domain's type and identifier by completing the following steps:

    1.   In the Exchange Admin Center, select Mail Flow in the Feature pane, and then select Accepted Domains. Next, select the accepted domain you want

to change, and then select Edit (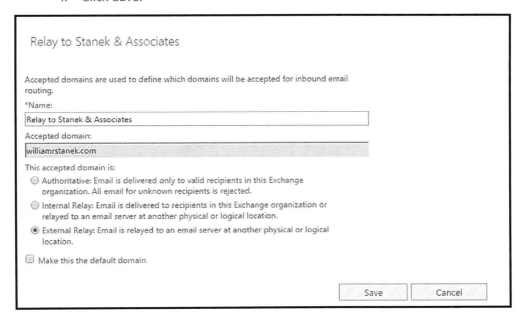). Or simply double-click the accepted domain.

2. In the Properties dialog box, enter a new identifier, use the options provided to change the accepted domain type as necessary.

3. Select the Make This The Default Domain checkbox to make the currently selected domain the default for the Exchange organization. The default accepted domain is used in the external postmaster email address and in encapsulated non-SMTP email addresses.

4. Click Save.

Relay to Stanek & Associates

Accepted domains are used to define which domains will be accepted for inbound email routing.

*Name:

Relay to Stanek & Associates

Accepted domain:

williamrstanek.com

This accepted domain is:

○ Authoritative: Email is delivered only to valid recipients in this Exchange organization. All email for unknown recipients is rejected.

○ Internal Relay: Email is delivered to recipients in this Exchange organization or relayed to an email server at another physical or logical location.

◉ External Relay: Email is relayed to an email server at another physical or logical location.

☐ Make this the default domain.

Save   Cancel

In Exchange Management Shell, you can use the Set-AcceptedDomain cmdlet to modify accepted domains. Listing 10-5 provides the syntax and usage. Use the – AddressBookEnabled parameter to enable recipient filtering for this accepted domain. You should set this parameter to $true only if all the recipients in this accepted domain are replicated to the AD LDS database on the Edge Transport servers. For authoritative domains and internal relay domains, the default value is $true. For external relay domains, the default value is $false.

LISTING 10-5 Set-AcceptedDomain cmdlet syntax and usage

Syntax

```
Set-AcceptedDomain -Identity AcceptedDomainIdentity
[-AddressBookEnabled <$true | $false>] [-DomainController DCName]
[-DomainType <Authoritative|InternalRelay|ExternalRelay>]
[-MakeDefault <$true | $false>] [-Name Name]
```

Usage

```
Set-AcceptedDomain -Identity "Relay to TV Press"
 -DomainType "ExternalRelay"
```

Removing Accepted Domains

You can remove an accepted domain that's no longer needed by completing the following steps:

1. In the Exchange Admin Center, select Mail Flow in the Feature pane, and then select Accepted Domains. Next, select the accepted domain you want to delete, and then select Delete ().

2. When prompted to confirm, click Yes.

warning

Are you sure you want to delete the accepted domain "Relay to Stanek & Associates"?

[Yes] [No]

In Exchange Management Shell, you can use the Remove-AcceptedDomain cmdlet to remove accepted domains. Listing 10-6 provides the syntax and usage.

Syntax

```
Remove-AcceptedDomain -Identity AcceptedDomainIdentity
[-DomainController DCName]
```

Usage

```
Remove-AcceptedDomain -Identity "Relay to TV Press"
```

Creating and Managing Remote Domains

In on-premises Exchange organizations, remote domain settings help you manage mail flow for most types of automated messages, including out-of-office messages, automatic replies, automatic forwarding, delivery reports, and nondelivery reports. Remote domain settings also control some automated message-formatting options, such as whether to display a sender's name on a message or only the sender's email address. Your Exchange organization has a default remote domain policy that sets the global defaults. You can create additional policies to create managed connections for specific remote domains as well.

Viewing Remote Domains

You can use the Get-RemoteDomain cmdlet to list remote domains or to get information on a particular remote domain. Remote domains are listed by name and the domain to which they apply. The Default remote domain applies to all remote domains, unless you override it with specific settings.

If you do not provide an identity with the Get-RemoteDomain cmdlet, configuration information for all remote domains is displayed. Listing 10-7 provides the syntax and usage, as well as sample output, for the Get-RemoteDomain cmdlet.

LISTING 10-7 Get-RemoteDomain cmdlet syntax and usage

Syntax

```
Get-RemoteDomain [-Identity DomainIdentity]
[-DomainController DCName] [-Organization OrgId]
```

Usage

```
Get-RemoteDomain -Identity "imaginedlands.com"
```

Output

Name	DomainName	AllowedOOFType
Default	*	External
The Magic Lands	*.imaginedlands.com	External

Creating Remote Domains

In Exchange Management Shell, you can use the New-RemoteDomain cmdlet to create remote domains. Use the -Name parameter to specify a descriptive name that identifies the purpose of the remote domain or simply enter the actual SMTP domain name.

Listing 10-8 provides the syntax and usage. The way you set the –DomainName parameter determines whether the remote domain includes subdomains. To manage connections for a specific domain, you simply provide the fully qualified name of the domain. You insert an asterisk and a period before the domain name to include the domain and all child domains of the domain.

LISTING 10-8 New-RemoteDomain cmdlet syntax and usage

Syntax

```
New-RemoteDomain -Name Name -DomainName DomainName
[-DomainController DCName] [-Organization OrgId]
```

Usage for parent domain only

```
New-RemoteDomain -Name "The Magic Lands Managed Connection"
 -DomainName "themagiclands.com"
```

Usage for parent domain and child domains

```
New-RemoteDomain -Name "The Magic Lands Managed Connection"
 -DomainName "*.themagiclands.com"
```

Configuring Messaging Options for Remote Domains

Remote domains are used to control how automated messages are used and to specify some types of messaging format options. In Exchange Management Shell, you can use the Set-RemoteDomain cmdlet to configure remote domains. Listing 10-9 provides the syntax and usage.

LISTING 10-9 Set-RemoteDomain cmdlet syntax and usage

Syntax

```
Set-RemoteDomain -Identity "RemoteDomainIdentity"
 [-AllowedOOFType <"External"|"InternalLegacy"|"ExternalLegacy"|"None">]
 [-AutoForwardEnabled <$true | $false>]
 [-AutoReplyEnabled <$true | $false>]
 [-CharacterSet "CharacterSet"]
 [-ContentType <"MimeHtmlText"|"MimeText"|"MimeHtml">]
 [-DeliveryReportEnabled <$true | $false>]
 [-DisplaySenderName <$true | $false>]
 [-DomainController DCName]
 [-LineWrapSize "Size"]
 [-MeetingForwardNotificationEnabled <$true | $false>]
 [-Name "Name"]
 [-NDREnabled <$true | $false>]
 [-NonMimeCharacterSet "CharacterSet"]
 [-TNEFEnabled <$true | $false>]
```

Usage

```
Set-RemoteDomain -Identity "The Magic Lands Managed Connection"
 -DeliveryReportEnabled $false
```

Use the -AllowedOOFType parameter to specify whether and how out-of-office messages are sent to the remote domain. The options are as follows:

* **None** Blocks all out-of-office messages.
* **External** Allows out-of-office messages to be received by the Exchange organization, but does not allow the organization's out-of-office messages to be sent.

- **ExternalLegacy** Allows out-of-office messages to be received by the Exchange organization and receipt of out-of-office messages generated by Microsoft Outlook 2003, Exchange 2003, or earlier.
- **InternalLegacy** Allows out-of-office messages to be sent from the Exchange organization and the sending of out-of-office messages generated by Outlook 2003, Exchange 2003, or earlier.

You also can specify how Exchange should format messages. Allow messaging options by setting the related parameters to $true, or disallow messaging options by setting the related parameters to $false. The options available are as follows:

- **-AutoReplyEnabled** Allows the sender to be notified that the message was received.
- **-AutoForwardEnabled** Allows Exchange Server to forward or deliver a duplicate message to a new recipient.
- **-DeliveryReportsEnabled** Allows Exchange Server to return delivery confirmation reports to the sender.
- **-MeetingForwardNotificationEnabled** Allows Exchange Server to forward or deliver a meeting notification to a new recipient.
- **-NDREnabled** Allows Exchange Server to return nondelivery confirmation reports to the sender.
- **-DisplaySenderName** Allows both the sender's name and email address to appear on outbound email messages.

By default, text word-wrapping is disabled, which means that Exchange does not enforce a maximum line length. If you'd like message text to wrap at a specific line length, you can set the -LineWrapSize parameter to the specific column position at which text wrapping should start, such as at 72 characters.

Use the -ContentType parameter to set the outbound message content type and formatting. The options are as follows:

- **MimeHTML** Converts messages to MIME messages with HTML formatting.
- **MimeText** Converts messages to MIME messages with text formatting.
- **MimeHtmlText** Converts messages to MIME messages with HTML formatting, except when the original message is a text message. Text messages are converted to MIME messages with text formatting.

If you want to send Transport Neutral Encapsulation Format (TNEF) message data to the remote domain rather than Exchange Rich Text Format, set -TNEFEnabled to $true.

Removing Remote Domains

In Exchange Management Shell, you can use the Remove-RemoteDomain cmdlet to remove remote domains. Listing 10-10 provides the syntax and usage.

LISTING 10-10 Remove-RemoteDomain cmdlet syntax and usage

Syntax

```
Remove-RemoteDomain -Identity RemoteDomainIdentity
[-DomainController DCName]
```

Usage

```
Remove-RemoteDomain -Identity "The Magic Lands Managed Connection"
```

Chapter 11. Implementing Exchange Policies and Rules

Exchange provides email address policies, journal rules and transport rules as a means to affect mail flow by modifying the transport pipeline. Email address policies allow you to generate or rewrite email addresses automatically for each recipient in your organization based on specific criteria you set. Microsoft Exchange Server uses email address policies in two key ways:

- Whenever you create a new recipient, Exchange Server sets the recipient's default email address based on the applicable email address policy.
- Whenever you apply an email address policy, Exchange Server automatically rewrites the email addresses for recipients to which the policy applies.

Journaling allows you to forward copies of messaging items and related reports automatically to an alternate location. You can use journaling to verify compliance with policies implemented in your organization and to help ensure that your organization can meet its legal and regulatory requirements. Enable journaling for the entire organization by using journal rules.

Transport rules, which apply to both on-premises and online Exchange organizations, allow you to screen messaging items and apply actions to those items that meet specific conditions. When you enable transport rules, all Mailbox servers in your Exchange organization screen messages according to the rules you've defined.

Creating and Managing Email Address Policies

Every Exchange organization has a default email address policy, which is required to create email addresses for recipients. You can create additional email address policies as well. For example, if your organization's internal domain name is different from its external domain name, you would need to create an accepted domain to match your external domain name and an email address policy that assigns your external domain name to user email addresses.

Working with Email Address Policies

To view the email address policies configured for your organization, complete the following steps:

1. In the Exchange Admin Center, select Mail Flow in the Feature pane, and then select Email Address Policies.

2. In the main pane, email address policies are listed by name, priority, last modified time, and status as shown in Figure 11-1. The status is listed as Applied for a policy that has been applied to recipients and Unapplied for a policy that has not been applied to recipients.

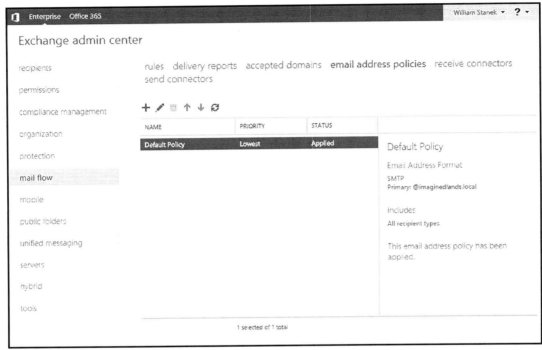

FIGURE 11-1 View the email address policies.

You can use the Get-EmailAddressPolicy cmdlet to list email address policies or to get information on a particular email address policy. If you don't provide an identity with this cmdlet, configuration information for all email address policies is displayed. Listing 11-1 provides the syntax and usage, as well as sample output, for the Get-EmailAddressPolicy cmdlet.

LISTING 11-1 Get-EmailAddressPolicy cmdlet syntax and usage

Syntax

```
Get-EmailAddressPolicy [-Identity PolicyIdentity]
[-DomainController DCName] [-Organization OrgId]
[-IncludeMailboxSettingOnlyPolicy <$true | $false>]
```

Usage

```
Get-EmailAddressPolicy | ft na me, priority, recipientfilter,
recipientfilterapplied, includedrecipients
```

```
Get-EmailAddressPolicy -Identity "Default Policy"
```

Output

Name	Priority	RecipientFilter
Default Policy	Lowest	Alias -ne $null
Rewrite Group Addresses	1	Alias -ne $null

Creating Email Address Policies

You can create email address policies for your organization by completing the following steps:

1. In the Exchange Admin Center, select Mail Flow in the Feature pane, and then select Email Address Policies. Next, click New (✚) to open the New Email Address Policy dialog box.

2. Use the Name text box to identify the email address policy. You can use a descriptive name that identifies the purpose of the email address policy or simply enter the actual SMTP domain name to which it applies.

3. Under Email Address Format, click the Add button (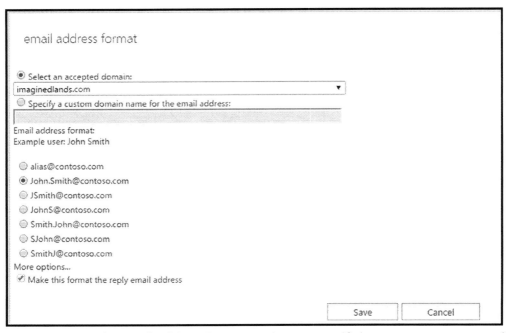). This displays the Email Address Format dialog box.

email address format

◉ Select an accepted domain:

imaginedlands.com   ▼

◯ Specify a custom domain name for the email address:

Email address format:
Example user: John Smith

◯ alias@contoso.com
◉ John.Smith@contoso.com
◯ JSmith@contoso.com
◯ JohnS@contoso.com
◯ Smith.John@contoso.com
◯ SJohn@contoso.com
◯ SmithJ@contoso.com
More options...
☑ Make this format the reply email address

Save   Cancel

4. Use the Email Address Format options to specify how to generate or rewrite email addresses automatically for each recipient to which the policy applies. You can use the Exchange alias or parts of the user name in various orders.

5. Use the Select An Accepted Domain drop-down list to select the email address domain. Only authoritative accepted domains are available for selection.

6. Although users can have multiple email addresses associated with their mailbox, only one email address, the default email address, is used for any sent messages. If you want the email address applied with this policy to be the default, select Make This Format The Reply Email Address.

7. Close the Email Address Format dialog box by clicking Save.

8. Specify the types of recipients to include in the policy. Select All Recipient Types, or select Only The Following Recipient Types, and then select the check boxes for the types of recipients to which you want to apply the policy.

Run this policy in this sequence with other policies:

| 2 | ∨ |

Specify the types of recipients this email address policy will apply to.

○ All recipient types

◉ Only the following recipient types:

    ☐ Users with Exchange mailboxes

    ☐ Mail users with external email addresses

    ☐ Resource mailboxes

    ☐ Mail contacts with external email addresses

    ☑ Mail-enabled groups

[save]   [cancel]

9. If you've previously created other email address policies, set the relative priority of this policy. Policies are run in priority order. A policy with a priority of one has the highest priority and runs before a policy with a priority of two, and so on.

10. You can create rules that further filter recipients. Each rule acts as a condition that must be met. If you set more than one rule, each condition must be met for there to be a match. To define a rule, click Add Rule. You can now set the filter conditions. The following types of conditions are available as well as conditions for custom attributes:

▪ **State Or Province**   Filters recipients based on the value of the State/Province text box on the Contact Information page in the related Properties dialog box. In the Specify Words Or Phrases dialog box, type a state or province identifier to use as a filter condition, and then press Enter or click Add. Repeat as necessary, and then click OK.

▪ **Department**   Filters recipients based on the value of the Department text box on the Organization page in the related Properties dialog box. In the Specify Words Or Phrases dialog box, type a department name to use as a filter condition, and then press Enter or click Add. Repeat as necessary, and then click OK.

▪ **Company**   Filters recipients based on the value of the Company text box on the Organization page in the related Properties dialog box. In the Specify Words Or Phrases dialog box, type a company name to use as a filter condition, and then press Enter or click Add. Repeat as necessary, and then click OK.

> ***IMPORTANT***   Although each rule acts as an OR condition for matches on specified values, the rules are aggregated as AND conditions. This means that a user that matches one of the values in a rule passes that filter but must be a match for all the rules to be included in the group. For example, if you were to define a state rule for Oregon, California, or Washington and a

department rule for Technology, only users who are in Oregon, California, or Washington and in the Technology department match the filter.

11. Get a complete list of the recipients to which this policy will be applied by clicking Preview Recipients The Policy Applies To. If the policy applies to the expected recipients, click Save to create the email address policy. Otherwise, repeat Steps 4 to 11 and ensure you configure options and rules to appropriately define the recipients to which the policy should apply.

12. The policy is not applied automatically. To apply the policy, select the policy Exchange Admin Center's main pane, and then click Apply in the details pane.

If you click More Options in the Email Address Format dialog box, you'll be able to specify a custom SMTP email address. With custom addresses, you use the following variables to specify how the email address should be formatted as well as manually entered text:

- *%d* Inserts the recipient's display name
- *%g* Inserts the recipient's given name (first name)
- *%i* Inserts the recipient's middle initial
- *%m* Inserts the recipient's Exchange alias
- *%s* Inserts the recipient's surname (last name)
- *%ng* Inserts the first *N* letters of the given name.
- *%ns* Inserts the first *N* letters of the surname.

For example, you could enter %g.%s@tvpress.com to specify that email addresses should be formatted with the given name first, followed by a period (.) and the surname.

In Exchange Management Shell, you create and apply email address policies by using separate tasks. You can create email address policies by using the New-EmailAddressPolicy cmdlet. Once you create a policy, apply it using the Update-EmailAddressPolicy cmdlet. Listings 11-2 and 11-3 provide the syntax and usage for these cmdlets. Use the -EnabledPrimarySMTPAddressTemplate parameter to specify the custom format for email addresses. Although the syntax for custom email addresses is the same as when you are working with Exchange Admin Center, you must use the SMTP: prefix before specifying the format, as shown in the example.

NOTE Any time you receive an error regarding missing aliases, you should run the Update-EmailAddressPolicy cmdlet with the –FixMissingAlias parameter set to *$true*. This tells Exchange to generate an alias for recipients who do not have an alias.

LISTING 11-2 New-EmailAddressPolicy cmdlet syntax and usage

Syntax

```
New-EmailAddressPolicy -Name PolicyName
-EnabledPrimarySMTPAddressTemplate Template
-IncludedRecipients RecipientTypes {AddtlParams} {ConditionalParams}


New-EmailAddressPolicy -Name PolicyName
-EnabledEmailAddressTemplates Templates -RecipientFilter Filter
[-DisabledEmailAddressTemplates Templates] {AddtlParams}


New-EmailAddressPolicy -Name PolicyName
-EnabledPrimarySMTPAddressTemplate Template
-RecipientFilter Filter {AddtlParams}


New-EmailAddressPolicy -Name PolicyName
-EnabledEmailAddressTemplates Templates
-IncludedRecipients RecipientTypes
[-DisabledEmailAddressTemplates Templates]
{AddtlParams} {ConditionalParams}


{AddtlParams}
[-DomainController DCName] [-Organization OrgId]
[-Priority Priority] [-RecipientContainer OUId]


{ConditionalParams}
[-ConditionalCompany CompanyNameFilter1, CompanyNameFilter2,... ]
[-ConditionalCustomAttributeN Value1, Value2, ...]
[-ConditionalDepartment DeptNameFilter1, DeptNameFilter2, ... ]
[-ConditionalStateOrProvince StateNameFilter1, StateNameFilter2, ... ]
```

Usage

```
New-EmailAddressPolicy -Name "Primary Email Address Policy"
-IncludedRecipients "MailboxUsers, MailContacts, MailGroups"
```

```
-ConditionalCompany "City Power & Light"

-ConditionalDepartment "Sales","Marketing"

-ConditionalStateOrProvince "Washington","Idaho","Oregon"

-Priority "Lowest"

-EnabledEmailAddressTemplates "SMTP:%g.%s@tvpress.com"
```

LISTING 11-3 Update-EmailAddressPolicy cmdlet syntax and usage

Syntax

```
Update-EmailAddressPolicy -Identity PolicyIdentity
[-DomainController DCName] [-FixMissingAlias <$true | $false>]
```

Usage

```
Update-EmailAddressPolicy -Identity "Primary Email Address Policy"


Update-EmailAddressPolicy -Identity "Primary Email Address Policy"
 -FixMissingAlias
```

Editing and Applying Email Address Policies

You can manage email address policies in several different ways. You can edit their properties or apply them to rewrite email addresses automatically for each recipient to which the policy applies. You can also change their priority to determine the precedence order for application in case there are conflicts between policies. When multiple policies apply to a recipient, the policy with the highest priority is the one that applies.

You can change the way email address policies work by completing the following steps:

1. In the Exchange Admin Center, select Mail Flow in the Feature pane, and then select Email Address Policies.

2. In the main window, select the email address policy you want to change, and then select Edit ( ). This opens the properties dialog box for the policy.

3. Use the options on the General page to set the policy name and relative priority.

4. On the Email Address Format page, you can use the options provided to specify how to generate or rewrite email addresses automatically for each recipient to which the policy applies. You can use the Exchange alias or parts of the user name in various orders as described in steps 4 through 8 in the "Creating Email Address Policies" section of this chapter.

5. On the Apply To page, you can use the options provided to specify the recipients to which the policy will apply. After you configure options, preview the recipients to which the policy applies to ensure you've configured the settings appropriately, as described in steps 9 through 12 in the "Creating Email Address Policies" section of this chapter.

6. The modified policy is not applied automatically. To apply the policy, select the policy Exchange Admin Center's main pane, and then click Apply in the details pane.

You can change priority in the Exchange Admin Center by selecting the policy, and then using the Increase Priority and Decrease Priority buttons to change the priority of the policy. The valid range for priorities depends on the number of policies you've configured. The Default Policy always has the lowest priority.

You can apply an email address policy by selecting the policy Exchange Admin Center's main pane, and then clicking Apply in the details pane.

In Exchange Management Shell, you can use the Set-EmailAddressPolicy cmdlet to modify email address policies, as shown in Listing 11-4. The Update-EmailAddressPolicy cmdlet, used to apply policies, was discussed previously.

LISTING 11-4 Set-EmailAddressPolicy cmdlet syntax and usage

Syntax

```
Set-EmailAddressPolicy -Identity PolicyIdentity
[-ConditionalCompany CompanyNameFilter1, CompanyNameFilter2,... ]
[-ConditionalCustomAttributeN Value1, Value2, ...]
[-ConditionalDepartment DeptNameFilter1, DeptNameFilter2, ... ]
[-ConditionalStateOrProvince StateNameFilter1, StateNameFilter2, ... ]
[-DisbledEmailAddressTemplates Templates] [-DomainController DCName]
[-EnabledEmailAddressTemplates Templates]
[-EnabledPrimarySMTPAddressTemplate Template]
[-ForceUpgrade <$true | $false>] [-IncludedRecipients RecipientTypes]
```

```
[-Name PolicyName] [-Priority Priority]
[-RecipientContainer OUId] [-RecipientFilter Filter]
```

Usage

```
Set-EmailAddressPolicy  -Identity "Primary Email Address Policy"
 -Name "Tvpress.com Email Address Policy"
 -IncludedRecipients "MailboxUsers"
 -ConditionalCompany "City Power & Light"
 -ConditionalDepartment "Sales"
 -ConditionalStateOrProvince "Washington"
 -Priority "2"
 -EnabledEmailAddressTemplates "SMTP:%g.%s@tvpress.com"
```

Removing Email Address Policies

You can remove an email address policy that is no longer needed by completing the following steps:

1. In the Exchange Admin Center, select Mail Flow in the Feature pane, and then select Email Address Policies.
2. In the main window, select the email address policy you want to delete, and then select Delete (   ).
3. When prompted to confirm, click Yes.

In Exchange Management Shell, you can use the Remove-EmailAddressPolicy cmdlet to remove email address policies. Listing 11-5 provides the syntax and usage.

LISTING 11-5 Remove-EmailAddressPolicy cmdlet syntax and usage

Syntax

```
Remove-EmailAddressPolicy -Identity EmailAddressPolicyIdentity
[-DomainController DCName]
```

Usage

```
Remove-EmailAddressPolicy -Identity "Tvpress.com
Email Address Policy"
```

Configuring Journal Rules

Exchange 2016 Setup creates a separate container in Active Directory Domain Services to store Exchange 2016 journal rules. If you are installing Exchange 2016 in an existing Exchange 2010 or Exchange 2013 organization, Setup copies any existing journal rules to this container so they will be applied to Exchange 2016. If you subsequently make changes to the journal rule configuration on your Exchange 2010 or Exchange 2013 servers, you must make the same changes on Exchange 2016 to ensure the journal rules are consistent across the organization (and vice versa). You can also export journal rules from Exchange 2010 or Exchange 2013 and import them to Exchange 2016.

Both Exchange Online and on-premises Exchange support a full set of compliance options for in-place eDiscovery and hold, auditing, retention policies, retention tags, and journal rules. These compliance options are configured in much the same way whether you are working with Exchange Online or Exchange 2016. If you are working in a hybrid configuration and have specific compliance requirements, you can ensure your on-premises compliance settings are applied to Exchange Online.

In a hybrid environment, inbound and outbound messages have separate routing configurations. If you enable centralized mail transport for inbound, outbound, or both types of messages in the hybrid configuration, messages sent by or to recipients in the online organization are set through the on-premises organization to ensure that compliance rules and any other processes or messaging requirements configured in the on-premises organization are applied. However, there is a noteworthy exception: Outbound messages sent from Exchange Online to other recipients in the same Exchange Online organization are delivered directly.

Setting The NDR Journaling Mailbox

When you first configure journaling, you'll need to specify an email address to receive any journal reports that are otherwise undeliverable. Typically, you'll want to create a new, dedicated mailbox to receive these reports so that the mailbox will not be journaled and also won't be subject to any transport rules or mailbox rule settings.

To specify the NDR journaling mailbox, complete the following steps:

1. In the Exchange Admin Center, select Compliance Management in the Feature pane, and then select Journal Rules.

2. If the journaling mailbox has already been specified, the email address is listed; otherwise, click Select Address.

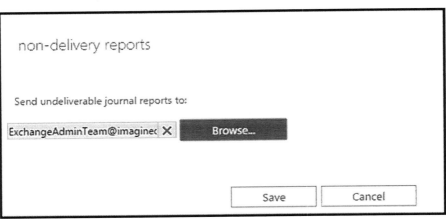

3. In the NDRs For Undeliverable Journal Reports dialog box, click Browse, select a destination mailbox, and then click OK.

4. Click Save.

5. A warning prompts lets you know the email address specified won't be journaled or use transport/mailbox rules. Click OK.

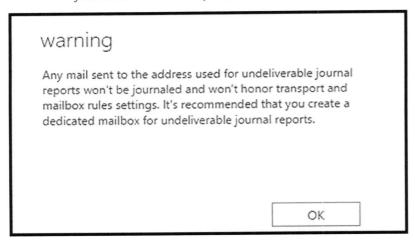

Creating Journal Rules

You create journal rules to record messages in your organization in support of email retention and compliance requirements. You can target journal rules for the following:

- **Internal messaging items**   Tracks messaging items sent and received by recipients inside your Exchange organization.
- **External messaging items**   Tracks messaging items sent to recipients or from senders outside your Exchange organization.
- **All messaging items**   Tracks all messaging items, including those already processed by journal rules that track only internal or external messaging items.

When you enable journal rules for one or more of these scopes, the rules are executed on your organization's Mailbox servers. Journal rules can be targeted to all recipients or to specific recipients. For example, you can create a rule to journal all messages sent to the AllEmployees distribution group.

You can create a journal rule by completing the following steps:

1.   In the Exchange Admin Center, select Compliance Management in the Feature pane, and then select Journal Rules. Next, click New to open the New Journal Rule dialog box (shown in Figure 11-2).

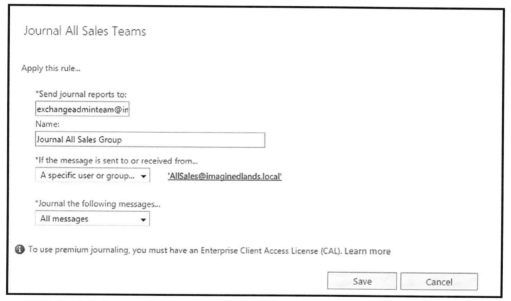

FIGURE 11-2 Create a journal rule.

2.   In the Name text box, type a descriptive name for the rule.

3.   In the Send Journal Reports To, provide the journal email address. This is the recipient to which Exchange should forward journal reports for this rule.

4.   Use the If The Message Is Send To Or Received From selection list to specify whether the rule should be applied to messages sent to or received from a

specific user or group, or to all messages. For a specific user or group, you'll then need to select the user or group.

5. Use the Journal The Following Messages selection list to specify the scope of the rule as either All Messages, Internal Messages Only, or External Messages Only.

6. Click Save.

Managing Journal Rules

When you are working with the Compliance Management area and select Journal Rules, the currently defined journal rules are listed in the main pane by status, name, user journaled, and journal report recipient.

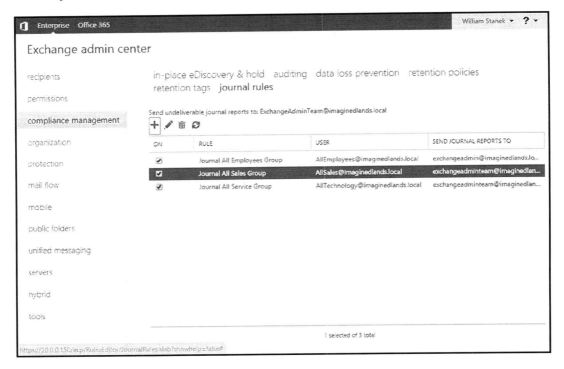

You can easily enable or disable a rule by setting or clearing the corresponding checkbox in the On column. If you select a rule and then select Edit (   ), you can modify the rule settings. If you select a rule and then select Delete (   ), you can delete the rule.

In Exchange Management Shell, you can manage journal rules by using the following cmdlets: New-JournalRule, Set-JournalRule, Get-JournalRule, and Remove-JournalRule.

Configuring Transport Rules

Transport rules have conditions, actions, and exceptions that you can apply. Conditions you can screen for include the following:

- **The sender is...**   Allows you to screen messages from specific senders according to their email address, group membership, account properties and more.
- **The recipient is...**   Allows you to screen messages being sent to specific recipients according to their email address, group membership, account properties, and so forth.
- **The subject or body...**   Allows you to screen messages that have specific words in their subject line or message body.
- **Any attachment...**   Allows you to screen messages with attachments for specific content, file names, file extensions, and password protection as well as when the attachment size is greater than or equal to the size limit that you set.
- **The message...**   Allows you to screen messages sent to or copied to specific recipients or specific groups as well as when the message size is greater than or equal to a size limit that you set.
- **The send and recipient...**   Allows you to screen messages sent between members of specific groups, messages sent by subordinates of a specific manager, and messages sent to a recipient who is a manager or direct report of the sender.
- **The message properties...**   Allows you to screen messages that have a spam confidence level (SCL) rating that is greater than or equal to a limit that you set. Also allows you to screen messages by classification, type, and importance level.
- **A message header...**   Allows you to screen messages that have a header field that includes specific words or matches specific patterns.

When a message meets all of the conditions you specify in a transport rule, the message is handled according to the actions you've defined. Actions you can apply to messages that meet your transport rule conditions include the following:

- Forwarding the message for approval to specific people or to the sender's manager.
- Redirecting the message to specific recipients, host quarantine or a specific outbound connector.

- Blocking the message by rejecting it with a specific return message and explanation or by deleting the message without notifying anyone.
- Adding recipients to the Bcc, To, or Cc fields or simply adding the sender's manager as a recipient.
- Applying a disclaimer to the beginning or end of the message.
- Modifying the message by removing a message header, adding a message header, adding a message classification, or setting the spam confidence level.
- Securing the message with rights protection or TLS encryption.
- Prepending the subject of the message with a specified text value.
- Generating an incident report and sending it to specific recipients.

Transport rules can also have exceptions. Exception criteria are similar to condition criteria. For example, you can exclude messages from certain people or from certain members of distribution lists. You can also exclude messages sent to certain people or to particular members of a distribution list.

Creating Transport Rules

You can create a transport rule by completing the following steps:

1. In the Exchange Admin Center, select Mail Flow in the Feature area, and then select Rules. Next, click New (**+** ▾), and then select Create A New Rule to open the New Rule dialog box.

2. In the New Rule dialog box, click the More Option link to display additional options.

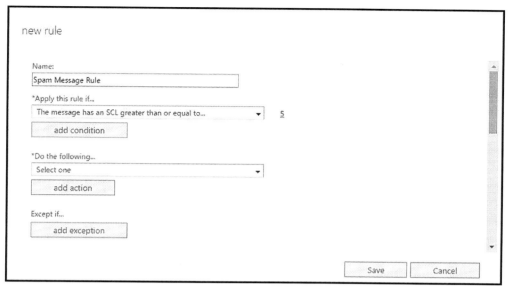

FIGURE 11-3 Create a transport rule.

3. In the Name text box, type a descriptive name for the rule and optionally enter a descriptive comment.

4. Next you need to specify the conditions for the rule by using the options under Apply This Rule If... Click in the selection list. Next, choose what part of the message to examine and then choose how the condition should be matched. Finally, in the selection dialog box, set the condition parameters by selecting an option or typing a value or values to match. For example, choose "The sender" and then choose "is this person." Finally, in the Select Members dialog box, select the sender to match in the rule and then click OK.

5. If you want to add another condition, click Add Condition and then click in the new selection list provided. Next, choose what part of the message to examine, and then choose how the condition should be matched. Finally, in the selection dialog box, set the condition parameters by selecting an option or typing a value or values to match. Repeat this step to add other conditions.

6. Use the options under Do The Following... to define the actions to take when a message meets the condition or conditions you specified. Click in the selection list. Next, choose the action, and then choose how the action should be performed. Finally, in the selection dialog box, set the action parameters by selecting an option or typing a value or values to match. For example, choose "Add recipients" and then choose "to the Bcc box." Finally,

in the Select Members dialog box, select the sender that should be added to the Bcc field of matching messages and then click OK.

7. If you want to add another action, click Add Action, and then click in the new selection list provided. Next, choose the action, and then choose how the action should be performed. Finally, in the selection dialog box, set the action parameters by selecting an option or typing a value or values to match. Repeat this step to add other actions.

8. You now need to specify any exceptions by using the options under Except If.... Click Add Exception, and then click in the new selection list provided. Next, choose the exception and then choose how the exception should be matched. Finally, in the selection dialog box, set the exception parameters by selecting an option or typing a value or values to match. For example, choose "The sender" and then choose "is this person." Finally, in the Select Members dialog box, select the sender to add as an exception to the rule, and then click OK. Repeat this step to add other exceptions.

9. By default, transport rules are audited and enforced. If you don't want the rule to be audited, clear the Audit This Rule... check box. If you want to test the rule rather than enforce it, select Test With Policy Tips or Test Without Policy Tips instead of Enforce.

10. Click Save to create the rule. If an error occurs during rule creation, note the error and then correct the issue before trying to create the rule again.

Managing Transport Rules

You can manage transport rules in several different ways including editing their properties or disabling them. When you've created multiple rules, you can also change their priority to determine the precedence order for application in case there are conflicts between rules. When multiple rules apply to a message, the rule with the highest priority is the one that your Mailbox server applies.

When you select a transport rule in Exchange Admin Center, you can manage the rule in the following ways:

- **Change Priority**   Use the Move Up or Move Down buttons to increase or decrease the relative priority of the rule. Rules are processed in priority order, with the rule listed first being the first one processed, the rule listed second being the second processed, and so on.
- **Disable Rule**   Use the checkbox in the On column to enable or disable the rule.
- **Remove**   Select Delete ( ) to remove the rule.
- **Edit Rule**   Select Edit ( ) to edit the properties of the transport rule.

In Exchange Management Shell, you can manage transport rules by using the following cmdlets: New-TransportRule, Set-TransportRule, Get-TransportRule, and Remove-TransportRule.

Chapter 12. Filtering Spam

Every minute users spend dealing with unsolicited commercial email (spam) or other unwanted email is a minute they cannot do their work and address other issues. To try to deter spammers and other unwanted senders, you can use message filtering to block these senders from directing messages to your organization. Not only can you filter messages that claim to be from a particular sender or that are sent to a particular receiver, you can also establish connection filtering rules based on IP block lists. The sections that follow discuss these and other anti-spam options.

As you configure message filtering, keep in mind that although Exchange Server is designed to combat most spammer techniques, no system can block all of them. Like the techniques of those who create viruses, the techniques of those who send spam frequently change, and you won't be able to prevent all unwanted email from going through. You should, however, be able to substantially reduce the flow of spam into your organization.

The way you configure message filtering depends on whether your organization uses Edge Transport servers:

* If your organization doesn't use Edge Transport servers and has only Mailbox servers, you can enable the anti-spam features on Mailbox servers that receive messages from the Internet and then configure message filtering options on those servers.
* If your organization is using Edge Transports, you can enable the anti-spam features on the Edge Transport servers and then and configure message filtering on those servers.

As discussed in "Enabling Anti-Spam Features" in Chapter 9 "Configuring Transport Services," Edge Transport servers have anti-spam features enabled by default and Mailbox servers do not. Generally, you want your Edge Transports to handle spam filtering before messages are routed into the Exchange organization. After your Edge Transport servers have filtered messages, there is no need to filter them again, which is why message filtering is disabled by default on Mailbox servers.

Filtering Spam by Sender

Sometimes, when you are filtering spam or other unwanted email, you'll know specific email addresses or email domains from which you don't want to accept messages. In this case, you can block messages from these senders or email domains by configuring sender filtering. Another sender from which you probably don't want to accept messages is a blank sender. If the sender is blank, it means the From field of the email message wasn't filled in and the message is probably from a spammer.

Sender filtering is enabled by default and is designed to filter inbound messages from non-authenticated Internet sources. You can view the current configuration of sender filtering by using Get-SenderFilterConfig. Use the -Enabled parameter of Set-SenderFilterConfig to enable or disable sender filtering. The following example disables sender filtering:

```
Set-SenderFilterConfig -Enabled $false
```

In Exchange Management Shell, you can use the Set-SenderFilterConfig cmdlet to configure sender filtering.

Listing 12-1 provides the syntax and usage. You can block individual email addresses using the -BlockedSenders parameters. If you want to filter all email sent from a particular domain, use the -BlockedDomains or -BlockedDomainsAndSubdomains parameter.

LISTING 12-1 Set-SenderFilterConfig cmdlet syntax and usage

Syntax

```
Set-SenderFilterConfig [-Action <StampStatus | Reject>]
[-BlankSenderBlockingEnabled <$true | $false>]
[-BlockedDomains <domain1,domain2…domainN>]
[-BlockedDomainsAndSubdomains <domain1,domain2…domainN>]
[-BlockedSenders <email1,email2…emailN>]
[-DomainController DCName]
[-Enabled <$true | $false>]
[-ExternalMailEnabled <$true | $false>]
[-InternalMailEnabled <$true | $false>]
[-RecipientBlockedSenderAction <Reject | Delete>]
```

Usage

```
Set-SenderFilterConfig -BlankSenderBlockingEnabled $true
```

```
Set-SenderFilterConfig -BlockedDomains contoso.com, margiestravel.com,
proseware.com
```

```
Set-SenderFilterConfig -BlockedDomainsAndSubdomains fineartschool.com,
wingtiptoys.com
```

```
Set-SenderFilterConfig -BlockedSenders tony@treyresearch.net,
ed@woodgrovebank.com
```

By default, sender filtering rejects messages from blocked domains and senders. This option ensures that Exchange doesn't waste processing power and other resources dealing with messages from filtered senders. If you want to mark messages as being from a blocked sender and continue processing them, set the -Action parameter to StampStatus instead. Here, a message header stamp will be added to the message and the message will be processed by other anti-spam agents. This stamp and any other issues found will then be used to set the spam confidence level as part of content filtering. A message that exceeds a spam confidence level is rejected, quarantined, deleted, or marked as junk mail. Set the -BlankSenderBlockingEnabled parameter to $true to block blank senders.

As shown in the previous examples, you can easily define the initial set of blocked domains and senders. If you want to modify these values, however, you must either enter the complete set of blocked domains or senders, or you must use a special shorthand to insert into or remove values from these multivalued properties. The shorthand for adding values is:

```
@{Add="<ValuetoAdd1>","<ValuetoAdd2>"...}
```

Such as:

```
Set-SenderFilterConfig -BlockedDomains
@{Add="imaginedlands.com","tvpress.com"}
```

The shorthand for removing values is:

```
@{Remove="<ValuetoRemove1>","<ValuetoRemove2>"...}
```

Such as:

```
Set-SenderFilterConfig -BlockedDomains
@{Remove="imaginedlands.com","tvpress.com"}
```

If you want to add values and remove others, you can do this as well by using the following shorthand:

```
@{Add="<ValuetoAdd1>","<ValuetoAdd2>"...;
Remove="<ValuetoRemove1>","<ValuetoRemove1>"...}
```

You can confirm that values were added or removed as expected by using Get-SenderFilterConfig. In this example, you view the currently blocked domains:

```
Get-SenderFilterConfig | fl BlockedDomains
```

By default, -InternalMailEnabled is set to $false and -ExternalMailEnabled is set to true which means authenticated internal email messages aren't processed by the Sender Filter whereas unauthenticated external email messages are processed by the Sender filter. An unauthenticated external email messages is one from an untrusted or anonymous source rather than a trusted partner.

Finally, when users in your organization add senders to their blocked sender list, the SafeList aggregation feature in Exchange 2016 adds these senders to the Blocked Senders List in Exchange 2016. By default, messages from these users are rejected rather than deleted. To delete these messages, set -RecipientBlockedSenderAction to Delete.

Filtering Spam by Recipient

In any organization, you'll have users whose email addresses change, perhaps because they request it, leave the company, or change office locations. Although you might be able to forward email to these users for a time, you probably won't want to forward email indefinitely. At some point, you, or someone else in the organization, will decide it's time to delete the user's account, mailbox, or both. If the user is subscribed to mailing lists or other services that deliver automated email, the automated messages continue to come in, unless you manually unsubscribe the user or reply to each email that you don't want to receive the messages. Unfortunately, some Exchange administrators find themselves going through this inefficient process. It's much easier to add the old or invalid email address to a recipient filter list and specify that Exchange shouldn't accept messages for users who aren't in the Exchange directory. Once you do this, Exchange won't attempt to deliver messages for filtered or invalid recipients, and you won't see related nondelivery reports (NDRs).

Recipient filtering is enabled by default. In Exchange Management Shell, you can use the Set-RecipientFilterConfig cmdlet to configure recipient filtering. Listing 12-2 provides the syntax and usage.

LISTING 12-2   Set-RecipientFilterConfig cmdlet syntax and usage

Syntax

```
Set-RecipientFilterConfig [-BlockedRecipients <email1,email2…emailN>]
[-BlockListEnabled <$true | $false>] [-DomainController DCName]
[-Enabled <$true | $false>] [-ExternalMailEnabled <$true | $false>]
[-InternalMailEnabled <$true | $false>]
[-RecipientValidationEnabled <$true | $false>]
```

Usage

```
Set-RecipientFilterConfig -RecipientValidationEnabled $true


Set-RecipientFilterConfig -BlockedRecipients tony@treyresearch.net,
ed@woodgrovebank.com
```

By default, recipient filtering rejects messages from blocked recipients but doesn't block users from sending messages to blocked recipients. If you set -BlockListEnabled to $true, users won't be able to send messages to blocked recipients. You also can specify whether Exchange 2016 validates recipients and then blocks messages sent to recipients who don't exist. Although Exchange 2016 doesn't validate recipients by default, you can have Exchange 2016 validate recipients by setting -RecipientValidationEnabled to $true.

Blocked list addresses can refer to a specific email address, such as walter@blueyonderairlines.com, or a group of email addresses designated with the wildcard character (*), such as *@blueyonderairlines.com to filter all email addresses from blueyonderairlines.com, or *@*.blueyonderairlines.com, to filter all email addresses from child domains of blueyonderairlines.com.

If you want to modify the blocked recipients, you must either enter the complete set of blocked recipients, or you use a special shorthand to insert into or remove values from this multivalued property. The shorthand for adding values is:

```
@{Add="<ValuetoAdd1>","<ValuetoAdd2>"...}
```

Such as:

```
Set-RecipientFilterConfig -BlockedRecipients
@{Add="mary@imaginedlands.com","gene@tvpress.com"}
```

The shorthand for removing values is:

```
@{Remove="<ValuetoRemove1>","<ValuetoRemove2>"...}
```

Such as:

```
Set-RecipientFilterConfig -BlockedRecipients
@{Remove="mary@imaginedlands.com","gene@tvpress.com"}
```

If you want to add values and remove others, you can do this as well by using the following shorthand:

```
@{Add="<ValuetoAdd1>","<ValuetoAdd2>"...;
Remove="<ValuetoRemove1>","<ValuetoRemove1>"...}
```

You can confirm that values were added or removed as expected by using Get-RecipientFilterConfig. In this example, you view the currently blocked domains:

```
Get-RecipientFilterConfig | fl BlockedRecipients
```

Filtering Connections with IP Block Lists

If you find that sender and recipient filtering isn't enough to stem the flow of spam into your organization, you might want to consider subscribing to an IP block list service. Here's how this service works:

- You subscribe to an IP block list service. Although there are free services available, you might have to pay a monthly service fee. In return, the service lets you query its servers for known sources of unsolicited email and known relay servers.
- The service provides you with domains you can use for validation and a list of status codes to watch for. You configure Exchange to use the specified domains and enter connection filtering rules to match the return codes, and then you configure any exceptions for recipient email addresses or sender IP addresses.
- Each time an incoming connection is made, Exchange performs a lookup of the source IP address in the block list domain. A "host not found" error is returned to indicate the IP address is not on the block list and no match was found. If there is a match, the block list service returns a status code that indicates the suspected activity. For example, a status code of 127.0.0.3 might mean that the IP address is from a known source of unsolicited email.
- If there is a match between the status code returned and the filtering rules you've configured, Exchange returns an error message to the user or server attempting to make the connection. The default error message says that the IP address has been blocked by a connection filter rule, but you can specify a custom error message to return instead.

The sections that follow discuss applying IP block lists, setting provider priority, defining custom error messages to return, and configuring block list exceptions. These tasks will need to be performed when you work with IP block lists.

Applying IP Block Lists

Before you get started, you need to know the domain of the block list service provider, and you should also consider how you want to handle the status codes the provider returns. Exchange allows you to specify that any return status code is a match, that only a specific code matched to a bit mask is a match, or that any of several status codes that you designate can match.

A list of typical status codes that might be returned by a provider service, include:

- 127.0.0.1   Trusted nonspam (on the "white" list). Code bit mask: 0.0.0.1.
- 127.0.0.2   Known source of unsolicited email/spam (on the "black" list). Code bit mask: 0.0.0.2.
- 127.0.0.3   Possible spam, like a mix of spam and nonspam (on the "yellow" list). Code bit mask: 0.0.0.3.
- 127.0.0.4   Known source of unsolicited email/spam, but not yet blocked (on the "brown" list). Code bit mask: 0.0.0.4.
- 127.0.0.5   Not a spam-only source, and not on the "black" list. Code bit mask: 0.0.0.5.

Rather than filter all return codes, in most cases, you'll want to be as specific as possible about the types of status codes that match to help ensure that you don't accidentally filter valid email. For example, based on the list of status codes of the provider, you might decide that you want to filter known sources of unsolicited email and known relay servers, but not filter known sources of dial-up user accounts, which might or might not be sources of unsolicited email.

Exchange 2016 allows you to configure multiple IP block list providers, with a relative priority assigned to a provider determining the order in which providers are checked. In Exchange Management Shell, you manage IP block list providers and their settings by using the following:

* Add-IPBlockListProvider   Adds an IP block list provider.

```
Add-IPBlockListProvider -LookupDomain SmtpDomain -Name ProviderName
[-AnyMatch <$true | $false>] [-BitmaskMatch IPAddressBitMask]
[-DomainController DCName] [-Enabled <$true | $false>]
[-IPAddressesMatch IpAddress1,IpAddress2…IpAddressN]
[-Priority Priority] [-RejectionResponse Response]
```

* Get-IPBlockListProvider   Displays the settings of a specific or all IP block list providers.

```
Get-IPBlockListProvider [-Identity SmtpDomain]
[-DomainController DCName]
```

* Set-IPBlockListProvider   Modifies the settings associated with the specified IP block list provider.

```
Set-IPBlockListProvider -Identity SmtpDomain
[-AnyMatch <$true | $false>] [-BitmaskMatch IPAddressBitMask]
[-DomainController DCName] [-Enabled <$true | $false>]
[-IPAddressesMatch IpAddress1,IpAddress2…IpAddressN]
[-Priority Priority] [-RejectionResponse Response]
```

* Remove-IPBlockListProvider   Removes a IP block list provider.

```
Remove-IPBlockListProvider -Identity SmtpDomain
[-DomainController DCName]
```

When you add a block list provider, you use the -Name parameter to set a descriptive name for the provider and the -LookupDomain to specify the domain name of the block list provider service, such as *proseware.com*. You can then specify whether to match any return code (other than an error) received from the provider service or to match a specific mask and return codes from the provider service. As shown in the following example, set -AnyMatch to $true to match any return code:

```
Add-IPBlockListProvider -Name Proseware -LookupDomain proseware.com
-AnyMatch $true
```

If you want to match a specific mask, use -BitmaskMatch to specify the bitmask to match, such as:

```
Add-IPBlockListProvider -Name Proseware -LookupDomain proseware.com
-BitmaskMatch 0.0.0.4
```

Alternatively, you can match specific values in the return status codes by using -IPAddressesMatch, such as:

```
Add-IPBlockListProvider -Name Proseware -LookupDomain proseware.com
-IPAddressesMatch 127.0.0.4, 127.0.0.5, 127.0.0.6, 127.0.0.7
```

Other commands you can use to manage and work with block lists include:

- Get-IPBlockListConfig   Displays information about the configuration of the Connection Filter agent.

```
Get-IPBlockListConfig [-DomainController DCName]
```

- Set-IPBlockListConfig   Modifies the configuration of the Connection Filter agent.

```
Set-IPBlockListConfig   [-DomainController DCName]
[-Enabled <$true | $false>] [-ExternalMailEnabled <$true | $false>]
[-InternalMailEnabled <$true | $false>]
[-MachineEntryRejectionResponse Response]
[-StaticEntryRejectionResponse Response]
```

- Set-IPBlockListProvidersConfig   Modifies the block list provider configuration used by Connection Filter agent.

```
Set-IPBlockListProvidersConfig [-DomainController DCName]
[-BypassedRecipients <email1,email2…emailN>]
[-Enabled <$true | $false>]
[-ExternalMailEnabled <$true | $false>]
[-InternalMailEnabled <$true | $false>]
```

* Test-IPBlockListProvider   Checks connectivity to the specified block list provider and then issues a lookup request for an IP address to verify.

```
Test-IPBlockListProvider -Identity SmtpName -IPAddress IPAddress
[-DomainController DCName] [-Server ServerID]
```

Configuring Block List Providers

You can configure multiple block list providers. Each provider is listed in priority order, and if Exchange makes a match by using a particular provider, the other providers are not checked for possible matches. In addition to being prioritized, providers can also be enabled or disabled. If you disable a provider, it's ignored when looking for possible status code matches.

In Exchange Management Shell, you can use Add-IPBlockListProvider and Set-IPBlockListProvider to manage provider priority and to enable or disable providers. If you don't specify a priority when you add a provider using Add-IPBlockListProvider, the order providers are added sets the priority, with the first provider added having a priority of 1, the second a priority of 2, and so on.

Use the -Priority parameter to set the relative priority of a provider and the -Enabled parameter to enable or disable a provider. In this example, you set the priority of Proseware.com to 2:

```
Add-IPBlockListProvider -Identity Proseware.com -Priority 2
```

Specifying Custom Error Messages

When a match is made between the status code returned and the filtering rules you've configured for block list providers, Exchange returns an error message to the user or server attempting to make the connection. The default error message says that the IP address has been blocked by a connection filter rule. If you want to override the default error message, you can specify a custom error message to return on a per-rule basis. The error message can contain the following substitution values:

- *%0* to insert the connecting IP address
- *%1* to insert the name of the connection filter rule
- *%2* to insert the domain name of the block list provider service

Some examples of custom error messages include the following:

- The IP address (%0) was blocked and not allowed to connect.
- %0 was rejected by %2 as a potential source of unsolicited email.

The custom error message can't be more than 240 characters.

In Exchange Management Shell, you use the -RejectionResponse parameter of Add-IPBlockListProvider and Set-IPBlockListProvider to set a custom error message on a per-provider basis. Use the -RejectionResponse parameter with the Set-ContentFilterConfig cmdlet to set the default custom response.

Defining Block Lists

Sometimes, you'll find that an IP address, a network, or an email address shows up incorrectly on a block list. The easiest way to correct this problem is to create a block list exception that indicates that the specific IP address, network, or email address shouldn't be filtered.

Using Connection Filter Exceptions

You can define connection filter exceptions for email addresses using the -BypassedRecipients parameter of the Set-IPBlockListProvidersConfig cmdlet. Define the initial set of exceptions simply by entering the email addresses in a comma-separated list, such as:

```
Set-IPBlockListProvidersConfig -BypassedRecipients joe@imaginedlands.com,
sarah@tvpress.com
```

If you want to modify the exceptions, however, you must either enter the complete set of exceptions, or use a special shorthand to insert into or remove values from this multivalued property. The shorthand for working with multivalued properties is:

```
@{Add="<ValuetoAdd1>","<ValuetoAdd2>"...}
```

```
@{Remove="<ValuetoRemove1>","<ValuetoRemove2>"...}
```

```
@{Add="<ValuetoAdd1>","<ValuetoAdd2>"...;
Remove="<ValuetoRemove1>","<ValuetoRemove1>"...}
```

Such as:

```
Set-IPBlockListProvidersConfig -BypassedRecipients
@{Add="tina@treyresearch.net","mark@contosso.com";
Remove="sarah@tvpress.com"}
```

Using Global Allowed Lists

Exchange will accept email from any IP address or network on the global allowed list. Before you can define allowed entries for IP addresses and networks you must be sure that the IP Allow List is enabled.

You use Add-IPAllowListEntry to add an IP address or IP address range to the IP Allow list. Listing 12-3 provides the syntax and usage.

LISTING 12-3 Add-IPAllowListEntry cmdlet syntax and usage

Syntax

```
Add-IPAllowListEntry -IPAddress IPAddress {AddtlParams}
```

```
Add-IPAllowListEntry -IPRange IPRange {AddtlParams}
```

```
{AddtlParams}
[-Comment Comment] [-ExpirationTime DateTime] [-Server ServerId]
```

Usage

```
Add-IPAllowListEntry -IPAddress 192.168.10.45
```

```
Add-IPAllowListEntry -IPRange 192.168.10.0/24
Add-IPAllowListEntry -IPRange 192.168.10.1-192.168.10.254
```

You use Get-IPAllowListEntry to list IP Allow List entries and Remove-IPAllowListEntry to remove IP Allow List entries. Listings 12-4 and 12-5 provide the syntax and usage.

LISTING 12-4 Get-IPAllowListEntry cmdlet syntax and usage

Syntax

```
Get-IPAllowListEntry [-Identity IPListEntryId] {AddtlParams}


Get-IPAllowListEntry -IPAddress IPAddress {AddtlParams}


{AddtlParams}
[-ResultSize Size] [-Server ServerId]
```

Usage

```
Get-IPAllowListEntry
Get-IPAllowListEntry -IPAddress 192.168.10.45
```

LISTING 12-5 Remove-IPAllowListEntry cmdlet syntax and usage

Syntax

```
Remove-IPAllowListEntry -Identity IPListEntryId
[-Server ServerId]
```

Usage

```
Get-IPAllowListEntry | Where {$_.IPRange -eq '192.168.10.45'} |
Remove-IPAllowListEntry


Get-IPAllowListEntry | Where {$_.IPRange -eq '192.168.10.0/24'} |
Remove-IPAllowListEntry
```

Using Global Block Lists

Exchange will reject email from any IP address or network on the block list. Before you can define blocked entries for IP addresses and networks, you must ensure that the IP block list is enabled.

You use Add-IPBlockListEntry to add an IP address or IP address range to the IP block list. Listing 12-6 provides the syntax and usage.

LISTING 12-6 Add-IPBlockListEntry cmdlet syntax and usage

Syntax

```
Add-IPBlockListEntry -IPAddress IPAddress {AddtlParams}
```

```
Add-IPBlockListEntry -IPRange IPRange {AddtlParams}
```

```
{AddtlParams}
[-Comment Comment] [-ExpirationTime DateTime] [-Server ServerId]
```

Usage

```
Add-IPBlockListEntry -IPAddress 192.168.10.45
```

```
Add-IPBlockListEntry -IPRange 192.168.10.0/24
Add-IPBlockListEntry -IPRange 192.168.10.1-192.168.10.254
```

You use Get-IPBlockListEntry to list IP block list entries and Remove-IPBlockListEntry to remove IP block list entries. Listings 12-7 and 12-8 provide the syntax and usage.

LISTING 12-7 Get-IPBlockListEntry cmdlet syntax and usage

Syntax

```
Get-IPBlockListEntry [-Identity IPListEntryId] {AddtlParams}
```

```
Get-IPBlockListEntry -IPAddress IPAddress {AddtlParams}
```

```
{AddtlParams}
[-ResultSize Size] [-Server ServerId]
```

Usage

```
Get-IPBlockListEntry
Get-IPBlockListEntry -IPAddress 192.168.10.45
```

LISTING 12-8 Remove-IPBlockListEntry cmdlet syntax and usage

Syntax

```
Remove-IPBlockListEntry -Identity IPListEntryId
[-Server ServerId]
```

Usage

```
Get-IPBlockListEntry | Where {$_.IPRange -eq '192.168.10.45'} |
Remove-IPBlockListEntry
```

```
Get-IPBlockListEntry | Where {$_.IPRange -eq '192.168.10.0/24'} |
Remove-IPBlockListEntry
```

Preventing Internal Servers from Being Filtered

Typically, you don't want Exchange to apply Sender ID, content or connection filters to servers on your organization's network or to internal SMTP servers deployed in a perimeter zone. One way to ensure this is to configure message delivery options for your organization's transport servers so that they don't apply filters to IP addresses from internal servers and your perimeter network.

In Exchange Management Shell, you prevent internal servers from being filtered by the Sender ID, content or connection filters by using the -InternalMailEnabled parameter of Set-SenderIdConfig, Set-ContentFilterConfig, and Set-IPBlockListProvider. By default, -InternalMailEnabled is set to $false for these cmdlets, which means authenticated internal email messages aren't processed by the Send ID filter, the content filter or the connection filter.

Chapter 13. Optimizing Web and Mobile Access

As you'll learn in this chapter, managing web and mobile access is a bit different from other tasks you'll perform as an Exchange administrator—and not only because you use the Microsoft Internet Information Services (IIS) Manager snap-in to perform many of the management tasks. In Exchange 2016, all client connections are handled by Mailbox servers. Mailbox servers provide front-end authentication and proxying, and also perform the actual back-end processing. Generally speaking, clients connect to front-end services and then are routed via local or remote proxy to the back-end endpoint on the Mailbox server that hosts the active copy of the mailbox database storing the user's mailbox.

When users access Exchange mail and public folders over the Internet or a wireless network, virtual directories and web applications hosted by Mailbox servers are working behind the scenes to grant access and transfer files. As you know from previous chapters, Outlook Web App (OWA) lets users access Exchange over the Internet or over a wireless network by using a standard web browser. Exchange ActiveSync lets users access Exchange through a wireless carrier using mobile devices, such as smart phones. Finally, MAPI over HTTP and RPC over HTTP let users access Exchange mailboxes using Microsoft Office Outlook from the Internet.

Navigating IIS Essentials for Exchange Server

On each Mailbox server there is a single instance of IIS that handles front-end and back-end processes. This IIS instance has a Default Web Site with a single virtual directory for each client protocol handled by the server and a corresponding Exchange Back End website with a single virtual directory for each client protocol handled by the server.

IIS handles incoming requests to a website within the context of a web application. A web application is a software program that delivers content to users over HTTP or HTTPS. Each website has a default web application and one or more additional web applications associated with it. The default web application handles incoming requests that you haven't assigned to other web applications. Additional web applications handle incoming requests that specifically reference the application.

Understanding Mobile Access via IIS

When you install an Exchange server, virtual directories and web applications are installed to support various Exchange services. Each web application must have a root virtual directory associated with it. The root virtual directory sets the application's name and maps the application to the physical directory that contains the application's content. Typically, the default web application is associated with the root virtual directory of the website and any additional virtual directories you've created but haven't mapped to other applications.

In the default configuration, the default application handles an incoming request for the / directory of a website as well as other named virtual directories. IIS maps references to / and other virtual directories to the physical directory that contains the related content. For the / directory of the default website, the default physical directory is %SystemRoot%/inetpub/wwwroot.

In most cases, you only need to open port 443 on your organization's firewall to allow users to access Exchange data hosted by IIS. Then you simply tell users the URL that they need to type into their browser's Address field or in their smart phone's browser. Users can then access Outlook Web App or Exchange ActiveSync when they're off-site. The URLs for Outlook Web App and Exchange ActiveSync are different. The Outlook Web App URL is *https://yourserver .yourdomain.com/owa*, and the Exchange ActiveSync URL is *https://yourserver .yourdomain.com/Microsoft-Server-ActiveSync*. Generally, however, the address users enter for both matches the OWA address.

As you configure web and mobile access, don't forget that the infrastructure has two layers:

- A front end that you can customize to control the way users access and work with related services and features
- A back end that handles the back-end processing but that you only modify to control the options that the front end uses for working with the back-end processes

Thus, although you typically modify front-end virtual directories to customize the environment for users, you rarely modify the back-end virtual directories. For example, when you first install Exchange services, Outlook Web App, Exchange

Admin Center, and other essential services can only be accessed by clients on the internal network. To allow external clients to access these services, you must specify an external access URL for Outlook Web App, Exchange Admin Center, and other essential services.

Maintaining Virtual Directories and Web Applications

When you install an Exchange server, Exchange Setup installs and configures virtual directories and Web applications for use. The virtual directories and web applications allow authenticated users to access their messaging data from the web. On Mailbox servers, you'll find a Default Web Site that provides front-end services and an Exchange Back End website that provides back-end services. Apps on the front end have corresponding back-end apps, with connections being proxied from the front end to the back end for processing.

In Exchange Management Shell, you can use the Get-OWAVirtualDirectory cmdlet to view information about OWA virtual directories, the New-OWAVirtualDirectory cmdlet to create an OWA directory if one does not exist, the Remove-OWAVirtualDirectory cmdlet to remove an OWA directory, and the Test-OWAConnectivity cmdlet to test OWA connectivity. There are similar sets of commands for ActiveSync, Autodiscover, ECP, OAB, Windows PowerShell, MAPI and web services.

Generally, any time you are working with Exchange via the shell, you should specify whether you want to work with the front-end virtual directory or backend virtual directory to ensure the directory you expect to be configured is the one created, modified or removed. Keep the following in mind:

- When you are working with related Get commands, only information about front-end directories is provided by default. To also display information about back-end directories, you must use the -ShowMailboxVirtualDirectories parameter.
- When you are working with the related New and Remove commands, you must use the -Role parameter to specify whether you are working with front-end or back-end directories. Set -Role to ClientAccess when you want to configure the front-end virtual directory. Set -Role to Mailbox when you want to configure the back-end virtual directory.
- With related Set commands, you must always specify the identity of the virtual directory that you want to work with. The identity points to the exact end point on the front-end or backend.

If you examine the virtual directory structure for the Default Web site or the Exchange Back End website, you'll find several important virtual directories and web applications, including:

- **Autodiscover**   Autodiscover is used to provide the Autodiscover service for all clients. By default, this directory is configured for pass-through authentication and the related app runs within the context of MSExchangeAutodiscoverAppPool. For troubleshooting non-configuration issues, use the Autodiscover, Autodiscover.Proxy, and Autodiscover.Protocol health sets. Check these health sets using:

```
Get-ServerHealth ServerId | ?{$_.HealthSetName -match "Autodiscover"}
```

- **ECP**   The Exchange Admin Center (ECP) is used for web-based administration of Exchange. By default, this directory is configured for pass-through authentication and the related app runs within the context of MSExchangeECPAppPool. For troubleshooting non-configuration issues, use the ECP and ECP.Proxy and OWA.Protocol health sets. Check the ECP health sets using:

```
Get-ServerHealth ServerId | ?{$_.HealthSetName -match "ECP"}
```

- **EWS**   Exchange Web Services (EWS) is used to enable applications to interact with Exchange mailboxes and messaging items using HTTPS. By default, this directory is configured for pass-through authentication and the related app runs within the context of MSExchangeServicesAppPool. For troubleshooting non-configuration issues, use the EWS, EWS.Proxy, and EWS.Protocol health sets. Check these health sets using:

```
Get-ServerHealth ServerId | ?{$_.HealthSetName -match "EWS"}
```

- **MAPI**   Mapi is the directory that provides MAPI over HTTP services to clients. By default, this directory is configured for pass-through authentication and the related app runs within the context of MSExchangeMapiFrontEndAppPool. For troubleshooting non-configuration issues, use the OutlookMapiHttp-related health sets. Check these health sets using:

```
Get-ServerHealth ServerId | ?{$_.HealthSetName -match "MAPI"}
```

- **Microsoft-Server-ActiveSync**   Microsoft-Server-ActiveSync is the directory to which Exchange ActiveSync users connect to access their Exchange data. By default, this directory is configured for pass-through authentication and the related app runs within the context of MSExchangeSyncAppPool. For troubleshooting non-configuration issues, use the ActiveSync, ActiveSync.Proxy and ActiveSync.Protocol health sets. Check these health sets using:

```
Get-ServerHealth Serverld | ?{$_.HealthSetName -match "ActiveSync"}
```

- **OAB** OAB is the directory that provides the offline address book (OAB) to clients. By default, this directory is configured for pass-through authentication and the related app runs within the context of MSExchangeOABAppPool. For troubleshooting non-configuration issues, use the OAB and OAB.Proxy health sets. Check these health sets using:

```
Get-ServerHealth Serverld | ?{$_.HealthSetName -match "OAB"}
```

- **OWA** OWA is the directory to which users connect with their web browsers to start an Outlook Web App session. By default, this directory is configured for pass-through authentication and the related app runs within the context of MSExchangeOWAAppPool. For troubleshooting non-configuration issues, use the OWA, OWA.Proxy, and OWA.Protocol health sets. Check these health sets using:

```
Get-ServerHealth Serverld | ?{$_.HealthSetName -match "OWA"}
```

- **PowerShell** PowerShell is the directory to which the Exchange Management tools connect for remote administration. Depending on whether you are working with the front-end or back-end, the related app runs within the context of MSExchangePowerShellFrontEndAppPool or MSExchangePowerShellBackEndAppPool. For troubleshooting non-configuration issues, use the RPS and RPS.Proxy health sets. Check these health sets using:

```
Get-ServerHealth Serverld | ?{$_.HealthSetName -match "RPS"}
```

- **RPC** RPC is the directory that provides Remote Procedure Call (RPC) services to clients. By default, this directory is configured for pass-through authentication and the related app runs within the context of MSExchangeRPCProxyAppPool. Whether the Rpc virtual directory on the front end connects to the Rpc virtual directory or the RpcWithCert virtual directory on the backend depends on whether an SSL certificate is used as part of authentication.
- **Public** Public is the directory to which mailbox users are connected to access the default Public Folders tree. This directory exists only on Mailbox servers and doesn't have a specifically configured application pool. For troubleshooting non-configuration issues, use the PublicFolders and OWA health sets. Check the PublicFolders health set using:

```
Get-ServerHealth Serverld | ?{$_.HealthSetName -eq "PublicFolders"}
```

For troubleshooting configuration issues with virtual directories, you might need to remove and recreate the front-end virtual directory first, and then check to see if this resolves the problem before removing and recreating the back-end virtual directory. As an example, if you've determined the OWA virtual directory is misconfigured, you can remove it by using Remove-OwaVirtualDirectory, and then recreate it by using New-OwaVirtualDirectory. You could remove and then recreate the OWA virtual directory from the Default Web Site on MailServer21 by using the following commands:

```
remove-owavirtualdirectory -identity "mailserver21\owa (Default Web Site)"
```

```
new-owavirtualdirectory -server mailserver 21
-websitename "Default Web Site"
```

By default, the New-OwaVirtualDirectory and New-EcpVirtualDirectory commands enable basic authentication and forms authentication but do not enable Windows authentication. As Windows authentication is required for OWA and ECP, you'll want to use the Set-OwaVirtualDirectory and Set-EcpVirtualDirectory commands to modify the default authentication settings. In the following example, you enable Windows authentication and disable basic and forms authentication:

```
set-owavirtualdirectory -identity "mailserver21\owa (Default Web Site)"
-WindowsAuthentication $True -Basicauthentication $false
-Formsauthentication $false
```

> **TIP** You can set properties on some or all virtual directories by piping the output of Get-OwaVirtualDirectory to Set-OwaVirtualDirectory. For example, the following command allows users to change their passwords by default for all Outlook Web App virtual directories:
>
> Get-OwaVirtualDirectory | Set-OwaVirtualDirectory -ChangePassword $true

After you recreate a virtual directory you should restart IIS services. You can do this in IIS Manager or by entering the following command at an elevated command prompt or shell:

```
iisreset
```

You can diagnose non-configuration problems with a particular feature as well as any related proxy and protocol features by using Get-HealthReport to check the status of the related health sets. Try to resolve the problem by using the following techniques while verifying the issue still exists each time you take a corrective action:

1. Try to isolate the problem to a specific server by running a health check for the feature on each Exchange server. If you find an Unhealthy status for the feature on a particular server, you've likely isolated the problem and identified the server experiencing the problem and can skip Steps 2 and 3.

2. If you are unable to isolate the problem to a specific server or servers, try to log on to OWA or ECP, and then use the feature using the URL for a specific Mailbox server. If this fails, try accessing and log on to a different Mailbox server. This should help you verify whether the problem is with a particular Mailbox server. Remember that the Mailbox server used is the one that contains the mailbox database where the mailbox for the user is stored.

3. Using the Services console, verify that all essential Exchange services are running on the Mailbox servers. If an essential service isn't running, select it and then click Start.

4. Verify network connectivity between the Mailbox servers. One way to do this is to log on to each server and try to ping the other servers. If you correct a connectivity issue, check to see if the issue is resolved. Most features require connectivity to domain controllers.

5. In IIS Manager, connect to the server that's reporting the health issue or otherwise experiencing a problem with the feature you are troubleshooting. Expand the Sites node and verify that the Default Web Site or Exchange Back End website is running as appropriate. If a required website isn't running, click Start in the Actions pane to start it. This should resolve the problem.

6. Under Application Pools, verify that the required application pools have been started. If a required application pool hasn't been started, select it and then click Start in the Actions pane.

7. If you suspect an issue with a required application pool on the front-end server, the back-end server, or both, select the application pool and then click Recycle in the Actions pane to recycle its work processes.

8. If the problem isn't resolved yet, restart the website in which the problem is occurring or the IIS itself. To restart a website, select the website in IIS Manager, and then select Restart in the Actions pane. To restart IIS, select the server node in IIS Manager, and then Restart in the Actions pane.

9. If the problem still isn't resolved, restart the server. If restarting the server doesn't resolve the problem, you likely have a configuration problem that can be resolved by removing and recreating the related virtual directories.

Starting, Stopping, and Restarting Websites

Websites run under a server process that you can start, stop, and pause, much like other server processes. For example, if you're changing the configuration of a website or performing other maintenance tasks, you might need to stop the website, make the changes, and then restart it. When a website is stopped, it doesn't accept connections from users and can't be used to deliver or retrieve mail.

The master process for all websites is the World Wide Web Publishing Service. Stopping this service stops all websites using the process, and all connections are disconnected immediately. Starting this service restarts all websites that were running when you stopped the World Wide Web Publishing Service.

You can start, stop, or restart a website by completing the following steps:

1. Start IIS Manager. In Server Manager, click Tools, and then select Internet Information Services (IIS) Manager.

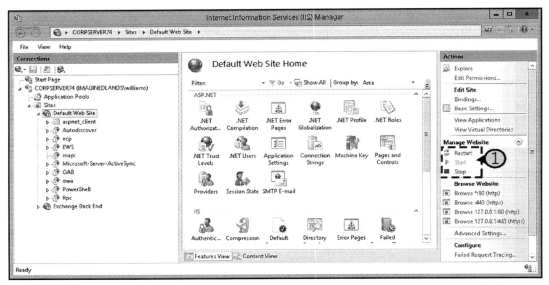

2. In IIS Manager, expand the server and related Sites node by double-clicking the entry for the server you want to work with, and then double-clicking Sites.

3. Select the website you want to manage. Using the options in the Actions pane, you can now do the following:

- Select Start to start the website.
- Select Stop to stop the website.

▪ Select Restart to stop and then start the website.

If you suspect there's a problem with the World Wide Web Publishing Service or other related IIS services, you can use the following technique to restart all IIS services:

1. Start IIS Manager. In Server Manager, click Tools, and then select Internet Information Services (IIS) Manager.

2. Select the entry for the server you want to work with, and then select Restart in the Actions Pane.

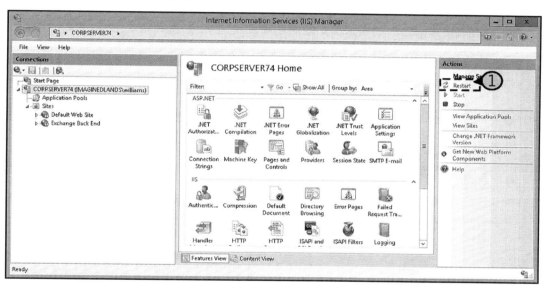

Configuring Outlook Web App Features

Microsoft uses the term *segmentation* to refer to your ability to enable and disable the various features within Outlook Web App. Segmentation settings applied to the OWA virtual directory control the features available to users. If a server has multiple OWA virtual directories or you have multiple Mailbox servers, you must configure each directory and server separately.

Managing Segmentation Features

A summary of the segmentation features that are enabled by default for use with Outlook Web App follows:

- **All Address Lists**   When enabled, users can view all the available address lists. When this feature is disabled, users can view only the default global address list.
- **Calendar**   When enabled, users can access their calendars in Outlook Web App.
- **Change Password**   When enabled, users can change their passwords in Outlook Web App.
- **Contacts**   When enabled, users can access their contacts in Outlook Web App.
- **Direct File Access**   When enabled, users can open attachments directly.
- **Email Signature**   When enabled, users can customize their signatures and include a signature in outgoing messages.
- **Exchange ActiveSync**   When enabled, users can remove mobile devices, initiate mobile wipe, view their device passwords, and review their mobile access logs.
- **Inbox Rules**   When enabled, users can customize rules in Outlook Web App.
- **Instant Messaging**   When enabled, users can access Instant Messaging in Outlook Web App.
- **Journaling**   When enabled, the Journal folder is visible in Outlook Web App.
- **Junk Email Filtering**   When enabled, users can filter junk email using Outlook Web App.
- **Notes**   When enabled, users can access their notes in Outlook Web App.
- **Premium Client**   When enabled, users can use the standard version of Outlook Web App (or the light version if that is the version supported by their browser). When this feature is disabled, users can only access the light version of Outlook Web App.
- **Public Folders**   When enabled, users can browse and read items in public folders using Outlook Web App.
- **Recover Deleted Items**   When enabled, users can view items that have been deleted from Deleted Items and choose whether to recover them.
- **Reminders And Notifications**   When enabled, users can receive new email notifications, task reminders, calendar reminders, and automatic folder updates.
- **Tasks**   When enabled, users can access their tasks in Outlook Web App.
- **Text Messaging**   When enabled, users can send and receive text messages and create text message notifications in Outlook Web App.
- **Themes**   When enabled, users can change the color scheme in Outlook Web App.
- **Unified Messaging**   When enabled, users can access their voice mail and faxes in Outlook Web App. They can also configure voice mail options.
- **Office Web Apps Viewing**   When enabled, users can view supported file types while using OWA in their web browser.

You manage segmentation features in several ways:

- In Exchange Management Shell, you can enable or disable segmentation features on a per server basis by running the Set-OWAVirtualDirectory cmdlet on Mailbox servers.

- In Exchange Admin Center and Exchange Management Shell, you can define Outlook Web App policies that enable or disable segmentation features and then apply these policies to users. Settings in Outlook Web App policies override virtual directory settings.
- In Exchange Management Shell, you can enable or disable segmentation features for individual users by using the Set-CASMailbox cmdlet. These settings override settings applied through policies and virtual directories.

To enable or disable segmentation features for a particular virtual directory, complete the following steps:

1. In the Exchange Admin Center, select Servers in the Feature pane, and then select Virtual Directories to view a list of the front-end virtual directories used by all Exchange servers in the organization. To streamline the view, select a specific server on the Select Server list and/or choose a specific directory type on the Select Type list.

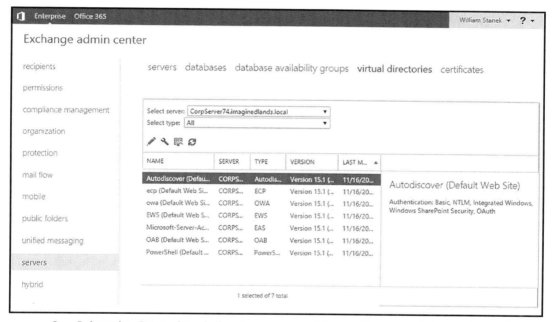

2. Select the OWA virtual directory you want to configure, and then select Edit ( ).

3. In the Virtual Directory dialog box, select the Features page. Scroll down and then click More Options to view all the features you can manage.

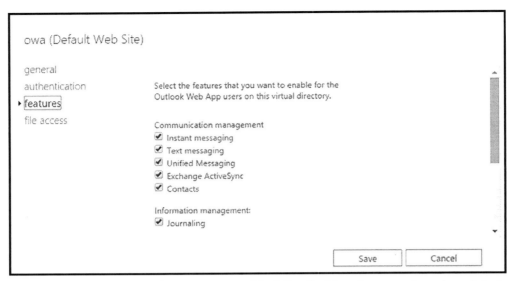

owa (Default Web Site)

general
authentication
▸ features
file access

Select the features that you want to enable for the
Outlook Web App users on this virtual directory.

Communication management
☑ Instant messaging
☑ Text messaging
☑ Unified Messaging
☑ Exchange ActiveSync
☑ Contacts

Information management:
☑ Journaling

[Save] [Cancel]

4. By default, all features are enabled. To disable a feature, clear the related checkbox.

5. By default users can view web-ready documents in their browser and open attachments directly whether they are using a public or private computer. As necessary, use the options on the File Access page to change the file access options.

6. Click Save to apply the settings.

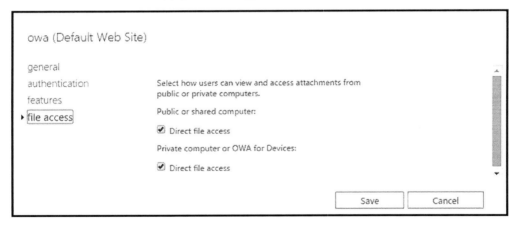

owa (Default Web Site)

general
authentication
features
▸ file access

Select how users can view and access attachments from
public or private computers.

Public or shared computer:

☑ Direct file access

Private computer or OWA for Devices:

☑ Direct file access

[Save] [Cancel]

Managing Outlook Web App Policies

In the Exchange Admin Center, select Permissions in the Feature pane, and then select Outlook Web App Policies to view the currently defined policies. Select a policy to view its settings in the details pane.

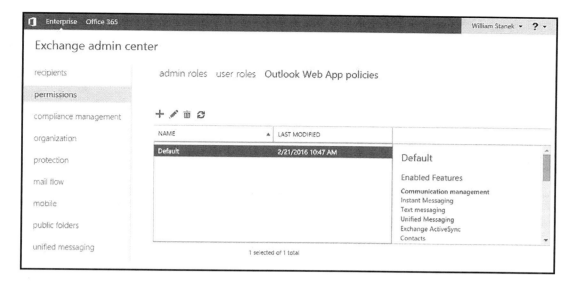

To create an Outlook Web App policy, follow these steps:

1. When you select Permissions > Outlook Web App Policies in Exchange Admin Center, you'll see a list of current policies. You can create a new policy by clicking Add ( ).

2. In the Policy Name text box, type a descriptive name for the policy, such as All Permanent Employees.

3. To view all of the features you can configure, click More Options.

4. By default, all features are enabled. To disable a feature, clear the related checkbox.

5. Click Save to create the policy.

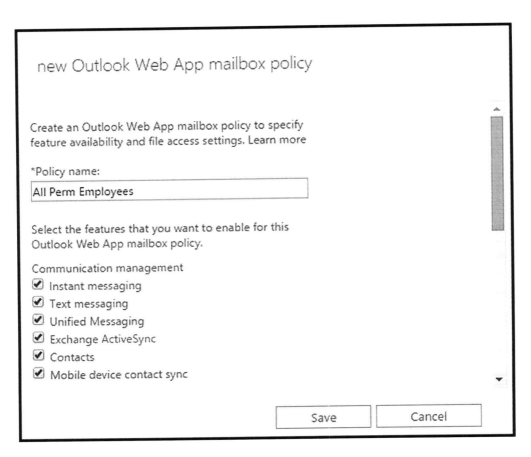

In Exchange Management Shell, you can create Outlook Web App policies by using New-OwaMailboxPolicy and then set the properties of the policy by using Set-OwaMailboxPolicy. The following example creates a policy called AllUsers and then configures its settings:

```
New-OwaMailboxPolicy -Name AllUsers
```

```
Set-OwaMailboxPolicy -Identity AllUsers -AllAddressLists $false
-ChangePasswordEnabled $false -AllowOfflineOn "NoComputers"
-ContactsEnabled $false -FacebookEnabled $false -LinkedInEnabled $false
-CalendarEnabled $true
```

Use Get-OwaMailboxPolicy to confirm that the properties of the policy are set as expected. Afterward, you can apply the policy to users by using the -OwaMailboxPolicy property of Set-CASMailbox. Listing13-1 shows various ways you can apply the policy.

LISTING 13-1 Techniques for applying OWA mailbox policies to mailbox users

Apply the policy to the mailbox user named HenryJ

```
Set-CASMailboxPolicy -Identity HenryJ -OwaMailboxPolicy "AllUsers"
```

Apply the policy to every mailbox in the Exchange organization

```
Get-Mailbox -ResultSize Unlimited | Set-CASMailboxPolicy
-OwaMailboxPolicy "AllUsers"
```

Apply the policy to every mailbox in the Sales database

```
Get-MailboxDatabase "Sales" | Get-Mailbox -ResultSize Unlimited |
Set-CASMailboxPolicy -OwaMailboxPolicy "AllUsers"
```

Apply the policy to all mailboxes in every mailbox database on MailboxServer18

```
Get-Mailbox -Server MailboxServer18 -ResultSize Unlimited
Set-CASMailboxPolicy -OwaMailboxPolicy "AllUsers"
```

Managing Bindings, Connections and Authentication

As you optimize IIS for your Exchange environment, you'll want to look at the configuration settings for bindings, SSL and connections. You might also need to redirect users to alternate URLs, control access and modify authentication settings. These topics are discussed in this section.

Optimizing the Mobile Access Websites

Each website hosted by IIS has one or more bindings. A binding is a unique combination of ports, IP addresses, and host names that identifies a website. For unsecure connections, the default port is TCP port 80. For secure connections, the default port is TCP port 443. The default IP address setting is to use any available IP address. The default host name is the Mailbox server's DNS name.

Normally, you wouldn't want to multihome a Mailbox server; however, when the server is multihomed, or when you use it to provide Outlook Web App or Exchange ActiveSync services for multiple domains, the default configuration isn't ideal. On a multihomed server, you'll usually want messaging protocols to respond only on a specific IP address. To do this, you need to change the default settings. On a server that provides Outlook Web App and Exchange ActiveSync services for multiple domains, you'll usually want to specify an additional host name for each domain.

When you are working with IIS, you can change the identity of a website by completing the following steps:

1. If you want the website to use a new IP address, you must configure the IP address on the server before trying to specify it on the website.

2. Start IIS Manager. In Server Manager, click Tools, and then select Internet Information Services (IIS) Manager.

> **NOTE** By default, IIS Manager connects to the services running on the local computer. If you want to connect to a different server, select the Start Page node in the left pane, and then click the Connect to a Server link to start the Connect To Server Wizard. Follow the prompts to connect to the remote server.

3. In IIS Manager, expand the server and related Sites node by double-clicking the entry for the server with which you want to work, and then double-clicking Sites.

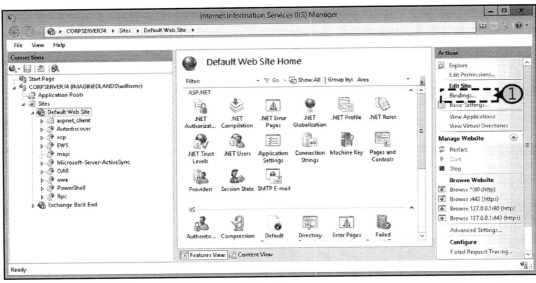

4. In the left pane, select the website that you want to manage, and then select Bindings on the Actions pane. You can now use the Site Bindings dialog box to configure multiple bindings for the website.

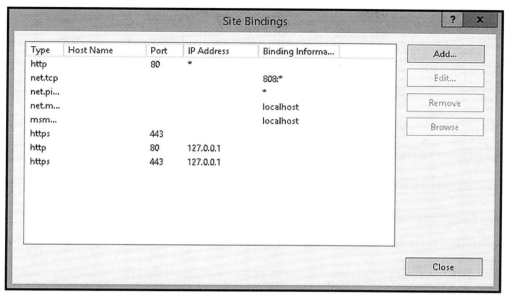

Type	Host Name	Port	IP Address	Binding Informa...	
http		80	*		
net.tcp				808:*	
net.pi...			*		
net.m...				localhost	
msm...				localhost	
https		443			
http		80	127.0.0.1		
https		443	127.0.0.1		

5. Use the Site Bindings dialog box to manage the site's bindings by using the following settings:

- **Add**   Adds a new identity. To add a new identity, click Add. In the Add Site Bindings dialog box, select the binding type, IP address, and TCP port to use. Optionally, type a host header name or select a Secure Sockets Layer (SSL) certificate as appropriate for the binding type. Click OK when you have finished.
- **Edit**   Allows you to edit the currently selected identity. To edit an identity, click the identity, and then click Edit. In the Edit Site Bindings dialog box, select an IP address and TCP port to use. Optionally, type a host header name or select an SSL certificate as appropriate for the binding type. Click OK when you have finished.
- **Remove**   Allows you to remove the currently selected identity. To remove an identity, click the identity, and then click Remove. When prompted to confirm, click Yes.
- **Browse**   Allows you to test an identity. To test an identity, click the identity, and then click Browse. IIS Manager then opens a browser window and connects to the selected binding.

6. Click Close.

Enabling SSL on Websites

SSL is a protocol for encrypting data that is transferred between a client and a server. Without SSL, servers pass data in readable, unencrypted text to clients, which could be a security risk in an enterprise environment. With SSL, servers pass data encoded using encryption.

Although websites are configured to use SSL on port 443 automatically, the server won't use SSL unless you've created and installed a valid X.509 certificate. When you install an Exchange server, a default X.509 certificate is created for Exchange Server 2016 and registered with IIS. In IIS Manager, you can view the default X.509 certificate by completing the following steps:

1. Log on to the Mailbox server. Start IIS Manager. In Server Manager, click Tools, and then select Internet Information Services (IIS) Manager.

2. In IIS Manager, expand the server node, and then double-click the Server Certificates feature.

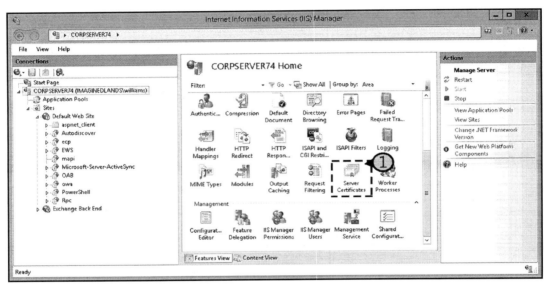

3. On the Server Certificates page, you'll see a list of certificates the web server can use. The default X.509 certificate for Exchange Server has the name Microsoft Exchange. Click the certificate entry, and then click View in the Actions pane to view detailed information regarding the certificate. By default, this certificate is valid for one year from the date you install the server.

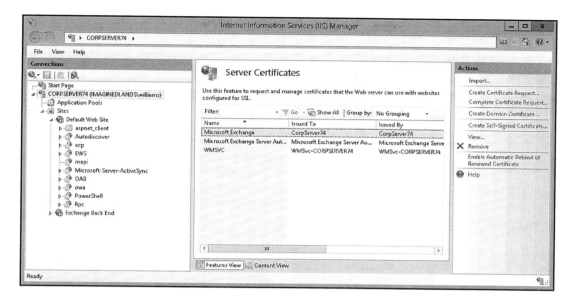

For a long-term solution, you need to create a permanent certificate for the server. This certificate can be a certificate assigned by your organization's certificate authority (CA) or a third-party certificate.

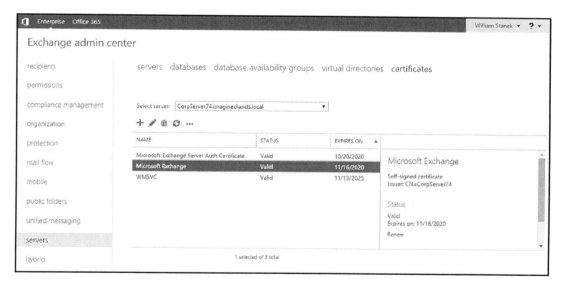

To create a certificate for use with Exchange and IIS, use the features provided by the Exchange management tools. In the Exchange Admin Center, you can view available certificates for Exchange servers by selecting Servers in the Feature pane, and then selecting Certificates. Next, on the Select Server list, choose the server you want to work with. You'll then see a list of available certificates for this server.

You can view the general settings for the certificate by selecting it and then selecting

Edit (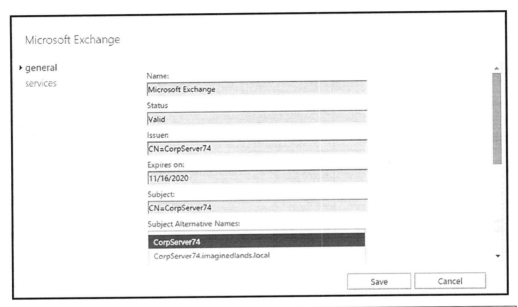). The subject alternative names associated with the certificate determines the names that can be used when establishing SSL connections. Typically, the subject alternative names include the host name and the fully-qualified domain name of the server.

Microsoft Exchange

▸ general

services

Name:

Microsoft Exchange

Status

Valid

Issuer:

CN=CorpServer74

Expires on:

11/16/2020

Subject:

CN=CorpServer74

Subject Alternative Names:

CorpServer74

CorpServer74.imaginedlands.local

[Save] [Cancel]

> **CAUTION** Don't make any changes to certificates as this could invalidate them. When you are finished viewing a certificate, click Cancel to exit the properties dialog box without saving any changes. The default certificates were created by using Exchange Management Shell and should only be modified or renewed by using Exchange Management Shell. The same is true for any other certificate created using the shell.

On the Services page, each selected option represents a service assigned to the certificate. By assigning a service to a certificate, you are allowing the certificate to be used to secure the service. After you are done viewing a certificate's properties, click Cancel (you don't want to inadvertently make any changes to a certificate).

To request and create a certificate from a certification authority, complete the following steps:

1. In the Exchange Admin Center, select Servers in the Feature pane, and then select Certificates.

2. On the Select Server list, choose the server with which you want to work.

3. Click Add to start the New Exchange Certificate Wizard.

4. Select Create A Request to use the wizard to create a certificate request file, and then click Next.

5. Type a descriptive name for the certificate, and then click Next.

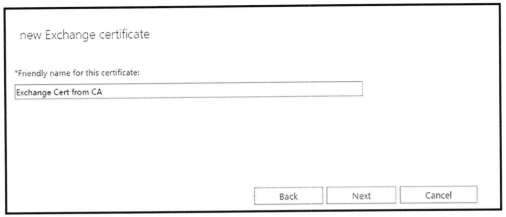

new Exchange certificate

*Friendly name for this certificate:

Exchange Cert from CA

| Back | Next | Cancel |

6.   Specify the root domain for the certificate. If you want the certificate to be usable for all subdomains of your root domain, select the Request A Wildcard Certificate checkbox, and then click Next.

new Exchange certificate

☑ Request a wildcard certificate. A wildcard certificate can be used to secure all subdomains under your root domain with a single certificate. Learn more

*Root domain:

imaginedlands.com

| Back | Next | Cancel |

7.   Click Browse. Choose the server where you want to store the request. Typically, this is the server where you will install the certificate. Click Next.

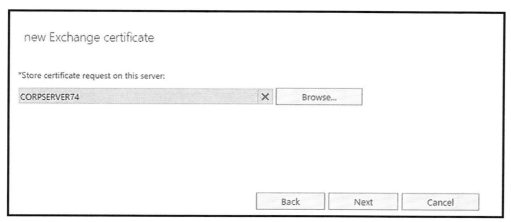

8. Identify your organization by entering the organization name, department name, city, state, and country. These values are all required and must be entered before you can continue. Click Next.

9. Specify the full file path for a network location where the certificate request file can be saved, such as \\CorpServer74\Data\CertRequest.req. Click Finish.

new Exchange certificate

*Save the certificate request to the following file (example:
\\myservername\share\mycertrequest.REQ):

\\CorpServer74\Data\CertRequest.req

You'll need to submit the contents of the file you entered to a certification authority.

After you receive the certificate file from the certification authority, you'll need to click
Complete in the Information pane to install it on your Exchange server. Learn more

| Back | Finish | Cancel |

Send the certificate request file to a third-party certificate authority or your
organization's CA as appropriate. When you receive the certificate back from the CA,
import the certificate. In the Certificates area, you'll see an entry for the certificate
with a status of Pending Request. Select this entry, and then select Complete in the
details pane.

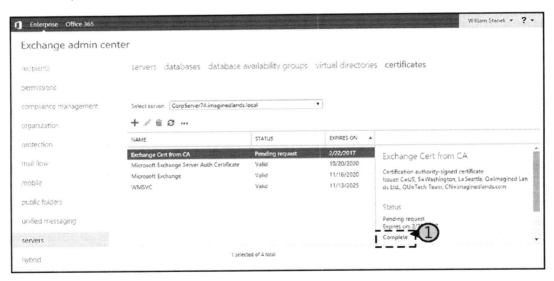

Next, in the Complete Pending Request dialog box, specify the full file path for a
network location where the certificate file is available to be imported, such as
\\CorpServer74\Data\MyCertificate.cer. Click OK.

If you have a certificate to install but don't have a pending request, you can import the certificate while working with the Certificates area in the Exchange Admin Center as well. To do this, complete the following steps:

1. Click the More button (•••), and then select Import Exchange Certificate to start the Import Exchange Certificate Wizard. Use the wizard to import the certificate file.

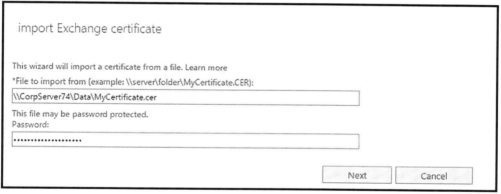

2. Specify the full file path for a network location where the certificate file is available to be imported, such as \\CorpServer74\Data\MyCertificate.cer. If the file is password-protected, enter the password. Click Next.

3. Click Add (+). In the Select A Server dialog box, select a server to which the certificate should be applied, and then click Add. Repeat this process to add additional servers. Click OK.

4. Click Finish to import the certificate.

import Exchange certificate

*Specify the servers you want to apply this certificate to. Learn more

+ −

NAME
CorpServer74.imaginedlands.local

| Back | Finish | Cancel |

After you've installed the certificate, you should test the certificate with an external client by accessing OWA from a remote computer. Clients won't automatically trust self-signed certificates or certificates issued by your CA; therefore, you might see an error stating that there is a problem with the website's security certificate. In this case, you'll need to configure the client to trust the certificate. One way to do this with Internet Explorer is follow these steps:

1. Click the Continue To This Website link. When you continue to the site, a Certificate Error option appears to the right of the address field.

2. Click the Certificate Error to display a related error dialog box, and then click View Certificates to display the Certificate dialog box.

3. On the General tab of the Certificate dialog box, you'll see an error stating the CA Root Certificate isn't trusted. Note the certificate details.

4. To enable trust, you must install this certificate in the Trusted Root Certification Authorities store on the computer. The browser will then trust the certificate, and you shouldn't see the certificate error again for this client.

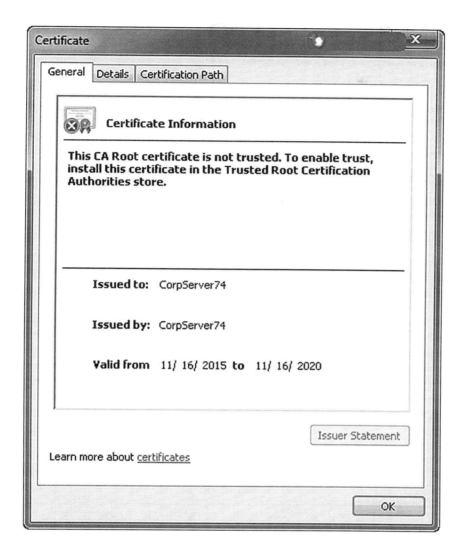

You also can test services supported by the certificate. Test web services by using Test-OutlookWebServices as shown in the following example:

```
test-outlookwebservices | fl
```

By default Test-OutlookWebServices, verifies the Availability service, Outlook Anywhere, Offline Address Book, and Unified Messaging. You can test OWA and ECP by using Test-OwaConnectivity and Test-EcpConnectivity respectively.

Another way to test connectivity is to use the Remote Connectivity Analyzer, which is accessed by entering the following URL in a web browser: **https://testexchangeconnectivity.com**.

Restricting Incoming Connections

You can control incoming connections to a website in several ways including setting a maximum limit on the bandwidth used, setting a limit on the number of simultaneous connections, and setting a connection time-out value. However, you typically wouldn't want to perform any of these actions for an Exchange server or OWA. OWA has its own timers based on whether the end user is on a public/shared or a private computer. These values are fixed and not affected by any restrictions or settings discussed in this section.

Normally, websites do not have maximum bandwidth limits and accept an unlimited number of connections, which is an optimal setting in most environments. However, when you're trying to prevent the underlying server hardware from becoming overloaded or you want to ensure other websites on the same computer have enough bandwidth, you might want to limit the bandwidth available to the site and the number of simultaneous connections. When either limit is reached, no other clients are permitted to access the server. The clients must wait until the connection load on the server decreases.

The connection time-out value determines when idle user sessions are disconnected. With the default website, sessions time out after they've been idle for 120 seconds (2 minutes). It's a sound security practice to disconnect idle sessions and force users to log back on to the server. If you don't disconnect idle sessions within a reasonable amount of time, unauthorized persons could gain access to your messaging system through a browser window left unattended on a remote terminal.

You can modify connection limits and time-outs by completing the following steps:

1. Start IIS Manager. In Server Manager, click Tools, and then select Internet Information Services (IIS) Manager.
2. In IIS Manager, expand the server and related Sites node by double-clicking the entry for the server with which you want to work, and then double-clicking Sites.

3. In the left pane, select the website that you want to manage, and then click Limits in the Actions pane. This displays the Edit Website Limits dialog box.

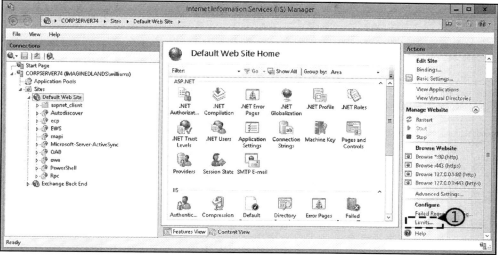

4. To remove maximum bandwidth limits, clear the Limit Bandwidth Usage check box. To set a maximum bandwidth limit, select the Limit Bandwidth Usage check box, and then set the desired limit in bytes.

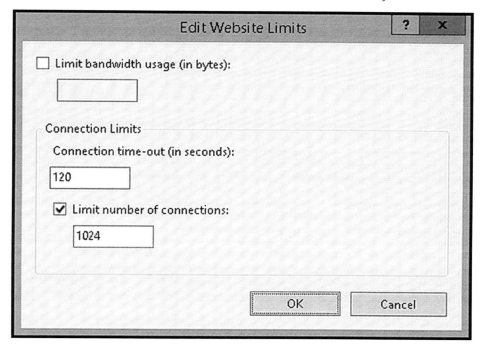

5. The Connection Time-Out field controls how long idle user sessions remain connected to the server. The default value is 120 seconds. Type a new value to change the current time-out value.

6. To remove connection limits, clear the Limit Number Of Connections check box. To set a connection limit, select the Limit Number Of Connections check box, and then type a limit.

7. Click OK.

Redirecting Users to Alternate Urls

You might occasionally find that you want to redirect users to alternate URLs. For example, you might want users to type **http://mail.tvpress.com** and get redirected to *https://mail.tvpress.com/owa*.

You can redirect users from one URL to another by completing the following steps:

1. Start IIS Manager. In Server Manager, click Tools, and then select Internet Information Services (IIS) Manager.

2. In IIS Manager, navigate to the level you want to manage. You manage redirection for an entire site at the site level, and redirection for a directory at the directory level.

3. In the main pane, double-click the HTTP Redirect feature. This displays the HTTP Redirect page.

> NOTE With IIS, HTTP redirection is an optional role service. Therefore, if the HTTP Redirect feature is not available, you need to install the related role service by using Server Manager's Add Roles And Features Wizard.

4. On the HTTP Redirect page, select Redirect Requests To This Destination.

5. In the Redirect Requests To This Destination text box, type the URL to which the user should be redirected. To redirect the user to a different server, type the full path, starting with http:// or https://, such as https://mailer2.tvpress.com/owa. To redirect the user to a virtual directory on the same server, type a slash mark (/) followed by the directory name, such as /owa. Click Apply to save your settings.

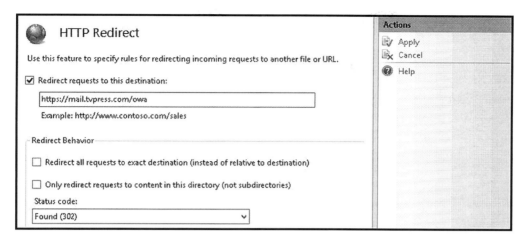

Controlling Access to the HTTP Server

IIS supports several authentication methods, including the following:

- **Anonymous authentication**   With anonymous authentication, IIS automatically logs users on with an anonymous or guest account. This allows users to access resources without being prompted for user name and password information.
- **ASP.NET Impersonation**   With ASP.NET Impersonation, a managed code application can run either as the user authenticated by IIS or as a designated account that you specify when configuring this mode.
- **Basic authentication**   With basic authentication, users are prompted for logon information. When entered, this information is transmitted unencrypted (base64-encoded) across the network. If you've configured secure communications on the server, as described in the section of this chapter titled "Enabling SSL on Websites," you can require that clients use SSL. When you use SSL with basic authentication, the logon information is encrypted before transmission.
- **Digest authentication**   With digest authentication, user credentials are transmitted securely between clients and servers. Digest authentication is a feature of HTTP 1.1 and uses a technique that can't be easily intercepted and decrypted.
- **Forms authentication**   With Forms authentication, you manage client registration and authentication at the application level instead of relying on the authentication mechanisms in IIS. As the mode name implies, users register and provide their credentials using a logon form. By default, this information is passed as cleartext. To avoid this, you should use SSL encryption for the logon page and other internal application pages.
- **Windows authentication**   With Windows authentication, IIS uses kernel-mode Windows security to validate the user's identity. Instead of prompting for a user name and password, clients relay the logon credentials that users supply when they log on to Windows. These credentials are fully encrypted without the need

for SSL, and they include the user name and password needed to log on to the network.

When you install IIS on a Mailbox server, you are required to enable basic authentication, digest authentication, and Windows authentication. These authentication methods, along with anonymous authentication, are used to control access to the server's virtual directories. A virtual directory is simply a folder path that is accessible by a URL. For example, you could create a virtual directory called Data that is physically located on C:\CorpData\Data and accessible by using the URL *https://myserver.mydomain.com/Data*.

The default authentication settings for important virtual directories are as follows:

- ActiveSync has basic authentication enabled for the front-end and back-end.
- Autodiscover has anonymous, basic, and Windows authentication enabled for the front-end and back-end.
- ECP has anonymous and basic authentication enabled for the front-end and back-end.
- EWS has anonymous and windows authentication enabled for the front-end and back-end.
- Mapi has Windows authentication enabled on the front-end; anonymous authentication enabled on the back-end.
- OAB has Windows authentication enabled for the front-end and back-end.
- OWA has basic authentication enabled on the front-end; anonymous and Windows authentication are enabled on the back-end.
- PowerShell doesn't have any authentication methods enabled on the front-end; Windows authentication is enabled on the back-end.
- Rpc has basic and Windows authentication enabled for front-end and back-end.

You should rarely change the default settings. However, if your organization has special needs, you can change the authentication settings at the virtual directory level.

The authentication settings on virtual directories are different from authentication settings on the Default Web Site and Exchange Back End website. By default, these websites allow anonymous access. This means that anyone can access the server's home page without authenticating themselves. If you disable anonymous access at the server level and enable some other type of authentication, users need to authenticate themselves twice: once for the server and once for the virtual directory they want to access.

The preferred way to manage authentication settings is to use the appropriate cmdlet in Exchange Management Shell:

- For ActiveSync, use Set-ActiveSyncVirtualDirectory
- For Autodiscover, use Set-AutodiscoverVirtualDirectory
- For ECP, use Set-EcpVirtualDirectory
- For OAB, use Set-OabVirtualDirectory
- For OWA, use Set-OwaVirtualDirectory
- For PowerShell, use Set-PowerShellVirtualDirectory
- For Exchange Web Services, use Set-WebServicesVirtualDirectory

As an example, to disable basic authentication on the default ActiveSync directory, you would enter:

```
Set-ActiveSyncVirtualDirectory -Identity "TVPRESS\microsoft-server-activesync" -BasicAuthEnabled $false
```

You can change the authentication settings for an entire site or for a particular virtual directory by completing the following steps:

1. Start IIS Manager. In Server Manager, click Tools, and then select Internet Information Services (IIS) Manager.

2. In IIS Manager, navigate to the level you want to manage, and then double-click the Authentication feature. On the Authentication page, you should see the available authentication modes. If a mode you want to use is not available, you need to install and enable the related role service using Server Manager's Add Role Services Wizard.

3. To enable or disable anonymous access, select Anonymous Authentication and then click Enable or Disable as appropriate.

> NOTE   With anonymous access, IIS uses an anonymous user account for access to the server. The anonymous user account is named IUSR_ServerName, such as IUSR_Mailer1. If you use this account, you don't need to set a password. Instead, let IIS manage the password. If you want to use a different account, click Edit, and then click Set to specify the user name and password for a different account to use for anonymous access.

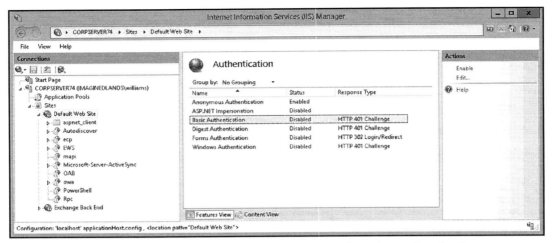

4. To configure other authentication methods, select the authentication method, and then click Enable or Disable as appropriate. Keep the following in mind:

- Disabling basic authentication might prevent some clients from accessing resources remotely. Clients can log on only when you enable an authentication method that they support.

- A default domain isn't set automatically. If you enable Basic authentication, you can choose to set a default domain that should be used when no domain information is supplied during the logon process. Setting the default domain is useful when you want to ensure that clients authenticate properly.
- With Basic and Digest authentication, you can optionally specify the realm that can be accessed. Essentially, a realm is the DNS domain name or web address that will use the credentials that have been authenticated against the default domain. If the default domain and realm are set to the same value, the internal Windows domain name might be exposed to external users during the user name and password challenge/response.
- If you enable ASP.NET Impersonation, you can specify the identity to impersonate. By default, IIS uses pass-through authentication, and the identity of the authenticated user is impersonated. You can also specify a particular user if necessary.
- If you enable Forms authentication, you can set the logon URL and cookies settings used for authentication.

Throttling Client Access to Servers

Every Mailbox server in your organization is subject to the default throttling policy. Throttling policies are designed to ensure that users aren't intentionally or unintentionally overloading Exchange. Exchange tracks the resources that each user consumes and applies throttling policy to enforce connection bandwidth limits as necessary.

The default policy is set in place when you install your first Mailbox server running a current version of Exchange Server. There is a single default throttling policy for the organization. You can customize the default policy or add additional policies as necessary.

To manage throttling policy, you use Exchange Management Shell and the Get-ThrottlingPolicy, Set-ThrottlingPolicy, New-ThrottlingPolicy, and Remove-ThrottlingPolicy cmdlets. Throttling policy applies to:

- Anonymous access
- Exchange Web Services (EWS)
- IMAP
- MAPI
- Microsoft Exchange ActiveSync (EAS)
- Outlook Web App (OWA)
- OWA Voicemail
- POP
- PowerShell
- PowerShell Web Services
- RPC Client Access

With all of these features except PowerShell, you can specify separate settings for the following:

- Maximum concurrency controls the maximum number of connections a user can have at one time, with $null removing the limit. The parameters are AnonymousMaxConcurrency, EASMaxConcurrency, EWSMaxConcurrency, IMAPMaxConcurrency, OWAMaxConcurrency, POPMaxConcurrency, and PowerShellMaxConcurrency as well as OWAVoiceMaxConcurrency for OWA voicemail, PsWsMaxConcurrency for PowerShell Web Services, and RcaMaxConcurrency for RPC Client Access.
- Maximum burst controls the amount of time in milliseconds that a user can use an elevated amount of resources before being throttled, with $null removing the limit. The parameters are AnonymousMaxBurst, EASMaxBurst, EWSMaxBurst, IMAPMaxBurst, OWAMaxBurst, POPMaxBurst, and PowerShellMaxBurst as well as OWAVoiceMaxBurst for OWA voicemail, PsWsMaxBurst for PowerShell Web Services, and RcaMaxBurst for RPC Client Access.

> NOTE   Each service also has a cutoff balance, such as
> AnonymousCutOffBalance, and a corresponding recharge rate, such as
> AnonymousRechargeRate. Both values are set in milliseconds. Cutoff
> balance controls the resource consumption limits for a service before a user is
> completely   blocked from performing operations on the related component.
> Recharge rate controls the rate at which the cutoff balance is recharged. For
> example, with anonymous access the cut off is 720 seconds (720000
> milliseconds) and the recharge rate is 420 seconds (420000 milliseconds).
> Thus, the maximum amount of time a user can use an anonymous connection
> is 12 minutes, but after seven minutes of idle time this cutoff value is fully
> recharged.

With PowerShell you can specify:

- Maximum number of concurrent PowerShell sessions per user using
  PowerShellMaxRunspaces.
- The time period for determining whether the maximum number of run spaces has
  been exceeded using PowerShellMaxRunspacesTimePeriod.
- Maximum number of cmdlets that a user can run in a given interval before their
  execution is stopped using PowerShellMaxCmdlets.
- The time period for determining whether the maximum number of cmdlets has
  been exceeded using PowerShellMaxCmdletsTimePeriod.
- The maximum number of operations allowed to be executed per user with the
  PowerShellMaxCmdletQueueDepth.
- Maximum number of concurrent Remote PowerShell connections for an Exchange
  tentant organization using PowerShellMaxTenantConcurrency.
- Maximum number of concurrent PowerShell sessions that an Exchange tent
  organization can have using PowerShellMaxTenantConcurrency.

> NOTE   Maximum concurrency controls the number of user sessions.
> Maximum cmdlets controls the number of cmdlets in each user session. The
> two valu es together are affected by the maximum queue depth allowed. For
> example, if five user sessions are allowed, and each can run four cmdlets in a
> given interval, the maximum queue depth to allow this is 20 (5 user session x
> 4 cmdlets each = 20). Any value less than 20 restricts the number of
> operations that can be performed in this scenario.

You can get the default throttling policy by entering: Get-ThrottlingPolicy default* or
Get-ThrottlingPolicy | where-object {$_.IsDefault -eq $true}. You can get the
throttling policy applied to a particular user by entering (Get-Mailbox
UserAlias).ThrottlingPolicy where UserAlias is the alias for a user, such as:

```
(Get-Mailbox jimj).ThrottlingPolicy | Get-ThrottlingPolicy
```

```
(Get-Mailbox jimj).RetentionPolicy | Get-RetentionPolicy

(Get-Mailbox jimj).SharingPolicy | Get-SharingPolicy

(Get-Mailbox jimj).AddressBookPolicy | Get-AddressBookPolicy

(Get-Mailbox jimj).RoleAssignmentPolicy | Get-RoleAssignmentPolicy
```

You can create a nondefault throttling policy by using the New-ThrottlingPolicy cmdlet. You can then assign the policy to a mailbox by using the -ThrottlingPolicy parameter of the Set-Mailbox and New-Mailbox cmdlets. In the following example, you apply TempUserThrottlingPolicy to AmyG:

```
Set-Mailbox -Identity amyg -ThrottlingPolicy (Get-ThrottlingPolicy

TempUserThrottlingPolicy)
```

You can modify default and nondefault throttling policies by using Set-ThrottlingPolicy. To have a user go back to the default policy, set the -ThrottlingPolicy parameter to $null as shown in this example:

```
Set-Mailbox -Identity amyg -ThrottlingPolicy $null
```

You can find all user mailboxes that currently have a particular policy applied by using Get-Mailbox with a where-object filter. In the following example, you look for all user mailboxes that have the TempUserThrottlingPolicy:

```
$p = Get-ThrottlingPolicy TempUserThrottlingPolicy

Get-Mailbox | where-object {$_.ThrottlingPolicy -eq $p.Identity}
```

To switch multiple users from one policy to another, you can do the following:

```
$op = Get-ThrottlingPolicy TempUserThrottlingPolicy

$ms = Get-Mailbox | where-object {$_.ThrottlingPolicy -eq $op.Identity}

$np = Get-ThrottlingPolicy RestrictedUserThrottlingPolicy
```

```
foreach ($m in $ms) {Set-Mailbox $m.Identity -ThrottlingPolicy $np;}
```

You can remove nondefault policies that aren't currently being applied by using Remove-ThrottlingPolicy. Simply enter Remove-ThrottlingPolicy followed by the name of the policy as shown in this example:

```
Remove-ThrottlingPolicy TempUserThrottlingPolicy
```

Optimizing Access for Web and Mobile Clients

When you deploy new Mailbox servers, you'll need to configure internal and external access URLs for client access protocols. While you are working with the related settings, you should also verify that the authentication settings are optimized for your environment. After you optimize these settings, you may need to double-check them as part of routine troubleshooting.

Configuring Access for OAB

Outlook 2010 and later clients can retrieve the offline address book (OAB) from a web distribution point. The default distribution point is the OAB virtual directory on the Default Web Site. Each distribution point has the following three associated properties:

- PollInterval   The time interval during which the Microsoft Exchange File Distribution service should poll the generation server for new updates (in minutes)
- ExternalUrl   The URL from which Outlook clients outside the corporate network can access the OAB
- InternalUrl   The URL from which Outlook clients inside the corporate network can access the OAB

You can configure web distribution points by completing the following steps:

1. In the Exchange Admin Center, select Servers in the Feature pane, and then select Virtual Directories to view a list of the front-end virtual directories used by Mailbox servers in the Exchange organization.

2. You'll see an entry for each OAB web distribution point. Select the distribution point you want to configure and then select Edit ( ). This opens the Properties dialog box.

3. Set the desired polling interval using the Polling Interval text box. The default interval is 480 minutes.

4. The current internal and external URLs are listed. If you want to change the current settings, enter the desired internal and external URLs in the text boxes provided. Click Save.

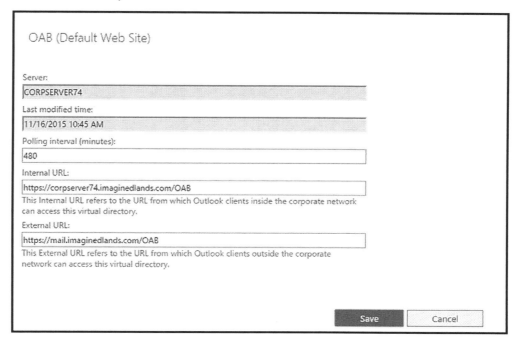

After you make changes to the OAB directory, you should verify that you can still access the OAB. If you can't access OAB or suspect there is a configuration problem, you can reset the OAB virtual directory by selecting it in the list of virtual directories, selecting Reset, and then confirming the reset by selecting Reset in the warning dialog box. When you reset a virtual directory, Exchange deletes the virtual directory and then recreates it with its default settings. Resetting a directory means any custom settings will be lost.

Configuring Access for OWA

When you install a Mailbox server, the server is configured with a Default Web Site and the virtual directories discussed previously. Through the OWA virtual directory, you can specify different URLs for internal access and external access to OWA. You can also configure various authentication options.

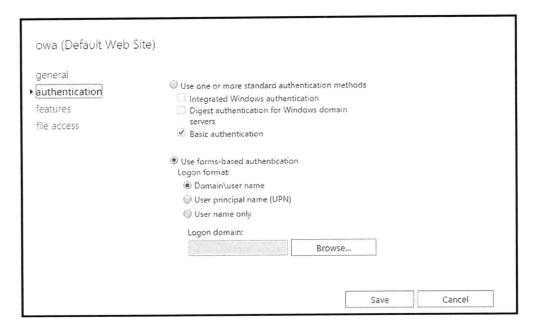

You can configure OWA virtual directory URLs and authentication options by completing the following steps:

1. In the Exchange Admin Center, select Servers in the Feature pane and then select Virtual Directories to view a list of the front-end virtual directories used by Mailbox servers in the Exchange organization.

2. You'll see an entry for each OWA virtual directory available. Select the OWA virtual directory you want to configure, and then select Edit ( ).

3. In the Properties dialog box, on the General page, the current internal and external URLs are listed. If you want to change the current settings, enter the internal and external URLs you want to use in the text boxes provided.

4. On the Authentication page, forms-based authentication is configured by default with the logon format set to Domain\User Name. Change this configuration only if you have specific requirements that necessitate a change.

5. Click Save to apply your settings.

After you make changes to the OWA directory, you should verify that you can still access Outlook Web App. If you can't access Outlook Web App or suspect there is a configuration problem, you can reset the OWA virtual directory by selecting it in the list of virtual directories, selecting Reset, and then confirming the reset by selecting

Reset in the warning dialog box. When you reset a virtual directory, Exchange deletes the virtual directory and then recreates it with its default settings. Resetting a directory means any custom settings will be lost.

Configuring Access for Exchange ActiveSync

When you install a Mailbox server, the server is configured with a Default Web Site that has a virtual directory for Exchange ActiveSync. Through this virtual directory, you can specify different URLs for internal access and external access to Exchange ActiveSync. You also can configure various authentication options.

You can configure the Exchange ActiveSync URLs and authentication options by completing the following steps:

1. In the Exchange Admin Center, select Servers in the Feature pane and then select Virtual Directories to view a list of the front-end virtual directories used by Mailbox servers in the Exchange organization.

2. You'll see an entry for each virtual directory available. Select the ActiveSync virtual directory you want to configure, and then select Edit ( ).

3. In the properties dialog box, on the General page, the current internal and external URLs are listed. If you want to change the current settings, enter the internal and external URLs you want to use in the text boxes provided.

4. On the Authentication page, basic authentication is enabled by default and client certificates are ignored. If your organization uses client certificates, you can clear the Basic Authentication check box and then select either Accept Client Certificates or Require Client Certificates as appropriate.

5. Click Save to apply your settings.

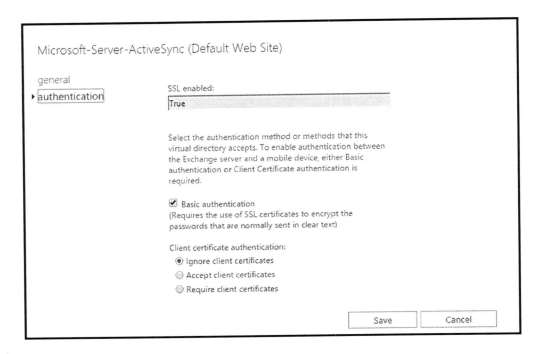

Microsoft-Server-ActiveSync (Default Web Site)

general

authentication

SSL enabled:

True

Select the authentication method or methods that this virtual directory accepts. To enable authentication between the Exchange server and a mobile device, either Basic authentication or Client Certificate authentication is required.

☑ Basic authentication
(Requires the use of SSL certificates to encrypt the passwords that are normally sent in clear text)

Client certificate authentication:
◉ Ignore client certificates
◯ Accept client certificates
◯ Require client certificates

Save   Cancel

After you make changes to the ActiveSync directory, you should verify that you can still access Exchange ActiveSync. If you can't access Exchange ActiveSync or suspect there is a configuration problem, you can reset the ActiveSync virtual directory by selecting it in the list of virtual directories, selecting Reset, and then confirming the reset by selecting Reset in the warning dialog box. When you reset a virtual directory, Exchange deletes the virtual directory and then recreates it with its default settings. Resetting a directory means any custom settings will be lost.

Configuring Access for ECP

When you install a Mailbox server, the server is configured with a Default Web Site and the virtual directories discussed previously. Through the ECP virtual directory, you can specify different URLs for internal and external access to Exchange Admin Center. You can also configure various authentication options.

You can configure ECP virtual directory URLs and authentication options by completing the following steps:

1. In the Exchange Admin Center, select Servers in the Feature pane, and then select Virtual Directories to view a list of the front-end virtual directories used by Mailbox servers in the Exchange organization.

2. You'll see an entry for each ECP virtual directory available. Select the ECP virtual directory you want to configure, and then select Edit (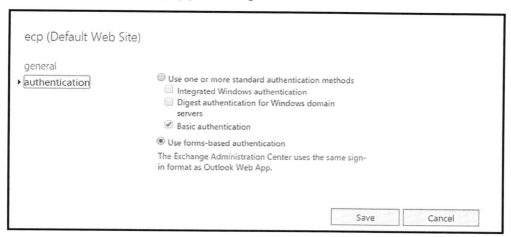).

3. On the General page, the current internal and external URLs are listed. If you want to change the current settings, enter the internal and external URLs you want to use in the text boxes provided.

4. On the Authentication page, basic authentication and forms-based authentication are configured by default. The logon format for forms-based authentication is the same as the format used for Outlook Web App. Change this configuration only if you have specific requirements that necessitate a change.

5. Click Save to apply your changes.

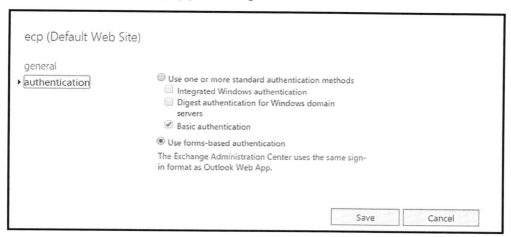

After you make changes to the ECP directory, you should verify that you can still access the Exchange Admin Center. If you can't access Exchange Admin Center or suspect there is a configuration problem, you can reset the ECP virtual directory by selecting it in the list of virtual directories, selecting Reset, and then confirming the reset by selecting Reset in the warning dialog box. When you reset a virtual directory, Exchange deletes the virtual directory and then recreates it with its default settings. Resetting a directory means any custom settings will be lost.

Chapter 14. Optimizing Client Access Protocols

Mail clients can use a variety of protocols to connect to Exchange server. Generally, Outlook clients will use either MAPI over HTTP or RPC over HTTP while other mail clients will use either POP3 or IMAP4. In this chapter, you'll learn techniques for optimizing these protocols for client access.

Managing RPC and MAPI over HTTP

Outlook clients can use either RPC over HTTP or MAPI over HTTP for connecting to their Exchange mailboxes, with MAPI over HTTP as the preferred option. Generally, these featured are enabled and configured automatically when you install Exchange services and no additional configuration is required (see Chapter 1 for exceptions). RPC and MAPI over HTTP also are secure by default, so unauthenticated requests from Outlook clients are blocked from accessing Exchange Server.

Working with RPC and MAPI over HTTP

The only requirement for RPC and MAPI over HTTP is that Exchange servers have properly configured SSL certificates. Because RPC and MAPI over HTTP requests use HTTPS, you must allow port 443 through your firewall. If you already use Outlook Web App with SSL or Exchange ActiveSync with SSL, port 443 should already be open and you do not have to open any additional ports.

As with other services, RPC and MAPI over HTTP have front-end components and back-end components on Mailbox servers:

- RPC over HTTP uses the Rpc virtual directory on the Default Web Site and the Rpc, RpcProxy and RpcWithCert virtual directories on the Exchange Back End website.
- MAPI over HTTP uses the Mapi virtual directory on the Default Web Site and the Mapi virtual directory on the Exchange Back End website.

You can use the Get-OutlookAnywhere cmdlet to list configuration details for RPC over HTTP. If you use the –Server parameter, you can limit the results to a specific server. If you use the –Identity parameter, you can examine a particular virtual directory on a server. Listing 14-1 provides the syntax, usage and sample output.

LISTING 14-1 Get-OutlookAnywhere cmdlet syntax and usage

Syntax

```
Get-OutlookAnywhere [-Server ServerName] [-DomainController DCName]


Get-OutlookAnywhere [-Identity VirtualDirId] [-DomainController DCName]
```

Usage

```
Get-OutlookAnywhere


Get-OutlookAnywhere -Server "MailServer42"


Get-OutlookAnywhere -Identity "MailServer42\Rpc (Default Web Site)"
```

Sample Output

```
RunspaceId                          : 035f41f8-7f92-4b3d-ac89-822b885de085
ServerName                          : MailServer42
SSLOffloading                       : True
ExternalHostname                    :
InternalHostname                    : mailserver42.imaginedlands.local
ExternalClientAuthenticationMethod  : Negotiate
InternalClientAuthenticationMethod  : Ntlm
IISAuthenticationMethods            : {Basic, Ntlm, Negotiate}
XropUrl                             :
ExternalClientsRequireSsl           : False
InternalClientsRequireSsl           : False
MetabasePath       : IIS://CorpServer74.imaginedlands.local/W3SVC/1/ROOT/Rpc
Path : C:\Program Files\Microsoft\Exchange Server\V15\FrontEnd\HttpProxy\rpc
ExtendedProtectionTokenChecking     : None
ExtendedProtectionFlags             : {}
ExtendedProtectionSPNList           : {}
AdminDisplayVersion                 : Version 15.1 (Build 225.42)
Server                              : CORPSERVER74
AdminDisplayName                    :
ExchangeVersion                     : 0.20 (15.0.0.0)
Name                                : Rpc (Default Web Site)

. . .
```

```
Id                            : CORPSERVER74\Rpc (Default Web Site)
OriginatingServer             : CorpServer91.imaginedlands.local
IsValid                       : True
ObjectState                   : Changed
```

Listing 14-2 provides the syntax, usage, and sample output for Get-MapiVirtualDirectory cmdlet, which you can use to list configuration details for MAPI over HTTP. When using this cmdlet, you can use the –Server parameter to limit the results to a specific server or the –Identity parameter to examine a particular virtual directory on a server. To get a complete listing, be sure to format the output as shown in the examples.

LISTING 14-2 Get-MapiVirtualDirectory cmdlet syntax and usage

Syntax

```
Get-MapiVirtualDirectory [-Server ServerName] [-DomainController DCName]


Get-MapiVirtualDirectory [-Identity VirtualDirId] [-DomainController DCName]
```

Usage

```
Get-MapiVirtualDirectory |fl


Get-MapiVirtualDirectory -Server "MailServer42" |fl


Get-MapiVirtualDirectory -Identity "MailServer42\Rpc (Default Web Site)" | fl
```

Sample Output

```
RunspaceId                    : 035f41f8-7f92-4b3d-ac89-822b885de085
IISAuthenticationMethods      : {Ntlm, OAuth, Negotiate}
MetabasePath  : IIS://CorpServer74.imaginedlands.local/W3SVC/1/ROOT/mapi
Path : C:\Program Files\Microsoft\Exchange Server\V15\FrontEnd\HttpProxy\mapi
ExtendedProtectionTokenChecking : None
ExtendedProtectionFlags       : {}
ExtendedProtectionSPNList      : {}
AdminDisplayVersion           : Version 15.1 (Build 225.42)
Server                        : CORPSERVER74
InternalUrl              : https://corpserver74.imaginedlands.local/mapi
```

```
InternalAuthenticationMethods  : {Ntlm, OAuth, Negotiate}
ExternalUrl                    :
ExternalAuthenticationMethods  : {Ntlm, OAuth, Negotiate}
AdminDisplayName               :
ExchangeVersion                : 0.10 (14.0.100.0)
Name                           : mapi (Default Web Site)
. . .
Id                             : CORPSERVER74\mapi (Default Web Site)
OriginatingServer              : CorpServer91.imaginedlands.local
IsValid                        : True
ObjectState                    : Changed
```

Configuring URLs and Authentication

When you install a Mailbox server, the server is configured with a Default Web Site and the virtual directories discussed previously. Through the Rpc and Mapi virtual directories on the front-end, you can specify different URLs for internal and external access to RPC and MAPI over HTTP. You can also configure various authentication options.

Although a graphical interface for setting Mapi virtual direction options isn't available, you can configure RPC virtual directory URLs and authentication options in Exchange Admin Center. To do this, complete the following steps:

1. Select Servers in the Feature pane, and then select the Servers tab to view a list of servers in the Exchange organization.

2. Select the server with which you want to work, and then select Edit (   ).

3. When you select the Outlook Anywhere page in the Properties dialog box, the current internal and external URLs are listed. If you want to change the current settings, enter the internal and external URLs you want to use in the text boxes provided.

CORPSERVER74

general

databases and database
availability groups

POP3

IMAP4

unified messaging

DNS lookups

transport limits

transport logs

▸ Outlook Anywhere

Outlook Anywhere allows your users to connect to their
Exchange mailboxes via Outlook. Learn more

Specify the external host name (for example, contoso.com)
that users will use to connect to your organization.

mail.imaginedlands.com

*Specify the internal host name (for example, contoso.com)
that users will use to connect to your organization.

corpserver74.imaginedlands.com

*Specify the authentication method for external clients to use
when connecting to your organization:

Negotiate ▾

☑ Allow SSL offloading

Save   Cancel

4. Select an available external authentication method. You can select Basic
Authentication, NTLM Authentication, or Negotiate. Although NT LAN
Manager (NTLM) authentication is more secure than basic authentication,
the most secure option is Negotiate, which configures Outlook Anywhere to
use Integrated Windows Authentication.

5. Select the Allow Secure Channel (SSL) Offloading check box only if you have
configured an advanced firewall server to work with Exchange 2016 and
handle your SSL processing.

6. Click Save to apply your settings.

You also can use the Set-OutlookAnywhere cmdlet to modify the RPC over HTTP
configuration. See Listing 14-3 for syntax and usage. The –IISAuthenticationMethods
parameter sets the authentication method for the /rpc virtual directory as either
Basic, NTLM or Negotiate and disables all other methods. The –
ExternalClientAuthenticationMethod and –InternalClientAuthenticationMethod
parameters set permitted authentication methods for external and internal clients
respectively. You can also control whether SSL is required for external and internal
clients using the -ExternalClientRequireSsl and -InternalClientRequireSsl parameters
respectively.

LISTING 14-3 Set-OutlookAnywhere cmdlet syntax and usage

Syntax

```
Set-OutlookAnywhere -Identity VirtualDirId [-DomainController DCName]
  [-DefaultAuthenticationMethod {AuthMethod}]
```

```
[-ExternalClientAuthenticationMethod {AuthMethod}]

[-ExternalClientRequireSsl {$true|$false}]

[-ExternalHostName ExternalHostName]

[-IISAuthenticationMethods <Basic | NTLM | Negotiate>]

[-InternalClientAuthenticationMethod {AuthMethod}]

[-InternalClientRequireSsl {$true|$false}]

[-InternalHostName InternalHostName]

[-Name Name]

[-SSLOffloading <$true | $false>]


{AuthMethod}

<Basic | Digest | NTLM | Fba | WindowsIntegrated | LiveIdFba |

LiveIdBasic | WSSecurity | Certificate | NegoEx | OAuth | Adfs | Kerberos

| Negotiate | LiveIdNegotiate | Misconfigured>
```

Usage

```
Set-OutlookAnywhere -Identity "CorpSvr127\Rpc (Default Web Site)"

 -ExternalHostName "mail.tvpress.com"

 -InternalHostName "mailserer21.tvpress.com"

 -ExternalAuthenticationMethod "Negotiate"

 -SSLOffloading $true
```

To configure MAPI virtual directory URLs and authentication options, you'll use the Set-MapiVirtualDirectory cmdlet. Listing 14-4 provides the syntax and usage. Use the -ExternalUrl and -InternalUrl parameters to set the external and internal Mapi URLs respectively.

LISTING 14-4 Set-MapiVirtualDirectory cmdlet syntax and usage

Syntax

```
Set-MapiVirtualDirectory -Identity VirtualDirId [-DomainController DCName]

 [-IISAuthenticationMethods <Basic | NTLM | Negotiate>]

 [-InternalUrl Url]

 [-ExternalUrl Url]
```

Usage

```
Set-MapiVirtualDirectory -Identity "CorpSvr127\Mapi (Default Web Site)"
 -InternalUrl "http://mailserver21.imaginedlands.com/mapi"
 -ExternalUrl "http://mail.imaginedlands.com/mapi"
```

Enabling the POP3 and IMAP4 Services

Clients that retrieve mail using POP3 or IMAP4 send mail using SMTP. SMTP is the default mail transport in Exchange Server 2016. To enable POP3 and IMAP4, you must first start the POP3 and IMAP4 services on the Exchange servers that will provide these services. You must then configure these services to start automatically in the future. You should also review the related settings for each service and make changes as necessary to optimize the way these services are used in your Exchange organization.

Because the client access infrastructure has two-layers with a front-end component and a back-end component, there are corresponding front-end and back-end services for both POP3 and IMAP4 running on Mailbox servers. You can enable and configure the front-end POP3 service for automatic startup by completing these steps:

1. Start the Services utility. In Server Manager, click Tools, and then select Services.
2. Right-click Microsoft Exchange POP3, and then select Properties.
3. On the General tab, under Startup Type, select Automatic and then click Apply.
4. Under Service Status, click Start, and then click OK.

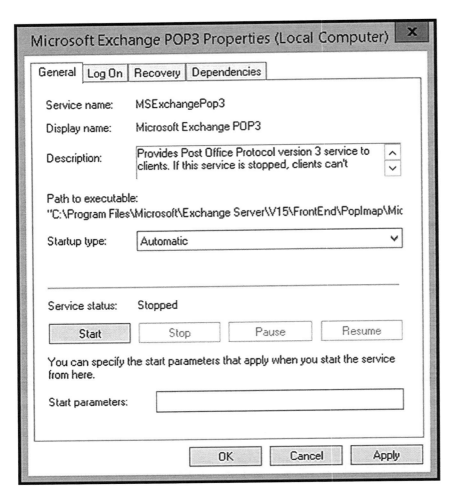

The corresponding back-end service is the POP3 Backend service. You can enable and configure the POP3 Backend service for automatic startup by completing the following steps:

1. Start the Services utility. In Server Manager, click Tools, and then select Services.

2. Right-click Microsoft Exchange POP3 Backend, and then select Properties.

3. On the General tab, under Startup Type, select Automatic and then click Apply.

4. Under Service Status, click Start, and then click OK.

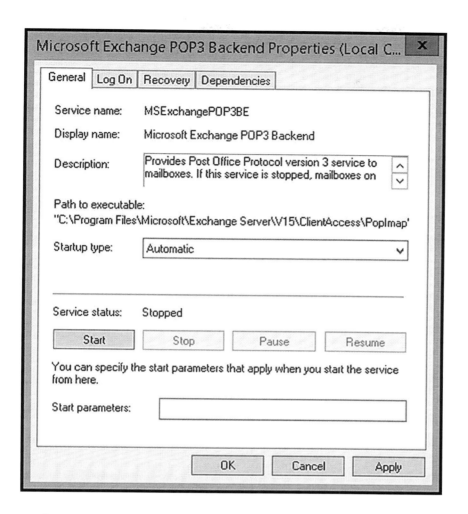

If you want to enable IMAP4, configure the Microsoft Exchange IMAP4 service as well as the Microsoft Exchange IMAP4 Backend service on your Mailbox servers for automatic startup and then start the services. Use the same techniques as discussed previously for POP3.

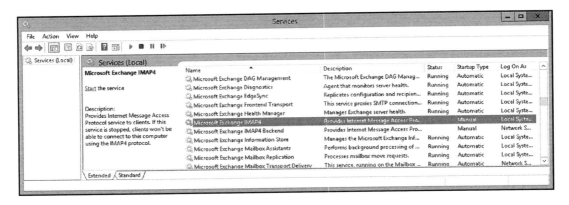

You can use the Set-Service cmdlet to enable and configure POP3 and IMAP4 as well. The identifiers for the services are as follows:

- MSExchangePop3 for the POP3 front-end service
- MSExchangePop3BE for the POP3 back-end service
- MSExchangeIMAP4 for the IMAP4 front-end service
- MSExchangeIMAP4BE for the IMAP4 back-end service

Use the –StartupType parameter to set the startup type as Automatic, Manual, or Disabled. Use the –Status parameter to set the status as Running, Paused, or Stopped. The following examples enable POP3 and IMAP4 for automatic startup and then start the services:

```
Set-Service –Name MSExchangePop3 –StartupType Automatic –Status Running
```

```
Set-Service –Name MSExchangeImap4 –StartupType Automatic –Status Running
```

The following examples enable the POP3 and IMAP4 back end services for automatic startup, and then start the services:

```
Set-Service –Name MSExchangePop3BE –StartupType Automatic –Status Running
```

```
Set-Service –Name MSExchangeImap4BE –StartupType Automatic –Status Running
```

Optimizing POP3 and IMAP4 Settings

As alternatives to RPC and MAPI over HTTP, Exchange 2016 supports Internet Message Access Protocol 4 (IMAP4) and Post Office Protocol 3 (POP3). IMAP4 is a protocol for reading mail and accessing public and private folders on remote servers. Clients can log on to an Exchange server and use IMAP4 to download message headers and then read messages individually while online. POP3 is a protocol for retrieving mail on remote servers. Clients can log on to an Exchange server and then use POP3 to download their mail for offline use.

By default, POP3 (version 3) and IMAP4 (rev 1) are configured for manual startup. Because other client access protocols offer so much more than POP and IMAP, they are the preferred way for clients to access Exchange Server. That said, if you still have users who want to use POP3 and IMAP4 to access Exchange Server, you can configure this, but you should try to move these users to other client access protocols.

As you configure POP3 and IMAP4 access don't forget that the client access infrastructure has two layers:

* A front end that you can customize to control the way users access and work with POP3 and IMAP4
* A back end that handles the back-end processing but that you only modify to control the options that the front end uses for working with the back-end processes

Thus, although you typically modify the front-end settings for POP3 and IMAP4 to customize the environment for users, you rarely modify the related back-end components.

Configuring POP3 and IMAP4 Bindings

POP3 and IMAP4 have related IP address and TCP port configuration settings. The default IP address setting is to use any available IP address. On a multihomed server, however, you'll usually want messaging protocols to respond on a specific IP address in which case you need to change the default setting.

The default port setting depends on the messaging protocol being used and whether SSL is enabled or disabled. For users to be able to retrieve mail using POP3 and IMAP4, you must open the related messaging ports on your organization's firewalls. The default port settings for key protocols used by Exchange Server 2016 are as follows:

- With SMTP, the default port is 25 and the default secure port is 587.
- With HTTP, the default port is 80 and the default secure port is 443.
- With POP3, the default port is 110 and the default secure port is 995.
- With IMAP4, the default port is 143 and the default secure port is 993.

In Exchange Management Shell, you can manage POP3 and IMAP4 by using the following cmdlets:

- **Get-POPSettings** Lists POP3 configuration settings
- **Set-POPSettings** Configures POP3 settings
- **Test-POPConnectivity** Tests the POP3 configuration
- **Get-IMAPSettings** Lists IMAP4 configuration settings
- **Set-IMAPSettings** Configures IMAP4 settings
- **Test-IMAPConnectivity** Tests the IMAP4 configuration

The bindings for POP3 and IMAP4 use a unique combination of an IP address and a TCP port. To change the IP address or port number for POP3 or IMAP4, complete the following steps:

1. In the Exchange Admin Center, select Servers in the Feature pane, and then select the Servers tab to view a list of servers in the Exchange organization.

2. Select the server with which you want to work, and then select Edit ( ).

3. In the Properties dialog box, select the POP3 or IMAP4 page as appropriate for the service you want to configure.

4. If you scroll down, you'll see the currently assigned IP addresses and ports used for TLS or unencrypted connections and SSL connections. The default configuration is as follows: POP3 and IMAP4 are configured to use all available IPv4 and IPv6 addresses, POP3 uses port 110 for TLS or unencrypted connections and port 995 for SSL connections, and IMAP4 uses port 143 for TLS or unencrypted connections and port 993 for SSL connections.

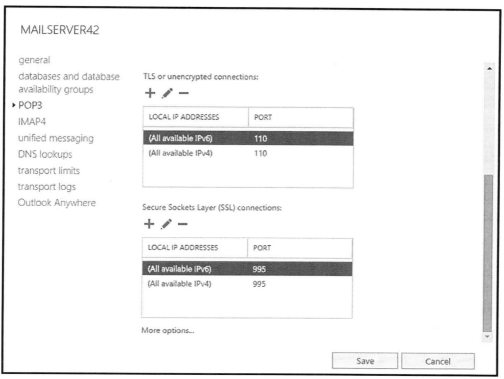

MAILSERVER42

general

databases and database
availability groups

▸ POP3

IMAP4

unified messaging

DNS lookups

transport limits

transport logs

Outlook Anywhere

TLS or unencrypted connections:

\+ ✎ −

LOCAL IP ADDRESSES	PORT
(All available IPv6)	110
(All available IPv4)	110

Secure Sockets Layer (SSL) connections:

\+ ✎ −

LOCAL IP ADDRESSES	PORT
(All available IPv6)	995
(All available IPv4)	995

More options...

Save   Cancel

5. To configure IP addresses and ports for TLS or unencrypted connections, use the following options on the TLS Or Unencrypted Connections panel:

- Add (   )   Adds a TCP port on a per-IP address basis or all unassigned IP address basis. Click Add, and then specify the IP address and port you want to use.

- Edit (   )   Allows you to edit the IP address and port settings for the currently selected entry in the Address list box.

- Remove (   )   Allows you to remove the IP address and port settings for the currently selected entry in the Address list box.

NOTE   The IP address/TCP port combination must be unique. You can assign the same port as long as the protocol is configured to use a different IP address. You can also assign the same IP address and use a different port.

6. To configure IP addresses and ports for secure connections, use the following options on the Secure Sockets Layer (SSL) Connections panel:

- Add (➕)　Adds a TCP port on a per-IP address basis or an all-unassigned IP address basis. Click Add, and then specify the IP address and port you want to use.

- Edit (✏)　Allows you to edit the IP address and port settings for the currently selected entry in the Address list box.

- Remove (➖)　Allows you to remove the IP address and port settings for the currently selected entry in the Address list box.

7. Click Save to apply your settings. When you add new ports, you must open the related messaging ports on your organization's firewalls.

8. Use the Services utility to restart the Exchange POP3 or IMAP4 service. Restarting the service applies the new settings.

Configuring POP3 and IMAP4 Authentication

By default, POP3 and IMAP4 clients pass connection information and message data through a secure TLS connection. A secure TLS connection requires the Exchange servers to have properly configured SSL certificates with POP3, IMAP4, or both as assigned services.

Secure TLS connections are the best option to use when corporate security is a high priority and secure communication channels are required. That said, you have two other options for configuring communications: plain-text authentication and logon using integrated Windows authentication. Configure these authentication options by completing the following steps:

1. In the Exchange Admin Center, select Servers in the Feature pane, and then select the Servers tab to view a list of servers in the Exchange organization.

2. Select the server with which you want to work, and then select Edit (✏).

3. In the Properties dialog box, select the POP3 or IMAP4 page as appropriate for the service you want to configure.

4. For Logon Method, do one of the following, and then click Save:

- Select Basic Authentication (Plain text) to use unsecure plain text for communications.
- Select Integrated Windows Authentication (Plain text) to use secure communications with Windows authentication.

5. Use the Services utility to restart the Exchange POP3 or IMAP4 service. Restarting the service applies the new settings.

When Exchange is configured to use SSL and secure TLS connections, mail clients also should be configured to use either SSL or secure TLS. You can configure an Outlook client to use SSL or secure TLS by completing the following steps:

1. Do one of the following:

- In Office 2010, click the Office button, click Account Settings, and then select the Account Settings option.
- In Office 2013 or Office 2016, click the File tab. Next, select the Account Settings option and then select Account Settings.

2. In the Account Settings dialog box, select the POP3/IMAP4 account, and then click Change.

3. In the Change E-Mail Account dialog box, click More Settings.

4. On the Advanced tab in the Internet E-Mail Settings dialog box, select SSL, TLS or Auto as the type of encrypted connection.

5. Click OK. Click Next, and then click Finish. Click Close.

Configuring Connection Settings for POP3 and IMAP4

You can control incoming connections to POP3 and IMAP4 in two ways. You can set a limit on the number of simultaneous connections, and you can set a connection time-out value.

POP3 and IMAP4 normally accept a maximum of 2,147,483,467 connections each and a maximum of 16 connections from a single user, and in most environments these are acceptable settings. However, when you're trying to prevent the underlying server hardware from becoming overloaded or you want to ensure resources are available for other features, you might want to restrict the number of simultaneous connections to a much smaller value. When the limit is reached, no other clients are permitted to access the server. The clients must wait until the connection load on the server decreases.

The connection time-out value determines when idle connections are disconnected. Normally, unauthenticated connections time out after they've been idle for 60 seconds and authenticated connections time out after they've been idle for 1,800 seconds (30 minutes). In most situations, these time-out values are sufficient. Still, at times you'll want to increase the time-out values, and this primarily relates to clients who get disconnected when downloading large files. If you discover that clients are being disconnected during large downloads, the time-out values are one area to examine. You'll also want to look at the maximum command size. By default, the maximum command size is restricted to 512 bytes.

You can modify connection limits and time-outs by completing the following steps:

1. In the Exchange Admin Center, select Servers in the Feature pane, and then select the Servers tab to view a list of servers in the Exchange organization.

2. Select the server with which you want to work, and then select Edit (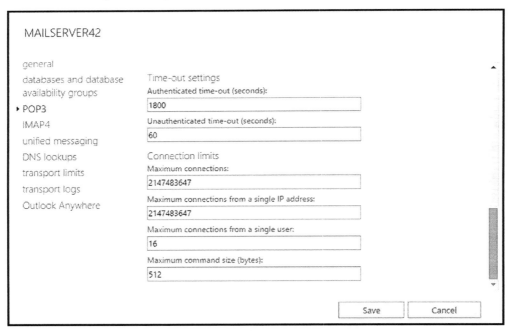).

3. In the Properties dialog box, select the POP3 or IMAP4 page as appropriate for the service you want to configure.

4. Scroll down and then click More Options to display the additional configuration options.

MAILSERVER42

general
databases and database availability groups
▸ POP3
IMAP4
unified messaging
DNS lookups
transport limits
transport logs
Outlook Anywhere

Time-out settings
Authenticated time-out (seconds):
1800

Unauthenticated time-out (seconds):
60

Connection limits
Maximum connections:
2147483647

Maximum connections from a single IP address:
2147483647

Maximum connections from a single user:
16

Maximum command size (bytes):
512

Save   Cancel

5. To set time-out values for authenticated and unauthenticated connections, enter the desired values in the Authenticated Time-Out and Unauthenticated Time-Out text boxes, respectively. The valid range for authenticated connections is from 30 through 86,400 seconds. The valid range for unauthenticated connections is from 10 through 3,600 seconds.

6. To set connection limits, enter the desired limits in the text boxes on the Connection Limits panel. The valid input range for maximum connections is from 1 through 2,147,483,467. The valid input range for maximum connections from a single IP address is from 1 through 2,147,483,467. The valid input range for maximum connections from a single user is from 1 through 2,147,483,467. The valid input range for maximum command size is from 40 through 1,024 bytes.

7. Click Save to apply your settings. Use the Services utility to restart the Exchange POP3 or IMAP4 service. Restarting the service applies the new settings.

Configuring Message Retrieval Settings for POP3 and IMAP4

Message retrieval settings for POP3 and IMAP4 control the following options:

- Message formatting   Message format options allow you to set rules that POP3 and IMAP4 use to format messages before clients read them. By default, when POP3 or IMAP4 clients retrieve messages, the message body is converted to the best format for the client and message attachments are identified with a Multipurpose Internet Mail Extensions (MIME) content type based on the attachment's file extension. You can change this behavior by applying new message MIME formatting rules. Message MIME formatting rules determine the formatting for elements in the body of a message. Message bodies can be formatted as plain text, HTML, HTML and alternative text, enriched text, or enriched text and alternative text.
- Message sort order   Message sort order options allow you to control the time sorting of messages during new message retrieval. By default, POP3 sorts messages in ascending order according to the time/date stamp. This ensures that the most recent messages are listed first. You can also sort messages by descending order, which places newer messages lower in the message list.

You can modify message retrieval settings by completing the following steps:

1. In the Exchange Admin Center, select Servers in the Feature pane, and then select the Servers tab to view a list of servers in the Exchange organization.

2. Select the server with which you want to work, and then select Edit (   ).

3. In the Properties dialog box, select the POP3 or IMAP4 page as appropriate for the service you want to configure.

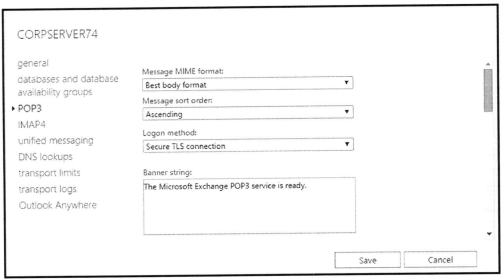

CORPSERVER74

general
databases and database
availability groups
▸ POP3
IMAP4
unified messaging
DNS lookups
transport limits
transport logs
Outlook Anywhere

Message MIME format:
Best body format ▼

Message sort order:
Ascending ▼

Logon method:
Secure TLS connection ▼

Banner string:
The Microsoft Exchange POP3 service is ready.

Save   Cancel

4. Use the Message MIME Format list to choose the desired body format for messages. As discussed previously, the options are Text, HTML, HTML And Alternative Text, Enriched Text, Enriched Text And Alternative Text, or Best Body Format.

5. If you are working with POP3, use the Message Sort Order list to specify the default sort order for message retrieval. Select Descending for descending sort order during message retrieval or Ascending for ascending sort order.

6. Click Save to apply your settings. Use the Services utility to restart the Exchange POP3 or IMAP4 service. Restarting the service applies the new settings.

Chapter 15. Configuring Mobile Messaging

In our increasingly connected world, users want to be able to access email, calendars, contacts, and scheduled tasks no matter the time or place. With Microsoft Exchange 2016 and Microsoft Exchange Online, you can make anywhere, anytime access to Exchange data a real possibility. Exchange 2016 and Exchange Online support wireless access for users with many types of mobile devices via Exchange ActiveSync and Outlook Web App for Devices.

Exchange ActiveSync allows users to link mobile devices to their Exchange accounts so that Exchange synchronizes mail data with the mobile device. Because mail and other data is stored on the device users can access their email, calendar, contacts, and scheduled tasks whether they are online or offline.

Outlook Web App for Devices allows users to access Outlook Web App on a tablet or smartphone simply by accessing the app in the device's browser and logging in. Unlike Exchange ActiveSync, Outlook Web App for Devices does not normally store mail and related data in a file cache on a user's mobile device.

Mobile access to Exchange Server is supported on smart phones and other mobile devices. Most mobile devices include extensions that permit the use of additional features, including

* Autodiscover
* Direct Push
* Remote Device Wipe
* Password Recovery
* Direct File Access
* Remote File Access

In Exchange Server, these features are all enabled by default. The sections that follow discuss how these features work and how related options are configured. Many additional options are available for fine-tuning the mobile access configuration as well, including mobile device mailbox policy and Outlook Web App policy. These policies are discussed as well.

Mastering Mobile and Wireless Access Essentials

Because sensitive data might be stored on a user's mobile device with Exchange ActiveSync, several safeguards are in place to prevent unauthorized access to this data. The first safeguard is a device password, which can be reset remotely by the user or by an administrator. The second safeguard is a remote wipe feature that remotely instructs a mobile device to delete all its Exchange and corporate data. A third safeguard is a data encryption requirement, which can be enabled and enforced.

Getting Started with Exchange ActiveSync

When you install Exchange 2016 or use Exchange Online, Exchange ActiveSync and Outlook Web App for Devices are automatically configured for use, which makes these features easy to manage. However, there are still some essential concepts you should know to manage them more effectively. This section explains these concepts.

Exchange ActiveSync allows users with smart phones and other mobile devices to initiate synchronization with Exchange to keep their data up to date and receive notices from Exchange that trigger synchronization through the Direct Push feature. *Direct Push* is a key feature about which you probably want to know a bit more. Direct Push works like this:

1. The user configures her mobile device to synchronize with Exchange, selecting specific Exchange folders that she wants to keep up to date.
2. When a new message arrives in a designated sync folder, a control message is sent to the mobile device.
3. The control message initiates a data synchronization session, and the device performs background synchronization with Exchange.

After synchronization, users can then access their data while they are offline. In Exchange 2016, Direct Push is either enabled or disabled as is Exchange ActiveSync itself. Because Direct Push uses HTTPS, TCP port 443 must be open on your firewall between the Internet and the Mailbox server to which the user is connecting.

Managing ActiveSync and OWA for Devices

With Exchange Online, Exchange ActiveSync and Outlook Web App for Devices are enabled by default and you cannot change this setting. With Exchange 2016, Exchange ActiveSync is enabled for each user by default, but you can disable Exchange ActiveSync for specific users as necessary by completing the following steps:

1. In Exchange Admin Center, select Recipients in the Feature pane, and then select Mailboxes.

2. You should now see a list of users with Exchange mailboxes in the organization. Double-click the user's name to open the Properties dialog box for the user account.

3. On the Mailbox Features page, the enabled mobile and web access features for the user are displayed.

- To disable Exchange ActiveSync for this user, under Mobile Devices, select Disable Exchange ActiveSync, and then click Yes.
- To enable Exchange ActiveSync for this user, under Mobile Devices, select Enable Exchange ActiveSync, and then click Yes.
- To disable OWA For Devices for this user, under Mobile Devices, select Disable OWA For Devices, and then click Yes.
- To enable OWA For Devices for this user, under Mobile Devices, select Enable OWA For Devices, and then click Yes.

4. Click Save.

> **REAL WORLD** Exchange ActiveSync notifications are sent over the
> Internet. The actual process of receiving synchronization requests and
> sending synchronization notifications is handled by Exchange. Exchange
> ActiveSync is, in fact, configured as an ASP.NET application on the web
> server. For Exchange ActiveSync to work properly, IIS server must be
> configured properly.

To define organization-wide security and authentication options, you can use mobile
device mailbox policies. When you install Exchange 2016 or use Exchange Online, a
default mobile device mailbox policy is created. Through mobile device mailbox
policy settings, you can precisely control mobile browsing capabilities for all users in
the enterprise, including:

* Whether Apple mobile devices can get push notifications
* Whether passwords are required, and how passwords must be configured
* Synchronization settings to include in addition to calendar and email items
* Permitted devices and device options, such as whether a device can use Wi-Fi,
  infrared, Bluetooth, storage cards, or its built-in camera
* Whether the device, its storage cards, or both must be encrypted

Although you configure many mobile device settings in Exchange Admin Center, you
will need to use Exchange Admin Shell to fully customize mobile device options.

Configuring Autodiscover

The Autodiscover service simplifies the provisioning process for mobile devices and
for Outlook 2010 and later clients by returning the required Exchange settings after a
user enters his or her email address and password. This provisioning eliminates the
need to configure mobile carriers in Exchange Server, as well as the need to
download and install the carriers list on mobile devices.

Understanding Autodiscover

Autodiscover is enabled by default. The Default Web Site associated with a particular
Mailbox server has an associated Autodiscover virtual directory that handles
proxying and authentication for Autodiscover. The Exchange Back End website
associated with the Mailbox server hosting the user's mailbox has an Associated
Autodiscover virtual directory through which devices can be provisioned. These
virtual directories handle Autodiscover requests:

- Whenever an Outlook client queries for service details
- Whenever a user account is configured or updated
- Whenever the network connection changes

Each Mailbox server is configured with a service connection point that contains an authoritative list of Autodiscover URLs for the associated Active Directory forest. The Autodiscover service URL for the service connection point is either https://*SMTPdomain*/autodiscover/autodiscover.xml or https://autodiscover.*SMTPdomain*/autodiscover/autodiscover.xml, where *SMTPdomain* is the name of the SMTP domain to which the client wants to connect, such as Imaginedlands.com.

ExServerName is the name of a Mailbox server in the site to which the client is connecting. For example, if the user's email address is tony@contoso.com, the primary SMTP domain address is contoso.com.

When the client connects to Active Directory, the client authenticates to Active Directory by using the user's credentials and then queries for the available service connection point objects. One service connection point object is created for each Mailbox server deployed in the Exchange organization. This object contains a ServiceBindingInfo attribute with the fully qualified domain name of the corresponding Mailbox server in the form https://*ServerFQDN*/autodiscover/autodiscover.xml, where *ServerFQDN* is the fully qualified name of the Mailbox server. After the client obtains and enumerates the service connection point instances, the client connects to the first Mailbox server in the enumerated list and obtains the profile information needed to connect to the user's mailbox. This profile is formatted with XML and also includes a list of available Exchange features.

Maintaining Autodiscover

When you install a Mailbox server, the server is configured with a Default Web Site that has a virtual directory for Autodiscover. Through this virtual directory, you can specify different URLs for internal access and external access to Autodiscover. You also can configure various authentication options.

In the Exchange Admin Center, select Servers in the Feature pane and then select Virtual Directories to view a list of the front-end virtual directories used by Mailbox servers in the Exchange organization, which includes an entry for each Autodiscover virtual directory available. If you've made any changes to an Autodiscover virtual directory, you should verify that you can still access Autodiscover. If you can't access Autodiscover or suspect there is a configuration problem, you can reset the Autodiscover virtual directory by selecting it in the list of virtual directories, and then selecting Reset. In the Warning dialog box, enter the full file path to a network share in which a settings file can be created to store the current settings for the Autodiscover virtual directory, such as \\mailserver21\updates\Autodiscoverlog.txt. Finally, confirm that you want to reset the virtual directory by selecting Reset. When you reset a virtual directory, Exchange deletes the virtual directory and then recreates it with its default settings. Resetting a directory means any custom settings will be lost. To complete the process, you must run the iisreset /noforce command on the affected server.

> **IMPORTANT** Only front-end virtual directories are listed in Exchange Admin Center and only the settings of front-end virtual directories are modified by the reset. If you also want to reset the corresponding back-end virtual directory after resetting a front-end virtual directory, you must do this in Exchange Management Shell.

In Exchange Management Shell, you have additional management options for the Autodiscover service. To get detailed information about the Autodiscover configuration, type the following command:

```
Get-AutodiscoverVirtualDirectory -Server MyServer | fl
```

where *MyServer* is the name of the Mailbox server you want to examine. Included in the detailed information is the identity of the Autodiscover virtual directory, which you can use with related cmdlets, and the authentication methods enabled for internal and external access. By default, Autodiscover is configured to use Basic authentication, NTLM authentication, integrated Windows authentication, Web Services security and Outlook Authorization Authentication. By using the Set-AutodiscoverVirtualDirectory cmdlet, you can enable or disable these authentication methods, as well as digest authentication. You can also set the internal and external URLs for Autodiscover. Neither URL is set by default.

By default, only information about the related front-end virtual directories is included. To add information about the related back-end virtual directories, you need to set -ShowMailboxVirtualDirectories to $true. Set -ADPropertiesOnly to $true if you want to only view the properties stored in Active Directory. The following example gets information for all Autodiscover virtual directories in the Exchange organization:

```
Get-AutodiscoverVirtualDirectory -ShowMailboxVirtualDirectories | fl
```

To disable Autodiscover, type the following command:

```
Remove-AutodiscoverVirtualDirectory -Identity ServerName\DirName
(WebSiteName)
```

where *ServerName* is the name of the Mailbox server on which this feature should be disabled, *DirName* is the name of the virtual directory to remove, and *WebSiteName* is the name of the web site you are configuring, such as:

```
Remove-AutodiscoverVirtualDirectory -Identity
"CorpMailSvr25\Autodiscover (Default Web Site)"
```

If you later want to enable Autodiscover, you can type the following command:

```
New-AutodiscoverVirtualDirectory -Identity -Identity
"CorpMailSvr25\Autodiscover (Default Web Site)"
```

where *MyServer* is the name of the Mailbox server on which this feature should be enabled for the Default Web Site.

Listings 15-1 to 15-4 provide the full syntax and usage for the Get-AutodiscoverVirtualDirectory, New-AutodiscoverVirtualDirectory, Set-AutodiscoverVirtualDirectory and Remove-AutodiscoverVirtualDirectory cmdlets, respectively.

LISTING 15-1 Get-AutodiscoverVirtualDirectory cmdlet syntax and usage

Syntax

```
Get-AutodiscoverVirtualDirectory [-Server ServerName | -Identity
VirtualDirID]

[-ADPropertiesOnly <$true | $false>] [-DomainController DCName]
```

```
[-ShowMailboxVirtualDirectories <$true | $false>]
```

Usage

```
Get-AutodiscoverVirtualDirectory

-Identity "CorpMailSvr25\Autodiscover (Default Web Site)"
```

LISTING 15-2 New-AutodiscoverVirtualDirectory cmdlet syntax and usage

Syntax

```
New-AutodiscoverVirtualDirectory [-ApplicationRoot RootPath]

[-AppPoolId AppPoolIdentity] [-BasicAuthentication <$true | $false>]

[-DigestAuthentication <$true | $false>] [-DomainController DCName]

[-ExternalURL ExternalURL] [-InternalURL InternalURL]

[-OAuthAuthentication <$true | $false>]

[-Path FileSystemPath] [-Role <ClientAccess | Mailbox>]

[-Server ServerName] [-WebSiteName WebSiteName]

[-WindowsAuthentication <$true | $false>]

[-WSSecurityAuthentication <$true | $false>]
```

Usage

```
New-AutodiscoverVirtualDirectory -WebSiteName "Default Web Site"

-BasicAuthentication $true -WindowsAuthentication $true

-OAuthAuthentication $true -WSSecurityAuthentication $true


New-AutodiscoverVirtualDirectory -WebSiteName "Exchange Back End"

-BasicAuthentication $true -WindowsAuthentication $true

-OAuthAuthentication $true -WSSecurityAuthentication $true

-Role Mailbox
```

LISTING 15-3 Set-AutodiscoverVirtualDirectory cmdlet syntax and usage

Syntax

```
Set-AutodiscoverVirtualDirectory -Identity DirectoryIdentity

[-BasicAuthentication <$true | $false>]

[-DigestAuthentication <$true | $false>]

[-DomainController DCName]

[-ExternalURL ExternalURL] [-InternalURL InternalURL]

[-LiveIdBasicAuthentication <$true | $false>]

[-LiveIdNegotiateAuthentication <$true | $false>]

[-OAuthAuthentication <$true | $false>]

[-WindowsAuthentication <$true | $false>]

[-WSSecurityAuthentication <$true | $false>]
```

Usage

```
Set-AutodiscoverVirtualDirectory

-Identity "CorpMailSvr25\Autodiscover(Default Web Site)"

-BasicAuthentication $false -DigestAuthentication $false

 -WindowsAuthentication $true
```

LISTING 15-4 Remove-AutodiscoverVirtualDirectory cmdlet syntax and usage

Syntax

```
Remove-AutodiscoverVirtualDirectory -Identity DirectoryIdentity

[-DomainController DCName]
```

Usage

```
Remove-AutodiscoverVirtualDirectory

-Identity "CorpMailSvr25\Autodiscover (Default Web Site)"
```

Using Direct Push

Direct Push automates the synchronization process, enabling a mobile device to make requests to keep itself up to date. When the website used with Exchange ActiveSync has SSL enabled, Direct Push allows a mobile device to issue long-lived Hypertext Transfer Protocol Secure (HTTPS) monitoring requests to Exchange Server. Exchange Server monitors activity in the related user's mailbox. If new mail arrives or other changes are made to the mailbox—such as modifications to calendar or contact items—Exchange sends a response to the mobile device, stating that changes have occurred and that the device should initiate synchronization with Exchange Server. The device then issues a synchronization request. When synchronization is complete, the device issues another long-lived HTTPS monitoring request.

Port 443 is the default TCP port used with SSL. For Direct Push to work, port 443 must be opened between the Internet and the organization's Internet-facing Mailbox server or servers. You do not need to open port 443 on your external firewalls to all of your Mailbox servers—only those to which users can establish connections. The Mailbox server receiving the request automatically proxies the request so that it can be handled appropriately. If necessary, this can also mean proxying requests between the mobile device and the Mailbox server in the user's home site. A user's home site is the Active Directory site in which the Mailbox server hosting his or her mailbox is located.

> TIP   On your firewall, Microsoft recommends increasing the maximum time-out for connections to 30 minutes to help optimize the efficiency of direct push.

Using Remote Device Wipe

Although passwords help to protect mobile devices, they don't prevent access to the device. You can protect the data on mobile devices in several ways. One such way is to apply a mobile device mailbox policy that controls access to the device and encrypts its content. Another way is to have a strict policy that requires users and administrators to remotely wipe lost or stolen devices. A remote device wipe command instructs a mobile device to delete all Exchange and corporate data.

Remotely Wiping a Device

An administrator or the owner of the device can prevent the compromising of sensitive data by initiating a remote device wipe. After you initiate a remote device wipe and the device receives the request, the device confirms the remote wipe request by sending a confirmation message and then removes all its sensitive data the next time it connects to Exchange Server. Wiping sensitive data should prevent it from being compromised.

The way remote wipe is implemented depends on the way the related protocol is implemented on the device. Although Exchange 2016 only requires that Exchange and corporate data be removed, most device operating systems wipe all data on the device and then return the device to its factory default condition. A complete wipe can also remove any data stored on any storage card inserted into the device. On the other hand, when you issue a remote wipe for a device that fully support Exchange, the wipe typically only affects Exchange and corporate data. For these devices, client application settings also can determine whether the wipe actually deletes the sensitive data or simply makes it inaccessible. As data on these devices is encrypted by default, any data remaining would be protected by encryption.

The easiest way to wipe a device remotely is to have the device owner initiate the wipe using Outlook Web App. When the device acknowledges the request, the user will get a confirmation email.

The device owner can wipe a device by following these steps:

1. Open your web browser. In the Address field, type the Outlook Web App URL, such as https://mail.tvpress.com/owa, and then press Enter to access this page.

2. When prompted, provide the logon credentials of the user whose device you want to wipe. Do not provide your administrator credentials.

3. On the Outlook Web App toolbar, click Settings ( ), and then click Options.

4. The left pane of the Options view provides a list of options. Click the General heading to expand it and then select Mobile Devices.

5. The user's mobile devices are listed in the details pane. Select the device you want to wipe, and then click Wipe Device.

6. Confirm the action when prompted.

7. Track the status of the device. When the status changes from Wipe Pending to Wipe Successful, the device wipe is complete.

NOTE   You can use Outlook Web App for remote device wiping only if the user has used the device previously to access Exchange Server and if you have enabled the Segmentation feature of Exchange Active Directory Integration (which is the default configuration).

CAUTION   Because wiping a device causes complete data loss, you should do this only when you've contacted the user directly (preferably in person) and confirmed that the mobile device has been lost and that he or she understands the consequences of wiping the device. If your organization has a formal policy regarding the wiping of lost devices that might contain sensitive company data, be sure you follow this policy and get any necessary approvals. Keep in mind that although a remote wipe makes it very difficult to retrieve any data from the device, in theory retrieval is possible with sophisticated data recovery tools.

Alternatively, an administrator can log on to Exchange Admin Center and initiate a remote wipe by completing the following steps:

1. In Exchange Admin Center, select Recipients in the Feature pane, and then select Mailboxes.

2. Select the mailbox for the user whose device you want to wipe. Next, in the details pane, under Mobile Devices, click View Details.

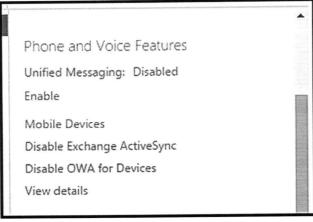

3. On the Mobile Device Details page, select the lost device, and then select Wipe Data.

4. Click Save to initiate the remote wipe.

5. Track the status of the device. When the status changes from Wipe Pending to Wipe Successful, the device wipe is complete.

In Exchange Management Shell, you can examine and filter through all of the mobile devices that have linked to Exchange by using Get-MobileDevice. You also can list the mobile devices registered as partners for a user's mailbox by using the Get-MobileDeviceStatistics cmdlet. In either case, the device identity you want is the DeviceId string. If the user has multiple mobile devices, also be sure to consult the DeviceModel and DeviceOperatorNetwork values.

After you know the mobile device identity, you can issue a remote device wipe command by using the Clear-MobileDevice cmdlet. You then need to confirm that you want to wipe the device when prompted by pressing the Y key. Listings 15-5 to 15-7 provide the syntax and usage for Get-MobileDevice, Get-MobileDeviceStatistics, and Clear-MobileDevice cmdlets, respectively. With Get-MobileDeviceStatistics, you can specify either the unique identity of the remote device or the user mailbox with which you want to work. The –GetMailboxLog parameter retrieves mailbox logs and usage information. Use the –OutputPath parameter to direct the statistics to a specific folder path or the –NotificationEmailAddresses parameter to email the statistics to specified email addresses.

> IMPORTANT   If you determine that you've made a mistake in issuing a remote wipe, you should immediately issue a cancellation request by using the Clear-MobileDevice cmdlet. In this case, set the –Cancel parameter to $true. The remote device processes the cancellation request only if the remote wipe has not yet been initiated.
>
> NOTE   Exchange also supports the Get-ActiveSyncDevice, Get-ActiveSyncDeviceStatistics and Clear-ActiveSyncDevice cmdlets, which have similar syntax and options as Get-MobileDevice, Get-MobileDeviceStatistics, and Clear-MobileDevice respectivly. As the ActiveSyncDevice cmdlets only work with ActiveSync devices and the MobileDevice cmdlets work with all supported devices, I prefer to use the MobileDevice cmdlets and you probably will too.

LISTING 15-5 Get-MobileDevice cmdlet syntax and usage

Syntax

```
Get-MobileDevice [-Identity MobileDeviceId] {AddtlParams}

Get-MobileDevice -Mailbox MailboxId {AddtlParams}
```

```
{AddtlParams}

[-ActiveSync <$true | $false>] [-DomainController FullyQualifiedName]

[-Filter FilterValues] [-Monitoring <$true | $false>]

[-Organization OrgId] [-OrganizationalUnit OUId]

[-OWAforDevices <$true | $false>] [-ResultSize Size]

[-SortBy AttributeName]
```

Usage

```
Get-MobileDevice -OrganizationalUnit Sales
```

LISTING 15-6 Get-MobileDeviceStatistics cmdlet syntax and usage

Syntax

```
Get-MobileDeviceStatistics -Identity MobileDeviceId {AddtlParams}

Get-MobileDeviceStatistics -Mailbox MailboxId {AddtlParams}

{AddtlParams}

[-ActiveSync <$true | $false>] [-DomainController FullyQualifiedName]

[-GetMailboxLog <$true | $false>] [-NotificationEmailAddresses

email1,email2,...emailN] [-OWAMobileApp <$true | $false>]

[-ShowRecoveryPassword <$true | $false>]
```

Usage

```
Get-MobileDeviceStatistics -Mailbox "David Pelton"
```

LISTING 15-7 Clear-MobileDevice cmdlet syntax and usage

Syntax

```
Clear-MobileDevice -Identity MobileDeviceId

[-Cancel <$true | $false>] [-DomainController FullyQualifiedName]

[-NotificationEmailAddresses email1,email2,...emailN]
```

Usage

```
Clear-MobileDevice -Identity "Mobile_DavidP"
```

```
Clear-MobileDevice -Identity "Mobile_DavidP" -Cancel $true
```

Reviewing the Remote Wipe Status

When you initiate a remote wipe, the mobile device removes all its data the next time it connects to Exchange Server. You can review the remote wipe status by using an alternate syntax for the Get-MobileDeviceStatistics cmdlet. Instead of passing the –Mailbox parameter to the cmdlet, use the –Identity parameter to specify the DeviceId string of the device you wiped. The statistics returned will include these output parameters:

- **DeviceWipeRequestTime**   The time you requested a remote wipe
- **DeviceWipeSentTime**   The time the server sent the remote wipe command to the device
- **DeviceWipeAckTime**   The time when the device acknowledged receipt of the remote wipe command

If there is a DeviceWipeSentTime timestamp, the device has connected to Exchange Server and Exchange Server sent the device the remote wipe command. If there is a DeviceWipeAckTime timestamp, the device acknowledged receipt of the remote wipe and has started to wipe its data.

Using Password Recovery

Users can create passwords for their mobile devices. If a user forgets his password, you can obtain a recovery password that unlocks the device and lets the user create a new password. The user can also recover his device password by using Outlook Web App.

Recovering a Device Password

To use Outlook Web App to recover a user's device password, complete the following steps:

1. Open a web browser. In the Address field, type the Outlook Web App URL, such as https://mail.tvpress.com/owa, and then press Enter to access this page.

2. When prompted, have the user enter her logon credentials or provide the user's logon credentials. Do not provide your administrator credentials.

3. On the Outlook Web App toolbar, click Settings ( ), and then click Options.

4. The left pane of the Options view provides a list of options. Click the General heading to expand it and then select Mobile Devices.

5. The user's mobile devices are listed in the details pane. Select the device for which you are recovering the password.

6. Click Display Recovery Password.

You also can display the device recovery password by completing the following steps:

1. In the Exchange Admin Center, select Recipients in the Feature pane, and then select Mailboxes.

2. Select the mailbox for the user whose device you want to wipe. Next, in the details pane, under Mobile Devices, click View Details.

3. The device recovery password is listed.

In Exchange Management Shell, you can display the device recovery password by using the –ShowRecoveryPassword parameter of the Get-MobileDeviceStatistics cmdlet. Listing 15-8 provides the syntax and usage.

LISTING 15-8 Recovering a device password

Syntax

```
Get-MobileDeviceStatistics -Mailbox MailboxIdentity

 -ShowRecoveryPassword $true {AddtlParams}


Get-MobileDeviceStatistics -Identity MobileDeviceIdentity

 -ShowRecoveryPassword $true {AddtlParams}
```

```
{AddtlParams}

[-ActiveSync <$true | $false>] [-DomainController FullyQualifiedName]

[-GetMailboxLog <$true | $false>] [-NotificationEmailAddresses

email1,email2,...emailN] [-OWAforDevices <$true | $false>]
```

Usage

```
Get-MobileDeviceStatistics -Mailbox "HelenB@tvpress.com"

 -ShowRecoveryPassword $true
```

Managing File Access and Document Viewing

Exchange 2016 includes many features designed to make it easier for users to work with files and documents. Users can access files directly, remotely and via Office Web Apps Server viewing. Each of which has separate configuration options.

Configuring Direct File Access

Exchange Server 2016 allows users to access files directly through Outlook, Outlook Web App, and related services by default. This means that users will be able to access files attached to email messages. You can configure how users interact with files direct file access by using one of three options in the Exchange Admin Center:

* **Allow**   Allows users to access files of the specified types, and sends the users' browser information that allows the files to be displayed or opened in the proper applications
* **Block**   Prevents users from accessing files of the specified types
* **Force Save**   Forces users to save files of the specified types prior to opening them

In a standard configuration, Exchange 2016 allows, blocks and force saves many file extensions and Multipurpose Internet Mail Extensions (MIME) values. Allowed files include .avi, .bmp, .doc, .docm, .docx, .gif, .jpg, .mp3, and other standard file types. Blocked files include that contain executables and scripts, such as .bat, .cmd,.exe, .ps1, .vbe, .vbs, and text/javascript. Forced save files include specific types of application files, such as .dcr, .dir, .spl, and .swf.

> NOTE   The related settings are applied to the Outlook Web App (OWA) virtual directory on Mailbox servers. If a server has multiple OWA virtual directories or you have multiple Mailbox servers, you must configure each

> directory and server separately. If there are conflicts between the allow, block, and force save lists, the allow list takes precedence, which means that the allow list settings override the block list and the force save list. As updates are applied to Exchange Server, the default lists can change. Be sure to check the currently applied defaults.

Exchange Server considers all file extensions and MIME types not listed on the allow, block, or force save list to be unknown. The default setting for unknown file types is force save.

Based on the user's selection, the configuration of her network settings, or both, Exchange divides all client connections into one of two classes:

- **Public or shared computer** A public computer is a computer being used on a public network or a computer shared by multiple people.
- **Private computer** A private computer is a computer on a private network that is used by one person.

For each Mailbox server, you can enable or disable direct access to files separately for public computers and private computers. However, the allow, block, and force save settings for both types of computers are shared and applied to both public and private computers in the same way.

You can configure direct file access on front-end virtual directories by completing the following steps:

1. In the Exchange Admin Center, select Servers in the Feature pane, and then select Virtual Directories to view a list of the front-end virtual directories used by Mailbox servers in the Exchange organization.

2. Select the OWA virtual directory on the Mailbox server you want to manage, and then select Edit ( ). Typically, you'll want to configure the OWA virtual directory on the Default Web Site because this directory is used by default for Outlook Web App.

3. In the Virtual Directory dialog box, select the File Access page.

4. To enable or disable direct file access for public computers, under Public Or Shared Computer, select or clear the Direct File Access check box, as appropriate.

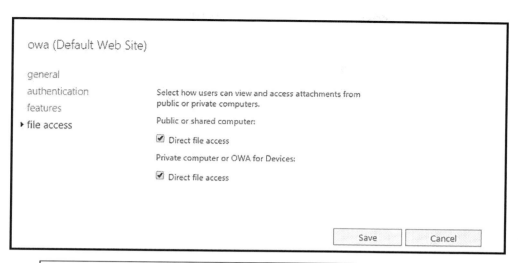

owa (Default Web Site)

general
authentication
features
▸ file access

Select how users can view and access attachments from public or private computers.

Public or shared computer:

☑ Direct file access

Private computer or OWA for Devices:

☑ Direct file access

Save   Cancel

> IMPORTANT   When you disable features in the front end, you prevent them from being used because the front end proxies connections to the back end and blocks disabled features from being used. However, if you enable a feature in the front end but the feature is disabled in the back end, clients also won't be able to use the feature.

5. Under Private Computer, you can select or clear the Direct File Access check box to enable or disable direct file access for private computers.

6. Click Save to apply your settings. As necessary, make corresponding changes in the related back-end virtual directory using Exchange Management Shell.

In Exchange Management Shell, you can use the Set-OWAVirtualDirectory cmdlet to manage the direct file-access configuration. Use the –Identity parameter to identify the virtual directory with which you want to work, such as:

```
Set-OWAVirtualDirectory –Identity "Corpsvr127\owa (Default Web Site)"
```

Then specify how you want to configure direct file access on the front-end and back-end virtual directory, such as:

```
Set-OWAVirtualDirectory –Identity "Corpsvr127\owa (Default Web Site)"
 –DirectFileAccessOnPublicComputersEnabled $false
 –DirectFileAccessOnPrivateComputersEnabled $true


Set-OWAVirtualDirectory –Identity "Corpsvr127\owa (Exchange Back End)"
 –DirectFileAccessOnPublicComputersEnabled $false
 –DirectFileAccessOnPrivateComputersEnabled $true
```

If you are unsure of the virtual directory identity value, use the Get-OWAVirtualDirectory cmdlet to retrieve a list of available virtual directories on a named server, as shown in the following example:

```
Get-OWAVirtualDirectory -Server "Corpsvr127" -ShowMailboxVirtualDirectories
```

Alternatively, you could get the OWAVirtualDirectory object for both the front end and back end and then set the desired options on both as shown in the following example:

```
Get-OWAVirtualDirectory -Server Corpsvr127 -ShowMailboxVirtualDirectories |
Set-OWAVirtualDirectory -DirectFileAccessOnPublicComputersEnabled $false
 -DirectFileAccessOnPrivateComputersEnabled $true
```

You could just as easily apply the changes to multiple Exchange servers throughout the organization. If you want to make changes across all servers, however, I recommend adding the -Whatif parameter to ensure the command is going to work exactly as expected before executing the command without the -Whatif parameter. In the following example, you disable direct file access on public computers on all front-end and back-end OWA virtual directories:

```
Get-OWAVirtualDirectory -ShowMailboxVirtualDirectories |
Set-OWAVirtualDirectory -DirectFileAccessOnPublicComputersEnabled $false
-WhatIf
```

You configure allowed file types and allowed MIME types by using the -AllowedFileTypes and -AllowedMIMETypes parameters respectively. As these are multivalued properties, you must either enter the complete set of allowed values or use a special shorthand to insert into or remove values from these multivalued properties. The shorthand for adding values is:

```
@{Add="<ValuetoAdd1>","<ValuetoAdd2>"...}
```

As you'll typically want to configure the front-end and back-end virtual directories in the same way, the following example sets the allowed file types on both the front-end and back-end OWA virtual directories:

```
Get-OWAVirtualDirectory -Server Corpsvr127 -ShowMailboxVirtualDirectories |
Set-OWAVirtualDirectory -AllowedFileTypes @{Add=".log",".man"}
```

The shorthand for removing values is:

```
@{Remove="<ValuetoRemove1>","<ValuetoRemove2>"...}
```

Such as:

```
Get-OWAVirtualDirectory -Server Corpsvr127 -ShowMailboxVirtualDirectories |
Set-OWAVirtualDirectory -AllowedFileTypes @{Remove=".log",".man"}
```

If you want to add values and remove others, you can do this as well by using the following shorthand:

```
@{Add="<ValuetoAdd1>","<ValuetoAdd2>"...;
Remove="<ValuetoRemove1>","<ValuetoRemove1>"...}
```

You can confirm that values were added or removed as expected by using Get-OWAVirtualDirectory. Because there are so many allowed file types, you won't get a complete list of file types if you examine the -AllowedFileTypes property as shown in the following example:

```
Get-OWAVirtualDirectory -Identity "Corpsvr127\owa (Default Web Site)" |
fl name, allowedfiletypes
```

A workaround to examine all the values of such a property follows:

```
$vdir = Get-OWAVirtualDirectory -Identity "Corpsvr127\owa (Default Web
Site)"

$data = $vdir.allowedfiletypes
$data | fl *
```

In this case, you store the virtual directory object in the *$vdir* variable. Next, you store the values associated with this object's AllowedFileTypes parameter in the *$data* variable. Finally, you list each allowed file type.

You can use similar techniques to work with

- **Blocked file types and blocked MIME types** The corresponding parameters are -BlockedFileTypes and -BlockedMimeTypes respectively.

- **Forced Save file types and forced save MIME types** The corresponding parameters are -ForcedSaveFileTypes and -ForcedSaveMimeTypes respectively.

Configuring Remote File Access

Exchange Server 2016 allows users to access files remotely through Outlook Web App (OWA) by default. This means users will be able to access Windows SharePoint Services and Universal Naming Convention (UNC) file shares on SharePoint sites. SharePoint sites consist of Web Parts and Windows ASP.NET–based components that allow users to share documents, tasks, contacts, events, and other information. When you configure UNC file shares on SharePoint sites, you enable users to share folders and files.

You configure remote file access by using configuration options for the ActiveSync virtual directory. The -RemoteDocumentsBlockedServers and -RemoteDocumentsAllowedServers parameters of the Set-ActiveSyncVirtualDirectory cmdlet specify the host names of servers from which clients are denied or allowed access respectively. If there is a conflict between the blocked servers list and the allowed servers list, the block list takes precedence.

As the -RemoteDocumentsBlockedServers and -RemoteDocumentsAllowedServers parameters are multivalued properties, you must either enter the complete set of allowed values or use the special shorthand discussed earlier in this chapter in the "Configuring Direct File Access" section to insert into or remove values from these multivalued properties. To add a server to the blocked or allowed servers list, use the fully qualified domain name of the server, such as *mailsvr83.tvpress.com*.

The following example adds two servers to the allowed servers list throughout the Exchange organization:

```
Get-ActiveSyncVirtualDirectory -ShowMailboxVirtualDirectories |
Set-OWAVirtualDirectory -RemoteDocumentsAllowedServers
@{Add="mailsvr83.tvpress.com","corpserver18.treyresearch.net"}
```

Servers that are not listed on either the allow list or the block list are considered to be unknown servers. By default, access to unknown servers is allowed. You can use the -RemoteDocumentsActionForUnknownServers parameter to specify whether to allow or block unknown servers. Set the parameter value to Allow or Block as appropriate. Here is an example:

```
Get-ActiveSyncVirtualDirectory -ShowMailboxVirtualDirectories |
Set-OWAVirtualDirectory -RemoteDocumentsActionForUnknownServers Block
```

Users have access only to shares hosted on internal servers. For a server to be considered an internal server, you must tell Exchange about the domain suffixes that should be handled as internal by using the -RemoteDocumentsInternalDomainSuffixList parameter. This is a multivalued parameter.

To add a domain suffix, specify the fully qualified domain name of the suffix. An example follows:

```
Get-ActiveSyncVirtualDirectory -ShowMailboxVirtualDirectories |
Set-OWAVirtualDirectory -RemoteDocumentsInternalDomainSuffixList
@{Add="tvpress.com","treyresearch.net"}
```

To remove a domain suffix, specify the suffix to remove, such as:

```
Get-ActiveSyncVirtualDirectory -ShowMailboxVirtualDirectories |
Set-OWAVirtualDirectory -RemoteDocumentsInternalDomainSuffixList
@{Remove="proseware.com","litwareinc.com"}
```

Integrating Office Web Apps Servers

Although earlier releases of Exchange included functionality for viewing documents directly in Outlook Web App, Microsoft has since developed separate server functionality to provide full viewing and editing functionality. The new architecture requires installing Office Web Apps servers which are then integrated into your Exchange organization to provide viewing and editing functions for Office documents.

After you install Office Web Apps servers on your network, you need to perform a series of steps to prepare your Mailbox servers to use the new architecture:

1. Use the -WacDiscoveryEndpoint parameter of the Set-OrganizationConfig cmdlet to specify the Discovery URL for Office Web Apps servers, such as:

```
Set-OrganizationConfig -WacDiscoveryEndpoint
https://MailServer85/hosting/discovery
```

2. Log on to the Mailbox server. Start IIS Manager. In Server Manager, click Tools, and then select Internet Information Services (IIS) Manager.

3. In IIS Manager, expand the base node for the server you want to work with and then select Application Pools.

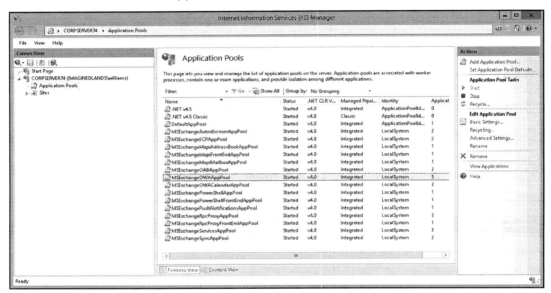

4. Click the MSExchangeOWAAppPool to select the application pool for OWA.

5. In the Actions pane, click Recycle to recycle the application pool. When the application pool restarts, OWA will detect the Discovery endpoint and then your Office Web Apps servers will be used for viewing and editing Office documents.

You can confirm integration and availability of the Discovery endpoint by entering the following command:

```
Get-OrganizationConfig | fl WacDiscoveryEndpoint
```

The output should include the URL you previously specified.

Once you've installed Office Web Apps servers and used the previous procedure to integrate them into your Exchange organization, OWA users will be able to view and edit Office documents without having the applications associated with those file types installed on their computing devices. Files types that WAC Viewing allows users to view and edit include:

- Microsoft Office Excel spreadsheets with the.xls, .xlsx, .xlm, and .xlsb extensions
- Microsoft Office Word documents with the .doc, .docx, .dot, .dotx, and .dotm extensions
- Microsoft Office PowerPoint presentations with the .pps, .ppsx, .ppt,.pptx, .pot, .potm, and .ppsm extensions

When there are conflicting settings between the direct file, remote file, and WAC Viewing settings, you can force clients to use WAC Viewing first, if you want. This ensures that the documents will be opened using Office Web Apps servers as helpers.

You can enable or disable WAC Viewing separately for public computers and private computers. However, supported document settings for both types of computers are shared and applied to both public and private computers in the same way.

In Exchange Management Shell, you can use the Set-OWAVirtualDirectory cmdlet to manage the WAC Viewing configuration. Use the –Identity parameter to identify the virtual directory you want to work, such as:

```
Set-OWAVirtualDirectory –Identity "Corpsvr127\owa (Default Web Site)"
```

Then specify how you want to configure WAC Viewing on the front-end and back-end virtual directory, such as:

```
Set-OWAVirtualDirectory –Identity "Corpsvr127\owa (Default Web Site)"
 -WacViewingOnPublicComputersEnabled $false
 -WacViewingOnPrivateComputersEnabled $true
 -WacEditingEnabled $true


Set-OWAVirtualDirectory –Identity "Corpsvr127\owa (Exchange Back End)"

 -WacViewingOnPublicComputersEnabled $false

 -WacViewingOnPrivateComputersEnabled $true

 -WacEditingEnabled $true
```

If you are unsure of the virtual directory identity value, use the Get-OWAVirtualDirectory cmdlet to retrieve a list of available virtual directories on a named server, as shown in the following example:

```
Get-OWAVirtualDirectory –Server "Corpsvr127" -ShowMailboxVirtualDirectories
```

Typically, you'll want to configure the front-end and back-end virtual directories in the same way.

Working with Mobile Devices and Device Policies

Mobile device mailbox policy makes it possible to enhance the security of mobile devices used to access your Exchange servers. For example, you can use policy to require a password of a specific length and to configure devices to automatically prompt for a password after a period of inactivity.

Each mailbox policy you create has a name and a specific set of rules with which it is associated. Because you can apply policies separately to mailboxes when you create or modify them, you can create different policies for different groups of users. For example, you can have one policy for users and another policy for managers. You can also create separate policies for departments within the organization. For example, you can have separate policies for Marketing, Customer Support, and Technology.

> NOTE   Mobile device mailbox policies replace ActiveSync mailbox policies. If your organization is still using ActiveSync mailbox policies, which are being phased out, you should transition to mobile device policies.

Viewing Existing Mobile Device Mailbox Policies

When the Mailbox role is installed on an Exchange server, the setup process creates a default mobile device mailbox policy, which allows enterprise mobile devices to be used without restrictions or password requirements. All users with mailboxes have this policy applied by default. You can modify the settings of this policy to change the settings for all users or create new policies for specific groups of users.

In the Exchange Admin Center, you can view the currently configured mobile device mailbox policies by selecting Mobile in the Feature pane, and then selecting Mobile Device Mailbox Policies. In the details pane, you'll see a list of current policies.

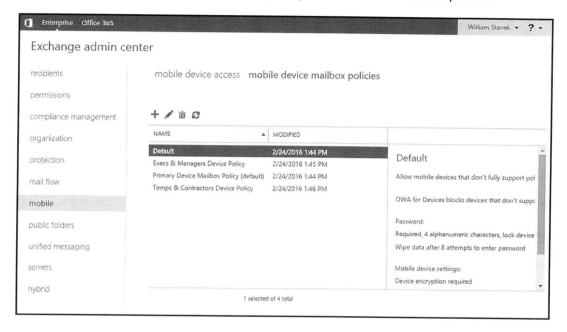

In Exchange Management Shell, you can list policies by using the Get-MobileDeviceMailboxPolicy cmdlet. Listing 15-9 provides the syntax, usage, and sample output. If you do not provide an identity with this cmdlet, all available mobile device mailbox policies are listed.

LISTING 15-9 Get-MobileDeviceMailboxPolicy cmdlet syntax and usage

Syntax

```
Get-MobileDeviceMailboxPolicy [-Identity MailboxPolicyId]

[-DomainController FullyQualifiedName] [-Organization OrgId]
```

Usage

```
Get-MobileDeviceMailboxPolicy

Get-MobileDeviceMailboxPolicy -Identity "Primary Device Mailbox Policy"
```

Output

```
RunspaceId                        :
AllowNonProvisionableDevices      : True
AlphanumericPasswordRequired      : True
```

```
AttachmentsEnabled                              : True
DeviceEncryptionEnabled                         : False
RequireStorageCardEncryption                    : False
PasswordEnabled                                 : True
PasswordRecoveryEnabled                         : False
DevicePolicyRefreshInterval                     : Unlimited
AllowSimplePassword                             : False
MaxAttachmentSize                               : Unlimited
WSSAccessEnabled                                : True
UNCAccessEnabled                                : True
MinPasswordLength                               : 4
MaxInactivityTimeLock                           : 00:15:00
MaxPasswordFailedAttempts                       : 8
PasswordExpiration                              : 90.00:00:00
PasswordHistory                                 : 5
IsDefault                                       : True
AllowApplePushNotifications                     : True
AllowMicrosoftPushNotifications                 : True
AllowGooglePushNotifications                    : True
AllowStorageCard                                : True
AllowCamera                                     : True
RequireDeviceEncryption                         : True
AllowUnsignedApplications                       : True
AllowUnsignedInstallationPackages               : True
AllowWiFi                                        : True
AllowTextMessaging                              : True
AllowPOPIMAPEmail                               : True
AllowIrDA                                        : True
RequireManualSyncWhenRoaming                    : False
AllowDesktopSync                                : True
AllowHTMLEmail                                  : True
RequireSignedSMIMEMessages                      : False
RequireEncryptedSMIMEMessages                   : False
AllowSMIMESoftCerts                             : True
AllowBrowser                                    : True
AllowConsumerEmail                              : True
AllowRemoteDesktop                              : True
AllowInternetSharing                            : True
AllowBluetooth                                  : Allow
MaxCalendarAgeFilter                            : All
MaxEmailAgeFilter                               : All
RequireSignedSMIMEAlgorithm                     : SHA1
RequireEncryptionSMIMEAlgorithm                 : TripleDES
AllowSMIMEEncryptionAlgorithmNegotiation        : AllowAnyAlgorithmNegotiation
MinPasswordComplexCharacters                    : 3
MaxEmailBodyTruncationSize                      : Unlimited
MaxEmailHTMLBodyTruncationSize                  : Unlimited
UnapprovedInROMApplicationList                  : {}
ApprovedApplicationList                         : {}
AllowExternalDeviceManagement                   : False
MobileOTAUpdateMode                             : MinorVersionUpdates
AllowMobileOTAUpdate                            : True
IrmEnabled                                      : True
AdminDisplayName                                :
ExchangeVersion                                 : 0.1 (8.0.535.0)
Name                                            : Default
DistinguishedName                               : CN=Default,CN=Mobile Mailbox"
Policies,CN=First Organization,CN=MicrosoftExchange,
```

```
CN=Services,CN=Configuration,DC=imaginedlands,DC=local
Identity                            : Default
. . .
Id                                  : Default
OriginatingServer                   : CorpServer91.imaginedlands.local
IsValid                             : True
ObjectState                         : Unchanged
```

Creating Mobile Device Mailbox Policies

The mobile device mailbox policies you create apply to your entire organization. You apply policies separately after you create them, as discussed later in this chapter in the "Assigning Mobile Device Mailbox Policies" section.

You can create a new policy by completing the following steps:

1. In Exchange Admin Center, select Mobile in the Feature pane, and then select Mobile Device Mailbox Policies to see a list of currently defined mobile device mailbox policies.

2. Click New (＋) to open the New Mobile Device Mailbox Policy dialog box.

3. Type a descriptive name for the policy. If you want the policy to be assigned to all users who are currently using the previously assigned default policy, select This Is The Default Policy.

4. By default, mobile devices that do not support all device mailbox settings can't synchronize with Exchange. This is by design to ensure strict security can be enforced. If you want to allow older devices to sync with Exchange regardless of whether they full support device policy, select the Allow Mobile Devices That Don't Fully Support... checkbox.

new mobile device mailbox policy

*Required fields

*Name:

Primary Device Mailbox Policy

☑ This is the default policy

☐ Allow mobile devices that don't fully support
these policies to synchronize

Save   Cancel

5. Before you can apply policy restrictions, you must specify that device passwords are required by selecting the Require A Password checkbox. If you do not select this option, you cannot specify password requirements.

6. Next, use the following options provides to specify the password requirements:

- **Allow Simple Passwords**   Allows the user to use a noncomplex password instead of a password that meets the minimum complexity requirements.
- **Require An Alphanumeric Password**   Requires that a password contain numeric and alphanumeric characters. If you do not select this option, users can use simple passwords, which might not be as secure. If you select this option, you can also specify the number of character sets that are required to be used in passwords. The four character sets are lowercase letters, uppercase letters, numbers, and symbols. You can require from one to four of these character sets to be used in passwords.

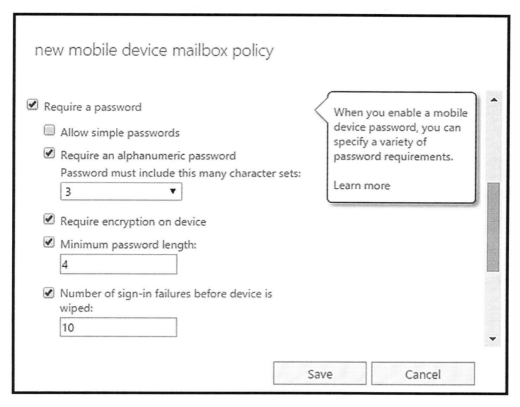

- **Require Encryption On Device**   Requires mobile devices to use encryption. Because encrypted data cannot be accessed without the appropriate password, this option helps to protect the data on the device. If you select this option, Exchange allows devices to download data only if they can use encryption (except when you allow mobile devices that don't fully support mobile device mailbox policy).
- **Minimum Password Length**   Allows you to set a minimum password length. You must select the related check box to set the minimum password length, such as eight characters. The longer the password, the more secure it is. A good minimum password length is between 8 and 12 characters, which is sufficient in most cases.
- **Number Of Sign-In Failures Before Device Is Wiped**   Allows you to specify the number of login failures before the device is wiped. If you select this option, be sure to set a high enough value so that mobile devices aren't accidentally wiped by users. For example, rather than setting a low value, such as 3, use a higher value, such as 9.
- **Require Sign-In After The Device Has Been Inactive For (Minutes)**   Allows you to specify the length of time that a device can go without user input before it locks. If you select this option, be sure to set an interval that allows for normal workflow and isn't disruptive. For example, if high security isn't a requirement, you

may want to require users to sign-in after 5 to 7 minutes of inactivity rather than having the device lock itself after 2 to 3 minutes of inactivity.

- **Enforce Password Lifetime (Days)** Allows you to specify the maximum length of time users can keep a password before they have to change it. You can use this option to require users to change their passwords periodically. A good password expiration value is between 30 and 90 days. This period is sufficient to allow use of the password without requiring overly frequent changes.

- **Password Recycle Count** Allows you to specify how frequently old passwords can be reused. You can use this option to discourage users from changing back and forth between a common set of passwords. To disable this option, set the size of the password history to zero. To enable this option, set the desired size of the password history. A good value is between 3 and 6. This helps to deter users from switching between a small list of common passwords.

7. Click Save to create the policy. Optimize the configuration, as discussed in the following section of this chapter, "Optimizing Mobile Device Mailbox Policies."

In Exchange Management Shell, you can create new mobile device mailbox policies by using the New-MobileDeviceMailboxPolicy cmdlet. Listing 15-10 provides the syntax and usage. There are additional policy settings you can access in the shell that you cannot access in the Exchange Admin Center.

LISTING 15-10 New-MobileDeviceMailboxPolicy cmdlet syntax and usage

Syntax

```
New-MobileDeviceMailboxPolicy -Name PolicyName
 [-AllowBluetooth <Disable | HandsfreeOnly | Allow>]
 [-AllowSMIMEEncryptionAlgorithmNegotiation <BlockNegotiation |
 OnlyStrongAlgorithmNegotiation | AllowAnyAlgorithmNegotiation>]
 [-ApprovedApplicationList AppList] [-DevicePolicyRefreshInterval
 Interval] [-DomainController FullyQualifiedName]
 [-MaxAttachmentSize MaxSizeKB] [-MaxCalendarAgeFilter <All | TwoWeeks |
 OneMonth | ThreeMonths | SixMonths>] [-MaxEmailAgeFilter <All |
 OneDay | ThreeDays | OneWeek | TwoWeeks | OneMonth>]
 [-MaxEmailBodyTruncationSize MaxSizeKB]
 [-MaxEmailHTMLBodyTruncationSize MaxSizeKB] [-MaxInactivityTimeLock
 InactiveTime] [-MaxPasswordFailedAttempts NumAttempts]
 [-MinPasswordComplexCharacters MinComplexChars] [-MinPasswordLength
 MinLength] [-MobileOTAUpdateMode <MajorVersionUpdates |
```

MinorVersionUpdates | BetaVersionUpdates>] [-Organization
OrgId] [-PasswordExpiration **PasswordExp**] [-PasswordHistory **HistLength**]
[-RequireEncryptionSMIMEAlgorithm <TripleDES | DES | RC2128bit |
RC264bit | RC240bit>] [-RequireSignedSMIMEAlgorithm <SHA1 | MD5>]
[-UnapprovedInROMApplicationList **AppList**] {OptionalTrueFalseParams}

{OptionalTrueFalseParams}

-AllowBrowser, -AllowCamera, -AllowConsumerEmail, -AllowDesktopSync,

-AllowExternalDeviceManagement, -AllowHTMLEmail, -AllowInternetSharing,

-AllowIrDA, -AllowMicrosoftPushNotifications, -AllowMobileOTAUpdate,

-AllowNonProvisionableDevices, -AllowPOPIMAPEmail,

-AllowRemoteDesktop, -AllowSimplePassword, -AllowSMIMESoftCerts,

-AllowStorageCard, -AllowTextMessaging, -AllowUnsignedApplications,

-AllowUnsignedInstallationPackages, -AllowWiFi,

-AlphanumericPasswordRequired, -AttachmentsEnabled,

-DeviceEncryptionEnabled, -IrmEnabled, -IsDefault, -PasswordEnabled,

-PasswordRecoveryEnabled, -RequireDeviceEncryption,

-RequireEncryptedSMIMEMessages, -RequireManualSyncWhenRoaming,

-RequireSignedSMIMEMessages, -RequireStorageCardEncryption,

-UNCAccessEnabled, -WSSAccessEnabled

Usage

New-MobileDeviceMailboxPolicy -Name "Primary Mobile Device Mailbox Policy"
 -AllowNonProvisionableDevices $true

 -PasswordEnabled $true

 -AlphanumericPasswordRequired $true

 -MaxInactivityTimeLock "00.15:00"

 -MinPasswordLength "8"

 -PasswordRecoveryEnabled $true

 -RequireDeviceEncryption $true

 -AttachmentsEnabled $true

Optimizing Mobile Device Mailbox Policies

When you create a mobile device mailbox policy, some additional settings are
configured automatically. You can modify policy settings by using the Set-

MobileDeviceMailboxPolicy cmdlet. By default, access to both Windows file shares and Microsoft Windows SharePoint Services is allowed. You can block access to file shares and SharePoint by setting the -UNCAccessEnabled and -WSSAccessEnabled parameters to $false.

If you specified that passwords are required, by default, simple passwords are not allowed. Additionally, by default, many device features are allowed. By using the TrueFalseParams shown in Listing 15-11, you can:

- Allow or disallow another device to share the device's Internet connection.
- Allow or disallow remote desktop connections.
- Allow or disallow the device to access email accounts other than Microsoft Exchange.
- Allow or disallow the device to access removable storage, such as memory cards.
- Allow or disallow the device to connect to a wireless network.
- Allow or disallow the device to connect to and synchronize with a desktop computer.
- Allow or disallow the device to connect to other devices using infrared.
- Allow or disallow the device to execute unsigned applications.
- Allow or disallow the device to install unsigned applications.
- Allow or disallow the device to use the built-in browser.
- Allow or disallow the device's built-in camera.

Use -MaxEmailBodyTruncationSize and -MaxEmailHTMLBodyTruncationSize to specify the maximum allowed size for email messages. Both parameter values are set in kilobytes. If a standard email message exceeds the MaxEmailBodyTruncationSize value, the message is truncated (clipped). If an HTML-formatted email message exceeds the MaxEmailHTMLBodyTruncationSize, the message is truncated (clipped).

If the policy allows devices to download attachments, the attachment has no default limit size. You can block attachment downloads by setting -AttachmentsEnabled to *$false*. If you allow attachments and you want to limit the size of attachments that users can download, you can specify the maximum allowed attachment size in kilobytes by using -MaxAttachmentSize.

For past calendar and email items, you can specify whether all calendar and mail items should be synced or only items from a specific period of time, such as the last two weeks. Use the -MaxCalendarAgeFilter and -MaxEmailAgeFilter parameters respectively. If you allow Bluetooth, you also can specify how the device can use

Bluetooth. Set -AllowBlueTooth to Allow if you want to allow mobile devices to use Bluetooth in any mode or HandsfreeOnly to allow mobile devices to use Bluetooth only in hands-free mode. Set -AllowBlueTooth to Disable if you want to prevent devices from using BlueTooth.

LISTING 15-11 Set-MobileDeviceMailboxPolicy cmdlet syntax and usage

Syntax

```
Set-MobileDeviceMailboxPolicy -Identity MailboxPolicyId
  [-AllowBluetooth <Disable | HandsfreeOnly | Allow>]
[-AllowSMIMEEncryptionAlgorithmNegotiation <BlockNegotiation |
OnlyStrongAlgorithmNegotiation | AllowAnyAlgorithmNegotiation>]
[-ApprovedApplicationList AppList] [-DevicePolicyRefreshInterval
Interval] [-DomainController FullyQualifiedName]
[-MaxAttachmentSize MaxSizeKB] [-MaxCalendarAgeFilter <All | TwoWeeks |
OneMonth | ThreeMonths | SixMonths>] [-MaxEmailAgeFilter <All |
OneDay | ThreeDays | OneWeek | TwoWeeks | OneMonth>]
[-MaxEmailBodyTruncationSize MaxSizeKB]
[-MaxEmailHTMLBodyTruncationSize MaxSizeKB] [-MaxInactivityTimeLock
InactiveTime] [-MaxPasswordFailedAttempts NumAttempts]
[-MinPasswordComplexCharacters MinComplexChars] [-MinPasswordLength
MinLength] [-MobileOTAUpdateMode <MajorVersionUpdates |
MinorVersionUpdates | BetaVersionUpdates>] [-Organization
OrgId] [-PasswordExpiration PasswordExp] [-PasswordHistory HistLength]
[-RequireEncryptionSMIMEAlgorithm <TripleDES | DES | RC2128bit |
RC264bit | RC240bit>] [-RequireSignedSMIMEAlgorithm <SHA1 | MD5>]
[-UnapprovedInROMApplicationList AppList] {OptionalTrueFalseParams}

{OptionalTrueFalseParams}
-AllowBrowser, -AllowCamera, -AllowConsumerEmail,
-AllowDesktopSync, -AllowExternalDeviceManagement, -AllowHTMLEmail,
-AllowInternetSharing, -AllowIrDA, -AllowMicrosoftPushNotifications,
-AllowMobileOTAUpdate, -AllowNonProvisionableDevices, -AllowPOPIMAPEmail,
-AllowRemoteDesktop, -AllowSimplePassword, -AllowSMIMESoftCerts,
-AllowStorageCard, -AllowTextMessaging, -AllowUnsignedApplications,
-AllowUnsignedInstallationPackages, -AllowWiFi,
-AlphanumericPasswordRequired, -AttachmentsEnabled,
```

```
-DeviceEncryptionEnabled, -IrmEnabled, -IsDefault, -PasswordEnabled,
-PasswordRecoveryEnabled, -RequireDeviceEncryption,
-RequireEncryptedSMIMEMessages, -RequireManualSyncWhenRoaming,
-RequireSignedSMIMEMessages, -RequireStorageCardEncryption,
-UNCAccessEnabled, -WSSAccessEnabled
```

Usage

```
Set-MobileDeviceMailboxPolicy -Identity "Device Policy for Executives"
-AllowNonProvisionableDevices $false -AllowBluetooth HandsfreeOnly
-DeviceEncryptionEnabled $true -PasswordRecoveryEnabled $true
-RequireDeviceEncryption $true -MaxAttachmentSize 5096
-MaxEmailBodyTruncationSize 10192 -MaxEmailHTMLBodyTruncationSize 10192
```

Assigning Mobile Device Mailbox Policies

The default mobile device mailbox policy is automatically applied by Exchange through implicit inheritance unless you assign a different non-default policy to a user. Any mailbox that has implicitly inherited policy automatically applies the currently-defined default policy and its settings. When you modify the default policy or configure a new default policy, you change the settings for all mailbox users that implicitly inherit the default policy.

To set a different policy as the default for new mailbox users, follow these steps:

1. In Exchange Admin Center, select Mobile in the Feature pane, and then select Mobile Device Mailbox Policies to see a list of currently defined mobile device mailbox policies.

2. The current default policy has the value (default) as a suffix. To make another policy the default, select the policy you want to be the new default, and then select Edit (✏).

3. In the Mobile Device Mailbox Policy dialog box, select This Is The Default Policy, and then select Save.

To explicitly assign a policy to a mailbox, complete the following steps:

1. In Exchange Admin Center, select Recipients in the Feature pane, and then select Mailboxes.

2. You should now see a list of users with Exchange mailboxes in the organization. Select the mailbox with which you want to work.

3. In the details pane, under Mobile Devices, select View Details.

4. In the Mobile Device Details dialog box, select Browse. Choose the policy to apply, and then select OK.

5. Click Save to apply your settings.

To explicitly assign a policy to multiple mailboxes, complete the following steps:

1. In Exchange Admin Center, select Recipients in the Feature pane, and then select Mailboxes.

2. You should now see a list of users with Exchange mailboxes in the organization. Select multiple mailboxes by using the Shift or Ctrl keys.

3. In the details pane, scroll down. Under Exchange ActiveSync, select Update A Policy.

4. In the Bulk Assign.... dialog box, select Browse. Choose the policy to apply, and then select OK.

5. Click Save to apply your settings.

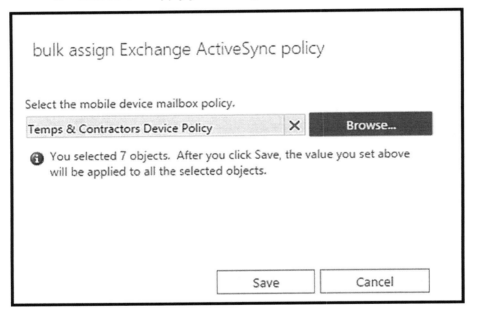

If you want mailbox users to use a mobile device mailbox policy other than the default, use the –ActiveSyncMailboxPolicy parameter of the Set-CASMailbox cmdlet to assign a policy directly to mailboxes. Listing 15-12 provides the syntax and usage.

LISTING 15-12 Assigning a Mobile Device Mailbox Policy to mailboxes

Syntax

```
Set-CASMailbox –Identity MailboxIdentity
  –ActiveSyncMailboxPolicy PolicyIdentity
```

Apply the policy to the mailbox user named MarkH

```
Set-CASMailbox -Identity "markh@tvpress.com"
 -ActiveSyncMailboxPolicy "Device Policy for Executives"
```

Apply the policy to every mailbox in the Exchange organization

```
Get-Mailbox -ResultSize Unlimited | Set-CASMailbox
-ActiveSyncMailboxPolicy "Device Policy for Executives"
```

Apply the policy to every mailbox in the Sales database

```
Get-MailboxDatabase "Sales" | Get-Mailbox -ResultSize Unlimited |
Set-CASMailbox -ActiveSyncMailboxPolicy "Device Policy for Executives"
```

Apply the policy to all mailboxes in every mailbox database on MailboxServer18

```
Get-Mailbox -Server MailboxServer18 -ResultSize Unlimited |
Set-CASMailbox -ActiveSyncMailboxPolicy "Device Policy for Executives"
```

Removing Mobile Device Mailbox Policies

When you no longer need a mobile device mailbox policy, you can remove it, provided that it isn't the current default policy. In the Exchange Admin Center, select the policy, and then select the Delete button. When prompted to confirm, click Yes to delete the policy. If users are assigned to the policy, they will stop using the policy and implicitly inherit the current default policy.

In Exchange Management Shell, you can remove a mobile device mailbox policy by using the Remove-MobileMailboxPolicy cmdlet. Listing 15-13 provides the syntax and usage.

LISTING 15-13 Remove-MobileMailboxPolicy cmdlet syntax and usage

Syntax

```
Remove-MobileMailboxPolicy -Identity Name [-DomainController DCName]
[-Force <$true | $false>]
```

Usage

```
Remove-MobileMailboxPolicy -Identity "Primary ActiveSync
Mailbox Policy"
```

Managing Device Access

To manage device access to Exchange, you can:

- Block device access
- Define access rules
- Set access levels
- Set blocking thresholds

Blocking Device Access

One way to prevent a device from synchronizing with Exchange is to put the device on the blocked mobile device list for the user's mailbox. The first step is to retrieve the ID of the device you want to prevent from syncing. Unfortunately, there's no way to retrieve the device ID before the user synchronizes the device with Exchange (unless you already know the device ID). If the user has synced the device already, you can get the device ID using:

```
Get-MobileDeviceStatistics -Mailbox ExchangeId
-ActiveSync | fl DeviceID
```

Where ExchangeId is the email address or Exchange alias of the user, such as:

```
Get-MobileDeviceStatistics -Mailbox KaraH
-ActiveSync | fl DeviceID
```

To prevent a device from synchronizing with Exchange, you must add the device to the -ActiveSyncBlockedDeviceIDs parameter list on the user's mailbox. To do this, run the following command:

```
Set-CASMailbox -Identity ExchangeID -ActiveSyncBlockedDeviceIDs
@{Add="DeviceID"}
```

Where *ExchangeID* is the email address or Exchange alias for the mailbox user you want to prevent from using certain mobile devices, and DeviceID is the ID of the device to prevent from synchronizing with Exchange. If the device was previously on the user's allowed ActiveSync device list, you can remove the device from this list as well by using the following syntax:

```
Set-CASMailbox -Identity ExchangeID -ActiveSyncAllowedDeviceIDs
@{Remove="DeviceID"}
```

> **NOTE**   As the blocked list has precedence over the allowed list, you technically don't have to remove the device from the allowed list. However, if someone accidentally resets the blocked list and you haven't removed the device from the allowed list, the user will be explicitly permitted to use the device to sync with Exchange.

Using Access Rules

Although you may sometimes want to manage device access for individual users, you'll probably prefer to define device access rules to control which device can and cannot sync with Exchange. To work with access rules, you'll use the following cmdlets:

* **Get-ActiveSyncDeviceAccessRule**   Lists an access group of Exchange mobile devices along with their access level

```
Get-ActiveSyncDeviceAccessRule [-Identity AccessRuleId]
[-DomainController FullyQualifiedName] [-Organization OrgId]
```

* **Get-ActiveSyncDeviceClass**   Lists mobile devices that have connected to Exchange by their type and model

```
Get-ActiveSyncDeviceClass [-Identity DeviceGroupId]
[-DomainController FullyQualifiedName] [-Filter FilterValues]
[-Organization OrgId] [-SortBy AttributeName]
```

* **New-ActiveSyncDeviceAccessRule**   Defines an access group of Exchange mobile devices along with their access level

```
New-ActiveSyncDeviceAccessRule -AccessLevel <Allow | Block |
Quarantine> -Characteristic <DeviceType | DeviceModel | DeviceOS |
UserAgent> -QueryString Devices [-DomainController FullyQualifiedName]
[-Organization OrgId]
```

- **Remove-ActiveSyncDeviceAccessRule**   Removes an existing device access rule

```
Remove-ActiveSyncDeviceAccessRule -Identity AccessRuleId
[-DomainController FullyQualifiedName]
```

- **Remove-ActiveSyncDeviceClass**   Removes a device class from the list of mobile devices synchronizing with Exchange

```
Remove-ActiveSyncDeviceClass -Identity DeviceGroupId
[-DomainController FullyQualifiedName]
```

- **Set-ActiveSyncDeviceAccessRule**   Sets the level of access for the ActiveSync Device Access rule

```
Set-ActiveSyncDeviceAccessRule -Identity AccessRuleId
[-AccessLevel <Allow | Block | Quarantine>]
[-DomainController FullyQualifiedName]
```

The following example creates access rules to block several different types of iOS 6.1 devices:

```
New-ActiveSyncDeviceAccessRule -querystring "iOS 6.1 10B142"
-characteristic DeviceOS -accesslevel block


New-ActiveSyncDeviceAccessRule -querystring "iOS 6.1 10B143"
-characteristic DeviceOS -accesslevel block


New-ActiveSyncDeviceAccessRule -querystring "iOS 6.1 10B144"
-characteristic DeviceOS -accesslevel block
```

Setting Access Levels and Blocking Thresholds

Another way to control device access is to define default access levels and blocking thresholds for ActiveSync devices. To do this, use the following cmdlets:

- **Get-ActiveSyncDeviceAutoblockThreshold**   Lists the Autoblock settings for Exchange ActiveSync mobile devices

```
Get-ActiveSyncDeviceAutoblockThreshold [-Identity RuleName]
[-DomainController FullyQualifiedName]
```

- **Set-ActiveSyncDeviceAutoblockThreshold**   Modifies the autoblocking settings for mobile devices

```
Set-ActiveSyncDeviceAutoblockThreshold -Identity RuleName
[-AdminEmailInsert MessageText] [-BehaviorTypeIncidenceDuration
TimeSpan] [-BehaviorTypeIncidenceLimit Limit]
[-DeviceBlockDuration TimeSpan] [-DomainController FullyQualifiedName]
```

- **Get-ActiveSyncOrganizationSettings**   Lists the Exchange ActiveSync settings for the Exchange organization

```
Get-ActiveSyncOrganizationSettings [-Identity ExchangeOrgId]
[-DomainController FullyQualifiedName] [-Organization OrgId]
```

- **Set-ActiveSyncOrganizationSettings**   Modifies the Exchange ActiveSync settings for the Exchange organization

```
Set-ActiveSyncOrganizationSettings [-Identity ExchangeOrgId]
[-AdminMailRecipients email1,email2,…emailN] [-DefaultAccessLevel
<Allow | Block | Quarantine>] [-DomainController FullyQualifiedName]
[-OtaNotificationMailInsert MessageText] [-UserMailInsert MessageText
```

Chapter 16. Tracking and Logging Exchange Server 2016

As part of routine maintenance, you need to monitor Exchange Server to ensure that services and processes are functioning normally. Key components of any monitoring plan should include messaging tracking and protocol logging.

You use message tracking to monitor the flow of messages into, out of, and within an organization. With message tracking enabled, Exchange Server maintains daily log files, with a running history of all messages transferred within an organization. You use the logs to determine the status of a message, such as whether a message has been sent, has been received, or is waiting in the queue to be delivered. Because Exchange Server handles postings to public folders in much the same way as email messages, you can also use message tracking to monitor public folder usage.

Tracking logs can really save the day when you're trying to troubleshoot delivery and routing problems. The logs are also useful in fending off problem users who blame email for their woes. Generally speaking, users can't claim they didn't receive emails if you can find the messages in the logs. That said, if you use third-party applications that integrate with Outlook, those applications could potentially delete messages before the user sees them.

Protocol logging allows you to track Simple Mail Transfer Protocol (SMTP) communications that occur between servers as part of message routing and delivery. These communications could include both Exchange servers and non-Exchange servers. When non-Exchange servers send messages to an Exchange server, Exchange does the protocol logging of the communications.

You use protocol logging to troubleshoot problems with the Send and Receive connectors that are configured on Mailbox and Edge Transport servers. However, you shouldn't use protocol logging to monitor Exchange activity. This is primarily because protocol logging can be processor intensive and resource intensive, which means that an Exchange server may have to perform a lot of work to log protocol activity. The overhead required for protocol logging depends on the level of messaging activity on the Exchange server.

Configuring Message Tracking

By default, all Edge Transport and Mailbox servers perform message tracking. By setting the –MessageTrackingLogEnabled parameter of the Set-TransportService cmdlet to $true or $false, as appropriate, you can enable or disable message tracking on a per-server basis.

The following example disables message tracking on MailServer96:

```
Set-TransportService -Identity "MailServer96"
-MessageTrackingLogEnabled $false
```

> **TIP** You can configure basic message tracking options in the Exchange Admin Center. To do this, select Servers in the Features pane, and then select the Servers tab. In the main pane, double-click the server you want to configure to display the related Properties dialog box. On the Transport Logs page select or clear the Enable Message Tracking Log check box. If you enable message tracking, you can enter the desired directory path for logging as well or accept the default setting.

Changing the Logging Location

Each Edge Transport and Mailbox server in your organization can have different message tracking settings that control the following:

- Where logs are stored
- How logging is performed
- The maximum log size and maximum log directory size
- How long logs are retained

By default, message tracking logs are stored in the %ExchangeInstallPath%\TransportRoles\Logs\MessageTracking directory. Generally, message tracking does not have high enough input/output activity to warrant a dedicated disk. However, in some high usage situations, you might want to move the tracking logs to a separate disk. Before you do this, however, you should create the directory you want to use and set the following required permissions:

- Full Control for the server's local Administrators group
- Full Control for System
- Full Control for Network Service

After you've created the directory and set the required permissions, you can change the location of the tracking logs by setting the –MessageTrackingLogPath parameter of the Set-TransportService cmdlet to the desired local directory. The following example sets the message tracking directory as G:\Tracking on MailServer96:

```
Set-TransportService -Identity "MailServer96"
 -MessageTrackingLogPath "G:\Tracking"
```

> **NOTE** When you change the location of the message tracking directory, Exchange Server does not copy any existing tracking logs from the old directory to the new one. If you want all the logs to be in the same location, you should manually copy the old logs to the new location before you use Set-TransportService to change the message tracking directory.

Setting Logging Options

By default, all Edge Transport and Mailbox servers perform extended message tracking, which allows you to perform searches based on message subject lines, header information, sender, and recipient. If you don't want to collect information on potentially sensitive subject lines, you can disable subject line tracking by setting the –MessageTrackingLogSubjectLoggingEnabled parameter of the Set-TransportService cmdlet to $false, as shown in the following example:

```
Set-TransportService -Identity "MailServer96"
-MessageTrackingLogSubjectLoggingEnabled $false
```

Exchange Server continues to write to message tracking logs until a log grows to a specified maximum size, at which point Exchange Server creates a new log and then uses this log to track current messages. By default, the maximum log file size is 10 megabytes (MB). You can change this behavior by setting the –MessageTrackingLogMaxFileSize parameter to the desired maximum file size. You must qualify the desired file size by using B for bytes, KB for kilobytes, MB for megabytes, or GB for gigabytes. The following example sets the message log file size to 50 MB:

```
Set-TransportService -Identity "MailServer96"
-MessageTrackingLogMaxFileSize "50MB"
```

Exchange Server overwrites the oldest message tracking logs automatically when tracking logs reach a maximum age or when the maximum log directory size is reached. By default, the maximum age is 30 days and the maximum log directory size is 1000 MB. You can use the –MessageTrackingLogMaxAge parameter to set the maximum allowed age in the following format:

`DD.HH:MM:SS`

where DD is the number of days, HH is the number of hours, MM is the number of minutes, and SS is the number of seconds. The following example sets the maximum age for logs to 90 days:

```
Set-TransportService -Identity "MailServer96"
 -MessageTrackingLogMaxAge "90.00:00:00"
```

You can set the maximum log directory size by using the –MessageTrackingLogMaxDirectorySize parameter. As with the maximum log file size, the qualifiers are B, KB, MB, and GB. The following example sets the maximum log directory size to 2 GB:

```
Set-TransportService -Identity "MailServer96"
 -MessageTrackingLogMaxDirectorySize "2GB"
```

Searching the Tracking Logs

The tracking logs are useful in troubleshooting problems with routing and delivery. In Exchange Management Shell, you use Get-MessageTrackingLog to search through the message tracking logs. The related syntax is:

```
Get-MessageTrackingLog [-Start DateTime] [-Server ServerId]
[-End DateTime] {AddtlParams}

{AddtlParams}
[-DomainController DCName] [-EventId {"BadMail" | "Defer" | "Deliver" |
"DSN" | "Expand" | "Fail" | "PoisonMessage" | "Receive" | "Redirect" |
"Resolve" | "Send" | "Submit" | "Transfer"} ] [-InternalMessageId
MessageTrackingLogId] [-MessageId MessageId] [-MessageSubject
```

Subject] [-Recipients **SMTPEmailAddress1, SMTPEmailAddress2,...**]
[-Reference **ReferenceField**] [-ResultSize **NumEntriesToReturn**]
[-Sender **SMTPEmailAddress**]

These parameters allow you to search the message tracking logs in the following ways:

* By date
* By event ID
* By message ID
* By message subject
* By recipients
* By sender
* By server that processed the messages

Beginning an Automated Search

To begin a search, you must specify one or more of the previously listed identifiers as the search criteria. You must also identify a server in the organization that has processed the message in some way. This server can be the sender's server, the recipient's server, or a server that relayed the message.

You set the search criteria by using the following parameters:

* **–End**   Sets the end date and time for the search.
* **–EventID**   Specifies the ID of the event for which you want to search, such as a RECEIVE, SEND, or FAIL event.
* **–InternalMessageID**   Specifies the ID of the message tracking log entries for which you want to search.
* **–MessageID**   Specifies the ID of the message for which you want to search.
* **–MessageSubject**   Specifies the subject of the message for which you want to search.
* **–Recipients**   Sets recipient's SMTP email address or addresses to return
* **–Reference**   Specifies the reference field value within the message for which you want to search.
* **–Sender**   Sets the sender's SMTP email address (listed in the From field of the message) to return.
* **–Server**   Sets the name of the Transport or Mailbox server that contains the message tracking logs to be searched.
* **–Start**   Sets the start date and time for the search.

Using the –Start and –End parameters, you can search for messages from a starting date and time to an ending date and time. Using the –Server parameter, you specify the server to search. Consider the following example:

```
Get-MessageTrackingLog -Start "05/25/2014 5:30AM" -End "05/30/2014 7:30PM"
-Server MailServer96 -Sender tonyj@imaginedlands.com
```

In this example, you search for a messages sent by Tonyj@imaginedlands.com between 5:30 A.M. May 25, 2014 and 7:30 P.M. May 30, 2014.

> **IMPORTANT** Keep in mind that only messages that match all of the search criteria you've specified are displayed. If you want to perform a broader search, specify a limited number of parameters. If you want to focus the search precisely, specify multiple parameters.

Reviewing Logs Manually

Exchange Server creates message tracking logs daily and stores them by default in the %ExchangeInstallPath%\TransportRoles\Logs\MessageTracking directory. For US-English, each log file is named by the date on which it was created, using one of the following formats:

- MSGTRKYYYYMMDD-N.log, such as MSGTRK20140325-1.log for the first log created on March 25, 2014 by the Transport service.
- MSGTRKMAYYYYMMDD-N.log, such as MSGTRKM20140325-1.log for the first log created on March 25, 2014 and used with moderated messages for tracking approvals and rejections.
- MSGTRKMDYYYYMMDD-N.log, such as MSGTRKM20140325-1.log for messages delivered to mailboxes by the Mailbox Transport Delivery service.
- MSGTRKMSYYYYMMDD-N.log, such as MSGTRKM20140325-1.log for messages sent from mailboxes by the Mailbox Transport Submission service.

The message tracking logs store each message event on a single line. The information on a particular line is organized by comma-separated fields. Logs begin with a header that shows the following information:

- A statement that identifies the file as a message tracking log file
- The version of the Exchange Server that created the file
- The date on which the log file was created
- A comma-delimited list of fields contained in the body of the log file

Although not all of the fields are tracked for all message events, message event fields and their meanings follow:

Client-hostname   The hostname of the client making the request

Client-ip   The IP address of the client making the request

Connector-id   The identity of the connector used

Custom-Data   Optional custom data that was logged

Date-Time   The connection date and time

Directionality   An indication of the source of the message

Event-id   The type of event being logged, such as Submit

Internal-message-id   An internal identifier used by Exchange to track a message

Message-id   The message identifier

Message-info   Any related additional information on the message

Message-subject   The subject of the message

Original-client-ip   The IP address for the original client

Original-server-ip   The IP address for the original server

Recipient-address   The email addresses of the message recipients

Recipient-count   The total number of recipients

Recipient-status   The status of the recipient email address

Reference   The references, if any

Related-recipient-address   The email addresses of any related recipients

Return-path   The return path on the message

Sender-address   The distinguished name of the sender's email address

Server-hostname   The server on which the log entry was generated

Server-ip   The IP address of the server on which the log entry was generated

Source   The component for which the event is being logged, such as StoreDriver

Source-context   The context of the event source

Tenant-id A tenant identifier

Total-bytes The total size of the message in bytes

You can view the message tracking log files with any standard text editor, such as Microsoft Notepad. You can also import the message tracking log files into a spreadsheet or a database. Follow these steps to import a message tracking log file into Microsoft Office Excel:

1. With Excel 2013 or Excel 2016, select File and then select Open. On the Open panel, select Computer and then select Browse.

2. Use the Open dialog box to select the message tracking log file you want to open. Set the file type as All Files (*.*), select the log file, and then click Open.

3. The Text Import Wizard starts automatically. Click Next. On the Delimiters list, choose Comma. Click Next, and then click Finish.

4. The log file should now be imported. You can view, search, and print the message tracking log as you would any other spreadsheet.

Searching the Delivery Status Reports

As part of message tracking, you can create delivery reports in Exchange Admin Center. Delivery reports allow you to search for the delivery status of messages sent to or from user's in your organization. In delivery reports, messages are listed by sender, recipients, and date and time sent. If subject line tracking is enabled, the subject line of messages is also included in reports.

You can track messages for up to 14 days after they were sent or received by completing the following steps:

1. In Exchange Admin Center, select Mail Flow in the Features pane, and then select Delivery Reports.

> **NOTE** Only messages sent using SMTP, RPC or MAPI over HTTP or Outlook Web App can be tracked. Mail sent using POP3 or IMAP mail clients cannot be tracked.

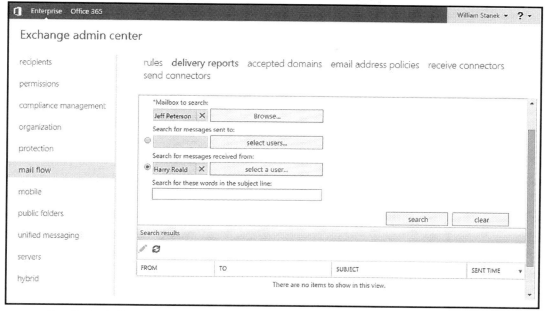

2. Each delivery report is for messages sent to or from a specific mailbox. Under Mailbox To Search, click Browse. Select the mailbox to search, and then click OK.

3. Use the options provided to specify whether you want to search for messages sent from or to the mailbox you're searching. Keep the following in mind:

- To find messages sent to specific users or groups from the mailbox you're searching, select Search For Messages Sent To, and then click Select Users. In the Select Users dialog box, select a user or group from the list, and then click Add. Repeat as necessary to add other users and groups. Click OK when you're finished.

- To find all messages sent from the mailbox you're searching, select Search For Messages Sent To and then don't select any specify users or groups. By leaving the field blank, you create delivery reports for messages sent from the mailbox to anyone.

- To find messages sent by a specific user to the mailbox you're searching, select Search For Messages Received From, and then click Select A User. In the Select Members dialog box, select a user from the list, and then click Add. Click OK when you are finished. If you choose this option, you must select a user and cannot leave the field blank.

4. Optionally, if subject line tracking is enabled, you can restrict the search to messages with specific keywords in the subject line. In the Search For These Words... box, type one or more keywords to search for in the subject line of

messages. To search for an exact phrase, enclose the phrase in quotation marks.

5. When you're ready to begin the search, click Search. If any matching messages are found, they are listed in the Search Results pane with the following fields:

- **From**   The display name, email address or alias of the person who sent the message.
- **To**   The display name, email address or alias of each message recipient.
- **Sent**   The date and time the message was sent.
- **Subject**   The subject line of the message.

6. View the delivery status and detailed delivery information for a message by selecting the message in the Search Results pane, and then selecting Details. When messages are sent to distribution groups, the details tell you the specific delivery status of each recipient in the group. When messages are moderated, the details tell you whether the moderator approved or rejected the message.

Configuring Protocol Logging

By default, protocol logging isn't enabled on custom connectors. As long as you know the identity of the custom connector with which you want to work, you can configure protocol logging for a specified connector. To retrieve a list of available Send and Receive connectors for a server, use the Get-SendConnector and Get-ReceiveConnector cmdlets, respectively. If you run either cmdlet without specifying additional parameters, a list of all available Send or Receive connectors is returned.

Enabling or Disabling Protocol Logging

You enable or disable protocol logging on a per-connector basis. For Send connectors, you use the Set-SendConnector cmdlet to enable protocol logging. For Receive connectors, you use the Set-ReceiveConnector cmdlet to enable protocol logging. Both cmdlets have a –ProtocolLoggingLevel parameter that you can set to Verbose to enable protocol logging or to None to disable protocol logging. Here is an example:

```
Set-ReceiveConnector -Identity "Corpsvr127\Custom Receive Connector"
-ProtocolLoggingLevel 'Verbose'
```

Associated with the Transport service and the Front End Transport service on every Mailbox server is an implicitly created Send connector, referred to as the intra-organization Send connector. The Transport service on Mailbox servers uses the intra-organization Send connector to relay messages to other Transport servers in the Exchange organization. By default, the Transport service doesn't perform protocol logging on the intra-organization Send connector. You enable or disable protocol logging for the intra-organization Send connector on a Mailbox server by using the -MailboxDeliveryConnectorProtocolLoggingLevel parameter of the Set-MailboxTransportService cmdlet. Use Verbose to enable protocol logging or to None to disable protocol logging. Here is an example:

```
Set-MailboxTransportService -Identity MailServer96
-MailboxDeliveryConnectorProtocolLoggingLevel 'Verbose'
```

The Frontend Transport service uses the intra-organization Send connector to relay messages to the Transport service on Mailbox servers. By default, the Front End Transport service performs protocol logging on the intra-organization Send connector. You enable or disable protocol logging for this Send connector by using the -IntraOrgConnectorProtocolLoggingLevel parameter of the Set-FrontEndTransportService cmdlet. Use Verbose to enable protocol logging or set to None to disable protocol logging. Here is an example:

```
Set-FrontEndTransportService -Identity MailServer26
-IntraOrgConnectorProtocolLoggingLevel 'Verbose'
```

Setting Other Protocol Logging Options

Although you enable protocol logging on a per-connector basis, you configure the other protocol logging parameters on a per-server basis for either all Send connectors or all Receive connectors by using the Set-TransportService cmdlet. As it does with message tracking logs, Exchange Server overwrites the oldest protocol logs automatically when tracking logs reach a maximum age or when the maximum log directory size is reached. If you decide to move the protocol log directories, you should create the directories you want to use and then set the following required permissions:

- Full Control for the server's local Administrators group
- Full Control for System

- Full Control for Network Service

Because the parameters are similar to those for message tracking, I'll summarize the available parameters. The Send connector parameters for configuring protocol logging include:

- **SendProtocolLogMaxAge**   Sets the maximum age for Send connector protocol logs. By default, set to 30.00:00:00.
- **SendProtocolLogMaxDirectorySize**   Sets the maximum size for the Send connector protocol log directory. By default, set to 250 MB.
- **SendProtocolLogMaxFileSize**   Sets the maximum size for Send connector protocol logs. By default, set to 10 MB.
- **SendProtocolLogPath**   Sets the local file path for protocol logging of Send connectors. By default, set to %ExchangeInstallPath%TransportRoles\Logs\ *ServerType*\ProtocolLogs\SmtpSend.

The Receive connector parameters for configuring protocol logging include:

- **ReceiveProtocolLogMaxAge**   Sets the maximum age for Receive connector protocol logs. By default, set to 30.00:00:00.
- **ReceiveProtocolLogMaxDirectorySize**   Sets the maximum size for the Receive connector protocol log directory. By default, set to 250 MB.
- **ReceiveProtocolLogMaxFileSize**   Sets the maximum size for Receive connector protocol logs. By default, set to 10 MB.
- ReceiveProtocolLogPath   Sets the local file path for protocol logging of Receive connectors. By default, set to %ExchangeInstallPath%TransportRoles\Logs\ *ServerType*\ProtocolLogs\SmtpReceive.

In the default path for logs, the ServerType can be FrontEnd, Mailbox, or Hub. On Maibox servers, you find these folders:

- Under FrontEnd\ProtocolLogs, you'll find logs for the Front End Transport service on Mailbox servers.
- Under Hub\ProtocolLogs, you'll find logs for the Transport service on Mailbox servers.
- Under Mailbox\ProtocolLogs, you'll find logs for the Mailbox Transport service on Mailbox servers.

> **TIP**   You can configure send and receive protocol log paths in the Exchange Admin Center. To do this, select Servers in the Features pane, and then select Servers. In the main pane, double-click the server you want to configure to display the related Properties dialog box. On the Transport Logs page, the Protocol log panel shows the current send and receive protocol log

paths. You can specify the log file path by entering the desired directory path for logging or accept the default setting.

Managing Protocol Logging

When protocol logging is enabled, a Mailbox server or a transport server creates protocol logs daily. The protocol log stores each SMTP protocol event on a single line. The information on a particular line is organized by comma-separated fields. Logs begin with a header that shows the following information:

* A statement that identifies the file as either a Send connector protocol log or a Receive connector protocol log
* The date on which the log file was created
* The version of the Exchange Server that created the file
* A comma-delimited list of fields contained in the body of the log file

Although not all of the fields are tracked for all protocol events, SMTP event fields and their meanings include:

* **Connector-id**   The distinguished name of the connector associated with the event.
* **Context**   The context for the SMTP event.
* **Data**   The data associated with the SMTP event.
* **Date-time**   The date and time of the protocol event in a locale-specific format. For U.S. English, the format is *YYYY-MM-DDTHH:MM:SSZ*, such as 2014-06-05T23:30:59Z.
* **Event**   The type of protocol event: + for Connect, – for Disconnect, > for Send, < for Receive, and * for Information.
* **Local-endpoint**   The local endpoint of the SMTP session, identified by the Internet Protocol (IP) address and Transmission Control Protocol (TCP) port.
* **Remote-endpoint**   The remote endpoint of the SMTP session, identified by the IP address and TCP port.
* **Sequence-number**   The number of the event within an SMTP session. The first event has a sequence number of 0.
* **Session-id**   The globally unique identifier of the SMTP session. Each event for a particular session has the same identifier.

You can view the protocol log files with any standard text editor, such as Notepad. You can also import the protocol log files into a spreadsheet or a database. Mailbox and transport servers store logs in either the %ExchangeInstallPath%\TransportRoles\Logs*ServerType*\ProtocolLog\SmtpSend or

%ExchangeInstallPath%\TransportRoles\Logs*ServerType*\ProtocolLog\SmtpReceive directory as appropriate for the type of server and connector being logged. For POP, IMAP, and other non-SMTP content aggregation, related logs are in the %ExchangeInstallPath%\TransportRoles\Logs\ProtocolLog\HTTPClient directory.

Each log file is named by the date on which it was created, using the format SENDYYYYMMDD-N.log or RECVYYYYMMDD-N.log, such as SEND20160805-1.log for the first Send connector log created on August 5, 2016. Additional protocol logs are found in subdirectories of the %ExchangeInstallPath%\Logging directory. In the AddressBook Service subdirectory, you'll find logs for the Address Book service. In the RPC Client Access subdirectory, you'll find logs for Remote Procedure Calls for Client Access services.

Optimizing Protocol Logging for HTTP

Mailbox servers have web-based applications and virtual directories that use Microsoft Internet Information Services (IIS) to provide the related services. In IIS, protocol logging for HTTP is a feature available when the HTTP Logging module is installed and logging is enabled. By default, this module is installed with IIS and enabled. The default configuration is to use one log file per website per day.

You can view and manage the logging settings by completing the following steps:

1. Start Internet Information Services (IIS) Manager. Start Server Manager, click Tools, and select Internet Information Services (IIS) Manager.

> **NOTE** By default, IIS Manager connects to the services running on the local computer. If you want to connect to a different server, select the Start Page node in the left pane, and then click the Connect To A Server link. This starts the Connect To Server Wizard. Follow the prompts to connect to the remote server. Keep in mind that the Windows Remote Management Service must be configured and running on the remote server.

2. When you install the Mailbox role, the default website is created (or updated) to include the virtual directories and web-based applications used to provide front-end services for Exchange Server. If a server has the Mailbox role, a website named Exchange Back End is created and has virtual directories and web-based applications used to provide back-end services for Exchange Server. In IIS Manager, double-click the entry for the server with which you want to work, and then double-click Sites.

3. In the left pane, select the website that you want to manage, and then double-click Logging in the main pane to open the Logging feature.

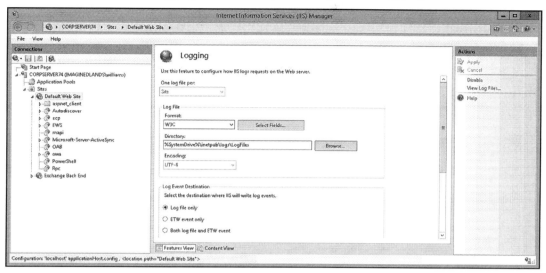

4. If all logging options are dimmed and the server is configured for per-site logging, you can click Enable in the Actions pane to enable logging for this site. Otherwise, if logging is configured per server, you need to configure logging at the server level rather than at the site level; the procedure is similar.

5. Use the Format selection list to choose one of the following log formats:

- **W3C Extended Log File Format**   Writes the log in ASCII text following the World Wide Web Consortium (W3C) extended log file format. Fields are space-delimited, and each entry is written on a new line. This style is the default. Using this option allows you to include extensive information about clients, servers, and connections.
- **Microsoft IIS Log File Format**   Writes the log in ASCII text following the IIS log file format. Fields are tab-delimited, and each entry is written on a new line. Using this option allows you to collect basic information about clients, servers, and connections.
- **NCSA Common Log File Format**   Writes the log in ASCII text following the National Center for Supercomputing Applications (NCSA) common log file format. Fields are space-delimited, and each entry is written on a new line. When you use this option, log entries are small because only basic information is recorded.

> **TIP**   W3C Extended Log File Format is the preferred logging format because you can record detailed information. Unless you're certain that another format meets your needs, you should use this format.

6. On the Log File panel, use the Directory text box to set the main folder for log files. By default, log files are written to a subdirectory of %SystemDrive%\inetpub\logs\LogFiles.

7. On the Log File Rollover panel, select Schedule and then use the related selection list to choose a logging time period. In most cases, you'll want to create daily or weekly logs, so select either Daily or Weekly.

8. If you selected W3C, click Select Fields, and then choose the fields that should be recorded in the logs. Click Apply.

Working with HTTP Protocol Logs

On Mailbox servers, HTTP protocol log files can help you detect and trace problems with HTTP, Outlook Web App, Microsoft Exchange ActiveSync, and Outlook Anywhere. By default, Exchange Server writes protocol log files to a subdirectory of %SystemDrive%\inetpub\logs\LogFiles. You can use the logs to determine the following:

* Whether a client was able to connect to a specified server and, if not, what problem occurred
* Whether a client was able to send or receive protocol commands and, if not, what error occurred
* Whether a client was able to send or receive data
* How long it took to establish a connection
* How long it took to send or receive protocol commands
* How long it took to send or receive data
* Whether server errors are occurring and, if so, what types of errors are occurring
* Whether server errors are related to Windows or to the protocol itself
* Whether a user is connecting to the server using the proper logon information

Most protocol log files are written as ASCII text. This means you can view them in Notepad or another text editor. You can import these protocol log files into Microsoft Office Excel in much the same way as you import tracking logs.

Log files, written as space-delimited or tab-delimited text, begin with a header that shows the following information:

* A statement that identifies the protocol or service used to create the file
* The protocol, service, or software version
* A date and timestamp
* A space-delimited or tab-delimited list of fields contained in the body of the log file

The name of the subdirectory used for logging depends on the number of websites hosted on a server. Typically, the W3SVC1 subdirectory is used for front-end logging and the W3SVC2 subdirectory is used for back-end logging.

Servers can have additional websites or may not have websites created in the expected order, such as when you deploy IIS prior to installing Exchange 2016. In this case, you'll want to confirm the identity of the logging subdirectory by using the following command:

```
Get-OwaVirtualDirectory -Server ServerID -ShowMailboxVirtualDirectories
|fl identity, metabasepath
```

Where ServerID is the host name or fully-qualified domain name of the Exchange server to check, such as:

```
Get-OwaVirtualDirectory -Server MailServer21 -ShowMailboxVirtualDirectories
|fl identity, metabasepath
```

The output will show the website identity and metabase path for the Outlook Web App (OWA) virtual directories created on the server. If the server has front-end and back-end virtual directories for OWA, the output will be similar to the following:

```
Identity      : MAILSERVER21\owa (Exchange Back End)
MetabasePath : IIS://MAILSERVER21.imaginedlands.com/W3SVC/2/ROOT/owa

Identity      : MAILSERVER21\owa (Default Web Site)
MetabasePath : IIS://MAILSERVER21.imaginedlands.com/W3SVC/1/ROOT/owa
```

In the output, note that the name of the associated website is shown in parenthesis as part of the identity and the subdirectory path can be extrapolated from the metabase path. Here, the back-end virtual directory is named Exchange Back End and has the associated subdirectory W3SVC2 (which is shown as W3SVC/2 in the metabase path). The front-end virtual directory is named Default Web Site and has the associated subdirectory W3SVC1 (which is shown as W3SVC/1 in the metabase path).

Using Connectivity Logging

Connectivity logging allows you to track the connection activity of outgoing message delivery queues. You use connectivity logging to troubleshoot problems with messages reaching their designated destination Mailbox server or recipient.

Configuring Connectivity Logging

By default, Exchange Server performs connectivity logging, creating connectivity logs when clients connect to the Front End Transport service on Mailbox servers and when clients are proxied or redirected to the Transport service on Mailbox servers where the related user's mailbox is stored. Exchange Server also creates connectivity logs for communications with the mailbox databases on a Mailbox server.

Generally, Exchange Server creates connectivity logs to track:

- When the Mailbox Transport Delivery receives SMTP messages from the Transport service and connects to local mailbox databases.
- When the Mailbox Transport Submission service connects to local mailbox databases to retrieve messages and submit them to the Transport service for delivery.

You manage connectivity logging for the Front End Transport service by using Set-FrontEndTransportService, the Transport service by using Set-TransportService, and the Mailbox Transport service by using Set-MailboxTransportService. With any of these cmdlets, you can enable or disable connectivity logging for the service by setting the –ConnectivityLogEnabled parameter to $true or $false, as appropriate. The following example disables connectivity logging for the Transport service on MailServer96:

```
Set-TransportService -Identity "MailServer96"
-ConnectivityLogEnabled $false
```

> **TIP** You can use the Exchange Admin Center to configure basic logging options for the Transport service (but not for other services). To do this, select Servers in the Features pane, and then select Servers. In the main pane, double-click the server you want to configure to display the related Properties dialog box. On the Transport Logs page select or clear the Enable Connectivity Logging check box. If you enable connectivity logging, you can specify the log file path, and then click OK.

The Front End Transport service, the Transport service, and the Mailbox Transport service can have different connectivity logging settings:

- Use the –ConnectivityLogMaxAge parameter to set the maximum log file age. The default maximum age is 30.00:00:00.
- Use the –ConnectivityLogMaxDirectorySize parameter to set the maximum log directory size. The default maximum log directory size is 250 MB.
- Use the –ConnectivityLogMaxFileSize parameter to set the maximum log file size. The default maximum log file size is 10 MB.
- Use the –ConnectivityLogPath parameter to move the log directory to a new location. The default logging directory depends on the service with which you are working.

As it does with other logs, Exchange Server overwrites the oldest connectivity logs automatically when tracking logs reach a maximum age or when the maximum log directory size is reached. If you decide to move the protocol log directories, you should create the directories you want to use and set the following required permissions:

- Full Control for the server's local Administrators group
- Full Control for System
- Full Control for Network Service

Working with Connectivity Logs

Exchange Server creates connectivity logs daily and stores them in the %ExchangeInstallPath%\TransportRoles\Logs*ServerType*\Connectivity directory. Each log file is named by the date on which it was created, using the format CONNECTLOGYYYYMMDD-N.log, such as CONNECTLOG20160319-1.log for the first connectivity log created on March 19, 2016.

The connectivity log stores outgoing queue connection events on a single line. The information on a particular line is organized by comma-separated fields. Logs begin with a header that shows the following information:

- A statement that identifies the file as a connectivity log
- The date on which the log file was created
- The version of Exchange Server that created the file
- A comma-delimited list of fields contained in the body of the log file

Although not all of the fields are tracked for all outgoing queue connection events, connectivity logging fields and their meanings are:

- **Date-time**   The date and time of the outgoing queue connection event.
- **Session**   The globally unique identifier of the SMTP session. Each event for a particular session has the same identifier. For Messaging Application Programming Interface (MAPI) sessions, this field is blank.
- **Destination**   The name of the destination Mailbox server, smart host, or domain.
- **Direction**   The direction of the event: + for Connect, – for Disconnect, > for Send, and < for Receive.
- **Description**   The data associated with the event, including the number and size of messages transmitted, Domain Name Server (DNS) name resolution information, connection success messages, and connection failure messages.

You can view the connectivity log files with any standard text editor, such as Notepad. You can also import the connectivity log files into a spreadsheet or a database, as discussed previously.

In the default path for logs, the ServerType can be FrontEnd, Mailbox, or Hub. On Maibox servers, you find these folders:

- Under FrontEnd\Connectivity, you'll find logs for the Front End Transport service.
- Under Hub\Connectivity, you'll find logs for the Transport service.
- Under Mailbox\Connectivity, you'll find a Submission subdirectory containing logs for the Mailbox Transport Submission service, and a Delivery subdirectory containing logs for the Mailbox Transport Delivery service.

Chapter 17. Maintaining Exchange Server 2016

You must maintain Microsoft Exchange Server 2016 to ensure proper mail flow and recoverability of message data. Routine maintenance should include monitoring event logs, services, servers, and resource usage as well as regular monitoring of Exchange queues. Mailbox and Edge Transport servers use queues to hold messages while they are processing them for routing and delivery. If messages remain in a queue for an extended period, problems could occur. For example, if an Exchange server is unable to connect to the network, you'll find that messages aren't being cleared out of queues. Because you can't be on-site 24 hours a day, you may want to set alerts to notify you when problems occur.

Monitoring Events, Services, Servers, and Resource Usage

As discussed in Chapter 18, "Troubleshooting Exchange Server 2016," Exchange 2016 includes a built-in monitoring and problem resolution architecture that can resolve many types of issues automatically. The automated responders will take recovery actions automatically, which can include restarting services and restarting servers. However, the automated processes won't detect all issues, which is why you must routinely monitor Exchange as well.

Viewing Events

System and application events generated by Exchange Server are recorded in the Windows event logs. The primary log that you'll want to check is the application log. In this log, you'll find the key events recorded by Exchange Server services. Keep in mind that related events might be recorded in other logs, including the directory service, DNS server, security, and system logs. For example, if the server is having problems with a network card and this card is causing message delivery failures, you'll have to use the system log to pinpoint the problem.

You access the application log by completing the following steps:

1. In Server Manager, click Tools, and then select Event Viewer.
2. If you want to view the logs on another computer, in the console tree, right-click the Event Viewer entry, and choose Connect To Another Computer

from the shortcut menu. You can now choose the server for which you want to manage logs.

3. Double-click the Windows Logs node. You should now see a list of logs.

4. Select the Application log.

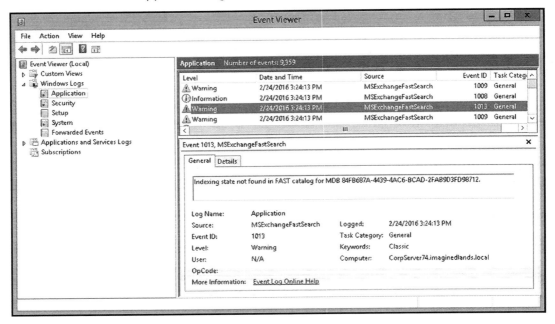

Entries in the main panel of Event Viewer provide an overview of when, where, and how an event occurred. To obtain detailed information on an event, select its entry. The event level precedes the date and time of the event. Event levels include the following:

- **Information** An informational event, generally related to a successful action.
- **Warning** Details for warnings are often useful in preventing future system problems.
- **Error** An error such as the failure of a service to start.
- **Critical** A critical error such as the failure of an essential clustering component.

In addition to level, date, and time, the summary and detailed event entries provide the following information:

- **Source** The application, service, or component that logged the event.
- **Event ID** An identifier for the specific event.
- **Task Category** The category of the event, which is sometimes used to further describe the related action.

- **User** The user account that was logged on when the event occurred.
- **Computer** The name of the computer on which the event occurred.
- **Description** In the detailed entries, this event entry provides a text description of the event.
- **Data** In the detailed entries, this event entry provides any data or error code output created by the event.

Use the event entries to detect and diagnose Exchange performance problems. Exchange-related event sources include the following:

- **ESE** Helps you track activities related to the Extensible Storage Engine (ESE) used by the Information Store. Watch for logging and recovery errors, which might indicate a problem with a database or a recovery action. For example, Event ID 300 indicates the database engine initiated recovery steps; Event ID 301 indicates the database engine has begun replaying a log file for a mailbox database; and Event ID 302 indicates the database engine has successfully completed recovery steps. If you want to track the status of online defragmentation, look for Event ID 703. Additional related sources include ESENT and ESE Backup.
- **MSExchange Antimalware, MSExchange Antispam, MSExchange Anti-spam Update** Helps you track activities related to anti-malware and anti-spam agents. When you've configured Microsoft Exchange to use Microsoft Update to retrieve anti-spam updates, watch for errors regarding update failure. You might need to change the Microsoft Update configuration or the way updates are retrieved.
- **MSExchange Assistants, MSExchangeMailboxAssistants** Helps you track activities related to the Microsoft Exchange Mailbox Assistants service. The Microsoft Exchange Mailbox Assistants service performs background processing and maintenance of mailboxes. Watch for processing errors, which can indicate database structure problems.
- **MSExchange EdgeSync** Helps you track activities related to the Edge Synchronization processes. The Microsoft Exchange EdgeSync service uses the Exchange Active Directory Provider to obtain information about the Active Directory topology. If the service cannot locate a suitable domain controller, the service fails to initialize and edge synchronization fails as well.
- **MSExchange TransportService, MSExchangeTransport** Helps you track activities related to the Microsoft Exchange Transport service and message transport in general. Watch for errors that can indicate issues with storage or shadow redundancy. Related sources include MSExchangeDelivery and MSExchangeTransportDelivery for tracking the Mailbox Transport Delivery service, and MSExchangeSubmission and MSExchangeTransportSubmission for tracking the Mailbox Transport Submission service.
- **MSExchangeADAccess** Helps you track activities related to the Exchange Active Directory Provider, which is used for retrieving information for Active Directory and performing the DNS lookups that Exchange uses to locate domain controllers

and global catalog servers. Watch for topology discovery failures and DNS lookup failures, which can indicate problems with the DNS configuration as well as with the Active Directory site configuration.

- **MSExchangeDiagnostics, MSExchangeHM**   Helps you track activities related to the Microsoft Exchange Diagnostics service and the Microsoft Exchange Health Manager, respectively. With diagnostics, watch for errors related to low disk space and low available memory. With the health manager, watch for errors related to the working processes. Also MSExchangeHMHost.
- **MSExchangeFrontEndTransport, MSExchange Front End HTTP Proxy**   Help you track activities related to Front End Transport service and Front End HTTP proxying of web applications, respectively. Related sources include MSExchange OWA for tracking the Outlook Web App, MSExchange Web Services for tracking Exchange Web Services, and MSExchange RPC Over HTTP Autoconfig for tracking the configuration of Outlook Anywhere.
- **MSExchangeIS**   Helps you track activities related to the Microsoft Exchange Information Store service and mailbox databases. If a user is having problems logging on to Exchange, you might see multiple logon errors. You might also see a lot of logon errors if someone is trying to hack into an Exchange mailbox. Watch also for errors related to high availability.
- **MSExchangeRepl**   Helps you track activities related to Active Manager and database failover. Watch for errors related to mounting, moving, or unmounting databases.

Managing Essential Services

Most of Exchange Server's key components run as system services. If an essential service stops, its related functionality will not be available and Exchange Server won't work as expected. When you are troubleshooting Exchange Server problems, you'll want to check to ensure that essential services are running as expected early in your troubleshooting process. To manage system services, you can use the Services console or the Services node in the Computer Management console. You can start and work with the Services console by completing the following steps:

1. In Server Manager, click Tools, and then select Services.

2. If you want to manage the services on another computer, right-click the Services entry in the console tree, and select Connect To Another Computer on the shortcut menu. You can now choose the system with which you want to work.

3. You'll now see the available services. Services are listed by:

- **Name**   The name of the service.
- **Description**   A short description of the service and its purpose.
- **Status**   The status of the service. If the entry is blank, the service is stopped.
- **Startup Type**   The startup setting for the service.
- **Log On As**   The account the service logs on as. The default in most cases is the local system account.

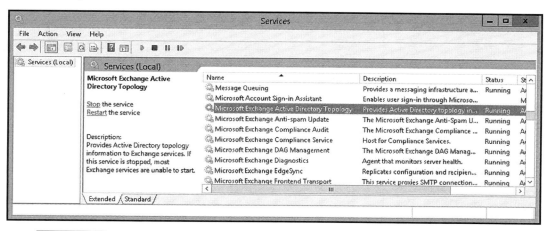

TIP   Any service that has a startup type of Automatic should have a status of Started. If a service has a startup type of Automatic and the status is blank, the service is not running and you should start it (unless another administrator has stopped it to perform maintenance or troubleshooting).

If a service is stopped and it should be started, you need to restart it. If you suspect a problem with a service, you can perform try to diagnose the problem as discussed in Chapter 18, "Troubleshooting Exchange Server 2016," and might also want to stop and then restart it. To start, stop, or restart a service, complete the following steps:

1.   Access the Services console.

2.   Right-click the service you want to manage, and then select Start, Stop, or Restart, as appropriate.

After you start or restart a service, you should check the event logs to see if there are errors related to the service. Any related errors you find might help you identify why the service wasn't running.

Keep in mind that Exchange 2016 automatically restarts services that are found to not be responding or otherwise need restarting as part of the Managed Availability architecture. The automated processes can also reset IIS and restart servers.

Although these automated processes work well, they won't always resolve service issues as quickly as you could by manually intervening.

Monitoring Messaging Components

When you are troubleshooting or optimizing a server for performance, you can use performance monitoring to track the activities of Exchange messaging components. Performance Monitor graphically displays statistics for the set of performance parameters you've selected for display. These performance parameters are referred to as *counters*. Performance Monitor displays information only for the counters you're tracking. Thousands of counters are available, and these counters are organized into groupings called *performance objects*.

When you install Exchange Server 2016 on a computer, Performance Monitor is updated with a set of objects and counters for tracking Exchange performance. These objects and counters are registered during setup in the Win32 performance subsystem and the Windows registry. You'll find several hundred related performance objects for everything from the Microsoft Exchange Active Manager to the Microsoft Exchange Journaling Agent to Microsoft Exchange Outlook Web App.

You can select which counters you want to monitor by completing the following steps:

1. In Server Manager, select Tools, and then select Performance Monitor. Next, select the Performance Monitor entry in the left pane.

2. The Performance Monitor tool has several views and view types. Ensure that you are viewing current activity by clicking View Current Activity on the toolbar or pressing Ctrl+T. You can switch between the view types (Line, Histogram Bar, and Report) by clicking the Change Graph Type button or pressing Ctrl+G.

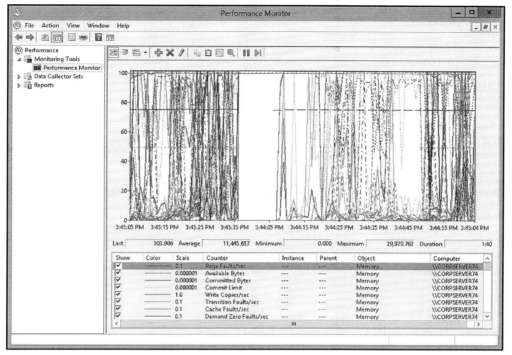

3. To add counters, click Add on the toolbar or press Ctrl+N. This displays the Add Counters dialog box.

4. In the Select Counters From Computer combo box, enter the Universal Naming Convention (UNC) name of the Exchange server with which you want to work, such as **\\MailServer96**, or leave it at the default setting of <Local computer> to work with the local computer.

NOTE You need to be at least a member of the Performance Monitor Users group in the domain or the local computer to perform remote monitoring. When you use performance logging, you need to be at least a member of the Performance Log Users group in the domain or the local computer to work with performance logs on remote computers.

---

5. In the Available Counters panel, performance objects are listed alphabetically. If you select an object entry by clicking it, all related counters are selected. If you expand an object entry, you can see all the related counters and you can then select individual counters by clicking them. For example, you can expand the entry for the MSExchangeTransport Database object and then select the DataRow clones/sec, Database Connections Current and MailItem new/sec counters.

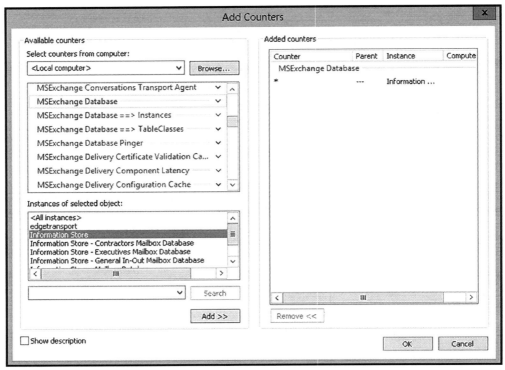

6. When you select an object or any of its counters, you see the related instances, if any. Choose All Instances to select all counter instances for monitoring separately. Choose _total to view a single combined value reflecting data for all available instances. Or select one or more counter instances to monitor. For example, when you select MSExchangeIS Store, you'll find separate instances for each database on the server and you could select an individual database to specifically track that database.

7. When you've selected an object or a group of counters for an object as well as the object instances, click Add to add the counters to the graph. Repeat steps 5 through 6 to add other performance parameters.

8. Click OK when you're finished adding counters. You can delete counters later by clicking their entry in the lower portion of the Performance window, and then clicking Delete.

Using Performance Alerting

Data Collector Sets are used to collect performance data. When you configure Data Collector Sets to alert you when specific criteria are met, you are using performance alerting. Windows performance alerting provides a fully automated method for monitoring server performance and reporting when certain performance thresholds are reached. You can use performance alerting to track the following:

- Memory usage
- CPU utilization
- Disk usage
- Messaging components

Using notifications, you can then provide automatic notification when a server exceeds a threshold value.

Tracking Memory Usage

Physical and virtual memory is critical to normal system operation. When a server runs low on memory, system performance can suffer and message processing can grind to a halt. To counter this problem, you should configure performance alerting to watch memory usage. You could then increase the amount of virtual memory available on the server or add more random access memory (RAM) as needed. However, keep in mind that increasing virtual memory isn't something you should do without careful planning.

You configure a memory alert by completing the following steps:

1. In Server Manager, select Tools, and then select Performance Monitor. Next, expand the Data Collector Sets node, and then select User Defined. You should see a list of current alerts (if any) in the right pane.

2. Right-click the User-Defined node in the left pane, point to New, and then choose Data Collector Set.

3. In the Create New Data Collector Set wizard, type a name for the Data Collector Set, such as **Memory Usage Alert**. Select the Create Manually option, and then click Next.

4. On the What Type Of Data Do You Want To Include page, the Create Data Logs option is selected by default. Select the Performance Counter Alert option, and then click Next.

5. On the Which Performance Counters Would You Like To Monitor page, click Add. This displays the Add Counter dialog box. Because you are configuring memory alerts, expand the Memory object in the Performance Object list. Select Available MBytes by clicking it, and then click Add.

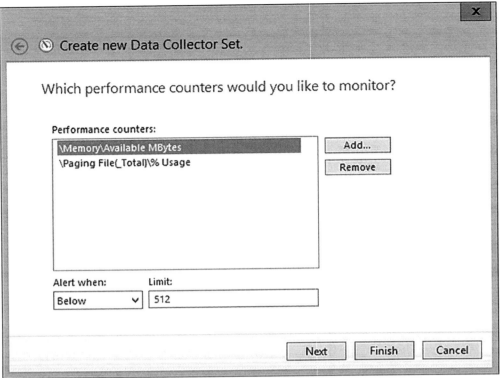

Create new Data Collector Set.

Which performance counters would you like to monitor?

Performance counters:

\Memory\Available MBytes
\Paging File(_Total)\% Usage

[Add...]
[Remove]

Alert when: Limit:
[Below ⌄]   [512]

[Next] [Finish] [Cancel]

6. Expand the Paging File object in the Performance Object list. Click %Usage. In the Instances Of Selected Object panel, select _Total, and then click Add. Click OK.

7. On the Which Performance Counters Would You Like To Monitor page, you'll see the counters you've added. In the Performance Counters panel, select Available MBytes, set the Alert When list to Below, and then enter a Limit value that is approximately 5 to 8 percent of the total physical memory (RAM) on the server for which you are configuring alerting. For example, if the server has 8 GB of RAM, you could set the value to 512 MB to alert you when the server is running low on available memory.

8. In the Performance Counters panel, select %Usage. Set the Alert When list to Above, and then type **98** as the Limit value. This ensures that you are alerted when more than 98 percent of the paging file is being used.

9. Click Next, and then click Finish. This saves the Data Collector Set and closes the wizard.

10. In the left pane, under User Defined, select the related Data Collector Set, and then double-click the data collector for the alert in the main pane. This displays the data collector Properties dialog box.

11. On the Alerts tab, use the Sample Interval options to set a sample interval. The sample interval specifies when new data is collected. Don't sample too frequently, however, because you'll use system resources and might cause the server to seem unresponsive. By default, Performance Monitor checks the values of the configured counters every 15 seconds. A better value might be once every 10 to 30 minutes. Generally, you'll want to track performance periodically over several hours at a minimum and during a variety of usage conditions.

12. If you want to log an event rather than be alerted every time an alert limit is reached, on the Alert Action tab, select the Log An Entry In The Application Event Log check box. Selecting this option ensures that an event is logged when the alert occurs but does not alert you via the console. Click OK to close the Properties dialog box.

By default, alerting is configured to start manually. To start alerting, select the User Defined node in the left pane, click the alert in the main pane to select it, and then click the Start button on the toolbar. If you later want to stop getting alerts, right-click the alert in the main pane, and then select Stop.

Tracking CPU Utilization

You can use a CPU utilization alert to track the usage of a server's CPUs. When CPU utilization is too high, Exchange Server can't effectively process messages or manage other critical functions. As a result, performance can suffer greatly. For example, CPU utilization at 100 percent for an extended period of time can be an indicator of serious problems on a server. To recover, you might need to use Task Manager to end the process or processes with high CPU utilization, or you might need to take other corrective actions to resolve the problem, such as closing applications you are running while logged on to the server.

You'll also want to closely track process threads that are waiting to execute. A relatively high number of waiting threads can be an indicator that a server's processors need to be upgraded.

You configure a CPU utilization alert by completing the following steps:

1. In Server Manager, select Tools, and then select Performance Monitor. Next, expand the Data Collector Sets node, and then select User Defined. You should see a list of current alerts (if any) in the right pane.

2. Right-click the User-Defined node in the left pane, point to New, and then choose Data Collector Set.

3. In the Create New Data Collector Set wizard, type a name for the Data Collector Set, such as **CPU Utilization Alert**. Select the Create Manually option, and then click Next.

4. On the What Type Of Data Do You Want To Include page, the Create Data Logs option is selected by default. Select the Performance Counter Alert option, and then click Next.

5. On the Which Performance Counters Would You Like To Monitor page, click Add. This displays the Add Counter dialog box. Because you are configuring CPU alerts, expand the Processor object in the Performance Object list. Click % Processor Time. In the Instances Of Selected Object panel, select _Total, and then click Add.

6. Expand the System object in the Performance Object list. Click Processor Queue Length, and then click Add. Click OK.

7. On the Which Performance Counters Would You Like To Monitor page, you'll see the counters you've added. Select % Processor Time. Then set the Alert When list to Above, and type **98** as the Limit value. This ensures that you are alerted when processor utilization is more than 98 percent.

8. In the Performance Counters panel, select Processor Queue Length. Then set the Alert When list to Above, and type **3** as the Limit value. This ensures that you are alerted when more than three processes are waiting to execute, which can be an indicator that a server's processors need to be upgraded.

9. Click Next, and then click Finish. This saves the Data Collector Set and closes the wizard.

10. Finish configuring the alert by following steps 10 through 12 under "Tracking Memory Usage" earlier in this chapter.

Tracking Disk Usage

Exchange Server uses disk space for data storage, logging, tracking, and virtual memory. To ensure ample disk space is always available, Exchange Server monitors free disk space. If free disk space drops below specific thresholds, Exchange will gracefully shut itself down. When Exchange is in this state, it is likely that data could get lost. To prevent serious problems, you should monitor free disk space closely on all drives used by Exchange Server.

You'll also want to track closely the number of system requests that are waiting for disk access. A relatively high value for a particular disk can affect server performance and is also a good indicator that a disk is being overutilized or that there may be some problem with the disk. To resolve this problem, you'll want to try to shift part of the disk's workload to other disks, such as by moving databases, logs, or both.

You configure disk usage alerting by completing the following steps:

1. In Server Manager, select Tools, and then select Performance Monitor. Next, expand the Data Collector Sets node, and then select User Defined. You should see a list of current alerts (if any) in the right pane.

2. Right-click the User-Defined node in the left pane, point to New, and then choose Data Collector Set.

3. In the Create New Data Collector Set wizard, type a name for the Data Collector Set, such as **Disk Usage Alert**. Select the Create Manually option and then click Next.

4. On the What Type Of Data Do You Want To Include page, the Create Data Logs option is selected by default. Select the Performance Counter Alert option, and then click Next.

5. On the Which Performance Counters Would You Like To Monitor page, click Add. This displays the Add Counter dialog box. Because you are configuring disk alerts, expand the LogicalDisk object in the Performance Object list. Click % Free Space. In the Instances Of Selected Object panel, select all individual logical disk instances that you want to track. Do not select _Total or <All Instances>. Click Add.

6. Expand the PhysicalDisk object in the Performance Object list. Click Current Disk Queue Length. In the Instances Of Selected Object panel, select all individual physical disk instances except _Total, and then click Add. Click OK.

7. On the Which Performance Counters Would You Like To Monitor page, you'll see the counters you've added. Select the first logical disk instance, set the Alert When list to Below, and then type **5** as the Limit value. This ensures that you are alerted when available free space is less than 5 percent. Repeat this procedure for each logical disk.

8. In the Performance Counters panel, select the first physical disk instance, set the Alert When list to Above, and then type **2** as the Limit value. This ensures that you are alerted when more than two system requests are waiting for disk access. Repeat this procedure for each physical disk.

9. Click Next, and then click Finish. This saves the Data Collector Set and closes the wizard.

10. Finish configuring the alert by following steps 10 through 12 under "Tracking Memory Usage" earlier in the chapter.

Working with Queues

As an Exchange administrator, it's your responsibility to monitor Exchange queues regularly. Mailbox and Edge Transport servers use queues to hold messages while they are processing them for routing and delivery. If messages remain in a queue for an extended period, problems could occur. For example, if an Exchange server is unable to connect to the network, you'll find that messages aren't being cleared out of queues.

Understanding Exchange Queues

Queues are temporary holding locations for messages that are waiting to be processed, and Exchange Server 2016 uses an Extensible Storage Engine (ESE) database for queue storage. Exchange Server 2016 uses the following types of queues:

- **Submission queue** The submission queue is a persistent queue that is used by the Exchange Categorizer (a transport component) to temporarily store all messages that have to be resolved, routed, and processed by transport agents. All messages that are received by a transport server enter processing in the submission queue. Messages are submitted through SMTP-receive, the Pickup directory, or the store driver. Each transport server has only one submission queue. Messages that are in the submission queue cannot be in other standard queues at the same time.

   Edge Transport servers use the Categorizer to route messages to the appropriate destinations. Mailbox servers use the Categorizer to expand distribution lists, to identify alternative recipients, and to apply forwarding addresses. After the Categorizer retrieves the necessary information about recipients, it uses that information to apply policies, route the message, and perform content conversion. After categorization, the transport server moves the message to a delivery queue or to the Unreachable queue.

- **Mailbox delivery queue** Mailbox delivery queues hold messages that are being delivered to a Mailbox server by using encrypted Exchange RPC. Only Mailbox servers have mailbox delivery queues, and they use the queue to temporarily store messages that are being delivered to mailbox recipients whose mailbox data is stored on a Mailbox server that is located in the same site as the Mailbox server. Mailbox servers have one mailbox delivery queue for each destination Mailbox server associated with messages currently being routed. After queuing the message, the Mailbox server delivers the messages to the distinguished name of the mailbox database.

- **Relay queue**   Relay queues hold messages that are being relayed to another server. Only Mailbox servers have relay queues, and they use the queue to temporarily store messages that are being delivered to mailbox recipients whose mailbox data is being relayed through a connector, designated expansion server, or non-SMTP gateway. Mailbox servers have one relay queue for each connector, designated expansion server, or non-SMTP gateway. After queuing a message, the Mailbox server relays the message.
- **Remote delivery queue**   Remote delivery queues hold messages that are being delivered to a remote server by using SMTP. Edge Transport servers can have remote delivery queues, and they use the queue to temporarily store messages that are being routed to remote destinations. On an Edge Transport server, these destinations are external SMTP domains or SMTP connectors. Edge Transport servers have one remote delivery queue for each remote destination associated with messages currently being routed. After queuing the message, the transport server delivers it to the appropriate server, smart host, IP address, or Active Directory site. Mailbox servers running Exchange 2016 do not have remote delivery queues.
- **Poison message queue**   The poison message queue is used to hold messages that are detected to be potentially harmful to Exchange Server 2016 after a server failure. Messages that contain errors that are potentially fatal to Exchange Server 2016 are delivered to the poison message queue. Each Mailbox server has one poison message queue, as does each Edge Transport server. Although this queue is persistent, it typically is empty and, as a result, is not displayed in queue viewing interfaces. By default, all messages in the poison message queue are suspended and can be manually deleted.
- **Shadow redundancy queue**   The shadow redundancy queue is used to prevent the loss of messages that are in transit by storing queued messages until the next transport server along the route reports a successful delivery of the message. If the next transport server doesn't report successful delivery, the message is resubmitted for delivery. This queue is nonpersistent. Mailbox and Edge Transport servers have one for each hop to which the server delivered the primary message.
- **Safety Net queue**   The Safety Net queue keeps a redundant copy of messages that have been successfully processed by a Mailbox server. If a message needs to be redelivered, a Mailbox server can resend the message from the Safety Net queue. Each Mailbox server has one primary Safety Net queue and one shadow Safety Net queue. These queues are nonpersistent.

- **Transport dumpster queue** The transport dumpster queue is used to hold messages that are being delivered. This queue is nonpersistent. Edge Transport servers have one queue for each Active Directory site. Mailbox servers do not have a transport dumpster queue.
- **Unreachable queue** The unreachable queue contains messages that cannot be routed to their destinations. Each Mailbox server has one unreachable queue, as does each Edge Transport server. Although this queue is persistent, it typically is empty and, as a result, is not displayed in queue viewing interfaces.

When a transport server receives a message, a transport mail item is created and saved in the appropriate queue within the queue database. Exchange Server assigns each mail item a unique identifier when it stores the mail item in the database. If a mail item is being routed to more than one recipient, the mail item can have more than one destination and, in this case, there is a routed mail item for each destination. A routed mail item is a reference to the transport mail item, and it is the routed mail item that Exchange queues for delivery.

Accessing the Queue Viewer

Using Queue Viewer, you can track message queues and mail flow. On any computer in which you've installed the Exchange management tools, you'll be able to access the Queue Viewer from the Exchange Toolbox. Open Exchange Toolbox from Start and then double-click Queue Viewer.

By default, the Queue Viewer connects to the queuing database on the local server (if applicable). To connect to a different server, on the Actions pane, select Connect To Server. In the Connect To Server dialog box, click Browse. Select the Exchange Server with which you want to work, and then click OK. Finally, click Connect.

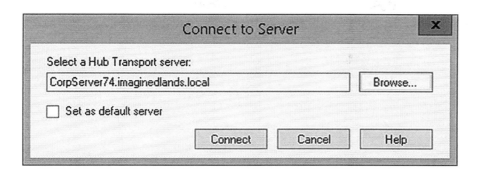

The Queue Viewer provides an overview of the status of each active queue, including the following information:

- A folder icon indicates an active state.
- A folder icon with a green check mark indicates the queue has a ready status.
- A folder icon with a blue button and a small down arrow indicates a retry state.
- A folder icon with a red exclamation point indicates a warning state, such as Not Available or Error.

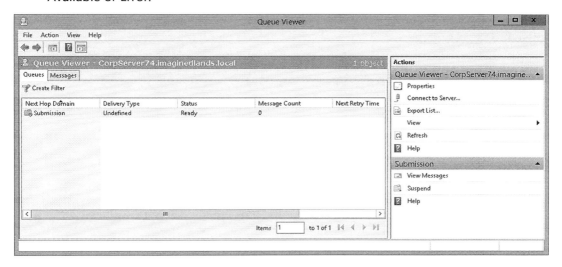

Managing Queues

You usually won't see messages in queues because they're processed and routed quickly. Messages come into a queue, Exchange Server performs a lookup or establishes a connection, and then Exchange Server either moves the message to a new queue or delivers it to its destination.

Understanding Queue Summaries and Queue States

Messages remain in a queue when there's a problem or if they have been suspended by an administrator. To check for problem messages, use the Queue Viewer to examine the number of messages in the queues. If you see a queue with a consistent or growing number of messages, there might be a problem. Again, normally, messages should come into a queue and then be processed quickly. Because of this, the number of messages in a queue should gradually decrease over time as the messages are processed, provided no new messages come into the queue.

Whenever you click the Queues tab in the Queue Viewer, you get a summary of the currently available queues for the selected server. Although queue summaries provide important details for troubleshooting message flow problems, you do have to know what to look for. The connection status is the key information to look at first. This value tells you the state of the queue. States you'll see include the following:

- **Active**   An active queue has messages that are being transported.
- **Ready**   A ready queue is needed to allow messages to be transported. When queues are ready, they can have a connection allocated to them.
- **Retry**   A connection attempt has failed and the server is waiting to retry.
- **Suspended**   The queue is suspended, and none of its messages can be processed for routing. Messages can enter the queue, but only if the Exchange Categorizer is running. You must resume the queue to resume normal queue operations.

Administrators can choose to enable or disable connections to a queue by right-clicking the queue and selecting Suspend. If a queue is suspended, it's unable to route and deliver messages.

You can change the queue state to Ready by right-clicking the queue and selecting Resume. When you do this, Exchange Server should immediately enable the queue, which allows messages to be routed and delivered. If a queue is in the retry state, you can force an immediate retry by using the Retry command.

Other summary information that you might find useful in troubleshooting include the following:

- **Delivery Type** Tells you what type of recipient messages are being queued for delivery.
- **Next Hop Domain** Tells you the next destination of a delivery queue. For mailbox delivery, relay, and remote delivery queues, this field tells you the next hop domain. Messages queued for delivery to an EdgeSync server list the associated site and destination, such as EdgeSync–Default-First-Site To Internet.
- **Message Count** Tells you the total number of messages waiting in the queue. If you see a large number, you might have a connectivity or routing problem.
- **Next Retry Time** When the connection state is Retry, this column tells you when another connection attempt will be made. You can click the Retry command to attempt a connection immediately.
- **Last Retry Time** When the connection state is Retry, this column tells you when the last retry attempt was made.
- **Last Error** Tells you the error code and details of the last error to occur in a particular queue. This information can help you determine why a queue is having delivery problems.

You can add or remove columns by using the Add/Remove Columns dialog box. Display this dialog box by choosing View in the Actions pane and then selecting Add/Remove Columns.

> **REAL WORLD** Queue Viewer uses Windows PowerShell to perform all actions, including displaying and refreshing queue data. To display the commands Queue Viewer is using, choose View in the Actions pane, and then select View Exchange Management Shell Command Log.

Refreshing The Queue View

Use the queue summaries and queue state information to help you find queuing problems, as discussed in the "Understanding Queue Summaries and Queue States" section earlier in this chapter. By default, the queue view is refreshed every 30 seconds, and the maximum number of message items that can be listed on each page is 1,000.

To change the viewing options, follow these steps:

1. In the Queue Viewer, on the View menu, click Options.

2. To turn off automatic refresh, clear the Auto-Refresh Screen check box. Otherwise, enable automatic refresh by selecting the Auto-Refresh Screen check box.

3. In the Refresh Interval text box, type a specific refresh rate in seconds.

4. Type the desired maximum number of messaging items to be displayed per page in the Number Of Items To Display text box. Click OK.

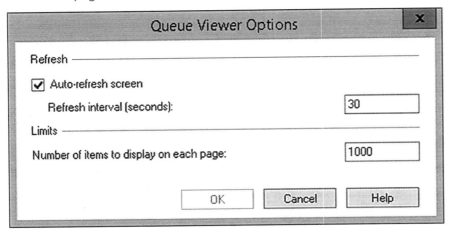

Working with Messages In Queues

To manage queues, you must enumerate messages. This process allows you to examine queue contents and perform management tasks on messages within a particular queue.

The easiest way to enumerate messages is to do so in sets of 1,000. To display the first 1,000 messages in a queue, follow these steps:

1. On the Queues tab in the Queue Viewer, you should see a list of available queues. Double-click a queue to enumerate the first 1,000 messages.

2. After you enumerate messages in a queue, you can examine message details by double-clicking the entries for individual messages. This enumerates the first 1,000 messages in the selected queue by filtering the message queues based on the queue identifier of the selected queue.

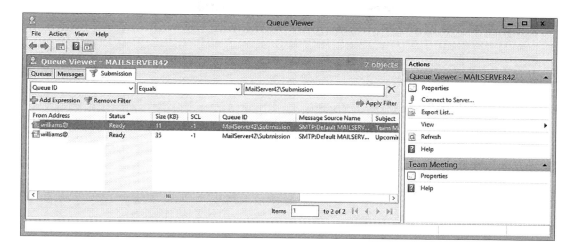

You can also create a filter to search for specific types of messages. To do this, follow these steps:

1. Double-click the queue with which you want to work. This enumerates the first 1,000 messages in the selected queue by filtering the message queues based on the queue identifier of the selected queue.

2. Click Add Expression. Use the first selection list to specify the field you want to use for filtering messages. You can filter messages by the following criteria: Date Received, Expiration Time, From Address, Internet Message ID, Last Error, Message Source Name, Queue ID, SCL, Size (KB), Source IP, Status, and Subject.

3. Use the second selection list to specify the filter criteria. The available filter criteria depend on the filter field and include Equals, Does Not Equal, Contains, Does Not Contain, Greater Than, and Less Than.

4. Use the text box provided to specify the exact criteria to match. For example, if you are filtering messages using the Status field, you might want to see all messages in which the Status field equals Retry.

5. To apply the new filter criteria, click Apply Filter.

Forcing Connections to Queues

In many cases, you can change the queue state to Ready by forcing a connection. Simply right-click the queue, and then select Retry. When you do this, Exchange Server should immediately enable connections to the queue, and this should allow messages to be routed to and delivered from the queue.

Suspending and Resuming Queues

When you suspend a queue, all new message transfer activity out of that queue stops and only messages being processed will be delivered. This means that messages can continue to enter the queue, but no new messages will leave it. To restore normal operations, you must resume the queue.

You suspend and resume a queue by completing the following steps:

1. On the Queues tab in the Queue Viewer, you should see a list of available queues. Right-click a queue, and then select Suspend.
2. When you're done troubleshooting, right-click the queue, and then select Resume.

| View Messages |
| Suspend |
| Help |

Another way to suspend messages in a queue is to do so selectively. In this way, you can control the transport of a single message or several messages that might be causing problems on the server. For example, if a large message is delaying the delivery of other messages, you can suspend that message until other messages have left the queue. Afterward, you can resume the message to resume normal delivery.

To suspend and then resume individual messages, complete the following steps:

1. On the Messages tab in the Queue Viewer, you should see a list of queued messages.
2. Right-click the message you want to suspend, and then select Suspend. You can select multiple messages by using Shift and Ctrl.
3. When you're ready to resume delivery of the message, right-click the suspended message, and then select Resume.

Deleting Messages from Queues

You can remove messages from queues if necessary. To do this, follow these steps:

1. On the Messages tab in the Queue Viewer, you should see a list of queued messages.

2. Right-click the message you want to remove. You can select multiple messages by using Shift and Ctrl, and then right-click. Select one of the following options from the shortcut menu:

- **Remove (With NDR)**   Deletes the selected messages from the queue, and notifies the sender with a nondelivery report (NDR)
- **Remove (Without Sending NDR)**   Deletes the message or messages from the queue without sending an NDR to the sender

3. When prompted, click Yes to confirm the deletion.

Deleting messages from a queue removes them from the messaging system permanently. You can't recover the deleted messages.

Chapter 18. Troubleshooting Exchange Server 2016

Microsoft Exchange Server 2016 is critically important to your organization and to be a successful Exchange administration you need to know how to diagnose and resolve problems as quickly as possible. Throughout this book, I've discussed techniques you can use to configure, maintain, and troubleshoot Microsoft Exchange Server 2016. In this chapter, I discuss additional techniques you can use to perform comprehensive troubleshooting.

Troubleshooting Essentials

Mailbox servers running Exchange 2016 can experience many types of issues that require troubleshooting to resolve. These issues can range from performance problems, to denied logins, to service outages. To help you resolve problems as they occur, you need a solid understanding of Exchange architecture, which I've covered throughout this book as part of the core discussion. Now let's look at architecture components specific to maintaining, diagnosing, and resolving Exchange services.

Tracking Server Health

In Exchange Server 2016, the Managed Availability architecture is used to automatically detect and correct many types of system problems with a goal of helping to ensure the overall availability of Exchange services. Managed Availability is implemented as part of the Mailbox server role. All servers running Exchange 2016 have this architecture.

As part of Managed Availability, hundreds of probes, monitors, and responders are running constantly on Exchange 2016 to analyze, monitor, and maintain services. If a problem is identified, it often can be fixed automatically. Managed Availability has three asynchronous components:

- **Probe Engine**   Takes measurements on the server and collects data samples. The collected data flows to the monitor engine.
- **Monitor Engine**   Uses the measurements and collected data to determine the status of Exchange services and components. The processed data flows to the responder engine.
- **Responder Engine**   Takes recovery actions based on unhealthy states reported by the monitor engine. If automated recovery is unsuccessful, escalates by issuing event log notifications.

By delving deeper into the Managed Availability architecture, you can get a better understanding of how the automated monitoring and response processes work. The workflow has three phases:

- **Sampling** The probe engine checks the state of Exchange services and components according to specific probes. Each probe has a top-level identifier and one or more related probe definitions. Each probe definition identifies the name of the associated probe, the health set to which the probe belongs, the target resource being tracked, a recurrence interval, and a timeout value.
- **Detection** The monitor engine analyzes the sampled data and issues alerts related to changes in the state of Exchange services and components according to specific monitors. Each monitor has a top-level identifier and one or more related monitor definitions. Each monitor definition identifies the name of the associated monitor, the health set to which the monitor belongs, and a sample mask that specifies the top level identifier for related probes.
- **Recovery** The responder engine responds to unhealthy states identified in alerts. Each responder has an associated responder definition that identifies the recovery action to be taken, the name of the responder, the target resource that will be acted on, and an alert mask that specifies the top-level identifier for related monitors.

> **NOTE** Rather than list each associated monitor or probe, Managed Availability components use name masking. Here, a top-level identifier is provided and then used as a mask to identify the related monitors and probes.

Collections of monitors are grouped together in health sets. Exchange 2016 has health sets for everything from Microsoft ActiveSync to User Throttling. Each health set has a number of associated monitors. As part of automated recovery, responders use the alerts issued by monitors to take recovery actions. There are three levels of recovery:

- **Tier 1** Provides the initial recovery response. As an initial response to an unhealthy state, responders typically will try to restart the service that uses the affected components.
- **Tier 2** Provides more advanced and customized recovery response. If restarting the service doesn't resolve the issue, the monitor state is escalated to the next level. The action or actions taken at this level to recover depend on the component but could include failover, bug checking, re-initialization of components to bring them back online, and more.
- **Tier 3** Uses the escalate responder to issue event log notifications regarding the problem. If you've installed the Exchange Server 2016 Management Pack,

escalated issues are sent to Microsoft System Center Operations Manager via the event logs as well.

Although designed to resolve many typical problems, Managed Availability cannot resolve every problem and this escalation is built into the architecture. As part of diagnosing and resolving problems, you can check the status of monitors and health sets by using:

- **Get-HealthReport**   Details the state and health of Exchange resources, monitors, and services.

```
Get-HealthReport -Identity ServerID [-GroupSize SizeOfRollup]
[-HaImpactingOnly <$true | $false>] [-HealthSet HealthSet]
[-MinimumOnlinePercent MinToDegraded>]
[-RollupGroup <$true | $false>]
```

- **Get-ServerHealth**   Returns the state of monitored resources as well as alert values.

```
Get-ServerHealth -Identity ServerID [-HaImpactingOnly <$true | $false>]
[-HealthSet HealthSet]
```

To check the state of resources, enter the following command:

```
Get-ServerHealth -Identity ServerID
```

Where ServerID is the host name or fully-qualified name of the Exchange server to check, such as:

```
Get-ServerHealth -Identity MailServer42
```

In the following sample, I've omitted the server name and server component columns from the default output:

```
State      Name                 TargetResource      HealthSetName    AlertValue
-----      -----                --------------      --------------   ----------
Online     AutodiscoverProxy... MSExchangeAutoDis... Autodiscover... Healthy
Online     ActiveSyncProxyTe... MSExchangeSyncApp... ActiveSync.P... Healthy
Repairing  ECPProxyTestMonitor  MSExchangeECPAppPool ECP.Proxy       Unhealthy
```

> **REALWORLD**   Often when you work with Exchange Management Shell, you'll find that the output is too long for the default screen buffer size or that the output has too many columns for the default window size. Because of this, I prefer to use a screen buffer height of 2999 and width of 120, along with a window width of 120 and height of 74. This makes Exchange Management Shell easier to work with. If you are using Windows 8.1 or later or Windows Server 2012 or later, you'll find that you can't customize all of these settings from the Start screen. Instead, right-click the tile for the shell on the Start screen, and then select Open File Location. This opens Windows Explorer to the folder in which the shortcut for Exchange Management Shell is located. Right-click this shortcut, and then select Properties. In the Properties dialog box, you'll then be able to use the options on the Layout tab to customize the shell.

From the State value you can determine the online status of a monitored resource that is used for transport, connections, or communications. State values you might see include:

- **Online**   All the components of the monitored resource are online.
- **Partially Online**   Some of the components of the monitored resource are not online.
- **Offline**   All the components of the monitored resource are offline.
- **Sidelined**   The monitored resource is sidelined and may not be in a fully online state.
- **Functional**   The monitored resource is functional but might not be in a fully online state.
- **NotApplicable**   An online or offline status is not applicable to this monitored resource.
- **Unavailable**   The monitored resource is unavailable.

From the alert value, you can determine the general health status of a monitored resource. Alert values you might see include:

- **Healthy**   All the components of the monitored resource are healthy.
- **Degraded**   Some of the components of the monitored resource are not healthy.
- **Disabled**   The components of the monitored resource have been disabled.
- **Unhealthy**   All the components of the monitored resource are not healthy.
- **Sidelined**   The monitored resource is sidelined and might not be in a fully healthy state.
- **Repairing**   The monitored resource is functional but is recovering from a degraded or unhealthy state.
- **Unavailable**   The monitored resource is unavailable.
- **Uninitialized**   The monitored resource hasn't been initialized.

If a health set has a status other than healthy or online, you can take a closer look at it by using the -HealthSet parameter. List the properties of the health set as shown in this example:

```
Get-ServerHealth -Identity MailServer42 -HealthSet ECP.Proxy | fl
```

You can get a formatted list of every monitor, target resource, and its related health set by entering the following command:

```
Get-ServerHealth localhost | ft name,targetresource,healthsetname
```

The output lists the name of the monitor, the target resource, and the name of the corresponding health set. You can store the output for later reference by redirecting the output to a file. In the following example, c:\data is the name of an existing folder, and Healthset-Reference.txt is the name of the file to create:

```
(get-serverhealth localhost|ft name,targetresource,healthsetname) >
c:\data\healthset-reference.txt
```

The output will look similar to the following:

Name	TargetResource	HealthSetName
ActiveSyncV2CTPMonitor	ActiveSync	ActiveSync
ActiveSyncCTPMonitor	ActiveSync	ActiveSync
ActiveSyncV2DeepTestMonitor	ActiveSync	ActiveSync.Protocol
ActiveSyncDeepTestMonitor	ActiveSync	ActiveSync.Protocol

Tracking User and Workload Throttling

Whenever you are trying to diagnose and resolve problems with Exchange 2016, you need to keep in mind how user and workload throttling may be affecting performance. All users with mailboxes on servers running Exchange 2016 are subject to user throttling policy.

The default user throttling policy is named the Global Throttling Policy. As the name implies, this policy has global scope and applies throughout the organization. User throttling policies also can have organization and regular scope. If you want to configure user throttling, you should create policies with these scopes rather than modify the Global Throttling Policy.

You can list currently defined user throttling policies by entering Get-ThrottlingPolicy at the shell prompt. To create and manage user throttling policies, you can use New-ThrottlingPolicy, Set-ThrottlingPolicy, and Remove-ThrottlingPolicy. You can view throttling policies assigned to users by using Get-ThrottlingPolicyAssociation, and assign user throttling policies to users by using Set-ThrottlingPolicyAssociation.

In addition to user throttling, Exchange Server manages workloads for protocols, features, and services using workload throttling policy. Workloads are automatically throttled to prevent overutilization of system resources and to try to ensure managed resources maintain a healthy state.

Each defined workload has an associated policy and classification. Workload policies are used to enable and configure workloads. Workload classifications set the default priority of the workload. Classifications that can be assigned to workloads include:

* Urgent
* Customer Expectation
* Internal Maintenance
* Discretionary

You can view the current workload policies and their associated workload classifications by entering Get-WorkloadPolicy at the Shell prompt. To create and manage workload policies, you can use New-WorkloadPolicy, Set-WorkloadPolicy, and Remove-WorkloadPolicy.

Managed resources have health indicators and resource thresholds. Health indicators are used to measure the relative health of the workload in terms of the resources used. Health indicators tracked include:

* Percent CPU utilization
* Mailbox database RPC latency
* Mailbox database replication health
* Content indexing age of last notification
* Content indexing retry queue size

Resource thresholds are used to configure usage limits for a system resource. Within each workload classification, one of three thresholds can be assigned: underloaded, overloaded, or critical. As an example:

- Discretionary workloads are considered underloaded at 70 percent utilization, overloaded at 80 percent utilization, and critical at 100 percent utilization.
- Internal Maintenance workloads are considered underloaded at 75 percent utilization, overloaded at 85 percent utilization, and critical at 100 percent utilization.
- Customer Expectation workloads are considered underloaded at 80 percent utilization, overloaded at 90 percent utilization, and critical at 100 percent utilization.

You can view the current resource threshold settings for each workload classification by entering the following command:

```
Get-ResourcePolicy | fl
```

To create and manage resource policies, you can use New-ResourcePolicy, Set-ResourcePolicy, and Remove-ResourcePolicy. Once you've defined custom workload and resource policies, you can create a policy object based on a particular policy by using New-WorkloadManagementPolicy. You then assign the workload management policy to a server using Set-ExchangeServer with the –WorkloadManagementPolicy and –Server parameters.

Tracking Configuration Changes

As part of your standard operating procedures, you should track changes in the configuration of your Exchange servers. Exchange Management Shell provides the following cmdlets for obtaining detailed information on the current configuration of your Exchange servers:

- **Get-ClientAccessService**   Displays configuration details for Client Access services on Mailbox servers.
- **Get-ExchangeServer**   Displays the general configuration details for Exchange servers.
- **Get-MailboxServer**   Displays configuration details for servers with the Mailbox services.
- **Get-OrganizationConfig**   Displays summary information about your Exchange organization.

- **Get-TransportService** Displays configuration details for transport services on servers with the Mailbox or Edge Transport server role.

To get related details for a specific server, you pass the Get-TransportService cmdlet the identity of the server you want to work with, as shown in the following example:

```
Get-TransportService mailserver23 | fl
```

To get related details for all servers, omit the –Identity parameter, as shown in the following example:

```
Get-TransportService | fl
```

When you finalize the configuration of your Exchange servers, you should use these cmdlets to store the configuration details for each server role. To store the configuration details in a file, redirect the output to a file, as shown in the following example:

```
Get-TransportService mailserver23 | fl >
c:\SavedConfigs\transport2016-0603.txt
```

If you then store the revised configuration, any time you make significant changes you can use this information during troubleshooting to help resolve problems that might be related to configuration changes. To compare two configuration files, you can use the file compare command, fc, at an elevated, administrator command prompt. When you use the following syntax with the fc command, the output is the difference between two files:

```
fc FilePath1 FilePath2
```

where *FilePath1* is the full file path to the first file and *FilePath2* is the full file path to the second file. Here is an example:

```
fc c:\SavedConfigs\transport2016-0603.txt c:\SavedConfigs\
transport2016-0603.txt
```

Because the files contain configuration details for specific dates, the changes shown in the output represent the configuration changes that you've made to the server.

Testing Service Health, Mail Flow, Replication and More

As part of troubleshooting, you'll often want to determine the status of required services, which can be done using Test-ServiceHealth. The basic syntax is:

```
Test-ServiceHealth [-Server ServerName]
```

Where ServerName is the name of the server to test. If you omit a server name, the local server is tested. As shown in the following sample output, Test-ServiceHealth shows you which required services are running and which aren't:

```
Role                      : Mailbox Server Role
RequiredServicesRunning : True
ServicesRunning           : {IISAdmin, MSExchangeADTopology,
MSExchangeDelivery, MSExchangeIS, MSExchangeMailboxAssistants,
MSExchangeRepl, MSExchangeRPC, MSExchangeServiceHost,
MSExchangeSubmission, MSExchangeThrottling, MSExchangeTransportLogSearch,
W3Svc, WinRM}
ServicesNotRunning        : {}


Role                      : Client Access Server Role
RequiredServicesRunning : True
ServicesRunning           : {IISAdmin, MSExchangeADTopology,
MSExchangeMailboxReplication, MSExchangeRPC, MSExchangeServiceHost, W3Svc,
WinRM}
ServicesNotRunning        : {}


Role                      : Unified Messaging Server Role
RequiredServicesRunning : True
ServicesRunning           : {IISAdmin, MSExchangeADTopology,
MSExchangeServiceHost, MSExchangeUM, W3Svc, WinRM}
ServicesNotRunning        : {}


Role                      : Hub Transport Server Role
RequiredServicesRunning : True
ServicesRunning           : {IISAdmin, MSExchangeADTopology,
MSExchangeEdgeSync, MSExchangeServiceHost, MSExchangeTransport,
```

```
MSExchangeTransportLogSearch, W3Svc, WinRM}
ServicesNotRunning    : {}
```

Although Exchange 2016 no longer has separate roles for Mailbox servers, Test-ServiceHealth continues to list separately the related required services and their status. As part of troubleshooting, you'll often need to test mail flow and replication. If you suspect a problem with mailflow, you can quickly send a test message by using Test-Mailflow. This cmdlet verifies whether mail can be successfully sent from and delivered to the system mailbox as well as whether email is sent between Mailbox servers within a defined latency threshold.

To test mail flow from one mailbox server to another or from one mailbox server to a target mailbox database, you can use the following syntax:

```
Test-MailFlow -Identity OriginatingMailServer [-TargetMailboxServer
DestinationMailServer | -TargetDatabase DestinationDatabase]
```

In the following example, a test message is sent from MailboxServer34 to MailboxServer26:

```
Test-MailFlow -Identity MailboxServer34 -TargetMailboxServer
MailboxServer26
```

As shown in this sample, the output of the command tells you whether the message was sent and received successfully:

```
TestMailflowResult : Success
MessageLatencyTime : 00:00:04.0077377
IsRemoteTest       : False
Identity           :
IsValid            : True
ObjectState        : New
```

If you suspect a problem with replication, you can quickly determine the status of replication components by using Test-ReplicationHealth. This cmdlet checks the status of all aspects of replication, replay, and availability on a Mailbox server in a Database Availability group. Use Test-ReplicationHealth to help you monitor the status of continuous replication, availability of Active Manager, and the general status of availability components.

The basic syntax is:

```
Test-MailFlow [-Identity MailboxServerId]
```

Such as:

```
Test-MailFlow MailServer19
```

As shown in this sample, the output of the command tells you the status of each replication component on the Mailbox server:

```
Server          Check                Result       Error
------          -----                ------       -----
MAILSERVER19    ReplayService        Passed
MAILSERVER19    ActiveManager        Passed
MAILSERVER19    TasksRpcListener     Passed
MAILSERVER19    DatabaseRedundancy   *FAILED*     Failures:...
MAILSERVER19    DatabaseAvailability *FAILED*     Failures:...
```

If errors are found, you'll want to get more details by formatting the output in a list, such as:

```
Test-MailFlow MailServer19 | fl server, check*, result, error
```

The error details should help you identify the problem. In this example, the Mailbox database doesn't have enough copies to be fully redundant:

```
Server           : MAILSERVER19
Check            : DatabaseRedundancy
CheckDescription : Verifies that databases have sufficient redundancy. If
this check fails, it means that some databases are at risk of losing data.
Result           : *FAILED*
Error            : Failures:
There were database redundancy check failures for database 'Engineering
Mailbox Database' that may be lowering its redundancy and
```

```
putting the database at risk of data loss. Redundancy Count: 1. Expected
Redundancy Count: 2.
```

In this example, the Engineering Mailbox Database does not have enough copies for
full redundancy. This could be because an administrator forgot to make a passive
copy of the database or because a Mailbox server hosting a copy of the database is
offline or otherwise unavailable.

Other useful cmdlets for checking the Exchange organization include:

- **Test-ActiveSyncConnectivity**   Performs a full synchronization against a specified
  mailbox to test the configuration of Exchange ActiveSync.
- **Test-ArchiveConnectivity**   Verifies archive functionality for a mailbox user.
- **Test-AssistantHealth**   Verifies that the Exchange Mailbox Assistant service is
  running as expected.
- **Test-CalendarConnectivity**   Verifies that calendar sharing as part of Outlook
  Web App is working properly.
- **Test-EcpConnectivity**   Verifies that the Exchange Admin Center is running as
  expected.
- **Test-EdgeSynchronization**   Verifies that the subscribed Edge Transport servers
  have a current and accurate synchronization status.
- **Test-ExchangeSearch**   Verifies that Exchange Search is currently enabled and is
  indexing new email messages in a timely manner.
- **Test-FederationTrust**   Verifies that the federation trust is properly configured
  and functioning as expected.
- **Test-FederationTrustCertificate**   Verifies the status of certificates used for
  federation on all Mailbox servers.
- **Test-ImapConnectivity**   Verifies that the IMAP4 service is running as expected.
- **Test-IPAllowListProvider**   Verifies the configuration for a specific IP allow list
  provider.
- **Test-IPBlockListProvider**   Verifies the configuration for a specific IP block list
  provider.
- **Test-IRMConfiguration**   Verifies Information Rights Management (IRM)
  configuration and functionality.
- **Test-MapiConnectivity**   Verifies server functionality by logging on to the
  mailbox that you specify.
- **Test-MRSHealth**   Verifies the health of the Microsoft Exchange Mailbox
  Replication Service.
- **Test-OAuthConnectivity**   Verifies that OAuth authentication is working properly.
- **Test-OutlookConnectivity**   Verifies end-to-end Microsoft Outlook client
  connectivity and also tests for Outlook Anywhere (RPC/HTTP) and TCP-based
  connections.

- **Test-OutlookWebServices**   Verifies the Autodiscover service settings for Outlook.
- **Test-OwaConnectivity**   Verifies that Outlook Web App is running as expected.
- **Test-PopConnectivity**   Verifies that the POP3 service is running as expected.
- **Test-PowerShellConnectivity**   Verifies whether Windows PowerShell remoting on the target Mailbox server is functioning correctly.
- **Test-SenderId**   Verifies whether a specified IP address is the legitimate sending address for a specified SMTP address.
- **Test-SmtpConnectivity**   Verifies SMTP connectivity for a specified server.
- **Test-UMConnectivity**   Verifies the operation of a computer that has the Unified Messaging installed.
- **Test-WebServicesConnectivity**   Verifies the functionality of Exchange Web Services.

Diagnosing and Resolving Problems

As discussed previously in this chapter in the "Troubleshooting Essentials" section, you can use Get-ServerHealth to list monitors, target resources, and corresponding health sets. Knowing which monitor, target resource, and health set you want to work with is important for troubleshooting. To diagnose and resolve problems, you often need to work backward from the reported problem to the source of the problem, as shown here:

1. Find recovery actions.
2. Trace recovery actions to their responder.
3. Use the responses logged by a responder to find the related monitor.
4. Find the probes for a monitor.
5. Locate the error messages being logged by probes.
6. Verify probe errors still exist.

The sections that follow examine the related procedures.

Identifying Recovery Actions

During recovery, the responder engine uses responders to take appropriate recovery actions, based on the type of alert and the affected target resource. Whenever a responder takes a recovery action, it logs related events in the Microsoft.Exchange.ManagedAvailability/RecoveryActionResults event log. An entry with an event ID of 500 indicates that a recovery action has started. An entry with an event ID of 501 indicates that the recovery action was completed.

Although you can view the events in Event Viewer, you can also view them at the Shell prompt. To collect the events in the RecoveryActionResults event log so you can process them, enter the following commands:

```
$Results = Get-WinEvent -ComputerName ServerName
-LogName Microsoft-Exchange-ManagedAvailability/RecoveryActionResults

$ResultsXML = ($Results | Foreach-object
-Process {[xml]$_.toXml()}).event.userData.eventXml
```

Where ServerName is the name of the Mailbox server that you want to work with. The first command collects the events. The second command formats the event entries so that they are easier to work with. These commands can be combined and shortened to:

```
$ResultsXML = (Get-WinEvent -ComputerName ServerName -LogName
Microsoft-Exchange-ManagedAvailability/RecoveryActionResults |
 % {[xml]$_.toXml()}).event.userData.eventXml
```

Next, you need to identify a response that you want to look at more closely. If you want to review corrective actions taken by Managed Availability, you'd look for events that occurred today and completed successfully. The following example parses the previously collected event data and looks for events from 2016-08-07 that have a successful result:

```
$ResultsXML | Where-Object {$_.Result -eq "Succeeded" -and $_.EndTime -like
"2016-08-07*"}| ft -AutoSize StartTime,RequestorName
```

As shown in this example, you also could look for events that occurred but where the responder failed to correct the issue:

```
$ResultsXML | Where-Object {$_.Result -eq "Failed" -and $_.EndTime -like
"2016-08-07*"}| ft -AutoSize StartTime,RequestorName
```

With either approach, you'll then get a list of issues by start time and requestor name, such as:

```
StartTime                    RequestorName
---------                    -------------
2016-08-07t21:00:10.1008312Z SearchLocalCopyStatusRestartSearchService
2016-08-07t21:00:06.1162578Z RWSProxyTestRecycleAppPool
2016-08-07t21:00:00.4597184Z ClusterEndpointRestart
2016-08-07t20:59:36.1601996Z RWSProxyTestRecycleAppPool
2016-08-07t20:57:17.8657794Z OutlookSelfTestRestart
2016-08-07t20:58:03.7958299Z RWSProxyTestRecycleAppPool
2016-08-07t20:55:24.6591276Z ServiceHealthActiveManagerRestartService
2016-08-07t20:57:11.2223574Z ClusterEndpointRestart
2016-08-07t20:55:06.9326525Z OutlookSelfTestRestart
2016-08-07t20:57:02.6438007Z RWSProxyTestRecycleAppPool
2016-08-07t20:54:34.5391633Z OutlookMailboxDeepTestRestart
2016-08-07t20:56:32.4360908Z RWSProxyTestRecycleAppPool
2016-08-07t20:54:41.4926429Z ClusterEndpointRestart
2016-08-07t20:53:34.1596832Z ActiveDirectoryConnectivityRestart
2016-08-07t20:52:11.0579430Z ClusterEndpointRestart
```

In this example, the value in the RequestorName column is the responder that took the action. To examine the properties of a recovery action, run a query for a specific responder, such as:

```
$ResultsXML | Where-Object {$_.Result -eq "Failed" -and $_.EndTime -like
"2013*" -and $_.RequestorName -eq "OutlookSelfTestRestart"}| fl
```

The output includes the details logged for events in which the recovery action initiated by the OutLookSelfTestRestart responder failed. Each entry will look similar to the following:

```
auto-ns2        : http://schemas.microsoft.com/win/2004/08/events
xmlns           : myNs
Id              : RestartService
InstanceId      : 130629.015717.86577.001
ResourceName    : MSExchangeRPC
```

```
StartTime            : 2016-08-07T20:57:17.8657794Z
EndTime              : 2016-08-07T20:59:19.4994266Z
State                : Finished
Result               : Failed
RequestorName        : OutlookSelfTestRestart
ExceptionName        : TimeoutException
ExceptionMessage     : System error.
Context              : [null]
CustomArg1           : [null]
CustomArg2           : [null]
CustomArg3           : [null]
LamProcessStartTime  : 8/07/2016 1:12:28 PM
```

Although the responder name and details will often help you identify the type of problem that occurred, you can keep working toward the exact problem that occurred by finding the monitor that triggered the responder.

Identifying Responders

Whenever the Health Manager service starts, it logs related events in the Microsoft.Exchange.ActiveMonitoring/ResponderDefinition event log that you can use to get properties of responders. To collect the events in the ResponderDefinition event log so that you can process them, enter the following command:

```
$Responders = (Get-WinEvent -ComputerName ServerName -LogName
Microsoft-Exchange-ActiveMonitoring/ResponderDefinition | %
{[xml]$_.toXml()}).event.userData.eventXml
```

Where ServerName is the name of the Mailbox server with which you want to work. If you examine the definition of a responder, the AlertMask property will identify the monitor associated with the responder. Thus, one way to display the required information is to look for the responder and list the responder name and the associated alert mask in the output as shown in this example:

```
$Responders | ? {$_.Name -eq "OutlookSelfTestRestart"} |
 ft name, alertmask
```

As the output will then be similar to the following:

```
Name                              AlertMask
----                              ---------
OutlookSelfTestRestart            OutlookSelfTestMonitor
OutlookSelfTestRestart            OutlookSelfTestMonitor
```

You'll know the related monitor is named OutlookSelfTestMonitor. Before examining the related monitor, you might want to display the full details for the responder to help you understand exactly how the responder works. To display the full details for a responder, simply list its properties in a formatted list as shown in this example:

```
$Responders | ? {$_.Name -eq "OutlookSelfTestRestart"} | fl
```

During recovery, the responder engine uses responders to take appropriate recovery actions based on the alert type and the affected target resource. The wait interval specifies the minimum amount of time a responder must wait before running again. As shown in this partial output, the definition details can help you learn more about the responder:

```
Id                        : 452
AssemblyPath              : C:\Program Files\Microsoft\Exchange
 Server\V15\Bin\Microsoft.Exchange.Monitoring.ActiveMonitoring
.Local.Components.dll
TypeName                  : Microsoft.Exchange.Monitoring
.ActiveMonitoring.Responders.ResetIISAppPoolResponder
Name                      : OutlookSelfTestRestart
WorkItemVersion           : [null]
ServiceName               : Outlook.Protocol
DeploymentId              : 0
ExecutionLocation         : [null]
CreatedTime               : 2016-08-07T20:02:32.2527661Z
Enabled                   : 1
TargetResource            : MSExchangeRpcProxyAppPool
RecurrenceIntervalSeconds : 0
TimeoutSeconds            : 300
StartTime                 : 2016-08-07T20:02:32.2527661Z
UpdateTime                : 2016-08-07T17:55:07.9754209Z
MaxRetryAttempts          : 3
```

```
ExtensionAttributes              : <ExtensionAttributes
AppPoolName="MSExchangeRpcProxyAppPool" MinimumSecondsBetweenRestarts="300"
MaximumAllowedRestartsInAnHour="3" MaximumAllowedRestartsInADay="-1"
DumpOnRestart="FullDump" DumpPath="C:\Program Files\Microsoft\Exchange
Server\V15\Dumps" MinimumFreeDiskPercent="15" MaximumDumpsPerDay="9"
MaximumDumpDurationInSeconds="180" />
AlertMask                        : OutlookSelfTestMonitor
WaitIntervalSeconds              : 30
MinimumSecondsBetweenEscalates : 0
NotificationServiceClass         : 0
AlwaysEscalateOnMonitorChanges : 0
```

Identifying Monitors

Monitor definitions are written in the
Microsoft.Exchange.ActiveMonitoring/MonitorDefinition event log. If you examine
the properties of events, you can learn more about monitors and learn their related
probes. To collect the events in the MonitorDefinition event log so that you can
process them, enter the following command:

```
$Monitors = (Get-WinEvent –ComputerName ServerName -LogName
Microsoft-Exchange-ActiveMonitoring/MonitorDefinition | %
{[xml]$_.toXml()}).event.userData.eventXml
```

Where ServerName is the name of the Mailbox server with which you want to work.
If you examine the definition of a monitor, the SampleMask property will identify the
probes associated with the monitor. List the monitor name and the associated
sample mask in the output as shown in this example:

```
$Monitors | ? {$_.Name -eq "OutlookSelfTestMonitor"} |
 ft name, samplemask
```

The output will then be similar to the following:

```
Name                                AlertMask
----                                ---------
OutlookSelfTestMonitor              OutlookSelfTestProbe
```

As shown in the output, probes related to this monitor have the top-level identifier: OutlookSelfTestProbe. To display the full details for a monitor, simply list its properties in a formatted list as shown in this example:

```
$Monitors | ? {$_.Name -eq "OutlookSelfTestMonitor"} | fl
```

During detection, the monitor engine uses monitors to analyze the sampled data. Whether a monitor issues an alert depends on the state of the target resource. As shown in this partial output, the monitor details provide a lot of information, including the exact definition of each transition state for the monitor:

```
Id                            : 339
AssemblyPath                  : C:\Program Files\Microsoft\Exchange
Server\V15\Bin\Microsoft.Exchange.Monitoring.ActiveMonitoring.Local.
Components.dll
TypeName                      : Microsoft.Exchange.Monitoring.
ActiveMonitoring .ActiveMonitoring.Monitors
.OverallConsecutiveProbeFailuresMonitor
Name                          : OutlookSelfTestMonitor
WorkItemVersion               : [null]
ServiceName                   : Outlook.Protocol
DeploymentId                  : 0
ExecutionLocation             : [null]
CreatedTime                   : 2016-08-07T20:02:32.2215111Z
Enabled                       : 1
RecurrenceIntervalSeconds     : 0
TimeoutSeconds                : 30
StartTime                     : 2016-08-07T20:02:32.2215111Z
UpdateTime                    : 2016-08-07T19:59:57.2971492Z
MaxRetryAttempts              : 0
ExtensionAttributes           : [null]
SampleMask                    : OutlookSelfTestProbe
MonitoringIntervalSeconds     : 300
MinimumErrorCount             : 0
MonitoringThreshold           : 2
SecondaryMonitoringThreshold  : 0
ServicePriority               : 0
```

```
ServiceSeverity                         : 0
IsHaImpacting                           : 1
CreatedById                             : 0
InsufficientSamplesIntervalSeconds      : 28800
StateAttribute1Mask                     : [null]
FailureCategoryMask                     : 0
ComponentName                           :
ServiceComponents/Outlook.Protocol/Critical
StateTransitionsXml                     : <StateTransitions>
<Transition ToState="Degraded" TimeoutInSeconds="0" />
<Transition ToState="Degraded1" TimeoutInSeconds="10" />
<Transition ToState="Degraded2" TimeoutInSeconds="240" />
<Transition ToState="Unhealthy" TimeoutInSeconds="300" />
<Transition ToState="Unhealthy1" TimeoutInSeconds="600" />
<Transition ToState="Unrecoverable" TimeoutInSeconds="1200" />
</StateTransitions>
Version                                 : 65536
```

Identifying Probes

To identify the probes associated with the OutlookSelfTestProbe identifier, you need to examine the probe definitions. Probe definitions are written in the Microsoft.Exchange.ActiveMonitoring/ProbeDefinition event log. If you examine the properties of events, you can learn more about each probe. To collect the events in the ProbeDefinition event log so that you can process them, enter the following command:

```
$Probes = (Get-WinEvent -ComputerName ServerName -LogName
Microsoft-Exchange-ActiveMonitoring/ProbeDefinition | %
{[xml]$_.toXml()}).event.userData.eventXml
```

Where ServerName is the name of the Mailbox server with which you want to work. Next, examine the associated probes to learn more about them as shown in this example:

```
$Probes | ? {$_.Name -eq "OutlookSelfTestProbe"} | fl
```

The output will then list the definition of each associated probe. Although many monitors have many associated probes, the OutlookSelfTestMonitor has only one associated probe. In this partial sample of the output, note the recurrence interval, timeout, and max retry values for this probe:

```
Id                       : 106
AssemblyPath             : C:\Program Files\Microsoft\Exchange
Server\V15\Bin\Microsoft.Exchange.Monitoring.ActiveMonitoring
.Local.Components.dll
TypeName                 : Microsoft.Exchange.Monitoring.ActiveMonitoring
.RpcClientAccess.LocalRpcProbe+SelfTest
Name                     : OutlookSelfTestProbe
WorkItemVersion          : [null]
ServiceName              : Outlook.Protocol
DeploymentId             : 0
ExecutionLocation        : [null]
CreatedTime              : 2016-08-07T20:02:32.2058880Z
Enabled                  : 1
RecurrenceIntervalSeconds : 10
TimeoutSeconds           : 8
StartTime                : 2016-08-07T20:02:41.2215111Z
UpdateTime               : 2016-08-07T19:59:57.2190196Z
MaxRetryAttempts         : 0
ExtensionAttributes      : <ExtensionAttributes AccountLegacyDN="
/o=First Organization/ou=Monitoring Mailboxes/cn=Recipients
/cn=HealthMailbox3d899a319e1e4c019f5362ead47f0185"
PersonalizedServerName="278c17fc-8adc-49d7-affa-90f0ea7679b6@
imaginedlands.com" StartupNotificationId="MSExchangeRPC"
StartupNotificationMaxStartWaitInSeconds="12
/>
CreatedById              : 0
Account                  : <r at="Kerberos"
ln="IMAGINEDLANDS\SM_fef8fb0aaba040c19"><s>S-1-5-21-1487214957-3235876329-
1606252878-1151</s><s a="7" t="1">S-1-5-21-1487214957-3235876329-
1606252878-513</s><s a="7" t="1">S-1-1-0</s><s a="7" t="1">S-1-5-2</s>
<s a="7" t="1">S-1-5-11</s><s a="7" t="1">S-1-5-15</s>
```

```
<s a="3221225479" t="1">S-1-5-5-0-8194354</s><s a="7" t="1">
S-1-18-2</s></r>
AccountDisplayName          : HealthMailbox3d899a319e1e4c019f5362ead47f0185
Endpoint                    : MailServer21.imaginedlands.com
SecondaryAccount            : [null]
SecondaryAccountDisplayName : [null]
SecondaryEndpoint           : MailServer21.imaginedlands.com
ExtensionEndpoints          : [null]
Version                     : 65536
ExecutionType               : 0
```

During sampling, the probe engine runs probes against target resources. How often a probe runs depends on its recurrence interval. How long a probe waits before reporting failure depends on its timeout value. Also listed in the output is the system account under which the probe runs and the authentication method used for that account.

Viewing Error Messages for Probes

Once you know which probes are associated with the issue you are tracking, you can get the error messages for the probes. Probe results are written in the Microsoft.Exchange.ActiveMonitoring/ProbeResult event log. As this log is quite extensive, you want to filter the logs for the exact information you are seeking. Properties for related events include:

- **ServiceName** Identifies the related health set.
- **ResultName** Identifies the name of the probe. When there are multiple probes for a monitor the name includes the monitor's sample mask and the resource it verifies.
- **Error** Lists the error returned by this probe, if it failed.
- **Exception** Lists the call stack of the error, if it failed.
- **ResultType** Lists an integer value that indicates the result type: 1 for timeout, 2 for poisoned, 3 for succeeded, 4 for failed, 5 for quarantined, and 6 for rejected.
- **ExecutionStartTime** Lists when the probe started.
- **ExecutionEndTime** Lists when the probe completed.
- **ExecutionContext** Provides additional information about the probe's execution context.
- **FailureContext** Provides additional information about the probe's failure.

Knowing this, you can collect the events in the ProbeResult event log and filter them. In this example, you look for failure results related to OutlookSelfTestProbe:

```
$Errors = (Get-WinEvent -ComputerName ServerName -LogName
 Microsoft-Exchange-ActiveMonitoring/ProbeResult -FilterXPath
"*[UserData[EventXML[ResultName='OutlookSelfTestProbe'][ResultType='4']]]"
 | % {[XML]$_.toXml()}).event.userData.eventXml
```

Where ServerName is the name of the Mailbox server with which you want to work. After you filter the log, you can display the results you want to see, such as:

```
$Errors | select -Property *Time,Result*,Error*,*Context
```

In this example, the output lists the time-, result-, error-, and context-related properties, which will help you identify the exact problem that occurred. Consider the following example:

```
ExecutionStartTime : 2016-08-07T21:24:26.9816420Z
ExecutionEndTime   : 2016-08-07T21:24:27.7508864Z
ResultId           : 644887342
ResultName         : OutlookSelfTestProbe
ResultType         : 4
Error              : The request was aborted: Could not create SSL/TLS
secure channel.
ExecutionContext   :      RpcProxy connectivity verification
Task produced output:
- TaskStarted = 8/07/2016 2:24:26 PM
- TaskFinished = 8/07/2016 2:24:27 PM
- Exception = System.Net.WebException: The request
was aborted: Could not create SSL/TLS secure channel.
- ErrorDetails = Status: SecureChannelFailure
                 HttpStatusCode:
                 HttpStatusDescription:
                 ProcessedBody:
                    - Latency = 00:00:00.5617493
- RpcProxyUrl = https://mailserver21.
imaginedlands.com:444/rpc/rpcproxy.dll?MailServer21.
```

```
imaginedlands.com:6001
                        - ResponseStatusCode = <null>
                    RpcProxy connectivity verification failed.
FailureContext      : Status: SecureChannelFailure
                    HttpStatusCode:
                    HttpStatusDescription:
                    ProcessedBody:
```

As you can see from the output, the probe error details provide a lot of information regarding the exact problem that occurred. In this example, an RPC Proxy error occurred that prevented creation of a secure SSL/TLS channel. If this was a problem preventing access to the server or causing other issues, you would then know that you need to look at related components to continue your troubleshooting. You would look at the RPC, RPC Proxy, SSL and TLS configuration in Internet Information Services (IIS) as well as the related settings in Exchange.

Tracing Probe Errors

Now that you know how to trace a reported problem to its source, let's take a look at additional ways in which you can put this knowledge to use. You view the overall health of a server by using Get-ServerHealth. As discussed earlier in this chapter, if a health set has a status other than healthy or online, you can take a closer look at it by using the -HealthSet parameter. List the properties of the health set as shown in this example:

```
Get-ServerHealth -Identity MailServer42 -HealthSet FrontEndTransport | fl
```

The Name property in the output of Get-ServerHealth lists the name of the monitor reporting the health status. Table 18-1 lists the health sets associated with key Exchange features and components.

TABLE 18-1 Health Sets Associated with Key Exchange Features and Components

FEATURE/COMPONENT	RELATED HEALTH SETS
ActiveSync	ActiveSync, ActiveSync.Protocol, ActiveSync.Proxy
Active Directory	AD
Anti-virus	Antimalware, AntiSpam

Autodiscover	Autodiscover, Autodiscover.Protocol, Autodiscover.Proxy
Mailbox databases	Clustering, Database, DataProtection, MailboxMigration, MailboxSpace, MRS, Store
Exchange Admin Center	ECP.Proxy
Exchange Web Services	EWS, EWS.Protocol, EWS.Proxy
Front-End Transport Service	FrontendTransport
Transport Service	HubTransport, MailboxTransport, Transport, TransportSync
Offline Address Book	OAB, OAB.Proxy
Outlook, Outlook Web App	Outlook, Outlook.Proxy, OWA.Protocol, OWA.Protocol.Dep, OWA.Proxy
Unified Messaging	UM.Callrouter, UM.Protocol
User Throttling	UserThrottling

You can quickly identify all the related probes, monitors, and responders for a health set by using Get-MonitoringItemIdentity. The basic syntax is:

```
Get-MonitoringItemIdentity -Identity HealthSetName -Server ServerName
```

Where HealthSetName identifies the health set to examine and ServerName is the name of an Exchange server. In the following example, you list items by type, item name, and target resource:

```
Get-MonitoringItemIdentity -Identity FrontEndTransport -Server mailserver38
| ft itemtype, name, targetresource
```

As shown in the following partial output, each associated probe, monitor, and responder is listed by name:

ItemType	Name	TargetResource
Probe	FrontendTransportServiceRunning	msexchangefrontendtransport
Probe	FrontendTransportRepeatedlyCrashing	msexchangefrontendtransport
Monitor	FrontendTransportServiceRunningMonitor	
Monitor	FrontendTransportRepeatedlyCrashingMonitor	
Responder	FrontendTransportServiceRunningEscalateResponder	Transport
Responder	FrontendTransportRepeatedlyCrashingResponder	Transport

If the name of the monitor reporting a status other than online or healthy is FrontendTransportRepeatedlyCrashingMonitor, you can analyze the problem by looking at errors for the FrontendTransportRepeatedlyCrashing probe. Collect events for this probe from the ProbeResult event log and filter them as discussed earlier in "Viewing error messages for probes." Here is an example:

```
$Errors = (Get-WinEvent -ComputerName ServerName -LogName
 Microsoft-Exchange-ActiveMonitoring/ProbeResult -FilterXPath
"*[UserData[EventXML[ResultName='FrontendTransportRepeatedlyCrashing']
[ResultType='4']]]" | % {[XML]$_.toXml()}).event.userData.eventXml
```

Where ServerName is the name of the Mailbox server with which you want to work. Remember, the result type can be 1 for timeout, 2 for poisoned, 3 for succeeded, 4 for failed, 5 for quarantined, or 6 for rejected.

After you filter the log, you can display the results you want to see, such as:

```
$Errors | select -Property *Time,Result*,Error*,*Context
```

Before you begin deeper troubleshooting, you might want to rerun the associated probe for the monitor to ensure its still not in a healthy or online state. You can rerun probes by using Invoke-MonitoringProbe. The basic syntax is:

```
Invoke-MonitoringProbe HealthSetName\ProbeName -Server ServerName | fl
```

Where HealthSetName is the name of the health set with which to work, ProbeName is the name of the probe within the specified health set, and ServerName is the name of the Exchange server to check, such as:

```
Invoke-MonitoringProbe FrontEndTransport\
FrontendTransportRepeatedlyCrashing -Server MailServer38 | fl
```

As shown in this partial sample of the output, the command returns a lot of information about the test:

```
Server               : MailServer38
MonitorIdentity      : FrontEndTransport\FrontendTransportRepeatedlyCrashing
RequestId            : 84dc68cd-c2f8-487f-a5e2-20b43f6f9207
ExecutionStartTime   : 6/5/2016 8:20:42 AM
ExecutionEndTime     : 6/5/2016 8:20:42 AM
Error                :
Exception            :
PoisonedCount        : 0
ExecutionId          : 18902819
SampleValue          : 2015
ExecutionContext     :
FailureContext       :
ExtensionXml         :
ResultType           : Succeeded
RetryCount           : 0
ResultName           : 84dc68cdc2f8487fa5e220b43f6f9207-
FrontendTransportRepeatedlyCrashing
IsNotified           : False
ResultId             : 1289896134
ServiceName          : InvokeNow
StateAttribute1      : No relevant crash events found for service
```

The ResultType value in the output will tell you whether the probe succeeded or failed. If the probe succeeded, the problem no longer exists. If the probe fails, the problem still exists and you'll need to continue trying to diagnose and resolve it. Step by step procedures for troubleshooting issues with Exchange services are provided in the "Troubleshooting Outlook Web App" section of this chapter and "Maintaining Virtual Directories and Web Applications" section of Chapter 13, "Optimizing Web and Mobile Access."

Troubleshooting Outlook Web App

As discussed in "Troubleshooting OWA, ECP, Powershell, and More" in Chapter 4, "Exchange 2016 Administration Essentials," sometimes users and administrators see a blank page or an error when they try to log on to OWA. This problem and other connection issues, such as those related to ECP, OAB, Autodiscover, and Windows PowerShell, can occur because of a wide variety of configuration issues, including:

- Invalid or missing TCP/IP settings.
- Corrupted or improperly configured virtual directories.
- Missing, expired, invalid, or improperly configured SSL certificates.

You resolve these issues by correcting the configuration problem as discussed in that chapter. Beyond configuration issues, Exchange servers can have connectivity, resource, and service issues. You can use Test-OwaConnectivity to test connectivity to Outlook Web App as part of troubleshooting connectivity; however, this cmdlet is deprecated and will be removed in a future release of Exchange Server.

Checking OWA Health

Exchange 2016 uses Active Monitoring to monitor essential services, connectivity, resources and the overall health of the messaging platform. Active Monitoring is performed by the Microsoft Exchange Health Manager service, which must be running on the Exchange server. As discussed in detail in "Managed Availability Components" in Chapter 6 "Implementing Availability Groups," Active Monitoring is itself part of the Managed Availability feature.

The overall health of Outlook Web App is tracked by the OWA health set. A health set includes a probe that takes measurements on the server and collects data, and a monitor that uses the collected data to determine whether a resource is healthy. OWA relies on the OwaCtpProbe to measure the health of Outlook Web App and the OwaCtpMonitor to determine the status of Outlook Web App. The OWA health is dependent on Active Directory Domain Services (AD DS) and the Microsoft Exchange Information Store service.

Alerts related to resources are logged in the event logs. You also can manually check the status of resources by using the Get-HealthReport and Get-ServerHealth. Whereas Get-ServerHealth provides the exact state and health of every Exchange resource, monitor, and service, Get-HealthReport returns the state of monitored resources. You can quickly check for unhealthy resources by entering the following command:

```
Get-ServerHealth -Identity ServerID | where ($_.AlertValue -eq
'Unhealthy')
```

Where ServerID is the host name or fully-qualified name of the Exchange server to check, such as:

```
Get-ServerHealth -Identity MailServer21.pocketonconsultant.com |
where ($_.AlertValue -eq 'Unhealthy')
```

Rather than check all resources and health sets, you can explicitly check the status of the OWA-related health sets by using the following command:

```
Get-ServerHealth ServerID | ?{$_.HealthSetName -match "OWA"}
```

Where ServerID is the host name or fully-qualified name of the Exchange server to check, such as:

```
Get-ServerHealth MailServer21.pocketonconsultant.com |
?{$_.HealthSetName -match "OWA"}
```

> **NOTE** Here, I've used a filter that looks for values that contain a match for OWA rather than a filter that looks for a value that equals OWA. In this way, you get the status of every OWA related health set rather than just the OWA health set.

Mailbox servers use IIS for front-end services, such as authentication and proxying, as well as back-end processing. You'll find front-end apps for OWA, ECP, PowerShell, OAB, and Autodiscover apps are configured on the Default Web Site. You'll find back-end apps for OWA, ECP, PowerShell, OAB, and Autodiscover are configured on Exchange Back End website.

Understanding Unhealthy Status

If the OWA health set reports an unhealthy status, an issue is present that might prevent users from accessing their mailboxes in Outlook Web App. Such issues include:

- The OWA application pool is not responding on the Mailbox server providing front-end proxy services
- The OWA application pool is not responding on the Mailbox server providing back-end services
- Network issues are preventing the Mailbox server from connecting to other Mailbox servers or a domain controller
- A domain controller or the Microsoft Exchange Information Store service is not responding
- The user's mailbox database is dismounted or otherwise inaccessible
- The credentials for the monitoring account are incorrect

Some of these problems can be resolved automatically by the responder engine, which is another Managed Availability component. When a problem exists with application pools or services on Exchange servers, the responder engine attempts to recover the resource by restarting the application pool or service that is causing the problem. The problem identification and recovery process can take several minutes. If you notice a problem with Outlook Web App that you suspect is related to application pools or services, you can, of course, perform the restart procedures yourself to try to restore access more quickly to Outlook Web App.

OWA.Proxy and OWA.Protocol also are related health sets. OWA.Proxy relies on OwaProxyTestProbe, OWAAnonymousCalendarProblem, and OwaProxyTestMonitor to track the status of proxy services and calendaring features. OWA.Protocol relies on:

- OwaSelfTestProbe and the OwaSelfTestMonitor. OwaSelfTestProbe performs connectivity tests by sending an HTTP request to *https://localhost:444/owa/exhealth.check*. If the probe gets back a status code of 200 OK, the MSExchangeOWAAppPool is responding. This probe doesn't depend on any other Exchange component.
- OwaDeepTestProbe and OwaDeepTestMontor. OwaDeepTestProbe checks each Mailbox database on the server to ensure that mailbox users can log on to the server using Outlook Web App. This probe depends on Active Directory for authentication and the Microsoft Exchange Information Store for mailbox access.

As with the OWA health set, an unhealthy status for OWA.Proxy or OWA.Protocol means an issue exists that might prevent users from accessing their mailboxes in Outlook Web App. The common issues for the OWA.Protocol health set are the same as those for the OWA health set. With OWA.Proxy, common issues may be related to the OWA application pool not responding on the Mailbox server providing front-end proxy services, a domain controller not responding, or the credentials for the monitoring account being incorrect.

Correcting Unhealthy Status

You can diagnose a problem with OWA by using Get-HealthReport to check the status of the OWA related health set. If the problem you are experiencing with Outlook Web App isn't a configuration issue, use the following techniques to try to resolve the problem while verifying the issue still exists each time you take a corrective action:

1. Try to isolate the problem to a specific server by running a health check for each server. If OWA.Proxy or OWA.Protocol for a particular server has an Unhealthy status, you've likely isolated the problem and identified the server experiencing the problem and can skip Steps 2 and 3.

2. If you are unable to isolate the problem to a specific server or servers, try to access and log on to Outlook Web App by using the URL for a specific Mailbox server. If this fails, try accessing and logging on to a different Mailbox server to help you verify whether the problem is with a particular server. Remember that the Mailbox server used in the one that contains the mailbox database where the mailbox for the user is stored.

3. Using the Services console, verify that all essential Exchange services are running on the Mailbox servers. If an essential service isn't running, select it, and then click Start.

4. Verify network connectivity between the Mailbox servers. One way to do this is to log on to each server and try to ping the other servers. If you correct a connectivity issue, check to see if the OWA issue is resolved.

5. In IIS Manager, connect to the server that's reporting the health issue or otherwise experiencing a problem with OWA. Expand the Sites node and verify that the Default Web Site or Exchange Back End website is running as appropriate. If a required website isn't running, click Start in the Actions pane to start it. This should resolve the problem.

6. Under Application Pools, verify that the required application pools have been started. If a required application pool hasn't been started, select it, and then click Start in the Actions pane.

   The main application pool for OWA is MSExchangeOWAAppPool. A single application pool with this name is used for both front-end and back-end services.

   For calendaring, OWA relies on MSExchangeOWACalendarAppPool. A single application pool with this name is used for both front-end and back-end services.

> **REAL WORLD**   As your messaging environment grows and usage of Outlook Web App increases, you may find that the basic application pool settings for MSExchangeOWAAppPool are insufficient. Specifically, if users are getting an HTTP 503 "Service Unavailable" response when they try to connect to OWA, you may need to increase the queue length so that a greater number of requests can be queued in the application pool. Although slow response times likely can be attributed to connection speed and latency on the network, they might also be because the application pool has to service too many users. If so, you may want to consider configuring the Maximum Worker Processes setting so that multiple worker processes can be used. In both cases, doing so, however, requires that additional system resources (primary memory resources) must be allocated to the application pool.

7. If you suspect an issue with MSExchangeOWAAppPool, select MSExchangeOWACalendarAppPool, and then click Recycle in the Actions pane to recycle its work processes.

8. If you suspect an issue with MSExchangeOWACalendarAppPool, select MSExchangeOWACalendarAppPool, and then click Recycle in the Actions pane to recycle its work processes.

9. If the problem isn't resolved yet, restart the website where the problem is occurring or the IIS itself. To restart a website, select the website in IIS Manager and then select Restart in the Actions pane. To restart IIS, select the server node in IIS Manager, and then click Restart in the Actions pane.

10. If the problem still isn't resolved, restart the server. If restarting the server doesn't resolve the problem, you likely have a configuration issue that needs to be resolved.

Index

About the Author

William R. Stanek (*http://www.williamrstanek.com*) has more than 20 years of hands-on experience with advanced programming and development. He is a leading technology expert, an award-winning author, and a pretty-darn-good instructional trainer. Over the years, his practical advice has helped millions of programmers, developers, and network engineers all over the world. In 2013, William celebrated the publication of his 150th book.

William has been involved in the commercial Internet community since 1991. His core business and technology experience comes from more than 11 years of military service. He has substantial experience in developing server technology, encryption, and Internet solutions. He has written many technical white papers and training courses on a wide variety of topics. He frequently serves as a subject matter expert and consultant.

William has an MS with distinction in information systems and a BS in computer science, magna cum laude. He is proud to have served in the Persian Gulf War as a combat crewmember on an electronic warfare aircraft. He flew on numerous combat missions into Iraq and was awarded nine medals for his wartime service, including one of the United States of America's highest-flying honors, the Air Force Distinguished Flying Cross. Currently, he resides in the Pacific Northwest with his wife and children.

William recently rediscovered his love of the great outdoors. When he's not writing, he can be found hiking, biking, backpacking, traveling, or trekking in search of adventure with his family! In his spare time, William writes books for children, including *The Bugville Critters Explore the Solar System* and *The Bugville Critters Go on Vacation*.

Find William on Twitter at http://www.twitter.com/WilliamStanek and on Facebook at http://www.facebook.com/William.Stanek.Author.

Exchange Server 2016 & Exchange Online
Essentials for Administration

William R. Stanek
Author & Series Editor

William R. Stanek, Jr.
Contributor

IT Pro
Solutions

Made in the USA
Middletown, DE
11 August 2016